Doing Member Care Well

Perspectives and Practices From Around the World

Edited by Kelly O'Donnell

William Carey Library
Pasadena, California

Technical editor: Susan Peterson
Cover art director: Jeff Northway
Cover art: Katy O'Donnell-Filson

Published by:
William Carey Library
PO Box 40129
Pasadena, CA 91114
626-798-0819

Printed in the United States of America

For information about other resources available from William Carey Library, visit our web site: www.WCLBooks.com.

Library of Congress Cataloging-in-Publication Data

Doing member care well : perspectives and practices from around the world / edited by Kelly O'Donnell.
p. cm.
ISBN 0-87808-446-0 (alk. paper)
1. Missionaries--Supervision of. I. O'Donnell, Kelly S.

BV2091 .D65 2002
266'.0068'3--dc21

2001058325

Contents

Section 3: Africa

Section 4: Latin America

Section 5: Arabic World

Part 3: Providing and Developing Member Care

Section 1: Master Care

Foreword

Caynumi rejjsishunqui llapan yachacojjnícuna cashgayquita, sichu charanquiman cuyapanacuyniquita juc jucnínhuan.

به همین همه خواهند فهمید که شاگرد من هستید اگر محبت یکدیگر را داشته باشید.

Si vous vous aimez les uns les autres, alors tous sauront que vous êtes mes disciples.

Kama mkipendana hivyo, watu wote watafahamu ya kuwa ninyi ni wanafunzi wangu.

你们如果彼此相爱，世人就会认出你们是我的门徒了。

Eğer birbirinize sevginiz olursa, benim şakirtlerim olduğunuzu bütün insanlar bununla bilecekler.

நீங்கள் ஒருவரிலொருவர் அன்புள்ள வர்களாயிருந்தால், அதினால் நீங்கள் என் னுடைய சீஷர்களென்று எல்லாரும் அறிந்துகொள்வார்கள் என்றார்.

En esto conocerán todos que sois mis discípulos, si os tenéis amor los unos a los otros.

Podle toho všichni poznají, že jste moji učedníci, budete-li mít lásku jedni k druhým.

አንትሙኒ ፡ ተፋቀሩ ፡ በበይናቲክሙ ። ወበዝንቱ ፡ ያአምረክሙ ፡ ኵሉ ፡ ከመ ፡ አርዳእየ ፡ አንትሙ ፡ እምከመ ፡ ተፋቀርክሙ ፡ በበይናቲክሙ ።

Dengan hal ini sekalian orang akan mengetahui bahwa kamu murid-muridku, jaïtu djikalau kamu menaruh kasih sama sendiri.

ἐν τούτῳ γνώσονται πάντες ὅτι ἐμοὶ μαθηταί ἐστε, ἐὰν ἀγάπην ἔχητε ἐν ἀλλήλοις.

In hoc cognoscent omnes quia discipuli mei estis, si dilectionem habueritis ad invicem.

Alla skall förstå att ni är mina lärjungar, om ni visar varandra kärlek.

بِهٰذَا يَعْرِفُ الْجَمِيعُ أَنَّكُمْ تَلَامِيذِي إِنْ كَانَ لَكُمْ حُبٌّ بَعْضًا لِبَعْضٍ

Le so aithnichidh na h-uile dhaoine gur sibh mo dheisciobuil-sa, ma bhios gràdh agaibh féin d'a chéile.

По тому узнают все, что вы Мои ученики, если будете иметь любовь между собою.

Ngalokho bonke bayakukwazi ukuthi ningabafundi bami, uma nithandana.

Si nou youn rinmin lòt, lè sa-a tout moun va konnin sé disip mouin nou yé.

너희가 서로 사랑하면 이로써 모든 사람이 너희가 내 제자인 줄 알리라

Se tiverem amor uns aos outros, toda a gente reconhecerá que vocês são meus discípulos.

Եթէ դուք միմեանց սիրէք, դրանով բոլորը պիտի իմանան, որ դուք իմ աշակերտներն էք։

O le mea lea e iloa ai e tagata uma lava o o'u soo outou, pe afai ua outou fealofani.

Als er liefde onder jullie heerst, zal iedereen kunnen zien dat jullie mijn leerlingen zijn.

もしあなたがたの互いの間に愛があるなら、それによって、あなたがたがわたしの弟子であることを、すべての人が認めるのです。

Sapos yupela i givim bel long ol brata, orait bambai olgeta man i save, yupela i disaipel bilong mi.

Агар орангизда муҳаббат ҳукмрон бўлса, сизлар Менинг шогирдларим эканингизни ҳамма шундан билиб олади.

Af því skulu allir þekkja, að þér eruð mínir lærisveinar, ef þér berið elsku hver til annars.

Air so aiṫéonaid na huile [ḋaoine] gur deisciobail ḋáṁsaiḃ, má ḃíoñ gráḋ aguiḃ [féin] dá ċéile.

Díí bee diné t'áá'ałtso shídahooł'aahii danohłį́įgo bił béédahózin doo, 'ayóó'áda'ahíínóh'nínígíí bee.

គេនឹងដឹងថា អ្នករាល់គ្នាជាសិស្សរបស់ខ្ញុំ ដោយសារសេចក្ដីនេះឯង គឺដោយអ្នករាល់គ្នាមានសេចក្ដីស្រឡាញ់ដល់គ្នាទៅវិញទៅមក

Po tym wszyscy poznają, żeście uczniami moimi, jeśli miłość wzajemną mieć będziecie.

यदि परस्परं प्रेमाचरथ, तर्ह्यनेन सर्व्वे ज्ञास्यन्ति यद् यूयं मम शिष्या इति ।

G'ouaiagi ađ-âqelen irkoul thellam đ-ṭoleba ou, ma thesaâm lmaȟibba b'ouai ḡar aoun.

בְּזֹאת יֵדְעוּ הַכֹּל שֶׁתַּלְמִידַי אַתֶּם: אִם תִּהְיֶה אַהֲבָה בֵּינֵיכֶם.

Daran wird jedermann erkennen, daß ihr meine Jünger seid, wenn ihr Liebe untereinander habt.

[illegible]

Lín nā sa^{n}-thià^{n}, chèng lâng beh tùi án-ni chai lín sī góa ê hák-seng.

Ant to kiekvienas numanys, jus mano mokįtinius esant, jei meilę tarp savęs turite.

اگر آپس میں محبت رکھوگے تو اس سے سب جانینگے کہ تم میرے شاگرد ہو۔

JESUS CHRIST

Preface

Human progress never rolls in on the wheels of inevitability; it comes from the tireless efforts of [people] willing to be co-workers with God, and without this hard work, time itself becomes an ally of the forces of social stagnation.
— *Martin Luther King, Jr.*
Letter from Birmingham Jail, 1963

This book explores how member care is being practiced around the world. There are guidelines, personal accounts, case studies, program descriptions, worksheets, and lots of practical advice. My goal is to further equip sending organizations as they intentionally support their mission/aid personnel. Like many of us, I yearn to see an ongoing, international "flow of care" directed towards those who compassionately toil as "co-workers with God." Such care is especially needed for those who seek to make "human progress" in places where complex humanitarian emergencies and social/spiritual needs abound.

This book is primarily intended for Christians: sending agencies/churches and their staff, training institutions, mission leaders and member care workers, and Christians living overseas in any capacity. Nonetheless, caregivers from the "non-faith-based" humanitarian aid and international health care sectors will find much of the content quite relevant. Religious belief and practice, of course, are extremely important factors in providing meaning and direction to one's life. How well we all know that personal spirituality is often challenged and strengthened as a result of overseas experience. Christian and non-Christian personnel alike often struggle with perplexing existential questions concerning human suffering, traumatic events, and one's understanding of God. So we have much in common as we look after the well-being and quality of life of staff—both local and international staff—regardless of how we approach spiritual matters. I thus ask those from a non-faith or non-Christian background to keep these perspectives in mind as they interact with the material in this book.

It is simply amazing to reflect upon the many developments in the care of mission personnel over the last 10 years. People have formed member care affiliations in different regions and nations around the world. There are various email networks, web sites, and consultations on member care. The Newer Sending Countries, in general, are becoming more actively involved in member care. And a growing body of literature and service organizations are helping to shape and further establish this field.

The overall result, I would say, has been a balanced, seasoned approach to caring for staff, acknowledging the need for supportive care and nurture, while embracing the reality of sacrifice and suffering. Yet in spite of all the advances, there are still organizations and regions which suffer from a dearth of member care understanding and resources. I would also point out the crying need for a more coordinated effort to focus supportive resources on behalf of personnel working among those groups and regions which have historically been the most neglected by the church's mission efforts.

A book of this scope could never be written or edited by just one person. The field is far too broad and the domains of specialist care far too deep. Accordingly, the book has included over 60 international colleagues who have written on topics within their areas of expertise. I feel so honored to have worked with several of them and to have them include their work in this book. Most of the authors had one to three colleagues review their articles. Hence, many eyes besides my own were able to look over and fine-tune the content. Together, we have scouted out and reported on the current international status of member care. The 50 chapters collectively enable us to both scan and gaze into this growing movement. I invite you now to explore the vast terrain of member care and to see how people all over the world are doing good to mission personnel—and doing it well.

Many people have helped me make this book a reality. I want to thank our staff at Le Rucher for their support and prayers during this book project. Specifically, I would like to thank Erik and Jeltje Spruyt, the Directors, for their encouragement; Renée Schudel, Véronique Guérard, Jan Pauw, and Ida Kouassi for their logistical help; and Henny Pauw, Michèle O'Donnell, Daniel Brill, and Denise Brill for their help with reviewing several articles. My sincere gratitude to our supporters too, many of whom have backed us over the past 15 years, especially friends at Calvary Community Church in Westlake Village, California, and Calvary Christian Fellowship in Uncasville, Connecticut.

Thanks also to Bill Taylor and Jonathan Lewis with the World Evangelical Alliance (WEA) Missions Commission for embracing this project. Steve Pillinger with Wycliffe in the United Kingdom—a true scribe of the multilingual Messiah—and the library resources at the World Council of Churches in Switzerland were instrumental in putting together John 13:35 for the Foreword. Eric Holloway, Dona Diehl, and Susan Peterson were all involved in creating and revising the main diagram for the book, which is presented in chapter 1, is included on the first page of each chapter, and is artistically portrayed on the book's front cover. In addition, Susan Peterson, in her usual meticulous and competent way, copy edited and did the final formatting for the whole book. And many thanks also to my colleagues who are part of the various regional member care affiliations, especially Dave Pollock with the WEA Global Member Care Task Force, Polly Chan with the Member Care/Asia Task Force, Harry Hoffmann with the Member Care/Europe group, Márcia Tostes with the COMIBAM Pastoral Care group, and Naomi Famonure with the Member Care Track of the Association of Evangelicals in Africa. What a privilege to work together with you!

Finally, I wish to express my deepest thanks to my family, who faithfully persevered with me during the many long days of compiling and editing this tome. Our girls, Erin and Ashling, and my wife, Michèle, were willing to give up many family times in order to see this book come into being. The Lamb and Shepherd, Jesus Christ, is worthy of our tireless efforts. I treasure being His co-workers with you.

Kelly O'Donnell
Geneva, Switzerland
February, 2002

Introduction

To the Ends of the Earth, To the End of the Age

KELLY O'DONNELL

Doing member care well helps us do missions well. This introduction looks at how member care is both a core strategy and a biblical responsibility for all those involved in missions. In addition to overviewing the book, it defines member care, offers some historical perspectives, reviews missionary attrition, and suggests several future directions for further developing this field. Close relationships, cooperation, sacrifice, and drawing on additional resources outside the mission community are key for supporting personnel around the world.

"I can handle the sickness and the poverty," the mother of four told me as tears welled up in her eyes. "And we are committed to live among this people that we truly love. But I am just not sure if I want my husband to tell me anymore when he receives death threats. Would it not be better if he just kept these to himself?"

There is nothing too glamorous about missions these days—especially missions which target the most historically neglected peoples and places in the world. Like the Muslims and Hindus in the impoverished and conflict-ridden areas of North India. Or the alienated Islamic/animistic Uighur people in the desolate borders of Northwest China. Or the Kurdish refugees who eke out an existence while walking the volatile tightrope between Iraq, Iran, and Turkey. Or in the case described above, in the dry lands of North Africa, where religious and political systems have endeavored to mute the Christian witness for over 1,200 years. Missionaries are committed to going to the ends of the earth to serve such needy people. And member care workers are committed to support them in their efforts as long as it takes, even until the end of the age.

I used to believe that "life was simply difficult," to paraphrase Scott Peck's catchy opener in *The Road Less Traveled* (1978). After 15 years of working overseas and observing some of the darker sides of human existence, I realize that these words are an understatement for many. The greater historical reality, the more accurate axiom, surely is, "Life is often traumatic." The dozens of "wars" that are currently being fought, the estimated 40–50 million refugees, and the countless children that die each year from diseases related to malnutrition give ample testimony to this fact.

It is not that life and missions are always so bleak, of course. Many, many good things are happening! Yet for those of us living in more secure and prosperous settings, the challenge is to counteract our own tendencies to deny or minimize the unpleasant aspects of our global community. We must regularly and soberly acknowledge that there really are large blocks of humankind that dwell beneath the dark shadows of poverty, war, and spiritual bondage: masses of distressed people who do not reside solely in our television sets, newspapers, magazines, counseling offices, or the bracketed-off recesses of our awareness.

As psychologists, my wife, Michèle, and I have been privileged to come alongside and support Christians who have purposefully crossed cultural and language borders in order to alleviate human misery through their compassion and skills, while sharing the hope of the gospel in a sensitive, contextualized manner. In the process, we have met many fine missionaries and member care colleagues, working together with them in several countries and learning from each other. This learning—this multicultural, consolidated learning about survival, health, and growth in challenging mission settings—is recorded in the chapters of this book.

Book Overview

Doing Member Care Well is a compilation of articles and updates on how different organizations and member care workers are doing member care around the world. By "doing" I really mean *proveloping*, a term that I use which is derived from two central processes of member care: *providing* and *developing* resources. Over 60 authors contributed to the book, from both the Newer Sending Countries (NSCs) and the Older Sending Countries (OSCs). I have been especially committed to include material from the NSCs and to use the book as a way to profile their issues and approaches to member care.

The book has 50 chapters and is organized into three parts:

- *The Member Care Context*—articles on the book's main model for member care, the flow of care, a missions review, and perspectives on suffering/martyrdom (five articles).
- *Regional Issues and Insights*—articles about mission personnel from Asia, South Asia, Africa, Latin America, and the Arabic World (15 articles).
- *Providing and Developing Member Care*—articles categorized in five sections according to the book's member care model: Master care, self/mutual care, sender care, specialist care, and network care (30 articles).

Many of these chapters overlap in content, a reflection of the way in which member care has developed and is practiced. Hence, several chapters could be easily placed in more than one section of the book. An example would be chapter 41 by Annemie Grosshauser, "Supporting Expatriate Women in Difficult Settings." The subject matter deals with single/married women's issues, spiritual warfare, counseling, and work in Asia. Thus, it could be included in the sections on Family/MKs, Pastoral/Spiritual, Counseling/Psychological, and Asia.

There are five "reflection and discussion" items at the end of most chapters. These are important helps for readers to interact with and apply the material. I especially want to encourage readers to select some of the most relevant articles for your setting and then read/discuss them with colleagues.

This volume builds upon several previous books, including *Honourably Wounded* (Foyle, 2001), *Helping Missionaries Grow* (O'Donnell & O'Donnell, 1988), *Missionary Care* (O'Donnell, 1992c), *Too Valuable to Lose* (Taylor, 1997), and *Raising Resilient MKs* (Bowers, 1998). It also builds upon various special journal issues dealing with member care, such as the *International Journal of Frontier Missions* (October 1995), the *Journal of Psychology and Theology*,

(1983, 1987, 1993, 1999), and the *Indian Journal of Missiology* (October 1998). These materials, when added to the dissertations/theses and the many articles from journals/conference proceedings, form a substantial body of knowledge which has significantly shaped this emerging field of missions. (See chapter 50 for an annotated listing of a number of member care books from around the globe.)

Although most of this written material has come from OSC authors, there is a steady stream of materials—mostly articles—coming from NSC regions. This book includes some of these articles, most of which are usually available only at the regional level, as well as new articles by both NSC and OSC authors alike. My goal is not to produce a comprehensive compendium, but rather a selective sampling of helpful member care perspectives and practices. The result, I believe, is a truly international work, filled with updates and practical applications, which is relevant for personnel from different organizations and different nations. As a whole, the book is a reflection of the many intertwining facets and faces of the growing field of member care.

I wish that there were more space for other fine articles, from NSC and OSC authors, from the field of human resource development, and from the experience of the Catholic and Eastern churches. It could be that the way forward is to share these and other articles through an international member care journal, both hardcopy and online. The field is broad, there are many practitioners, and we need some new forums for regularly sharing important news and ideas.

Some More Distinctives of *Doing Member Care Well*

In addition to the NSC and international emphases in developing this book, I was also guided by the idea of the non-primacy of any single specialty domain for member care. Mental health has an essential role, as do medical care, logistical support, personnel management, and pastoral nurture. Hence, this book intentionally includes material from a variety of member care colleagues, including pastors, personnel development specialists, church leaders, physicians, psychologists, and missionaries themselves. Further, many authors not only share about their respective topics, but they also add a personal touch as they share their hearts for mission personnel, national Christians, and the unreached.

Another distinctive of the book stems from my concern that any good movement, such as the international member care field, can stagnate or become "institutionalized." To avoid or at least help minimize this process, I have long sensed a need to incorporate new voices and fresh input for member care from both inside and outside the evangelical missions community. I thus earnestly endeavored to launch into and learn from new areas as I prepared this book, pushing the usual borders of member care into several additional realms:

- The international health care communities and non-government organizations in the humanitarian aid sector.
- Spiritual warfare as it relates to the personal life and ministry of member care workers as well as to mission personnel.
- The member care needs of nationals/locals who are the focus of missionary service.
- Applications from personnel programs within the military.
- Emphases on human rights and religious liberty advocacy.
- Trauma care and contingency management approaches.
- Information from the field of human resource development.
- Perhaps above all, a balanced perspective on the cost of missions, including martyrdom, informed by 2,000 years of the church's sacrificial commitment to take the gospel compassionately to the unreached.

There is one final feature which marks this book. Perhaps I am saving what I think is the best for the last! It is the five-sphere model of care that has been used to categorize the 30 articles in Part 3 of the book. This model is described in detail in chapter 1, and it is reproduced on the first page of each chapter. It is also artistically represented on the cover of the book (embedded in generic motifs from different macro-cultures). I believe this model reflects a close approximation of a truly *trans-cultural tool* (one which is relevant across organizational and cultural boundaries) as well as a *trans-conceptual tool* (one which is relevant across member care philosophies and member care programs). It reflects the breadth of member care (e.g., the five spheres of care discussed in this book), as well as the depth of skills needed to provide specialist services well (including character and compassion in addition to competence). Over the last two years, the model has been reviewed and adjusted by several colleagues around the globe. It also appeared in two issues of *Evangelical Missions Quarterly* (January and April 2001). Does it meet up to its trans-cultural and trans-conceptual aspirations? Time will tell. Undoubtedly, though, it will be built upon and further contextualized in the days ahead.

There are, then, several core, intertwining distinctives of the book. These include the international platform for the NSCs and OSCs to share their experiences; the pooled wisdom from a wide variety of member care practitioners; the refreshing sense of the authors sharing their hearts with us; the timely venture into additional areas of member care which take into consideration current socio-political and historical realities; and a comprehensive model applicable to many settings. The articles collectively provide a clear picture of how the member care field is maturing as an interdisciplinary, international, and indispensable handmaiden to missions.

Background Perspectives for Member Care

The development of member care really has its origins in the biblical admonitions to "love one another" (John 13:34-35), "bear one another's burdens" (Gal. 6:2), and scores of similar "one another" verses that fill the New Testament (see Jones & Jones, 1995, pp. 160-162). Member care, in this sense, is nothing new. Yet what is new is the more organized attempt to develop comprehensive, sustainable member care approaches to support cross-cultural Christian workers.

I define member care in this way:

> *Member care is the ongoing investment of resources by mission agencies, churches, and other mission organizations for the nurture and development of missionary personnel. It focuses on everyone in missions (missionaries, support staff, children, and families) and does so over the course of the missionary life cycle, from recruitment through retirement.*

Member care is also the responsibility of everyone in missions—sending church, mission agency, fellow workers, and member care specialists. The word "member" implies belonging. So member care includes the sense of community, along with the attendant mutual responsibility for care between those who belong to a group (e.g., a sending organization or colleagues in a specific setting).

Another key source of member care is the mutually supportive relationships which missionaries form with those in the host culture. Whatever the source, the goal is to develop godly character, inner strength, and skills to help personnel remain effective in their work. Member care, then, is as much about developing inner resources within individuals as it is about providing external resources to support them in their work.

At the personal level, each individual must find a balance between the realities of suffering/sacrifice and the normal desires for personal growth/fulfillment. At the agency level, we must harmonize the organizational emphasis on "achievement/task" with the staff needs for "support/member care." For some, the greatest stress results from a poor fit between one's background and preferences with the type of agency ethos—the "established way of doing things." For others, it is from the more common or anticipated stressors, such as cross-cultural adjustment. Different cultures/settings emphasize different aspects of member care too, such as the role of mutual support in a community context or the need for self-support/fortitude for those in demanding or isolated locations.

Some brief examples will give us an appreciation of the significance and diversity of the member care field:

■ Doing team building sessions in Central Asia to help a multinational team work through conflict in their goal differences, decision making preferences, and worship style.

■ Setting up an interagency missionary health care team in India to provide counseling, medical screening, and consultation to national and expatriate missionaries.

■ Encouraging missionary families in Indonesia to avail themselves of local hospitality and to form supportive friendships with at least two national families.

■ Running a reentry program for missionary children who will be returning to Europe in order to attend university.

■ Inviting two trusted pastors to a missionary center in South America for several days of ministry through Bible teaching and encouragement.

■ Meeting regularly for prayer and mutual support as part of a commitment between two missionary couples living in a large city of North Africa.

■ Organizing a team of caregivers in Europe to resource a mission agency's annual conference via counseling, seminars, and consultation.

■ Offering an informal retreat for "workers" from different Christian aid agencies in a safe and relaxing location outside a war zone in the Middle East.

■ Consulting with the missions departments of local churches in NSCs such as Singapore, Brazil, or Nigeria, as they develop logistical support for their missionaries, including help with visas, children's education, medical insurance, and travel arrangements.

Some Personal Perspectives

A pivotal point in my own member care involvement was at the Mental Health and Missions Conference, held each November in Indiana (USA). This conference has been an oasis of inspiration for me and many others over the last three decades. Here, at a beautiful inn set in a national park, mental health professionals along with missionaries, church/mission leaders, graduate students, and member care workers come together for networking, training, and mutual support. This conference has sparked many a vision to work in member care and has served as a tangible rallying point for this field within the United States. Over the years, many have yearned to see similar gatherings take root in other places of the world—and indeed this is happening!

It was during the 1990 conference when I was most deeply touched. The conference theme that year dealt with intervention models for helping missionaries, and the presentations were excellent. Surprisingly, though, as the conference was drawing to a close, I found myself becoming uneasy. Something was stirring within me which was hard to put into words. By the end of the last presentation, I was able to clarify my sense of unsettledness. It was an awareness that something important needed to be added to the methods and models we were discussing—not just there at the conference, but in the general member care community as well. And then suddenly, from my heart shot out a verbal plea to all of us there: *"We must move beyond the individual, family, and agency approaches to care, and develop a more systematic, global, cooperative approach to providing member care. We must develop a **macro-model** for member care."*

Shortly after the conference, I began to write down my thoughts concerning this macro-model—of how to further develop member care globally. In the summer of 1992, I published my ideas in an article for the *International Journal of Frontier Missions* (O'Donnell, 1992a) and in the book *Missionary Care* (O'Donnell, 1992b). I called the article, "An Agenda for Member Care in Missions." Following are a few excerpts from the final section (O'Donnell, 1992b, pp. 296, 297). These principles continue to have a profound influence on me, and they have guided my work in "proveloping" member care in missions.

- "The member care momentum in missions today is most heartening. Yet there must be a direction for this momentum: to prioritize and channel member care resources towards those working among the least evangelized."
- "Further developing this field is not something to be left up to chance. Neither is it the responsibility of a single conference nor a periodic meeting where member care issues are addressed. Rather, mutual consultation, coordinated efforts, perseverance, and interdependency are to be the guiding principles."
- "Member care must keep in stride with current missions thinking and realities. The missions force is rapidly expanding, a fact which is especially true for missionaries from the Two-Thirds World. This expansion must be mirrored within the global missions community by developing appropriate, comprehensive member care programs and services."
- "Finally, I am convinced that the time has come to actively pull together the various pockets of member care workers around the world. It is also time to systematically train and mobilize many others for this strategic ministry. And the time is here for anointed leaders to step forward and help steer this field in response to the Lord's direction."

These visionary comments were neither unrealistic nor without precedent. Cooperative endeavors were and have been on the rise. In fact, this book is a tangible expression of the above aspirations for coordinated efforts, comprehensive programs, mobilization, and leadership which I shared some 10 years ago! To get a better historical feel for some of the member care developments, refer to chapter 48 of this book, as well as chapter 22 in Bill Taylor's (1997) edited work on missionary attrition, *Too Valuable to Lose*.

Will We Depart in Peace or in Pieces? Revisiting Attrition

As a prelude to launching into the 50 chapters of this book, it would be important to summarize some of the major findings of the World Evangelical Fellowship's (WEF—now called the World Evangelical Alliance) attrition study upon which *Too Valuable to Lose* was based. *Doing Member Care Well* is a natural extension of *Too Valuable to Lose*, and together they represent some of the best international sources of information on missionary adjustment and member care strategies.

The Three Ps of Attrition

Basically, the WEF study found the overall annual attrition rate to be 5.1% for the 453 mission societies that were surveyed. When items such as normal retirement and possible transfer to another agency were ferreted out, the bottom line figure becomes 3.1%—attrition that is "undesirable" because it is *premature*, *preventable*, and likely *permanent*. Think of this as the *3Ps of the 3%*, to help remember the findings.

In real person terms, this may mean that over 12,000 missionaries are lost each year out of the global missionary pool of about 425,000 (both Catholic and Protestant) (Barrett & Johnson, 2001). Such undesirable attrition also spills onto others, negatively impacting thousands of family members and friends in the home and host communities.

More Results

So why do missionaries leave the field? In the WEF study, the main reasons were, in order, normal retirement (9.4%), children's issues, change of job, health problems, lack of home support, problems with peers, personal concerns, disagreement with agency, lack of commitment, and lack of call (4.1%). Note that those surveyed in this study were mission administrators such as personnel directors, rather than the actual missionaries themselves.

Several important comparisons were also made between different groups of missionaries:

■ Missionaries from the NSCs (e.g., Korea, Brazil, Nigeria) were a bit more at risk for "preventable" attrition than those from the OSCs (e.g., UK, USA, Australia).

■ Reasons for overall annual attrition between NSCs and OSCs were very different. For NSCs, the top reasons were reported to be lack of home support (8.1%), lack of call (8.0%), inadequate commitment (7.3%), disagreement with agency (6.1%), problems with peers (5.7%), and health problems (5.1%). For OSCs, the top reasons were normal retirement (13.2%), children (10.1%), change of job (8.9%), health problems (8.4%), problems with peers (6.0%), and personal concerns (5.2%).

■ In general, the larger and older the mission society, the lower the preventable attrition rate.

■ Those who worked in their own culture versus cross-culturally had almost the same preventable attrition rates.

■ Workers in pioneer/church planting settings had lower preventable attrition rates than those in relief and development settings.

To continue, the most important factor in preventing attrition was reported to be the missionary having a clear call. This was then followed by having a supportive family, healthy spirituality, cultural adaptation, good relationships, pastoral care, and financial provision. Interestingly, a key component of pastoral care was the "regular communication" that occurred for field workers, which was rated even higher than pastoral visits or pre-field training (which are also very important).

Some Suggestions

How can we best make use of these findings? And how do we reduce our attrition rates? This is where "the rubber meets the road" and what *Too Valuable to Lose* and *Doing Member Care Well* are all about. There's no way around it: We in missions must commit ourselves to more comprehensive, culturally sensitive approaches to sustain and nurture our personnel over the long haul. This means we must prioritize time and finances for our personnel. It also calls for serious reflection on our member care approaches, mutual consultation on developing our care, and participative reviews of the quality of life for/by our mission personnel.

Who will do all this care? Leaders (church and mission) who make time for their people. People like personnel development specialists, field directors, pastors, strategy coaches, and cross-cultural trainers, who are available to support and further equip our workers. And finally, colleagues and friends—you and me—whose mutual encouragement provides the backbone for effective member care programs.

The findings from the WEF study, along with the material in this book, highlight the need for sending groups to support mission personnel in these ways:

■ Clarify and grow in the sense of call.

■ Prepare realistically through good pre-field selection and training.

■ Cultivate their walk with the Lord.

■ Stay connected with supportive friends and family.

■ Care for their children's educational and developmental needs.

■ Improve interpersonal, conflict resolution, and ministry-related skills.

■ Raise finances for long-term involvement.

■ Maintain good communication with leaders and peers.

■ Understand service opportunities and career development possibilities.

■ Prioritize language/culture learning.

■ Connect with leaders/mentors who can help them negotiate the missions world.

■ Receive helpful member care resources during the course of their missionary lives.

■ Go through exit interviews/follow-up for greater closure on their missions experience.

Attrition, historically, has been part of the cost the church has paid for penetrating the Enemy's darkness. People in battle are vulnerable and inevitably get hurt. Our weaknesses as people and as sending agencies also make us vulnerable. So let's put attrition in perspective. Whether it be considered preventable or unpreventable, desirable or undesirable, *missionary* attrition happens as we work together to prevent the *eternal* attrition which hovers over the unreached peoples of the earth.

Too bad there is no attrition vaccination. However, discussing the above issues and suggestions with others will definitely help. Why not review the WEF study and a few chapters of the book *Too Valuable to Lose* with your colleagues? It would be good to do this as you are reading through the various chapters of this present book. Keep at it until you find practical ways to apply the material. This will be one of your greatest aids for preventing undesirable attrition!

Future Directions: PACTS

There is a purpose to human history—it is not random—and there will be a conclusion to this age, for the glory of God. God is at work in history to redeem people from every nation, tribe, and tongue (Rev. 5:9-10). Member care, as a service ministry which supports the missions task, is a means to this end.

Developing member care well is a process. We cannot expect, for example, younger sending groups to develop in just a few years what has taken other sending groups several years to achieve. It will take time and toil to "knit the net"—the net of caregivers, the net of concepts, the net of organizational member care culture, the net of communication, the net of centers/hubs, and the net of consultations. But it is happening!

I believe that there must be an intentional and Spirit-led direction as to how this global member care net is developed. Here are five such directions—PACTS—which will help us to work together and further "provelop" member care. PACTS involve forming close relationships with colleagues as we pursue cooperative tasks with each other.

Pioneering. Is it time to break out of some member care and missions bubbles? Yes indeed! We must go to places with relatively few member care resources. Prioritize those working among the least evangelized peoples. Innovate! Stretch! Help set up interagency member care teams, for instance, in Central Asia, India, or Africa. Sure, it would be challenging, but why not? Or how about helping to connect culturally sensitive member care workers with the many interagency partnerships ministering within the 10/40 Window? For some examples, see chapters 12, 14, and 41.

Affiliations. Bring together member care workers for mutual projects, mutual support, and mutual consultation. Purposefully affiliate! Set up regional or organizational networks of caregivers. Specialists can likewise band together for personal and professional support—physicians in travel/tropical medicine, personnel directors, crisis caregivers, etc. Form short-term teams with members from different agencies or service groups. Encourage their members to track with mission personnel over time. In addition, convene and attend strategic consultations of mission personnel and/or member care workers to discuss ways to coordinate services further. These can be small and informal or larger and more formal. Prioritize these for regions of the world where coordination is still really needed. Africa is a prime example. Finally, consider forming a national or regional member care task force within your organization or interagency, similar to the various ones that are described in chapters 13 and 48.

Continuing Growth/Care. Member care is an interdisciplinary field, requiring considerable effort to keep abreast of new developments and to maintain one's skills. Prioritize time to read, attend seminars, and upgrade (see the materials listed in chapter 50). Grow! It would be helpful for some to link with a few of the secular umbrella agencies like the World Health Organization and the International Union of Psychological Science as a way to network and keep abreast of current trends (see Pawlik & Ydewalle, 1996). Build connections and bridge gaps between the "faith-based" and "non-faith-based" organizations involved in international health, exchanging information on the management and support of personnel. Some examples would be attending conferences, reading journals, and reviewing the peer support network and psycho-social support program for staff offered by humanitarian aid organizations (see chapters 27 and 35). We must not become isolated by interacting solely with the evangelical community. Also, member care can be a burnout profession. So we must maintain accountability with others, pace ourselves, find ways to "refuel" emotionally, seek God, and practice what we preach!

Training. Resource missionaries and member care workers alike via workshops at conferences. Impart both your skills and your life (1 Thess. 2:8)! Include member care tracks at major conferences. Teach member care courses, seminars, and modules at key graduate schools/seminaries, including the Bible colleges in Africa and India and the missionary training centers in Asia and Latin America. Training in peer counseling, marriage enrichment, family life, team building, spiritual warfare, and crisis intervention are especially important (see chapters 15, 16, and 37 for examples). Further, help mission personnel from both NSCs and OSCs develop member care skills (e.g., by attending the "Sharpening Your Interpersonal Skills" courses that are taught in many places). Also assist in developing member care programs which are culturally relevant. There could be opportunities to join with groups such as Youth With A Mission and Operation Mobilization, which offer counseling courses in different locations to train their missionaries in helping skills, or the Operation Impact program at Azusa Pacific University, which provides various field-based courses in the area of leadership development.

Special Projects. Based on strategic needs and common interests, pursue some short-term and longer-term projects together. Fill in member care gaps! Some current projects that are being done include maintaining and updating a global referral base of member care organizations (chapter 49) along with a global member care website (www. membercare.org); supporting the efforts of groups such as Trans World Radio's "Member Care Radio," which broadcasts encouraging programs for field workers; doing joint research/articles; and setting up member care hubs/groups in needed areas (e.g., Thailand, Cyprus, India, Africa). Let us be sure to pursue some projects together where we get a bit "dirty"—and take some risks. A cutting-edge example would be to provide supportive services—critical incident debriefing, counseling, reconciliation seminars—to people who have been traumatized by war and natural disasters (see chapters 20, 25, 43, and 47). In short: be proactive; do not reinvent the wheel; pursue God's heart for the unreached peoples; and prioritize time to work on strategic, doable, field-related projects.

Final Thoughts

Doing member care well helps us to do missions well. It strengthens missionaries so that they can effectively love, evangelize, and disciple people groups; endure hardship; and grow as people. It is a pioneering, practical, and deeply personal ministry. Doing member care well is a direct and strategic way to fulfill the Abrahamic Covenant of Genesis 12, along with both the Great Commandment and the Great Commission. That is to say, God blesses us and thus we bless others, especially those who bring the blessings of God to the unreached.

Tolkein (1965, p. 325) has said it well:
"Everything that is gold does not glitter.
Not all those who wander are lost.
The old that is strong does not wither.
Deep roots are not reached by the frost."

In the world of missions and member care, some of the choicest servants are unheard of, not necessarily professionally trained, and not usually invited to be plenary speakers at conferences. But they are solid gold—they sparkle internally, privately, out of the limelight; and they are sturdy folk, with deep roots in God, putting into practice the biblical call to "love one another." It is not the member care specialists—as important as these are—who are the main practitioners of member care, even though some of them might be leading the member care charge. Rather, it is the missiological equivalent of "the average person on the street"—the missionary on the field. Herein lies the backbone and the future of member care: mutual support and spiritual nurture among missionaries, and between missionaries and the people to whom they are called. We member care workers primarily polish the gold that is already there. May God give us grace to follow their examples of sacrifice. And may we do our part in supporting them in their most holy work, serving with them unto the ends of the earth and until the end of the age.

References

Barrett, D., & Johnson, T. (2001). Status of global mission. *International Bulletin of Missionary Research, 25*, 24-25.

Bowers, J. (Ed.). (1998). *Raising resilient MKs*. Colorado Springs, CO: ACSI.

Foyle, M. (2001). *Honourably wounded: Stress for Christian workers*. London, UK: Monarch Books.

Indian Missiology Association. (1998, October). *Indian Journal of Missiology*. Special issue on "Care of the Missionary Family."

International Journal of Frontier Missions. (1995, October). Special issue on "Member Care."

Jones, G., & Jones, R. (1995). *Teamwork*. London, UK: Scripture Union.

Journal of Psychology and Theology. (1983, 1987, 1994, 1997). Special issues on "Mental Health and Missions."

Neely, A. (1995). *Christian mission: A case study approach*. Maryknoll, NY: Orbis Books.

O'Donnell, K. (1992a). An agenda for member care in frontier missions. *International Journal of Frontier Missions, 9*, 95-100.

———. (1992b). An agenda for member care in missions. In K. O'Donnell (Ed.), *Missionary care: Counting the cost for world evangelization* (pp. 286-298). Pasadena, CA: William Carey Library.

———. (Ed.). (1992c). *Missionary care: Counting the cost for world evangelization*. Pasadena, CA: William Carey Library.

———. (2001a). Touring the terrain: An international sampler of member care literature. *Evangelical Missions Quarterly, 37*, 18-29.

———. (2001b). Going global: A member care model for best practice. *Evangelical Missions Quarterly, 37*, 212-222.

O'Donnell, K., & O'Donnell, M. (Eds.). (1988). *Helping missionaries grow: Readings in mental health and missions*. Pasadena, CA: William Carey Library.

Pawlik, K., & Ydewalle, G. (1996). Psychology and the global commons: Perspectives of international psychology. *American Psychologist, 51*, 488-495.

Peck, S. (1978). *The road less traveled*. New York, NY: Simon & Schuster.

Taylor, W. (Ed.). (1997). *Too valuable to lose: Exploring the causes and curês of missionary attrition*. Pasadena, CA: William Carey Library.

Tolkein, J. (1965). *The fellowship of the ring*. New York, NY: Ballantine Books.

*Portions of this introduction were adapted from "Member Care in Missions: Global Perspectives and Future Directions" (**Journal of Psychology and Theology**, 1997, vol. 25, pp. 143-154) and "Will We Depart in Peace or Pieces?" (**International YWAMer**, October 1998, p. 18). Used by permission.*

Part 1
The Member Care Context

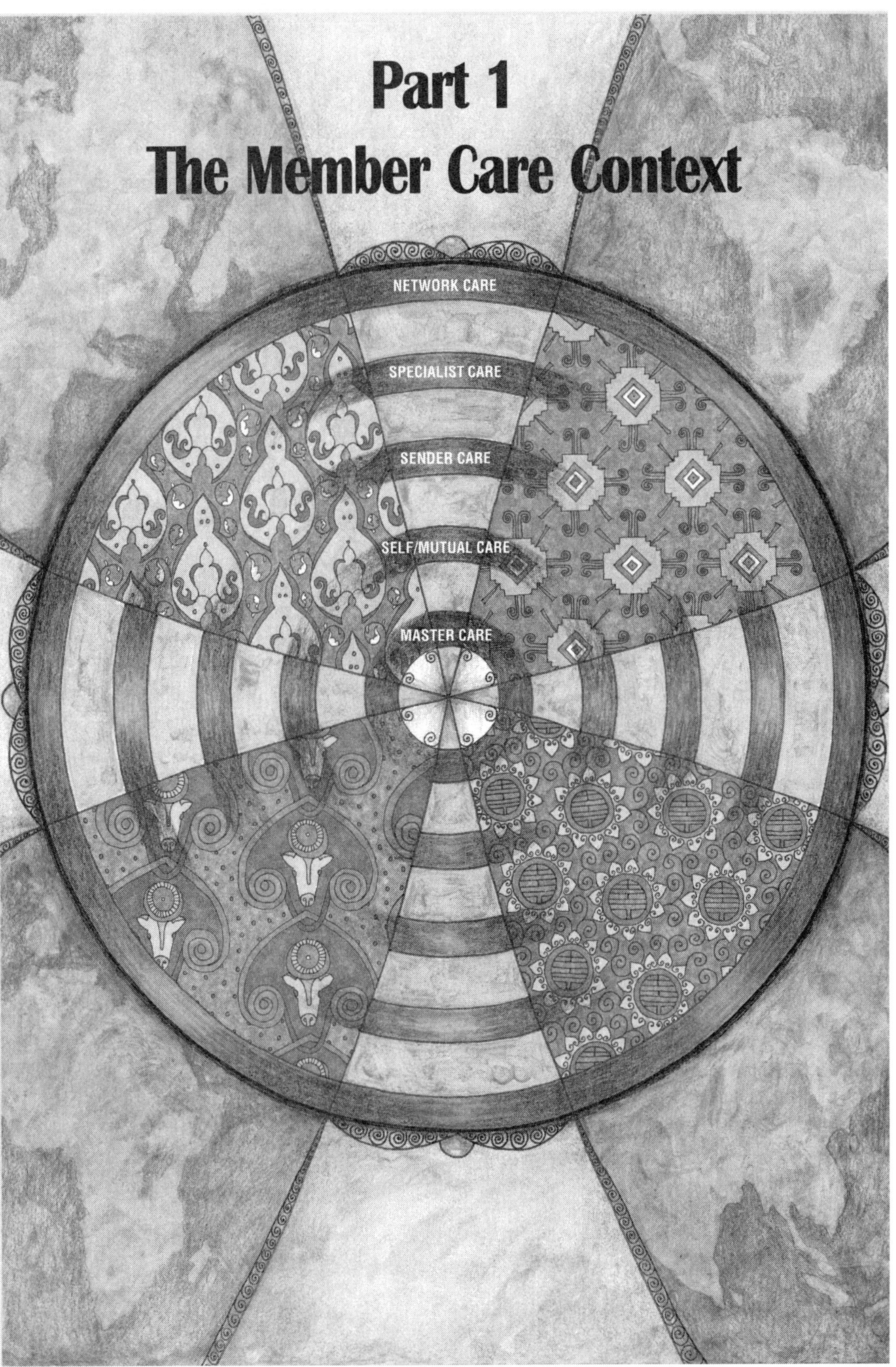

1

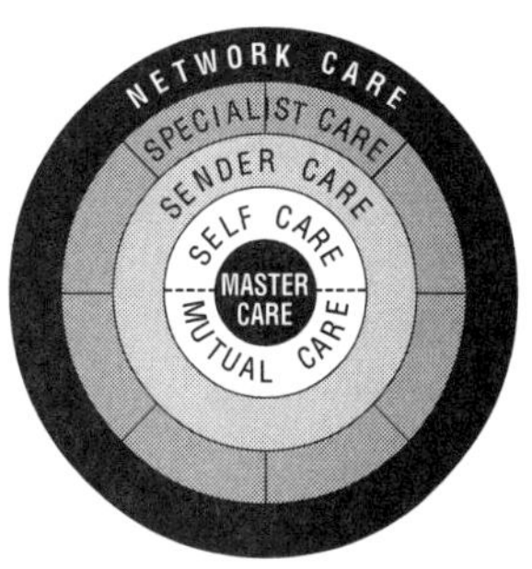

Going Global: A Member Care Model For Best Practice

KELLY O'DONNELL

Is a user-friendly, transcultural framework possible for understanding and practicing member care? And what are some of the core best practice principles that are relevant across many national and organizational cultures? I launched out to explore these questions, pulling together some of the consolidated learning in this field and calling upon 25 reviewers from around the globe to help refine the resulting best practice model for member care. This model can serve as "a grid to guide and a guide to goad."

Member care is going international! Over the past five years (1997–2001), for example, interagency consultations on missionary care have taken place in India, Pakistan, Singapore, Malaysia, the Philippines, the Netherlands, Germany, France, Hungary, Côte d'Ivoire, Cameroon, New Zealand, USA, Peru, and Brazil. It is especially encouraging to see caregivers emerging from the Newer Sending Countries and their efforts to develop culturally relevant resources. Email forums, web sites, written materials, interagency task forces, and missions conferences enable these and other member care personnel around the globe to communicate and contribute. The member care field is truly maturing. It is developing as an interdisciplinary and international handmaiden to promote the resiliency and effectiveness of mission personnel, from recruitment through retirement.

Best Practice and Member Care

In this article, we will take a fresh look at the basic contours of care needed in missionary life. The aim is to present a practical, "best practice" model to support mission personnel from different organizations and nations. The ideas that I present are based on the shared, practical experience of many colleagues working in this field. Although the article is conceptual in nature, most readers will find the material easily applicable.

"Best practice" is a term used by many human service organizations. An equivalent term also in use is "good practice." The term refers to recognized principles and performance standards for the management and support of staff. These principles are written, public statements which are formed, adopted, distributed, and reviewed by several organizations. Each organization voluntarily signs and holds itself accountable to these principles. Organizations can further adjust the principles according to their settings and ethos. "Key indicators" are also identified which serve as criteria to measure the extent to which each principle is being put into practice.

As an example, consider two of the seven principles from the People In Aid's (1997, pp. 9, 10, 23) *Code of Best Practice*. A few key indicators follow in parentheses.

> **Principle 1:** The people who work for us are integral to our effectiveness and success.... Human resource issues are integral to our strategic plans. (The Chief Executive or Chair has made a written and public commitment to the Code; the agency allocates resources to enable its managers to meet staff support, training, and development needs.) ...
>
> **Principle 7:** We take all reasonable steps to insure staff security and well-being. We recognize that the work of relief and development agencies often places great demands on staff in conditions of complexity and risk. (Programme plans include written assessment of security and health risks specific to country or region; the agency maintains records of work-related injuries, accidents, and fatalities and uses these records to help assess and reduce future risk to field staff.)

Best practice per se has been spearheaded by various sources, one of them being the humanitarian aid community. It emerged from the felt need for agreed-upon guidelines to raise the work quality of non-governmental organizations (NGOs) as they provide relief services, relate to one another, and care for their staff—often in stressful/dangerous situations (Leader, 1999; McConnan, 2000). Best practice also arose within the national and international health care communities, where guidelines for providing health care services were needed, based on research and expert consensus (Beutler, 2000). One example is the *Guidelines for Assessing and Treating Anxiety Disorders* (1998) by the New Zealand National Health Committee. Another is the *Practice Guidelines for the Treatment of Patients With Schizophrenia* (1997) by the American Psychiatric Association.

Best practice is a relatively new term within Evangelical missions, although the underlying emphasis on the quality of care has been part of Evangelical missions thinking and practice for some time. Specific examples would be the emphasis on providing proactive care to all mission personnel (e.g., Gardner, 1987) and the need to develop ethical guidelines for member care practice (e.g., Hall & Barber, 1996; O'Donnell & O'Donnell, 1992). What is new and quite helpful, though, is the emphasis on publicly stating specific commitments to staff care in the form of written principles and evaluation criteria (key indicators), to which a sending agency voluntarily subscribes and is willing to be held accountable. This, in my estimation, is the greatest contribution of the current best practice context to member care in missions.

One example of best practice in missions is the best practice document (consisting of 15 principles and several key indicators) which emerged from the 2000 Roundtable Discussion in Toronto, sponsored by the Evangelical Fellowship of Canada Task Force for Global Mission and the Tyndale Intercultural Ministry Centre (see chapter 26). Another good example is the *Code of Best Practice in Short-Term Mission*, developed in 1997 by Global Connections, the main association for Evangelical missions in the United Kingdom. This code has been embraced by several mission agencies in the United Kingdom. Being a signatory is not an indication of current achievement in meeting the code, but rather of one's aspirations to fulfill the principles. Table 1 is taken from section 3 of the code (see chapter

Table 1
Field Management and Pastoral Care Principles*

- Clear task aims and objectives and, where appropriate, a job description will be provided.
- There will be clear lines of authority, supervision, communication, responsibility, and accountability. Communication and reporting will be regular.
- Pastoral care and support structures will be established. The respective responsibilities of the sending church, sending organization, host organization/local church, and team leader/job supervisor/line manager/pastoral overseer/mentor will be made clear to all parties.
- Opportunities for personal and spiritual development will be provided.
- Participants will be given guidelines on behavior and relationships.
- With reference to above items, culturally appropriate ways of fulfilling these matters will be sought.
- Procedures covering health care and insurance, medical contingencies, security and evacuation, stress management and conflict resolution, misconduct, discipline, and grievances will be established, communicated, and implemented as appropriate.

* Global Connections, 1997.

26), covering field management and pastoral care.

I see best practice as being rooted in the example of the loving care offered by Christ, the "Best Practitioner" (O'Donnell, 1999a). Our Lord's model of relationship with us serves as a foundation for our interaction with others and for the best practice principles that we develop for member care (see Figure 1). The middle two dimensions of being comforted and challenged are normative for us and reflect many of Christ's encounters with disciples in the New Testament. Jesus is both tender and at times tough in His relentless love for us. The extremes on the continuum would represent "worst practice" and do not represent Christ's relationship with His people. Likewise, they should not reflect our relationship with mission personnel—that is, overly protecting them and not sufficiently challenging them (coddling) or blaming them for having needs and frailties (condemning). Member care, then, is as much about comfort as it is about challenge. It involves lots of hugs with some kicks (culturally appropriate forms) and lots of affirmation with some admonition (1 Thess. 5:11, 14).

Overview of the Member Care Model

The basic member care model was developed by Dave Pollock and me, with some initial help from Marjory Foyle. It consists of five permeable spheres which are able to flow into and influence each other (see Figure 2). At the core of the model are the two foundational spheres of *master care* and *self/mutual care*. These are encircled by a middle linking

Figure 1
Christ's Love Relationship With Us: A Foundation for Best Practice

	JESUS CHRIST AS BEST PRACTITIONER		
Coddler	COMFORTER	CHALLENGER	Condemner
Placater	PEACE-GIVER	PROVOKER	Punisher
(worst practice)	(best practice)	(best practice)	(worst practice)

Figure 2
A Best Practice Model of Member Care

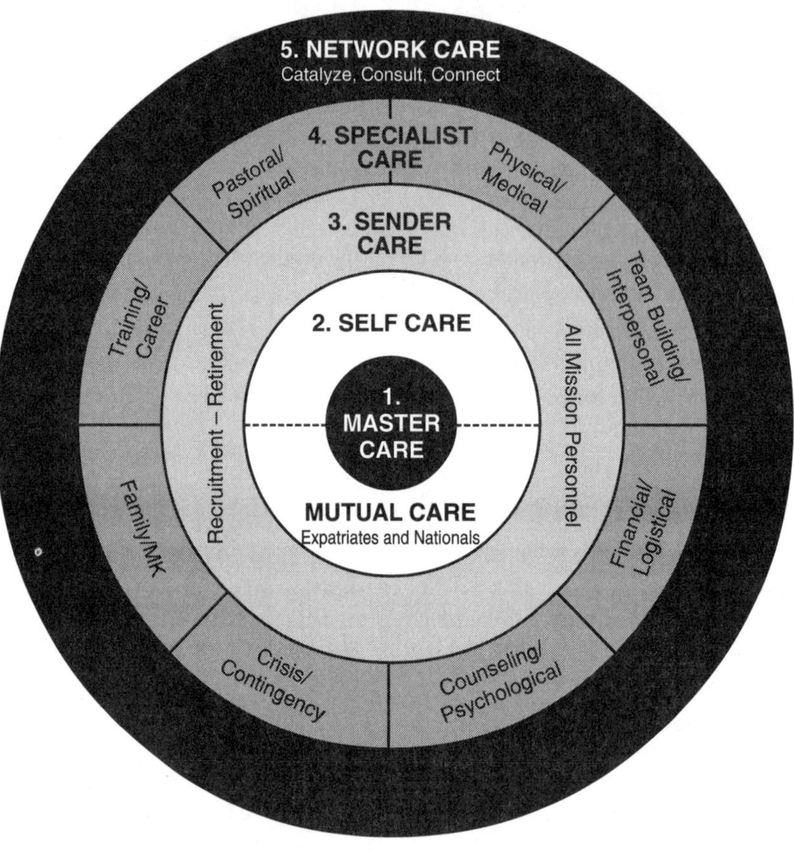

sphere called *sender care* and then surrounded by the two outer spheres of *specialist care* and *network care*. Member care specialists and networks stimulate the care offered by the other spheres.

Each sphere includes a summary best practice principle related to the overall "flow of care" needed for staff longevity (Pollock, 1997): *the flow of Christ, the flow of community, the flow of commitment, the flow of caregivers, and the flow of connections*. Note that the flow of care is initiated by both oneself and others and that it is always a two-way street. Supportive care thus flows into the life of mission personnel, so that effective ministry and care can flow out from their lives. Such a flow of care is needed due to the many cares and the assortment of "characters" in mission life!

The model includes the *sources* of member care, such as pastors from sending churches and mutual care between colleagues, and the *types* of member care, such as medical and debriefing care. Think of it as a tool that can be used by individuals, agencies, service organizations, and regions. The model is a flexible framework to help raise the standards for the appropriate care and development of mission personnel. Use it as "a grid to guide and a guide to goad." Here is an overview of the model along with the five best practice principles:

Sphere 1: Master Care

Care from and care for the Master—the "heart" of member care.

■ *From the Master*—the renewing relationship with the Lord and our identity as His cherished children, cultivated by the spiritual disciplines (e.g., prayer, worship) and Christian community, which help us run with endurance and enter His rest (Heb. 12:1, 2; Heb. 4:9-11).

■ *For the Master*—the renewal and purpose that derive from trusting/worshipping the Lord, serving Him in our work, often sacrificially, and knowing that we please Him (Col. 3:23, 24).

Best Practice Principle 1: The Flow of Christ

Our relationship with Christ is fundamental to our well-being and work effectiveness. Member care resources strengthen our relationship to the Lord and help us to encourage others in the Lord. As we serve/wait on Him, He in turn promises to serve/wait on us (Luke 17:5-10; Luke 12:35-40). A "look to God only/endure by yourself" emphasis for weathering the ups and downs of mission life is not normative, although it is sometimes necessary (2 Tim. 4:16-18).

Sphere 2: Self and Mutual Care

Care from oneself and from relationships within the expatriate, home, and national communities—the "backbone" of member care.

■ *Self care*—the responsibility of individuals to provide wisely for their own well-being.

■ *Expatriate, home, and national communities*—the support, encouragement, correction, and accountability that we give to and receive from colleagues and family members (see the "one another" verses in the New Testament—a list of these is in Jones & Jones, 1995) and the mutually supportive relationships that we intentionally build with nationals/locals, which help us connect with the new culture, get our needs met, and adjust/grow (Larson, 1992).

Best Practice Principle 2: The Flow of Community

Self care is basic to good health. Self-awareness, monitoring one's needs, a commitment to personal development, and seeking help when needed are signs of maturity. Likewise, quality relationships with family and friends are necessary for our health and productivity. Relationships require work, and they are not always readily available nor easy to develop in various settings. Nonetheless, staff are encouraged to form/maintain close and accountable friendships with those in one's home culture and in the host culture. Colleagues who love and are loved form a key part of the "continuum of care" needed for longevity, ranging from the informal care offered by peers to the more formal care provided by professionals.

Sphere 3: Sender Care

Care from sending groups (church and agency) for all mission personnel from recruitment through retirement—"sustainers" of member care.

■ *All mission personnel*—includes children, families, and home office staff, in addition to the "primary service providers" such as church planters, trainers, and field-based administrators.

■ *Recruitment through retirement*—includes specific supportive care coordinated by the sending church/agency throughout the life span and significant transitions:

- Pre-field—recruitment, selection/candidacy, deputation, training
- Field—first term, additional terms, change in job/location/organization
- Reentry—furlough, home assignment, returning to the field later in life
- Post-field—end of service, retirement

Best Practice Principle 3: The Flow of Commitment

An organization's staff is its most important resource. As such, sending groups—both churches and mission agencies—are committed to work together to support and develop their personnel throughout the missionary life cycle. They demonstrate this commitment by the way they invest themselves and their resources, including finances, into staff care. Sending groups aspire to have a comprehensive, culturally relevant, and sustainable approach to member care, including a commitment to organizational development, connecting with outside resources, and effective administration of personnel development programs. They thus root member care in organizational reality and vice versa. Sending groups also solicit input from staff when developing/evaluating policies and programs related to member care.

Sphere 4: Specialist Care

Care from specialists which is professional, personal, and practical—"equippers" of member care.

■ *Specialists*—missionaries have a special call, need special skills, and often require various specialist services to remain resilient and "fulfill their ministry" (2 Tim. 4:5).

■ *Eight specialist domains of care*—these can be understood and remembered under the rubric: **PP**ractical **TT**ools **FF**or **CC**are. These domains and specific examples are as follows:

- **P**astoral/spiritual (retreats, devotionals)
- **P**hysical/medical (medical advice, nutrition)
- **T**raining/career (continuing education, job placement)
- **T**eam building/interpersonal (group dynamics, conflict resolution)
- **F**amily/MK (MK education options, marital support group)
- **F**inancial/logistical (retirement, medical insurance)
- **C**risis/contingency (debriefing, evacuation plans)
- **C**ounseling/psychological (screening, brief therapy)

Best Practice Principle 4: The Flow of Caregivers

Specialist care is to be done by properly qualified people, usually in conjunction with sending groups. Specialists need to capitalize on their strengths—working within their competencies and maximizing contributions. They also need to capitalize on their "stretches"—going beyond familiar/convenient comfort zones in order to provide services in challenging contexts within professional ethical limits. Specialist services are "investments" which build character (virtue/godliness), competence (cross-cultural/professional skills), and compassion (love/relationships) in culturally relevant ways. The goal is not just care but empowerment—to help personnel develop the resiliency and capacities needed to sacrifice and minister to others. Specialist services collectively include four dimensions of care: prevention, development, support, and restoration. They are essential parts of an effective member care program and complement the empowering care that staff provide each other.

Sphere 5: Network Care

Care from international member care networks to help provide and develop strategic, supportive resources—"facilitators" of member care.

■ *Networks*—the growing body of interrelated colleagues and groups which facilitate member care by serving as catalysts, consultants, resource links, and service providers.

■ *Resources*—the network is like a fluid that can flow into the other four spheres and different geographic regions to stimulate and help provide several types of resources:

- Sending groups—special member care services/personnel from churches/agencies.

- Member care affiliations—national, regional, or special task forces, such as Member Care/Europe and Member Care/Asia (see chapter 48 and O'Donnell, 1999b).
- Consultations/conferences—examples include the national member care consultations in Malaysia and India, the Pastor to Missionaries Conference and the Mental Health and Missions Conference in the USA, and the European Member Care Consultations.
- Service organizations—see chapter 49, updated from the listing of member care organizations in *Too Valuable to Lose* (Taylor, 1997).
- Workshops/courses—interpersonal skills, crisis response, pastoral care, etc.
- Email forums/web sites—the European and Asian member care email forums and the World Evangelical Alliance web site for member care (www.membercare.org).
- Facilities/hubs of member care—Link Care and Heartstreams in the USA; Le Rucher, Bawtry Hall, and InterHealth in Europe; the care networks in Chiang Mai, Thailand, and Singapore, etc.
- Additional resources.

Best Practice Principle 5: The Flow of Connections

Member care providers are committed to relate and work together, stay updated on events and developments, and share consolidated learning from their member care practice. They are involved in not just providing their services, but in actively "knitting a net" to link important resources with areas of need. Partnerships and close working relationships are required among member care workers, service organizations, sending agencies, and regional member care affiliations. Especially important is the interaction between member care workers from different regions via email, conferences, and joint projects.

Applications

This best practice model is relevant for two main reasons. First, it is biblical in its core concepts, with its emphasis on our relationship with Christ and with each other, along with the role of self care. Second, the model is general enough to be both culturally and conceptually applicable across many national and organizational boundaries.

Different sending groups will emphasize different aspects of this model, yet each sphere is important to consider. There is so much to learn from each other with regards to how we "do" member care! Sending groups, for example, represented by Sphere 3 in the diagram, play a significant intermediary role in linking staff with the resources from the other four spheres. Other groups emphasize different mixes between the self care and mutual care which comprise Sphere 2. Some opt more for the individual's responsibility for his/her well-being, and others emphasize the community's role. For many sending groups, there is much overlap between self care and mutual care; hence, both have been listed in the same sphere.

The importance of mutual care cannot be overstated. Social support and good relationships come out in the research over and over again as being key to adjustment. Mutual care, though, can be a two-edged sword. When done well, it pays rich dividends. But when done poorly or not at all—especially in cultures where there is a high expectation for such care—it can break the relational bank! In addition, mutual care in international settings is tricky, especially if a person/family is part of the less dominant culture. For example, there can be a hesitancy to share concerns and needs because of language limitations (especially where the main language of the setting is one's second or third language) and because of cultural differences (especially where one's values of harmony and respect take precedence over the prevailing setting ethos of openness and directness or vice versa).

Perhaps the biggest potential disparity between member care approaches lies in the use of and emphasis on a variety of specialized resources (Sphere 4). These can be viewed as being too Western, an excessive luxury, or just not possible to develop in one's situation. For instance, it has been difficult for financial reasons in some of the Newer Sending Countries to fully provide medical insurance, MK educational options, and retirement provisions. It can also be hard to think in terms of things like possible pension plans, when the villagers in one's setting do not even have enough to survive on a daily basis. Perhaps a more reasonable and helpful goal, then, would be to ensure that a certain standard of care is being provided, rather than a whole host of resources which may not be relevant/possible in various settings. In this sense, the better term would be something like "basic" practice rather than "best" practice.

As for training, many "specialist" caregivers may be qualified more from on-the-job experience than from formal academic study/certification. A corollary is that many professionals, with all due respect for their expertise "at home," would be better equipped to serve in missions if they had additional cross-cultural and missions experience.

Challenges for Developing Member Care

The main challenge continues to be providing the appropriate, ongoing care necessary to sustain personnel for the long haul (O'Donnell, 1997). A common practice is to share member care resources creatively with other groups and also tap into the growing international network of caregivers. Help with pre-field training, crisis care, tropical medicine consultation, and MK education needs are examples. Sharing resources can be especially important for personnel from Newer Sending Countries and smaller sending groups with limited funds and/or experience, as well as for those serving in isolated settings. It is thus not necessarily up to one organization to provide all of its own member care by itself. In spite of any group's best practice efforts, though, we must realistically expect that at least a few gaps will be present in the overall flow of care that it provides for its staff.

Another challenge is to help discern when it might be time to "attrit"—to find a new position in missions or to leave missions altogether. Longevity is not always a desirable goal. Thankfully, both life and God's will are bigger than the Evangelical missions world!

Still another challenge is simply to raise the awareness of member care needs in certain sending churches and agencies, along with the responsibility to help provide jointly for these needs. Unfortunately, there are still a number of settings where member care is either overlooked or misunderstood. Towards this end, it is my hope that this model will serve as a framework to help assess and address member care issues and that it will be a robust, fluid model for fostering staff resiliency. The model's five spheres and five best practice principles can be used as both a "guide and a goad" to better care. As a further aid, Figure 3 lists some strategies that can help develop member care in different settings.

Another help is to review periodically one's involvement in member care. As an example, here are four best practice "check points" that can be used by member care workers, sending groups, national mission associations, and regions/partnerships (O'Donnell, 1991).

- *Acceptability*. How available/accessible are our member care resources—are we meeting felt needs in relevant ways?
- *Building*. To what extent are we building member care into our settings—forming sustainable, comprehensive resources and an ethos of mutual support and spiritual vitality?
- *Cooperation*. In what ways are we networking with others who are involved in member care—sharing resources, ex-

Figure 3
Strategies and Settings for Developing Member Care

Member Care Strategies	Member Care Settings
	Church/Agency, Interagency, Nation, Region, Global
■ Write/conduct research	
■ Do needs/resource assessment	
■ Resource conferences	
■ Provide training	
■ Convene consultations	
■ Participate in email forums	
■ Form service teams	
■ Form service organizations	
■ Set up resource centers/hubs	
■ Connect with "secular" resources	

changing information/updates, working on joint projects?

■ *Priorities.* To what extent have we identified our guiding principles and priorities for member care—best practice statement, clear focus, at-risk groups, designated budget?

Final Thoughts

Life does not always work according to our best practice models. Likewise, our best efforts for providing a flow of care can only go so far. We must remember that God is sovereign over any member care model or approach. His purposes in history often take precedence over our own personal desires for stability and order in our lives (Jer. 45:1-5). This is frequently the case for missionaries, where hardship, disappointment, and unexpected events have historically been part of the job description.

Irrespective of the struggles and strains of life in general and of missionary life in particular, we know that there is still much joy in the Lord! Joy and pain are not mutually exclusive. Joy is refined by and often flows from life's challenges and pains.

Member care is important not because missionaries necessarily have more or unique stress, but rather because missionaries are strategic. They are key sources of blessing for the unreached. Member care is also important because it embodies the biblical command to love one another. Such love is a cornerstone for mission strategy. As we love, people will know that we are His disciples.

Reflection and Discussion

1. How is your sending group's approach to member care similar to and different from the model presented in this article?
2. List a few of the greatest issues/struggles for mission personnel in your setting, organization, and/or region.
3. Identify how you could work with others in order to improve member care in your setting—e.g., review your member care approach, form/apply best practice principles and key indicators, develop additional specialist resources, read/discuss additional materials.
4. In what ways do your skills/gifts and interests/preferences fit into the model presented—how do you contribute to member care?
5. Which parts of the model seem most relevant across national and organizational cultures?

References

American Psychiatric Association. (1997). Practice guidelines for the treatment of patients with schizophrenia. *American Journal of Psychiatry*, *154*, 1-64.

Beutler, L. (2000). David and Goliath: When empirical and clinical standards of practice meet. *American Psychologist, 55*, 997-1007.

Gardner, L. (1987). Proactive care of missionary personnel. *Journal of Psychology and Theology*, *15*, 308-314.

Global Connections. (1997). *Code of best practice in short-term mission*. London: Author.

Hall, M., & Barber, B. (1996). The therapist in missions contexts: Avoiding dual role conflicts. *Journal of Psychology and Theology*, *24*, 212-219.

Jones, G., & Jones, R. (1995). *Teamwork*. London, UK: Scripture Union.

Larson, D. (1992). Closing space: De-alienation in missionary orientation. *Missiology: An International Review*, *20*, 513-523.

Leader, N. (1999, March). Codes of conduct: Who needs them? *Relief and Rehabilitation Network Newsletter* (pp. 1-4). London, UK: Overseas Development Institute.

McConnan, I. (2000). *The sphere project: Humanitarian charter and minimum standards in disaster response*. Oxford, UK: Oxfam Publishing.

National Health Committee, New Zealand. (1998). *Guidelines for assessing and treating anxiety disorders*. Wellington, New Zealand: Author.

O'Donnell, K. (1991). An agenda for member care in frontier missions. *International Journal of Frontier Missions*, *9*, 107-112.

———. (1997). Member care in missions: Global perspectives and future directions. *Journal of Psychology and Theology*, *25*, 143-154.

———. (1999a). *Developing best practice guidelines*. Paper presented at the Second European Member Care Consultation, June 10-13, 1999, Le Rimlishof, France.

———. (1999b). Developing member care affiliations: Personal reflections and community psychology contributions. *Journal of Psychology and Theology*, *27*, 119-129.

O'Donnell, K., & O'Donnell, M. (1992). Ethical concerns in providing member care services. In K. O'Donnell (Ed.), *Missionary care: Counting the cost for world evangelization* (pp. 260-268). Pasadena, CA: William Carey Library.

People In Aid. (1997). *Code of best practice in the management and support of aid personnel*. London, UK: Overseas Development Institute.

Pollock, D. (1997, October). Developing a flow of care. *Interact*, pp. 1-6.

Taylor, W. (Ed.). (1997). *Too valuable to lose: Exploring the causes and cures of missionary attrition*. Pasadena, CA: William Carey Library.

Kelly O'Donnell is a psychologist working with Youth With A Mission and Mercy Ministries International, based in Europe. He co-chairs with Dave Pollock the Member Care Task Force (MemCa), which is part of the World Evangelical Alliance's Missions Commission. Kelly studied clinical psychology and theology at Rosemead School of Psychology, Biola University, USA. Specialties include personnel development, setting up member care affiliations, team building, and crisis care. Together with his wife, Michèle, he has published several articles in the member care field, along with editing **Helping Missionaries Grow** *(1988) and* **Missionary Care** *(1992). They have two daughters: Erin, aged 12, and Ashling, aged 8. Email: 102172.170@compuserve.com.*

This is a revision of an article that first appeared in **Evangelical Missions Quarterly** *(2001, vol. 37, pp. 212-222), PO Box 794, Wheaton, IL 60189, USA. Used by permission.*

Many thanks to the 25 colleagues from different regions and organizations who reviewed this article in an effort to make it as widely applicable as possible. Thanks also to Dona Diehl with EMIS for her help with the diagram of the member care model.

2

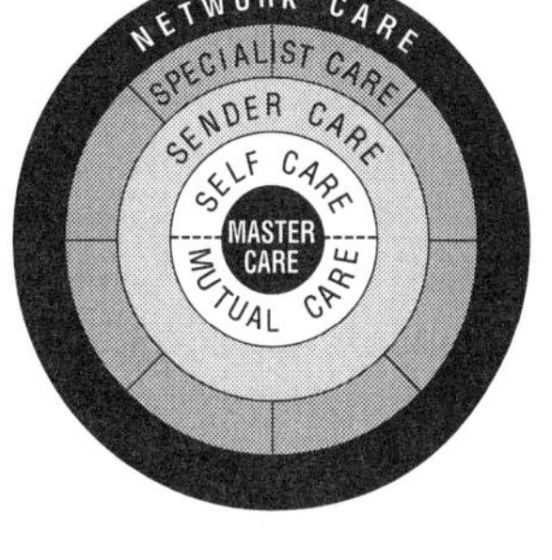

Developing A Flow of Care And Caregivers

DAVID POLLOCK

This article explores the need to develop a steady stream of care on behalf of mission personnel. The essence of this care is best understood as a "flow of love." Such love permeates the good programs, the competent practitioners, the mutual support between mission personnel, and the supportive resources needed throughout missionary life. Our love and unity demonstrate that we are His disciples.

Two themes converged in the Word.
And we should be doing both.
And that would make all the difference.

The *Great Commandment* and the *Great Commission* are inseparable. The second cannot be done without the first. Obedience to the Great Commandment is the motivation, message, and methodology in fulfilling the Great Commission. "For God so loved ... that He gave" (John 3:16). "God demonstrated His love toward us in that while we were yet sinners Christ died for us" (Rom. 5:8). The key motivating force for all that is good is God's love toward us, in us, and through us. Fulfilling the Great Commission is unthinkable without the love of Christ compelling us (2 Cor. 5:14). Our struggle to see the Great Commission fulfilled, however, may be in our struggle to believe that Jesus' command of John 13:34 is also His strategy in reaching the world (John 13:35).

The command of John 13:34 comes in the context of the last evening before the crucifixion of Jesus Christ. It may be that what we see in John chapters 13–17 is in fact the shorter catechism of all He had taught His friends over their three-year journey of discipleship. That which is recorded includes *demonstration* of His love for them in the process of washing their feet and predicting His crucifixion through the bread and wine. This was followed by His *proclamation* of what He was about to do, what the future of the disciples would be, and how through His Spirit their care would be safeguarded and their ministry implemented. He concludes with *supplication* as He reviews the essence of His journey on earth: "that they may have eternal life ... this is eternal life, that they may know You and Jesus Christ whom You have sent ... that they may glorify Me ... that they may be one as we are one, *that the world may know* that You have sent Me" (John 17).

This unity for which Jesus prays confronts the world with the truth that "God was in Christ reconciling the world to Himself." This unity is the product of obedience to the Great Commandment, and the fulfillment of the Great Commandment demonstrates the very character of God. The demonstration of His character *is* the glory of God—it is how we glorify Him!

Following the coming of the Holy Spirit, we have a snapshot of the church in Acts 2:42ff. In this description, nothing is said of evangelism as proclamation, yet the closing line states, "And the Lord added to the church daily." Clearly, a demonstration of the functional love of God in His people was a convincing basis for proclamation. This body of believers, in their lifestyle and relationship to each other, shouted to the world that something had occurred in them—normal human beings—that could be explained in no other way except that God had invaded their lives and changed them to reflect who He is. These early Christians were fulfilling John 13:34 and 17:21.

The Epistles have far more to say about demonstrating Christ than about proclaiming Him. This demonstration is referred to throughout the New Testament as a body with different parts that strengthen, support, nurture, and care for each other under Christ, who is the head (Rom. 12, 1 Cor. 12, Eph. 4). Out of this demonstration, proclamation comes naturally and makes sense to a watching world.

The Apostle Paul, addressing the problem of division in the church in Corinth (which reflected the opposite of Jesus' prayer of John 17), clearly identifies the solution to be a combination of "faith, hope, and love, but the greatest of these is love" (1 Cor. 13:13). Paul's description of love in 1 Corinthians 13 leaves little to the imagination regarding what love looks like and how it works itself out in the support and care of a healthy community.

Jesus was clear in defining the essence of God's commandments in Matthew 22:36-40. "Love the Lord your God with all your heart and with all your soul and with all your mind. This is the first and greatest commandment. And the second is like it: love your neighbor as yourself." It is the same issue—loving God and one another—which is at the heart of His strategy for fulfilling the Great Commission.

The eternal God of the universe in His mission plan has, according to Paul, revealed Himself through:

- Creation (Rom. 1:19-20)
- Conscience (Rom. 2:12-15)
- Commandment (Rom. 2:17-20)
- Christ (Rom. 3:21–5:21; Heb. 1:1-4)
- Christians (Rom. 6:1–16:27; Heb. 13:20, 21)

With regards to the last means of revelation, God uses Christians to reveal His character via the love they show. It is behavioral demonstration, not just verbal proclamation. It bears repeating that perhaps our frustration in fulfilling the Great Commission is related to our failure to concentrate on fulfilling the Great Commandment. The simplicity of the community of Acts 2:42-47 often seems too elementary, and our world and its demands seem so complex that a return to this model appears impossible. It was the growing complexity of body life even in the first century that made the directives to the churches in Corinth, Galatia, Ephesus, and Rome necessary. Encouragement and instruction to Timothy, Titus, and Philemon indicate the need for advice on how best to conduct oneself and manage the churches, but the principle and motivation remained the same. The advice consistently goes back to Jesus' simple and profound instructions: we are to love God and love one another, demonstrate God's love, and thus proclaim the identity and activity of the eternal God.

The church is a body—a community—not a business. The direction given in the Epistles is abundant and clear for the well-being of this living demonstration in community. The atrocities committed within "evangelized" countries such as Rwanda, Liberia, and Sierra Leone (as well as in Western "Christian" countries) confront us with the fact that the Great Commission is not fulfilled by planting branch offices called churches and making them an ecclesiastical statistic. The Great Commission is not complete until we have made disciples, "teaching them to obey everything I have commanded you." The Great Commandment is the essence of what we are to teach, how we are to disciple, and the way to develop Christian community.

The model in Acts 2:42-47, the life of Barnabas, the "one another" verses of the Epistles, and the relationships reflected in the book of Acts and the apostles' writings give us basic insight into the task before us. The same love requirement is incumbent upon the church of the 21st century with our own complex and ever-changing challenges. This is why we must prepare a *flow of care* for those whom God has moved to be the mobile, global proclaimers of the good news. Member care in this sense is really an embodiment of love. The flow of care is actually the flow of love. It is not simply an accommodation to stem the tide of attrition. It is not done simply to make people more effective, efficient, and enduring. It is the response to the Master's mandate.

In the international business world, there is a growing awareness of the need to heed the "people issues" of cross-culturally mobile personnel. According to researchers Grant-Vallone and Ensher (2000), premature home returns for Americans occur in 10-20% of expatriate assignments. Some statistics quote percentages as high as 40%. The extra financial loss to the company is $100,000 to $500,000. In addition, 20% of employees leave their company within three years after repatriation. The high attrition has many reasons, including couples with dual careers where one is unable to pursue his/her career, problems with children's care and education, and responsibility for elderly relatives in the home country. Some of the reasons are more subtle, including the sense of being sidetracked from one's career flow by being away from the home office, not being valued for what one has learned on the international assignment, and generally not being cared for by those in charge of personnel. The financial loss in all of this is only a part of the problem. One executive reflected, "In the 30 years of sending employees abroad, I have always known the financial loss, but I have considered it part of the price of doing international business. Now, however, as I retire I am asking myself, 'What was the cost in terms of broken families and destroyed lives of those for whom we have not sufficiently cared?'"

In the missions community, care of personnel is the fulfillment of our mandate and the natural expression of our fellowship. It is, of course, more than just protection against financial loss or safeguarding our investments. Such care is not an event, nor is it necessarily automatic. Rather, it is an intentional, planned, and ongoing flow which occurs throughout missionary life.

The Flow of Care and Caregivers

The flow of care begins with the prospective missionaries' relationship to the local body of believers and moves to the relationship with the sending agency, whether it be the same local body or a mission agency. Ideally, the local church has nurtured the individual and family and has thus functioned as a visible caring community. Basic spiritual and personal growth has been promoted through mentors as well as through the general life of the body. Now comes a new level of intentional care, requiring a variety of caregivers and moving from stage to stage in the life cycle of the missionary and the missionary family—from recruitment through retirement/end of service.

Stage 1: Recruitment

The "call" must be from God, not from slick promotion. We must expose and even confront people with the needs of the real world, but the decision to go must be in response to the question of the individual, "Lord, what do You want *me* to do?" This approach recognizes that all Christians are called to *Him,* that they might be with Him and that He might send them (Mark 3:14). Each has a role in the Great Commission, but not all have the same role. Some are sent to "Jerusalem" and some to "a distant place." Some are sent to their own cultures and others to different cultures. Each needs to hear an assignment from the Lord and obey. And each person needs to understand that the fundamental call is first to be with the Lord Jesus (1 Cor. 1:9) and then, from this place of fellowship, to launch out.

Key to good recruitment is "honesty in advertising." The likely cost must be spelled out, as well as the needs and rewards. Jesus directs His disciples to count the cost before building a tower. This does not mean that a high cost precludes building the tower, but rather by counting the cost one avoids discouraging and destructive surprises. There are many questions and considerations: Should a family go with teenagers or if there are needy, elderly parents? Should one move into a limited access and/or potentially dangerous situation with all the uncertainties? Do both spouses agree? Is there a sense of call for both? Do older children have a sense that this is God's direction for them? What are the details of the task? Are the new recruits gifted in these areas? Are they equipped? Is the entire family prepared to respond to the call? What are the issues for single people? Is celibacy for the sake of the kingdom feasible? The list of considerations is long.

Asking the appropriate questions of these potential missionaries is key for starting well. Inquirers are usually not in a position to raise all of the essential questions about themselves; they need the guidance of people who from experience know what questions to ask and how to evaluate the responses. At the same time, it is also critical for candidates to ask the right questions about the sending agency. Giving permission to ask questions, even encouraging questions and providing objective sources for answering those questions, sets the right tone for healthy communication over the long haul. Providing an accurate picture of the mission agency, prospective candidate, task, and ministry environment is all part of "honesty in advertising." Senders must realistically communicate that there will be many unknowns and that much of the journey is one of faith, not sight. The caring recruiter/mobilizer, pastor, and friends are some of the main caregivers at this time.

Stage 2: Screening

It is important to determine who the "client" is when one is doing both recruitment and screening. In the first stages of both processes, the sending agency is the primary client as we seek to find personnel to do the tasks required and desired. Nevertheless, love always requires that we keep the potential candidate clearly in mind as the subject of both God's love and ours.

The agency should be seeking the best possible people to do the task. Candidates need to meet basic requirements, but the agency should acknowledge that recruits will grow and learn with time and experience. The agency needs to be protected from bad choices for the sake of itself and its existing teams, as well as for the sake of those who will be served. Sometimes the most loving response to those who are not qualified, prepared, or otherwise ready is a "no" stated in genuine concern for the potential candidates as well as all the others involved. The "GP" seen in the clouds by the candidate may indeed mean "Go Plow" at home as opposed to "Go Preach" overseas. Screening out should be done as early as possible with great care and sensitivity before public announcements have been made, resignations from jobs submitted, or houses sold. In most cases involving a "no" or a "not yet," counseling should be advised to assist the individuals in moving ahead with their lives.

For those who are probable candidates and potential personnel, there is also an important screening process that is called "screening in." At this point, the primary client is the candidate. Screening in is designed to discover as much as possible about each individual, in order to direct and place each one (and the entire family) wisely and then to deliver appropriate care and support throughout their entire life experience, both overseas and upon return to the passport country. Medical history is key in being able to predict possible needs, as are family history, psychological evaluation, and social and cross-cultural abilities. It is important that these areas of examination be integrated in order to get a composite and accurate picture of strengths and weaknesses. Physical problems may have a psychological basis, and social background, including family dynamics, may have a profound impact on the development of cross-cultural adjustment. The competent input from special caregivers at this stage—physicians, mental health professionals, personnel officers—is an early and essential part of the flow of care.

Stage 3: Preparation and Pre-Departure Orientation

Proper education and training are obviously an important consideration. Professional competency must be closely examined from the perspective of both education and a practical track record. Untested education is always a danger when sending someone into a new and unfamiliar situation where the environment, tools, and details of the task require one to be able to adapt abilities to meet new demands. If abilities have not been mastered in one's "home" territory, it is difficult to customize them to new circumstances. Lack of ministry experience in one's home culture is not a good indicator of success elsewhere.

Spiritual formation prior to going overseas is critical. Usually nothing dynamic of a spiritual nature occurs during the flight across an ocean. It can be a great disappointment to discover that the person entering the airport in a new country is basically the same person who left the old. Neither the name "missionary" nor the new geographical location produces the spiritual maturity that may be needed. The preparation process is in one sense the process of a lifetime. On the other hand, there are aspects of preparation, even fine-tuning, that must take place in the period of time prior to embarkation.

Pre-departure orientation may vary from agency to agency in length of time, people invited to participate as teachers and resources, and even content. Unfortunately, some agencies question the importance of this type of orientation and leave such preparation to the discretion of people who often are not in a position to know that there are issues and questions to explore, let alone having a sense of need to get answers. As a result, there may be dangerous gaps in the awareness, preparation, and ability to respond appropriately in the overseas ministry setting. Inappropriate expectations leave the sojourner open to deep disappointment and perhaps failure.

Pre-departure orientation, properly developed, should accomplish several objectives. First, it should assist people in "leaving right." Leaving right is key to entering right and to the correct process of reentering when one returns to the place of origin. Secondly, this experience should assist in developing and defining expectations that are both realistic and sufficiently positive. Thirdly, the orientation should help develop a frame of reference that provides basic understanding of one's own reactions and responses to the new environment and helps to develop a positive attitude toward good adjustment and ability to learn. It should inform one's perspective and produce patience with oneself as well as others. Good decisions are based on good preparation. Key caregivers at this stage include cross-cultural trainers, seasoned missionaries, and others who can further prepare the new missionaries.

Stage 4: Departure

An important aspect of the pre-field experience is the opportunity for proper farewells. The commissioning of missionaries is an important step in the process, but often the less formal aspects of departure are just as critical. Being certain that a "RAFT" is built to help one get to the new location is important. Reconciliation of any unresolved conflicts, as much as possible, is the first section of the transition raft. Affirmations are next, for both the departing and the remaining, in order to express appreciation to each other. The Farewells from family, friends, and body of believers need to be done at different times and in culturally appropriate ways, and these represent the third part of the raft. Finally, there is the exercise of Thinking about one's destination: developing expectations that are both realistic and positive will minimize disappointment and will enhance resilience. Friends and family are especially important caregivers at this time.

Stage 5: Arrival

Probably the most important aspect of arriving is to have healthy, proactive mentors. A mentor, who is an important type of caregiver, performs two tasks. First of all, mentors introduce the culture to the newcomer. They answer questions that are asked and questions that should have been asked. They make suggestions, correct errors, and generally guide through the uneasy experience of being foreign. The second task of mentors is to introduce the newcomer to the community. Sometimes this is accomplished automatically by virtue of the mentor's reputation, which can open relationships to others, while at other times the mentor must actively introduce the newcomer.

The meeting of initial needs within the first few hours/days provides a sense of peace and well-being. For the sojourner, the basics of a reasonably comfortable place to sleep, eat, and relax are critical. Transportation and basic instruction and guidance in getting around are next in order of need, closely followed by the need for sufficient funds to meet personal and family requirements. Health care and information about safety are other important issues. A good mentoring program is prepared with information and help in these areas.

After a few days, the issues of schedule, job description, cultural practices, and relationships beyond the mentors begin to impress themselves on newcomers. A basic orientation addressing these issues and reminding newcomers of the elements in the pre-orientation that are now relevant allows them to know that they are normal, and they can be patient with themselves and others during these days of initial adjustment.

Stage 6: Field Life

This stage involves the ongoing flow of care on-site. Support systems for physical, psychological, and emotional health will vary in usefulness and importance from person to person and time to time. Quality relationships formed with team members along with nationals/locals are essential sources of support. Colleagues and nationals become the building blocks for mutual care.

Crisis care in the face of traumatic experiences becomes increasingly critical in our age of growing anarchy and the chaos it produces. In 2000, Karen Carr and Darlene Jerome with other teammates initiated the Mobile Member Care Team in Abidjan, Côte d'Ivoire (see chapter 12). It is hoped that this will be the first of many locations/centers from which quick response can be launched to meet the needs of those confronted with severe crisis. In addition, such centers can provide crisis response and interpersonal skills training as well as counseling services. Often a crisis situation allows the members of the body of Christ to activate their ability and interest to be supportive in Christ's love for one another. A supportive Christian community and the input from professional caregivers are a powerful combination for the flow of care.

Another aspect of the flow of care is how the organization handles its personnel on the field. On the down side, often the organizational *system*, removed from the conscious obedience to the Master's directives, can act more like a company than a community. The organization may become very impersonal, and even those "in charge" can blame poor decisions and destructive behavior on the "system." Getting the job done in missions also involves assessing and acknowledging the impact on the lives of those involved. Leaders at every level must thus be evaluated on the basis of how they view and treat the people for whom they are responsible. The flow of care, though assisted by intentional member care programs, is in reality dependent upon person-to-person consideration and care.

One issue in particular that is near and dear to my heart is the well-being of missionary children. Accomplishing the goals of a mission cannot be done while knowingly "sacrificing" children. This is still happening far too frequently! The response of Jesus to the self-centered question of Peter (Matt. 19:27-30, What do I get by leaving family for the sake of the gospel?) does not negate the powerful admonition and warnings related to the care of children that Jesus gave earlier (Matt. 18:1-14, Woe to the person causing one of these little ones to stumble!). Sending organizations thus do well to prioritize care for all members of the mission family. MK caregivers (e.g., educational consultants, teachers, dorm parents, reentry facilitators) are becoming an increasingly important part of missions today.

Home churches and mission agencies have a responsibility to maintain communication on behalf of mission personnel. There should be clear understanding of expectations of all concerned—the agency's expectations of the church, the church's expectations of the agency, the missionary's expectations of the church/agency, and vice versa. Ongoing three-way communication, visits from the church leadership to the missionary, support in crisis situations from the sending groups, and regular signs of genuine interest and concern contribute significantly to the health of mission personnel.

Specialists with knowledge and experience in the international and missions community are critical in providing a flow of adequate care. A flow of caregivers who can deliver care through their specialties of medicine, psychology, crisis intervention, pastoral care, team building, conflict management, education, training, fiscal support, and career development across mission agency lines is necessary. Personnel and human resource directors as well as mission specialists in local churches need to build relationships with these specialists (and vice versa) and facilitate the connection with their mission personnel. Such a pool of specialists that are supported, promoted, and used by a variety of agencies reduces cost, assures availability of care when needed, and reduces the stress on the individual agency by making it unnecessary to maintain its own group of specialized support personnel.

Stage 7: Preparation for Returning "Home"

For many, the process of returning to one's "home" country is more challenging than moving to a new one. Also, for many, the first such transition comes as a shock. Preparation for this change is both loving and necessary. The same process of leaving right via a "RAFT" is necessary for returning right. Personnel need to be assisted and at times admonished to reconcile and be reconciled; to affirm and be affirmed; to bid farewell to people, places, pets, and possessions; and to think ahead in developing realistic expectations and strategies for reentry and re-adjustment. Materials, seminars, exit interviews, and peer counseling may all be employed to assist personnel of all ages to leave/return right. Building the RAFT is as important in leaving the overseas assignment as it is in the original "home" departure.

Another part of repatriation includes the preparation of those receiving the overseas sojourner. Neal Pirolo (2000) in his book *The Reentry Team* uses the model of the church of Antioch as the basis for forming both right perspectives and right plans for healthy missionary reentry. The anticipation and planning for missionaries' return raise expectations of the "home team." Although surprises are sometimes nice, it is important that returning missionaries receive realistic information about the basics of the reentry process and support. They must know who will meet them at their point of entry, where they will be staying initially, and what provision there is for transportation, schooling for the children, money for immediate use, and other necessary living issues. It is critical that "promises" made are fulfilled.

Stage 8: Reentry

As with the previous stage of preparation, reentry care (for furlough, end of service, or retirement) is a team effort involving the mission agency, the primary supporting church or churches and, it is hoped, the family. The mission agency, in most cases, must take the position of "coach" in identifying what must and should be done and then coordinating the process. The better the communication has been between mission agency and church, the simpler this process becomes. Some churches have formed "home teams" made up of several families to support the missionaries throughout their career. These teams interface with the mission agency, the church body as a whole, the missionary family, and the missionary as a key source of support, including in the reentry process. Such proactive commitment minimizes miscommunication and prevents important issues from being ignored and people "slipping through the cracks."

Mentors are vital to reentry support. The healthiest and most helpful people should be invited to be mentors for adults and young people alike. The role of mentors is to inform, answer questions, and give guidance to returnees. They also are the representatives of returnees in introducing new people to them (sometimes including new church or community leaders) and representing their needs to those who may be able to help. They function as advocates on behalf of the returnees. Their task is to help returning missionaries reestablish themselves as deeply and as quickly as possible. This does not mean that mentors are the sole caregivers, but they are often the main points of contact for the care team.

Transition or reentry seminars are often a key source of support. Not only are the content and process of such seminars valuable, but meeting others and listening to their experience of reentry is also helpful. Returnees usually end up feeling more "normal" and become more patient and relaxed about the reentry process.

Two types of debriefing are helpful around the time of reentry. The first is *operational debriefing*, which primarily reviews the work-related experiences and issues for the missionary. This type of debriefing is done by the sending agency and/or the sending church. The second is *emotional debriefing*, which explores the feelings and personal experiences of the missionaries. This debriefing is done more privately to allow the missionary to express him/herself freely and explore his/her life and work. Children and families benefit from this type of debriefing too.

In general, both types of debriefing should be designed to help the missionary and the sending groups better understand the missionary's experience. Debriefing should be an opportunity to hear both the good and the bad without defense (or offense). Its goal should be to discover ways to contribute to support, healing, and preparation for the future. Thus, those who conduct the debriefing should be individuals who have some knowledge of the people involved. In the case of operational debriefings, they should be in places of sufficient leadership where appropriate actions can be taken when necessary.

Which caregivers are the debriefers? Depending on the type of debriefing, they could include a counselor, the head of the missions department at the missionary's church, a trusted/skilled friend, a pastor, or a personnel officer.

Stage 9: Ongoing Support

There are at least three special categories of people in the missions community who should have specialized and ongoing support. They are the "beginners," the "finishers," and the "injured."

Beginners. Third-culture kids (TCKs) can be considered "beginners" when they experience significant transitions as young adults: from living abroad to living in one's passport country, from secondary education to university or the work force, from being close to parents to distance from them with few or no familiar faces. Transition seminars, networking through the Internet, publications, reunions, return visits to the family and the "home" country, and coaching/counseling support are all important.

Once again, healthy, helpful mentors are critical not only upon reentry but through the ongoing growth and development of these TCKs. To realize their potential, young adult MKs need people who can validate their TCK experience and serve as coaches to help them into appropriate places of development and leadership. Mentors may begin the process by helping to meet very mundane needs such as attaining a driver's license, getting a job, buying a used vehicle, and getting registration and insurance for the first time without the help of their parents.

Finishers. The second area of ongoing care is for the finishers. Retiring missionaries or those who conclude their career because their particular task is finished or due to health reasons are not throwaways. Too often, people who have consciously sacrificed economic security for the cause of the gospel find themselves in desperate need because there is little or no provision for retirement (including government-supported supplements) in their closing years. Too often, the church rejects the responsibility to continue to support because the person is "no longer a missionary."

Beyond the issue of finances, however, there is the issue of continued significance. Missionaries may return or retire, but they may live many years beyond the termination of their overseas assignment. They may be healthy and sharp-minded and still have a heart for kingdom business. Helping returnees or retirees reinvest themselves at a reasonable level of involvement is part of the support process.

Retirement support needs to begin long before retirement, through the encouragement and support of both mission agency and church. Financial planning, retirement housing, and useful post-retirement activity are too often ignored until it is too late to provide for these things. Once again, the mission agency and the church need to communicate with each other about expectations and provisions.

Injured. The third area of continuing care involves those who are injured, whether physically, psychologically, or spiritually. Barnabas separated from a rewarding, positive, long-term relationship with Paul in order to care for a wounded disciple named John Mark. The latter ultimately recovered to become "profitable" to Paul (Acts 15:36ff; 2 Tim. 4:11). Such a model of care in the early church is instructive. Personal growth takes time, as does helping someone who is weak or injured. There are consequences to our kingdom work, and oftentimes there are significant injuries. We must thus prioritize, budget, and take the time necessary to walk mission personnel through the healing process and see them restored. This is applicable not only to active mission personnel, but also to those who are leaving mission service.

Summary Thoughts

The flow of care is made possible only with a flow of caregivers. And missionaries themselves, along with their mutually supportive relationships with nationals/locals, are surely a major part of the care needed for longevity. But that is not, of course, all that is required. Personnel/human resource directors and church-based mission leadership, coupled with specialists in fields of medicine, mental health, education, crisis and conflict management, pastoral care, finance, and so on, must coordinate and integrate their activity. Training is required to hone the skills of people in these disciplines to the specific needs of the interculturally mobile mission population. A network for communication is required to coordinate efforts, cross-pollinate the care disciplines, and communicate availability and accessibility of these services. It is encouraging to see the ongoing development of such networks within and between the Newer Sending Countries from Asia, Africa, and Latin America, and the Older Sending Countries.

It has been my conviction over the last four decades of my work in missions that member care is by its very nature the tangible expression of the love of Christ for us and of our love for Him. It is not simply a program or a plan; it is the product of who we are because of our relationship to Him and our being His "new creation." He is Emmanuel, God with us, and it is Christ in us who is the hope of glory. The flow of caregivers, cooperating together to support mission personnel, is one more demonstration to the world of the unity for which Jesus prayed. Providing the flow of care is a body effort of mission agencies, sending churches, supporting families, and committed caregivers who realize that the Great Commandment and the Great Commission are inseparable.

Reflection and Discussion

1. What is the rationale for stating that "the Great Commandment and the Great Commission are inseparable"?
2. List a few ways that the flow of care might be different for Newer and for Older Sending Countries.
3. List some ways that the flow of caregivers might be different for Newer and for Older Sending Countries.
4. Who should coordinate/oversee each phase of the flow of care?
5. What are appropriate expectations for care that missionaries should have for their mission agency, sending church, field leadership, other missionaries, and themselves?

References

Grant-Vallone, E., & Ensher, E. (2000). An examination of work and personal life conflict, organizational support, and employee health among international expatriates. *International Journal of Intercultural Relations, 25,* 261-278.

Pirolo, N. (2000). *The reentry team.* San Diego, CA: Emmaus Road International.

***David Pollock** is the director of Interaction, an organization committed to support and care for interculturally mobile families and third-culture kids. He was a missionary with his wife, Betty Lou, in Kenya as part of the Africa Inland Mission. They have four children and five grandchildren. Earlier ministry included work with Youth for Christ and pastoring a church in New Jersey for seven years. Dave has been the director of the Intercultural Studies Program at Houghton College, New York, where he serves as an adjunct professor. He is also the co-coordinator of the WEA Missions Commission Member Care Task Force and has written extensively, including co-authoring the book **The Third Culture Kid Experience: Growing Up Among Worlds**. Email: 75662.2070@compuserve.com.*

*This chapter is an expanded version of an article that first appeared in **Interact** (1997, October, pp. 1-6). Used by permission.*

3

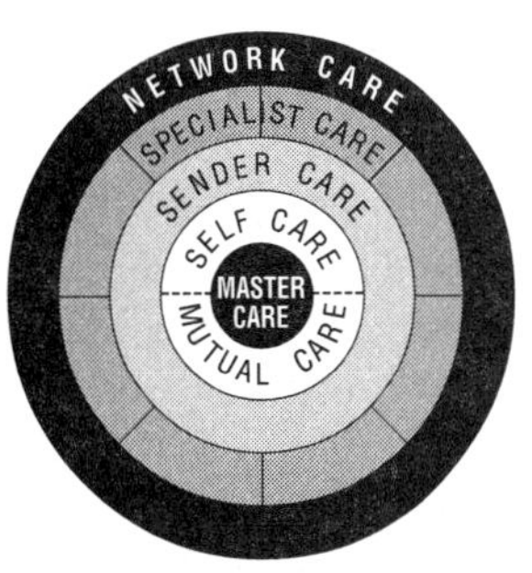

Christianity at 2000: Changes Today, Challenges Tomorrow

Todd M. Johnson

How has the church fared with regards to its endeavors to fulfill the Great Commission? Here are some historical perspectives, current realities, and future trends to consider seriously. It is within this broader context that we are providing and developing member care on behalf of the missions community.

At the end of the 20th century, just over 33% of the world's population profess to be Christians. Contrary to the optimistic outlook 100 years ago of a "Christian century," this percentage is actually slightly lower than it was in 1900. Some might conclude that Christians have made virtually no progress in enlisting followers in the past 100 years.

But such a point of view would miss the radical changes that have impacted the world Christian movement in the 20th century. First of all, in 1900, over 80% of all Christians were white. Most were from Europe and North America. Today that percentage is only 45%. The demographic weight of Christianity is now found in Latin America, Africa, and Asia. Over the next 25 years, the white portion of global Christianity is expected to continue to decline dramatically.

Second, in 1900, only a handful of Christians were involved in renewal movements. By AD 2000, over 500 million or 25% of all Christians were participants in renewal. Over the century, the first wave of renewal, the Pentecostal Movement, grew into 750 denominations in 225 countries with 65 million members. Later, a second wave, the Charismatic Renewal, hit the mainline churches, encompassing 6,500 denominations in 235 countries with over 175 million members. Finally, a third wave, or the rise of Neocharismatics, emphasizing a break with denominationalism, spread into over 18,800 networks in 225 countries, claiming over 295 million members. The majority of these are in Africa and Asia. Altogether, these three waves of renewal mark a radical transformation of Christianity in the 20th century.

Third, Christians of all major traditions have grown increasingly committed to the Great Commission of Jesus

Christ. One out of three Christians in the world is active in obedience to this Commission. The number has grown from 78 million in 1900 to over 650 million in AD 2000. As a result, hundreds of new mission agencies have been formed and thousands of new missionaries sent out. The independent churches, barely a factor in mission in 1900, are now providing a new infusion of workers, as many of the more traditional sending bodies continue to decline. An almost entirely unexpected surge of workers has emerged from the non-Western world—thousands of new churches and agencies sending foreign and home missionaries.

Fourth, Christians have stepped up their evangelistic efforts, particularly in line with advances in communications technology, beginning with the radio early in the century and progressing to satellite networks today. In 1900, it is estimated that Christians generated enough evangelism on earth for every person to hear the gospel six times every year. By 2000, that figure had skyrocketed to 155 times—a gospel presentation for every person on earth every other day all year long.

Social Trends and the Impact of the Gospel

Remarkably, these dramatic changes have not achieved a fundamental goal of Christian mission—proclaiming the good news to every people in the world. A major study by Samuel Zwemer was commissioned by the Edinburgh Missionary Conference in 1910 and then published the following year as *The Unoccupied Mission Fields of Africa and Asia*. Zwemer clearly outlined the unfinished task and the opportunities the churches had for contacting the unevangelized. He even emblazoned an early version of the "10/40 Window" on the cover. This call was largely ignored. Similar clarion calls were made throughout the 20th century, culminating with a global concerted effort in the 1990s with a now-popularized 10/40 Window. Nonetheless, at the end of the 20th century, 1.6 billion people in several thousand ethnolinguistic peoples are still without access to a culturally relevant church community.

This shortfall is largely the result of where missionaries went to work during the 20th century. Nine out of 10 missionaries who were sent out went to work among peoples already contacted with the Christian message and, in some cases, already heavily Christian. This pattern is being repeated today by the new independent missionaries and, to a large extent, by non-Western missionaries. The result is that over 95% of all Christian effort today is directed at the Christian world.

The lack of contact between Christians and non-Christians must also be viewed in the context of the world's great social problems. The 20th century was one of the bloodiest on record with over 200 major conflicts, including two world wars. These conflicts are largely responsible for a record 40 million displaced persons (internal and external exiles). One-third of these are environmental refugees, with 300,000 a year dying as the result of environmental disasters. Some 800 million individuals—mainly women, children, and the elderly—are chronically malnourished. Every year, 15 million die from diseases related to malnutrition. Two million children die each year through lack of immunization against preventable diseases. Every year, nearly 600,000 children are newly infected with the AIDS virus. The global total of HIV-positive individuals now exceeds 40 million. 2.2 billion people do not have access to safe water. The urban poor have mushroomed to 1.4 billion (half of all urban dwellers). 120 million children live or work on the streets of the world's cities. 10 million children are forced into prostitution, and another 200 million children are forced into child labor. These and hundreds of similar statistics paint a stark picture of reality—a reality that Christians ignore at great peril.

Another unanticipated trend has been the tremendous resistance non-Christians have shown to Christians and Christian missions in the 20th century. The rise of Communism early in the century provided most of this dynamic. For over 70 years, not only were Christians in Communist lands under intense persecution, but millions lost their lives prematurely as a result of their witness—the standard definition of Christian martyrs. With the collapse of Communism in the latter part of the century, one would think that martyrdom and persecution would now be rare. Unfortunately, this is not the case. Outside of the Communist world, governments that now persecute Christians are run by secularists, Muslims, Hindus, and, surprisingly, other Christians. In fact, the 20th century has been the bloodiest on record, not only for all of humanity but for Christians as well. In these 100 years, more Christians lost their lives as martyrs than in all the previous centuries combined. The current rate is a staggering 165,000 Christian martyrs each year.

Challenges of the 21st Century

The challenges faced by the new missions force of the 21st century are legion. The world of AD 2000 is radically different from that of 1900. The overconfidence exhibited early in the 20th century by secular leaders of the Enlightenment Project has been completely deflated by the collapse of Communism and a general loss of faith in science and the idea of inevitable progress. Christian theologians and mission leaders who borrowed heavily from this paradigm find themselves at a crossroads. Although some advocate an even stronger "modern" approach, many see the changing times as a corrective to the overconfidence of 20th century strategies.

With this in mind, some see the ethos of 20th century mission creeping into 21st century initiatives. First is the tendency to convene big conferences with impressive slogans, in which the implications of the slogans are not always seriously addressed. Second, the hoped-for century of church union has become instead one of schism and lack of cooperation. If anything, hundreds of new organizations have emerged, each with its own independently stated plans. Third, the number of missionaries available for frontier missions may be impacted by an increasing uneasiness over the efficacy of Christianity in "already discipled" peoples—Rwanda being a premier example. As a result, more mission effort is advocated among the 141 countries already 60% or more Christian and already the locus of current missionary deployment. Fourth, short-term missions are now a driving force in missions. Although this means that more Christians are exposed to mission fields, it seems to be having the effect of injecting a short-term emphasis into long-term church planting strategies. Fifth, although much has been learned about contextualization of the gospel, emerging short-term mentalities foreshadow a de-emphasis on language and culture learning, which are still the backbone of the foreign missionary enterprise.

Nonetheless, positive developments in 20th century mission are also being appropriated in the new century. First and foremost has been the formation of two kinds of partnerships. First, we see increasing cooperation between Western and non-Western missions. There have been many false starts along the way, but valuable lessons have been learned with regard to the use of money and the sharing of control of personnel and funds. Second, strategic partnerships between mission agencies have been formed specifically around unreached peoples. For example, a Bible translation agency might work closely with church planting efforts and radio broadcasters. These partnerships are growing and represent a major step forward in frontier mission strategy. Closely related to this is the rise of strategy coordinators. A new breed among missionaries, these individuals step back far enough from a specific people group to enumerate all the possible ways the people might be reached. They then choose 10 or so of the best strategies and advocate among specialized agencies (such as media ministries) for their accomplishment.

Perhaps the most astonishing development in frontier missions in the 20th century has been the unanticipated rise of the non-baptized believer in Christ. Akin to the fabulous growth of the Chinese house churches or African Independent churches in the latter half of the 20th century, several million Hindus, Muslims, and Buddhists have given their primary allegiance to Jesus Christ but have chosen not to leave their cultural traditions to join Christian churches. Their growth and development as individual believers and as movements must not be taken for granted. Understanding the implications of this kind of radical contextualization may rest largely with key leaders within the Christian church. Their role as ambassadors will be to try to anticipate how these new believers interact with Christian churches. They may also be able to unlock contextualized strategies in reaching peoples currently beyond the gospel.

All of these developments underscore the fact that missionaries of the 21st century will likely have a much greater load to bear than their predecessors from the 20th century. Today's missionaries are faced with information overload in a networked environment; multiple agencies from multiple countries taking multiple approaches; the impact of globalization and postmodernism on seemingly remote peoples; an increased need for cultural, ethnic, and religious sensitivity; the emergence of almost-unrecognizable new forms of Christianity; and a host of other new factors. More than ever, missionaries will need to be well prepared and well cared for in the 21st century. Only then will the churches of the world be able to fulfill the initial requirement of the Great Commission—the effective penetration of all peoples with the gospel message.

Reflection and Discussion

1. How is the Christian world in AD 2000 substantially different from what it was in 1900?

2. What are two major explanations for why Christians have not evangelized the world?

3. How should the world's social problems impact Christian mission strategies, including member care emphases?

4. What are some cautions for 21st century missions?

5. What positive developments can impact 21st century missions and the ability to do member care well?

Todd M. Johnson *has been a missionary with Youth With A Mission (YWAM) since 1978. He has traveled in 30 countries performing various ministry tasks, including relief work among Cambodian refugees in Thailand, inner city work in San Francisco, evangelism in villages in Guatemala, and language study in the Soviet Union. Since 1983, Todd has been involved in the long-term church planting arm of YWAM exclusively focused on the unreached peoples. In 1989, he began his current position as a full-time missionary researcher and is presently Director of the World Evangelization Research Center (WERC) in Richmond, Virginia, USA. Email: ToddMJohnson@sprynet.com.*

Note: All statistics in this article are documented in Barrett, D., Kurian, G., & Johnson, T. (2001). ***World Christian encyclopedia: A comparative survey of churches and religions in the modern world*** *(2nd ed.). Oxford, UK: Oxford University Press. For an annual global summary table of statistics, see www.gem-werc.org.*

4

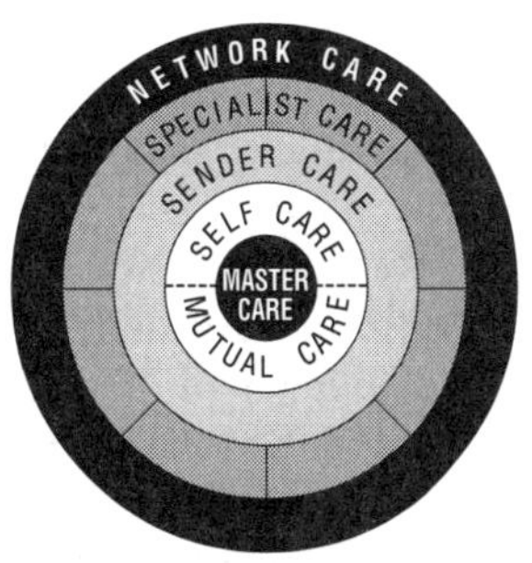

Humanitarianism With a Point

JOHN L. AMSTUTZ

To whom was Christ referring when He spoke about "the least of My brothers" in Matthew 25? The answer to this question has profound implications for the church's approach to missions—and member care.

"Inasmuch as you have done it to one of the least of these My brothers, you have done it to Me" (Matt. 25:40). Few verses are used more frequently than this verse by Christian humanitarian organizations. Whether the appeal is to invest in a ministry to prison inmates or to give to a ministry to feed the hungry and clothe the needy, this is the "John 3:16" of the charitable organizations. It is the verse which validates and underscores the biblical basis of such ministries to the less fortunate people of any society.

Understanding God's Heart for the Poor and Needy

Let there be no doubt about it: the Bible makes clear a Christian's responsibility toward the poor and needy. Jesus was anointed of the Spirit to "preach good news to the poor" (Luke 4:18). He seemed to show special concern for those who lacked life's essentials, the poor and the oppressed. Thus He instructed His disciples to "sell your possessions and give to the poor" (Luke 12:33). He affirmed the Jewish practice of almsgiving, placing it on a level with practices of prayer and fasting (Matt. 6:1-4). In the parable of the Good Samaritan, Jesus clearly identified one's obligation to "go and do likewise" for a neighbor in need, irrespective of ethnicity or socioeconomic standing (Luke 10:25-37).

By such teaching, Jesus identified with God's concern for the poor in the Old Testament, where the God of Israel is described as "a stronghold to the poor, a stronghold to the needy in his distress" (Isa. 25:4). Howard Snyder (1975, p. 41) is right when he concludes that "there is biblical evidence for God's particular concern for the poor ... if one takes the trouble to look for it."

Understanding the Parable of the Sheep and the Goats

But is unconditional humanitarianism the point of the parable of the sheep and the goats in Matthew 25? Perhaps we need to take a second look at what Jesus intended to teach, in light of the context in which the parable is found, namely, the Olivet Discourse. Matthew 24:4-35 outlines Jesus' remarks concerning when the temple of Jerusalem and its buildings will be destroyed and what will be the sign of His coming and of the end of the age (v. 3). Since no one knows the exact day or hour of His coming, not even Jesus Himself, the need for "watching" is imperative (vv. 36ff). To underscore the meaning and significance of such alertness, Jesus told several parables. The parable of the sheep and the goats is the final parable and concludes the Olivet Discourse as found in Matthew.

Simply stated, the parable of the sheep and the goats pinpoints the basis of judgment of the nations. Jesus, when He comes in His glory as the Son of Man, will separate the nations (*ethne*) of the earth into two groups, sheep and goats. The basis of this division will be their response to "the least of these My brethren." Those identified as sheep responded positively. They fed, gave drink, provided hospitality, clothed, cared for, and visited Jesus' brethren when they were in prison. The goats, on the other hand, did none of these things. In both cases, neither the sheep nor the goats were aware of when they had so responded, and they asked the question, "When did we see You hungry or thirsty or a stranger or needing clothes or sick or in prison...?" (vv. 37, 44). Thus, the identity of "the least of these My brethren" is crucial for a proper understanding of the basis of judgment.

A survey of commentators indicates that the majority hold "the least of these My brethren" to be oppressed and suffering humanity. Typical of the comments of such writers is the comment of R. V. G. Tasker (1977, p. 238): "In virtue of the divine compassion and the infinite sympathy shown in His life on earth, the Son of Man has come to feel the sorrows and afflictions of the children of men as though they were His own. He can, therefore, in a real sense refer to the suffering men and women as His brethren."

In light of such interpretation, no wonder contemporary Christian humanitarian organizations use Matthew 25:40 as they do. But again, we ask, is such unconditional humanitarianism the point of the parable?

Matthew 12:46-50 clearly states that Jesus' "mother and brothers" (i.e., His family) is "whoever does the will of My Father in heaven." The parallel passage in Luke 8:21 describes the "brothers" of Jesus as those who "hear God's word and put it into practice." Who are Jesus' brothers? Those who are hearers and doers of His word, namely, those who are His disciples and who continue in His word (John 8:31). Such close identification of Jesus with His disciples is clearly taught in Matthew 10:40-42: "He who receives you receives Me, and he who receives Me receives the one who sent Me. Anyone who receives a prophet *because* he is a prophet will receive a prophet's reward, and anyone who receives a righteous man *because* he is a righteous man will receive a righteous man's reward. And if anyone gives a cup of cold water to one of these little ones *because* he is *My disciple*, I tell you the truth, he will certainly not lose his reward" (italics added).

Therefore, one's response to Jesus' disciples is one's response to Jesus Himself and to the Father who sent Him. Is not this reality the basis of Jesus' question to Saul on the Damascus road, "Why do you persecute Me?" (Acts 9:1-5)? Had not Saul's persecution of believers in Jerusalem, in fact, been a persecution of Jesus Himself? It seems so.

If this is a proper interpretation of the word "brethren," then the point of the parable of the sheep and the goats is even more pointed. Earlier in the Olivet Discourse, Jesus had said that "this gospel of the kingdom shall be preached in all the world for a witness to all nations" (*ethne*) before the end comes (Matt. 24:14). Apparently this parable assumes such a worldwide witness to all nations through Christ's disciples. Therefore, the basis of judgment of the nations rests on their response to these disciples and thus to Jesus Himself. A positive response indicates a sheep; a negative response indicates a goat, for accompanying this worldwide witness also would be persecution, for Jesus Himself also had told His disciples that they would be "hated by all nations" (Matt. 24:9).

Apparently the universal proclamation of the gospel of the kingdom will be accompanied by a universal positive and negative response to that proclamation, in that some will show kindness to persecuted believers/disciples while others will not. Some will give them something to eat and drink and take them into their homes, caring for the sick and even visiting those in prison for their witness to Christ. Others will do just the opposite. Such response to Christ's messengers indicated their response to their message and to the One who had sent them, Jesus Himself.

Rejection of "the least of these Jesus' brethren" is in reality a rejection of Him. It was this point of identity with Jesus that apparently occasioned the question of surprise on the part of both sheep and goats: "When did we do this *to you*?" The element of surprise was *not* their treatment of followers of Jesus. Rather it was in their treatment of Christ Himself, who was identified with such disciples. The issue was *not* unconditional humanitarianism to mankind generally or even unconscious humanitarianism to Christ's disciples specifically. The issue was unconscious kindness to Christ Himself... or the lack of it. The parable of the sheep and goats teaches humanitarianism, but with a point.

Understanding the Implications of the Parable

The implications of such an understanding of this parable are significant. First, the parable assumes the universal preaching of the gospel is not optional in the plan of God. "Missions" is not an appendage on the church's agenda. It is essential. A worldwide witness is the foundation for the judgment of the nations.

Second, accompanying this universal witness to Jesus Christ will be persecution. Indeed, "All who desire to live godly in Christ Jesus will be persecuted" (2 Tim. 3:12). Opposition for one's faith in Christ is not just for believers in the Middle East and Asia. Christ's disciples will be "hated by all nations" because they are *in* all nations.

Third, the place of hospitality and kindness toward followers of Jesus Christ is no small matter, particularly toward those who are being persecuted for their faith in Him. "Remember those in prison as if you were their fellow prisoners, and those who are mistreated as if you yourselves were suffering" (Heb. 13:3). "By this shall all men know that you are My disciples if you have love for one another" (John 13:35). In the words of the Apostle Paul, "Let us do good to all men, *especially* to those of the household of faith" (Gal. 6:10, italics added).

Is it not time we free this pointed parable of the sheep and the goats to speak clearly and fully of the crucial place of the universal preaching of the gospel to *every nation* (*ethne*) and the opposition and persecution that will attend such preaching? And is it not time we free this pointed parable to speak clearly and fully of the essential need of intentional humanitarianism—member care—toward those who have chosen to suffer loss for their witness to Christ in these nations?

Humanitarianism with a point is the point, and the point is, "Inasmuch as you have done it to one of the least of these My brothers, *you have done it to Me*"! And never has a proper understanding of this pointed parable been more important than it is as we enter the new millennium, in which the church increasingly focuses on the final frontiers, many of which are in risky and resistant areas.

Reflection and Discussion

1. Do you agree with the author's understanding of the identity of "the least of these My brethren"? Why or why not?

2. What is your understanding of God's promise that those who bless His people will be blessed, but those who curse them will be cursed (Gen. 12:3)? Can you think of any illustrations in Scripture showing that the way a people/nation responded to God's people determined how God responded to them? Can you think of any examples of this today?

3. What are some of the implications of the author's understanding of the parable of the sheep and the goats, both for missions and for member care?

4. What accounts for such different responses to Christ's messengers? Is the problem with the messengers, the message, the host culture, and/or other factors?

5. What has been your response to persecuted followers of Christ?

References

Snyder, H. (1975). *The problem of wineskins*. Downers Grove, IL: InterVarsity Press.

Tasker, R. (1977). *The Gospel according to St. Matthew: Tyndale New Testament commentaries*. Grand Rapids, MI: Eerdmans Publishing Company.

John L. Amstutz *is currently an associate pastor at Valley Christian Center in Fresno, California, and a consultant with Foursquare missions. He has been a missionary, pastor, missions professor, and missions trainer. He has written numerous missions articles which have appeared in* ***Emphasis Magazine, Foursquare World Advance, Pneuma****, and the* ***International Journal of Frontier Missions****. Email: jlamstutz@earthlink.net.*

This article first appeared in the ***International Journal of Frontier Missions*** *(1992, vol. 9, pp. 131-132). Used by permission.*

5

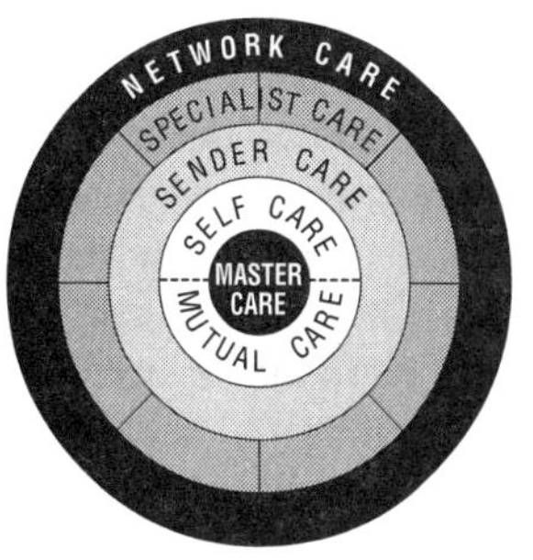

Commemorating The Witnesses To the Faith

JOHN PAUL II

This homily was delivered by John Paul II during a special ecumenical gathering, 7 May 2000, to honor all those Christians killed for their faith during the 20th century. It was given at a unique memorial service at the Coliseum in Rome, the ancient site where so many early Christians and others gave their lives for their faith.

"Unless a grain of wheat falls
into the earth and dies, it remains alone;
but if it dies, it bears much fruit."
John 12:24

With these words on the eve of His Passion, Jesus foretells His glorification through His death. We have just heard this challenging truth in the Gospel acclamation. It resounds forcefully tonight in this significant place, where we remember the "witnesses to the faith in the 20th century."

Christ is the grain of wheat who by dying has borne fruits of everlasting life. And down the centuries, His disciples have followed in the footsteps of the crucified King, becoming a numberless multitude "from every nation, race, people, and language": apostles and confessors of the faith, virgins and martyrs, bold heralds of the gospel and silent servants of the kingdom.

The Christian Legacy of Suffering

Dear brothers and sisters united by faith in Jesus Christ! I am especially happy today to offer you my brotherly embrace of peace, as we commemorate together the witnesses to the faith in the 20th century. I warmly greet the representatives of the Ecumenical Patriarchate and of the other Orthodox Sister Churches, as well as those of the ancient Churches of the East. I likewise thank the representatives of the Anglican Communion, of the worldwide Christian Communities of the West, and of the Ecumenical Organizations for their fraternal presence.

Gathered as we are at the Coliseum for this meaningful jubilee celebration, our coming together this evening is for all of us a source of great emotion. The monuments and ruins of ancient Rome speak to humanity of the sufferings and persecutions endured with fortitude by our forebears in the faith, the Christians of the first generations. These ancient remains remind us how true are the words of Tertullian, who wrote: *"sanguis martyrum semen christianorum"*—the blood of the martyrs is the seed of new Christians.

The experience of the martyrs and the witnesses to the faith is not a characteristic only of the church's beginnings but marks every epoch of her history. In the 20th century, and maybe even more than in the first period of Christianity, there has been a vast number of men and women who bore witness to the faith through sufferings that were often heroic. How many Christians in the course of the 20th century, on every continent, showed their love of Christ by the shedding of blood! They underwent forms of persecution both old and new; they experienced hatred and exclusion, violence and murder. Many countries of ancient Christian tradition once more became lands where fidelity to the gospel demanded a very high price. In our century, the witness to Christ borne even to the shedding of blood has become a common inheritance of Catholics, Orthodox, Anglicans, and Protestants.

The generation to which I belong experienced the horror of war, the concentration camps, persecution. In my homeland, during the Second World War, priests and Christians were deported to extermination camps. In Dachau alone, some 3,000 priests were interned. Their sacrifice was joined to that of many Christians from other European countries, some of whom belonged to other churches and ecclesial communities.

I myself am a witness of much pain and many trials, having seen these in the years of my youth. My priesthood, from its very beginning, was marked by the great sacrifice of countless men and women of my generation. The experience of the Second World War and of the years following brought me to consider carefully and with gratitude the shining example of those who, from the beginning of the 20th century to its end, met persecution, violence, and death because of their faith and because their behavior was inspired by the truth of Christ.

And there are so many of them! They must not be forgotten; rather, they must be remembered and their lives documented. The names of many are unknown; the names of some have been denigrated by their persecutors, who tried to add disgrace to martyrdom; the names of others have been concealed by their executioners. But Christians preserve the memory of a great number of them. This is shown by the numerous replies to the invitation not to forget, received by the New Martyrs Commission within the Committee for the Great Jubilee.

The Commission has worked hard to enrich and update the church's memory with the witness of all those people, even those who are unknown, who "risked their lives for the sake of our Lord Jesus Christ" (Acts 15:26). Yes, as the Orthodox Metropolitan Benjamin of Saint Petersburg, martyred in 1922, wrote on the eve of his execution, "The times have changed and it has become possible to suffer much for love of Christ...." With the same conviction, from his cell in Buchenwald, the Lutheran Pastor Paul Schneider asserted once more in the presence of his prison guards, "Thus says the Lord: 'I am the resurrection and the life!'"

The presence of representatives of other churches and ecclesiastical communities gives today's celebration particular significance and eloquence in this Jubilee Year 2000. It shows that the example of the heroic witnesses to the faith is truly precious for all Christians. In the 20th century, almost all the churches and ecclesiastical communities have known persecution, uniting Christians in their places of suffering and making their shared sacrifice a sign of hope for times still to come.

These brothers and sisters of ours in faith, to whom we turn today in gratitude and veneration, stand as a vast panorama of Christian humanity in the 20th century, a panorama of the "Gospel of the Beatitudes," lived even to the shedding of blood.

"Blessed are you when they insult you and persecute you and utter all kinds of evil against you falsely on my account. Rejoice and be glad, for your reward is great in heaven" (Matt. 5:11-12). How well these words of Christ fit the countless witnesses to the faith in the last century, insulted and persecuted, but never broken by the power of evil!

Where hatred seemed to corrupt the whole of life, leaving no escape from its logic, they proved that "love is stronger than death." Within terrible systems of oppression which disfigured man, in places of pain, amid the hardest of privations, through senseless marches, exposed to cold and hunger, tortured, suffering in so many ways, they loudly proclaimed their loyalty to Christ crucified and risen. In a few moments, we shall hear some of their striking testimonies.

Countless numbers refused to yield to the cult of the false gods of the 20th century and were sacrificed by Communism, Nazism, by the idolatry of state or race. Many others fell in the course of ethnic or tribal wars, because they had rejected a way of thinking foreign to the gospel of Christ. Some went to their death because, like the Good Shepherd, they decided to remain with their people, despite intimidation. On every continent and throughout the entire 20th century, there have been those who preferred to die rather than betray the mission which was theirs. Men and women religious lived their consecration to the shedding of blood. Men and women believers died, offering their lives for love of their brothers and sisters, especially the poorest and the weakest. Many women lost their lives in order to defend their dignity and purity.

"Whoever loves his life loses it, and whoever hates his life in this world will keep it for eternal life" (John 12:25). A few minutes ago, we listened to these words of Christ. They contain a truth which today's world often scorns and rejects, making love of self the supreme criterion of life. But the witnesses to the faith, who also this evening speak to us by their example, did not consider their own advantage, their own well-being, their own survival as greater values than fidelity to the gospel. Despite all their weakness, they vigorously resisted evil. In their fragility, there shone forth the power of faith and of the Lord's grace.

Our Precious Heritage

Dear brothers and sisters, the precious heritage which these courageous witnesses have passed down to us is a patrimony shared by all the churches and ecclesial communities. It is a heritage which speaks more powerfully than all the causes of division. The ecumenism of the martyrs and the witnesses to the faith is the most convincing of all; to the Christians of the 21st century it shows the path to unity. It is the heritage of the cross lived in the light of Easter: a heritage which enriches and sustains Christians as they go forward into the new millennium.

If we glory in this heritage, it is not because of any partisan spirit and still less because of any desire for vengeance upon the persecutors, but in order to make manifest the extraordinary power of God, who has not ceased to act in every time and place. We do this as we ourselves offer pardon, faithful to the example of the countless witnesses killed even as they prayed for their persecutors.

In the century and the millennium just begun, may the memory of these brothers and sisters of ours remain always vivid. Indeed, may it grow still stronger! Let it be passed on from generation to generation, so that from it there may blossom a profound Christian renewal! Let it be guarded as a treasure of consummate value for the Christians of the new millennium, and let it become the leaven for bringing all Christ's disciples into full communion!

It is with a heart filled with deep emotion that I express this hope. I pray to the Lord that the cloud of witnesses which surrounds us will help all of us who believe to express with no less courage our own love for Christ, for Him who is ever alive in His church: as He was yesterday, and is today, and will be tomorrow and forever!

Reflection and Discussion

1. Where are some of the main regions of the world today where Christians are being persecuted for their faith?
2. Church history is full of martyrs. Which ones do you admire the most and why?
3. What role could member caregivers play in supporting the persecuted church?
4. At what point and to what degree should persecution be resisted?
5. What are some reasons that the Lord allows persecution and martyrdom?

***John Paul II**—Karol Wojtyla—is the Pope of the Roman Catholic Church. He is internationally respected for his personal piety and, among other areas, his commitment to human dignity and religious freedom.*

This homily is in the public domain and is part of a larger written treatise on the topic.

Note: The World Evangelical Alliance's Religious Liberty Conference shares information on the state of religious liberty and persecution around the world. For information, contact the moderator—MarkAlbrecht@xc.org. Other helpful groups are Compass Direct (www.compassdirect.org); Keston Institute (www.keston.org); Open Doors (www.odusa.org); and US CIRF (www.uscuirf.gov).

Part 2
Regional Issues and Insights

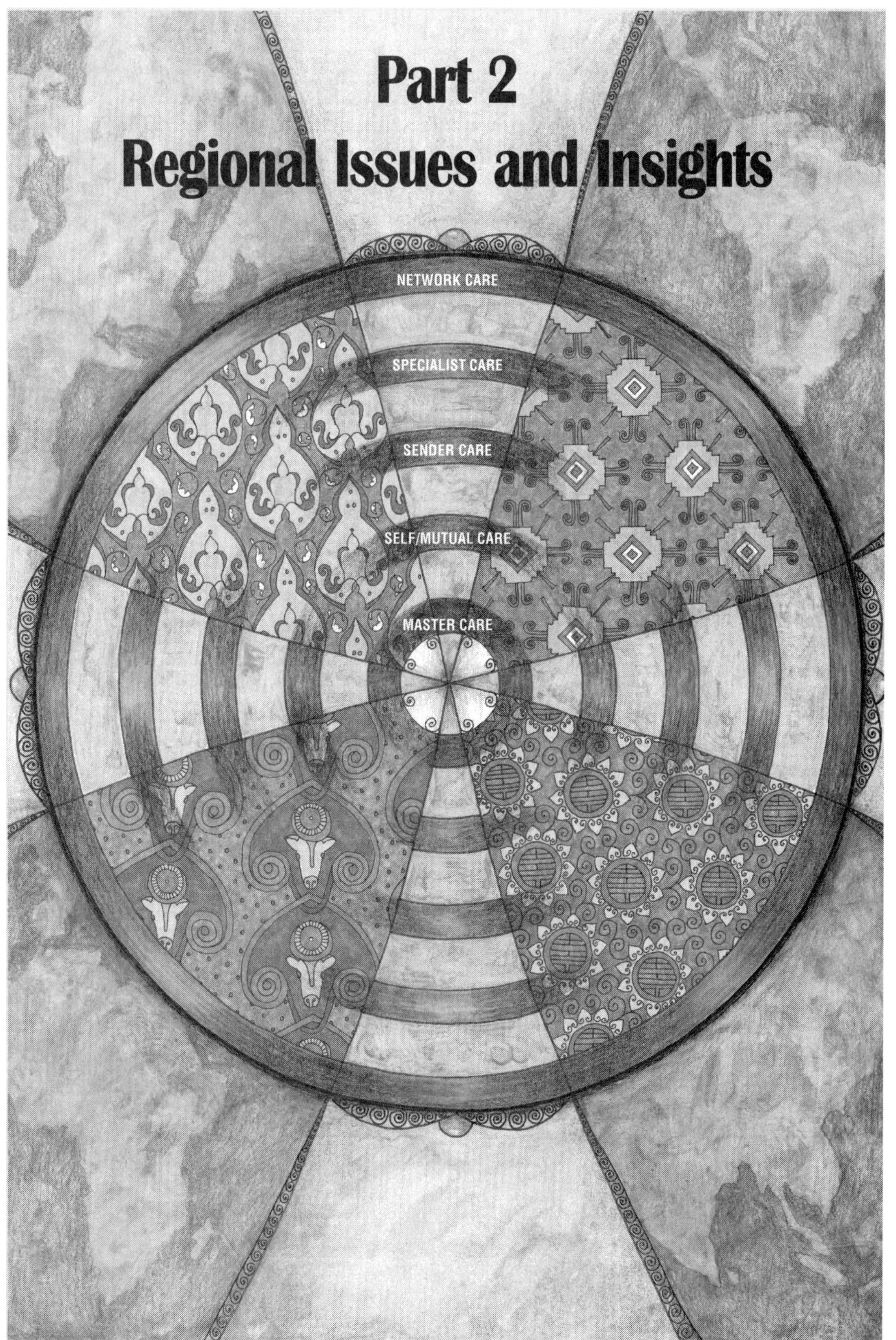

6

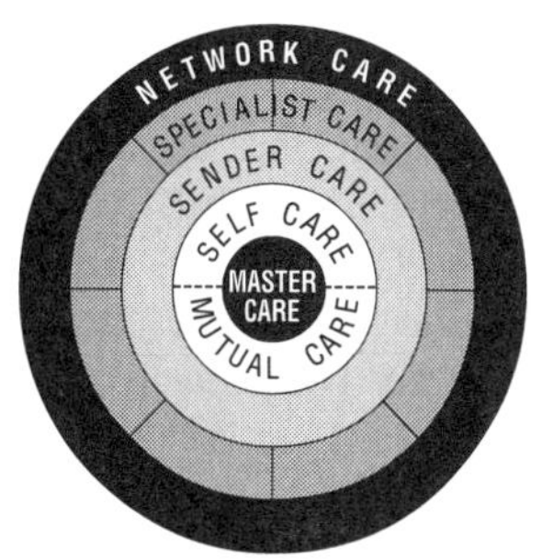

Challenges and Care For Asian Missionaries

Gracia Wiarda

This chapter focuses on some of the common issues facing Asian missionaries when they are on the field and on home assignment. These issues can differ in some measure from those confronted by Western missionaries. It is my hope that the various areas addressed in this article will lead to more action on the part of mission agencies and churches, as they seek to provide appropriate member care for Asian mission personnel.

It is my privilege to be in touch with many Asian missionaries through my work as a therapist at the Counselling and Care Centre in Singapore. Several mission agencies and churches in Singapore refer their candidates and missionaries to me for assessments, counselling, and debriefing. My perceptions are therefore based on feedback from a relatively broad base of missionaries working in different Third World countries. The people I work with tend to be in their late 30s to mid-50s. The issues they face may be peculiar to their generation. They are primarily Singaporeans but also include Taiwanese, Japanese, Nepalese, Koreans, Indonesians, Hong Kong Chinese, and Chinese Malaysians. The majority of them are first-generation Christians.

Field-Side Issues

Concern for the Family

Respecting and understanding the Asian culture will involve an appreciation of the strong sense of filial piety and family loyalty—an obligation to meet parental and familial needs and wants—in the Asian psyche. There is generally a lesser sense of entitlement, but rather a keen awareness of the need to repay relational debts. However, this trait may lessen as the socio-economic and cultural background changes with the onslaught of globalization and technological advances and as the emotional hold of family life breaks down. Many Chinese Asian missionaries continue to give their parents a monthly allowance while they are away. It represents a token of their gratitude for their parents' care and provision for them when they were young. Most parents expect this token even if they may not openly ask for it. It reflects well on the family when adult children express their gratitude in monetary terms, as well as in frequent home visits and practical caregiving. Thus, the attempts of mission personnel to visit or contact parents and relatives on behalf of the missionary mean a great deal to both missionaries and their family members. Often Christian friends and church members act as proxies in the discharge of filial duty by visiting (particularly during important festivals and events) and making phone calls to the parents.

The idea of an adult child going away to serve other people instead of staying back to take care of parents is still unacceptable to some Asian parents. If the adult child goes away for money-making purposes, advancement of career, or because of a lack of other work choices, it may be deemed prudent or necessary. In the case of missionaries, there may be a mutual understanding between them and the family that they should compensate in the form of financial contributions or return when the parents (for health or other reasons) need their service. The exception may be for those who have sufficiently well-to-do siblings who support their overseas ministry.

Language Learning

There is a general consensus that Asians find learning another Asian language easier than their Western counterparts. Most have already been exposed to more than one language or dialect from a young age. Some of them have gone straight into field ministry without needing a language-learning program—for instance, a Singaporean Mandarin speaking Chinese going to Taiwan or China. Some breeze through a language program, while others plod along perseveringly. One missionary experienced undue stress when there was an inner expectation to master another Asian language faster because of his Asian background. A few mentioned feeling rather embarrassed when making language blunders and causing misunderstanding, being themselves sensitive to the Asian tendency of not asking for clarification or correcting someone's mistakes. This Asian "politeness" is adopted so as to avoid causing the other person to "lose face" (experience shame). Nevertheless, Asian missionaries feel embarrassed when they fumble, knowing that blunders are noted even though they are not addressed.

Those who have grown up in countries where they had little exposure to English find themselves needing to learn the English language in order to become members of international missionary organizations. Many missionary candidates from Korea, Japan, Hong Kong, and Indonesia are sent for English language courses so that they can take courses in cross-cultural studies or participate in the orientation programs of their organizations. For them, the period of preparation for service is lengthened by at least a year. Many Asians already speak fluent English and have graduated from colleges and seminaries overseas. Those who had learned the language only for communication within their missions often find themselves at a disadvantage. Particularly during their first term, when bonding and mutual understanding with their international colleagues are quite critical, they usually do not have sufficient mastery of the language to help negotiate all the nuances inherent in cross-cultural communication. Apart from learning and working at mastering the national language, they need to continue learning and improving in English. Otherwise, they will not be able to benefit as much from mission conferences and seminars and will be unlikely to move into leadership positions, even though they may be very competent.

Adjusting to the New Culture

Many have expressed that, as Asians, they are able to bond more easily with nationals, whether in Africa or in Asia, because of their cultural affinity. Statements such as, "The nationals tend to open up to us and share more deeply with us than with Western missionaries," "The nationals treat us like family," and, "They confide in us and we can say things to them," are made. One missionary to Africa believed that what bridges the gap is the high value placed on the family and the extended family that Asians and Africans tend to share. She felt that most Western missionaries found it very hard to appreciate and understand the invisible family loyalty bonds that influence individual behavior. Another missionary shared that she was told by an African national that she was "family," but the Western colleague was more like an employer.

In some cases, Asian missionaries feel triangulated because they identify with the nationals as Asians and with the Westerners as team members. A national may criticize a Western colleague and expect the Asian missionary to understand and take sides. Though rarely framed very explicitly, the negative aspects of what Westerners stand for are often alluded to in the criticism. A national might say, "You know the Westerners, they...," or comparisons might be made between "them" (the Westerners) and "us" (the Asians) in the context of how things are done. Asians may not be aware of their own racial prejudice coloring their views of Western colleagues or of identification with the sentiments of the nationals. However, Western colleagues are still teammates with similar goals and calling, and Asian missionaries sometimes find themselves caught between two loyalties. On the other hand, one Asian family felt second class because the nationals preferred to host a Western family, since that was more prestigious. Among Asians themselves, there is racism based on the degree of lightness of skin color, cultural heritage, economic status of the country of origin, and other factors.

A common perception is that Western missionaries tend to be treated with more deference and outward respect, but Asian missionaries know the nationals better. Several have remarked that they are able to pick up signals when things are amiss. They feel that they can better read the nonverbal and verbal cues, what was said and not said, what was hinted at and meant. One person said, "You just know. I can pick up when they are just being polite, when to stop pushing."

A Singaporean Chinese expressed that sometimes the similarity she shares with the Taiwanese Chinese in both features and spoken language becomes a disadvantage. Although fluent in Chinese, she was raised in a multi-cultural context and in an English-medium school. She felt that the Taiwanese expected her to be more "Chinese" in her outlook and were less forgiving when she made mistakes in the use of the language or in interpreting some cultural cues and customs. Although educated in English, she would probably never see herself as "Western" in orientation by any means.

Asian countries share many similar cultural and religious expressions, including the wearing of school uniforms, the practice of having several generations and units of the extended family living nearby or under one roof, open markets, the offering of incense, the presence of shrines in homes, the use of talismans, and the celebration of Buddhist festivals and rites. The buildings of major religions are common sights: ornate Hindu and Buddhist temples, mosques, and Catholic cathedrals. While there are significant differences between countries and while Asians do experience some measure of cultural shock, on the whole they may be exposed to less shock in terms of an overload of differences. It seems that the Asian missionary, once settled, tends to move faster in establishing relationships and ministry with the nationals. The adjustment struggles may be more related to areas of lifestyle, standard of living, and understanding the deeper nuances of the particular culture of the country.

Collegial Relationships

Asians, particularly those for whom English is a second or third language, have to work harder to communicate with colleagues. Those who cannot hold their own with fluent English may minimize social contacts with Western or other Asian colleagues. It is natural to seek out homogeneous groups for social and emotional support. Often Koreans will look for other Koreans and Singaporeans for other Singaporeans when seeking fellowship.

A general belief is that working as an international team is enriching and a good testimony to the gospel message, but it is often stressful. Western missionaries, while mentally prepared to work with the nationals, are often not oriented to the cultural background of their Asian colleagues. The Asian colleague, though similar in some ways to the nationals, is quite different in other ways. Sometimes Western colleagues may have difficulty understanding where the Asian colleague is coming from. There are stories aplenty about miscommunication between the two, primarily as a result of differences in use of the language and style of expressions. Asian colleagues, in particular perhaps the Koreans, tend to value the spiritual disciplines and hard work, and they arrive on the field with very high expectations concerning the spirituality of their Western colleagues. One Asian was nonplussed by what he perceived as lack of dedication and Christian love. Some have expressed disappointment at what seems to be a vestige of colonialism. When inconsistencies of treatment and preference are perceived, these are often not verbalized. Thus, perceptions are often not clarified because of the sensitivity of the issues and sometimes because of the language barrier. Over time, the accumulation of such perceptions, whether accurate or inaccurate, leads to distancing and disillusionment.

When Asian missionaries are asked why they do not request help from Western missionaries when it is needed or would be appreciated, the frequent answer is, "I don't want to impose." This sensitivity towards being an imposition seems quite prevalent. There is a strong belief that Western colleagues value their time and space very highly. When help is proffered, Asians may still be hesitant to accept until they are certain that no inconvenience will be caused. Unfortunately, this dance may not be familiar to Western colleagues, and the number of steps back and forth may vary considerably among Asians themselves. Some look for non-verbal cues, while others listen for repeated offers before accepting.

On the other hand, it is interesting to note that quite a number of Asian missionaries who have been on the field for more than one term mention that they have changed as a result of interacting with their Western colleagues. They believe that they are now more open in their style of communication. One revealed that, being Asian, she had tended to be reticent in sharing, but she had learned to be more self-disclosing towards the latter part of the first term. Another said she learned to speak up so as to be heard and get what she needed. She had initially expected to be looked after, but she found that she did not receive because she did not ask her team leader. Several shared that they had learned to be more assertive when dealing with their team members. However, they tend to moderate their approach and engage in socially understood but more indirect ways when dealing with Asians. It seems that they generally prefer to have help offered by Western colleagues rather than request help directly. Although they may have learned new behaviors, their preference may not have changed.

Some find the fellowship meetings difficult to cope with because of the speed at which English is spoken. The various accents of spoken English make listening hard work as well. Since Asians are still the minority in most international mission bodies, they continue to find that they have to accommodate more to the prevalent Western culture. A single lady mentioned that fellowship suppers often cater to Western palates. Another tried to be part of her international team by hosting her colleagues and cooking special Chinese meals. After the meals, however, she was left out of the table games and general conversation, where cultural references were made that only the majority group would understand. She ended up feeling like a maid, serving food and doing the dishes while her colleagues sat around the table, played Scrabble, and chatted. She became very upset and felt discriminated against. She thought the others would try to come halfway to meet her social and inclusion needs. To cope with the situation, she stopped entertaining and distanced herself from others.

Children's Education and Welfare

Some Asian parents whose children go to boarding schools experience difficulty relating to their children as they grow older. This may be compounded by the fact that the culture of boarding schools tends to be more Western, and the longer the children are in boarding, the more fluent they become in English as compared to the mother tongue. This poses a greater problem for those parents who learned English only in order to be part of the mission organization. Unless they continue to make significant progress in English, they may find themselves becoming more distant from their children because of language problems. Unless the children are encouraged to read in their mother tongue when they are home on vacations, they may never be as fluent in it as needed.

Some parents try to get around this problem by serving in cities where there are international schools and where the children can stay at home with them. This is impossible for those working in isolated villages or other areas without such options. Most Asian school systems are such that home schooling is not a viable option. Even if possible, home schooling poses a greater challenge for children whose educational medium is an Asian language, as it would mean more isolation for them, as well as isolating the parent from the mission community. One Japanese family placed their children in the Indonesian school system while homeschooling them in Japanese and later moved to another field where there was a Japanese school when the children finished primary-level studies.

One parent expressed that his children tend to be more assertive, expressing their preferences and knowing their rights, than they would have been if they were raised in their home culture instead of a boarding school. One child was reported to have said, "You need to take my views into consideration as well." Some parents find the children more independent in their decision making than they are prepared for. Several families indicated that having siblings together at the boarding school helped them feel more assured. The parents expect the oldest child to keep an eye on the younger ones and to maintain the sense of family. Asian children are still in a minority in boarding schools, and parents may be more concerned about their acceptance and integration.

A ubiquitous parental concern is reintegration of older children into tertiary schools of the home country. There are two main fears: the children's potential struggle with cultural re-adaptation and their difficulty with the educational system. The situation is particularly difficult when the home country's educational system does not use English as a medium of instruction. This puts Asian families in a predicament if they ever desire to return home halfway through their children's schooling. Boarding schools are attempting to expose Asian MKs to their mother tongue, but not at the level of proficiency that is needed for re-entrance to a school back home. It may be very difficult for an Asian MK to enter an Asian non-English university.

Going outside Asia for higher education is an option, but it is more expensive for the Asian missionary family. Generally, an overseas education is a highly valued commodity for Asians, as it often means better educational input, status, and employment prospects for the graduate. It is unlikely that church members will be eager to fund missionary children abroad if they themselves can afford to send their own children only to local universities. Also, it is unlikely that young people will have relatives living overseas to help them adjust there. If Asian MKs do go to university abroad, they may return to their own country and culture an additional three to four years later than the typical Western MK. It may be more difficult for Asian MKs to feel "Asian" when all their education, from kindergarten to college, is done away from the home country. The majority of their peers throughout their schooling life will not be from their own country of origin. It may be quite a task for these MKs to fit in when they return to their home countries as young adults.

Singapore presents a unique problem in its very structured, pressurized system, its two-language policy, and its requirement for a cash bond for males of 11 years and older who reside outside the country. Looking into educational and housing arrangements for middle school children needs to be high on the MK care agenda.

Leadership Styles and Opportunities

The two preferred leadership styles seem to be the benevolent authoritative and the consultative styles. Generally there is a strong loyalty towards and respect for the authority figure. It is often expected that the authority figure should have one's interests and welfare at heart. The Asian tends to avoid challenging a leader out of respect for both the person and the position held. Therefore, Asian workers struggle when they feel that they have been wrongfully treated or that partiality has been shown towards others. To deal with the issue directly may come across as challenging leadership, being self-seeking, or owning up to feelings of hurt. This may be considered too threatening and perhaps unspiritual. The affected individuals feel anger, disappointment, and guilt simultaneously. They may berate themselves for having negative feelings and for harboring inner complaints towards the leader. It becomes an emotional and spiritual crisis for some, and they often try to process their feelings internally. They may be more open to talking to someone outside the system or to another trusted colleague rather than leveling with the leader.

One person bemoaned, "How can I submit when he has made such an obviously wrong decision? But not to submit is not respecting authority." Another lady asked, "He is my leader. How can I feel this way and complain like the Israelites and not be sinning?" There is a tendency to have high expectations about the character of the leader as well, that the person be mature spiritually and emotionally. A high level of emotional control in public is expected, and if a person explodes in anger, it brings much shame and loss of face. There tends to be more willingness to forgive for incompetence than for perceived lack of patience, humility, integrity, or spiritual disciplines.

There has also been a shift among the Asians towards wanting a consultative leadership style. Some have felt hampered in their work because leaders had goals that did not take into consideration the gifting and individual goals of the missionary. Here the feeling expressed was that leaders did not trust them in the pursuit of their ministry focus. This is particularly true for those who have to work closely as a team. They feel that they have very little say in their own direction and job fit. Asians who are given free rein to develop in their ministry focus tend to express appreciation.

Team leadership opportunities within the field require a good command of English. Members from certain Asian countries are disadvantaged unless they have had the opportunity of tertiary education in English abroad and have gained fluency in the language, both spoken and written. Leadership roles also require that the person be able to communicate well with the usually larger group of Western colleagues. The homogeneity principle tends to motivate group behavior and so may work against the minority members in a mixed team. The reverse would be true if Asians dominate in numbers, and the leader chosen would then more likely be an Asian.

Pastoral Care on the Field

Most Asian missionaries value a strong connection with the home base and express a desire for pastoral care. They welcome official visits from the staff of the mission home office or from the pastor or members of their home church. Perhaps they feel that they can better share with other Asians, using their own language or slang, or perhaps they long periodically for a taste of home away from home. Little indicators that the missionary is being remembered—such as birthday cards, postcards, letters, the occasional phone call, or small packages—are valued, particularly by singles, who admit feeling lonely and isolated at times. Some share that they feel more able to process their feelings and thoughts with a pastoral person who is outside the "system." One missionary requested a pastor to visit her and act as her mediator to resolve some team issues, as she was the only Asian member and she felt that having another Asian would be a great support for her.

The proximity of and relatively cheap airfares to Asian countries allow for frequent mission trips organized by some Singaporean churches to expose their members to missions, as well as to visit their missionaries. These trips nurture vital contact between missionaries and their church during their years on the field, and they permit church members to share in the ministry. The latter are better able to pray for and promote continued interest in the work when they return.

Home-Side Issues

Reentry Stress

A Singaporean missionary couple once remarked, "The Singapore Dream is but a dream for us. We sometimes feel like paupers among princes. Singapore has become very comfortable and seemingly or really affluent. The difference in lifestyles between Singapore and what we are used to [on the field] is almost Grand Canyon-wide. Many of our friends have upgraded to bigger and better housing, own club memberships, and dine in fancy places. Coming back from the field, it has become increasingly difficult for us to conform and adjust to the present standard of living."

Exposure to the good life attained by some contemporaries often brings about mixed feelings. The contrast in financial standing and spending between these individuals and the missionary may be experienced as a rude shock. One of the Asian ways, in particular among the Chinese, of welcoming a person back from a long stay away is to take him/her out for fancy meals in fancy restaurants. A Singaporean missionary said that she ate her way back into the country and then out of the country. Also, the missionary may be heaped with special monetary gifts, taken to posh clubs, and even treated to short vacations. Since it is generally expected that missionaries are "poor" and have "sacrificed to serve overseas," Christian friends are quick to take the tab. While it is wonderful to experience abundance, some struggle with the disparity of the two worlds they straddle—perceived as poor in one and as rich in the other. Some struggle with the sense of being patronized; others, with the sense of being put on a pedestal. The question of one's identity apart from one's role as a missionary may trouble the sensitive soul.

Those who have been able to make more frequent visits to their home countries during their terms on other Asian fields may be less impacted by the rapid changes of technology and lifestyle. It seems that missionaries from the richer Asian countries are able to make more frequent and shorter home assignments as well as take vacations in their home countries. This is helped by the relatively cheaper airfares they have to pay compared to their Western colleagues returning home. While this may be an advantage, it challenges the expectation still held by the majority of Asian Christians that missionaries should be sacrificial and careful with money. Some missionaries feel compelled to explain their plans and actions to ward off misunderstanding and jealousy. It is not uncommon to hear a missionary quickly respond, "This was given to me," or, "This was a hand-me-down dress from my lawyer friend," when complimented for having an expensive belonging or for wearing a beautiful dress.

Housing for Singles

Single missionaries are often expected to stay at the home of their parents or a sibling while on home assignment. However, there are several reasons why this may not be a good arrangement. Family members may find it difficult to understand the single's need for separateness and space.

Most Asian families (unless particularly well to do) do not leave the bedroom of the missionary empty during the person's term on the field. The room may have been rented out for economic reasons. One single lady had to sleep on a couch in the living room. What was more stressful was that her bedroom had been rented out to a male boarder. In other situations, the room may have been taken over by siblings or other members of the family, or, for practical reasons, it may have been converted into a study room. Single missionaries may feel less at home in their own home country than in an apartment on the field. It requires extra energy to readjust to sharing a room in crowded conditions, with disrupted family members feeling unhappy about the imposition. Sometimes the close proximity causes unresolved issues and conflicts to resurface. Several missionaries have highlighted how they feel more comfortable on the field. One heaved a sigh of relief as she neared the end of home assignment, saying, "I am glad to return to my country of service and rest up."

For some, there is the psychological stress of adjusting to living with parents, who may revert to treating the adult as a child. Asian parents often continue to expect child-like deference and respect when one is under their roof. Chinese parents use the phrase, "I have eaten more salt than you have rice," to silence any dissenting opinion. Singles, who have experienced living competently abroad, find this stressful. Since many Asians find it hard to apply conflict management principles when it comes to handling differences with their parents, they feel the tension all the more. It is also difficult to bring new rules or activities into established family life. For instance, the bedroom doors in some homes are seldom closed or locked, and family members enter at will. Having savored what it means to have boundaries respected, the missionary may now feel the "invasion" to be very intrusive. One missionary found that although all her siblings had married and moved out, the parental home remained like Grand Central Station. The parents were babysitting several of the grandchildren, and her siblings and their spouses would take their evening meal at the home before taking their children home. This provided an excellent setting to reconnect with the extended family, but it left the missionary feeling frazzled.

Even with understanding parents, there may still be stress. The missionary may want to contribute financially towards the household expenses. Among traditional Asian Chinese, it is often the cultural expression of a filial and gainfully employed adult to give a token sum to the parents, even more so if the person stays with them. However, this contribution may not have been factored into the missionary's home assignment stipend.

Increasingly in Singapore, single missionaries are advised to buy their own apartments, more to resolve a future retirement housing problem than for home assignment housing. This option is not always affordable, especially for Asian counterparts whose government does not provide subsidized public housing.

Housing for Families

Most Singaporean missionary families buy their own homes before they go overseas. However, their apartments are usually rented out so that the income can go towards paying the mortgage. If a family wants to use the apartment, arrangements will have to be made to ensure that tenancy completion coincides with their return from the field. Thereafter, there will be further paperwork involved to get new tenants. Most Singapore families choose home assignment options that suit their older children's overseas school calendar; for those electing shorter but more frequent home assignments, this arrangement becomes impractical.

Those who have personal resources, either through well-endowed families or friends, will have their housing needs adequately met. Resources available within their home church can make a big difference. One family moved into the new and empty apartment of a church couple who were getting married later in the year. However, there are families who do not have access to a large support network and have to camp out with relatives.

Since to my knowledge none of the mission agencies in Asia keeps apartments for missionaries on home leave, appropriate and restful housing arrangements continue to present a challenge for most.

Parental Expectations and Needs

Asian families are likely to expect the missionary to do his/her part to fulfill family obligations while on home leave. Since the siblings and other relatives have been assuming the familial responsibilities and duties during the missionary's absence, the balance of relational fairness calls for the missionary to pull as much weight as possible while at home. One lady became solely responsible for taking her father to medical appointments and handling his physical care. Another cleared the financial morass created by another family member. Where there are tensions between family members, the missionary may be roped in to resolve the issues. Often a previous family role is reassumed, such as peacemaking, caregiving, or overfunctioning. Much time and energy are expended in these roles, and little is left for rest, self-care, and reconnecting with supporters and friends. Resultant feelings may include a sense of burden, guilt, fatigue, emotional drain, and being stretched at the end of home assignment.

It is common for older Asian parents to continue maintaining the hierarchical posture in relating to their adult children. They often continue to tell the adult what is good for him/her and what ought to be done, sometimes in seemingly offhand comments and sometimes very directly. Single missionaries are subtly and sometimes not so subtly pressured to get married. Marriage is seen as a means of ensuring security for the future. One lady in her 50s was still pressured to get a husband, any man, and settle down. On the other hand, since singles are supposedly less encumbered than their married siblings, they are often the ones "assigned" to care for aging and frail parents. Although traditional-minded parents generally prefer to be with their eldest son, many of them live with and are cared for by the single child. Some families tend not to see missions as a worthy enough profession to place before family obligations. The culture still defines filial piety as financially and physically supporting aged parents. Perhaps in a couple of decades this mindset will change, as young adults and parents are encouraged to do financial planning for their retirement.

There are those who are blessed with supportive and understanding family members who respect them and their calling and seek in all ways to facilitate the readjustment at home. Often these members are from richer backgrounds or have Christian siblings who have since moved up in life and are willing to support them or who are second-generation Christians.

Financial Considerations

Asian missionaries tend to be very careful about how they are perceived by others in their financial management and lifestyle. Most of them tend to be frugal and are often hesitant to ask directly for what they need. There is a reluctance to talk about financial matters for fear of appearing unspiritual. (The Campus Crusade Asian missionaries may be different in their approach because of the culture of the mission.) When they do ask, it is often out of necessity. Missionaries are more likely to express their financial concerns only when directly approached. Some may feel financial pressure and not express it, but they would appreciate having the mission or church leadership check with them. Generally, they prefer being asked rather than to have to ask or inform leadership and others about the sensitive issue of money.

Some struggle with finances more when they are on home leave. The many social obligations to family and friends can make quite a dent in the monthly stipend. Monetary gifts to the bereaved at wakes, birthday gifts, wedding gifts, transport, and other miscellaneous costs add up. There is often an expected increase in contribution to the parents when staying with them. It cannot be assumed that parents or siblings, particularly those who are non-Christians and not too well off financially, will take care of the missionary's needs. One missionary reported that she was able to save money on the field but not while on home leave. Another reported that he was shocked at how much money he spent on social obligations and transport costs going to the various functions and church meetings.

Many reported, however, that they were amply supplied by monetary gifts slipped to them by friends and supporters. Many receive practical gifts like clothes, books, and toys. This may be one reason that church and mission leaders do not check on how missionaries are faring financially, as they expect them to be getting extra support from outside the official system. One missionary was not paid for three months because the church treasurer was too busy to sign the checks and did not think that the missionary would be financially strapped. Those who have not nurtured a good social support system before leaving for the field tend to be those who do not have as many supplementary gifts.

As far as I know, there are no retirement homes provided for Asian missionaries, and most Asian countries are not welfare states. Singaporean missionaries are encouraged to purchase government subsidized public housing for their retirement needs. Unless they have worked for some time before becoming a missionary or have helpful and well-to-do relatives, not all of them can afford the down payment. Other Asian missionaries may not have access to subsidized housing or the financial resources to purchase retirement housing. Some mission agencies provide guidance and help in developing retirement plans, while others leave missionaries to buy their own insurance policies or handle their own financial planning. One missionary jokingly responded, "Well, I hope I die quickly," when asked whether she had enough money put aside to live on after retirement.

Children's Schooling Needs

One unique problem of Asian parents is the reintegration of their children into schools in the home country. In most Asian countries, the medium of instruction in the schools is not English. The school system also tends to be more structured and intense and operates with a class size of about 40 pupils to a teacher. Having a child above kindergarten age fit easily into the system halfway through the school year is nearly impossible, unlike in the Western system. To enter a Singaporean school for just a year while the family is on home assignment requires herculean effort, incessant prayer, and the goodwill of many levels of officials in the Ministry of Education and the school. Unless the schooling issue is creatively handled, most Asian families with primary and secondary level school children will have to make short home assignment stays.

The solution of short but frequent home assignments may become a problem in the future. Short stays feel more like extended vacations. It is difficult to experience one's culture when one is mostly observing but not intensely participating. A worrying thought is that Asian MKs may have even less of a sense of rootedness in their home country than Western MKs. When mother tongue usage is not developed at boarding school and the school culture is likely to be Western, children shift imperceptibly but surely towards Western frames of reference. Unlike their Western counterparts, however, Asian MKs do not return to the West but to an Asian country when their schooling is done. Most parents are delighted with the educational system of international schools, which tend to be less pressured than Asian schools. They feel that their children are getting a better education. They appreciate the care and spiritual guidance provided in mission-run boarding schools. Few are thinking of the adjustment issues that their children may experience when their entire school and dorm life is within a Western orientation. There are now attempts to recruit Asian teachers to teach Korean and Chinese students in some boarding schools and to set up a dormitory catering to Asian MKs. However, there are still teething problems.

Home Church Expectations

It appears that many Asian churches are still expecting their missionaries to fit right back into church ministry while on long home assignment, such as administrative work at the church office or extensive pastoral or teaching duties. This is particularly true when the church is a fully supporting one, a smaller congregation, or a non-English-speaking one. Members may ask awkward questions like, "How is it that you are doing nothing?" and, "Why don't you...?" to a missionary who took home leave to reintegrate the children into the local schools. Some pastors may look forward to having the missionary on home assignment share their heavy work load, but they frame it as, "I want to give you opportunities to reacquaint yourself with the members." While some missionaries may have the energy to take on ministry duties, others arrive home already exhausted from long periods of learning and serving in a different language and culture. They may return to the field not feeling adequately rested and revitalized, and some actually return more tired and drained than when they left. A couple who were able to take a vacation just before resuming their field duties reported that it helped them recoup enough to start the new term without feeling depressed.

It seems that Asians do less deputation work, on the whole, than their Western counterparts. They are more likely to take on ministry duties and to attend as many of the regular meetings of their supporting churches as possible. In Singapore, it is common to have one church, the home church, providing fully for a missionary's support. Because the support sum can be quite substantial, the church members may expect more from their missionaries in terms of ministry results or service when they are on home leave. In some international mission organizations, missionary families may have to raise a monthly support figure amounting to more than what most of their church members earn monthly. This is due to the high cost of living in some Asian countries, and included in the support package are the mission's administration costs, children's overseas educational expenses, transport allowances to and from the field, medical and retirement funds, and other items. There is generally a willingness to support the individual who is leaving a high-paying job to go into missions or who has good qualifications that would command a good salary in the secular world. In such cases, the high support amount that has to be raised by the home church is still less than the real or potential earning power of the missionary, and the missionary is perceived as making the greater sacrifice. However, if a missionary is getting more financial support than would be gained from a job or from professional training, more seems to be demanded from the individual to merit the financial investment of the church.

Some Recommendations for Asian Member Care

Field-Side Issues

Pastoral care and help for the family

Mission agencies and churches may want to give serious consideration to the importance of providing pastoral care to the parents of missionaries as part of their commitment and support of each missionary. Visiting the parents during festivals, calling on them to inquire about their welfare, treating them to special dinners or events, and praying for them when they are ill are small gestures that mean a lot culturally. These things create positive feelings towards the church and predispose non-Christian parents towards Christ. The financial support raised by missionaries may need to include an amount that goes towards parents, who expect such a contribution from their adult children. Missionaries cannot say "Corban" like the Pharisees and expect to avoid supporting their parents. One agency hosted a special Chinese New Year dinner to honor the parents and gave them the traditional gifts of oranges and "red packets" on behalf of their missionaries on the field.

Flexible language program

Tailoring language programs according to factors such as aptitude, learning style, number of languages spoken and written, and similarity of the new language to the individual's mother tongue (for instance, Japanese writing and Chinese writing are quite similar) is a step towards acknowledging the advantages some Asians possess language-wise. Structured programs developed with the Western learner in mind may require adaptation to fit the peculiarities of the Asian learner.

Bonding with the mission team

It is important for Asians to experience bonding with the mission agency through the team members on the field. Even those who already speak the national or local language when they first arrive on the field need to be oriented and helped in the transition. Perhaps assigning a "big brother" or "big sister" from the team would be helpful for those who do not go through the usual language and orientation program. It cannot be assumed that knowledge of a language is equivalent to knowledge and understanding of the culture and way of life. The national believers, if there are any in that field, will probably be the best informers and helpers for the new missionary. However, the mission is supposed to be the "family," and it is important that the initial caregiving comes from the team. This will contribute to more cohesiveness between the Asian and Western missionaries.

Team building

Working with an international team will demand extra sensitivity on the part of the majority group to the needs of the minority group. It may require greater attentiveness to including the one who is most different from the group, helping those who struggle with English, and avoiding any semblance of unfair treatment.

Efforts need to be made to challenge racial stereotypes, enhance the personal growth of missionaries within the international team, and strengthen personal and corporate identity. Having lectures or presentations on the general differences between various nationalities is educational and informative, but it is insufficient for promoting mutual understanding and acceptance. Reflective and experiential group exercises that increase awareness of the latent or unconscious racial beliefs that missionaries may have imbibed from their cultural background are necessary as the first step to change. These beliefs can then be challenged and discarded. Building a cohesive team of culturally sensitive and mature individuals will go a long way toward reducing attrition from interpersonal conflicts on the field.

Boarding school for older children

Asian parents may want to seriously consider and try other options of schooling to keep their children with them until they are at least in their teens before sending them away to boarding school. This will give the children more time not only to bond with the family but also to embrace cultural values from the parents. However, this may not be possible, as there may not be any international schools nearby, some local schools are just not suitable, and home schooling does not work for every family. Mission agencies and Asian missionary families must take equal responsibility in providing for their MKs an environment that encourages and maintains some measure of their own national identity. Eating with chopsticks (for the Chinese, Japanese, or Koreans) or eating with fingers (for the Indians) once a week at the cafeteria in the boarding school is really not good enough.

Home-Side Issues

Home assignment coordinator

It may be helpful to appoint a home assignment coordinator. This person acts as a resource and pastoral person and actively looks into the various needs of the missionary during the home assignment period. Duties may include:

- Debriefing and counseling or referring for professional counseling as needed.
- Looking into orientation for reentry, housing, and cultural induction programs for the children.
- Researching schooling possibilities for children who are on a year-long home assignment.
- Planning with the missionary a personalized plan for rest and relaxation, self and relational growth programs, programs for upgrading skills, spiritual retreats, and deputation meetings.
- Collaborating with the missionary and the supporting churches regarding the kind and extent of church involvement during home assignment.
- Monitoring the missionary throughout the home assignment to ensure that the purpose and personalized plan for home assignment are accomplished.
- Supplying updates on trends in the church and society, immigration, education, and other national policies.
- Educating Asian church leaders and members as to the purposes of the home assignment.
- Processing the home assignment experience before the missionary returns to the field.

There is a special advantage to having a coordinator shared by several mission agencies or churches. Such a person knows when there are large enough numbers of missionaries back on home assignment at any one time so special growth groups, MK meetings, or marital enrichment seminars can be held.

Housing coordinator

There are several ways to resolve housing needs of singles and families for up to one year in length. The most effective is to build and maintain a broad network with the Christian community so that resources, whether financial or housing, can be tapped when needed. There are many Asian Christians who are generous and desirous of sharing their resources for the use of God's ministers. There are many churches in Asian cities that have members in the educated and well-to-do classes, and they are often very willing to offer their furnished, empty apartments/houses free or at minimal rent for short-term stays. What may be needed is a person who is respected and known in the community to take on the administrative task of coordination and management of needs and resources and to see this service as a vital contribution to member care.

Flexible arrangements for home assignments

Missionaries serving in nearby fields may wish to consider frequent and shorter home assignments and even vacations in their home country. This reduces major disruption for the children in their schooling and increases the satisfaction of extended family members to have more frequent contact. However, missionaries may also want to take into consideration the sensibilities of their compatriots, who may view this solution as an easy life with more holidays than workdays. One church member commented enviously, "Only the missionary can travel as much as the rich and famous." Several factors will need to be weighed carefully in this matter, including the degree of hardship on the field, the stage of the family life cycle, the children's sense of rootedness in the culture, the financial burden on the church, and other considerations.

Retirement plans

International mission agencies must take into consideration that Asian countries are not welfare states that provide public health and retirement services for their citizens (as in the UK) or that have a system for social security payments after retirement (as in the USA). It is important that mission agencies and churches plan with their missionaries to consider retirement needs and encourage them to raise support either for pension plans or endowment policies.

Conclusion

In this article, I have discussed some specific issues for Asian missionaries and have made recommendations for providing these workers with member care. It must be highlighted that contextual variables such as differing economic, cultural, religious, political, and educational structures exist among various South East Asian countries, creating different experiences and challenges for each group. Asian missionaries are therefore not a homogeneous group, and differences among them must also be addressed. With the trend of increasing response to missions from Asians, sending churches and mission organizations can no longer ignore Asians' special concerns and challenges.

Reflection and Discussion

1. What are some of the main strengths of Asian missionaries that the author describes? In what ways do the strengths enhance their ministry?

2. Respond to the notion that Asian missionaries would usually be more effective if they worked together as a homogeneous group under an Asian organization.

3. In what ways can the cultural gap between Asian and Western missionaries be minimized, so that cross-cultural teamwork can be enhanced?

4. What are some possible changes in organizational structure that mission agencies may want to adopt to meet the challenge of internationalization of staff?

5. How can we sensitively address the issue of racism among missionaries and work towards removing the unconscious barriers to deeper trust and acceptance?

Gracia Wiarda *is Senior Therapist at the Counselling and Care Centre in Singapore. She is married to Dr. Timothy James Wiarda, a lecturer at Singapore Bible College. They have two children. Together they served with Arab World Ministries in Algeria and in the Sultanate of Oman (1980–1992). Gracia received her B.A. in psychology in 1975 from Wheaton College and an M.A. in interpersonal communications in 1976 from Wheaton Graduate School. She also holds a Marriage and Family Therapy degree (1989) from Hahnemann Graduate School in the USA. Email: wiarda@singnet.com.sg.*

Special thanks to Mr. Patrick Lim of WEC, Mrs. Belinda Ng of SIM, and Mr. Kenneth Tan of OMF for their helpful comments on this paper.

7

MK Education and Care: Lessons From Asia

POLLY CHAN

Asian sending countries are gradually becoming more involved in MK care. As more information, training, and support are offered, the result will be healthier families and more resilient MKs. This chapter looks at some of the ups and downs of Asian MK life, interspersed with three case studies. It concludes with several practical exercises and resources to help MKs and their families—both Asian and non-Asian.

I started my work with MKs in 1990 at an MK school in Japan. I was surprised to find that half of the students in the school were Asians—from Korea, Singapore, and Hong Kong! In December 1996, during the Missionary/Christian Overseas Schools (MCOS) Regional Rally in Manila, teachers and boarding home parents from different MK schools approached me and sought advice on how to help Asian children attending their schools. It was on that occasion that I became more aware of the increasing concern for Asian children at MK schools. A further concern was how MKs attending international or local schools on the field were struggling to readjust to school and life in their home country. Personnel in MK schools were becoming aware of the urgency of these needs. The relevance of MK support services and the need for MK workers are also being understood more and more on the Asian home side.

During the past decade, I have been grateful to see that both Western and Asian mission personnel and educators have responded positively to the dramatic increase of Asian MKs. The development of the two groups, though, has progressed at a different rate, with the Western response being earlier and quicker. The Asian mission community, however, is slowly but steadily catching up!

Some Background Perspectives

Asia has been the largest missionary sending continent in the Two-Thirds World (Barrett and Johnson, 2001; Pate, 1991, p. 29). Korean research in 1994, for example, has confirmed that country's continuous and dramatic growth in mission. Compared with the 93 Korean missionaries in 1979, the number had jumped to 3,272 by the end of June 1994 (Lee, 1994, p. 1). Excluding cross-cultural missionaries reaching other peoples in their home country, Korea now ranks fourth in terms of overseas missionaries, following the USA, UK, and Canada. Some current estimates put Korean missionaries at about 8,000. Estimates of Indian missionaries working within India itself (often cross-culturally) are put at about 15,000 (Rajendran, 1998).

The number of Asian MKs is also growing, understandably! Research from 1988 through 1998 in my organization, Overseas Missionary Fellowship (OMF), for example, shows that the number of Asian MKs in OMF has more than quadrupled in the last 10 years and that the number of Asian sending countries has increased from five to eight. Besides Hong Kong, Japan, Korea, the Philippines, and Singapore, we now also have missionaries with children from Malaysia, Taiwan, and India. Other research (Chan, 1999) reveals that in the period 1988–1998, the number of MKs from Korea more than tripled, from 13 to 46.

As we look at these figures, we are excited to know that many Asians have joined the global mission force. With the relatively sudden increase in the number of Asian missionaries in the past decade, the concern is not only in sending out these missionaries, but also in how to take good care of them and their families. We are grateful to have our Western counterparts who have gone before us in this ministry. There are valuable experiences we can learn from them so as to avoid repeating previous mistakes in the ministry.

Nevertheless, there are also areas that are unique to the Asian culture and situation, and Asians need to invest personnel and resources in developing the ministry. For instance, recent research conducted by the Hong Kong Association of Christian Mission (HKACM) found that missionary parents reported that concern for their children ranked second among reasons for leaving the field, whereas it was seventh from the mission organization's perspective (Hung, 2000). For Singaporeans, a minimum bond of S$75,000 has to be paid to the government if parents choose to continue with overseas schooling for boys after they have reached the age of 11 (Taylor, 1993). Such a national policy has become a major hurdle for some families who would like to continue their ministry overseas after their boys turn 12. The next few years will be a critical period in the history of Korean missions, as the majority of Korean MKs pass through adolescence, work through identity issues, and possibly return "home" (Moon, 1997). A similar concern can be applied to other Asian countries with a monocultural and monolinguistic background, such as Japan, Taiwan, and even Hong Kong. There is a certain inflexibility in the culture and educational system in many Asian countries, which requires proactive care of Asian children, especially upon their reentry or at the time of the family's return.

Potential of Asian MKs

Asian MKs have great potential, and investing in the lives of these children is worth the effort. In the book *Kids Without Borders: Journals of Chinese Missionary Kids* (Chan, 2000), Chinese MKs of different ages, whose parents originally came from Hong Kong, Singapore, Taiwan, and North America, shared their MK experiences. All of these Asian MKs spent their childhood on the mission field, such as in Africa, South America, and different Asian countries. Many of them had an English education in MK schools, while others studied in local schools on the mission field. All these children are fluent in at least two or three languages, including English, their mother tongue, and the field language. They have interests in the world that are not limited to their parents' country, and many of them also enjoy making international friends. Some of them even inherited their parents' vision and have become second-generation missionaries or are preparing to serve in overseas missions. MKs who have received an English education in MK/international Christian (IC) schools are usually able to bring out the best of both Western and non-Western values and become fine examples of world Christians and cross-cultural workers (Loong, 2000).

Below is a short account written by a Singaporean MK who grew up in Africa. As you read, you will be amazed at the maturity and potential of these Asian MKs.

I Love Africa

*by Joel Ng Kuang-Jong**

Missionary kids (MKs) are a funny breed. I've often found that what is true for me is true for an MK who lives in India, South America, or elsewhere. We may come from the four corners of the earth, yet when we share our experiences with other MKs, we find ourselves saying, "That sounds just like what I did," or, "That's exactly how I feel." It's funny because we find so much in common among ourselves yet so little in common with our fellow countrymen.

Why is this so? I guess we view the world differently from the people at home. We are more in tune with what we have experienced during our formative years. As a child, I saw victims of a myriad of diseases nearly every day in the hospital where my father worked. Having seen such suffering, I felt I had no other choice as a fellow human being than to help these people who were no less made in God's image than I was. I made it a point to return to Africa, initially because I felt that I did not fit into the Singaporean way of life, but later because I realized that life would be so much more fulfilling there. This has prompted me to study Third World Development when I enter university in England this September.

As a member of a missionary family, I have learned to put my trust in God as I have seen Him perform miracles during my time in Africa. One of the many miracles we experienced was during a hot season in Africa. The rainy season was late that year, and we knew that the Africans would not have enough time to grow their crops if it did not rain soon. As we closed our nightly family devotions, we each prayed for rain, and as my father prayed, a heavy thunderstorm broke loose. Perhaps the most glorious sound in the world—raindrops on zinc roofing—continued through the night.

The comforts of Singapore have never left me at ease. The ugliness of materialism here is magnified by what I have seen in the Third World. We who have so much only want more, and we fail to recognize our blessings. It is difficult, then, to think of those who have so little, yet who rejoice in the little they do have. I guess I want to be like that—having little, yet each day thanking God for His blessings and relying on Him for the future.

It is even more amazing when the Africans, who have so little, freely give of what they have to visitors, even strangers, not thinking of what they may get in return. In Kefa Sempangi's testimony of life under Idi Amin's reign in Uganda, "Reign of Terror, Reign of Love," he recounts how a Dutch friend once told him, "Giving is not a two-way street, but to tell the truth it is a flowing river. It does not stop or return, but only passes on."

To me, working with the people of Africa is both a calling and a blessing. Their daily victories are the important ones we sometimes take for granted—life over death, health over sickness and disease, a bountiful harvest over starvation. Living close to them only heightens one's sense of blessing. Working in Africa is also something I have been very sure about. God has blessed me with the potential to do anything I want. In return, I find the most appropriate response is to pass on the gifts he has blessed me with to the people of my birthplace—Africa.

Challenges for Asians

Raising children overseas among different cultures has its challenges, some of

* Used with permission from *Intercom*, SIM Issue 141, September/October 1999.

which are unique to Asians. For instance, missionary parents may have to handle pressure from their extended family and friends, make changes in their Asian lifestyle, and broaden their monocultural mindset. For Asian MKs, growing up overseas has many privileges, but returning to live and study in the parents' home country, where people have low tolerance of cultural differences, can be very difficult. The education of MKs has been a pressing issue for Asians, and it will take time before some good Asian MK educational options can be more fully developed. Besides facing unique challenges as Asians, many Asian MKs also share with their non-Asian counterparts the challenge of making frequent transitions. Saying hellos and good-byes to people and places can be very hard, not only for adults, but for children as well. Many adult Asian MK caregivers and even parents may not be aware of the effect that unresolved grief may have on these children.

Sacrifice in Missions

Asians value relationships, and they are closely tied to their extended family. Missionary parents may face pressure from relatives, friends, and even other Christians who do not understand missions and who discourage them from taking their young children to "suffer" in disadvantaged places. In response to such opposition, it is important for parents to have a clear sense of calling from the Lord. Parents also need to have a balanced view of the gains and losses of being an MK. They need to count the cost of bringing up children on the mission field but also believe that the overseas experience will bring blessings to their children. In times of trial, they need to trust that God has good plans for their children—plans to prosper and not to harm them (Jer. 29:11).

Balance Between Family and Ministry

Having both quantity and quality time with children is important. Some Asian parents are so involved in their work that they have neglected the needs of their children. Others understand the importance of spending time with the family, but they struggle to put their head knowledge into practice. Once a Korean MK in our boarding school shared that during the summer holiday, 17 mission teams visited his family, and his mother was busy all the time cooking for the visitors. Parents may need to be more assertive in protecting their family time, as well as in taking adequate rest time for their own physical and mental health. They may also need to help mission leaders and supporting churches understand their family needs and establish a work schedule together, including vacation time for the family.

It is healthy and important for children to be involved in their parents' ministry. A teenage Chinese MK shared that because of the relocation of her parents' ministry, she had to move with the family and had studied in nine different schools, with no more than two years in each school. Nevertheless, she was grateful for her parents' efforts to help her understand their work and its importance. She then added that it was also through difficult times that the Lord had enabled her to experience more of His love and faithfulness. Family and ministry are both important, and wisdom is needed to maintain a good balance.

MK Identity Issues

Parents from a monocultural background often struggle with how to help their children maintain their national identity and at the same time remain international. I once heard a Korean MK saying that her father was racist, because he forbade her to date a Caucasian fellow. The truth was that the girl's parents cared deeply for her, and they understood the challenges that cross-cultural marriage would bring, along with the pressure their daughter would face in Korean society if she ended up marrying a non-Korean.

Many Asian families who have sent their children to MK/IC schools, where Western culture prevails, struggle with the fear of their children being Westernized.

However, they are also pleased that their children can learn good English and get an international flavor in these schools. There is no easy solution to the national/ international identity challenge. Parents must think things through carefully when making decisions about their children's schooling. As they try to stretch their children to be more international, they in turn may need to stretch themselves. They may need to improve their English and learn more about Western culture, so as to narrow the gap between themselves and their children who are educated in an international school setting.

A Korean mother was very concerned about her son's cultural identity. After attending a seminar and hearing about the gains and losses of being a third-culture kid (TCK), her eyes sparkled as she shared, "Instead of changing my son, I should change myself!" Asian MKs who come from a monocultural and monolinguistic background will anticipate more challenges as they return to their home country. But as the world shrinks into a global village, these monocultural Asian countries are becoming more and more open to the rest of the world. We anticipate that the adjustment challenges during MK reentry will be reduced in the days to come.

Long-Term Educational Planning

Frequent moves significantly impact children's education, not to mention their social world! It is difficult switching from one school to another and from one educational model to another. It is an advantage to learn different languages, but if the child does not stay in one language system long enough, she/he will not be able to consolidate the language. Academically, there will be gaps in learning as the MK changes from one educational system to another. These are only a few examples of the costs of frequent moves when parents do not have a long-range plan for their children's education.

Schooling in the Asian home country during the parents' home assignment and when the family returns home due to unexpected reasons is a big challenge for Asian MKs. It is especially difficult for older MKs who have not acquired much academic language in the mother tongue and do not know much about the home culture. In many Asian countries, the local educational system is pressurized and competitive. Peer pressure is also intense. Parents are advised to make a long-term educational plan for their children, including schooling during the parents' home assignment as well as tertiary education. Parents need to decide when will be the best time to send their children back to settle in the home country, if it is their wish. For families who are considering sending their children to North America or Europe for tertiary education, the financial implications must be considered. Many mission agencies and churches only support MK education until high school.

Transition to the parents' home country is also a big challenge. It is very helpful if parents and teachers, both on the field and in the home country, can be in close communication and work together to find ways to prepare the children for transitions. Parents need to prepare to give extra time and support to their children during the process. Sometimes one of the parents may even have to put aside the ministry for a while so as to stay at home full-time to help the children settle. Despite the difficulties upon reentry, there are more and more successful cases of Asian MKs returning to Asia for high school and even for university.

Making Transitions

Making transitions is another big issue closely related to frequent moving and changing schools. It is emotionally draining for a child to have developed friendships in one place and then have to say good-bye in a year's time and make new friends in another place. Children can feel the pain, and they do not need to wait until they grow up to reflect on the experience and do something about the wounds. The book *The Third Culture Kid*

Experience (Pollock & Van Reken, 1999), helps parents understand separation as well as how to prepare for and work through transitions.

Sometimes moving is inevitable, and it is part of the cost in missions. Besides helping children understand the presence of God in the moves, it is important for parents to strengthen their relationship with their children. Many MKs claim that "home" is wherever the family is. It is marked with a sense of relational belonging rather than geographic location. A stable and healthy family gives children a sense of security in the midst of transitions. Parents can be more sensitive to children's reactions to moving and can encourage them to share both positive and negative feelings about the moves. Asians are more reserved in sharing emotions openly. This is an area that parents can first work on themselves and set an example for their children.

Reentry

Besides academic challenges, the social and cultural adjustments that MKs face upon reentry cannot be underestimated. No wonder some MKs are not so keen about returning "home"! Relatives, friends in school, and even people at church may tease MKs about their accent when they try to speak in the mother tongue. They may regard them as strange, since these children do not fit into the cultural norm. For instance, MKs may walk barefoot in the house, and they may not bow properly to the elders and teachers. Asian MKs who studied in an international school generally speak excellent English, and the teenage girls may dye their hair and color their nails. Reentry will be a particular challenge for teenage MKs who have few friends in the home country.

Close ties with the extended Asian family can be a big support for MKs. I know some MKs who have kept in close touch with their cousins in the home country and who look forward to seeing them when they return home. In Korea, one church has set up an MK care group to support their returning MKs. Older brothers and sisters in the church reach out to these MKs and become good mentors for them. In Hong Kong, an MK care group has been established to provide intermission services to care for all missionary families sent out from Hong Kong.

Below is an account based on an interview with a Chinese MK who grew up in Japan. It will help us understand some of the challenges these MKs face as they grow up among different cultures.

Gains and Losses as an MK

*by Karen Wong Chiao-Lin**

Many people may wonder how different an MK is from other children who grew up in their parents' country. What are the gains and losses of being an MK? Perhaps I can share my experience to help you understand more about the life of an MK.

I was born in Hong Kong and left for Japan with my parents and younger sister when I was seven. Before we went to Japan, we also spent some time in Singapore. At that time, my parents were in cross-cultural training. I remember going to kindergarten in Hong Kong and Singapore. I was very young then, so my memories of kindergarten are vague. After we settled in Japan, my sister and I first went to a Chinese school near Tokyo. We only studied there for a few months and then changed to a local Japanese school. I studied in two different Japanese schools for a total of three years. My experience in Japanese school was not that exciting at the beginning. I still remember being bullied by Japanese classmates. Nevertheless, we were grateful to have a good teacher. One time, she told the class that Japanese *kanji* (characters) originated from Chinese writing. She then introduced me to the class. After that, my classmates started

* Used with permission from *Kids Without Borders: Journals of Chinese Missionary Kids*, 1999.

addressing me as Chinese *sansei* (teacher) and even asked me to write their names in Chinese!

Because of my parents' work, our family moved again. We moved to Tsukuba, and I started attending a small international school there. That was where I started my English education. Since it was an elementary school, I stayed there for just two years before changing to the Christian Academy of Japan (CAJ) for middle school. I liked CAJ very much. It was the first time I felt at home in school. The teachers were very understanding, and many of my friends were MKs. Unlike in the local school, I did not feel very different from others. Unfortunately, I didn't study there for long. After one year, my family had to leave Japan. At that time, my parents sent my sister and me to board at Dalat School in Malaysia. Adjusting to Dalat was difficult for me. I think it was mainly because I missed Japan so much. I am 14 this year, and I have spent seven years, which is half of my life, in Japan. Japan is really my home! When I first started school in Malaysia, I always compared Dalat with CAJ. After the first school term, however, I started to develop a sense of belonging to this school and have made many friends here. Dalat is the ninth school I have attended. Sometimes I joke with my friends, saying that I just want to experience what it would be like to study in a school for more than two years!

People might wonder how I felt about moving from one place to another and changing schools so many times. Sometimes I found moving to be quite difficult. I told myself that if I were a parent, I would not want my children to be MKs. It's tiring making new friends all the time. In spite of this, I am thankful that I enjoy making new friends. Now I have friends in many different places, and we still keep in touch through email. I am also grateful that I can speak Japanese, English, and Chinese. A few months ago, Dalat had an exchange program with a Japanese school in Penang. My sister and I were very honored to be asked by our teachers to be the interpreters during the school visits. Although we are studying in an English language school, my sister and I like to talk to each other in Japanese so that we won't forget the language.

There are gains and losses being an MK. Moving is not easy. Nevertheless, if I were given a choice, I would still choose to live the way I am instead of being stuck in one place all the time. It is really a privilege to be able to move around and see more of the world! I am very thankful to my parents for helping me understand what they are doing and the importance of their work. Sometimes, life can be difficult. But when I think about the souls that my parents have gained for Christ, the losses I have experienced being an MK become insignificant. It is also through difficult times that I understand God better and have been able to experience more of His faithfulness.

Some Updates and Strategies for Asian MK Education

MK education is a pressing need that usually draws immediate attention. Western and Asian educators have felt the urgency to provide suitable support for Asian children in their schools, fearing these children would become too Westernized. Many attempts have been made to cater to the educational needs of Asian MKs, as seen in the type of curriculum offered, the publications of groups such as the Association of Christian Schools International (ACSI), and several significant conferences. These conferences, in particular, have helped boost the awareness among Asians of Asian MK care.

Western/Asian Partnership

Partnership with individual MK schools. In the early 1970s, the Mother Tongue Studies (MTS) program was set up at Ukarumpa International School in Papua New Guinea, run by the Summer Institute of Linguistics (SIL). Students whose mother tongue is not English can learn in their mother tongue and develop their national identity within the context of international education. At present, the school offers MTS programs to five language groups: Dutch, Finnish, Swedish, Japanese, and Korean. Trained teachers from each national group are recruited to serve on the international team. The MTS program is not only a program to serve the Asian community, but a truly international effort in MK education.

In recent years, more and more Asian countries are becoming aware of the need to send and support teachers to serve Asian nationals and other students in MK schools. For instance, there are Korean and Japanese teachers at Ukarumpa International School in PNG, and a Hong Kong teacher at Dalat School in Malaysia.

Although not all MK schools offer international education to such an extent, creative attempts have been made in different MK schools to meet the needs of the international student body. Since there is a growing number of Asians in these schools, more and more MK schools, originally dominated by Western culture, have now become more culturally sensitive to the needs of these Asian students. The Murree Christian School in Pakistan is a good illustration of what some MK schools have attempted to do in Asian MK care (Billing, 1998). Dialogue started between school staff and the Asian parents; as a result, the school curriculum was adapted, and even the menu in the boarding homes became more international. Nevertheless, despite the efforts of some MK/IC schools in making significant changes in their schools, there is still much variation regarding the truly international nature of international schooling.

International consultations and conferences. In response to the increasing number of Asian students in MK/IC schools in Europe, 38 MK educators and caregivers met for the first time at the Asia Forum in Germany, April 19-21, 1999. The forum was organized by ACSI and sponsored by Black Forest Academy in Germany, with the goal of preparing recommendations, guidelines, and strategies for better serving Asian students and their families in MK/IC schools. Issues related to understanding Asian culture, educational systems, educational philosophy, and parents' and missions' expectations were discussed. Asian mission leaders shared their hope that schools could help Asian MKs make the transition back to their home country. Subsequently, 12 consensus statements were written and shared with other MK/IC schools around the world. MK educators also gave suggestions for Asian sending countries about how they can support MK/IC schools in the education of Asian MKs.*

The Missionary/Christian Overseas Schools (MCOS) conference, sponsored by ACSI and held in Korea in November 1999, further strengthened what had been discussed in Germany earlier that year. Since the conference took place in Korea, it also provided a marvelous opportunity for many Korean educators and mission leaders to interact with experienced Western MK personnel. Because Korea has the largest number of Asian MKs, the conference helped to fire the ministry in the country. It has been exciting to see the launch of an educational project for Koreans in Eastern Europe, with strong Western/Korean partnership. Another result is that 12 Korean mission organizations are now meeting regularly to share experiences and resources in the MK ministry.

Developments in Asian MK Education

In contrast to the enthusiasm of Western counterparts in the care of the educational needs of Asian MKs, the rate of development in the different Asian countries varies, depending on the pace of their mission growth. In order to make MK education viable, we need to have a cluster of children from the same ethnic group who

* Details of the Asia Forum, the consensus statements, and the wish list are included in ACSI's *World Report*, September/October 1999.

share the same need. If such a cluster or critical mass does not exist, it is hard to convince mission agencies to invest. Nevertheless, we are encouraged to see that different Asian countries are working at their own speed, and more and more helpful MK educational projects have been launched in recent years.

National MK schools and hostels. Some Asian countries, such as Korea, have enough MKs to set up their own school. The first Korean MK school, Hankuk Academy, was established in Manila in 1994. The school has recently set up boarding facilities to cater to the needs of children from families who live too far away to commute to school. In 1998, the first Korean MK hostel was set up near an IC school in Chiang Mai, Thailand, to serve Korean families in other parts of Thailand and those who live across the borders. At present, some Korean educators in Korea are in the process of setting up a high school with boarding facilities to serve families who would like to send their children back to Korea for education.

Proposed hostel projects. At present, and with the view of supporting missionaries with boys over age 11, mission and church leaders in Singapore have proposed setting up a hostel in Singapore to enable parents to continue their service on the field. In Hong Kong, some mission leaders are thinking of a similar project in order to encourage MKs to stay in Hong Kong for their tertiary education.

Resources and advice for parents. In some Asian countries, more and more home-schooling materials, especially on learning the mother tongue, have been produced. Handbooks and books on MK education have been published or are in the process of being published by different Asian countries, to guide parents regarding children's education, as well as to provide information on educational resources (see Appendix 2 at the end of this article). At present, these handbooks are available for Koreans, Filipinos, Hong Kongese, and Malaysians. Also, several Asian advisors on MK education and family care are available to provide consultation services within their mission agency and for parents in other mission organizations as well.

Today, more and more overseas Asian schools set up by the government are found on different mission fields, located mainly in major cities. Some examples include the Japanese School in Taipei, the Taiwanese School in Bangkok, and the Korean and Singaporean International School in Hong Kong. Some of these schools are well established and can be a good resource for Asian missionary families. For the mission community, most of the educational projects, such as the Korean MK school in Manila, the American/Korean dual track model in Eastern Europe, and the field and home hostel projects are still at an experimental stage. It will take some time to evaluate the effectiveness of these models. Nonetheless, it is very encouraging to see Asians initiating various creative educational projects.

Case Study: HKACM MK Care Group

Following is a description of the Hong Kong Association of Christian Mission (HKACM) MK Care Group. It illustrates the kind of support that has been provided for missionary families and how education about MK care is taking place for mission agencies and sending churches.

History and Composition of the MK Care Group

Twenty years ago, some mission leaders and missionary parents in Hong Kong started voicing concern about MK education. At that time, there were only a few school-age MKs, and these families were scattered in many different countries around the world. Unfortunately, at that time, very little was done for these children. In 1995, in response to the increasing number of Hong Kong MKs, an MK Care Group was set up under HKACM, an organization which provides inter-mission support services in Hong Kong. Since none of the mission agencies in Hong Kong had done anything about the care of missionaries' children at that time, the MK Care Group maximized resources and provided inter-mission services to all missionary families sent out from Hong Kong. The group is now composed of mission personnel, MK parents, a church pastor, a Christian educational psychologist, and a professional counselor. All members of the group are part-time volunteers.

Since its inception, the group has done various projects, and we have been able to gain the trust of parents, mission agencies, and sending churches. Since many of the ideas originated in the West, we have had to make some modifications to meet our own needs.

Educating Mission Leaders and Supporting Churches

Seminars. Missionary parents have been encouraged and invited to share about MK care during seminars with mission leaders and churches. Previously, missionaries had shared about their ministry but seldom talked about the joys and struggles in their families. Many people claimed that this was the first time they had heard about the need of MK care.

Short-term mission trips. Several trips for church and mission leaders to visit MK boarding schools have been organized. Running an MK hostel or boarding school is something very new to us. The visits to these boarding schools and hostels have helped leaders and supporters better understand the ministry of boarding home parenting. In response to the expressed desire of some parents to provide supplementary language teaching in their mother tongue to their children at home, some of the sending agencies and churches have mobilized teachers to use their summer vacation in tutoring these MKs on the mission field.

Publications. Literature is a powerful means of education. As the ministry develops, more books, articles, and leaflets are being published. Most of them are written by local missionary parents and MKs, while some were translated from English MK literature.

Training. Recently, a 12-session training course has been offered to mission leaders on general missionary/member care. Two of these sessions focused on MK care and education. In-depth discussions on marital relationships, family planning, views on boarding, etc., were included. The participants also discussed MK care and education policies at different stages of child development, ranging from the pregnancy of the mother to options for funding MKs' tertiary education. Expectations of workers at different stages of ministry, such as during language learning and home assignment, were also presented. We hope that this course will help mission/church leaders as they formulate MK policy for their organizations.

Parental Support

Pre-field orientation (PFO). It is very important for parents to be aware of cross-cultural parenting and MK issues before they leave for the field. The first PFO for parents was held in June 2000 and the second one in October of the same year. Topics covered included issues related to third-culture kids, MK education, and parenting and child development. We plan to offer this kind of PFO on a regular basis in the future.

Consultation. We offer consultation services to parents in the area of MK education, parenting, and reentry. Currently most of the adult missionary candidates undergo psychological screening with our professional counselor in the HKACM. The HKACM counselor and the educational psychologist in the MK Care Group are in close communication to help families who need advice on child development and parenting issues. Many parents have found this service especially helpful. Our psychologists also visit missionary families on the field.

Fellowship. Whenever there is a group of parents in transit in Hong Kong, we try to organize seminars or meetings so these parents can meet together, have fellowship, talk, and pray with each other. A column in the HKACM quarterly journal for missionaries has been reserved for parents to share their experiences on family issues.

Resource center. We have a resource center on MK care and education which is part of the HKACM library. Updated changes in the local educational policies, teaching resources, and MK books and articles are available for parents.

MK Education

Home-school curriculum. A three-year curriculum is available with teaching materials to help parents teach Chinese to their Hong Kong pre-school MKs .

Dalat/Hong Kong project. In 1998, HKACM started an educational project with Dalat School, an MK school in Malaysia, to help Hong Kong students in the school maintain their mother tongue and culture. In 1999, a Hong Kong teacher was sent to help in the school.

Hong Kong MK hostel project. Encouraged by the education project in Malaysia, a local mission agency is considering a pilot project to set up an MK hostel in Hong Kong, to provide an option for parents who wish to send their children back to Hong Kong for education. It is encouraging to see that more options for educational support are being discussed and made available to families.

Tertiary education. Several Hong Kong MKs are studying in MK/IC schools on the field. In the coming years, many will likely further their education by attending universities in North America. Mission and church leaders have become more and more concerned about financing tertiary education for these children if they go overseas. We have set up a study group to explore the possibility of subsidizing the education of these MKs.

MK Care

This is an area that we would like to develop in the near future. Our MKs vary from pre-school ages to high school and college young adults. The need to care for teenage and young adult MKs is especially apparent. We need to help develop a support system for these MKs, as well as help to provide suitable career guidance for them.

When the MK Care Group was first set up in Hong Kong, most people were frankly skeptical about the necessity of MK care in mission. As the ministry develops, more people are becoming convinced of its importance and have shown more appreciation of our work. Our two biggest challenges since we started the MK Care Group are the need to have a full-time person coordinating the group and finding viable ways to finance the ministry. Nevertheless, we trust that the Lord will meet our needs as we keep the vision and continue to be faithful in the ministry.

Future Directions

Asian/Western Partnership

Asian/Western partnership in MK education and care needs to be strengthened continually. We are grateful that the partnership is happening, and there is much that Asians can learn from the rich experience of our Western counterparts. On the other hand, as we know, the cultures and educational philosophies of East and West are quite different. The dialogue between MK personnel from these two parties needs to continue, so that both groups understand the best ways to educate and care for MKs.

Asian/Asian Partnership

Another area of partnership is inter-mission collaboration between different Asian countries. In some Asian countries, there is still a lot of room for the ministry to be developed. In order to maximize resources and reduce the duplication of work, inter-mission partnership and partnership with and among churches should be encouraged, at least at the beginning stage. As with international partnerships, working together with mission agencies and churches of different backgrounds can be a big challenge. However, as we share common goals in world evangelism and

MK care, we believe that many barriers can be overcome.

Asian/North American Asian Partnership

There are many resources among Asian churches in North America. Many overseas Asians are bilingual and bicultural. They can be effective bridges between Asians and Westerners in MK schools. I know an American Korean who used to mobilize Korean teachers in the USA and has now become a teacher in the Korean MK school in the Philippines. A Chinese couple from Canada are serving at Black Forest Academy in Germany. There are multitudes of resources among overseas Asian churches that are just waiting to be tapped!

Demography of Asian MKs

We need some more good research in mapping out the demography of missionary families sent from each Asian country. The findings will be a strategic tool in helping to allocate resources in the ministry. Needs of MKs in different age groups are different. It will be helpful for mission leaders and educators to find out the number of MKs in each age range, their location, and their educational needs. Such data will help leaders make plans to support families in ministry. For example, if mission leaders anticipate a cluster of school-age MKs from the same ethnic group in a particular location, they can be more proactive in planning to meet their educational needs.

Asian MK Educational Models

The existing MK/IC schools set up by Western colleagues have attracted many Asian families. However, families who would like their children to have a more national-based education may not be content with the international education offered by these schools. We are encouraged to see the establishment of the first Korean MK boarding school in Manila and Korean MK hostel in Chiang Mai. However, we need further improvement in the curriculum of our Asian MK schools and the care in our boarding homes. How special it would be to set up an Asian-based international school where the beauty of multiculturalism can be celebrated in school! We also hope to see home-side high school options created to meet the educational needs of returning MKs. Traditional MK educational models may not be able to meet the different needs of MK families. Asian educators must create educational models for this new generation. For instance, the one-room classroom, the online school, and other non-traditional models can be explored.

Recruiting MK Teachers and Caregivers

As the number of Asian MKs has increased drastically, more and more MK schools around the world are requesting Asian teachers to teach in their schools. Mission agencies can be more proactive in recruiting qualified and well-supported Asian and North American Asian teachers to serve in these overseas schools. We need experienced and creative teachers with a heart for missions to be involved in the ministry of MK education. Boarding home parents are also needed. As many Asian countries are planning to start their own MK boarding homes, the vision needs to be shared in Asian churches. Many Asians have not heard about such needs, and so they must be informed about the opportunities, qualifications, and preparation for this type of ministry. One idea is to send Asians to help in existing boarding homes run by Western colleagues in order to gain some on-the-job experience.

Care for MK Personnel

Practical investment in equipping MK educators and personnel is a must. First, the status of MK educators, boarding staff, and caregivers needs to be raised. Although these are staff in support roles, they are of the same importance in the mission team. They are not "second class" mission personnel and thus should be recognized like missionaries and get the same kind of support as those doing church planting on the mission field. These MK personnel also need to have a mission call and be equipped for cross-cultural living and ministry. Support and supervision for MK boarding home staff are essential. As personnel in boarding or hostel parenting have a great impact on the lives of MKs, it is important for them to have special pre-field and on-the-job training in their ministry, clear guidelines and supervision, as well as good pastoral care and support.

It is often a challenge for our MK teachers and caregivers to commit themselves for long periods in this ministry. We so appreciate those who can serve as teachers for families on the field for one summer or those who can serve for one to two years in an MK school. However, it will be even better if we can have well-supported teachers who are prepared to be committed for long-term ministry. I know some Western teachers who have taught MKs on the field for almost 40 years, until their retirement. What a powerful testimony their service is to the mission community!

Conclusion

More and more Asians are becoming committed to MK care. Providing such care is a strategic way to support missionaries in fulfilling the Great Commission, and it is worth doing because Asian MKs are precious and of great value. These children have immense potential. We need people who can love, care for, and understand them, as well as advocate, protect, support, and nurture them so that they can develop their potential. Lord willing, many of them will become second-generation missionaries and effective ambassadors for Christ in the international field.

In 1995, when I started mobilizing Asians in this ministry, I was very frustrated by the slow response in the Asian countries. An experienced Asian missionary trainer, who is an MK himself with two adult MKs of his own, gave me a great deal of encouragement. He also helped me understand that our Western colleagues have spent several decades doing MK care and that Asians have just begun this ministry. We need more patience. I can testify that since the ministry started, the Lord has worked many miraculous things in Asian MK care and has brought about many breakthroughs. The Lord cares for our Asian MKs, and so does our mission community. There is now a good sense of momentum in MK care. As we persevere, I do not think we will have to wait long before we see this ministry really take off and become established.

Reflection and Discussion

1. Do you see MK education and care as a priority in missions? What has been done in your country to show that it is a priority, and in what ways can the ministry be improved?

2. Imagine you are a mission or church leader. List five important questions about family and MK educational issues to ask a couple with two children, aged five and seven, who are going to apply to be missionaries.

3. How would you respond when non-Christians, or even Christian relatives and close friends, question why you as a prospective missionary couple are going to take your children to "suffer" in disadvantaged countries?

4. You are parents of a missionary family that will be returning for a year of home assignment in three months' time. How would you prepare your children to return to the home country for high school or tertiary education, and what kind of support (educational, social, cultural, etc.) is available to make their return smoother?

5. In what ways can the supporting church be involved in MK care? For instance, how could the church help with meeting the educational needs of MKs; strengthening the family relationship; supporting the family during preparation, field work, and reentry; and in general developing MK potential?

Appendix 1
Some Practical Exercises for MK Families

Preparation for Transitions

- Despite busy schedules, parents are encouraged to cultivate a tradition in the family to spend time regularly with the children. For instance, the whole family can go out for ice cream or walk in the park once every week. These outings provide a good way to strengthen relationships and encourage communication in the family.
- Talk to the children about the place where the family is moving. Parents are encouraged to involve their older children in the decision making. Do a project with the children on the country where the family is going. It can include pictures and newspaper clippings of the country and descriptions about the people, climate, food, houses, etc.
- Help children arrange a farewell party. Encourage them to make a list of people whom they would like to invite. Help them understand that they can maintain friendships through correspondence.
- Ask the children what places they would like to visit and whom they would like to see before they leave a place, and take them for a last visit. Make sure to take along a camera and take photos of these places and with these people.
- Spend time with the children and encourage them to talk out their feelings of moving. Sometimes, parents can first start talking about their feelings, such as their excitement, sadness, fears, and anxieties about the move.
- Encourage children to do the packing with parents. They can pack the toys they would like to take, and with the help of parents, they can decide what to do with things that they cannot take with them.
- Parents will be extremely busy during the last few weeks before the family departs. Be careful not to tire young children out too much by taking them to a lot of meetings. One parent can stay home with the children while the spouse attends these meetings.
- Encourage children to develop some bridge-building skills which do not require the use of language, such as sports and music. These skills will make it easier for MKs to fit into a new culture and will enable them to make friends in a new place.

Maintaining the Mother Tongue and Culture

- Always talk to children in the mother tongue at home.
- Take the children to a bookstore in the home country and ask them to choose story books and tapes they like. These will be the teaching materials in the mother tongue when they are on the field.
- Encourage the extended family to write, email, phone the children, and send them little gifts when the family is overseas. It will be even better if the relatives can make short visits to the mission field and stay with the family.
- Make a big picture of the family tree, with photos of the relatives, and post it in the house. Encourage the children to send birthday cards to each of the relatives and cousins and encourage them to keep in contact.

Preparation for Reentry

- Have friends send news and magazines of the home country while the family is overseas. This information will be very helpful in preparing the family for reentry.
- Spend more time with the children, especially the first couple of months after arrival. Listen to their excitement and worries. The parents' home may be a foreign place to the children.
- Help relatives, friends, and teachers understand the overseas experiences of MKs so that they will be more tolerant of these children, as they may not readily conform to the norm in the home culture.
- Set up a buddy system at home. It would be ideal to have another MK take

care of returning MKs and tell them the do's and don'ts in the "home" culture.

MK Education

■ Parents are encouraged to make a long-range plan for their children's education. The plan should include where to go to school during furlough in the home country and MKs' tertiary education.

■ The education system in many Asian countries is changing rapidly. Have friends at home inform parents of the changes in the education system and schooling policies.

■ If parents are planning to send their children back to the home country for further education, they should make sure that their children will have a chance to learn the academic language in the mother tongue while they are overseas. Teaching can be done by parents or a tutor.

■ If non-English-speaking Asian parents are planning to send their children to MK or international schools, they should be prepared to learn more English themselves and gain a better understanding of Western culture. Also, it is important to prepare the children with more English before school.

Appendix 2
Asian Books and Handbooks

Korean

Park, N. (1999). *Korean MK handbook: A comprehensive resource book for parents and caregivers*. Seoul, Korea: GMF Press.

MK Journal (quarterly magazine). Seoul, Korea: GMF Press.

Pre-field orientation seminar for MK parents (manual and nine audiotapes).

Daily quiet time – Grades 4-6 (available in Korean and English), Yejoung Com.

➤ Orders for the above can be made through MKNEST Korea, www.mknest.org.

Chinese

Chan, P. (Ed.). (1997). *Nurturing missionaries' children*. Hong Kong: HKACM.

———. (2000). *Kids without borders: Journals of Chinese missionary kids*. Hong Kong: HKACM and OMF HK.

Fung, J. (Ed.) (2000). *Harold and Stanley say good-bye*. Hong Kong: OMF HK.

Sojourners: The family on the move. Taiwan Chinese Christian Mission, 1999.

➤ Orders for the above can be made through HKACM, Hong Kong, hkacm@hkacm.org.hk.

Philippines

Manzano, J., & Manzano, R. (1999). *Filipino MKs: Which schooling option?* OMF Philippines.

➤ Orders can be made through OMF Philippines, ph-gs@omf.net.

Malaysia

Kumar, B. (2000). *Member care handbook: A guide to caring for our missionaries.*

➤ Orders can be made to Beram Kumar, sbks@pc.jaring.my.

Japan

➤ For matters on Japanese MKs, contact Toshio Nagai of Wycliffe Japan: toshio_nagai@wycliffe.org.

Other Useful Resources and Websites

Educator teaching overseas. CHED Family Services Department of Wycliffe Bible Translators (WBT) USA.

Educational options: Europe and Christian international schools. S.H.A.R.E., 1996.

Interact (periodical on MK issues), www.tckinteract.net.

Parents teaching overseas. CHED Family Services Department of WBT USA.

World Report. Association of Christian Schools International (ACSI), www.acsi.org.

www.mknet.org.

References

Barrett, D., & Johnson, T. (2001). *World Christian encyclopedia: A comparative survey of churches and religions in the modern world* (2nd ed.). Oxford, UK: Oxford University Press.

Billing, P. (1998, February/March). Special report. Serving the Korean community: Caring enough to learn, learning enough to care. *World Report*. ACSI.

Bowers, J. (Ed.). (1998). *Raising resilient MKs: Resources for caregivers, parents, and teachers*. Colorado Springs, CO: ACSI.

Chan, P. (1999, September/October). Working toward the internationalization of MK/IC schools from an Asian perspective. *World Report*. ACSI, pp. 2-11.

Chan, P. (Ed.). (2000). *Kids without borders: Journals of Chinese missionary kids*. Hong Kong: HKACM and OMF.

Fan, S. (2000). Going to school in Brazil. In P. Chan (Ed.), *Kids without borders: Journals of Chinese missionary kids*. Hong Kong: HKACM and OMF.

Hung, V. (2000, October–December). Report on missionary attrition. *Go unto all nations*. Hong Kong: HKACM, pp. 9-11.

Lee, T. (1994). *The pabalma*. Korea Research Institute for Missions.

Loong, T. (2000, Summer). Educating and discipling the Asian TCK: The role of the international Christian school. *World Report*. ACSI.

Moon, S. (1997). Missionary attrition in Korea: Opinions of agency executives. In W. Taylor (Ed.), *Too valuable to lose: Exploring the causes and cures of missionary attrition* (pp. 129-142). Pasadena, CA: William Carey Library.

———. (1998). *Korean mission handbook*. Seoul, Korea: GMF Press.

Pate, L. (1991). The dramatic growth of Two-Thirds World missions. In W. Taylor (Ed.), *Internationalizing missionary training: A global perspective* (pp. 26-39). Grand Rapids, MI: Baker Book House.

Pauls, D., & Pauls, N. (1993). Looking at yesterday for tomorrow's clues: Summary of MK CART/CORE research findings on adult MKs. *Parents teaching overseas*. Dallas, TX: CEFD WBT USA.

Pollock, D., & Van Reken, R. (1999). *The third culture kid experience: Growing up among worlds*. Yarmouth, ME: Intercultural Press.

Rajendran, K. (1998). *Which way forward Indian missions? A critique of twenty-five years 1972–1997*. Bangalore, India: SAIACS Press.

Taylor, B. (1993, September 20-23). *Perspectives on global attrition: Examining the iceberg*. Paper presented at EFMA/IFMA Triennial Leadership Conference, Orlando, FL.

Taylor, W. (Ed.). (1997). *Too valuable to lose: Exploring the causes and cures of missionary attrition*. Pasadena, CA: William Carey Library.

Polly Chan *joined OMF in 1990 and served two years at Chefoo School, an OMF MK boarding school in Japan. She then furthered her studies at Wheaton College in USA in 1993, graduating with a master's degree in education in ministry, with a focus on MK education and care. She received a bachelor's degree in psychology from Canada, and she is also a certified high school teacher in Hong Kong. In 1995, Polly was appointed by OMF International in her current ministry to coordinate the care of Asian MKs. In the same year, she also helped to set up and coordinate the MK Care Group in HKACM. Polly has co-chaired the Member Care/Asia Task Force, an interagency ministry of the Evangelical Fellowship of Asia's Missions Commission, since its inception in 1997. Email: ChanPolly@omf.net.*

The author is grateful for the helpful review of this article by Barry McKessar (OMF International MK Coordinator), Ruth Baek (GMF MK NEST Director), and David Wilcox (ACSI Assistant to the Vice President, International Ministries).

8

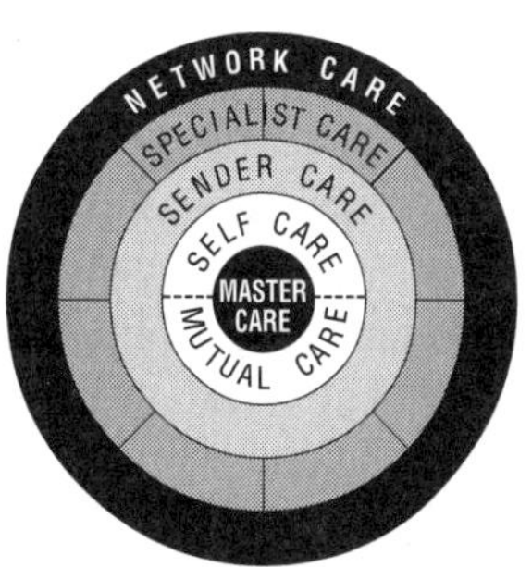

Care for Christian Workers In India: Dark Obstacles And Divine Opportunities

K. K. RAJENDRAN

Christian workers in India are called to serve in some very challenging places. Over the last few years, we have seen the good hand of the Lord at work both in and through His servants, as they minister to fellow Indians and beyond. This article focuses on the various pastoral care structures, people, and programs that are emerging to provide support to Indian workers as they minister to others. There are, in fact, many good things into which the Lord is guiding us—divine opportunities—to enable us to care well for His sheep (John 21).

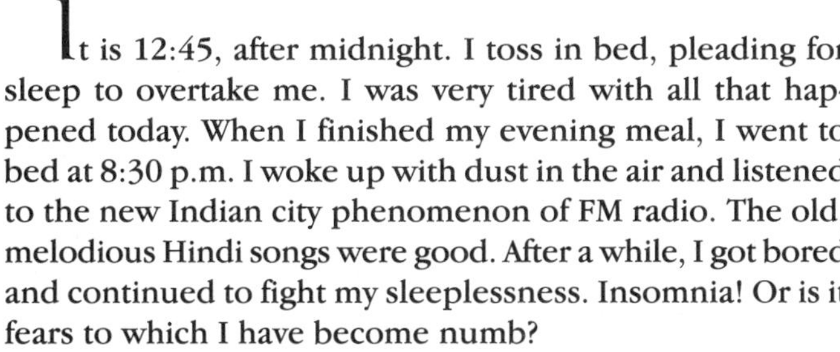

It is 12:45, after midnight. I toss in bed, pleading for sleep to overtake me. I was very tired with all that happened today. When I finished my evening meal, I went to bed at 8:30 p.m. I woke up with dust in the air and listened to the new Indian city phenomenon of FM radio. The old, melodious Hindi songs were good. After a while, I got bored and continued to fight my sleeplessness. Insomnia! Or is it fears to which I have become numb?

It is now 1:15 a.m. I toss in bed, yearning again for sleep to overtake me. The opportunities for communicating Christ in India are fantastic. There are 141 member missions with the India Missions Association (IMA). Persecution of Christians is daunting in the country, and fanatics are acting like Nazis, even though India, as a country, is moving forward. As Christians, we are trying to be positive with a belief in the sovereignty of God. There is a rat race, as so many groups are trying to be the definitive voice of Christians. There are tendencies to attract the "global Christian market" by the distinctiveness of our organizations. If possible, we add spice—*masala*—to increase the flavor of our organizational descriptions. Or to use another metaphor, we are willing to play different types of chords to attract outside interest:

- Regional chords such as South, North, and North East Indians.
- The chord of the despicable caste tantrum.
- The chord of the church versus parachurch organizations.
- The chord, "North India is needier than the South."
- The chord of sending Christian workers versus using native workers.
- The chord of Christian workers feeling that "there are no good local people to train and carry on the work"

versus the locals feeling that "there are no good Christian workers, and they are exploiting us."

■ The chord that the Dalits (the lower caste people in the Hindu ladder of castes) are neglected, while the upper caste Christians "rule" over them.

■ The chord of some saying that the Dalits are lazy and incompetent.

■ The chord of male chauvinism and a forced submission of women, while 50% of the nation of India consists of unreached women who will never be reached by men.

We can add many more chords to our organizational music. Such practices, though, will continue to keep us disunited and will carry us through the next millennium without making a dent in sharing the love of the Lord Jesus Christ in India.

We are asking many questions: Where are we going as the church, as missions, as Christian workers, and as human beings who want to follow Christ? Who will share Christ with the growing urbanites and the emerging educated class, 30% of whom are women? Who will go to the rural people, who comprise 60% of our overall population of one billion people? Who is teaching the gospel-sharers? Who is teaching the emerging new Christians, some of whom dare to go to churches in areas where there is potential persecution?

Who is training people to share Christ with different sectors of the Indian masses? There are several Bible colleges, seminaries, and missiological and cross-cultural "pedagogues"—what are they up to? Do they have the whole picture of India? What is their philosophy of training, and for what do they train people? What are the end results envisioned? Is the training simply for the purpose of maintaining the existing churches and winning a few more token converts? Where are the trainers for the grassroots workers? Where are the workers who will go to the income-tax payees and the yuppie Indians who are moving to other parts of the world and perpetuating stronger "Indian culture"?

We are also asking about the vision of Indian Christians for India. Often, Indian Christian churches and missions are puny-minded and have very little challenge to harness the politics, art, culture, and imagination of Indians. No wonder we are minorities forever. Christians are not mainstreamers but peripheral onlookers who are highly trained to be critical of both the secular and the sacred. Our pet theologies (not the Pauline theology of Christ) have made us critical of everything.

These questions meander through my mind and nearly overwhelm me until 2:20 a.m. Although all these are "high, legitimate, and honorable" thoughts, I start to become worried about different "earthly, no good" thoughts too. Where should my children go to school? My daughter faxed her application forms today, paying 1,260 rupees, trying to find admission in a college for her post-graduate studies. What do I do with my son in 11th grade, who is growing bigger than I am! I am 49. Where will I end up if I get a stroke or cancer or a heart attack? By God's providence, so far so good.

With all these overwhelming good as well as useless thoughts coursing through my mind, I think of IMA and the limited skills we have as individuals and as a team. I almost panic. It is now 2:30 a.m.

Here are some commitments to make us at IMA uneasy. We have *Indian Missions*, a quarterly magazine that is always rushed, and I am always unhappy with the mistakes we continuously make. We try to produce some "interesting" IMA brochures, but the results are often unsatisfactory. We are trying to make a video of IMA's work, which so far has resulted in a major fiasco of scripts. Our research needs help. We are trying to upload information about member missions and IMA into our developing website, but we are pretty slow. I am not sure how well my teammates are coping with the demands or whether they understand the urgency. Should we continue to fire people who don't perform satisfactorily, or should we help them develop? Do we have the time to fool around and dilly-dally in all that we are supposed to do? And where are the competent, dedicated men and women of God who will work for such a small amount—Rs. 6,000 per month—while they can fetch Rs. 16,000 in the market? With their Rs. 6,000 income, after paying a monthly house rent of 3,000, what else do they do with their salaries? Eat, pay insurance, spend on education for their children, pay for transportation, and have some entertainment, such as buying some good books to read or some music tapes for relaxation (why should they relax; they are supposed to be "dedicated" men and women of God!). How do they manage? Well, their wives can work, and the young children can look after themselves! What if the wife is not trained too much and/or cannot get a job? Ah! Should I go to sleep now? It is 2:45 a.m.

We have felt that many missions in India, which do not have a voice apart from their immediate region, must be helped in their needs, in the event of an emergency such as persecution, famine, and flood. So we have organized a Project Manager, who continuously receives project proposals and who serves as a liaison with prospective donors.

We have also organized many networks that are supposed to be serving the missions and interconnecting each other. There are prayer initiative networks, pastoral care networks for Christian workers and the CEOs, a Bible translation network, a leadership training network, a student mobilization network, a missiology network, a research network, a welfare network for Christian workers, and others. But we lack the time, the leaders, and the funds to get these networks moving. We are constantly saying that the church should be mobilized. But very few realize how big the task is and how small the church in India is. It is easier for a parochial group to scrounge for money from their constituencies, but this is hardly enough even to scratch the surface of the mammoth missions task. I roll over yet again in my bed and wonder how we could be better impacting India as a whole.

IMA has a vision to expand to Delhi, North East, and other places, because we want to be the uniting force among missions in the country. This desire is very legitimate. There have also been underlying fears that if we do not do the job, there will be several regional missions associations claiming their legitimacy and uniqueness—saying that they are more spiritual and are more focused for the global and local marketers. These groups are fine, but we will continue to fractionalize.

Now I consider the financial strength of IMA. This subject not only adds to my insomnia, but also makes my stomach acidic. The member missions give contributions of about 0.2% of their income. Most missions give the minimum—that is, Rs. 3,000. Most of these contributions, when combined, cover the existence of IMA for two to three months. The IMA staff also have to visit member missions, sort out many difficulties, represent them to many bodies inside and outside the country, run leadership training programs for the missions, keep in touch with the CEOs and with the emerging second generation of leaders in missions, guide the missions in the country, and be the consultants of Christian worker welfare for the missions. How do we do it?

The executive members of IMA have been very sympathetic, but what do we do? Shall I go to sleep now? It is 3:00 a.m.

Maintaining Perspective

The reason that I share this account with you is *not* that I am so frustrated that I want to quit. It is to ask you to pray, to understand the task ahead better, to stand with us in the ministry, and, for my colleagues, to learn to work together better. I write in case you are having trials similar to mine, to assure you that you are not alone. Many CEOs and other leaders have many similar sleepless nights. Yet there is a sense that God is in control in the midst of chaos. God is also at work in me and in you. Let Jesus be praised for the movement of His Spirit among us. Yes, there are many dark obstacles in India, but His light is far brighter, turning the enemy's ploys into divine opportunities for His people. Let us not lose this crucial perspective!

Obstacles for Indian Missions

Christian workers face many obstacles, such as demonic forces and opposition from those who have chosen not to believe in Christ. There are also internal struggles. Some workers go to the mission field carrying many unwanted habits and significant unresolved issues from the past. Some struggle with a deep sense of insecurity or incompetence, the backlash of their family background, pressures from both their immediate family and their parents, peer pressure from friends, and the temptation to compromise to find an easier road in life. Thus, Christian workers have a tremendous task of disciplining themselves to become a special agent of the gospel. In the words of Marjorie Collins (1986, p. 25): "For some it is easy to adjust.... Others feel the whole adjustment is interesting.... But one thing that does not radically change is you. And because you have to live with you the rest of your life, it is well to consider some of the little things (and big things, too) in your personal life which can be or ought to be adapted, adjusted, deleted, or enhanced. And it is never too early to begin!"

One mission leader shared with me some of his struggles as a Christian worker and as a mission leader. What he is going through sounds so familiar! He has to find a balance between ministry and family, work and health care, personal relaxation and giving time to others in the mission, direct soul winning and leading a soul-winning agency, choosing priorities and non-priorities, being big-hearted and knowing that he was being taken advantage of, taking time off to evaluate himself and constantly working in ministry, having time with God and fulfilling work demands, and having the home and office together in the same house. Apart from all these stresses, he said there were financial struggles, especially following his marriage, together with the need for hospitality due to constant visitors.

Discouragement and Loneliness

The roots of discouragement are many. Poulose from Kerala was a Christian worker in Bihar. Being the only son in his house, he felt responsible to arrange the marriages of his two sisters. Heavy dowry burdens weighed him down with worries. In this situation, he found it hard to concentrate. Devan, a weaving technologist and now a Christian worker, was the first Christian in his family. He struggled to send Rs. 300 as a monthly remuneration to help his family. As an Indian, he is normally expected to provide for his parents' needs. He was constrained with a big responsibility and was reluctant to spend anything on himself beyond his own food expenses.

Some workers become discouraged when they have to live in primitive places, without modern equipment or facilities, in the midst of the computer and email age. The pressures to keep pace with new scientific developments and the new communication techniques challenge those working in cities and towns and with middle and upper class people.

Marjorie Collins (1986, p. 216) describes loneliness as "a fog which arrives out of nowhere to envelop the soul and cause it to feel lost or wayward.... If loneliness lasts for a long period of time, it erodes the ability to work well and produces a number of problems, both in relation to personal matters as well as in the area of ministry. Loneliness often turns to self-pity. [Christian workers] often carry burdens, many heartaches, and discouragement. Because of a fear of being misunderstood, very few ... speak of their difficulties."

Organizational Issues

There are also pressures within agencies in the form of difficult relationships with coworkers, poor leadership, clan-ruled authority structures, unorganized plans, and inadequate training for accomplishing the task. In the organizational structure, too much accountability is expected of some workers, while others are not required to be as accountable due to favoritism. These factors can kill the zeal of Christian workers over a period of time.

Even 40-year-old Christian workers can feel frustrated when senior members of the organization do not trust them because of their younger age. Young workers are forced to hear stories of how their elders have suffered, and so they should also expect to suffer and sacrifice, even though the times have changed. Yet sacrifice is an attitude of the heart. It cannot be forced upon people by legalisms. Thus, there has to be sensitivity in embracing the new ways, both in the area of technology and in adapting to a new generation of people in the mission, in order to enhance the work of missions.

When one worker was married, the mission insisted that the new wife quit her job, so as to help her husband in the ministry. The wife did not feel that she should give up a profession for which she was trained. She felt that she could serve the Lord by remaining in her profession. Eventually, the mission asked both the husband and the wife to resign. Such tension has been seen in many agencies.

Financial Issues

A prominent, well-educated, Christian leader in his mid-50s, who could have made it well in the secular world, could not make ends meet as a Christian worker. His children were very disappointed and felt that their parents were useless, because they could not provide many of the basic needs of the family. The parents, though prominent leaders, felt quite heartbroken. The whole family asked the same question, "Was this the right thing to have done with our lives?"

Another man, working with an unreached people group in the North, said that his mission, 10 years back, paid him a monthly salary of Rs. 400. After 10 years, he received around Rs. 1,000 a month. Financially he and his wife could not survive. Therefore, he resigned and left the mission. He wondered, "How has it come about that we use the noble name 'evangelist' for the lowest category of church worker—workers who are half-trained, half-paid, and half-starved? And how is it that respectable Christians feel uncomfortable with the very idea of evangelism?"

One particular mission has 87 workers, although it does not have a regular pay structure for them. Each worker was paid Rs. 200-300 per month. The workers struggled to survive. For example, living in a one-bedroom house in the North cost a man, his wife, and two school-aged children Rs. 4,000 per month in 1991. Today it would cost Rs. 4,000-6,000 in large cities and Rs. 6,000-10,000 in cosmopolitan cities and commercial townships (Daniel, 1997). Because of such financial pressure, many turn away from service and choose not to join mission work at all.

Medical Issues

M. C. Matthew (1995), a noted medical doctor in Vellore Christian Hospital, conducted an informal survey of two sending organizations. Many of the workers suffered from frequent illnesses. "There are some who experience exhaustion because of the nature of the work. The average age of [Christian workers interviewed] may be crossing 35 years, with at least 25% ... in their mid-40s. This makes them vulnerable to illnesses of middle age like hypertension, diabetes, backaches, arthritis, acid-peptic disease, psychosomatic dysfunction, etc."

An important concern in Indian missions is the payment of major medical bills. Even many minor medical bills can mount up. Missions have many different methods to pay off the medical bills of their Christian workers. Most struggle with the systems. There is no one system which is satisfactory.

Most Christian workers in India have no medical insurance, and when they fall ill they struggle to pay the bills. The mission agencies may be willing to pay the large bills, but they have no money to do so. The worker feels a burden to the mission when he falls ill. His own self-worth and security have deteriorated. This situation has to change. Workers should not feel that they are a burden to the agency, or this will affect their families, and eventually the children will never want to come back to the mission field. Not only the children, but also others who consider missions will hesitate when they know a worker is not taken care of adequately.

In the new Indian scene, the cost paid is too high for many Christian workers. The cost includes deficient medical care, insufficient salary, inadequate schooling facilities for children, meager retirement benefits, complete lack of housing for the future, and no provision for decent insurance coverage. Several workers that I have interviewed agreed that Christian workers did not have much savings nor any health insurance, retirement benefits, or death relief schemes. The consensus was that this state of affairs resulted from the false theology called "faith," until some disaster such as a heart attack struck. One man's wife became mentally ill, and the mission could not treat her because of the lack of funds. Eventually the man died, and his wife was left homeless.

Ongoing Educational and Spiritual Input

Christian workers need ongoing training and opportunities for personal growth and spiritual refreshment. The larger missions have been dealing with this situation, due to their size and recurring requests from their workers. They have also realized the value of investing in the lives of their workers as a part of enhancing their effectiveness and in preparation for future leadership. The leaders wisely envision expansion and the passing of the mantle to future generations. Thus, the aspect of studies at the midpoint of a Christian worker's life has consciously been planned.

The smaller missions struggle to provide such ongoing input. In general, this is because they have not experienced much numerical growth and have very limited funds. The workers have felt inadequate and worn out and have wanted to catch their breath. While the mission leaders have struggled and made positive and negative decisions, the workers have been caught in the middle, and some have become victims of delayed decisions or wrong decisions. The result is that Christian workers suffer from a lack of motivation and a sense of inadequacy.

Missions will have to cope with more and more people wanting to go for studies in the middle of their careers, to enhance their efficiency and improve their focus so as not to get into a perpetual rut. If such a provision is not made, then workers simply quit the mission and go to another mission which is able to help, or they give up Christian work altogether. Two or three years of mid-term training for workers are well worth considering, in light of the future 15-20 years of service.

Pension and Retirement Benefits

The issue of the future is not easy for any Christian worker of any nation if it is not planned well. The mission leaders, as part of pastoral care for their workers, should plan pension/retirement matters with their personnel and not avoid facing such weighty issues. There may not be easy answers, but they have to be found.

Slowly, the mission agencies are becoming aware of the needs of the Christian workers who will retire. Most workers do not feel comfortable living "in the shadows" of their children, as is the case for many Indians in the country. Very few of the present Christian workers have any income from ancestral properties. Thus, there have been anxieties both on their part and on the part of the mission. Credible mission agencies have been progressively aware of the pension needs of retiring workers to assure a regular income for these faithful servants. The workers who will retire in the next few years have not prepared for their retirement and pension. The younger workers have been encouraged to contribute money for a pension. The Executive Committee of IMA has requested that all IMA staff be put under a pension scheme as soon as possible to provide a regular income in the future. In the same way, many missions are planning to get into pension schemes.

The best years of a worker's life are spent in winning people to Christ, but when the person retires, he/she has nowhere to go. There is not any pension plan, or a house to live in, or a plot of land upon which to build a house. Patrick Joshua commented, "When a [Christian worker] retires, he has to live the rest of his life with dignity." Home is a place of rest and care, of belonging and security. A home for the Christian worker is a blessing, and it is not unspiritual to have a house.

Rev. Diraviam of the CSI diocese mentioned that this used to be a problem among the clergy also. Most retired bishops and pastors lived with their children in cities like Chennai. There were some who thought about housing for the clergy back in 1984. In 1991, a decision was made to buy a plot of land for the clergy at Chengelpet, 60 kilometers away from Chennai, but the program fell through. Coimbatore Diocese had a scheme. In the diocese compound itself the retired pastor could rent a house for a small amount until he passed away. However, Diraviam recognized the need for one's own house where the pastor's wife and children could continue to live. This could be worked out if, from the time the pastor entered ministry, a sum of Rs. 1,000 a month allocated for his housing could be set aside to get him a good house when he retired in 30 years' time. The allocated Rs. 1,000 a month could be used for a house built with a housing loan. A similar plan could be worked out for Christian workers also.

Children's Education

Many missions, especially the smaller ones, have made very little allowance for the education of the children. The problem increases when the children enter college for higher education. It is difficult to get the large sum of money needed for higher education. Some children, in the worst case scenarios, have reacted very negatively to this situation, resenting the "sacrifice" which parents/others have demanded of them.

Most parents who live in the city manage to keep their children with them, even though they might not get the full support needed for the city education of their children. But some parents have to send their children far away to a hostel. They have no choice, as there are insufficient funds for children to go to a closer but more expensive hostel or school. If only they had more funds, they would have preferred to have their children near their working place in a hostel where they could see them more often and where they felt comfortable with their children's education. The mission leaders must plan in such a way that the Christian workers are not coerced into sending their children only to the schools which the agencies recommend 1,000 kilometers away!

We must not lose the opportunity to invest in our children. They deserve good care and a good education if they are to grow and positively impact their society. Further, if the children of Christian workers are neglected, neither they nor others who may consider mission work will likely come into the missions.

Persecution

There has been some persecution in India for Christians in the past few years. Houses have been burned, people have been forced to move, and there have been some deaths. However, the persecution is not as much as in Indonesia and other parts of the world. It comes largely from some religious fanatics who are opposed to thc idea of the equality of human beings and who believe in the superiority of their religion. The minority religions in India are still largely considered "foreign." Christianity is especially seen as being Western and an attempt to "colonize" the religion and culture. These fanatics, like many others, erroneously believe that the Hollywood culture, as portrayed in the media, is in fact the Christian culture. Thus Christianity is perceived as a threat to the integrity and unity of India as a Hindu nation.

Another factor affecting the persecution scenario is that mission efforts have mostly impacted tribal groups rather than the "thinkers and influencers" of the country. Thus, when the fanatics verbally or physically assault Christians, the secular thinkers do not support Christians. In fact, often the Indian political parties make use of the accounts of persecution for their own advantage, rather than sympathizing with those being persecuted.

Persecution has a psychological effect on Christian workers, with ongoing fear being a major result. The IMA tries to help in any way possible when there is persecution. This includes practical support and care. The IMA also tries to encourage Christian workers to communicate the gospel to the whole of India, not just to certain groups, and to do so in culturally appropriate ways. We hope that this approach will produce more sympathizers (not to mention more disciples of Christ, of course!), who will at least view Christ and His teachings positively. Nonetheless, when the uniqueness of Jesus is being proclaimed as the only way to salvation, many will be offended, and persecution can ensue, a historical fact for both India and many other parts of the world.

Opportunities for Member Care and the Gospel

Christians need systematically to care for their workers who carry the good news of Christ to all. Workers need training to give them good tools. They need care to relate to their own coworkers. They need to provide adequately for family needs, including their children's education. Preparation for crises and for possible persecution is necessary. Christian workers also need a good salary comparable to the normal secular ones, accompanied by planning for their housing and pension after their retirement. A large percent of the success of the mission depends on the care we give to workers. A good strategy for the work is not the only reason for the mission's success. Care of the worker and strategy go hand in hand.

In the IMA, we realize that India will never hear about and respond to Christ unless there is healthy care of Christian workers. Therefore, the need of member care for Christian workers has become critical in order to take the gospel forward. The leaders of the IMA have organized member care-related seminars and consultations and have written on several pastoral care topics concerning Christian workers, the CEOs, and leaders; families of Christian workers and their children; and the medical/financial welfare of Christian workers. There have been networks established on member care, counseling, welfare, children's education, and others. We are thus doing our best to raise the profile and awareness of member care.

The IMA in particular has held several meetings for people involved in different aspects of pastoral care, from rest/renewal home directors to psychiatrists involved in missions. The idea is to help member care workers link together and develop complementary roles in caring for Christian workers. We hope that member care departments within organizations will be created/strengthened, that regional care centers will be formed, that additional rest/renewal houses will be set up, and that there will be a greater understanding of the ongoing needs of Christian workers.

A network of member care centers/hubs is also key. Since India is so vast and diverse, with the mission agencies and workers being geographically so spread out, we will need many centers which will cater to Christian workers from their regions. This is not to abdicate the role of each mission in caring for its own people, but rather it is a complement to what the missions are already doing/developing. Many times, agencies need outside specialist support—for example, when there are cases of severe mental disorder, physical disorders affecting health and mind, and special educational and behavioral issues for children. Specialists located at or associated with such centers could help immensely.

The IMA, in conjunction with other groups, is working to help develop an ethos of member care within missions today. We want to support mission leaders and sending groups as they care for their people. Our approach is becoming more proactive, and there are many opportunities which we believe the Lord is giving us. We fully expect to see Christian workers become more effective as we work together to nurture them and their families for the long haul. And we fully expect a splendid harvest of people for the Lord as a result of commitment and care for Christian workers.

Reflection and Discussion

1. The author lists many struggles for Indian Christian workers. Which ones relate the most to your context?
2. In what ways can these obstacles be turned into opportunities for the kingdom of God? Give a few examples.
3. In what ways can these obstacles actually obliterate Christian missions? Give a few examples.
4. Where can leaders go to find help for some of their struggles, such as the types of personal issues that the author recounts at the beginning of the article?
5. How does your organization provide for the member care needs of its personnel? Also describe how member care is part of the organization's thinking/ethos.

References

Collins, M. (1986). *Manual for today's missionary: From recruitment to retirement.* Pasadena, CA: William Carey Library.

Daniel, R. (1997, April). Missionary's cost index. *Insight India—Assembly Testimony Journal.*

Matthew, M. (1995). *IMA health care support for missionaries: A proposal.* Unpublished paper.

Appendix
Some Member Care Resources in India

We believe the Lord is giving us understanding and opportunities for raising the quality of life for Christian workers. One of the main ways for us is to create a network of partners who could help in different aspects of the pastoral care for these workers. Here are some of the member care resources of people and places available in India. This is not an exhaustive list, and we hope that additions will be made to it in the days ahead as the network grows.

We are in the process of creating web pages to describe these and other member care resources. For further information, contact my wife, Pramila Rajendran, at: IMA, 48, First Main Road, East Shenoy Nagar, Chennai 600 030, India. Tel: (0)44-6444602/6444603/6448944/6448945; Fax: (0)44-6442859; Email: rajpramila@eth.net or imahq@vsnl.com.

Counselors and Places for Care

- Mr. Samson Gandhi, Person-to-Person (PP), Hyderabad, Andra Pradesh.
- Dr. Gnanamuthu, Counselling Centre at Bangalore, Karnataka.
- Mr. John Zechariah, Grace Counselling Centre, Kerala.
- Mr. Marcus Chacko and Mr. Alfy Franks, Pastoral Care Department, OM, Hyderabad, AP.
- Christian Medical College, Pastoral Care Department, Vellore, Tamil Nadu.
- Dr. M. C. and Annie Mathew, Christian Medical College, Vellore, Tamil Nadu.
- Noor Manzil Hospital, Lucknow, UP.

■ South Asia Institute for Advanced Christian Studies, Bangalore (counseling course).

■ Mr. and Mrs. Tim and Carol Svoboda, YWAM, Chennai, Tamil Nadu (member care course).

■ Mr. and Mrs. Rod and Ruth Gilbert, Corner Stone, Mahapalipuram, Chennai (counseling in marriage and family).

■ Dr. and Mrs. Theodore and Dianna Srinivasagam, IMA, Bangalore, Karnataka.

■ Rev. and Mrs. J. N. Manokaran, India Missions Association, Chennai.

■ Mrs. and Mr. Kasturba and Hansraj Jain (marriage seminars/counselors; also involved with home schooling for MKs in Nagpur, Maharastra).

■ Dr. and Mrs. Bijoy and Premi Koshy, InterServe, Delhi.

■ Mr. Ravi David, Scripture Gift Missions, Bangalore, Karnataka.

■ Mr. John Amalraj, India Missions Association, Delhi.

■ Mrs. Joyce Joshi, India Missions Association, Delhi.

■ Rev. Sushanto Patra, National Fellowship, Calcutta, West Bengal.

■ Dr. Rajesh Agarwal, RSP, Barreilly, UP.

■ Mr. Augustine Jebakumar, GEMS, Dehri-on-sone, Bihar.

■ Mrs. Pramila Rajendran, India Missions Association, Chennai, Tamil Nadu.

■ Miss Evangeline Stanley, Blessing Youth Mission, Vellore, Tamil Nadu.

■ Mrs. and Mr. Sneha Lata and David, Lucknow, UP (marriage counselors/seminars).

■ Mr. and Mrs. Ray and Christa Eicher, Shanti Kunj, Landour, Mussorie, UP (a place for MKs to come and relax and share their problems; some families also come).

■ Dr. Daniel Sathiaraj, India Missions Association, Hyderabad.

■ Mr. James Kaiser, India Missions Association, Chennai.

■ Mr. Chacko Thomas, OM, UK.

■ Mr. Ashok Kumar, India Ministries, Singapore.

■ Mr. J. J. Rathnakumar, MUT, Vellore, Tamil Nadu.

■ Mr. David Meengs, Biblical Counselling Trust India, R. A. Puram, Chennai.

Some Guest Houses and Retreat Centers

■ Deodars Retreat Centre, Mussorie, UP.

■ Landour Guest House, Mussorie, UP.

■ Rod and Ruth Gilbert, Corner Stone, S.U. Mahapalipuram, Chennai.

■ Scripture Union Camp Centre, Mahapalipuram, Chennai.

■ J. J. Rathnakumar, MUT Rest House, Vellore, Tamil Nadu.

■ Mr. and Mrs. Wilson, Brookland Guest House and Retreat, Koonoor, Nilgiris, Tamil Nadu.

■ Mountaben Guest House, Ooty, Tamil Nadu.

***K. Rajendran**, a pioneer Christian worker and trainer, has been in Christian leadership both in India and abroad. Originally from Tamil Nadu, he has 30 years of experience in missions with over 25 years in Operation Mobilization. Currently he is the General Secretary of the India Missions Association, one of the largest mission associations in the world, representing over 25,000 Christian workers to other peoples. Rajendran is married to Pramila, who has a master's degree in counseling and is also actively involved in member care. Rajendran earned his doctorate in missiology from the South Asia Institute for Advanced Christian Studies at Bangalore. He is an Executive Committee member of the WEA Missions Commission.*

Email: rajendranwwf@eth.net.

Note: The India Missions Association is the national federation of missions in India, which assists missions and churches in the proclamation of the gospel and in making disciples of Christ among the various unreached peoples, languages, and postal codes. IMA members partner to share resources, research, and training, and they are committed to accountability and care of their personnel. IMA today has 141 missions and evangelistic organizations in its membership, representing over 25,000 Christian workers, who work in about 1,500 locations across India and in 10 other nations beyond India.

9

Field Care For Asian Missionaries In South Asia

Ah Kie Lim

In recent years, there has been a dramatic increase in the number of Asian missionaries working at home and abroad. How do we care for the new and growing wave of Asians who are counting the cost to take the gospel to the unreached? This chapter reviews five areas of need, focusing on the situation in South Asia: finances, singles, families, children's education, and vacation/home leave. Several suggestions are offered for meeting the challenges of care in this immense and diverse region.

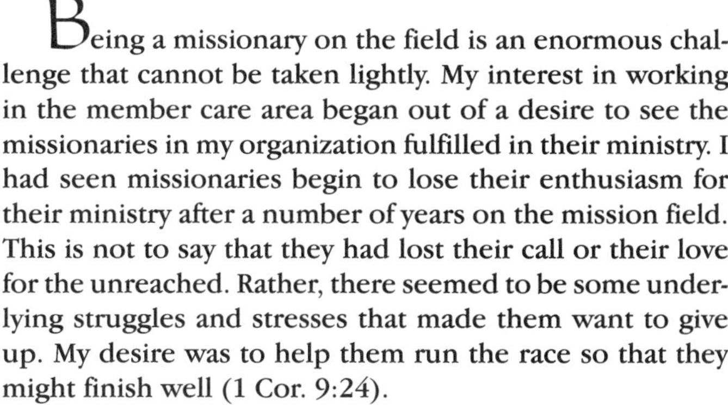

Being a missionary on the field is an enormous challenge that cannot be taken lightly. My interest in working in the member care area began out of a desire to see the missionaries in my organization fulfilled in their ministry. I had seen missionaries begin to lose their enthusiasm for their ministry after a number of years on the mission field. This is not to say that they had lost their call or their love for the unreached. Rather, there seemed to be some underlying struggles and stresses that made them want to give up. My desire was to help them run the race so that they might finish well (1 Cor. 9:24).

Asians tend to view member care very differently from their Western counterparts. Asian churches and mission organizations are often afraid that "too much" care from them will "spoil" their missionaries. Some are even of the philosophy that missionaries should be willing to suffer all for Jesus and for the sake of carrying the gospel. "There are others that believe too much care can become a distraction and ultimately make workers less resilient and effective" (O'Donnell & O'Donnell, 1992, p. 13). Because of this mindset, Asian churches and mission organizations are very cautious when giving care to their missionaries. Missionaries who genuinely need care are afraid to ask, because they could be branded as "not self-sacrificial in their ministry" or, even worse, "not fit to be on the mission field." Often they live with unmet needs and suffer disappointments with their mission organizations or sending churches.

It is a challenge to know exactly what should be considered as adequate member care for such a diverse group. The needs of Asian missionaries are very different from those of Western missionaries or those from the Middle East or Latin America. How or where does one even begin?

What I write in this article is the result of some of the successes and failures from providing care for our missionaries who are on the frontlines working as church planters among the unreached peoples of South Asia. Many of the issues faced by our national missionaries are also common for Asians working in other Asian countries. Working in South Asia, as a Malaysian, has challenged me to look at different ways to provide better care for Asian missionaries in general.

Issues Faced by National Asian Missionaries

Stress of Financial Needs

"My wife has been sick for two years, and we do not have enough money for her to seek better treatment. We barely have enough monthly financial support to meet our family needs," says one missionary. Some workers do not have enough money to travel to their ministry locations if they are working in several villages. "In many of the prayer meetings, the missionaries pray for their financial needs to be met. If they waited for all their needs to be met, India and the world would never be reached with the gospel" (Rajendran, 1998, p. 108). These workers took a step of faith and trusted that God would indeed meet all their needs. "We need to realize that the lack of money is just as definitely from God as the provision of money" (Cunningham, 1991, p. 51). So the basic perspective, for better or worse, is that the lack of finances should never deter or stop us from serving God.

When we visit our church planters in their ministry locations, we are constantly confronted by the reality of their financial needs. These are genuine needs. Some of them do not have enough finances to send their children to school or have regular monthly support to meet their family necessities. How I wish I had answers to their dilemmas! The ideal would be for the sending churches to offer financial support, yet some churches in South Asia are not in a position to support themselves, let alone a missionary from their church. Some of these churches are also hesitant to support missionaries who are working with parachurch organizations.

A common expectation is that the sponsoring church or mission will financially provide for the missionary, but there is often a problem with asking for such support. Asian missionaries often have a mentality that to ask for money for their monthly support is equal to begging. They believe that if God has called them, then He will provide. One missionary told me that she had no problem raising money for others but not for herself. It is much easier to speak for the needs of someone else than to tell the church of one's own needs. In the Asian culture, it can be shameful to ask money for oneself, but it is an honor to help someone else raise support.

In our organization, we are working closely with our church planting teams to help them with income-generating projects to earn income for themselves. Some of these small businesses are making Indian pickles, greeting cards, etc. These micro-enterprises allow our workers to be more independent of outside support, as well as being a testimony to the community. We are in no way saying that we do not trust God to provide for all of our needs or that the sending churches/agencies do not need to take more responsibility for missionaries' support. But we need to be creative with whatever means we have, in order that we might continue to stay on the field. The Apostle Paul himself was a tentmaker, working to support himself in the ministry (Acts 18:1-3).

We also help workers raise support from other interested organizations and their local sending churches. A key to this effort is writing and visiting their pastors in order to build relationships. We also help missionaries write prayer letters to people who are looking to support missionaries but do not know whom to support.

Recently we were able to network with a South Asian organization called Missionary Upholders Family (MUF). This organization links missionaries with individuals and families who are interested in supporting missionaries. The interested group will then adopt a missionary and pray for that person and his/her work. The MUF group also supports the missionary financially each month. This involvement is a positive sign that South Asian churches and Christians are taking part in reaching the lost with the gospel through their giving and prayers. The India Missions Association has also published a timely book called *Management of Indian Missions* (Sunder Raj et al., 1998). A chapter is dedicated to helping missionaries save money by showing the different savings plans that are available in India.

Single Men and Women on the Mission Field

To be single in the South Asian context can sometimes bring shame both on the individual and on his/her immediate family. For example, sometimes single men and women are not respected in the communities where they are working. Workers are only considered "adults" if they are married and have the responsibility of taking care of a family of their own, thus demonstrating that they are able to handle life. For parents, the marriage of their children means that they have done their duty as parents. For a woman, marriage means that her future is secure, with someone to care for her. For a man, it means that his position is secure, with recognized authority.

Arranged marriages are common in the Asian culture. One young woman in our mission was asked by her family members to leave the ministry, because they had arranged a life partner for her. She felt obligated to submit, even though the proposed husband was not a believer. This cultural norm may seem strange and even repulsive to cultures that believe in individual freedom to choose a life partner. In many South Asian cultures, though, matchmaking is an area that mission organizations need to take into account, and possibly, although arguably, it is a role they should provide for their missionaries.

Mission organizations in many ways act as parents to the single missionaries in their organization. This can include looking for a life partner for them. It is a big step for single missionaries to leave their homes and serve on the mission field. For many, it involves a form of "giving up their family" and belonging to another one. In this case, they become a part of the "family" in the organization where they are working. I believe that as mission agencies look after the future life partner of their single missionaries, these workers will not be forced by their families to return home to get married. One idea is that mission agencies could partner with other mission agencies and act as "marriage bureaus" for their missionaries. This is a need especially for the frontline missionaries, who face the shame of being single in the community where they are working and who also receive pressure from their non-Christian families to be married.

Aside from the usual struggles of feeling alone and not fulfilled, single missionaries who are working in South Asia need to be careful in relating to members of the opposite sex. Men and women in this culture do not mix freely in public, and to do so raises great suspicion. "Living in a marriage-oriented society poses peculiar problems for singles" (Foyle, 1987, p. 29). Can a person be in ministry and still be single in a society that looks at marriage as the norm for everyone? One solution is that in our mission we work in teams, with both singles and married couples working alongside each other. The married couples provide a "covering" for the singles, which is accepted in the South Asian context. In this way, one can reasonably mix without the fear of being questioned or frowned upon.

Family Commitment

"My parents are old and they need my help, as there is no one at home who can take care of them. I am afraid that I have to leave the mission field, although this is not my choice." "I am the oldest son in my family. It is my duty to care for my parents. I have to earn enough money to take care of them and my younger brothers and sisters." These issues are very common in Asian cultures, where children are expected to care for their family. It is considered a dishonor to the parents if their children do not care for them in their old age. Honoring parents includes providing for their material needs. I have seen many missionaries leave the mission field because their parents needed their help. Are we to abandon our parents for what we or others may perceive as the "higher" calling that God has for us? This is a tough decision that most Asian missionaries have to face and answer.

I believe that we can find some alternative solutions. For example, is there a place on the mission field for parents? In one case, a missionary's mother moved to the field location to live with her son and his family. There, she was able to help care for the grandchildren, thus freeing both parents to continue their work.

In another case, one of our national missionaries had to raise extra monthly support to provide for his parents. His parents released him to the mission field, but they were not financially independent. His Western coworkers did not understand why he gave money to his parents when he did not have enough for himself. Another missionary gives monthly support to her parents primarily out of respect and honor to them. I believe that helping to provide for the parents of missionaries will not only bless the parents, but will show the community that we practice what we preach. If we want to see more Asian missionaries released into the mission field, mission agencies need to make room for changes in policies, such as having parents of missionaries joining their offspring in the field. The question is, are we ready for such radical changes? Is this also part of our call to mission?

Children's Education

Many missionaries wrestle with schooling options for their children. For Asian missionaries, the concern is often that they do not have the money to send their children to school. "Some missions have no money earmarked for children's education, and thus children and parents suffer. The struggle has at times made the missionaries leave mission work" (Rajendran, 1998, p. 114). There is no easy solution. A large percentage of missionary children are not able to pursue higher studies due to either poor social skills, lack of finances, or lack of access to schools or colleges near where the missionaries are working. "We cannot neglect the education of the children of the missionaries, as they are an integral part of their parents' ministry. One of the reasons why missionaries leave the field is because of the education of their children" (Jones, 1995, p. 101).

There are a number of boarding schools that are available for the children of national missionaries in Asia. The issue here is not just the type of boarding schools that are available but the costs involved. In an international volunteer organization like ours, there is room for partnership in helping Asian missionaries to raise support for the education of their children. We have churches that adopt and support missionaries. I believe it is time for us to explore the idea of "adopting" the education of missionaries' children. This will ease the burden of the missionaries, and they will be able to concentrate on their ministry. Inter-mission agencies need to work together in this area to find a better solution to help provide better education for the children of our national missionaries. As member care providers, we can assist our missionaries and our organizations in finding available resources.

Vacation and Home Leave

Vacation and home leave for many means going to a beach resort or another nice place for rest and refreshment. Such breaks are necessary, and they help missionaries return to the field ready to continue. One Indian missionary told me that it is so nice that the foreign missionaries are able to take a vacation or go on home leave, but she has nowhere to go nor the funds to do so. For her to take a holiday means going to stay with her non-Christian family, which is not a conducive place to rest. For some missionaries who are from non-Christian backgrounds, going home for a holiday might mean having to endure idol worship in the home and the rituals associated with it. One of our missionaries is mocked by her family members each time she goes home, because she chose to be a missionary. For others, going home really is a holiday. One man gets to be spoiled by his mother's cooking and watch television when he goes home. After a week of these luxuries, he is refreshed and ready to get back to work.

The ministry of hospitality can provide vacation alternatives for missionaries. As member care providers, we can periodically open our homes to frontline workers who need a break. These individuals may not have the finances to take a holiday, but for them to leave their location for a week and be "spoiled" by member care providers can be most refreshing. Another example was when a group of my friends raised some money and sent me on a holiday. Their generosity blessed me and gave me the desire to do the same for other missionaries who are isolated and need a break. Finally, mission agencies could seriously consider opening mission guest houses that are affordable and easily available, designed especially for Asian missionaries.

Other Suggestions for Practical Member Care

As the number of missionaries grows, so also does the need for more member care providers. This is especially true for the teams that are working in remote or sensitive areas. These places are not easy to get to on a regular basis. In some sensitive locations, though, to have an "outsider" visiting the team may attract more attention and raise suspicion. In such areas, the member care providers are not allowed to visit the team. What do we do in situations like these? Here are some strategies:

Further Training

Missionaries are often so busy with their work that they do not take the time to receive personal input. Some of them do not have the funds to do so, or the sending churches do not see the need. A friend told me that he had been on the mission field for 10 years without a study break or an opportunity to receive teaching input into his life. What missed opportunities! Our need for ongoing learning, be it formal or non-formal, stays with us as long as we live.

Member care providers can play a part in helping missionaries to find a training location or options for training. This does not necessarily mean that they must leave their field location for an extended period of time. There are a number of institutes that provide distance learning for those who are motivated. In our organization, we have numerous training programs that are three months long. These programs enable missionaries to have a short break from the field and at the same time receive input into their lives. We also make available ongoing training that lasts for a week, designated for our frontline church planters. The ongoing training is held twice a year, thus enabling the missionaries to put into practice what they have learned. At the same time, they are refreshed spiritually and physically by the break in routine.

I believe that we can learn from corporations who seek to increase the productivity of their company by sending their workers for further training on a regular basis. The company's purpose is to motivate and upgrade their workers. It is a good investment, in hope that the workers will bring more quality and productivity to the company. We have a number of good examples from the business world concerning the management and care of personnel. Company staff are given good incentives, often with big bonuses and attractive vacation packages. Yet in Christian organizations, sometimes we are not even willing to send our workers for more training to be further equipped. This must change!

Ongoing Member Care

Field visits

One missionary said that no one had visited him in the four years he had been on the field. On occasion, he and his team did receive letters from their field office, but that was all. When I first heard about this state of affairs, I was saddened, and I was reminded that most sending mission agencies and sending churches do not visit their missionaries on a regular basis. This is not to say that they are at fault or do not care for their missionaries. The distance, travel time to remote areas, and finances make such visits difficult.

Nevertheless, contact between member care providers and missionaries is crucial for the effectiveness of frontline missionaries. On his missionary journeys, the Apostle Paul never failed to encourage the believers wherever he went. His is a good example to follow. As member care providers in our organization, we set up a regular schedule to visit each church planting team on location at least once a year. We also bring our missionaries to a central location for further training, refreshment, and refueling two or three times a year. In this way, the missionaries are not left alone too long without outside contact and input.

Tapes

Phil Parshall's (1988, p. 75) article, "How Spiritual Are Missionaries?" gives a sobering insight into the spiritual state of some missionaries. Devotional time and prayer life, Parshall found, are often short and inconsistent. I believe that member care providers can help meet some of the spiritual needs of missionaries by sending good Bible teaching tapes. In addition to visiting our teams, we also send them teaching tapes or articles each month. These servants give out so much, and they need renewing and refueling. One of our team leaders thanked me a few years ago for sending teaching tapes and teaching notes to his team. He said that as a team they wait eagerly each month for these materials. They listen to the tapes as a team and then discuss them at length. The team leader files all the teaching notes he receives and occasionally uses them as a tool to teach new believers.

Cards

It is so important to remember the birthdays and wedding anniversaries of missionaries. "My wife was ready to quit and go home because she felt so alone and was very discouraged. She began to wonder if anybody really cared. That same day when she was ready to quit, she received a birthday card from a member care team. Just a simple card encouraged her so much, and she began to have a change in attitude towards people and her work." Don't underestimate the blessing that a card or a letter can have. It communicates loud and clear that others—friends—really care. And anyone can send a card or write a letter!

Prayer

Workers on the frontlines need to be surrounded with prayer. Member care providers can be a channel to raise prayer support, especially for church planting teams who are isolated without many outside contacts. We can link the teams with churches, interest groups, and resources to support them in prayer. A few churches and interest groups have contacted us and have expressed a keen interest in praying for South Asia. As member care providers, we have written to these groups and have suggested a few teams for them to choose from. We have had the joy of linking a number of our church planting teams with interest groups who will stand alongside our workers in prayer as well as in some financial support.

Members Caring for Each Other

Missionaries are great sources of mutual care, especially in isolated areas. Barry Austin (1992, p. 60) in his article, "Supporting Missions Through Pastoral Care," wrote that in difficult settings we need to find creative ways to support our people. He said that ultimately the primary resource for care rests with those who are actually working together. We need each other for support and growth. In Hebrews 10:24, we are encouraged to spur each other to love and good works. We encourage our teams to find a prayer partner with someone from their team or outside. We also encourage them to find someone to whom they can be accountable personally and spiritually, in addition to their team leader. Regular fun time, outings, and sharing of meals are some of the team-building activities that we encourage our teams to maintain.

Area Member Care Providers

Missionaries in our organization are located all over South Asia. The vast area makes it a real challenge for member care providers to assure adequate care. To deal with this geographic reality, we have set up a program for training area member care personnel in different regions. They are thus physically located closer to the church planters. These member care providers are appointed by their leaders, and they receive ongoing training at least once a year from the main member care department in Pune, India. Our goal is for each church planting team to have a member care provider that is close to their ministry location, and especially to train Asian member care providers.

Although we have the burden and the heart to care for our missionaries, we still lack the "professional" training. This includes the areas of counseling, mental health professionals, crisis care, and others, as discussed in an article by Richard and Laura Mae Gardner (1992, p. 315), "Training and Using Member Care Workers." I would especially like to see member care providers be better equipped in crisis care and mental health counseling. The current political atmosphere in the Asian region raises the need for us to be prepared for the crises that could arise.

National and International Member Care Partnerships

Member care is not the work of one organization or church but the ministry of the body of Christ providing care for all of our missionaries. We in South Asia are still at the beginning stages of working together with agencies, both nationally and internationally. There is a great need for more networking between agencies, churches, and other mission organizations.

During the past few years, our organization has been able to partner with a few national mission agencies. We have been able to share resources and counselors, as well as provide counseling and crisis care training for our member care workers. Member care forums have been organized to provide a place for member care personnel to meet each other, discuss issues, and share resources and ideas. The India Missions Association has set up a member care consultation group to meet the growing needs of Indian missionaries. Our organization is part of this group. We have the joy of inviting one of the members of the consultation group to teach at our training program. Our member care workers have also attended some of the member care training programs that are offered by other mission organizations. We are young, but we are on the right track.

Conclusion

In closing, I would like to encourage Asian and especially South Asian member care providers to embrace the call to nurture the missionaries that are being raised up by God. But we must do this together.

The challenges and needs are before us. At times they may seem overwhelming, but we have a great God who enables those who trust in Him.

Reflection and Discussion

1. In what ways does your mission organization practically support single missionaries? How important is finding a life partner for your missionaries?

2. What types of provisions are made for the parents of missionaries in your organization? What would it take for a missionary from your culture to return to be with his/her parents?

3. How does your organization help with the financial needs of missionaries, especially those from Newer Sending Countries? Are income-generating projects viable options?

4. What are some of the needs that member care providers have? How does your organization care for the caregivers?

5. In what ways could networking with other groups further support your missionaries? How could other groups benefit from partnering with you?

References

Austin, B. (1992). Supporting missions through pastoral care. In K. O'Donnell (Ed.), *Missionary care: Counting the cost for world evangelization* (pp. 60-68). Pasadena, CA: William Carey Library.

Cunningham, L. (1991). *Daring to live on the edge: The adventure of faith and finances*. Seattle, WA: YWAM Publishing.

Foyle, M. (1987). *Honourably wounded: Stress among Christian workers*. London, UK: Monarch Books.

Gardner, L., & Gardner, R. (1992). Training and using member care workers. In K. O'Donnell (Ed.), *Missionary care: Counting the cost for world evangelization* (pp. 315-331). Pasadena, CA: William Carey Library.

Jones, M., & Jones, E. (1995). *Psychology of missionary adjustment*. Springfield, MO: Logion Press.

O'Donnell, K., & O'Donnell, M. (1992). Perspectives on member care in missions. In K. O'Donnell (Ed.), *Missionary care: Counting the cost for world evangelization* (pp. 10-23). Pasadena, CA: William Carey Library.

Parshall, P. (1988). How spiritual are missionaries? In K. O'Donnell & M. O'Donnell (Eds.), *Helping missionaries grow: Readings in mental health and missions* (pp. 75-82). Pasadena, CA: William Carey Library.

Rajendran, K. (1998). *Which way forward Indian missions? A critique of twenty-five years 1972-1997*. Bangalore, India: SAIACS Press.

Sunder Raj, E., Shyam, W., Dhanapal, M., & Lynda, S. (Eds.). (1998). *Management of Indian missions* (rev. ed.). Chennai, India: India Missions Association.

***Ah Kie Lim** is from Malaysia and has been working with Youth With A Mission for 16 years. Her main focus is providing member care for church planters working in South Asia. She has pioneered and directed the member care ministry in YWAM South Asian frontier missions for the past seven years. Ah Kie is currently working on her M.Div. at Fuller Theological Seminary in California. Email: ahkie@pqsa.net.*

10

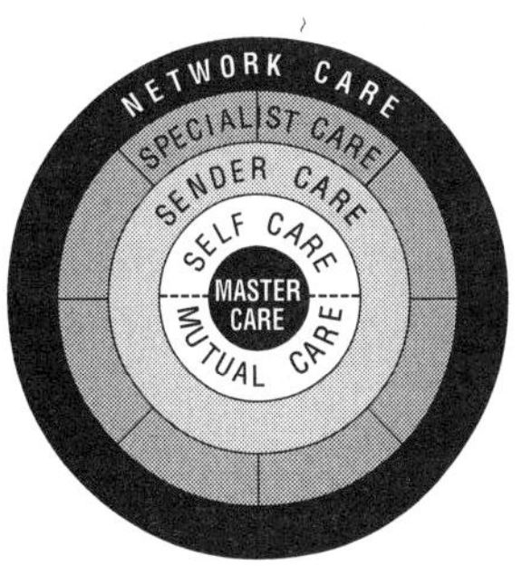

Member Care For African Mission Personnel

Naomi Famonure

Africa is a fascinating continent, rich in natural resources and abounding in cultural diversity. It is also a continent which wrestles with incapacitating problems: widespread HIV/AIDS, poverty, war, famine, financial and government corruption, and minimal infrastructures for health care and social services. In the midst of its beauty and its bleakness, the Lord is stirring the church to raise up and send out mission workers. As with any new mission movement, the African sending groups are having to come to terms with the need for ongoing supportive resources to sustain their workers. This chapter addresses some of the current realities in African missions, focusing on some of the main needs and resources for member care.

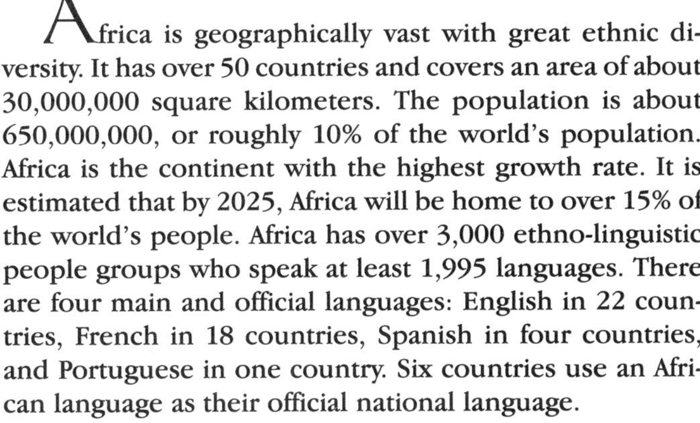

Africa is geographically vast with great ethnic diversity. It has over 50 countries and covers an area of about 30,000,000 square kilometers. The population is about 650,000,000, or roughly 10% of the world's population. Africa is the continent with the highest growth rate. It is estimated that by 2025, Africa will be home to over 15% of the world's people. Africa has over 3,000 ethno-linguistic people groups who speak at least 1,995 languages. There are four main and official languages: English in 22 countries, French in 18 countries, Spanish in four countries, and Portuguese in one country. Six countries use an African language as their official national language.

Africa has an abundance of natural and human resources, yet no other continent in the world has suffered such a series of natural, political, and economic disasters. Food production over the past 30 years has been on the decline and has been unable to keep pace with the rapid population growth. As a result, several places on the continent have had and still suffer from acute famine. As rich and well-endowed as this continent is, 32 of the 40 poorest nations in the world are there. Africa generates only 1.2% of the world's total earnings. Other factors affecting the African economy include corrupt government policies, foreign debts, and unending senseless wars that have claimed millions of innocent lives.

Into this context, the African church has, in spite of the odds, continued to forge forward sacrificially. Much has happened to God's glory, through both African and non-African mission personnel. But as we look at how the work has been done, we see the lamentable need to have managed our human resources better. Thankfully, I believe this situation is changing.

For example, the Association of Evangelicals of Africa (AEA) was founded in 1966 with the purpose of "fostering unity and cooperation among evangelicals in Africa for the furtherance of God's kingdom." The AEA at the initial stages began two commissions that have helped make a difference: the Theological and Christian Education Commission (TCEC) and the Evangelism and Missions Commission (EMC). The TCEC straightway founded two theological institutions for the purpose of training ministers and other Christian workers. The EMC initiated a missions training program and also began helping churches and mission agencies to develop their own missions training programs.

With this background in mind, we now approach the subject of member care of African mission personnel. I will look at training and selection issues, family and MK issues, MK education, physical health, spiritual warfare, and some ways forward for African missions. The various case studies that I use are all true, although the names mentioned are fictitious.

Training and Selection

Indigenous mission societies that sprang up as offshoots of Western missionary efforts in Africa either saw little need for relevant missionary training or did not have the know-how to prepare their staff adequately before sending them out to the mission field. The practice was to send everybody who had a call for ministry—regardless of the nature of the ministry—to a Bible school for training, where available. In most cases, the students of the Bible schools and seminaries were equipped for pastoral work in organized church denominations, rather than in the rugged missionary work which the African mission field demands. The effect was that Christian workers who were trained in Bible schools plunged into missions and were ill equipped for the challenges they faced on the field.

A large denominational church in the central African region was jolted into the practical reality of the need for effective pastoral care. One of its trusted, proven, and reliable workers was sent out as a missionary but had to return home, devastated, broken, and possibly never to go back to the field. Recently, a member of the mission board was asked to attend the AEA/EMC Member Care Consultation that took place in Cameroon in July 2001 (described more fully later). As you can imagine, the board member was very eager to learn more about member care, and he brought back many insights into what needs to be done to sustain missionaries on the field. He told me that this missionary had never received any form of training to prepare him and his family for what they would face on the field. It was assumed that he was sufficiently prepared, since he had known the Lord and served in the church as a worker for years. That was a costly mistake.

Another participant at the consultation, from a French-speaking country, recalled with sadness how he had gone through Bible school training without ever having been asked at the point of entry if he had been born again or had had a conversion experience in the Lord Jesus Christ. The choice of students enrolled for training in that denomination in preparation for ministry, including missionary work, was never based on a conversion experience or on a conviction of a call into ministry. In some denominations, it is based on the pastor's recommendation (who was trained through the same process) and on the candidate's educational qualifications. Depending on his qualifications, a candidate, after training, is either employed as a pastor with a parish or as an evangelist to assist the pastor, or he is posted to a remote village for church planting. In many parts of Africa, pastoral ministry is regarded with the highest esteem, but in general this is not the case with missions ministry.

The new sending agencies in Africa, mostly from the Pentecostal background as a result of the charismatic revival in the institutions of higher learning, were modeled after the faith missions of the early European missions. These African missions, like their predecessors, did not grasp the need for training or for the patient, careful selection of the missionary candidates. Many of these new sending agencies were being led by directors who themselves did not go through any form of training to prepare and equip them for their work, especially in cross-cultural settings. Most agencies did not require any form of training, but rather saw the training period as a waste of time, while souls were perishing in heathen lands. They felt that all that missionaries needed was a knowledge of the Bible, to be able to tell sinners that Jesus loves them and that He came to save them from their sins. Armed with this Bible knowledge, Christian workers moved out in faith.

Out of zeal to send many hundreds of workers to mission fields in and around Africa, some agencies have recruited indiscriminately, without reference to individual qualifications or the home church and without relevant missionary training. Many missionaries have gone out not only without the necessary skills, but also without adequate field supervision, mentoring, and appropriate care. In fact, in some cases missionaries went out by themselves to unreached and very difficult areas.

This approach has done more harm than good. Some of these untrained missionaries crashed woefully and returned home broken. Others who managed to weather the storms and who stayed on "spoiled" the work and shut the door to subsequent mission efforts among the people groups they served.

Positive Changes

After many faltering steps, the mission enterprise in Africa over the years has looked back in retrospect to see the "potholes" into which they stumbled and fell, and they have taken far-reaching measures in ensuring that the mistakes of the past are corrected. At least in the areas of training and selection, many mission agencies are now not only looking into the area of relevant cross-cultural training, but they are also seeking to work with church leaders to ensure that the right people are selected, trained, sent out to the field, and supported. Working together, churches are now relying on the recommendations of the training institutions to determine whether or not candidates are suitable, the type of ministry in which they will likely be most effective, and whether or not they are likely to thrive in a pioneering situation. It is a slow process, because some African church pastors do not yet see missions as the priority of the church, but we are progressing!

The EMC of AEA initiated a missionary training program in the early 1990s called the School of Missions Eastern Region (SOMER), in which key trainers were further equipped to go back to their home countries to start schools of missions. At least 18 missionaries were trained to be trainers. This was very effective, and as a result of the EMC initiative, many schools of missions sprang up. African sending countries are putting a lot of effort now into training their missionaries and especially into preparing and equipping them for the harsh realities of the African mission fields. For instance, the main sending countries, such as Nigeria, Democratic Republic of Congo, Ghana, Côte d'Ivoire, South Africa, and Kenya, now have training schools for missions. Here are some examples:

- Agape School of Missions for Training in Discipleship and Missions – Nigeria
- Calvary Ministries (CAPRO) School of Missions – Nigeria
- Nigerian Evangelical Missionary Institute (NEMI) – Nigeria
- Christian Missionary Foundation – Nigeria
- Foursquare School of Missions – Nigeria
- Sheepfold Ministries Missions Training – Kenya
- Africa Inland Missionary Training – Kenya
- World Mission Center – South Africa

- Ecole de Mission Inter-Africain au Benin – Republic of Benin
- Adonai International Missions School – Central African Republic (CAR)
- CERFEM – Chad
- Ghana Evangelical Missionary Institute – Ghana

The development of better training, to some extent, has served to reduce the occupational hazards of African missions. Churches with genuine and authentic missionary thrusts, which have hitherto used only their Bible schools to prepare their missionaries, have been able to take advantage of these new missions training centers to better train and equip their workers.

In August 1996, the AEA TCEC and the EMC jointly organized a workshop on missions training in Africa, held in Jos, Nigeria. Those who were invited to attend were theologians, primarily from accredited theological schools, along with missionaries involved in training from 10 different African countries and the United Kingdom. The workshop centered on the need for integration between missions and theology. It emphasized that in order for Africans to be won to the Lord Jesus Christ, "It is not only necessary to encourage enthusiastic Africans into missions, but also to give them solid, biblically based theological foundations for that mission." A careful look at the curriculum of the theological institutions in Africa revealed that in most cases they did not reflect what could be considered an adequate program of missions and missionary training, even though "the spread of the gospel" frequently forms a part of the mission statements of these institutions. Many of the theological training institutions did not have much missions content. Some did not have any course on missions at all. Pastors being produced by these institutions had little or no understanding of nor interest in missions.

The workshop, therefore, saw an urgent need for our theological schools to include missions as an integral part of their programs. Likewise, there is a need for the missions schools to include theological foundations in their training. With this sort of balanced training and preparation, every theological college graduate will have a "missionary sense and understanding, and every missions-trained graduate will have an adequate theological foundation." In this case, it is hoped that both the missionary and the pastor will make disciples who will be mature, balanced Christians who will make a difference on the African continent and in the world as a whole. One of the many practical outcomes of the workshop was the compendium *Training God's Servants* (1997), jointly edited by my husband Bayo, myself, and Alan Chilver.

Another positive example is the EMC training track's launching of the Council of Missions Training in Africa (COMITA). The EMC has discovered that whereas a good number of schools of missions are emerging, many still need to improve their curriculum, use qualified trainers and teachers, and develop their philosophy of missions training. The result is that people are still being sent out ill equipped. Training issues were further addressed at an all-African consultation that was held in April 1998 in Accra, Ghana. The participants at this consultation agreed that the EMC should set up a body that could help all mission training programs improve in their quality, that could serve as a medium to exchange ideas and faculty, and that could help produce and distribute quality resource materials for missions training. This body, in effect, is serving as a regulatory body for missions training in Africa.

Other advances are seen in the training programs of two denominations. One large denomination in West Africa, the Evangelical Churches of West Africa (ECWA), which was pioneered by the Sudan Interior Mission (SIM), targeted the rural areas through its mission organization called the Evangelical Missionary Society. It began to train vernacular evangelists and preachers in its Bible Training Schools (BTSs), with the sole aim of reaching the local villages. The same thing has been going on in the Africa Inland Church (AIC), which was founded by the Africa Inland Mission (AIM).

Some Selection Procedures

Each training institution has its own selection procedures and criteria. Most require applicants to fill out a series of forms. The Agape School for Training in Discipleship and Missions, for example, requires candidates to fill out forms, obtain references from pastors and sometimes from other respected Christian leaders, write exams, and undergo oral interviews before they are accepted for enrollment for training. Once in the school, the new students are given a full week of intensive orientation to prepare them for the rigors of the training. The orientation allows them to know what to expect and the rationale for each course.

The training is three-pronged: formal, non-formal, and informal. Evaluations based on all three methods of training are given midway and at the end of training by a team of trainers made up of not less than five people. The non-formal and informal training areas carry more weight than the actual academic work, although that too is very important. A great deal of importance is laid on character building. With recommendations from the training center, a formal interview is conducted by the leaders of the mission to determine whether or not a candidate should be accepted into the mission. A missionary is accepted on probation for one year initially and then full time after the period of probation is over, if found suitable.

Family and MK Issues

The typical African culture and religions have little regard for women and children. They are to be seen and not heard. They are usually not reckoned with when important decisions are made. And yet we know that strong nations are made up of strong family units, which include wives, mothers, and children. Healthy family units make healthy churches and healthy nations. A church or a nation that does not care for or have plans for its families, and especially for its children, is doomed to have problems of divorce, delinquency, crime, and other undesirable things to grapple with. The same will be true of any mission agency involved in sending out missionaries, if it does not take much thought for the family.

As inroads are being made in the areas of selection and training, so also is the African mission agency slowly advancing in the area of the family. One especially important issue is the needs of children and the effect that these needs have on the mission as a whole. Some mission organizations in Africa consider only the man or the husband as the bona fide missionary, and they post him to the field without any consideration for his wife and children. Experience has shown that either the wife or the children can destabilize work on the field, unless the needs of the entire family are met.

A prime example of the care a missionary family needs is the kind of care Messiah College is giving. My husband Bayo and I were both missionaries before our three children were born. We had our first two children in a little village where we were serving. Vehicles could only go in there once a week—on market days only. There was no kindergarten except a low standard public school some miles away, too far for a child to walk. And Bayo and I had no means of transportation. The only option left was for me to teach our children basic reading and writing skills at home (there wasn't any home school program in Nigeria then). This difficult experience led us to start a boarding secondary school for MKs a few years ago called Messiah College. It is our attempt to meet some of the teeming needs of MKs in Africa, starting with Nigeria. We of course were not the only missionary and ministry family facing the predicament of lack of provision for our children's education!

Provision for widows is another issue. "This church does not know how to appreciate people. It does not value its staff. I left for training, and no one remembered that I had served here for so many years. It is not that I expect much, but just that they could have at least showed that I came out from among them and that they care. Now the church is doing the same with my friend who needs help with her children." These words were spoken to me by Danuba, a quiet, soft-spoken, and unassuming brother who had just enrolled for missions training. He had been serving with one of the leading Evangelical churches in Nigeria in the area of education and had been nursing a vision of serving in cross-cultural church planting work. He subsequently resigned his job and enrolled for missions training, although with little support from his church.

I wondered why he was telling me these things. He had just introduced me to his friend, a widow, who wanted two of her children to attend our MK school, Messiah College. Apparently Danuba had tried to help enroll this lady's children in Messiah College the previous year, but for lack of sufficient funds they could not be enrolled. Danuba decided to help her again with the process and to enable her to talk with us in Messiah College.

The woman was despairing because of her inability to give quality education to her fatherless kids. "And their father died while in active service with the church," she said. She despaired also because the church had not come to her aid with the welfare of the children. And yet she herself is still on staff at the church, serving under this same organization in which her husband served and died. She and her children survive on a meager salary from the church (which is far from being enough), supplemented by proceeds from the sales of buns and donuts that she makes herself, which her children sell on the streets.

While her son Dubai, 11 years old, was being interviewed for placement in Messiah College, he was asked if he would prefer to attend a public school near home so he could be with his mother. His answer was, "I will spend most of my time hawking donuts, and I don't enjoy doing that." He said he misses his father more when he has to hawk in order to earn money for the family.

Separation Issues

Ryang is a little 12-year-old girl who came to Messiah College in the year 2000. When she was asked about her parents during the interview preceding her admission, she began to sob. She continued crying for quite a while, so pathetically that the panel was helpless and simply allowed her to weep. Even when she later regained composure, she still would not talk about her family.

Messiah College then decided to make contact with the mission agency with which her parents serve, and we made a startling discovery. We found that Ryang does not get to see her parents often because they serve in a distant mission field. The last time she saw her family was when she was eight. Messiah College may not be able to solve this problem; nevertheless, we began to work at it. We said we were going to offer Ryang admission only on the condition that at least one of her parents comes with her on reporting day. This was an attempt to ensure some kind of security for Ryang, at least emotionally. She would at least see one parent, and she would be assured that her family knows exactly where on earth she is.

Another case is that of Tope, who is 17 now and is graduating from Messiah College this year, 2001. When his father brought him to Messiah College in 1995, he was only 11. And for the next three years that followed, he never set eyes on his family. He was constantly lonely, withdrawn, and quiet. He would not play like other youngsters in the school. When the time was drawing near for his class to write the Junior Secondary Certificate Exams, we felt we had to do something quickly so as not to jeopardize Tope's academic performance in the external exams. We had noticed that whenever he was withdrawn, he was weeping. We later learned that he was crying because he assumed that his parents and family must all be dead! If not, he could not understand why he hadn't seen them. He concluded everyone was hiding the facts from him and not telling him the truth. To deal with this situation, the school decided to facilitate the process of getting Tope to visit his family during one of the Christmas holidays before the external exams his class was about to write.

As I have spoken with missionary parents and leaders about separation issues, I have been surprised and sometimes shocked by some of the things I have heard. For example, many denominational church-based missionaries get posted for missions not necessarily based on call or convictions. They are usually trained in vernacular schools as pastors, then become missionaries, and then are posted to remote, usually government-forsaken villages with no basic amenities for survival. Some pastors manage to lobby for better and favorable postings by playing and dancing along to the tune and dictates of their leaders. Those who do not satisfy their leaders risk getting sent to difficult areas without consideration of their families' needs, such as schooling for the children, health matters, etc. These missionaries end up sending their children to live with relatives or friends who agree to help keep them while they attend school.

While I was working on this chapter, a missionary from one of the leading agencies came to my office to talk about his children and the possibility of enrolling his son in Messiah College. Talking with him, I found out that while he was serving in a church planting situation, his children's education needs were not well met. This understandably bothered him and his wife a great deal. His solution was to find a way to be re-posted to a more favorable location, with access to good schools. Somehow he managed to get elected (done by ballot) as a coordinator of several fields. This position required him to relocate to a city from which he could coordinate the work of the mission. It was from this "favorable" location he heard of Messiah College and came to see me. More often than not, many people get "favorably posted" by lobbying!

Some Issues for Missionary Wives

Very few mission agencies prepare and make use of the wives of the men who have been accepted and sent out as missionaries. It is only the men that are recognized as genuine missionaries. If the wife cannot accompany her husband, then the family is forced to separate. The wife remains in a nearby town or city with the children, so she can keep her job and so the children can go to school. In addition, the majority of the wives of missionaries are unschooled. While their husbands were being trained, they were usually tending the children and caring for their husbands.

Thankfully, there are some changes happening. The trend now among agencies is to try to train the illiterate wives. Many of them are taught how to be better wives and mothers, better home keepers, and better supporters of their missionary husbands. Some training institutions have added evangelism and other relevant courses to the training program for pastor/missionary wives.

Agape Missions and Calvary Ministries, for example, will not allow a married man or woman to enroll in the training program apart from the spouse. The two must both have a call, must both go through training, and must both be sent out as missionaries in their own right, though as a couple. Agape Missions has developed a curriculum for basic training of missions candidates who have no educational background. This includes a literacy program, from which the wives of missionary candidates have benefited a great deal. These women have been graduated and sent out with their husbands as full partners in ministry.

The new sending agencies are generally not prepared for unexpected and untimely deaths of serving missionaries. There are cases of missionary families (as in the case described above) where the husband/father and breadwinner has died, and the wife/mother and children are left alone and forgotten. Because no plan had been made for such an unforeseen time as this, sending groups do not seem to know what to do or how to handle the family in their grief and need. Many missionary widows and their children get forgotten. Of necessity, they pull out of the mission and the missions community in order to survive. Very few remain to continue with the ministry following their husband's death.

A successful mission director in Cameroon was sharing about the tragic loss of two of his missionaries. One died of a prolonged illness, leaving a wife and two small children. The other was killed in a ghastly motor accident, leaving a wife and seven children. In the first case, the two little ones were taken over by the non-Christian family of the deceased, to be placed among the relatives for care. But the missionary had denounced idols and had in turn been denounced by his family before his untimely death. Knowing this, the director of the mission went to the dead man's village and single-handedly negotiated to retain the children and to secure them for their mother. The wife and children of the missionary who died in the motor accident were all brought to live with the director's family. The mission director is still wrestling with how to help them with their loss and their practical support, as the mission has no policy in place yet to guide in the area of bereavement and care.

MK Education

Along with their children, missionary parents also struggle greatly with separation. Noel, for example, submitted his resignation letter to his mission board over this very issue. Upon receiving the letter, the leadership of the board wisely invited Noel to the mission headquarters for a chat with the director. Noel had been an outstanding and very successful evangelist and church planter who was penetrating the rural areas of an unreached people group and was reaching out to the local people with the Jesus Film. He had won several people into the kingdom of God.

The "thorn in his flesh," though, was the issue of quality education for his children. In the search for good education, he and his wife had distributed the children to the homes of relatives in different towns, some of whom were not Christians. Unfortunately, Noel's wife was not educated, although Noel himself was a graduate of a theological seminary. She might have been of some help to the children's education if she had had some education herself. What kept gnawing at Noel's heart and conscience was the fact that whenever he made his rounds to visit his children, he never liked what he saw of them. They were imbibing habits and traits their parents had never taught them. The second child was beginning to steal, lie, and curse. Such things broke Noel's heart and prompted him straightway to submit his letter of resignation at the mission. He did it with tears in his eyes—not because he no longer had a call to continue in service, but because of his children's needs.

In talking with the mission director, Noel openly shared what he was going through. At this, the director sent Noel with a letter to us at Messiah College. It was that simple trip to Messiah College that sent Noel singing and rejoicing back to the mission field and to his ministry. His children were admitted into Messiah College at a huge discount. The college solicited help from friends and supporters to supplement the children's fees. After all, Noel never really wanted to quit the field. He was doing a fantastic job. But he felt a deep sense of responsibility and an obligation to his own children. The story is not over, though. We at Messiah College must still grapple with the issue of separation and with the fact that the children are not growing up under the care and Christian influence of their parents.

Another person who comes to mind is Mallam Adamu. This man has a wonderful ministry reaching out to the desert/ nomadic people of northern Nigeria, Niger, and Chad. He and his wife are both powerful evangelists who have been able to impact Muslim villages. But the itinerant nature of their ministry can never allow their children to have a stable school life. This is because most of the areas they cover have no schools apart from Koranic ones. Even if suitable schools are available, the parents work in very hostile environments where their lives are not always safe. Adamu's relatives are all Muslims, so he would not want to send any of his children to any of them. He was in a dilemma until he was directed to Messiah College.

One of the most unusual cases is that of Obi and Janet, who are serving in Swaziland. They have three children. The oldest is schooling in Nigeria and speaks English and a Nigerian language (the mother tongue) very well. The second child is schooling in Mozambique, because Obi and Janet served there for a couple of years. The schooling there is all in Portuguese. When the parents moved to Swaziland, they had to leave this child behind with a colleague's family to continue his education. The third child is with them in Swaziland and can speak some English and the Swastika language.

Many African missionaries serving in countries where the *lingua franca* is different from the one spoken in their home countries (and usually where the educational systems are different too) are not able to afford international school fees for their children. The children either attend national schools and then cannot fit in when they go back home, or they are sent away to live with relatives.

The most painful thing here with the family of Obi and Janet is not the separation, but the fact that the three children cannot communicate with one another when they come together! The parents were not willing to talk this issue over with the mission board that sent them out, nor did they want us to talk to their leaders on their behalf. They did not want to be seen to be complaining or gossiping about their leaders. They would rather suffer and endure in silence or figure out their problems on their own. Likewise, many if not most African missionaries prefer to remain silent over their pains and traumas, or else they quietly resign or withdraw from the mission agency without stating what the reason for withdrawal really is.

Another couple, Joe and Pam, were serving in Liberia, when war broke out and they had to escape. On their return to Nigeria, they felt a call to go to Central African Republic (CAR), a French-speaking nation. Now, the question was what to do with the children, who had already started school in Liberia, an English-speaking country. The system of education in CAR is totally different. Their decision to enroll the children in Messiah College and to go to the mission field without them was a hard one. But the hardest part of the separation was the inability of the parents to afford air tickets for the children to be able to spend holidays with their parents in CAR. In trying to work out a solution to this in order to ease the pain of separation, Messiah College approached the leadership of the mission agency, soliciting some assistance for this family to unite at least once a year. But the leaders felt that it was Joe's family affair and that the family ought to be able to work through the problems in a way that would suit them without the "interference" of the mission.

Six years ago, my husband and I met two families in Togo who were doing an excellent job of planting churches. Today, however, they are no longer on the mission field. The first family had a 19-year-old son who had dropped out of school at the age of 16. He had gone through the French system of education until the junior year of secondary level. The parents then felt he needed to continue in an English school, but because they could not afford the fees for an international school, they sent him to Nigeria. His French schooling background did not allow him to fit into the English system of education in Nigeria. Inevitably, he dropped out and was also jobless. His younger sister had a similar problem and just settled into an early marriage.

The second family, who had been instrumental in the planting of about 50 churches in northern Togo, had an equally heart-rending experience. Knowing that they could not afford international school fees, they decided to keep their children in a city in Nigeria a couple of hours' drive away from the capital city of Togo. They rented an apartment for their children, where the children lived all by themselves—about five of them of primary and secondary school ages. Each parent was paying a bi-monthly visit alternately. Eventually, they understood the dangers and the negative consequences of this arrangement. Their best recourse, regrettably, was to resign their service as church planters and go back home.

I was talking with an adult MK from Chad recently as he reminisced about how he went through school. He shared how he had to ride horseback on a three-day journey from the mission station to the nearest school. Because of the hassle of going to school that way, his younger brothers could not attend school. Instead, they became shepherd boys and are now illiterate adults. Did it have to be that way?

Some mission agencies and a few denominational mission boards are looking into the area of MK education and are offering what they call a "children's education allowance" to missionary families. In some cases, these allowances offset most of the schooling bills of the MKs, depending on their grade levels. But in many cases, the parents have to make up whatever differences there may be. Messiah College, for example, as a service ministry to missionary families, is always giving discounts ranging from 30% to 80%. This is always done in faith, trusting that God will provide the rest.

Another positive development is that three years ago, an Evangelical group (ECWA) opened a children's hostel in West Africa. There are about 75 MKs of different age groups and grade levels presently being accommodated. Most go to nearby schools, including the ECWA staff school, while some go through the pre-school and primary school programs using the Accelerated Christian Education (or the School of Tomorrow) curriculum.

Physical Health

The health of African missionaries has not yet received much attention in many quarters. In general, there is no organized, consistent, ongoing provision for health care. However, in an emergency, "fire brigade" attention will be given to the need. The African continent is largely a rural continent, and basic amenities such as health delivery services are luxuries in many areas. This is especially true in the rural areas where missionaries are mostly found. Most missionaries hardly ever go for routine medical check-ups unless they are ill. Even then, if the problem is something that they can manage on their own with self-medication, they will not hesitate to do so, unless it becomes an emergency.

Malarial fever, typhoid fever, and dysentery are some of the common diseases in Africa with which missionaries have to contend. Malaria is so common that many people just treat themselves with over-the-counter drugs. Regular health check-ups are not common practice by agencies, so in many cases agencies do not have a physician specifically assigned to do such check-ups on missionaries. There may be Christian physicians in private practice who may volunteer their clinics or their time to help missionaries, and they will often offer discounts for consultancy and treatment. Some mission agencies may have particular hospitals, clinics, or mission-owned hospitals where they will refer their missionaries for consultations and treatment, but I am not aware yet of a hospital or a clinic in Africa set up solely for missionaries and their families.

The most threatening factor to the health of missionaries and their families is stress. This is so because most African missionaries do not take leave or vacations. They work and continue to work until they are no longer able to work. Many African missionaries work under very austere conditions, and often they are stressed by many factors, including long years of work without vacation, lack of adequate provision, family and children's issues, trauma from civil or religious wars, communal clashes, and so on.

The children of a Nigerian missionary family who served in Sierra Leone still become hysterical at the mere mention of the name "Sierra Leone." They went through a number of traumatic experiences during the country's rebel war, before they were rescued and evacuated by the United Nations peacekeeping corps. No one thought of doing any kind of therapy to help these children overcome the trauma that they experienced. The family never went back to Sierra Leone. They are in another country still serving as missionaries, but their children live in constant fear of anything that sounds like gunshots or war.

It is not uncommon to find one missionary doing the jobs of five people. Because of this, missionaries need to go on vacation at regular intervals, in order to maintain their physical, mental, and spiritual health and to avoid burnout. Most do not do this. Some consider themselves too busy to take a vacation or break. The work is too important. And where there are not enough people to cover the work, there is the fear that the work will collapse. Some think it is unspiritual to go on vacation when souls are perishing. It is never surprising to hear a missionary (and even his/her leader) boast of having not gone on any break for the past 10 years of ministry! And yet there are some who would be happy to have a vacation if only they could afford to do so with their families.

Mission leaders who have had cases of burnout in personnel are beginning to think of the general health of the missionary. As a start, some leaders are recalling their missionaries for "refresher" courses. It is hoped that this input/break will help missionaries develop and improve themselves intellectually and spiritually, as well as provide rest by getting them out of their work domain. For example, member groups of the Nigerian Evangelical Mission Association (NEMA) send their missionaries for short courses or conferences organized by the NEMA-owned institute, the Nigerian Evangelical Missionary Institute. These courses run for a couple of weeks or a few months. They are long enough to enable missionaries to learn but short enough to allow them to get back to their base on the mission field without being gone too long from the work.

Spiritual Warfare

Spiritual warfare is commonplace in any typical mission field in Africa. In many cases, the sending agencies or mission boards endeavor to set up consistent and effective prayer support for their missionaries (prayer support is covered more than financial support). Churches along with cell groups of various sizes and age groups have effectively mobilized for the prayer support of missionaries in the major sending countries. Women's prayer groups are in the forefront of this kind of support.

Missionaries from Pentecostal church backgrounds are nowadays being trained to engage in spiritual warfare, praying against the territorial spirits that rule the regions or the tribes in which the missionaries serve. In fact, some schools of missions include spiritual warfare or power encounter as a course in the curriculum. Prayers with long days of dry fasts (i.e., fasting with no eating and no drinking of water or other fluids) are part and parcel of the missionary work in Africa. Missionaries whose church background has not prepared them for power encounter have had to learn the hard way. Some sending agencies and churches have learned from their casualties as a result of demonic attacks. They had no choice but to believe and to take action in the area of adequate preparation for power encounter and spiritual warfare.

An example of spiritual warfare is a team of five missionaries (a couple and three singles) who were serving in Senegal, when suddenly their health came under severe attack. The team leader developed inexplicable and excruciating pain all over his body. He could neither sit nor lie down. All the doctors he saw could not diagnose anything. His wife had persistent and bitter migraines. One of the men, a very effective cross-cultural missionary, went out of his mind with depression. The only team member still able to function was a young lady, a short-termer. The team leader, sensing the danger they were all in, decided that the surviving missionary, the short-termer, who was also a novice on the field, should be sent with an SOS back to the mission headquarters. She also took along with her the depressed colleague.

The moment she stepped into the headquarters office with her sick colleague, she burst into tears (tears that had been suppressed throughout their journey), and it took her a few moments to be able to explain what was going on in Senegal. A hasty prayer summons was sent to all prayer partners, while the director of the mission along with two others made a quick trip to Senegal to visit the team and pray. Within a week, everyone on the field had recovered with no medical intervention or explanation. But the man who was brought back home could not get back to the field for a long while. In fact, it took over 10 years before he could return to the field, and even then it was not to the same field but to another. And that was after receiving professional counseling for several months. This whole incident involved spiritual warfare—genuine physical and emotional problems, but stemming from the enemy.

The Way Forward

In May 2000, a continental missions conference in Abidjan, Côte d'Ivoire, called "Mission Africa" brought together missions and church leaders from around the continent. During this conference, the Evangelism and Missions Commission (EMC) of the AEA launched the member care track for Africa. The track works to increase awareness about member care needs and resources, especially among mission leaders. A main strategy is to hold member care awareness seminars and consultations in each region of the continent for mission executives and leaders. Initially, communication between members of the track (and in general) posed a huge hindrance to achieving some of the goals. It is still difficult, especially in areas where telephone services are not very efficient and where the postal service is very slow.

In July 2001, the EMC convened a member care consultation in Cameroon for the central African region. It was attended by mission and church leaders, pastors, and some missionaries. It was a very valuable time, and there was a lot of brainstorming on what should be done on the issue of the care of missionaries in Central Africa. We decided to organize a special awareness seminar for 2002, where many more leaders—the decision makers—will be invited to come and hear and also contribute. A regional member care committee has been set up for this region. The members will work together, looking into the needs of the care of the African missionaries in the region. Also in the pipeline for 2002 is member care training for mission executives and/or personnel managers of mission agencies and boards for the West African region.

Travel within the continent is expensive, especially by air—probably more so than anywhere else in the world. So it is a challenge financially to meet together. In addition, the instability of some African countries makes planning and attending member care/missions events difficult. For example, at the time the Cameroon consultation was held, there were no participants from Central African Republic (CAR), because of the uncertainties caused by a rebel war and an attempt to topple the ruling government.

In conclusion, African missions have come a very long way. There is a growing member care awareness, and I believe that some significant changes will soon take place to provide better support for mission personnel. We are praying for more people to become involved in member care and to raise the standard of care. Our mission efforts will thus improve because our staff will be better prepared and cared for as they serve the Lord in missions.

Reflection and Discussion

1. What are some of the main logistical obstacles to developing member care in Africa?

2. What does a typical member care program/approach include for an African sending church/agency? How does it compare with the member care program/approach from your sending group?

3. Review some of the challenges of African missionary wives or missionary children. What could be done to support them further and to help them contribute to missions?

4. List some ways that non-Africans could work with Africans to develop member care within organizations and at the regional level.

5. Recall some of the case examples in this article—positive or negative. Which ones affected you the most and why?

References and Suggested Readings

Adeyemo, T. (1997). *Is Africa cursed?* Christian Learning Material Centre.

Anyomi, S. (1997). Mission agency screening and orientation and effect of attrition factors: Perspective of the new sending countries. In W. Taylor (Ed.), *Too valuable to lose: Exploring the causes and cures of missionary attrition* (pp. 229-239). Pasadena, CA: William Carey Library.

Famonure, B. (1989). *Training to die: A manual for discipleship*. Jos, Nigeria: CAPRO Media Services.

Famonure, B., Famonure, N., & Chilver, A. (Eds.). (1997). *Training God's servants*. Nairobi, Kenya: Association of Evangelicals of Africa.

Johnstone, P. (1993). *Operation world*. Carlisle, Cumbria, UK: OM Publishing.

Newto, A. (1992). *West Africa: A travel survival kit*. South Yarra, Victoria, Australia: Lonely Planet.

Olande, T. (2000). *Equipping for the harvest*. Jos, Nigeria: CAPRO Media Services.

Richmond, Y., & Gestrin, P. (1998). *Into Africa: Intercultural insights*. Yarmouth, ME: Intercultural Press.

***Naomi Famonure** is a missionary with Agape Missions and Evangelistic Network (AMEN) with headquarters in Nigeria. She heard the call of God for missions when she was in high school. She has served in various capacities, including running schools of missions and training and conducting a women's ministry. She is currently working with African MKs at Messiah College. Naomi coordinates the member care track of the Evangelism and Missions Commission of the Association of Evangelicals of Africa. She is married to Bayo, and they have three biological children, Sharon Ife, John-Daniel Adua, and James Ayo, along with several others whom they adopted. Email: naomi_messiah@hotmail.com.*

Special thanks to Bayo Famonure, Clement Anegbe, Andrew Abah, and Esther James for their helpful review of this chapter.

Editor's note: Just before the book went to press, the boys dormitory at Messiah College was burned down by an antagonistic religious/terrorist group which opposes Christians and Christian schools. This college, like other Christian schools in the country, has received threats to kill students too.

11

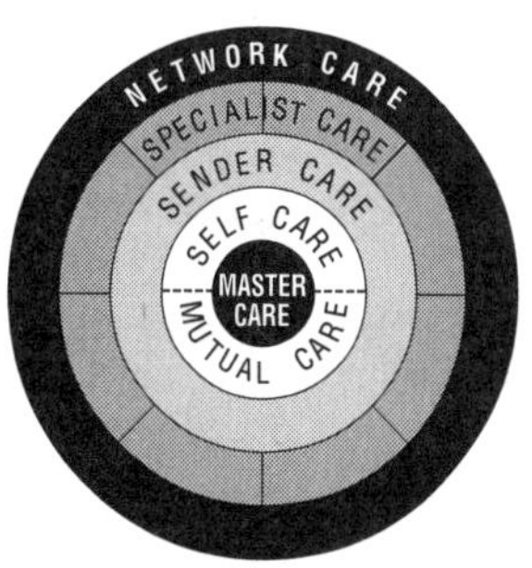

Member Care In North Africa: Finding Life in the Desert

ANKE TISSINGH

Timely field visits, healthy teams, proper orientation, and good relationships are like cool water to a thirsty soul. This is especially true for expatriate and national Christians living in spiritually desolate and often isolated regions like North Africa.

If someone asked me what my most favorite sound is, my thoughts would immediately go to something I often hear on my member care travels in North Africa. It is the sound of the wheels on my little suitcase clicking over the tiles at the railway stations. That suitcase would hold a few changes of clothes but mostly mail and "goodies" to be taken to our workers. My member care trips give me tremendous joy as I become part of the lives of those serving in and around the deserts of North Africa. These dear people, like their national brethren, have such wonderful determination and a sacrificial commitment, with hope in their hearts that one day the church in this spiritual desert will again blossom.

Some Background

Although North Africa is certainly not all covered in desert, it is known for the vast Sahara Desert. This desert dominates most of the area and is greater in size than the United States. Within and surrounding the desert are cities, towns, camps, and villages where over 100 million people live. About 98% of the people of North Africa are Muslims who have had little or no witness of the gospel in a way that they can understand. The people in this area are hospitable and often open to talk about spiritual matters. Just as the desert literally flourishes when there is water and when seed is in the ground, so too we believe that North Africa will spiritually flourish in God's timing. God's promise is sure: The desert *will* bloom (Isa. 35:1).

Mission efforts have occurred in this area for 100 years. We stand on the shoulders of those who have given *all* to see North Africa reached. Some of them have never seen any fruit for their efforts. Currently, though, there is an emerging joy, growth, and maturation in the North African church. In some nations, the church is just beginning to see its own potential and strengths. In other countries, the need for training is receiving much attention, and the North African believers choose the topics and write the curriculum. It is interesting to note that inner healing and right relationships are on that list, as well as understanding the importance of prayer for deliverance. Many have been involved in the occult before embracing Christianity, either through folk Islam or via widely practiced forms of superstition.

My husband Garry and I began taking short-term teams into North Africa in the early 1980s. Our main role was that of facilitation. We began helping others in their vision, setting long-term goals, getting established on the field, and remaining there effectively. This has evolved to include our supportive roles of pastoral care as well. We have often been deeply moved by the gratefulness that is expressed because of a visit from us or from something as seemingly small as a written message of encouragement. The Lord uses such visits and notes as timely reminders that the workers are indeed remembered, both by their colleagues and leaders and especially by their Comforter and Shepherd.

During a recent field visit, I took a 10-hour train ride to the southern part of the country. The next day, I was off on a five-hour bus ride over the mountains to reach a small team of women, all working in health care in the town. I felt so happy to have made it to them and, above all, just to be in their midst! As we shared a lovely meal together, I asked how we could best use our time together—how to make it worthwhile. With that comment, we all looked at each other, and I saw the answer all over their faces. Just the fact that I had come from so far on their behalf was the greatest thing I could have done. My presence was more valuable than any words that I could communicate.

Stressors and Strategies

Our workers encounter a plethora of stressors that affect their physical, spiritual, emotional, and relational health and also the quality of their work. Coping strategies are not always that simple to find.

Physical Health

Remaining healthy in our part of the world may prove to be a real challenge. Workers, like locals, are faced with the lack of fresh fruit and vegetables, the high price of meat, the unreliable provision of clean water or water at all, plus the presence of diseases such as malaria, cholera, typhoid, and meningitis. There is also insufficient or even no medical care in a number of locations where our workers have made their homes.

We try to teach our workers the basics of health care in this environment and creative ways to fix nutritious meals. We encourage them to consult by phone with a qualified nurse located at our home office in a nearby country. Werner's (1992) *Where There Is No Doctor* has been an invaluable tool. We also encourage them to have regular medical check-ups.

Language Stress

Language learning is a major stressor. In North Africa, workers need to learn at least two languages and sometimes three: French, Arabic, and a tribal language. Additional stress occurs when the children (because of their schooling) do not learn the language in which the parents are ministering. For example, the children may go to a French-speaking school, and the parents will lead a home-group with nationals in Arabic.

Work Stress

The fact that one needs to find "a reason for being there"—some acceptable job which would eventually give residency status for the person and his/her family—has proven to be one of the most challenging issues. One of the workers explained: "It's almost like leading a double life. You live with the "secret" of being there to share the good news. But then there is your public life and your job, which should give you the reason to stay in the country. How do you balance the two with integrity?"

The red tape in dealing with bureaucracy can become very wearisome and overwhelming, particularly if a worker is trying to start a legitimate business. Along with work concerns may come a long season of trying to sort out ministry options. "How can I/we best contribute to the building of the church in North Africa?" can be quite a perplexing question.

Workers often feel pressured to "look legitimate." For example, they may feel compelled to leave the house in the morning and spend a full day at "work," concerned that neighbors are checking up on them. They may spend so much time and energy at work that little time remains for what they really yearn to do—sensitively share their faith, disciple, church plant. There are no set guidelines as to how to work or connect with the culture. Workers need to consult with colleagues with more experience and come to terms with what God tells them to do, even when team members or other colleagues might question their priorities.

Spiritual Health

It is essential for workers to have learned to have a healthy relationship with God, before settling in a harsh, spiritually dry environment. It is axiomatic yet so true: our self-worth and identity need to be deeply rooted in our assurance that God loves us at all times. I have found that those who do have and prioritize their *loving* relationship with their Heavenly Father, which includes a disciplined devotional lifestyle, seem to have the greatest longevity. This is especially true for families that worship and sing together.

Relational Health

Loneliness may affect us all, even in the midst of a good team with healthy relationships. It can occur when our lives are too busy and when we allow our work/ministry to become too demanding. We miss or even avoid the nurture of friends that is so necessary to maintain our emotional balance and sense of well-being. There are cultural expectations and restrictions which can limit one's opportunities for recreation, such as going out for a nice dinner, taking a walk in the park or along the beach, or going to see a movie. Married women with children are the most isolated and most prone to experience loneliness. They come with strong convictions to do ministry, and although they accept their limitations because of children, language, and culture, they want to have deep soul friendships for sharing and intercession. Very few are in a location that allows such friendships to develop.

Although we would so like to see strong, mutually accountable relationships within teams, the reality is that very few examples exist. It can be very hard to share your weaknesses and be vulnerable with your team members when you know that each one of them already has so much to carry. I encourage each individual to have one "accountability relationship," i.e., someone who can ask the hard questions at any time, such as: How is your thought life? Are you relaxing? Are you keeping to your set goals? Are you eating well, sleeping well? How is your social activity? Are you lonely? How is your walk with God? How is your marriage? Some field workers have this type of relationship with me, others share with a close friend locally, and still others share with confidants via email. Email may be the only real option in many cases.

These issues concerning friendships, loneliness, and accountability are not unique to this part of the world. Nor are they unique to missions. I've found, though, that it is a long and sometimes heart-breaking process to build long-lasting friendships that are free from expectations or hurts. Further, in trying to build friendships with North Africans, one often wonders, What do they really want from me? Perhaps vice versa too! Do they like me as a friend, or are they hoping I will help them procure some form of legal residency in the West, or find them a suitable companion, or even help them financially?

Couples and Children

Since much time needs to be spent on language learning, building relationships with nationals, and building the team, married couples should not forget to keep their relationship as a priority. Communication skills in one's marriage should be learned before couples come into this part of the world. It is essential to have walked through right ways to resolve conflicts. Under stress, we all tend to blame our spouses or our fellow workers. Couples spending time with trusted couples has been a good way to provide mutual support and strengthen marriages.

There is no perfect option for a child's education. Parents must read, talk to other parents, and sometimes consult with education specialists. In general, it is important to communicate to one's children that they are in no way deprived. They may not have all the gadgets or opportunities their friends overseas have, but at the very least, they certainly have a much wider knowledge of the cultures of the world. Parents need to be careful to communicate by their actions that they trust God and that He gives the best, even though it may not be what they choose. Parents can trust Him also to build their children's characters in ways they are not ordinarily able to because of the new and challenging setting.

Singles

Singles on the field have a special place in missions. Single women, for example, usually have more time to build relationships and minister than their married counterparts. Their service as nurses, social workers, and healthcare teachers has sown thousands of seeds of the love of God in people's hearts. One particular challenge for the single ladies is that they have to come to terms with the fact that they can almost never be alone, except in their own little apartment. Creativity is needed for both men and women on how to maintain a healthy social life, pursue hobbies, and nurture strong and lasting friendships, especially with nationals. Singles need to be assertive at times to ask for their particular emotional and spiritual needs to be met. Team leaders or couples are not always aware or in tune with the specific needs of singles and vice versa.

Teams

North Africa attracts pioneers. These are highly motivated people with noble ideas, determined to carry out their vision and calling. By and large, they are wonderfully committed workers who are prepared to pay a high price to remain. Not all of them, though, have great people skills or have taken the time to develop their skills in leadership or to be a good team player.

Much wisdom is needed in helping teams work through areas of conflict. Conflict of some type is endemic on any team. Some strong visionaries, for instance, might be quite unaware of the tensions created by their leadership or interpersonal styles. New workers coming with high expectations of what team life will be like may be in for some real surprises, once they are "stuck" in a small group of co-workers. The bottom line is that relationships with fellow Christians, even those with the same vision and calling, are not necessarily easy.

Conflict in a relationship can persist, even after intervention and counsel. People may just prefer to separate. In a frontier mission setting, we must be realistic and not expect that these draining conflicts take all the energy of the workers. Some can struggle with a heavy sense of guilt or sin in not being able to resolve a breakdown in relationship. All of this, of course, is a very difficult and painful process.

We see an increasing need for teaching leaders and mentoring them while on the field. At times, we might need to ask leaders to take time out to further develop their leadership style, sharpen their administrative skills, or be in a safe place where they can receive correction, instruction, and healing. There is often a great deal of loyalty among workers towards their superiors, not wanting to say anything negative about their leaders. Team members may take a long time to share about their unmet expectations. New workers do not easily share their concerns which may be seen as criticism.

As caregivers, it is vitally important that we create a safe place where each worker can freely share about personal stresses and concerns. Not all relationships in our teams need to result in deep, intimate friendships. So we also encourage workers to develop meaningful friendships with folk outside their team, work, and agency.

Orientation

Teams and team members need proper pre-field orientation, regardless of their length of service. A good orientation should include a cultural briefing, time to explore one's lifestyle/work expectations, one's previous experiences with language learning and cross-cultural living, and preferences for privacy, hospitality, raising children, etc. Sensitively probing for deeper issues is a must: In what areas could I improve in relating to people? Do I carry bitterness or have unresolved, broken friendships? Have I suffered under abusive leadership? Do I have a good, deep understanding of a God of justice? How do I deal with suffering? How do I handle fear? (Fear is at the foundation of most of society in this part of the world, and Islam operates this way too.) Have I come to terms with fear of loneliness, loss of loved ones, imprisonment possibilities, singleness, etc.? Not all of these issues need to be "resolved" before going to the field, but they need to be considered seriously before committing oneself.

For single women in their first term, careful placement is required with other families or with other women on the team. They should not be placed alone. The same advice holds for single men. We need to help them stay connected to others.

The orientation package should include discussion on how to respond to poverty, such as beggars at your door, and the possibility of your host country suffering drought. Decide in advance as singles and as a family how much you are willing to contribute daily, monthly, and yearly, so that in your own mind you have a sense of peace about contributions and are not influenced so much by guilt.

New workers, therefore, need to look at their own lives, know about the stresses they will face, and understand the possible pitfalls of life in a new society. Along with these things, though, we need to let them know that the North Africans are lovable people, people who can greatly enrich their lives, people who may become their brothers and sisters in the Lord. And we want each of our workers to know that we are right there with them, committed to help carry their burdens.

One "mechanism" that helps us support our field workers is the Member Care Working Group. This is an interagency affiliation of member care colleagues, currently representing eight organizations, which is under the umbrella of the North Africa Partnership. It provides a wonderful platform where we encourage each other, pray, join together in member care efforts, and plan visits/seminars for workers on the field. This group meets about four times a year and has been in existence for eight years.

Moving On and Debriefing

When for whatever reason, folk leave the field, it is so important to plan enough time to talk with them about their experience. I suggest a week of daily one- to two-hour sessions. Some things that could possibly be discussed include the following: What was good/bad about your experience? What successes/failures did you have? What lessons did you learn? What could we as leaders have done differently/better? What good did you leave behind? How have you said your good-byes and to whom/what? Have you thanked people and they you? Do you sense God's "smile" on your time? How much time do you need to unwind, rest, and recover? What awaits you in your next location or back in your passport country? What thoughts do you have about a new assignment? When closure is brought to field experience, it is much easier to move on, look to the future, and trust God for the next assignment.

This Holy Seed

Life for North African believers, especially young converts, is tough. There is immense pressure from the family not to leave Islam. Much rejection follows when they choose to obey Jesus. Our brothers and sisters very much need our prayers: prayer that they will find the strength to keep standing in their faith; prayer that they will experience deep joy as they persevere; prayer that their example would encourage others to come to faith in Jesus too. Their courage spurs us on. In fact, to see the price they pay—to lose family relationships, to be an outcast in the strongly knit community, to lose their job—is an encouraging challenge for each of us as workers to even stronger commitment to the Lord and His service.

What a privilege we have in sitting together at the Lord's feet with these special expatriate workers and the national brethren. May He use us, each other, and His Word to speak comfort and hope to each of them. May we see in our days the fulfillment of God's promise to pour out His Spirit upon North Africa, so that this holy seed of the church, which has lain dormant for nearly 13 centuries, will once again abundantly sprout and bring forth much fruit.

Case Study: Team Life, Team Strife

Following is a case study of a fictitious team working in North Africa. The issues, though, are common to many teams.

Elizabeth, a career missionary from Germany, joined a team in North Africa about four months ago. Her job had not been defined, and the hot, dusty, uninviting town made it hard for her to find any way to relax—be it going out for coffee, riding a bike, or just taking a walk to enjoy the sunset. Nonetheless, she feels very strongly about her call, and she wants to "make it on the field." She is also well aware that culturally she cannot develop friendships with men. The team is made up of three single women and two American couples and their children.

Tensions with her two flat mates, a young lady from Korea named Hayyong, and Conchi, a highly qualified social worker from Chile, have been there from the beginning. Lately, though, they have become "too much to bear," as Elizabeth wrote in her last accountability email to her home office. Hayyong keeps smiling and trusting the Lord to work things out, in spite of Conchi's frequent negative comments about Hayyong's culture, Elizabeth's being "so different," and the sense that Elizabeth really does not try to understand the Latino mindset. Elizabeth thinks it is much more an issue of personality than of culture, and she is prepared to talk and work through the personality clashes. Conchi has no time for that. With her many social commitments, she can only prioritize going to the team meetings, which mostly involve prayer and discussions about work assignments. Meals were initially agreed to be the time for relationship building, but Hayyong prefers her own cuisine, and Conchi has only twice sat down for a meal with her flat mates.

Elizabeth had wanted to focus on bonding with the culture, along with her team. Her ministry leader, however, felt that she was too vulnerable to be initially placed in a local family. So she would have to find other options to become familiar with the "ways of the land" and to be immersed in the local dialect.

The timing of Elizabeth's placement was not ideal, a fact recognized by the ministry leader. Both families will be leaving in the next few weeks, to be replaced by a family from Argentina and one from Mexico. These families are in language study right now. All team discussions are about the upcoming changes for the team and closure, not about Elizabeth's entry! The team's language is French, since it is the only language they all have in common. It is no one's first language, though.

Elizabeth would like to live with a missionary family from another agency, that has just moved to this town. They have given her a warm invitation to stay with them and to have her own room, and they hope that Elizabeth could help lighten the burden of home schooling their children. The idea of the move has been met with strong negative responses by her team mates. "Such a move would really destroy our testimony here in the neighborhood," Conchi and Hayyong say, "because people would never understand it and would think that we are not getting along well."

Elizabeth wants to stay strong, but she cannot see how she can cope much longer with these pressures, especially with the "underlying criticism" of Conchi. Something has to change!

Reflection and Discussion

1. Based on the case study and the information in the article, what are some of the main stressors for the three single women?

2. What might be some creative ways for these women to "unwind" after a demanding day at work and ministry?

3. How could a field visit from a trusted leader help this team and improve relationships?

4. The author describes several stressors and coping suggestions in the North African context. Which of these are the most relevant for your setting?

5. How do expatriate and national workers differ in the types of challenges that they face?

Suggested Readings

Daniel, R. (1993). *This holy seed*. Harpenden, UK: Tamarisk Publications.

Farmaian, S. (1996). *Daughter of Persia*. London, UK: Transworld Publisher.

Hargraves, O. (1995). *Culture shock! Morocco*. Portland, OR: Times Editions.

Mallouhi, C. (1994). *Mini-skirts, mothers, and Muslims: Modeling spiritual values in Muslim cultures*. Carlisle, UK: Spear Publications.

Mernissi, F. (1988). *Doing daily battle*. London, UK: The Women's Press.

———. (1996). *The harem within*. London, UK: Transworld Publishers.

St. John, P. (1990). *Until the day breaks*. Harpenden, UK: OM Publishing.

———. (1995). *Patricia St. John tells her own story*. Carlisle, UK: OM Publishing.

Werner, T. (1992). *Where there is no doctor*. London, UK: MacMillan Press.

***Anke Tissingh** was born and raised in Holland, where she received training as a nurse. She joined YWAM in 1976 and moved to North Africa in 1983. Together with her husband, Garry, she co-leads the YWAM work in North Africa. Much of her attention is given to the pastoral needs of YWAM teams on the field, as well as providing assistance to other agencies. She currently coordinates the Member Care Working Group for North Africa. Email: 100767.527@compuserve.com.*

Special thanks to Gail Whitney, Andy Lee, and Michele Martindale for their helpful review of this article.

12

Mobile Member Care Team West Africa: Our Journey and Direction

DARLENE JEROME

What does it take to set up member care well in an unstable region? Consultation with colleagues, careful planning, compatible skills, teamwork, an advisory board, clear values and objectives, financial stability, and a commitment to quality and sacrificial service. This crisis response team is exemplary and is paving the way for similar groups in other high-risk areas.

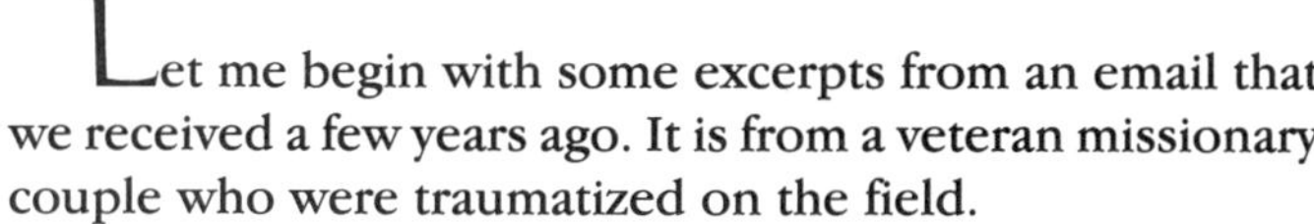

Let me begin with some excerpts from an email that we received a few years ago. It is from a veteran missionary couple who were traumatized on the field.

"Ask me how many times we have thought about you since the armed robbery! We sure wished that you had been in place here in West Africa. We could have been your first candidates. Without being ugly, we have had the worst field member care. We were shocked at the things that were said, not said, done, and not done for us. We aren't bitter about it at all, but it is something that we have a heart for, and it upsets us to think that this could be repeated on someone else. West Africa needs you! We wish that we could see you for a good, quality debriefing. We have been angry with our leadership but also praised God that something is coming together next year. It is such a need. The first thing I would recommend that you do is train the leadership of all these missions in what to say and do when one of their people has a trauma."

What Is the Mobile Member Care Team?

Mobile Member Care Team (MMCT) is a cooperative, inter-mission ministry that provides training, consultation, and direct crisis response for missionaries on the field. It seems that traumatic events such as evacuation, civil war, kidnapping, car jacking, armed robbery, rape, theft, assault, and severe medical illness are increasingly a common experience for missionaries these days. MMCT exists because we believe that member care that is proactive and compassionate can help missionaries remain in effective service, even after going through crises. Our purpose is to strengthen the mission community in West Africa for healthy, loving service in the midst of challenge, change, and crisis.

The first regional MMCT team (MMCT West Africa), launched in May 2000, serves West Africa (14 countries from Senegal to Nigeria) with a central location of Abidjan, Côte d'Ivoire. The MMCT staff is a multidisciplinary group of counselors and trainers that responds to crises by providing coaching and consultation for peer responders and mission administrators, debriefings, assessment, and referral. The team provides training in the areas of interpersonal skills and crisis response, with the goal of equipping missionaries to provide the initial response to crisis as volunteer peer responders.

Our ultimate goal is to establish MMCTs in several strategic locations of the world to provide training and crisis response for members of any mission group. We are developing a model in Côte d'Ivoire that might be contextualized in other regions of the world.

"Standing on the shoulders of the giants before us" is very much the case for the Mobile Member Care Team. Blessed by the vision, experience, and wise counsel of several of the founders and developers of member care as a specialty in missions, we find ourselves launched into an exciting venture. We'd like to share a bit of our journey and vision, as well as some specific strategies that we sense the Lord is blessing as we begin this ministry.

Our Journey From Concept to Service

In mid-1997, several leaders in the member care movement gathered as a "think tank" to consider how missions might work together to enhance the delivery of member care services. Primary concerns expressed were lack of accessibility and the increasing need to support missionaries who experience trauma. It seemed that a mobile member care team might be able to address these concerns. Dr. Karen Carr, a clinical psychologist with a specialty in crisis response, who had served as a part-time consultant for several missions, was identified as a potential leader for this kind of team. Later that year, at the Mental Health and Missions Conference in Indiana, USA, the "think tank" brainstormed with a larger group about what this team might look like and the kinds of services and strategies it might develop.

In March 1998, a core group again met and worked towards a vision statement, values, and more specific strategies. This group agreed to form itself into a Global Advisory Board to ensure that this vision would be fulfilled. Karen Carr was asked to give full-time leadership to the mobile member care team concept. Karen then asked me to join her in this leadership role. (I am a member of Wycliffe Bible Translators and served as Personnel Director with the SIL Cameroon group for nine years. I hold a master's degree in intercultural training and management.) In 1999, Marion Dicke became part of the team as well. Marion served with the Christian and Missionary Alliance/Canada in Zaire for over 15 years in midwifery, leadership training, mission administration, and member care. Currently Karen serves as Clinical Director, I am the Personnel and Training Director, and Marion is a Trainer/Debriefer. This combination of key disciplines—mental health, mission administration, and training—is foundational to the MMCT values and strategy.

Based on advice given by SIL leadership in Africa, we decided to focus on one region of the world so as to ensure our ability to respond. If we spread ourselves too thin, we would set up expectations for service that could not be met. It was suggested that we begin in West Africa for several reasons: lack of member care resources in that area, the increasing incidence of violence and crisis in the region, the missions infrastructure already in place that could help launch a new ministry, and the fact that I was already familiar with life in Africa and had natural connections there.

In August 1998, Karen and I traveled to Abidjan, Côte d'Ivoire, to explore the possibility of basing there. Abidjan offers a well-developed communications system and is a transportation hub for West Africa. Several missions base regional personnel in Abidjan, and the country traditionally has been politically stable. Twenty-four mission leaders from 14 mission organizations gathered one afternoon to discuss this possibility. We had done a needs survey before the meeting that confirmed our impressions: traumatic events were very common, and crisis response services were non-existent.

We were very encouraged when a group of 11 people, representing eight missions, emerged from this meeting as a Liaison Committee. We related and made plans with them over the next 20 months, until we moved to Abidjan in May 2000. This group was the confirmation from the Holy Spirit that we needed. The Liaison Committee group eventually gave birth to a regional Governing Board of nine people from several missions. The Board provides the MMCT West Africa team leadership, advice, accountability, and networking within the mission community.

As the focus has shifted to issues more specific to West Africa, the Global Advisory Board has passed its oversight role on to the local Governing Board. Currently, the Global Advisory Board is considering where the next regional MMCT might be launched. During the 20 months of transition, the Advisory Committee continued to give wise counsel, support, and strategic input as we fine-tuned the MMCT vision statement, spelled out our values, and developed strategy documents.

Vision Statement

We envision communities of missionaries who are able to withstand life's traumas and challenges, supported by a network of peers and administrators able to respond to crises, with a mobile team providing training, mentoring, consultation, on-site crisis response, and referral.

Our Values

- *Servanthood.* We are servants of our Lord, and our lives are devoted to loving others with humility.
- *Partnership.* We serve in partnership with organizational leadership, churches, and member care providers.
- *Integrity.* We are committed to quality, truth, and the fulfillment of promises.
- *Proactive care.* We provide training and care to promote the strength and resilience of communities and to lessen the negative impact of crises.
- *Accessibility.* We are committed to being available to respond to crises or requests for help in a timely manner.
- *Community development.* We are committed to facilitate peer support networks, resource sharing, and local ownership of member care programs.
- *Diversity.* We believe that a multicultural and multidisciplinary team is the best way to meet the needs of the community we serve.
- *Mutual support.* We are committed to maintaining the health and stability of the team by caring for each other in practical ways, so that we can serve with enduring joy.

MMCT Distinctives

The values expressed above naturally yielded some program distinctives that later led to specific strategies. I would like to comment briefly on some of the distinctive aspects of the MMCT approach to member care.

Proximity

We are committed to our services being accessible to the mission community in a defined service area. This means living in the region and being ready to travel as needed.

Focus on crisis

While some of our strategies contribute to other aspects of member care, our primary focus is on crisis care. Although our specialty is narrow, our geographical service area of the 14 countries of West Africa is large, and travel in this area is challenging. We must stay focused on crisis response, or our resources will be spread too thin. Keeping this focus is difficult, since our team has the only missionary clinical psychologist that we are aware of in the region.

As missions become aware of Karen's presence and ask her to help with their crises, our definition of crisis is being challenged. Having anticipated this, we had developed a grid to assess and prioritize what others might present to us as crisis situations. But even with such a tool, it is very hard to limit our services when our saying "no" necessitates either a return to the home country, having a mental health professional travel to the field at great expense, or no help at all.

This dynamic means that we are ideally placed to collect data and offer some consultation about the need of a counseling or member care center for this region. Several missions are considering this possibility, and we welcome that development.

Multidisciplinary

Foundational to the MMCT concept is a team of mental health professionals, mission administrators, and trainers serving together with mutual respect and appreciation for the others' roles and contributions. We feel very blessed to have a team of three that reflects this combination now, but we are definitely asking the Lord to increase our numbers.

Partnering with mission leadership

Mission administrators ultimately hold much of the responsibility for member care, especially in crisis situations. They make the initial needs assessment, allocate resources, monitor the situation, and make decisions that significantly impact the effects of traumas. Our desire is to help mission leaders be more successful by intentionally building supportive relationships with them, equipping them, and being available for consultation.

The political unrest in Côte d'Ivoire during the year 2000 gave us numerous opportunities to come alongside mission leaders and consult concerning what member care concerns needed to be addressed before, during, and after episodes of political unrest, violence in the streets, and the ongoing stress of uncertainty. We convened an Inter-Mission Forum on Contingency Planning and Crisis Management at a very strategic point in the period of unrest, that brought together 31 leaders from 19 different organizations. We shared concerns, resources, and strategies, and we strengthened the inter-mission network of support. It was thrilling to facilitate such a gathering and to pass on to them some fundamentals of member care in crisis situations.

Facilitation role

Rather than developing a separate ministry that offers a specialized service parallel to the mission community, we desire to strengthen and equip mission communities to fulfill their mutual care responsibilities as the body of Christ, cutting across organizational boundaries. Larger missions may have personnel available to respond to crises, but many smaller missions do not. Surely the Lord intends for us to serve one another on the frontlines. MMCT is committed to help facilitate inter-mission cooperation toward that end. Seeing these relationships start and grow in the context of inter-mission forums and workshops is very satisfying.

Training emphasis

One-on-one crisis response service by professionals is a luxury in this setting. Our research tells us that there are 5,000 missionaries (and their children) in this region from missions based in North American alone. We know there are many more missionaries from organizations based in other parts of the world: Europe, Asia, Latin America, and other African countries as well. Considering these numbers and the increasingly unstable and violent environment here, it is essential that we train administrators and peers to respond to crisis situations and that we make a commitment to mentor and coach them in the future.

Proactive care

Traumatic events require immediate and appropriate loving care from the surrounding mission community. We are finding, however, that there is some resistance to seeking or accepting help before someone is visibly struggling, which is not always the case immediately following a trauma. We expect it will take some time and increased awareness through education before proactive care is considered to be normal protocol by leaders and the mission community at large.

MMCT Strategies

Our vision statement, values, and distinctives have contributed to the development of several strategy statements. These include personnel, crisis response, training, partnership, and financial strategies.

Personnel Strategy

So as to meet our personnel needs adequately, we have developed several ways to serve as staff of the Mobile Member Care Team.

Resident personnel

A multidisciplinary staff resides in Abidjan. Their function is to provide administrative leadership to MMCT, training and consultation for mission administrators and peer responders, debriefing, psychological assessments, and brief therapy after crisis events.

Associate personnel

Part-time associate staff may reside in the region or elsewhere in the world (currently, we have a group of about 20, primarily in North America and Europe). Available for short periods of service, from two weeks to a couple months, these individuals serve as workshop staff, give direct post-trauma care, assist with research, serve as consultants, or offer a technical service. We especially appreciate these folks because of what they bring to fill in the staff picture: professional expertise in areas such as with children or in psychiatry, access to research, language abilities in French, German, and Dutch, as well as a variety of cultural backgrounds. In addition, since the resident staff members are presently all single females, it is good to have several men and married couples in the larger staff group.

Peer responders

Because of the sheer size of the task (geographically as well as numbers of mission personnel), trained peer responders are essential to meet the need. Often individuals in formal or informal member care roles already serve as peer debriefers in crisis situations. Our strategy is to train missionaries identified as peer responders within their own missions so that they can better handle the "ordinary" crisis events.

Inter-mission peer responders

From the peer responder group, we select and further train some who are made available by their organization to the wider mission community. Their training further prepares and qualifies them to respond to more difficult crisis situations and to serve other missions at the request of MMCT staff. These teams have an ongoing mentoring, coaching, and training relationship with MMCT staff.

Consultants

Professional consultant input, especially from psychiatrists, is a necessary part of our personnel strategy. Even when performed from a distance via phone or email, this support enhances our effectiveness.

Crisis Response Strategy

According to each situation, MMCT offers several levels of response as described below.

Training

The first response is to prepare mission leaders and peer responders before crises happen, so as to enable their good response when needed. Recognizing that for many years mission leaders and colleagues have responded to members' needs in crisis situations, we desire to enhance the quality of response and care that is already in place.

Indirect response

When a crisis occurs, but its effects are not severe enough that MMCT staff are needed to respond directly, a predetermined indirect response plan is implemented. This includes long-distance consultation with the mission leadership and local peer responders in their specified roles via email or phone. Peer responders are responsible to assess those affected by the trauma, defuse (meet briefly to support) the victims, debrief the group involved, and report back to the mission leadership and the MMCT staff. Protocols are in place for these procedures, and the MMCT staff supervise and mentor the peer responders from a distance via email and phone.

Direct response

When a crisis and its effects are severe enough that mission leaders along with the peer responders do not have the resources to provide the care needed, MMCT staff do their best to respond directly. Circumstances may prevent arrival until several days later, but all efforts are made to expedite the response. In the meantime, local peer responders are responsible for emotional first aid care. Upon arrival of MMCT staff, an assessment of the victims and the affected community is made, direct care is given to those affected, consultation and mentoring are given to mission leadership and the peer responders, and a long-term care plan is determined.

Referral

At times, the best response is a referral to outside services. This could be for various reasons, such as anticipation that long-term care will be required, psychological needs of a specialized nature for which the MMCT has no adequate expertise or resources, and inadequate MMCT staffing or staff already responding to another crisis situation. Although we hope that we can be of help in most situations, there are some for which referral is the best and most responsible contribution we can make.

Rather than rely entirely on a list of member care organizations or individual providers, which may become outdated, we also rely on the referral services of regionally based Christian organizations and individuals familiar with the needs of missionaries.

Training Strategy

MMCT/WA desires to strengthen the mission community and train and equip peer responders and mission leaders to care well for members in crisis. To meet this goal, we offer five workshops, as outlined below, with possibilities for a sixth and seventh as well. Our workshop designs are based on adult learning principles and seek to build on the knowledge, skills, and attitudes each participant brings to the training context.

Sharpening Your Interpersonal Skills (SYIS)

Developed by Dr. Ken Williams of Wycliffe Bible Translators/SIL, this workshop is used worldwide by missions that desire to equip and encourage their members in biblical relational skills such as listening, managing conflicts, and living in community. In a supportive training environment, with an emphasis on Scripture and prayer throughout, participants are guided through four and a half days of skills-building practice in a group of up to 28 missionaries from several different agencies. We offer this workshop as a means of strengthening the mission community life, believing that this will result in better mutual member care throughout the community.

Understanding Crisis (UC)

This one-day workshop introduces missionaries to the basics of crisis care, so that they can be better friends and colleagues when crises happen. Participants learn what is a normal response to a crisis and how to help someone through the necessary stages of grief after loss or trauma.

Member Care While Managing Crises (MC/MC)

This two-day workshop, following the UC, gathers interested leaders of missions in a particular region to share and learn about the strategic role they play in member care while managing crisis situations. Building on the UC material, topics include the impact of crisis on groups; helpful policies, procedures, and protocols; confidentiality and communication; assessment of vulnerable members; leadership style in crisis; the when, why, and how of debriefings; crisis committees; and how MMCT and local Peer Response Teams can be of service to missions in West Africa. We also offer parts of the MC/MC when we convene a half-day or one-day "Inter-Mission Forum on Contingency Preparation and Crisis Response."

Peer Response Training (PRT) Level 1

This is a six-day workshop that prepares missionaries to serve as peer responders within their own organizations. Participants review and go into more depth with the UC material. In addition, they learn how to debrief someone in crisis one-on-one and how to assess the impact of a traumatic event. The workshop includes opportunities to practice these skills in a supportive context with personal coaching. Participants are also encouraged to further develop their own theology of suffering through Bible studies and times of reflection. People are invited to this workshop based on an application, completion of the SYIS, evaluations by SYIS facilitators, and referrals from mission leadership and peers.

Peer Response Training (PRT) Level 2

This five-day workshop further prepares peer responders and qualifies them to respond to situations for other missions at the request of MMCT staff. Participants have an ongoing mentoring, coaching, and training relationship with MMCT staff. Emphasis in the workshop is placed on further developing screening and assessment skills, skills in working with children, advanced one-on-one debriefing skills, and group debriefings. Prerequisites for PRT Level 2 include successful completion of PRT Level 1, demonstration of competence with the PRT Level 1 skills on the field, an invitation from the MMCT staff for advanced training, and agreement from their mission administration regarding suitability and availability to serve other missions.

MKs and Crisis

This topic is currently being discussed by MMCT and other interested parties. There is potential for two workshops: one for MKs themselves and the other for parents and MK school staff.

Partnership Strategy

A primary value of MMCT/WA is our desire to facilitate and work in partnerships. We are in several strategic partnerships, both formal and informal, with other organizations involved in member care. Some of our partners include Mercy Ministries International and Le Rucher near Geneva in France; Missionary Health Institute in Toronto, Canada; and Headington Research Center of Fuller Seminary and Narramore Christian Foundation, both in California, USA.

We are talking with some Christian educational institutions that have graduate programs in clinical psychology regarding the possibility of MMCT becoming an internship site for graduate students seeking to develop skills of crisis response for the mission community. We also anticipate providing data for students and others conducting research in trauma and missions.

Team members can be loaned to MMCT from another sponsoring organization, whether it be an established mission or a sending home church. We receive these personnel based on a memorandum of understanding drawn up between the sponsoring agency and the MMCT Governing Board.

Financial Strategy

Besides our commitments to the principles of accountability, integrity, and internal responsibility, we have certain financial strategies to facilitate our ministry and make our services accessible to those who need them.

Strategies related to staff finances

- MMCT staff members come with their own personal support needs fully covered (living expenses, furlough travel, professional training, personal and professional insurance, retirement savings, etc.).
- Each staff member contributes a monthly "administrative contribution" to support the MMCT office as it facilitates each one's personal ministry.
- Associate staff are encouraged to raise funds to cover the cost of their short-term service (in particular, air fares).
- Honorariums received by staff while representing MMCT are allocated to the group account.

Strategies related to services

- Participant fees cover workshop costs.
- The missions being served cover crisis response costs, including a suggested per diem honorarium, as they are able.
- MMCT counsels mission leadership to budget for crisis response.
- There is a subsidy fund for crisis response. Those unable to reimburse full costs may apply to this fund, and financial help is provided as available.
- There is a subsidy fund for workshop scholarships. Those unable to pay full workshop registration fees may apply to this fund, and financial help is provided as available.

Strategy for capital purchases

Large capital purchase needs are presented to the regional and home country MMCT/WA constituencies by the staff, regional Governing Board, and Global Advisory Board. The Lord has blessed us with several grants and large donations towards capital purchases.

Blessing others

The first tenth of MMCT/WA non-designated income is given to other ministries with whom MMCT shares common vision, with special consideration to member care development for national missions.

Thanks Be to God

I would like to share a story with you that illustrates some of the key values, distinctives, and strategies that I have presented. While Karen and I were still in French study in early 2000, we received news of a car hijacking involving a young family in their first term of service in West Africa. We were unavailable for direct response at that time, but the Lord had already provided a way for this family to receive care quickly and without having to return to their home country.

Their field leader and his wife quickly drove to where they had been stranded and supported them in practical ways. They also ministered to them using member care skills they had recently enhanced through a Sharpening Your Interpersonal Skills workshop that we had led a few months before on a visit to Côte d'Ivoire. In addition, one of our Associate Staff, who is a mental health professional and works in another West African country as a school counselor, was able to go to them and spent five days debriefing the car hijacking, as well as working through some other traumatic events and issues that had developed during their first term. It was very clear that this sort of intervention made the difference in how this family was able to process this crisis. Rather than having a devastating impact on this family, the crisis actually created the opportunity for them to move forward with more insight and resilience than they had going into it. What was meant for evil turned out for good.

As we look back over the past three years at how the Lord has led, nurtured, and provided for the development of the Mobile Member Care Team, we are very thankful. He has blessed us beyond what we could have imagined or dreamed. The Global Advisory Board and local Governing Board are two very tangible examples of His abundant provision for us. In His sovereignty, He has led us, in consultation with our advisors, to make decisions based on what we understood at the time, only to find out later that He had other reasons in mind.

A good example of this is our choosing to base the MMCT in Abidjan, Côte d'Ivoire, because of the city's reputation for being economically healthy and politically stable, which would mean less stress for us as a team in our living situation. While that was true when we visited here in August 1998, over the next two years things quickly deteriorated with a successful coup, other attempted coups, a very rocky election process, inter-ethnic conflicts surfacing into violence in the streets, and a general atmosphere of uncertainty. That is our current situation at the time of this writing, and we are finding it stressful. But the Lord is bringing good out of all this, as we have been able to minister to our immediate community, as well as grow in our personal understanding of what it means to go through these crises and live with these stresses. We are finding Him trustworthy and a very present comfort in the midst of it all.

Future Directions for MMCT

As we develop MMCT in one region of the world, we wonder how the Lord is going to move next. What region of the world is on His heart for the next Mobile Member Care Team? What might that team look like? Who will be on it? What needs to happen to get it going?

At the same time, we can see the need for MMCT here in West Africa to expand to include national church leaders. Our current vision includes national African missionaries from and in this region, but the church leadership is also in need of this kind of care. Might we be able to encourage the development of a ministry with their needs in focus?

The need for a more comprehensive member care center for this region also comes up frequently. Our research tells us that there are 5,000 missionaries (and their children) in this region from missions based in North America alone. We know there are many more from missions based in other parts of the world. Could we help facilitate the development of a multi-service center that supports missions in their efforts to develop member care services for this large group of God's servants? With an emphasis on training, especially of mission leaders and member caregivers, a member care center would be able to make a significant impact in this region, helping God's servants to stay spiritually strong and continue in His service with joy.

Please pray with us as we seek the Lord and join Him in what He is doing here in West Africa in member care, as well as in crisis response across the world of missions.

Reflection and Discussion

1. What regions of the world are most in need of a Mobile Member Care Team?
2. How would the MMCT concept need to be adapted for a particular region?
3. What would it take to get an MMCT started in your region?
4. How could you/your organization contribute to the development of an MMCT?
5. How could the needs of non-expatriate Christian workers be met through an MMCT?

Darlene Jerome *resides in Abidjan, Côte d'Ivoire, and is the Director of Personnel and Training of MMCT/WA, which is her current SIL assignment. She served for nine years as the Personnel Director of the SIL (Wycliffe) Cameroon Branch and brings experience in training, member care, administration, and team building. Darlene worked for two years in primary health care/community development in Liberia as part of her master's degree in intercultural management and training prior to service with SIL. Email: darlene_jerome@sil.org.*

Thanks to my MMCT/WA teammates, Marion Dicke and Karen Carr, for their contributions to this article. Thanks also to my mother, Catherine Jerome, for her editorial input.

13

Member Care Development In South Africa

MARINA PRINS
BRAAM WILLEMSE

The past few years in South Africa have been characterized by major shifts within the government, society, the church, and missions. Many more local churches have started to send out missionaries, either on their own or in partnership with mission agencies. Sending groups in South Africa need to be further equipped as they prepare and support their mission personnel. This chapter looks at strategies for the pre-field, on-field, and reentry stages of mission life. It also describes the recent formation of an inter-agency affiliation and a network of colleagues.

According to the 1996 Census Report, South Africa has a population of just over 40 million people, consisting of Africans (76.7%), Whites (10.9%), Coloureds (8.9%), Indians (2.6%), and Others (0.9%). Over 16 million (40.1%) are reported to be church members, with the Afrikaans Reformed churches being the largest Protestant group, followed by the Pentecostal, Anglican, Methodist, Lutheran, Charismatic, and Presbyterian churches. However, nearly three-quarters of the total population associate themselves with a specific Christian denomination (Froise & Hendriks, 1999, pp. 1, 35, 48).

Our ethnic diversity poses new challenges to the whole society, including the church. To a large degree, South Africa is two worlds in one. On the one hand, we are a developing world, with the poverty and social problems normally associated with this. On the other hand, we are a more developed world. The church has a major role to play in a society where 61% of the population is living in poverty and where it is expected that in two years' time, 250,000 people will be dying of AIDS each year (Froise & Hendriks, 1999, pp. 19, 22).

Over the past decade, the number of missionaries sent out from South Africa has increased six-fold, from 309 in 1990 to 1,870 in 1999 (Froise & Hendriks, 1999, p. 39). The majority of these missionaries come from churches that are attended by those of European descent. These churches have undergone a remarkable growth in missions awareness over the past few years, particularly among Afrikaans-speaking churches. At the same time, there is a significant awakening to missions among churches from disadvantaged communities. According to Froise and Hendriks (1999, p. 41), 41% of South African missionaries are working in

Africa, 25% in Western countries, 19.5% in countries in the 10/40 Window, and the rest in various locations all over the world.

Another interesting phenomenon on the South African missionary landscape is the shift in the type of missionary agencies that are active. Agencies that fit the "traditional model" can still be found, but a new generation of missions agencies is now flourishing as well, including Operation Mobilization (OM), Youth With A Mission (YWAM), South African Action for World Evangelization (SAAWE), Member Care Southern Africa, and others.

In the traditional model, the control of what is happening on the field is strongly in the hands of the agency. These agencies also tend to put less emphasis on the role of the local sending church. In South Africa, it appears that many of these agencies struggle to recruit new missionaries, and some have amalgamated with other traditional agencies.

The sending church has historically had a rather narrow, though vital role: financial and prayer support, occasional contact via letters, field visits, support during furlough, and some supply of clothing and other material needs. "Over the years, we have witnessed the missions enterprise becoming increasingly sophisticated and relatively autonomous from the local church.... Much of the responsibility for the preparation and the spiritual and emotional support of missionaries has been assumed to be the domain of the mission organization" (Strauss & Narramore, 1992, p. 299).

In the past, we have experienced the same trend in South Africa. Most missionaries were sent out by organizations or denominational mission boards with little or no involvement by or responsibility given to the local church. One of the major shifts worldwide—and one that has also taken place within the church in South Africa over the last few years—is that local churches have started to take to heart the task of sending out their own missionaries. Today an increasing number of local churches are sending out missionaries, either on their own or in partnership with organizations.

Member Care Within the South African Church

The term "member care" is relatively new in the South African context, but if we look at the core meaning, the concept is nothing new. Member care simply means caring for the members of the body of Christ. This includes members sent out by the church to reach the unreached. According to O'Donnell (1997, p. 144), member care in this sense is not new. It is a New Testament practice. What is new is the more organized attempt to develop comprehensive, sustainable member care approaches to support cross-cultural Christian workers.

The growing involvement in missions has confronted the church with unique challenges. Because so many of the local churches in South Africa are sending out their own missionaries and are taking full responsibility for them, member care in a South African context not only focuses on the care of the missionary as a total human being, but also has a strong emphasis on *equipping local churches* to be effective in member care. To a large degree, member care is like the dog that chased the car—and caught it—and now it does not know what to do with it. The churches have taken responsibility for their missionaries, but they are not always certain what that responsibility entails.

This leaves us with the challenging task of equipping local churches to send and care for their missionaries effectively. The aim is twofold: firstly, to ensure effective care for the missionary and, secondly, to find ways in which a larger proportion of church members can be involved in the Great Commission. Often it is only a small number of people within a church who are involved or have any interest in missions. At the core of this is the problem that so many church members do not know what their spiritual gifts are, or they are not given the opportunity to minister in the church according to their gifts and ministries. This is often due to the "clergy-laity apartheid" that still prevails in the church, where the priesthood of all believers is not recognized practically. Often church members who are very competent, well-trained people in civilian life act like zombies the moment they participate in church life, because of the prevalent notion that only those who are ordained have any real say in the church.

In member care in South Africa, a lot of emphasis is therefore put on establishing and training "support teams" (described later) for every missionary sent out by the local church. This should be done not only for missionaries who work outside the borders of South Africa, but also for those who work within South Africa among poor and disadvantaged communities and for those who serve on the home office staff of mission organizations. We want church members to see missions as an extension of the ministry of the local church. We want them to understand that by sending out and caring for their missionaries, they themselves are also reaching the unreached to the ends of the earth.

Local churches have a lot to offer in terms of support for their missionaries. This does not mean that the contributions of missions agencies are overlooked or downplayed. Over the years, agencies have gained experience in matters such as liaison with other organizations and with churches both at home and on the field. They are familiar with arrangements for entering the host country and for transferring money to foreign countries, among other things. The role of missions agencies cannot and must not be overlooked, but that does not mean that local churches should not get involved and gain experience in these areas. Rather, missions agencies should be willing to share their expertise with local churches. At the same time, the local churches must be willing to accept their responsibility and be equipped in the process, so that in the end they will all work together to give effective care and support to the missionary on the field. A partnership is needed between the missionary, the local church, and the mission organization, in which both the local church and the organization have a commitment and responsibility towards the missionary on the field.

Although South African local churches are beginning to understand that missionary support involves much more than just "pay and pray," it still happens that missionaries are being sent out without proper backing and care. As Pirolo (1991, p. 15) puts it, "There is a tremendous need for senders. And the need goes beyond the traditional token involvement of showing up for a farewell party or writing out a cheque to missions. A cross-cultural worker needs the support of a team of people while he is preparing to go, while he is on the field, and when he returns home."

The Missionary Cycle

In order for local churches to develop a proper member care strategy, they need to understand the stages and challenges of missionary life. In our Member Care Southern Africa group, an important part of the teaching that we do covers three main phases in the missionary's cycle: pre-field, on-field, and reentry.

The Pre-Field Phase

The pre-field phase includes four areas: selection, personal preparation, formation of the support team, and field orientation. Simply stated, during the selection process, information about the missionary candidate is gathered by questionnaires, references, and psychometric evaluation. The purpose of this process is to get relevant information and a profile of a candidate's functional skills, personality, and behavioral characteristics. This information can be used to:

- Identify emotional problems and personality disorders.
- Assess areas of strength.

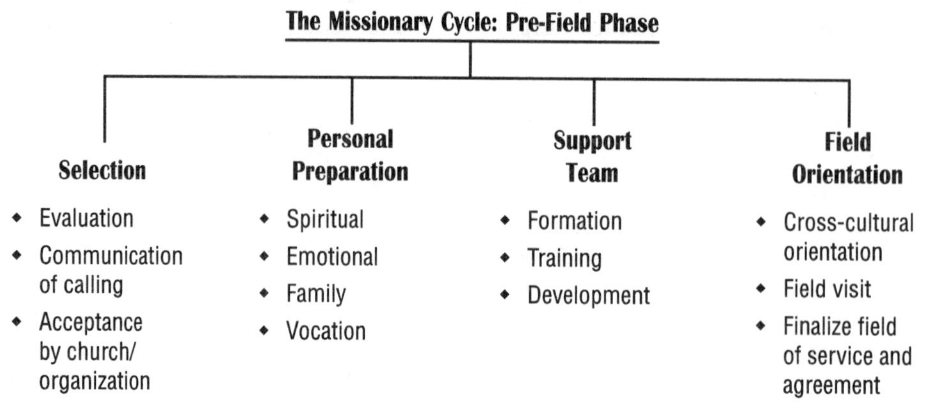

- Identify and address areas of personal development.
- Assist in career planning.
- Determine if a candidate is suitable for a specific environment, culture, or position.

The missionary should be well prepared spiritually, emotionally, and practically. Where needed, additional skills should be acquired. When a family is evaluated, it is essential that the wife and children be included in the evaluation. The missionary candidate and family should then communicate their calling to the leadership of the church and/or the agency (if involved). After prayer and discussion, the candidate and family are accepted by the different parties as their missionaries.

Proper evaluation is one of the most neglected areas before missionaries go to the field. It is only recently that local churches (and the mission community) in South Africa have started to realize the value of psychometric evaluation. But this has created other problems, such as the need for an evaluation battery that is suitable for the South African population, and the need for specialists who are not only qualified to conduct an evaluation but also have experience in cross-cultural missions.

During the pre-field phase, a support team should be formed and equipped and should start to function within the local church. A support team is a group of friends and supporters of a missionary and his family, who work together as a team to ensure that the missionary receives the necessary care. This is done under the leadership of a ***support team coordinator*** or ***advocate***. On the team, there are different areas of responsibility or ***portfolios***, which could include the following: morale support, logistical support (including medical care), prayer support, communication support, financial support, occupational support (if the missionary is a tentmaker), and reentry support.

According to Froise and Hendriks (1999, p. 42), "The number of people in [theological] training, both full-time and part-time, has risen appreciably over the past decade." Because many of these theological institutions offer training in missions, this also gives us an indication of trends in missionary training. What is interesting, however, is that the method of training is changing from full-time to part-time. The number of full-time students peaked in 1997, then started to decline. There are probably several reasons for this:

- Financial constraints.
- Lack of accommodation for students' families.
- The time that students have to spend away from their homes/ministry.

Formal institutions are therefore not always a solution for these problems, particularly if the students come from a previously disadvantaged community. Some

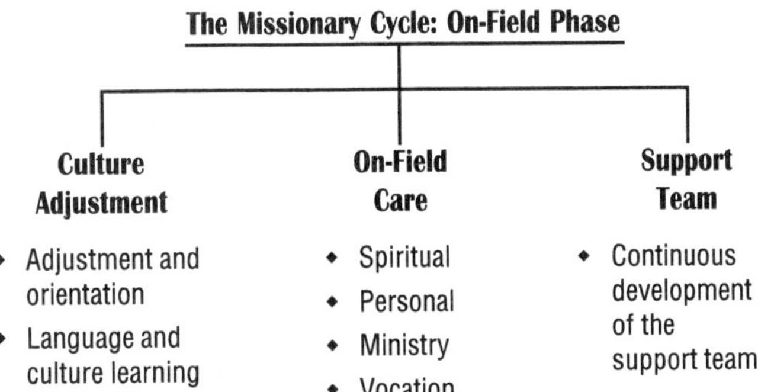

churches have introduced theological training as part of their church program in an attempt to address the problem. Unfortunately, few church based Bible schools offer courses in missions. Organizations such as YWAM and OM offer their own training in missions to their recruits.

It is also important that missionaries-in-training should visit their field of service in advance. In this way, they can get first-hand information on conditions on the field, as well as a better idea of their roles.

The On-Field Phase

During the on-field phase, the missionary has to adjust to and become part of a new environment and lifestyle. It is important for the support team back home to understand what the missionary is experiencing (e.g., culture stress, language learning), in order to provide the necessary support. One of the best ways to achieve this is through regular visits by members of the support team. If missionaries know that their supporters actually understand the living conditions in which they minister and that they have met some of those with whom they are ministering, it will be much easier for mutual trust to develop. On the other hand, a missionary will feel much less comfortable with supporters who have never visited the field and who do not actually understand the environment. Regular communication via email and phone calls with the missionary is also essential.

During this phase, the support team must continuously develop and expand their member care strategy to meet the needs of the missionary. Where the support team itself cannot give the necessary support, alternatives should be found. For example, if someone from the support team cannot visit the field or does not have the expertise to give the necessary member care support on the field, other organizations that are already operating on the field might be asked to help the missionary on their behalf.

The Reentry Phase

In many cases, the missionary returns to the sending church during reentry. Because reentry is usually a difficult and stressful time for the missionary, it is extremely important that the local church will be able to help in the process. So many times, neither the missionary nor the

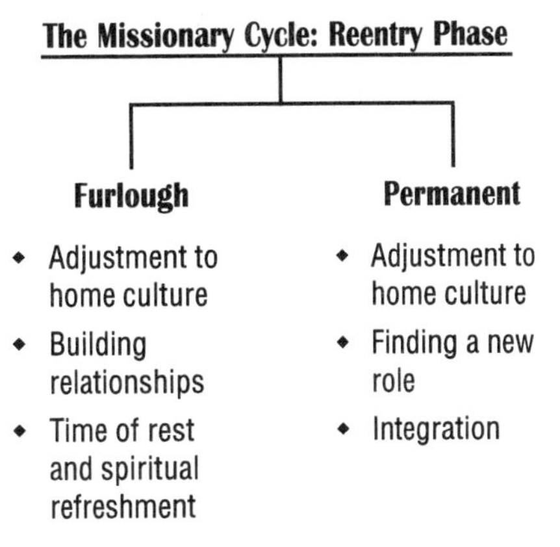

sending church is properly prepared for this phase. Often the missionary is not seen as the church's responsibility after the return home, and financial support is cut the moment one arrives back home. In other cases, churches are willing to assist their missionaries, but they simply do not know how to care for them during reentry. In the past, the church assumed that the missions agency sent the missionary out and that the agency should therefore take care of the missionary during reentry (which in many cases did not happen). It is often difficult for a large organization to give the necessary personal attention to each missionary during reentry. In this sense, the local church's structure and functioning make it easier to look after the missionary's specific reentry needs. The missionary can, for example, become part of a cell or care group. The members of these groups can be briefed as to the specific needs of a returning missionary.

Member Care Developments in South Africa

In 1999 and 2000, there were two significant member care developments in South Africa. These were the formation of an interagency affiliation called Member Care Southern Africa and the formation of a network of colleagues called the Member Care Forum.

Member Care Southern Africa

Preparation for the founding of Member Care Southern Africa started in March 1999. Initially, research was done, general member care literature was gathered, and national and international member care networks were contacted. In September 1999, a member care work group was formed, which developed during 2000 into the organization Member Care Southern Africa, of which we (the authors) are a part. We are a missions support organization, involved in the development of member care within and from South Africa. We have five focus areas: evaluation of missionaries, training and equipping of churches, on-field care, reentry care, and research.

Evaluation of missionaries

The aim of the evaluation procedure is to get an overall profile of missionary candidates. Information is gathered about their personality, work style, contribution in a team, and spiritual gifts by means of different measuring instruments. These items, in combination with personal interviews that are focused on spiritual maturity and the person's calling, give a good indication of where and in what position the person can be used optimally by the Lord.

During the past year, a preliminary evaluation battery has been compiled which is suitable for use with the South African population. Evaluation has already been done on a small scale by a psychologist with experience in missions and in psychometric evaluation of missionaries. In the future, Member Care Southern Africa would like to expand this service by providing a service to evaluate missionary candidates in the Western Cape, and by extending this service by identifying suitable psychologists in all the major cities of South Africa.

Training and equipping churches

We have developed material that we present as a workshop for local churches. The following topics are covered in this material:

- Definition, biblical basis, and importance of member care.
- Role of the local church in the preparation and sending of a missionary.
- Phases in the missionary's life.
- Phases in the preparation, sending, and care of the missionary.
- Evaluation of the missionary.
- Support team within the local church.
- Attrition, on-field care, and reentry.

This material is available in the handbooks *Member Care for Missionaries: A Practical Guide for Senders* (Prins & Willemse, 2001a; also in Afrikaans) and *The Support Team* (Prins & Willemse, 2001b; also in Afrikaans). At this stage, the care of missionaries' children is not addressed as a separate section, although it is mentioned where applicable in the other sections. The workshops are also suitable for use at conferences.

On-field care

It is important for missionaries to be backed up and cared for while on the field. This type of care consists of two parts. The first is *day-to-day care*, with the emphasis on practical, spiritual, and emotional needs. Here, Member Care Southern Africa can act as consultants on what is available in terms of courses for spiritual and emotional care, e.g., team building, interpersonal skills, and marriage and family enrichment.

The second type of care involves *crisis management* to help during potentially traumatic experiences—e.g., during wars, armed robbery, or emotional struggles such as serious depression. Again, we can act as consultants on what is available in terms of the availability of specialized crisis care teams.

Reentry care

If reentry is not handled with wisdom and care, the result can be a missionary who is spiritually and emotionally so wounded and disillusioned that it can take years to recover—if ever. Reentry is one of the topics that is addressed in the workshop for local churches. The aim is to help the missionary and the sending church to understand the reentry process and to give guidelines on reentry care. Member Care Southern Africa also presents a short workshop on reentry.

Research

Research is an inseparable part of the development of each of the other four areas. Member Care Southern Africa, therefore, spends a lot of time on networking nationally and internationally with individuals and organizations specializing in member care. We gather, compile, distribute, and let others know about both newer and older member care materials that are available.

Two years ago, when Member Care Southern Africa was started, the term "member care" was hardly known in South Africa. Initially, it was difficult to convince people that member care was an important aspect of missions. Funding in general is difficult in South Africa, because of the pressing national needs, and finding funding for a relatively unknown aspect of missions is even more difficult. However, there were a few individuals and local churches who were very faithful in their support—both morally and financially.

It was Walter Henrichsen who said, "Grow into business; do not go into business." Kelly O'Donnell reminded us, "Function brings people together; fellowship keeps them together." This is exactly what happened with our member care group. We were aware of the hand of the Lord, not pushing or forcing, but constantly urging us on through His love and care for His church, including those on the front line of the battle. Step by step, He opened the doors, gave us the right contacts (nationally and internationally), and at the right time He fanned the flame of interest in what we were doing. Now, after two years, we can look back and see the fruit of our labor—a growing ministry that came about according to His will and at His time. One of the outstanding things was the moral and spiritual support we could give each other as a team. It is not possible to be effectively involved in any care ministry without giving care to each other.

If there is one thing that other existing or aspiring member care groups can learn from us, it is to have patience—even if the first phase takes time. "Do not despise the small beginning, for the eyes of the Lord rejoice to see the work begin" (Zech. 4:10, LB). In God's own timing, He will complete His work. "In all my prayers for all of you, I always pray with joy because of your partnership in the gospel from the first day until now, being confident of this, that he who began a good work in you will carry it on to completion until the day of Christ Jesus" (Phil. 1:4-6, NIV).

Member Care Forum

The Member Care Forum was officially formed in June 2000 in Cape Town, in response to the felt need of many to organize a member care network in South Africa. The Forum functions as a partnership with a facilitator, Marina Prins, and different working groups. The participants include members from different organizations and churches, as well as individuals involved in the sending and caring of missionaries. The Forum meets every three to four months. The purpose of the Forum is to enhance the development of member care resources within and from South Africa.

At the formation meeting, participants identified several member care issues which they felt needed attention. At the next meeting, three working groups were formed to address the most important of these issues, as identified by the participants. The three groups are equipping the local church, a database for member care resources, and reentry care. It is hoped that other issues identified at the first meeting will develop into working groups as the Forum develops. These include intercession, evaluation, and MK care.

At this stage, most of the participants are from the Western Cape (in the south, in the vicinity of Cape Town), but a sister member care group has already started to develop in Gauteng province (located in the north around Johannesburg/Pretoria). There are people in other provinces who are also interested in becoming part of this development. In the future, we hope to establish a national member care network within South Africa.

Conclusion

A great deal of member care development still needs to be done in South Africa. However, a start has been made as churches, organizations, and individuals begin to work more intentionally together. The challenge in South Africa today is not just to send out more missionaries. The challenge is also to get local churches and agencies to partner together to ensure that missionaries are effectively cared for, from the pre-field phase right through to reentry.

Reflection and Discussion

1. List some of the challenges that your local church/organization is faced with in terms of the sending and caring of your missionaries. Which are the main ones at this time?
2. List some practical ways in which members of your church can be involved in missionary support. Which specific people could be/are involved in a support team?
3. What resources are available for the care of your missionaries on the field? And for reentry? How can this type of care be improved?
4. What resources could your church/organization offer to enhance member care development within your region/country?
5. How might the experiences/approach of Member Care Southern Africa apply to member care development in your region/country? Could a similar group be started?

References

Froise, M., & Hendriks, J. (1999). *South African Christian handbook 1999-2000*. Welkom, South Africa: Christian Info.

O'Donnell, K. (1997). Member care in missions: Global perspectives and future directions. *Journal of Psychology and Theology*, *25*, 143-154.

Pirolo, N. (1991). *Serving as senders: Six ways to care for your missionaries.* San Diego, CA: Emmaus Road.

Prins, M., & Willemse, B. (2001a). *Member care for missionaries: A practical guide for senders* (also in Afrikaans: *Sendelingversorging—'n praktiese gids vir stuurders*). Cape Town, RSA: Member Care Southern Africa.

———. (2001b). *The support team* (also in Afrikaans: *Die Ondersteuningspan*). Cape Town, RSA: Member Care Southern Africa.

Strauss, G., & Narramore, K. (1992). The increasing role of the sending church. In K. O'Donnell (Ed.), *Missionary care: Counting the cost for world evangelization* (pp. 299-314). Pasadena, CA: William Carey Library.

***Marina Prins** holds a M.Sc. Agriculture degree from the University of Stellenbosch (South Africa). From 1991 to 1997, she served as a missionary of the Dutch Reformed Church Mission in Malawi. She is currently director of Member Care Southern Africa and is responsible for member care development. This includes writing member care material, presenting workshops, and networking both nationally and internationally. She is also the facilitator of the Member Care Forum. Email: mcsa@xsinet.co.za.*

***Braam Willemse** holds an Honours B.A. degree from the University of Stellenbosch (South Africa), as well as a L.Th. from Cape Town Baptist College. He and his wife, Marianne, a medical doctor, were missionaries to the Yao People in Malawi for six years. He was also Director (Church Liaison) with Global Careers and one of the Directors of Member Care Southern Africa. Braam died shortly after this article was written. He will be dearly missed.*

We would like to express our appreciation to Professor H. J. Hendriks (Department of Practical Theology and Missiology, University of Stellenbosch, South Africa) and Rev. J. H. Theron (Hofmeyr Mission Centre, Tygervalley, South Africa) for their input and comments on this article.

14

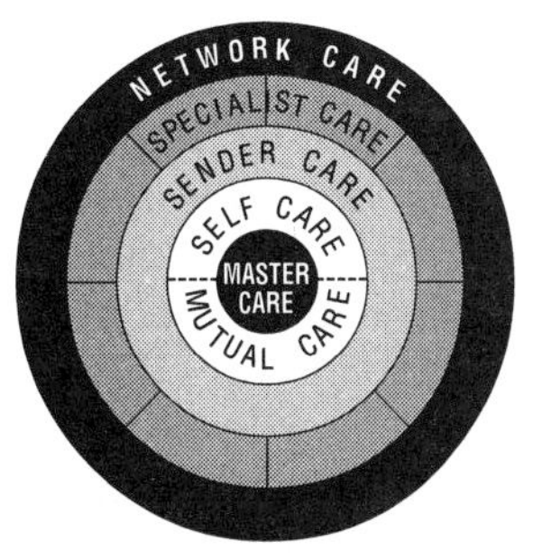

Tumaini Counselling Centre: Ten Years In/From East Africa

Roger K. Brown
Shirley M. Brown

In this chapter, we will look at the operation of a field-based missionary care center, with a specific focus on the Tumaini Centre. We will explore the relevance of field counseling, the types of services that are offered, how the center is managed, future directions, and several other related areas. Five brief case studies conclude the chapter.

Missionaries are normal people who serve in some very challenging situations. They may face political crises, hostilities, or physical assault. The stresses of cross-cultural adjustment can bring out unsettled past issues or raise new concerns. Missionaries can face depression, burnout, anxiety, marital difficulties, or interpersonal struggles. Their children may deal with learning difficulties, bed-wetting, eating disorders, or acting-out. Just like the Christian populations whom they represent in their respective sending countries, missionaries are not exempt from the cares and troubles of this fallen world.

Missionaries from past generations were generally more familiar with hardships and fewer luxuries. Many came from hard-working rural backgrounds and from strong Christian homes. They are sometimes perceived as having exhibited greater stress-hardiness than today's missionaries. Yet some of the stalwart missionaries of earlier generations were not permitted to express their very human hurts and needs within their Christian home cultures. Some families grew in God's grace during hardships, and others suffered deeper hurts and wounds. The emotional and family sacrifices of these servants cannot be fully tallied in this world.

Missionary service has always been challenging. Political instability, crumbling infrastructures, rampant crime, hostile environments, isolation, separation from familiar support systems, financial pressures, and family needs are just some of the common stressors experienced by missionaries. As more honest expressions of hurts and needs are being permitted in the Christian community, church workers and missionaries have ventured forth to share their own struggles. This increasingly candid acknowledgment of the emotional side of life has led to more candidates with emotional struggles applying to serve as missionaries. These candidates often expect and need more emotional and spiritual support, even on their field of service.

In general, missionaries returning to many Western countries have been able to receive emotional, physical, and spiritual care from specialized missionary providers such as Link Care in the United States, InterHealth in the United Kingdom, and Missionary Health Institute in Canada. Christian mental health professionals with special interest and skills are often available to provide helpful counseling and therapy. Missionaries on the field, however, usually have few options to receive professionally trained Christian counseling or therapy. Basically, the demand for care far exceeds the available care.

Several organizations have placed counselors at missionary boarding schools (Rift Valley Academy, Kijabe, Kenya; Faith Academy, Manila, Philippines). Their function has been primarily to care for the emotional needs of the students of these schools, but many have also been called upon to counsel staff or even other missionaries who have come to see them. Some organizations have had a pastoral counselor travel from mission station to mission station to provide a listening ear, guidance, or intervention. While helpful at times, this technique can be limited in adequately addressing long-term issues or major problems. Other organizations have placed an individual counselor in a field setting on a more permanent basis. For example, SIL began field placement of missionary counselors in 1983. Some of these counselors have faced pressures relating to being overloaded with requests for their services, professional isolation, and being stretched beyond their areas of expertise. They may or may not be available to missionaries outside their own organization.

When missionary crises or concerns arise, mission organizations may spend inordinate amounts of time, energy, and finances to provide support for their missionaries and field administrators. That support may be too little, too late, or off-target. Administrators can feel overwhelmed or perplexed as they work through a crisis. Despite the best efforts by a mission agency, missionaries do not always feel heard and understood. Both the mission and the missionary may express a need for professional expertise to provide support and intervention. All too often, the outcome may not be so positive for the missionary, the mission agency, and the ministry. When the needs for care have been urgent, these missionaries have had to "uproot" themselves from their place of service and home in order to go elsewhere for help.

Mission organizations often send administrators, pastors, or counselors to their fields for crisis intervention. They may speak at field conferences with the option of short-term counseling. More recently, some organizations have begun placing professional counselors in field settings as short- or long-term missionaries. This is true for Older Sending Countries (OSCs) and to a lesser extent for Newer Sending Countries (NSCs).

Tumaini Counselling Centre

In the mid-1980s, missionaries of Africa Inland Mission International (AIM) and Wycliffe Bible Translators/SIL began discussing the possibility of shared office space for their missionary counselors located in East Africa. This cooperation led to the opening of Tumaini Counselling Centre in Nairobi, Kenya in late 1990. Tumaini (pronounced *to my ee' nee*) is a Swahili word for "hope," reflecting the hope for healing and care that is given at the center.

Tumaini Counselling Centre is the only counseling center of its kind on the African continent. Based in a regional hub for missionary activity which includes field mission offices, MK schools, and medical and transportation services, it is dedicated to the care of missionaries and their families. The center is staffed by a multidisciplinary team of missionary therapists. These missionary caregivers are well-trained and experienced professionals who are able to integrate their Christian faith with their counseling, consultation, and training. The staff members prioritize their own mission agencies, AIM and SIL. However, they also see missionaries from other mission agencies serving across Africa. Approximately 100 different Protestant mission organizations have made use of Tumaini services.

The primary users of Tumaini are missionaries who work in Kenya, Tanzania, Uganda, Democratic Republic of Congo, and Sudan. However, Tumaini also regularly serves missionaries working in more distant countries throughout East and Central Africa, including Ethiopia, Burundi, Rwanda, Mozambique, Malawi, Zimbabwe, Namibia, Lesotho, Comoros, Madagascar, and Chad. Additionally, 11 West African countries are covered by administrative consultations. Missionaries from these countries occasionally fly to Nairobi for evaluations, and the therapists at times fly there for teaching or crisis intervention.

Missionaries utilizing the center originate from about 20 sending nations. These have included missionaries coming from North and South America, Western Europe, East Asia, Africa, Australia, and New Zealand. Although most clients are non-Africans, there has been a recent increased contact with this particular underserved missionary community. Most clients are self-referred. Friends or peers are often the source of information about the helpfulness of the counseling ministry. The majority of the users come voluntarily for assistance; only rarely are evaluations required by an individual's organization.

Types of Services

A variety of services are provided within and from Nairobi. The main ones are counseling (individual, group, family, child, and marital); critical incident stress debriefings; consultation with mission administrators and faculty/administration of MK schools; team-building workshops and conflict management; seminars on topics such as marriage enrichment, parenting, stress management, and interpersonal skills; speaking at schools or churches; writing articles; and lending out library books relating to individual, group, couple, or family growth and spiritual life.

Field emergencies may require the counselors to travel internationally. In many cases, the missionaries affected come to Nairobi for evaluation and possible ongoing treatment, since lasting interventions often require more time and resources than the counselor is able to provide in a brief interaction.

Occasionally the missionary counselors are able to respond to international requests for speaking during field conferences or presenting seminars. However, such travels have necessarily been limited due to the time commitment, disruption to the Nairobi-based ministry, and family needs.

Types of Problems

For the most part, the counseling issues seen at Tumaini have been remarkably similar to those experienced in the West. Political instability, spiritual warfare, and cross-cultural transitions can create or amplify problems.

Trauma victims. Individuals who have experienced significant trauma are seen. Violent assaults, car hijackings, accidents, war, and evacuations are significant dynamics for many missionaries.

Boundaries. Because missionaries often have a high work ethic and a great deal of compassion, and because they are surrounded with endless needs, some may struggle with keeping a healthy balance in their own work and personal needs.

Adjustment difficulties. Many missionaries live in harsh conditions, whether in deserts, remote villages, or sprawling cities. Culture shock, homesickness, financial pressures, and prolonged separations from loved ones are a part of most missionaries' lives. Consequently, there are significant stress issues of work and even daily living.

Spiritual issues. Missionaries are not immune from struggling with distorted images of God or themselves. Issues of acceptance, significance, and security inhibit some individuals in their spiritual growth. This can cut short their missionary service if not adequately addressed when the distortion becomes evident.

Interpersonal difficulties. Relationships with team members often involve multiple cultures, different expectations, and interdependent living in close quarters. Personality clashes, difficulties with confrontation and conflict resolution, unspoken expectations, and misunderstanding of cultural cues can complicate interpersonal relationships.

Past issues. Every missionary comes to the mission field influenced by past experiences, whether positive or negative. Even the best screening and orientation cannot guarantee that past personal struggles will not resurface in the intense situations on the mission field. More young missionaries are coming from broken or abusive homes. Many are first-generation believers who are learning to establish Christ-like homes and marriages. The lack of familiar support systems on the field can weaken the buffer which protects individuals during times of difficulty. Stress is then experienced with greater intensity, leading to a possible breakdown in the missionary's stability and functioning.

Substance abuse and addictions. Unlike Western counseling groups, the Tumaini counselors rarely see substance abuse among adults or teens. Workaholism can be an issue for some missionaries. Recent availability of the Internet heightens the risk for pornography for both MKs and missionaries.

Developmental disorders. Attention Deficit Disorder and learning disorders occur in the same frequency as in the West. However, they cannot be adequately recognized, understood, or treated in much of Africa. Professional services provided by or coordinated through Tumaini have proven essential for many missionary families to remain on the field.

Services on the Field or Services Back Home?

In the early stages of Tumaini, several counselors attempted to provide therapy for individuals struggling with sexual abuse, severe early trauma, personality disorders, or severe eating disorders. In the process, the counselors found that inordinate amounts of time were spent helping just a few people in crisis. This did not allow time or energy to assist greater numbers of other missionaries who were struggling with less entrenched problems. It has subsequently been recognized that severe needs cannot be dealt with in depth, even in a specialized field care center such as Tumaini. Counselor involvement with more severe diagnoses is limited to crisis intervention, evaluation, and facilitating transfer to a sending country that can provide services.

These more deeply affected clients can tend to be unstable and require significant amounts of time from the counselors, as well as their administrators and fellow missionaries. This can distract from the ongoing ministries of fellow missionaries and administrators and can even harm missionary reputations. In addition, their healing may necessitate the availability of ancillary support services, hospitals, close friends, or family members near at hand.

Nonetheless, when a family or individual missionary is known to have a problem which will require return to a sending country for assistance, there are recognized benefits to a limited number of sessions with one of the field counselors. This can be an important opportunity to discuss transition, anger, and grief issues that might hinder addressing underlying problems once the person has relocated.

The Tumaini professional staff strongly recommend against mission organizations sending missionaries with known emotional problems to the field, with the assumption that they can utilize Tumaini for providing ongoing care. Field resources remain limited, and the staff members at the center are committed to careful allocation of their energy and resources. It is imperative that each missionary candidate be fully screened psychologically and physically. Missionaries should not be sent to the field unless they have adequately addressed psychological and medical concerns raised in the selection process. The candidate with unresolved emotional and relational problems is more likely to be successful on the field if he/she has had time in the home country after completing counseling to consolidate the gains made during therapy. Adjustment tasks of being a new missionary can overwhelm or set back previous progress in dealing with deep-seated issues. It should be the mutual goal of the missionary and the sending and receiving unit to facilitate successful transition and ministry.

The premature sending of candidates to the field is not helpful to the missionary family, their supporters, the receiving ministry, nor the overall missionary goal. Field missionaries and churches need new colleagues who are able to join in partnership after appropriate field orientation. They are expected to begin taking on responsibilities, rather than requiring inordinate amounts of emotional support. The national church needs mature believers as role models, not missionaries who might distract with unhealthy coping or relationship patterns.

How Did Tumaini Counselling Centre Develop?

The formation of Tumaini Counselling Centre can only be described as miraculous in God's design and leading. Each of the original counseling staff was called independently to serve in a counselling ministry in East Africa.

In 1983, David Dunkerton, a veteran AIM church planter, returned to Kenya with a counseling degree and took an assignment as professor and chaplain at Daystar University in Nairobi. Missionaries began to come to his office for counseling in increasing numbers as trust was built with missionaries and administration. AIM subsequently adopted Dave's vision for field counseling support and approved a new department named AIM Care.

In 1983, God also called Roger Brown, a medical doctor, to train in general and child and adolescent psychiatry, with the intent to work in a missionary support ministry somewhere in the world. The Browns discussed ministry proposals with several mission agencies, and it became very clear that AIM was ready to move forward with a missionary counseling center that was very much in line with their vision for ministry.

David Dunkerton also developed a relationship with the SIL International Counseling Department as staff members passed through Nairobi. Roger Brown was developing a mutually supportive relationship with the Dallas-based SIL counseling office as he completed his training and prepared to join AIM Care. Thus, both organizations were ripe for greater interaction when God led veteran SIL missionary counselors Harry and Pat Miersma to a new counseling ministry assignment in Nairobi in 1989. Harry (M.A., M.F.C.C.) and Pat (M.N., C.S.) had first seen the need for field missionary counselors while serving as Reformed Church in America (RCA) missionaries in Ethiopia during the Communist revolution (1973–1976). Following graduate work in their respective fields, they joined the counseling staff of Wycliffe Bible Translators in 1980. They served with Wycliffe's sister organization, SIL, as counselors for three years in Papua New Guinea before accepting their current Africa assignment in 1989. As they discussed with Dave Dunkerton the details of a cooperative SIL/AIM ministry, both organizations gave their consent and blessings, and common office space was rented in late 1990. This cooperative location was called Tumaini Counselling Centre.

The Browns arrived in Nairobi in 1991 to join the counseling ministry under AIM.

The Dunkertons later returned to the States at the end of 1992 to assume a pastorate. SIL psychiatrist Dr. Richard Bagge and his family arrived in 1993. Several veteran missionaries with pastoral or other counseling experience also helped at the center on a part-time basis. In 1998, AIM added veteran counselors John (M.A., M.F.F.C.) and Karen (M.A.) Zilen to the team. Nancy Crawford, a clinical psychologist, and Doug Ghrist, psychiatrist, joined the AIM staff in 2001.

A key to the acceptance of a counseling ministry by the missions community was the groundwork laid by Dave Dunkerton. His prior church planting years validated him as a "real missionary" and allowed fellow missionaries to know that he could identify with their experiences. Dave was a respected spiritual leader within the community and a friend to many, so that potential misgivings against counseling were lessened. The counsel he provided was culturally sensitive, wise, and godly. As other Tumaini counselors arrived, Dave perceptively introduced them to the missionary community. Thus he facilitated new counselors' sensitivity to fellow missionaries, as well as the missionaries' acceptance of these counselors.

How Does Tumaini Counselling Centre Function?

Tumaini is not a formal organization per se, but rather a location where missionary counselors work together and provide mutual support, both professional and personal. The staff shares resources such as auxiliary personnel, office equipment, utility and security expenses, a lending library, and a professional library. The key to this cooperation has been a high commitment to staff relationships, as well as viewing respective ministries as ultimately belonging to the Lord and not to an organization. The counselors meet weekly for mutual support and case discussions, as well as daily informal interactions. Tumaini is not a formal entity, but rather a place where each mission headquarters its counseling ministry. This also allows each organization to maintain its distinct character and philosophy and minimizes professional and organizational liability concerns.

The AIM and SIL counseling departments receive ministry direction from their respective administrative boards or councils. The counseling staff also contribute direction and recommendations for ministry emphases. Historically, the requests for services have nearly always exceeded staff capabilities. The counselors have wrestled over the years with ways to provide crisis care, ongoing therapies, and preventative care, yet still protect themselves from being too overwhelmed to be effective. In the recent past, staff members were able to get away for a staff retreat to discuss direction and focus. The time investment was helpful to strategize together on potential interventions and proactive services. It was also an invaluable mutual support.

Africa Inland Mission has historically had a vision to provide services for the broader missions community of like-minded mission agencies in East Africa. The counseling ministry is a good fit for the AIM International Services Department, which also provides bush flights, freight shipping and clearing, a guesthouse, financial services, etc. AIM has also been involved in developing and managing institutions such as Rift Valley Academy and Kijabe Medical Center. Thus, AIM has been designated to help oversee the general office management of the counseling center. The SIL staff members have contributed from the wealth of many years of experience in member care, and they assist in office management responsibilities when coverage is needed. The entire counseling staff and office manager meet regularly to discuss policies and direction which affect the office as a whole.

All of the counselors are missionaries who raise their own support from churches and individuals in their home countries, so that none of the donations go to the professional staff. Suggested donations are charged only to cover operating expenses of rent, utilities, security, Kenyan staff, etc. Operating expenses have been proportionately divided according to the number of counselors representing each of the sponsoring organizations. The two organizations differ in how they receive their income. The AIM counselors suggest a small donation from each individual who receives services. SIL expenses are met through a portion of their missionaries' field allocation, with a similar donation being charged to non-SIL missionaries.

Future Directions

We are trusting the Lord for additional staff. We are also hoping to expand into several important areas.

Field-based pastors for the missionary community. A missionary pastor would visit various mission stations, attend field conferences, encourage ongoing spiritual growth, and focus on raising the level of mutual care within the body of Christ.

Involvement in the orientation and follow-up of new missionaries. The first months on the field for new missionaries can be a critical time, as they grieve the loss of close contact with family and go through cultural adjustments. The care by trained counselors can assist in the transition, through supportive counseling and practical workshops on life skills.

Greater encouragement of African national missionaries. The African church is becoming more involved in its own missionary efforts. Tumaini staff members desire to remain open to ways in which the center might support equipping and caring ministries within the African church.

Networking and collaboration in developing other centers on the continent. This would then make care more readily accessible to other missionaries.

Internship program. This would provide clinical field experiences and mentoring for future counselors to missionaries as they disperse throughout the world.

Mission leadership training in interpersonal and personnel management skills.

Consultation with missionaries working to develop biblically sound materials for ***training African church leaders***. The psychological, emotional, and spiritual impact of the AIDS crisis and ethnic conflicts in Africa might be a few of the areas that could be addressed.

With the blessing of much-needed additional staff, the current Tumaini facility has been stretched beyond its limit. The center has been housed in a rented four-bedroom apartment with a small rooftop office, large living room that serves as a lobby, and enclosed veranda that is a part-time seminar room/office. AIM Care has been involved in a capital development project to construct a new counseling center that would be designed to meet counseling criteria for privacy, quiet, space, and adequate parking. The center will have 10 offices, a group room, professional library, public lending library, and seminar facility. It is set on an attractive plot just outside of Nairobi, which will also offer landscaped gardens as a haven from the bustling city. The goal is to provide a counseling facility that will support missionary activities within a professional and pleasant setting.

Benefits of a Field-Based Counseling Center

There are many benefits to the missionary community from the presence of a well-organized counseling/member care center on the field.

Benefits to Mission Personnel

- Counseling is professional and godly.
- Counseling is in close proximity to the field of service for prompt care.
- Counseling on the field helps preserve the family continuity.

■ Counseling on the field is more likely to be utilized.

■ Counseling on the field can be cost-efficient in both finances and time.

■ Counseling on the field provides care for some nationalities of missionaries who may not have counseling available in their countries of origin.

■ Counselors on the field provide referrals and can facilitate inter-mission cooperation and sharing of resources and knowledge.

■ Counseling provided by those who are missionaries themselves enhances insight into the struggles of missionary service.

Benefits to Mission Organizations

■ A counseling center provides professional care for mission members to maximize their service and capabilities.

■ It can be an attractive benefit in missionary recruitment.

■ It can assist in maintaining a healthy working environment and positive attitudes.

■ It can assist field administration concerning staff problems, screening, required evaluations, and personnel policies.

■ It can assist in long-term staff development, leadership training, and further training for national counselors.

■ It can be a change agent for growth within the mission body.

Benefits to Missions Work

■ The missions community is strengthened to serve the Lord in the face of many pressing needs and struggles.

■ The support from readily available counselors can protect the precious investment of a missionary's call, training, and culture and language acquisition.

■ The counselors of Tumaini see themselves as encouragers of missionaries on the front lines to enable them to minister in healthy ways to their families, colleagues, and focus group.

Case Examples

The following cases are for illustrative purposes only. Although they are essentially true, the identifying features have been altered or combined in order to protect the identity of the individuals and missions involved.

Case 1

An ever-present danger for missionaries living in much of Africa is hazardous road conditions. Over the past few years, a number of missionaries have been involved in accidents, some involving significant injuries or even fatalities. Several mission organizations have made use of the Tumaini counselors for such accidents, as well as for missionaries who have inadvertently hit and injured or killed pedestrians.

Judy and Joe had invested years of effort in learning the culture and language of an unreached tribal group. Joe was tragically killed in a road accident. Judy received counseling support at Tumaini as she worked through her grief. While involved in the on-site field counseling, Judy was also able to complete a major church project, which had been a mutual effort with her husband before he died.

Case 2

Living in an isolated setting can be difficult for anyone. Many missionaries in East and Central Africa are located many hours or days away from anyone of a familiar culture.

Mary and John lived in a remote setting with their two children. They were involved in church planting and discipleship. There was a very strong religious presence (non-Christian) in this community, which they described as having a spiritually oppressive atmosphere. One day while her husband was away, a man forced his way into their home and bound Mary with ropes. In front of her children, the man made terrible threats but eventually left, after stealing a number of items.

Mary and John met with a field counselor for several sessions of debriefing and assessing the impact of this trauma. As Mary had pre-existing emotional issues that complicated her treatment, the counselor encouraged the couple to return to their home country for a medical leave of absence. While on home assignment, Mary sought professional counseling and was diagnosed with Post-Traumatic Stress Disorder (PTSD). Her treatment progressed fairly well. They were anxious to return to their field assignment and left their home country shortly after the counseling was completed, now with three children.

Work initially went well. However, Mary began to find it more and more difficult to manage her African home, care for an infant, and home school their children. Mary had a set back with her PTSD and also developed a major depression. She became incapable of functioning and was suicidal. The entire family was evacuated by plane to Nairobi so that she could be evaluated further at Tumaini. Over a course of eight weeks, Mary made significant progress. However, the family realized that they would not be able to return to their previous remote setting, in light of her need for further treatment. The family made the difficult but necessary decision to return to their home country. They expressed their gratitude to Tumaini for helping them to work through their crisis and clarify future plans.

Case 3

Mr. and Mrs. Greene served the national church in an important support capacity. Their teenage son Peter developed a significant obsessive-compulsive disorder. He spent hours daily washing his hands and was continually preoccupied with how others responded to him. Peter became depressed and at times suicidal. His parents sought treatment at Tumaini. As treatment required their close support and medication management, they relocated to Kenya for a temporary work assignment until his condition stabilized. He has done well and now receives periodic follow-up for medication management. His parents have been able to return to their previous assignment.

Case 4

Judy was a 30-year-old missionary nurse who came to Africa to work in a war-torn country whose population was facing starvation. Her organization realized the tremendous stress each of their missionaries endured under war and famine conditions and required them to come to Nairobi every six weeks for a time of debriefing and rest. Judy recognized that she was not coping well and sought counseling at Tumaini. She was able to recognize and work through her anger at the tremendous injustices around her. In addition, she and her colleagues were a part of a debriefing at Tumaini that followed a mortar shell being fired into their home. She was able to continue her work in a stressful assignment with the support of Tumaini.

Case 5

John, an 11-year-old MK, had difficulty completing his work at school and was often restless. His mother had previously home schooled him. This restlessness and inattention had not been a significant problem while he was home schooled. Now that he was attending a boarding school, it was apparent that he was also developing a problem with his peer relationships and suffering academically. At the recommendation of his teacher, his parents brought him to Tumaini for an evaluation. At that time, he was diagnosed as having an Attention Deficit Hyperactivity Disorder. The child psychiatrist at Tumaini instructed the parents and the child about this disorder, suggested behavioral interventions for the family and school, and prescribed medication. In addition, the boy was referred to an educational psychologist. Further testing revealed that John also had a learning disorder. John's medication, school progress, and family interactions continue to be monitored at Tumaini, while his parents remain in their place of ministry.

Reflection and Discussion

1. Based on the authors' description, what are some of the main reasons for Tumaini's success?
2. Which skills and qualities are needed to work as a counselor in a field center?
3. What are some additional ways that a field missionary care center might support field missionaries or national counselors?
4. What concerns and risks should a mission organization or a group of service providers consider before establishing a field missionary care ministry as described in this chapter?
5. Where would be some strategic locations to locate missionary/member care centers?

Roger Brown *and* ***Shirley Brown*** *have worked in Nairobi, Kenya, with AIM since 1991. Roger is a physician and board certified in general psychiatry with a further specialization in child and adolescent psychiatry. He is also a graduate of Moody Bible Institute. Shirley is a registered nurse and holds a master's degree in biblical studies from Dallas Theological Seminary. Both Roger and Shirley had short-term missions experiences as singles. They have two daughters, Rachel and Hannah. Email: roger-shirley_brown@aimint.org.*

15

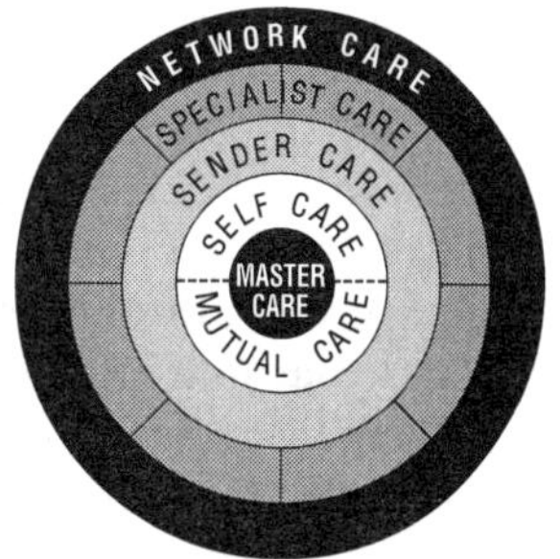

Awakening Pastoral Care In Latin American Missions

CHRISTOPHER SHAW

A steady increase in the numbers of Latins leaving their countries as missionaries to other continents encourages me to believe they will soon be major partners in the task of making disciples of every nation. But learning from the struggles of the first waves of workers from this region will be important to truly impact the unreached.

Nobody shows quite as much zeal as the person who has belatedly embraced a cause that, in days gone by, was considered of little importance or even as unnecessary. The same passion to see the gospel preached in the remotest corners of the earth, modeled for so long by nations in the northern hemisphere, has now gripped Latin America. With an enthusiasm sometimes bordering on desperation, the church has shown itself eager to make up for lost time. In the first heady rush to fill the front lines with excited young volunteers, hundreds of Latins have been sent everywhere from Peru to the Philippines. It was time to arise and shine for the Lord!

This conversion to missions, however, is a fairly recent occurrence. For years, the insistent message preached by a handful of isolated leaders throughout the continent, advocating involvement in the missionary task, fell largely on deaf ears. It was only in the 1987 missions conference sponsored by COMIBAM (Iberoamerican Missions Cooperation) in São Paulo—the first continental gathering of its kind—that a turning point was finally reached. At COMIBAM, the trumpet call to join in advancing the kingdom to the ends of the earth was sounded with unusual conviction. More than 3,500 delegates from virtually every country in Central and South America collectively understood that the region had a vital role to play in the cause of missions. The subsequent response of the church has far exceeded the expectations of many denominational leaders. Today, an estimated 4,000 Latin American missionaries from every country on the continent are serving the Lord in different parts of the world, including the 10/40 Window (Limpic, 1997).

A Growing Need for Pastoral Care

In the early days of this movement, it was not uncommon to hear regional leaders expounding on the particular potential that Latins possessed for missions. And there is no doubt that Latins bring a particular mix of cultural and social characteristics that make them suited to enter and serve in countries now closed to missionaries from the northern hemisphere. Confident assertions were made that the mistakes missionaries from the Older Sending Countries (OSCs) had made would not be repeated by the Latins. It was believed that a painful awareness of some of the consequences of these mistakes would be enough to ensure that Latins did not tread along the same path.

It was perhaps this feeling of over-confidence, coupled with a lack of experience, that led pastoral care to be regarded as not a very important aspect of the task before the church. The push was on to get as many people as possible recruited, trained, and out onto the field. Undoubtedly some leaders expected the Latins to advance unimpeded where others had experienced grave difficulties. A poor understanding of the cost of doing missionary work led other leaders to consider suffering on the field as the price to be paid for being involved in missions. There was little time to evaluate which suffering was avoidable and which suffering was unavoidable.

Fifteen years have elapsed since that first continental missions conference. National and regional conferences have been held throughout Latin America, and the theme of missions has become a part of the vision of many local congregations. Christians are gaining exposure to the issues related to recruiting, training, and sending missionaries, even as an ongoing number of casualties from these early days have begun to filter back to their home countries. Some organizations, based on a private survey that I conducted, have lost as many as 40% of their workers in the past decade. The worst of these cases have even turned their backs on the church.

Concern for those who have fallen by the wayside has had a sobering effect on church leaders. Uncomfortable questions beg answers from organizations that have continued to push ahead while encountering increasing problems with the missionaries working on the fields. The time is ripe for re-evaluation, as a growing awareness of the importance of pastoral care for missionaries is developing in key leaders in the region.

This growing concern can be seen in the fact that missionary conferences and gatherings in recent years have begun to include workshops and plenary sessions on offering pastoral care to those on the field. Congregational leaders are also beginning to assign members of their staff to take responsibility for this particular aspect of the missionary task. Slowly, we have seen the appearance in Christian literature of articles, brochures, and books on the subject. Efforts are being made to establish networks of caregivers who can share resources and experience with congregations, sending agencies, training schools, and other organizations involved in missions.

All of these developments are most welcome, especially if the enthusiasm of Latins for missions is not to be dampened by some of the stories of suffering and defeat coming from the field. Efforts must be redoubled to direct emerging missionary movements towards specific ways that both preventive and restorative pastoral care can be offered to those serving Christ in other countries.

Some Contributing Factors to Latin American Attrition

There are, no doubt, a whole series of factors related to some of the difficulties that Latins experience on the field. Some of these are common to missionaries the world over, and in this regard Latins have become one with generations from every people who have struggled with similar issues throughout the history of the church. Other elements, however, are peculiar to the Latin mindset. Some of these are of special interest to those involved in pastoral care.

Pablo Carrillo (1995), for example, in a seminal article in this area, has discussed some of the major problems of Latin Americans in missions. Drawing on his 20 years of experience in several regions of the world, he lists three broad areas of problems. These struggles are still highly relevant today.

- *Problems within the worker*—deterioration in personal relationships with other workers; inability to adapt to a new culture and learn a new language; unresolved problems affecting one's emotional stability; lack of tools for spiritual survival.
- *Problems in the participating church*—lack of adequate financial resources; organizational differences; inability to help missionaries find meaningful work.
- *Problems in the mission agency*—lack of planning and strategy development; lack of cooperation with other agencies.

A Weakness in Existing Congregational Structures

Pastoral care does not come easy to many of the organizations working in missions. Latins in general are a people who have strong social ties to family, friends, and even co-workers, and relations develop within this natural network. The context for much that goes on in the local congregation, therefore, is built around providing opportunity for these ties to develop. There is an underlying conviction that problems will take care of themselves if a person has a network of support. Much of the spiritual life of the church members, therefore, revolves around attending meetings. Deliberate pastoral care is often replaced by abundant teaching provided from behind a microphone.

The strong commitment to providing as many meetings as possible for Christians and their growth interferes with the time that pastors need to provide individual care for church members. As new leaders develop, they too are pulled into the never-ending cycle of formal activities. Pastors assume that those who are serving within specific ministries naturally possess a level of maturity that makes pastoral care unnecessary. Leaders are expected to take care of their own personal needs without being cared for by their pastors.

These two aspects combine to make potential missionaries especially vulnerable when breakdown experiences occur on the field. Their traditional reliance on meetings for spiritual growth will often be replaced with a sense of isolation, as missionaries grow roots in countries where it is difficult or impossible to join existing congregations. At the same time, their own experience before leaving for the field can lead them to deny the existence of problems, struggles, and hurts in their own lives, because they assume that leaders/missionaries are not supposed to experience them. Denial is a great way to reinforce self-defeating patterns on the field, while doing nothing to deal with the underlying problem.

For example, a missionary couple on the field may begin to experience a breakdown in their marital relationship, or they may face issues of conflict arising with team members. Whereas the appropriate course of action might be to stop and address these problems or even seek help from leaders back home before things deteriorate beyond control, this couple may feel that anything not specifically related to their "missionary" task is of a lesser concern. They might thus "sit tight" and hope that the problems will not interfere with their work, or even that the Lord will take care of things as they demonstrate their loyalty to His service. Their experience and training have simply not prepared them to deal correctly with these or a host of other problems they may face on the field.

An Emphasis on Individual Effort

The fact that many leaders choose or are pressured into ministry responsibilities without adequate support often leads to ministers becoming overly concerned with protecting their own interests. In the absence of adequate pastoral care, many feel that they must ensure success by their own means. This leads to a strengthening of individualism in the leaders themselves. Others in ministry are frequently viewed as potential competitors for scarce resources. Each person must move forward as best as possible while taking care that others do not threaten their personal projects. Cultural gravitation towards strong, authoritarian types of leaders aggravates the situation. This attitude is not only prevalent in many individuals involved in ministry, but it can also be found in hundreds of congregations throughout the continent. Strong denominational pressure has often led different congregations to view others outside the intimate circle of relationships with attitudes of suspicion or even hostility.

Although much has happened in recent years to break down some of the stronger barriers dividing different groups, Latins in general are not well-equipped to work in teams. The strong emphasis on individual effort is not conducive to dialogue or negotiation. Disagreement is sometimes seen as an attitude of open rebellion towards those who are in authority. With this kind of background, it is not surprising that many conflicts in the lives of missionaries develop quickly on the field. As missionaries are put in teams in a variety of destinations, they find that differences with other team members become major obstacles to ministry. The tools for conflict resolution are not always available, and the tensions rise to intolerable levels as individual members compete for primacy within the team structure.

This particular difficulty holds an element of irony to it, for it is also a strong inclination to developing relationships that stands out as a quality in the lives of many Latins. It is when these relationships are taken to a level where deep exchanges of ideas and passions occur that conflicts arise. A potential strength, therefore, loses its value for enhancing the missionary experience. Again, Latins need to learn how to take this quality to greater depths than they would normally experience within the framework of the local congregation.

A Shortened Training Experience

A general tendency to move away from the more formal, academic models of training has become common in Latin America. A large part of the effort is to find more personal, relevant, and efficient ways to train missionaries. The new models which have arisen have paid much more attention to such things as character development, community experience, and practical training in evangelism, church planting, and discipleship. These changes have brought much-needed renewal to the whole area of ministry preparation. The changes, however, have also tended to reduce drastically the time allotted to training. The four-year course traditionally advocated by formal institutions has been replaced by highly compressed training experiences that may last as little as four months. Although these programs are often part of a larger project where a practical field experience is necessary, this latter part of the training often lacks the supervision needed to make it an effective learning experience.

The rushed nature of much of this training usually means less time to identify and deal correctly with issues in the lives of candidates that will most certainly cause problems on the field. An alarming number of candidates with a desperate need for inner healing or with serious character problems are being allowed to leave without receiving adequate ministry. These untreated areas of their lives come to the fore under the normal pressures of the field, often when it is very difficult to reach them with adequate help.

A Low Commitment to Pastoral Care

As previously noted, congregational leaders are often hard pressed to provide pastoral care for their own people at home. A lack of resources and time, inadequate training, and a host of other factors contribute to the poor quality of pastoral care in many congregations. But even more important than these elements is the fact that there is much pressure in Evangelical circles to provide proof of effective ministries through numerical increases in church attendance. Literature highlighting the glittery ministries of mega-churches in different parts of the world has spawned countless imitators throughout Latin America. This means that much effort is spent on seeking to enlarge congregations without providing the adequate support structures to ensure that new converts develop into mature disciples of Christ.

This particular focus of pastoral work often transfers to the missionaries who are working on the field. Teams who have been sent out to difficult countries feel a particular sense of frustration as their efforts to develop growing congregations produce pitifully small results by comparison with their home churches. Even when the missionaries themselves begin to understand that they are in a setting where the rules are different, it is difficult for the sending congregations to grasp the same concept. Because of this, it is often hard for denominational leaders to understand how missionaries can be experiencing personal problems or team conflicts when they seem to be doing so very little on the field. As well as this, the few resources available for the cause of missions seem to be ill-spent if they are not directed at activities that make a significant contribution to the cause of spreading the gospel. To invest time and money in providing pastoral care for the missionaries on the field is not always understood as a good investment by the church leaders.

When missionaries return home, they are naturally received with great expectation and are invited on whirlwind tours to recount their experiences on the field. They are expected to provide "rewarding" results to supporters, to motivate and mobilize new candidates for the cause, and to secure further support for the future. A long list of engagements is often planned for them well in advance of their return home. People do not expect to hear from missionaries that they are hurting, frustrated, or angry. The same denial that has been a problem on the field accompanies them back home. It is rare, therefore, to find a congregation that takes time for debriefing or that helps missionaries to work through some of their pain and reentry needs.

Too Few Resources

Even when church and mission leaders fully understand the need for providing pastoral care, they often run into a frustrating lack of resources that make every move in this direction difficult. Funds are usually already stretched to the limit and often scarcely cover the basic needs of those who are on the field. Lack of funds, however, is not the only problem. There is also only a handful of men and women who are gifted and equipped to offer the right kind of pastoral care overseas. Missionaries often complain that in the few visits they do get, the people visiting them are more interested in tourism than in ministering to their needs.

The experience of the past decade, therefore, provides an emerging picture of the kind of person who is needed for this work. First, people are needed who can actually get out onto the field. These are people with strong pastoral gifts, with a special orientation to the healing of emotional wounds and the resolution of interpersonal conflicts. Second, age is also important. Latin missionaries often relate better to older people who can also provide a father/mother figure from which they can receive comfort and support in times of crisis.

These characteristics often leave out a number of people who could help but are lacking the experiential framework to be able to make a significant contribution in this area. Even when this reduced group of people can be identified, there remains the ever-present problem of raising the funds to mobilize them and get them to the right places when needed. Personal time constraints have to be considered, as some of these people may have job responsibilities from which they cannot easily take leave.

Creative Ways to Provide and Develop Pastoral Care

The particular mix of challenges that have been outlined in my previous comments calls for a special quota of creativity in resolving the issue of pastoral care for missionaries. It seemed unimaginable two decades ago to be speaking of Latins as major partners in missions. Yet today they have become important participants in the process, enriching the experience of the missionary community in many parts of the world. The unthinkable actually materializing encourages us to admit no defeat when thinking about pastoral care. The flow of missionaries out of Latin America *must* continue. While encouraging Latins to rise up and take their place in the Lord's harvest, we must not cease in our efforts to build into this movement the support structures necessary for the healthy pastoral care of its laborers. As our experience grows, so too will we become wiser about the ways in which we can take better care of our missionaries.

The doors are obviously closed to pursuing the comprehensive kind of pastoral care offered by many organizations in the OSCs. These nations enjoy the advantages of long experience in the equipping and sending of missionaries, as well as the solid financial situation of their home economies. The approach to pastoral care shown by many organizations in the northern hemisphere testifies to the particular characteristics of their own cultures, such as strong emphasis on holistic models of ministry, avoiding burnout through balanced priorities, conflict resolution through team dialogue, and the sense of security that comes from strong financial support. The Lord has blessed them within this context.

Latin Americans are very new to the world of missions, and they bring with them a whole new mindset with its own set of cultural traits. It is, therefore, a wonderful time to explore and find the means to care for missionaries, especially in ways suited to Latins. So how creative and culturally relevant can we Latin Americans be? Here are some ideas.

Training Teams for Pastoral Care

It is common to insist that people who will provide pastoral care should have themselves had experience in some field. The principle is sound, for surely nobody can understand the particular needs of missionaries better than those who have experienced firsthand what it means to be a missionary. It does not always follow, however, that a person with mission experience is capable of providing adequate pastoral care for other missionaries. In truth, providing pastoral care for missionaries has much more to do with giftedness than with the experience, though there is definitely a plus to possessing the latter.

A more serious problem with this principle, however, is that years will go by before there is a sufficiently large pool of Latin people with missions experience available to help in this area. The need for adequate pastoral care is urgent today and therefore requires immediate steps. The required skills, like the needs themselves, are extensive: team building, conflict resolution, marriage enrichment, children's education, family life, crisis care, stress management, and so on. An interesting alternative may be to include training in pastoral care as part of the overall missions program of a denomination or organization. Such training need not rely on centralized programs but could also be delivered through extension/correspondence courses, although ongoing hands-on experience and supervision are usually needed.

It seems to me that a good way forward would be to carefully select small groups of people to be equipped and exposed to the particular needs of those who are serving on the field in different parts of the world. The selection could be done by those involved in providing pastoral care today, in conjunction with church/agency leaders and field leaders. Initially this program would concentrate on giving these people tools to develop basic counseling skills, providing practical experience within the local church setting. Eventually these people could travel with missionary leaders and caregivers to become familiar with field conditions. The process of developing this team of ministers would take time, but it would be a definite improvement on requiring the exhausted handful of people currently taking care of missionaries to continue shouldering all the burden indefinitely. As in all pioneer situations, the early stages of development are the ones that take the greatest amount of energy and effort.

Ideally, such a team of people would become part of a growing network of pastoral caregivers available to a wide range of missionary organizations. Those sending agencies or congregations not able to provide adequate care could use the services of such a team. Less experienced caregivers in the team could be called on to make routine visits to different fields, while the crisis situations could be left to those who have more experience.

Creating Awareness in Local Churches

A second area where much work can be done is in helping local church leaders to understand the need for pastoral care of their missionaries. Those with a burden for the pastoral care of missionaries would have to work alongside the recruiting and sending agencies, taking advantage of the natural bridges that exist to the local church to bring awareness to missionary leaders and pastors. Congregations that are involved in mission projects can be informed about the stress and difficulties, the trials as well as the joys and accomplishments, that many missionaries experience on the field. Seminars, literature, and personal talks with the leaders responsible for the missionaries will go a long way towards helping local congregations understand in what ways they can be particularly useful in supporting their people serving in other regions. Even where there is little literature on the topic, simple articles can be extremely useful in helping leaders who know very little about the subject, and who are generally surprised to hear that missionaries often experience breakdowns on the field.

Mission agencies can help sending congregations to understand some of the specific needs that returning missionaries have. Through careful planning, those who return can be shielded from the effects that a well-meaning, though otherwise insensitive congregation can have on their missionaries. Special training is not needed for this. Some basic guidelines can be very useful in providing the necessary tools for church leaders to be instruments of healing and blessing in the hands of God.

Making Pastoral Care a Part of Training

Training has made enormous steps in moving away from highly intellectual models that leave the heart untouched. Community living often gives candidates a foretaste of what it will mean to live and work with a team of people on the field. An emphasis on the devotional life helps develop some of the habits that will be much in need on the field.

The most significant aspect of the new training models, though, is that it often provides firsthand knowledge of problem areas and character weaknesses in the lives of candidates. These priceless insights are too valuable to let slip by without more than a cursory observation by training leaders. Often these particular weaknesses, such as lack of discipline, inability to work in a team, unresolved conflicts from the past, or inability to accept orders or submit to a set of rules, are only patched up sufficiently for the candidate to reach the field.

Instead of concentrating so much effort in overloading candidates with information on a whole variety of topics related to the missionary experience—which they hardly can understand because they do not have the experiential framework with which to interpret it—time could be better used if candidates were not only ministered to in a more personal way, but also helped to reflect on the process of resolving personal problems and interpersonal conflicts. In one program I have been involved with, for example, the very nature of the intense schedules—with very little free time—tends to separate couples from one another and rob them of valuable time for sharing together during the training process. Unwittingly, we are setting them up to continue with this pattern on the field, instead of teaching vital skills in caring for their marital relationship.

The presence, therefore, of qualified pastoral staff during part or all of the training experience is essential. These people could be fully devoted to helping candidates work through these issues, even while the program leaders continue to work on developing other traits important for the missionary task. Unfortunately, trainers often expect the process of healing and conflict resolution to take place on its own, simply because people are thrown together to share the same experience for a period of time.

Training should also provide candidates with a basic understanding of the mechanisms needed to resolve conflict situations in their own and in group settings. Those candidates who show the right qualities to provide adequate pastoral care could be further equipped with the basic tools needed to provide pastoral care for other team members. In this way, missionaries would be better equipped to deal with stress and interpersonal conflicts without outside help.

Sharing Resources

The resources available in NSCs for pastoral care may be relatively scarce, but this can and will, I believe, change. History leaves us this valuable lesson, however. The success of the missionary task has never depended on the abundance of available resources, but rather on the wise and intelligent use of whatever was available—more often than not, very little, "so that His grace may be sufficient in us, for His strength is made perfect in our weakness" (2 Cor. 12:9). In this sense, we Latins are exceedingly well-equipped to take on our missionary role! And, indeed, many Latins have once again placed faith—a realistic, informed faith—at the center of their missionary endeavors.

I am convinced that it is not so much a matter of resources, but rather of creating sensitivity in the body of Christ towards the needs of the workers in front-line trenches. It is a matter of seeking ways to bring about the natural caring that should exist within the church. Once the sensitivity exists, the resources will be mobilized much more readily.

I envision congregations and organizations involved in better recruiting practices, equipping and sending laborers to the field who are healthier and better prepared. But to do this, we must lay aside the inherited tendency to work alone and instead team up with others who have similar interests and needs to our own. The pool of pastoral experience and resources is growing and must be shared between groups. Attitudes of suspicion or self-serving plans must become a defunct cultural accretion from the church's past. We must continue to create networks of mutual cooperation, including networks of counselors, trainers, debriefers, an affiliation of caregivers, and missionary care consultations.

The availability of a network in itself, though, will rarely convince pastors and leaders to make use of the resources offered. In the context of Latin culture, it is the personal recommendation that goes a long way to break down mistrust and hesitation in approaching others. Encouraging leaders to make use of a network in the region will therefore depend largely on the endorsement of key leaders who have access to different parts of the missions community. These leaders must take advantage of their natural contacts and the authority that they have within the community to introduce leaders to new individuals who can contribute in offering pastoral care in given situations without being committed to any one group alone.

This kind of resource sharing will take time to build. Yet it is the only way forward in a continent where the level of poverty in the population is increasing year by year and where the possibilities of small, individual missionary ventures become increasingly difficult. Such adversity, though, rather than a hindrance, is an opportunity for unprecedented generosity and growth. What a wonderful moment to ignore the tug of selfishness and explore the unlimited resources of the whole of the body of Christ!

Conclusion

For years, we Latins saw ourselves as a missionary field, the target of the missionary projects of other nations. Indeed, we often convinced ourselves that we had little to contribute to the spread of the gospel to the ends of the earth, and we grew used to the idea that mission was something that others did. The last two decades have brought wonderfully good news to the church in our region. We too can be missionaries! How exciting it has been to see a whole army of people begin to share long-treasured dreams of serving Christ in other lands and slowly witness the coming about of these dreams.

The way forward has been filled with all sorts of experiences, both good and bad. In our youthful eagerness, we have made many mistakes. But we are rapidly growing up, and we hope to capitalize on all that we have experienced to this point. One thing is clear to us: there is no turning back. We have joined the great missionary enterprise, and we intend to make that particular contribution for which God created us Latins!

Reflection and Discussion

1. The experience of the church in Latin America has been one of rapid growth. The same is true for the flow of Latin missionaries leaving for other fields. What steps need to be taken to ensure that this progress does not ride on the wings of enthusiasm alone?

2. Communication and effective links with the sending church are vital to help missionaries fight off the feeling of loneliness on the field. In what ways can a local congregation with a limited budget work to keep these links healthy?

3. If you were asked to head up a project to develop a team of caregivers throughout Latin America, how would you go about developing such a project? What specific steps would you take to get the project started?

4. The need for literature on pastoral care, from a Latin American perspective, is great. What are some ways in which regional member care workers and mission leaders could be involved in producing the kind of literature which would be helpful to all those working with missions projects?

5. Training new missionaries is essential to the task ahead. Some of the pitfalls in both traditional and new models of missionary development have been outlined in this chapter. What elements would you consider vital to include in the missionary training experience, if you were trying to practice preventive pastoral care?

References

Carrillo, P. (1995). Struggles for Latin Americans in frontier missions. *International Journal of Frontier Missions*, *12*, 195-198.

Limpic, T. (1997). *Ibero-American missions handbook*. COMIBAM/OC International.

***Christopher Shaw** was born and raised in Argentina. He graduated from the Buenos Aires Bible Institute in 1982, and later completed a doctorate in missiology at Fuller Theological Seminary, in California. He has been involved in pastoral ministry for over 20 years. Since 1992, Christopher has been involved as a guest lecturer with Kairos, a Brazilian missionary agency which recruits, trains, and sends Latins to work among the poor in the great urban centers of the world. In offering support to graduates who are on the field, he has traveled to Peru, Chile, Spain, and the Philippines. He is the author of several articles on the subject of character development and pastoral care of missionaries. Christopher is married to Iris, and they have three children. He currently lives in Buenos Aires, Argentina. Email: fliashaw@sinectis.com.ar.*

16

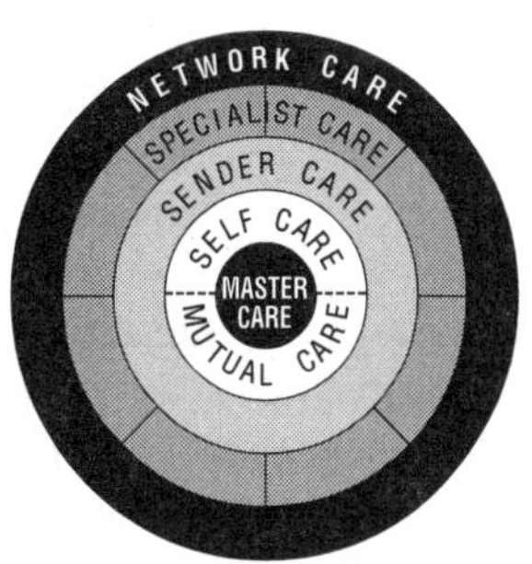

Pastoral Care From Latin America: Some Suggestions For Sending Churches

PABLO CARRILLO LUNA

The Latin sending churches play a crucial role in supporting their workers well. Here are some reflections and suggestions on pastoral care from an experienced Latin leader.

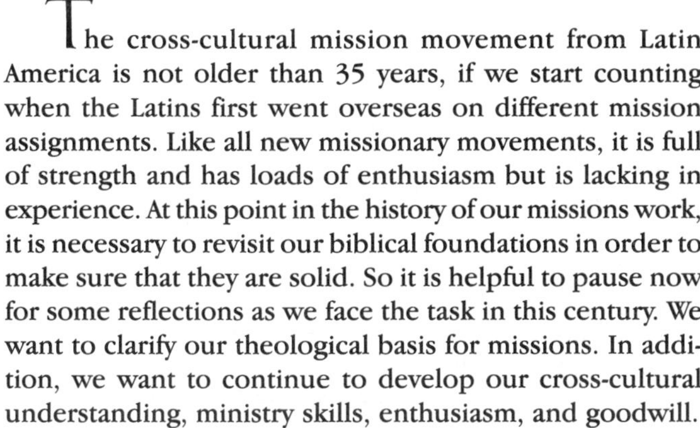

The cross-cultural mission movement from Latin America is not older than 35 years, if we start counting when the Latins first went overseas on different mission assignments. Like all new missionary movements, it is full of strength and has loads of enthusiasm but is lacking in experience. At this point in the history of our missions work, it is necessary to revisit our biblical foundations in order to make sure that they are solid. So it is helpful to pause now for some reflections as we face the task in this century. We want to clarify our theological basis for missions. In addition, we want to continue to develop our cross-cultural understanding, ministry skills, enthusiasm, and goodwill.

How do we understand the mission of the Latin American church? It seems to me that the way we are answering this question is at the root of many of the problems that Latin workers face on the mission field.

Limitations in Our Understanding of Mission

It is interesting to observe the way a young missionary candidate might respond to the appeals made at local mission conferences. Often without the knowledge of the church leadership and many times without the parents' consent, a decision is made to go to the ends of the earth with the message of the gospel. Being a person who has been there myself and done that very thing many times, and who has interviewed hundreds of young Latin candidates during the last 18 years, let me point out two main areas of concern about this approach for missions involvement. First, it is the wrong way of recruiting for missions, and second, it involves the wrong motivations in some of these young people.

We have relentlessly used a couple of verses which we consider to be the ones that best express the mission of the Lord: in the Old Testament, Isaiah 6:8 ("Here I am. Send me!"), and in the New Testament, Matthew 28:18-20 ("Go into all the world..."). If these verses are the primary ones that we emphasize, no wonder people are reluctant to respond to the missionary call. Or those who do respond end up with an incomplete understanding of what the mission is all about. There is so much more to missions and to Scripture! We need to look for a fresh approach to reviewing and presenting the *entire* Scriptures. We also must try to rediscover what the Spirit is saying to the Latin church on the matter of reaching the nations and obeying God's will. May true knowledge be added to our well-intentioned zeal!

The missionary conference is still the main motivational platform to recruit young candidates for the mission task. The problem with this model is that the people who often respond to the missions summons in these conferences are the *sanguines*, the more emotional and spontaneous. The *phlegmatics*, who seem better suited for the long haul, do not respond to all the emotional hype. I know this is a general statement, but in many cases I have seen it to be accurate.

Moreover, when some candidates try to explain why they want to go to certain places, the answer is often, "I feel called." Having such a "call" usually translates into the message, "This is the end of the discussion, and anyone probing more into this call might be found to be contradicting the Lord!" Of course, there is a subjective element in a missionary call, but God has also provided objective ways of confirming His word. In the New Testament, that confirmation always came through the local church. It is very rare—and I think non-existent, frankly—to find a person being called to a mission task without someone from the church, often a person in a leadership position, confirming that call. Even the Apostle Paul, who received his unmistakable call on the road to Damascus (Acts 9:3-7), later submitted to objective screening by members of the church (Acts 9:10-18, 27, 30; 13:1-3).

In general, the least becoming idea of "mission" that we have in Latin America is that of an organization—many times a foreign one—that comes to snatch our young people from the local churches in order to do the missionary task. Later, that same missionary organization comes to our church to ask for money to support these same young people. It is a way of doing missions in which the local church adopts a *passive* role and the mission agency the *active* one. We urgently need more reflection in the church on the function and reason of being the church. We need a serious study on the *ecclesia* and her true identity in the midst of a postmodern world.

Some Struggles for Latin Americans on the Field

Many struggles that the missionary faces on the field are a direct result of minimal missions understanding in the Latin church. For example, the lack of finances for missionary support in some cases is because the church is not totally convinced of the missionary task. In other cases, it stems from the entrepreneurial approach to missions, whereby the local church demands results, numbers, and a return in the investment. That puts pressure on the missionary to perform, with the likely result of a fruitless and stressful activism, accompanied by exaggerated prayer reports from the field. Sometimes guilt and depression are the symptoms of not being able to perform to expectations from back home.

Fortunately, some of the Latin missionaries have seen improvement in this area through diversifying their constituency and through redefining their mission task as new opportunities open for them on the field. Realistic approaches to building relationships and obtaining "results" are being taken more frequently among Latins. But this does not solve the ongoing lack of understanding of the mission task on the part of the local church. Orientation about missions and visits to the field by the church leadership are some practical solutions.

Another recent issue is that of children's education on the field. As the Latin American missions movement develops, so do the families that comprise it. Missionary *families* have thus become a growing part of the missions scene. The presence and needs of children have begun to affect the capability of some people to stay on the field. Following the lead of other sending countries, one strategy has been to bring a Latin teacher for a short-term commitment until a more definite solution is found. Another option is to consider home-schooling, yet this must be carefully reviewed, since it is still such a "foreign" practice and might not be recognized by the education authorities back in one's home country. In general, most of the workers have mainstreamed their children in local schools or, in some cases, in schools which use a more international language, such as French or English. However, the implications of sending a family with older children to an area where the education options are few needs to be considered before the family steps into the airplane. The home-based mission agencies and local Latin churches need orientation in this area from some experienced Latins.

One of the most significant problems has been that of convincing some of the local churches to provide medical insurance for their missionaries. Back home, local pastors hardly have such coverage themselves. Hence, how can they afford to pay insurance for some young missionaries from the same church? There are no quick solutions, and the expected time of departure of some candidates is often delayed until this item is fully covered by some other source. Many missionaries choose to go to the field with no medical insurance. There are many risks in sending people to politically unstable and volatile countries even with full medical and life insurance. However, these hard decisions must be seriously considered by the church and the candidates before leaving for the field. The question is: Are they aware of the total implications of this decision? Who will help them to understand the risks?

Church Orientation and Involvement

It is clear that many problems that Latin workers face on the field could be solved before they leave for their missionary assignments. A healthy local church is the key place to address these issues.

If the recruitment is done carelessly or without the church leadership's approval and significant involvement, we will continue with some of the same old problems. Workers will go out with inadequate preparation, they will struggle to relate to and respect their colleagues, they will not discipline themselves to learn the local language, and they will misunderstand spiritual authority and be hesitant to submit to leadership. The church in which biblical community is practiced is the best place to assess the emotional and spiritual stability of candidates. Questionnaires and interviews from sending agencies have their place too, of course, but nothing is better than observing someone's behavior and growth over time.

If the church or denomination allocates in the budget an adequate amount for the support of their candidates, the financial stress would be reduced considerably. The sending base should be open to cooperate with the rest of the body of Christ too. The antithesis to this would be repeating the "old" ways of denominational parochialism, which in the name of guarding "sound" doctrine seeks to reproduce replicas of itself in the resulting field churches. Lack of cooperation gives birth to lone rangers and isolated missionaries.

Some Helpful Directions

In a previous article on this subject, I overviewed three main areas of struggle for Latin American missionaries (Carrillo, 1995). These areas were the missionaries themselves, the sending church, and the mission agency. These are not three separate entities having isolated problems. Yet as I have pointed out in this chapter, it is in the church where we can see both the source and the solution of many problems that the Latin worker faces.

Needless to say, there is a glaring need to provide basic and specific orientation as to how to go about doing the missionary task. The role of the local church is more important than we have allowed in theory and practice. The sending church should be aware that the missionary task is to be done with excellence, as unto the Lord Himself. Part of excellence involves clearly defining the biblical basis for missions as well as the common issues facing Latin countries. The orientation program should include some basic information regarding the mission fields to be reached, the missionary project being undertaken, job expectations for the workers, expectations and commitments of the sending groups, and the type of accountability. There are already several training courses and well-meaning systematic approaches available. These in my experience tend to be very pragmatically oriented, yet they do not adequately address the Latin American context or the questions that the Latin church is raising.

One practical tool to help church leaders understand the biblical basis of missions and the practical steps in sending out workers is the Raymond Lull Seminar (SRL). Ramon Lull, one of the first proponents of missions to the Muslim world, lived in Spain in the 14th–15th centuries. This seminar bearing his name was birthed while we were trying to develop a pastoral care program for Latin workers in restricted areas. We first discovered that some of the usual approaches among the Older Sending Countries were irrelevant to the growing numbers of Latin workers, many of whom were coming on their own with minimal advice about what to expect. They started to return frustrated to their home churches. The churches then questioned what went wrong and who was to blame, and there was much discouragement.

The seminar is structured in three main sections. The first section reviews the *biblical and historical foundations of mission*. The idea is to help the Latin leaders and candidates maintain the biblical perspective and to be faithful and sensitive to what the Lord is trying to say to us. Moreover, we do not need to re-invent the wheel but rather need to learn from mission history and from our predecessors. The second section of the seminar deals with the *world of Islam*, emphasizing the necessity for understanding the peoples we are trying to reach with the gospel and their felt needs. The third section comes to grips with the *practice of mission*. In order for the Latin church to assume her responsibilities in the missionary task, it is necessary to understand what the missionary process is and the role of the church and the candidate.

SRL is our response to the problem, and the enthusiastic reception to the first presentations in Chile, Argentina, and Mexico has confirmed that there is a need for such a tool and that the seminar is the right tool to address the problem. SRL fills a critical need of the Latin American church at this crucial time in her growth.

It is not too late to avoid more casualties and the discouragement that the churches will experience in their mission work. We sense the Lord is moving the Latin church at this time to responsibly embrace her role in world missions, but the church needs to be assisted in a wise way. There is now enough experience among seasoned Latin missionaries and leaders to provide significant help.

Reflection and Discussion

1. List some of the main challenges that the author mentions for Latin sending churches. How do these challenges compare to those from your own sending church/country?

2. What are a few practical ways that a sending church can cooperate with a sending agency in supporting the mission personnel that they both send out?

3. How would you begin to plan for a coordinated effort to orient the Latin American church concerning missions involvement?

4. Compare and contrast some of the Latin American issues/struggles for field care with those from the Older Sending Countries.

5. What are some other ways to recruit Christian young people into missions besides missions conferences?

Suggested Reading

Bertuzzi, F. (Ed.). (1994). *Ríos en la soledad.* Alcántara, Argentina: Unilit.

Bosch, D. (Ed.). (1999). *La misión transformadora.* Grand Rapids, MI: Eerdmans.

Bowers, J. (Ed.). (1998). *Raising resilient MKs.* Colorado Springs, CO: Association of Christian Schools International.

Carrillo, P. (1995). Struggles of Latin Americans in frontier missions. *International Journal of Frontier Missions, 12,* 195-198.

Gnanakan, K. (1993). *Kingdom concerns: A theology for missions today.* Downers Grove, IL: InterVarsity Press.

Manning, B. (1994). *Abba's child.* Colorado Springs, CO: Navpress.

Minirth, F., Hawkins, D., Mier, P., & Flournoy, R. (1986). *How to beat burnout.* Chicago, IL: Moody Press.

Padilla, R. (1986). *Misión integral.* Buenos Aires, Argentina: Nueva Creación.

Snyder, H. (1978). *La comunidad del rey.* Downers Grove, IL: InterVarsity Press.

Steuernagel, V. (Ed.). (1996). *Obediencia misionera y práctica histórica.* Grand Rapids, MI: Eerdmans.

Tournier, P. (2000). *El sentido de la vida.* Tarrasa, Barcelona, Spain: Publicaciones Andamio. Ed. CLIE.

Worthington, E. (1989). *Marriage counseling.* Downers Grove, IL: InterVarsity Press.

Pablo Carrillo Luna *was born in Mexico City. He has a Bachelor of Science in industrial engineering from the Instituto Politécnico Nacional. He was involved with OM in the Middle East, North Africa, and Spain from 1971 to 1974. Pablo is married to Jane, and they have three children: Natasha, 24, Yusef, 20, and Yamila, 18. They have made Granada, Spain, their base of operations since 1979. Founder and former President of PM Internacional, Pablo is at present developing the Raymond Lull Seminar, a tool designed to give orientation and to encourage biblical reflection on the Latin mission to the Muslim world. Email: saulus1030@cs.com.*

Special thanks Jane Carrillo for her helpful review of this article, as well as other colleagues who have helped shape my thinking in this area: Marcos Amado, President of PMI; Tim Halls; and Susana Malcolm.

Note: This article builds upon the author's previous article in the special member care issue of the ***International Journal of Frontier Missions*** *(1995, vol. 12, pp. 195-198), "Struggles of Latin Americans in Frontier Missions."*

17

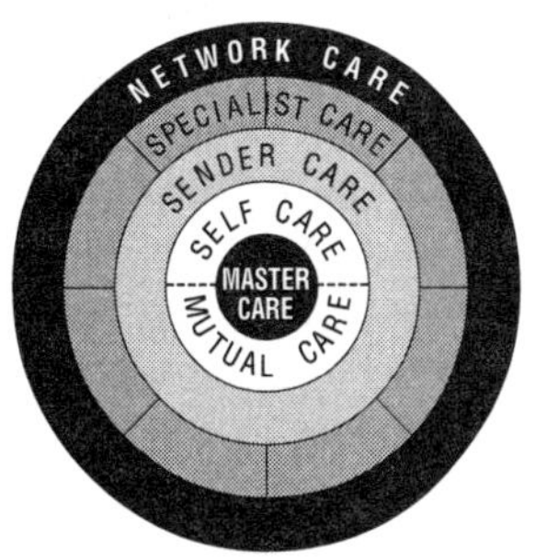

Preparing to Persevere In Brazilian Missions

MÁRCIA TOSTES

"Blessed, happy, to be envied is the man who is patient under trial and stands up under temptation, for when he has stood the test and been approved, he will receive the victor's crown of life which God has promised to those who love Him" (James 1:12, Amplified). This chapter looks at how this verse is becoming a reality in the lives of mission personnel from Brazil. The author offers practical encouragement on how the Brazilian church can take the next step forward—the step of perseverance—in its global missions efforts.

"My goodness, how luxurious your suitcase is!"

"Well, you are welcome to have this suitcase if you are ready to go through all I went through in order to have it."

Such was the brief exchange between a Brazilian missionary and a member of a church she was visiting on her deputation program, as her host unloaded the car. The suitcase, in fact, was quite impressive, especially when compared to the ones that missionaries used to have. That man, though, was getting the wrong idea that missionary life was very easy. The suitcase had actually been a gift of the Brazilian consulate to that missionary as she and three other missionaries arrived for a brief stay in Portugal, worn out after the long process of negotiation for their release. They had spent eight months as hostages in an African city that had been taken by rebels.

The four missionaries had the chance to leave as others did on the day of the occupation. They decided to remain, though, convinced that God wanted them to stay. At the moment of their quick decision, they could not foresee all they would have to go through. The righteous will live by faith, for sure, but was this being naïve and presumptuous, or was it courageous and wise?

Fortunately, some days before the attack, the Brazilian missionary had received a large shipment of medicines. As the local people were hurt, she was able to care for them, and the church became a center for help, hope, and safety. The missionary became a leader in that time of horror. Miraculously, several individuals were healed with the simple treatments she provided, even when the injured required much more help, such as amputation of limbs.

One day during an attack, many people swarmed into the church, filled with fear and desperation. The missionary had to cry out in a commanding voice, "Lie down, lie down." She then turned her head so that nobody could see the tears that were streaming from her eyes.

Attack followed attack, and some of the missionary's friends fell wounded or lifeless close by her. The cries of those people remained vivid in her mind, along with other horrible memories, long after her safe return eight months later to her home country. She lost weight, and she wrestled with the relentless question, "Could I have done anything else to have saved these people?"

Negotiations were made with the help of the United Nations, and the missionary and some other hostages were released. The four missionaries were then carefully taken out of the country, with just the clothes they were wearing. Because of their poor health, they spent three days in Cabo Verde for medical help. Next was a week in Portugal, where they received care from the Brazilian consulate to help them recuperate further before traveling on to Brazil. It was at that time that they each received nice clothes along with a new suitcase. What a price to pay for a stylish suitcase!

As I reflect on this story, two questions come to my mind. First, was this Brazilian missionary adequately prepared for this experience? And the corollary, are our other missionaries prepared for what they are going to face? In this chapter, I will look at these questions by reviewing how pastoral care is developing in the Brazilian missionary movement. I will also reflect on how far we have come and what else we need to do.

Review of Brazilian Missions and Member Care

The Brazilian missionary movement is relatively new, especially when compared to that of the Older Sending Countries. The oldest Evangelical Brazilian missionary agency, Antioch Mission, was founded in 1976. Nevertheless, our history is already full of beautiful stories, many of which contain accounts of suffering. Missionaries often just persevered without fully understanding the kind of suffering they were going through.

In the beginning of the movement, missionaries were sent out almost as one sends a parcel in the mail. In some ways, it seems that this was the price that zealous but missions-inexperienced Christians had to pay in order to build a foundation. These early missionaries—like the current ones—needed a lot of faith to be able to overcome things like the lack of financial support, the unknown, culture shock, and difficult communication between the home country and the field. Many of those who were sent in the beginning persevered, and they are still on the field today, 20 years later. But some were seemingly not strong enough and had to return. Nowadays there are still many missionaries being sent out without adequate care. These people and those connected with them continue to pay a high price.

The growth of the church in Asia, Africa, and Latin America has been tremendous. There are more Evangelicals in these regions than in North America and Europe. The increasing number of mission personnel being sent from these regions is also amazing. In Latin America, the missions movement came into full view in 1987, when a large congress (COMIBAM 87—Iberoamerican Missions Cooperation) was held in São Paulo, Brazil. Over 3,000 delegates attended. One of the main purposes was to discuss how Latin Americans could be more involved in world evangelization.

After this congress, much happened. Many other missionary conferences were held, new missions began, and many missionaries were sent. After 10 years of work, another congress (COMIBAM 97) was convened in Acapulco, Mexico. Here, over 3,000 mission personnel and church leaders evaluated what had transpired and considered future opportunities. Balance and realistic appraisals were sought. Yes, a lot had happened in terms of sending missionaries, but some mistakes had also been revealed. One of the main errors was that many missionaries had been sent out without proper preparation and without enough care in the field.

Somewhere in the midst of such excitement, with the church rejoicing in being part of such a great work, a distressing estimate was circulated that three out of every four missionaries from Brazil remained less than five years on the field. This news got our attention! Research on missionary attrition in Brazil was then conducted in 1995 by Ted Limpic with SEPAL/OC International, together with the World Evangelical Alliance's Missions Commission. The new and more carefully researched estimate was considerably lower, but it was still worrying. Some 7% of the missionaries from Brazil were returning home each year for various reasons, not too far from the 5% average figure for other countries in the study.

This research also explored the reasons that missionaries were leaving the field. The findings are discussed at length in the book *Too Valuable to Lose*, edited by Bill Taylor and translated into Portuguese and Spanish (Taylor, 1998). Among the principal reasons for the premature return of missionaries sent from Brazil were personal problems which were related to the character of the missionary.

These findings made an impact on the mission movement in Brazil. Three organizations—the Brazilian Association of Transcultural Missions (AMTB), the Brazilian Association of Mission Teachers (APMB), and the Association of Church Mission Departments (ACMI)—began to discuss openly the issues of missionary care and attrition, via articles, presentations, and consultations.

Two interagency member care affiliations were also subsequently formed. The first one was started in 1999 and focuses on Brazilian missions. This group has the aim of raising pastoral care awareness among the sending churches and agencies, giving specific training in pastoral care areas and also offering specialized help through professionals who understand the needs of missionaries. The Brazilian group is also linked to the second affiliation, the Pastoral Care Program of COMIBAM.

The aim of the COMIBAM program is to help the national mission movements in Iberoamerica develop member care resources in their own countries, through appropriate literature, consultations, and communicating/sharing experiences. In October 2000, the first continental pastoral care consultation took place, held in Lima, Peru. This resulted in the formation of a working group which oversees and develops the objectives of the Pastoral Care Program.

The result of all this understanding and activity regarding pastoral care is that there is no turning back. Sending churches and mission agencies are becoming more aware of the care that is needed from recruitment through retirement.

A Proposed Model of Missionary Care

Here is a three-stage model of missionary care currently being used by many mission groups as a framework for understanding missions. It spans the life cycle of the missionary and his/her family, focusing on the supportive care and training needed during pre-field, on-field, and post-field stages. It emphasizes the coordinated care that the local church, training center, and agency need to provide. There is also a growing appreciation for the place of the mental health professional and cross-cultural trainer.

Pre-Field

This stage includes the selection process, logistical help to secure visas and medical insurance if possible, and preparation/orientation to develop emotional, physical, theological, and missiological areas. Antioch Mission, for example, accepts candidates who are involved in their local churches and recommended by their pastors. In the Mission Training Course, there are classes, presentations, and exams to assess whether the candidates are emotionally prepared to face stressful situations. This is a sifting process which releases some to go and requires others to take more time to develop their skills and/or deal with things from the past. Better to grow now at home than to fall apart later on the field. Some missionary organizations in Brazil, such as Kairos and Antioch Mission, require their candidates to go through an intermediate transcultural experience prior to placement on the field. In this setting, candidates are exposed to stressors that are similar to those in their future field locations.

On-Field

Live and learn, as the saying goes. We Brazilians have learned firsthand how much missionaries on the field need supervision and pastoral care. We are making strides in a number of areas through the involvement of field leaders within the regions, visits from leaders from the sending country, organizing retreats, email communication and phone calls, and encouraging the sense of community and mutual support among missionaries themselves. It is important for missionaries to know that people back home and on the field care about them. They are not forgotten.

Post-Field

The needs of missionaries and their children during reentry are being better understood, wheher the reentry is for a brief return, furlough, retirement, or end of service. Supportive care includes housing arrangements, transportation, health and medical check-ups/treatment, educational options for children, and debriefing. It is also very important to help the missionary think ahead and make proper arrangements for pension and retirement.

A Step Forward

Another concern, in addition to those mentioned above, is increasingly tugging at our hearts: *Are we preparing our candidates to persevere?* This concern was the subject of a master's thesis by a well-known mission teacher in Brazil, Margaretha Adiwardana (1999). It was presented at the Brazilian Mission Teachers Association Consultation in April 2000.

It is hard to say whether we as a Newer Sending Country are in our infancy or adolescence with regards to the development of missionary care. Possibly we are somewhere in between. We feel it is time for us to take the next step forward. All that we have learned and tried to apply in terms of missionary care is essential, but we need to go further. We need to train our workers to persevere through suffering and difficulties, as faithful witnesses of Jesus Christ.

First of all, candidates need to have a biblical understanding of suffering. This subject can be taught from many texts in the Bible, such as 1 Peter 4:12-19. Peter understood that suffering for Christ was normal and that suffering is part of the Christian experience. Christ suffered, and the invitation He makes to His followers is to share with Him in this. It is totally contrary to what the world teaches, and it can come as a shock to us who are not at all used to suffering. "For whoever wishes to save his life shall lose it; but whoever loses his life for My sake shall find it" (Matt. 16:25).

Our candidates come from a generation in which enduring through suffering without giving up is not the order of the day. Being from a developing country does not necessarily mean that one is able to handle life's challenges any better. Many candidates have never experienced significant suffering in their lives. Wars, floods, oppression, and other extreme stressors are part of the news that comes from "far away."

Brazilian culture, speaking in general terms, has a high regard for beauty and the enjoyment of life. The "here and now" is usually more important than planning ahead. Even though there is suffering, especially due to widespread poverty, a Brazilian person takes life as it comes, making jokes of his/her own condition. This way of seeing life can help a person to adapt to new situations. Yet this approach will not usually serve the Brazilian missionary so well, especially in places where poverty is devastating, made worse by natural catastrophes such as droughts, floods, and earthquakes, as well as by manmade disasters such as wars and oppression.

Wars and ethnic conflicts seem to be everywhere, putting missionaries under great stress. Considering whether to stay or leave the country becomes part of everyday life. Many choose to stay, even with all the cost involved, as in the case described at the beginning of this article. Najua Diba, for instance, a Brazilian missionary in Albania, felt so much a part of that country that departure or evacuation during the times of instability was virtually unthinkable. How could she leave behind all the brothers and sisters that she had won for Christ?

Workers in closed countries face oppression. The simple act of using the special clothes and manners that are required in those countries (especially for women) can produce much pressure and loneliness. Are missionaries able to embrace these challenges, adapt as needed, and continue whole-heartedly in their work?

Seeing limited results is something that can be very wearing, especially for those coming from countries where the church is flourishing. Is one willing to work in a country for several years without seeing tangible evidence of his/her labor?

And then there is disease. Malaria is one of the worst enemies missionaries face in certain African countries. Aldacyr Motta, a Brazilian missionary leader who lives in South Africa, concurs: the greatest nemesis is carried by the little mosquito. Many missionaries have been attacked by this disease, suffering through the pain. And some, just like missionaries from the past and like the people they are serving, have died.

So these are some of the realities—the adversities. Not all is negative, of course. There are many joys and rewards in serving the Lord! Yet candidates who are accustomed to the comforts of life, minimal suffering, and a mindset and lifestyle that elevate personal success, richness, and quick answers are particularly prone to struggles and failure. Good news is best presented—and often only presented—in the package of perseverance.

Equipping Missionaries for Adversity

Being involved myself in missions training for some years, I have come to the conclusion that training needs to be as thorough as possible. There are no shortcuts. Everything is part of the learning process: classroom lectures, homework, everyday chores, living together, evangelistic teams, and even parties. Group exercises, simulations which reflect field stress, and just our life together sheds so much light on our strengths and weaknesses, such as our creativity, independence, conflict styles, leadership skills, listening ability, and so on. It is so important to understand and improve our reactions under stress.

There are many important aspects of training to consider, including formal and non-formal approaches for language and culture learning, technical skills, etc. My emphasis here, though, is on the need to train our workers to persevere during trials and suffering, especially while on the field. This is a crucial area in which we as trainers and administrators also need to grow!

Practical Understanding of Suffering

As I have shared, missionary candidates need to understand biblical principles about suffering, perseverance, and trust in God. All these were part of Jesus' teaching and life. The preaching of the gospel frequently involves suffering, rejection, and persecution. Training should include general as well as specific challenges of the mission field, so that candidates can begin to adjust some of their expectations and coping strategies. Cultural and sociological studies will help them to understand their own weaknesses and their strengths to persevere. They also must understand their own culture and how it can impact their longevity either positively or negatively. They need to be exposed to the reality of suffering, by actually being at the place where it is happening (visiting hospitals, slums, etc.) and also by seeing it through videos or other forms of media. The ability to appraise a situation realistically is also an important cross-cultural and life skill. The important thing is that candidates need to think ahead about suffering and about how they will cope with it once they are exposed to it.

I remember visiting a Brazilian couple in Eastern Europe, prior to the collapse of Communism. They worked with an organization that supported the suffering church, bringing literature and encouragement. Part of their training included a simulated interrogation that was so real that some participants could not handle it. I believe that we need more of this kind of training. Theory can become practice, before one even sets foot in the new culture.

Seeing and living among people who are suffering great pain are bound to produce inner reactions and behavioral responses. Suffering can produce apathy, fear, irritability, and depression, along with physical and psychosomatic pains. With apathy comes an inner bleakness, a lack of interest in oneself and one's surroundings, and finally, a lack of energy to do one's job. Personal losses which are part of missions (e.g., many farewells, relocation) can have similar effects. The same can be said of team conflicts.

A missionary from Brazil, working in a village in Eastern Africa, lived through a brief civil war. She faced daily fear, insecurity, and lack of basic things such as food. In retrospect, she said, "I was there, I lived in situations of great pain, but it was worthwhile!" She was not focused on herself. Rather, what was really meaningful to her was being able to help others. She felt that all the suffering that she experienced was compensated by the support and love she received from others. She worked hard and took risks, but nothing could deter her from her commitment to seeing a school being built and people being saved. I believe that finding meaning in life, in part through caring for others, is one of our basic needs as humans. It is a core asset for cross-cultural coping too!

Models and Mentors

Missionary training must be done in a context where teachers and students can develop a relationship that goes beyond the classroom. This is more of an informal approach to learning. Teachers are friends, partners, and at times counselors. It is a discipleship process in which the teacher is a model. Values, interests, and attitudes become more transparent and can be held up to the light of biblical teaching. The candidates are trained to be agents of change, in the same way the teachers need to be agents of transformation in the lives of the candidates.

This approach brings a great deal of responsibility to the leaders. Teaching is more than transmitting knowledge. Teachers must also demonstrate in their own lives what they teach. Mission teachers need to have experienced the challenges of the mission field. They also need to have a good understanding of the areas in their own culture and life that had to change in order for them to be effective.

Spiritual Growth

I see spiritual growth as mostly involving informal training which aims to strengthen important habits, especially spiritual habits. The spiritual disciplines need to be cultivated, since they help a person to live a life devoted to God and to good deeds. Prayer, worship, simplicity, giving, solitude, Scripture, and fasting are important in our everyday life. It is through these practices, both on the field and off the field, that the abundant life that Jesus taught will be a reality.

The Valley of Blessing is a missionary training center in Brazil, located where Antioch Mission has its headquarters. This is a good example of a place where devotional life is strongly emphasized. In the heart of the property is a prayer center, where a prayer vigil is maintained. The students are included in this program, and each person regularly sets aside 90 minutes to pray there. Inside the chapel, there are seven small rooms for individual prayer. In each of these rooms, there are two books, one containing prayer requests for the Valley of Blessing itself and the other containing requests for the missionaries who are serving around the world. Missionaries who have been sent from this center testify that the lessons they learned from this prayer experience have been a blessing in their life on the field. Prayer makes a difference.

Conclusion

It is very important to consider how we are training our mission candidates. Missionary training must include the Christian teaching about suffering and perseverance. Candidates need to be exposed in advance to stressful situations along with healthy community life. Training needs to include all areas: cognitive, affective, spiritual, and behavioral. Teachers contribute best by mentoring through their lifestyles, as true disciples of Christ themselves. May we trust God to help us as trainers to prepare missionaries as best as possible to face the many challenges on the field. May they persevere with God's help and the help of friends, in their calls to the unreached.

You might be curious to know about what happened to the missionary mentioned at the beginning of the chapter. She went back to the same African country where she had been held hostage. She returned one year later, after having received physical, emotional, and spiritual support and refreshment. She serves with a local church and has developed an important work in the areas of health care and teaching. To answer my question at the beginning, I would say, "Yes, by the grace of God, she *was* prepared to persevere!"

Reflection and Discussion

1. List a few principles and key verses on the biblical teaching of suffering and perseverance. How do these relate to your experience?
2. Which aspects of your own culture/upbringing could contribute either positively or negatively to the adjustment of the missionary in situations marked with much suffering?
3. What are some practical ideas mission teachers could use in their training centers to increase the awareness of the candidates towards suffering?
4. What recommendations would you make to candidates—singles and couples with children—who will likely experience significant suffering during their ministry?
5. What resources are available to your mission to help those who return from fields where they faced suffering?

References and Suggested Reading

Adiwardana, M. (1999). *Missionários: Preparando-os para perseverar (Preparing to persevere)*. São Paulo, Brazil: Descoberta.

O'Donnell, K. (Ed.). (1992). *Missionary care: Counting the cost for world evangelization*. Pasadena, CA: William Carey Library.

Taylor, W. (Ed.). (1998). *Valioso demais para que se perca (Too valuable to lose)*. London, UK: Descoberta.

***Márcia Tostes** is a missionary with Antioch Mission, a Brazilian missionary organization, where she serves as the Director for Pastoral Care. She and her husband, Silas, were trained at All Nations Christian College in England. Her vision for pastoral care began in the UK while at this college, and since then she has been specializing in the subject. At the moment, she is studying family therapy. She is a member of the WEA Missions Commission and helps to coordinate the Brazilian Pastoral Care Working Group and the COMIBAM Pastoral Care Working Group. Márcia and Silas have two boys and are living in Brazil. Email: antioquiabrasil@uol.com.br.*

I appreciate the help of Durvalina Bezerra, Margaretha Adiwardana, and Rosimeire Lopes de Souza, who reviewed this article and offered suggestions.

18

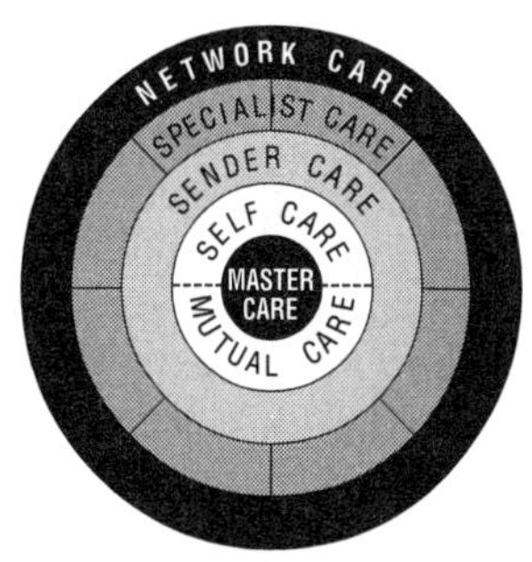

Holding On to the Good: A Short Experience For Emotional Debriefing

ESLY CARVALHO

This chapter describes a group debriefing session that lasts about three hours and that is useful for missionaries returning from the field. It is aimed at processing gains and losses on the field, expectations for furlough, and the eventual return (or not) to the missionary field. It offers a quick and practical evaluation of the past, present, and future regarding missionary work. This approach is useful for Latin American missionaries and others as well.

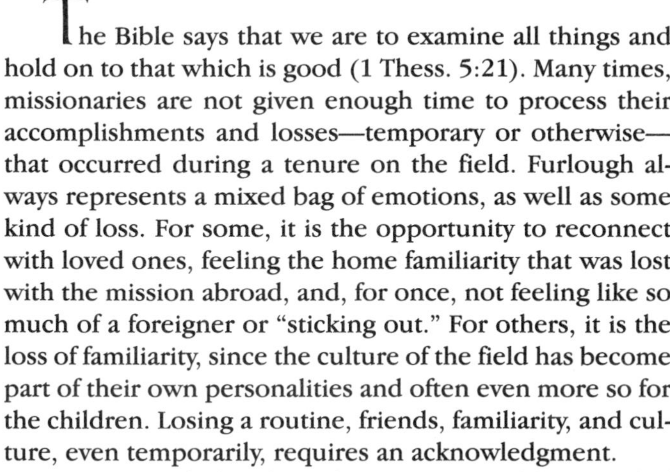

The Bible says that we are to examine all things and hold on to that which is good (1 Thess. 5:21). Many times, missionaries are not given enough time to process their accomplishments and losses—temporary or otherwise—that occurred during a tenure on the field. Furlough always represents a mixed bag of emotions, as well as some kind of loss. For some, it is the opportunity to reconnect with loved ones, feeling the home familiarity that was lost with the mission abroad, and, for once, not feeling like so much of a foreigner or "sticking out." For others, it is the loss of familiarity, since the culture of the field has become part of their own personalities and often even more so for the children. Losing a routine, friends, familiarity, and culture, even temporarily, requires an acknowledgment.

In contrast, furlough is often a very unstable period of visits and fundraisers, traveling from town to town, home to home, oftentimes dragging unwilling teenagers along. Younger children miss the daily routine of home. At other times, furlough means spending a year in a new school environment with new challenges, both in academics as well as social skills. Latin American missionaries especially struggle with raising financial support for a return to the field or even making ends meet at home. This is due to the concept that missionaries should live as poor as church mice, as well as to poor follow-through on pledges made. And then there are the issues of changes in child education. Home schooling is not an option at this point, and children on furlough will usually go to school in a different language/culture than they had been studying in on the field.

Finally, there are expectations, often unspoken, about the future return to the field. Sometimes missionaries do not return to the same place of service, which *really* entails an enormous loss to be processed. Other times, there will be new assignments within the mission itself, even if returning to the same locale. It is a good idea to bring up these expectations as soon as possible, in order to figure out which ones are realistic, scary, or comforting, so that missionaries can have a better sense of stability in a very uncertain environment.

Debriefing Workshop

The following short workshop provides an opportunity to begin to look at all of these issues. The exercises will be presented with accompanying comments. In ideal terms, many of the issues that come out of such a debriefing procedure will already have been discussed in some fashion within the family and the mission structure. It is hoped that the missionary organization has in place means of communicating missionary needs in acceptable and safe ways, while the workers are still on the field.

Many organizations do have certain structures that show pastoral care and concern for their missionaries, but oftentimes the focus is limited to operational debriefing. This type of debriefing has its merit, of course. (*How many people were led to the Lord? What were your specific activities on the field? etc.*) A common complaint of missionaries, though, is that they do not have a "place" where they can unwind about what is going on and not risk retaliation or rejection for their feelings. Being able to open up and share about one's feelings is an important aspect of missionary "health care." (*How did you feel about certain decisions? What would have been better for your family? How does this impact your relationship with the mission? etc.*) It is interesting to note that Jesus debriefed the apostles on their return from their "missionary incursions" (Luke 9:10; 10:17). Suffice it to say that this particular exercise has emotional debriefing as its primary goal in the context of bridging missionary needs and organizational needs.

It would be good to provide this framework for returning missionaries as soon as possible upon their return. It will ease furloughs, as well as give the missionaries and leadership at headquarters an opportunity to discuss relevant issues. Obviously, a three-hour workshop is not sufficient to cover the whole reentry process. One would hope that the missionary organization has already offered guidelines and materials prior to missionaries' return. As missionary agencies in Latin America mature, these issues are becoming more and more important in avoiding missionary burnout and subsequent resignation.

These debriefing workshops were developed in the framework of trust and confidentiality among returning missionaries, and they are basically for the benefit of the participants. Children and teenagers can benefit from such an exercise as well and need it just as much as the adults. Leadership at headquarters was not privy to the information that came out of these workshops, which was one of the reasons for success. Missionaries were free to "let down their hair" in a private and caring atmosphere, without fear of retaliation for not "performing" according to the expectations put on them. Obviously, they were free to use the information gleaned from the workshop about themselves as they pleased, but they were also kept to confidentiality regarding their peers who participated. Not all missions will be willing to allow for this level of transparency, but it is essential for the good outcome of this particular process. Participants felt encouraged when they realized that they were not the only ones struggling with certain issues or decisions. The exercise gave them a reality check, as well as perspective and insights into their experiences.

The leader of these workshops (a trained and experienced group psychotherapist) was not part of the mission and had no emotional stake regarding what went on or regarding future decisions relating to the missionaries. This was a completely neutral and outside person, with no prior knowledge of the participants, brought in specifically for this task, which also heightened the trusting atmosphere. No report was given to the mission headquarters about what went on, but many participants were encouraged to discuss certain hurts and painful decisions with the missionary organization. This workshop was offered in the framework of a week-long reentry and debriefing exercise provided by the missionary organization, through which their returnees were normally routed.

Instructions

What follows is a sample of the instructions given at the start of the session:

"This workshop will enable you to evaluate the years that each of you has just spent on the field and to sort out the things that you want to hold on to. We will also look at expectations for the furlough and focus a bit on future hopes.

"This will be done through a few action exercises, drawings, and sharing with each other about the wealth of experiences each has had. Hopefully, we will leave the workshop with a sense of closure and perhaps new insights regarding the experience.

"We expect that everyone present will maintain confidentiality about what may be shared here from a personal perspective regarding any of the others.

"Please feel free to share as much or as little as you desire. There is no obligation to disclose anything. However, you will get as much out of the workshop as you put into it. If you feel unable to adhere to these rules, we ask that you discreetly leave now." (No one has ever left.)

The Workshop

Step 1

The participants are asked to introduce themselves, where they are from, and where they served on the field during their last term. (The leader introduced herself first, emphasizing her own cross-cultural experiences, which helped put the members at ease.) Oftentimes, the participants already know each other, but this is not always the case and should not be taken for granted. Nametags are helpful (especially for the workshop leader!). Usually the leader knows very little about the participants. It is helpful to know which ones will not be returning to the field (for example, due to retirement), so that introductions can include those aspects.

Step 2

The participants are given white sheets of paper and boxes of crayons and asked to draw a picture of their experience on the field during this last term. Mention is made of what they left behind. Some people will always protest that they can't draw and will ask if they can write about their experience instead. It is explained to the group that most people cannot draw better than a five-year-old and that this is not an artistic competition. Writing is not an acceptable alternative, since the idea is to access the symbolic part of the brain that is fast, creative ("a picture is worth a thousand words"), and more connected to the emotions. It is also the part of the brain that helps change behavior.

Once the pictures have been drawn, the group is asked to share them in small groups of four or five people (couples should be separated). Pictures usually include significant friends and situations they have left behind, a special pet, and/or religious symbols (such as the Bible, God, etc.). After the small groups are finished sharing, they are asked to pray for one another.

Often this is a very emotional time as participants begin to share about what they have gone through in the last term and what they have left behind. Boxes of tissue should be available to the groups, since tears are commonplace. This is an important part of the process, and the emotions, often strong, are not to be stifled nor suppressed. It may be the only opportunity that participants will have to let out some of the strong feelings they have had regarding this past experience. Prayer for each other usually brings adequate closure to the exercise. Participants are encouraged to acknowledge the enormity of some of their losses and to allow themselves to grieve.

Step 3

Once again in the large group, participants are asked to symbolically "pull out" of the picture what they would like to hold on to: things they have learned, people they have come to love, things they care about, etc. They are asked to place the item on the part of their body where they would like to keep it forever. For example, a woman may pull out the friendships she has made and place them over her heart. Or perhaps someone will pull out what he has learned and will put it on his head for future reference. One participant pulled out his family and put them in his hand. ("They are engraved in the palm of my hand.")

This is often a very touching and moving exercise, done in the big group, where others have an opportunity to see what each one would like to "hold on to" from their previous experience. Usually only positive experiences are pulled out and kept.

Step 4

Finally, a "start" and a "finish" line are drawn with masking tape on the floor, about five meters apart. Participants are asked to take off the shoe of the foot that will symbolically take the next step into their future, to show what they envision furlough, retirement, or leaving the field will be like in the ensuing months. All together, they line up at the starting line and move their own shoe the way they feel that the next few months will be like, until they reach the finish line.

It is very interesting to see how different people envision their futures in such different ways. Once, a participant took both shoes with him, saying, "I go into everything with both feet." Another time, one person went round and round and wondered if she would ever arrive at the finish line. Others made beelines to the finish: they knew where they were going. Still others took faltering steps, uncertain of what lay ahead. Some did the exercise in silence; others maintained a running commentary. In some groups, participants do the activity one at a time; most do it all together.

Step 5

This is the time for final sharing and closure. The participants are asked to share about what they learned during the exercises, as well as what this opportunity to debrief emotionally meant to them.

Conclusion

It is hoped that this simple exercise will encourage sending groups, from Latin America and elsewhere, to invest in the emotional debriefing of their field personnel. Note that children can also benefit from the exercise and have a lot of fun with it. It is common for missionaries to be debriefed regarding what they have done, including their accomplishments and difficulties, but few get the opportunity to share from the heart about their experiences. And "heart" experiences can be quite different from the "head" experiences. Sometimes they can even be at odds with each other. Even though believers "know" what has happened, it is important to let the feelings come out, whatever they may be. Unresolved feelings and unsatisfied or unrealistic expectations can lead to future problems for both mission and missionary, which is why this exercise can be so valuable. If necessary, participants are discreetly encouraged to seek out counseling, give themselves time in their grieving process, share certain aspects of the exercise with their supervisors, or follow other procedures which might be helpful to them.

Action exercises tend to draw out a lot of information very quickly. In Latin cultures, they have been especially helpful because of the "dramatic quality" of the

Latinos. Women tend to be more comfortable sharing their feelings, but it was amazing to see how many men also opened up, given the chance. The men especially like the shoe exercise. All of the participants commented positively on having been given an opportunity to *do* it instead of having to listen to long lectures on the reentry process itself. It was a good way of getting them "off and running" into furlough and reentry.

Reflection and Discussion

1. Why is emotional debriefing important? What type of experiences have you had with debriefing?
2. How should confidential information be handled in group debriefing sessions?
3. In what ways could children be involved in their own debriefing sessions?
4. What are the advantages and disadvantages of having an outside person do the debriefing?
5. How can sending organizations include debriefing in their member care toolbox?

***Esly Regina Carvalho** is a Brazilian-American licensed psychotherapist, specializing in group therapy and psychodrama. She maintains a practice (Plaza del Encuentro) in Quito, Ecuador, where she lives with her husband, Ken Grant, an MK raised in China, and her daughter, Raquel. Esly is the author of many articles on counseling, recovery, and emotional healing and is fluent in three languages, Portuguese, English, and Spanish. She is presently leading Christian counseling training workshops through action methods. Email: plazadelencuentro@attglobal.net.*

19

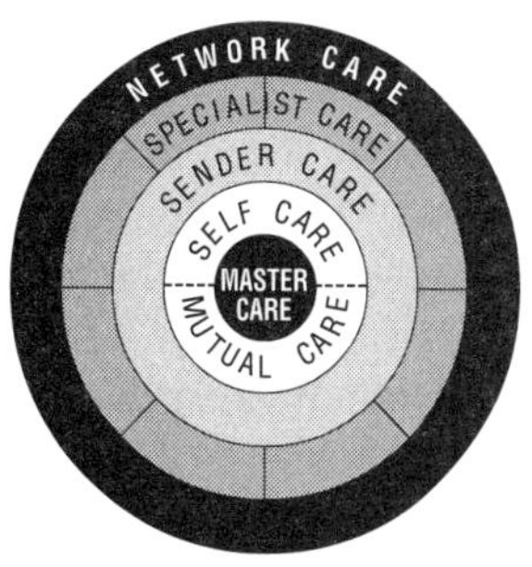

Ministering Wisely in the Middle East: Christian Service Under Pressure

Naji Abi-Hashem
Anneke Companjen

Understanding the social and historical context of the Middle East, along with the cultural and religious values of the people, is key to working effectively in this region. Pastors, missionaries, and national Christians must live wisely and righteously as they seek to shine the light of Christ, often in the midst of intense pressures. They face serious struggles, and at times they may go through suffering and persecution, as the cases at the end recount. Naji writes the first part of this chapter and Anneke the second part.

The Middle East is a vast and diverse area of the world. Its people are friendly and hospitable, and in most places life is beautiful, easy, meaningful, and tranquil. In other troubled areas, though, life is marked by tension, stress, conflicts, and hostility. The region has a wide variety of subcultures, norms, traditions, and customs. It is a place where ancient civilizations meet modern lifestyles. The Middle East serves as the gateway to three major continents. Its people are still rooted in the land, as they deeply cherish their traditions, values, faiths, and cultures. Most urban people operate well within the modern, Western lifestyle, without losing their cultural heritage or religious identity. Christian workers in the Middle East encounter many rewards and joys. At the same time, they face serious challenges and struggles. Depending on the situation and location, Christian service is limited and shaped by the surrounding circumstances, traditions, subcultures, social norms, and political climate.

Presently, the Christian presence in many quarters of the Middle East is being diminished and weakened. Unfortunately, as we enter the third millennium, the Christian communities are decreasing in number, in presence, and in influence. In some areas, serious persecution is taking place. These are alarming signs. Many church leaders, both in the East and in the West, are deeply concerned about these new developments. Many provinces, communities, and towns that were predominantly Christian in the recent past are now gradually losing ground and becoming equally mixed or predominantly non-Christian (mostly Muslim). There are numerous reasons for this current phenomenon, including political tension, economic hardship, civil unrest, and religious oppression.

All of these factors are causing migration in large numbers, especially for those who can afford to leave. Migration is high among the young and educated, particularly those from unfortunate and less established communities.

Christian families are traditionally smaller, and many young adults opt to remain single, which is a little more acceptable within the Christian communities and in urban settings than in other places. In addition, there are scores of young priests and nuns who dedicate themselves to celibacy and ecclesiastical life (which means fewer offspring).

So, the Christian community and the Christian presence in the Middle East are shrinking! My (Naji's) homeland, Lebanon, for example, used to be predominantly a Christian nation, with about 85% Christians and the rest a mix of Druze and Muslims. Now the Christian community counts for about 35% and is declining.

Lebanon is as old as the biblical times. It was once prosperous and successful and a model of co-existence. It was a place where culture, education, ethnicity, religion, civilization, and political persuasion met and formed a successful democratic republic, manifesting a balanced harmony and healthy integration. The country was hospitable and free, modern in function, and open to the East, the West, and the international community. Currently, it has a rich variety of subcultures, socioeconomic classes, and traditions. Its population is about 3.5 million, with another 13 million Lebanese of all generations living outside the country.

Since Lebanon reflects the miniature Middle East and the gate to the Arabic and European worlds, most religious sects and subcultures are represented in it in some measure. The Maronite, Catholic, Greek Orthodox, and Eastern churches are all strong. Protestants are a minority. The Jews were established in many cities. But since the political turmoil started, the majority of Jews reluctantly migrated from Lebanon and neighboring countries, leaving behind their homes, Arabic heritage, and synagogues. The Shiites are the larger Muslim group. They are, however, socially and economically less established than the Sunnis. The Arabic and old Middle Eastern way of life are still observed in villages and rural areas in the mountains, valleys, and deserts—less in Lebanon now and more in the surrounding countries.

All these dynamics, together with the rapid changes in the Middle East, are affecting the local churches and missionary work. Churches of all types are struggling to adjust and, at times, readjust over and over again to the new developments and emerging needs. They have to adapt quickly to new regimes, political systems, social trends, and religious realities. They have to change approaches, switch places, apply new labels, and carefully guard their ministries or else completely stop their activities. At times, they must sit and wait patiently until the dust settles down again after each turbulence. In vulnerable and changing areas of the Middle East, nothing is taken for granted.

Historically, the Middle East has been the birthplace of most civilizations and religions. There are several groups in the Arab world that are religiously radical (zealous to the cause of Islam as the only true religion) and politically angry (because of the invasion of Western imperialism and culture and also because of the presence of Israel and its behaviors in the region). Some individuals would fight anybody anywhere, using any means to press their ultimate cause. Some are paid or indoctrinated to do so, as is the case in any troubled spot in the world. However, the vast majority of the Arabic people are friendly, moderate, peaceful, God-fearing, and hospitable.

Although Christians are declining in influence both politically and financially in most areas of the Middle East and North Africa, they are gaining spiritually. There seems to be a kind of renewal and return to the fountains of faith and to Christian churches. There is a fresh sense of collaboration and camaraderie among Christian groups, which has often been the case throughout history when believers have faced pressure, opposition, or persecution. The churches have to unite and mobilize their efforts and energy, in order to face the challenges and reach out to those in need. Unfavorable conditions are gradually drawing Christians together and sharpening their faith, witness, and service. This is the current situation in the Middle East, and this is where hundreds of pastors and missionaries are faithfully trying to serve, respond to ever-changing conditions, provide care, maintain a presence, and, at times, merely survive in an unpredictable climate and under unfriendly circumstances.

Common Misperceptions

There are a number of misunderstandings and misconceptions regarding the Arabic world and the Middle East in general, especially in the Western mind and media. Such ideas often take the form of inaccurate impressions or sociocultural stereotypes which can be very misleading and, at times, dangerous (Abi-Hashem, 1992). They need to be corrected, especially in the minds of Western Christians who are interested in supporting churches and ministries in the Middle East.

All Arabs Are Muslims

Although the majority of Arabs are Muslims, there are significant Christian communities in the region, in some countries more than others. Middle East historians have documented the presence of Christianity in the Arabic peninsula centuries before Islam. Early church missionaries spread east from Jerusalem to the deserts, reaching multitudes of local tribes and Bedouin Arabs, and then continued to the Far East until they reached the tip of India. Many of the Christians in Arabia converted to Islam, either under direct threat of repeated holy Muslim raids or through indirect pressure which made conversion a matter of necessity for survival. Since then, Islam has kept expanding to become one of the major religious and political systems in the world. It is, today, one of the fastest growing religions in the world. Islamic strategists are mobilizing intense missions and evangelistic efforts to reach both the contemporary/affluent world and the developing/underprivileged countries with the message of the Quran.

Some Muslims, just like Christians, are such by affiliation and heritage only. They are not necessarily "practicing" or committed Muslims. However, religious affiliation is still an integral part of people's sense of community and part of their social identity. In the Middle East, there is usually no sharp division between religion and government. Both are intertwined, along with the cultural heritage and social customs. Therefore, people and leaders are not afraid of referring to God or making room for their faiths or respecting each other's practices and customs in private, in public, in business, or in politics.

Presently, the largest Christian presence in the Arabic world is found in Egypt, although it is still considered a minority when compared to the total population of that country. It is mainly represented by the historic, yet active Coptic church, a North African form of the Eastern Orthodox. Other mainline Christian denominations, parachurch organizations, and other bodies and institutions are present as well. But lately, most of them have been under serious pressure and even persecution. The rise of Islamic fundamentalism and the residual effects of the Gulf War in 1991 strongly fed into the anti-West, anti-Christianity movement in the Arabic world.

In most Muslim countries, Christian gatherings and activities are restricted. In Jordan, Syria, Iraq, and Egypt, where the system is moderate, churches have limited freedom as the state keeps an eye on them. Depending on the religious system of the particular country, the day of worship for the churches is normally Friday, because Sunday is a regular business day. Preachers and church leaders have to monitor carefully what they say, because a secret intelligence agent may be present at any church service or activity.

In Saudi Arabia, Libya, Qatar, Yemen, Bahrain, Morocco, and Kuwait, where the state law is mostly Islamic, few or no church buildings are allowed. In some cases, meeting houses or worship halls are permitted to foreigners only. Approaching a local resident in any form of direct evangelization or persuasion is against the law and is severely punished. Punishment may take the form of withdrawing hard-to-obtain permission to meet as a religious group or even deportation of the people involved. In highly restricted countries, national believers meet secretly for Bible study and prayer, while closely monitoring doors, windows, and telephone lines.

The most free and democratic country in the whole region has been Lebanon. Up until the last decade, Lebanon used to be known as the Christian nation in the Middle East, because the vast majority of its population were Christians. It has been the home of many Christian organizations, seminaries, agencies, and publication houses which have been serving the needs of the church communities in the area. The presidency and most of the key posts in the government, army, and judicial system were held by figures from the Christian community. Other countries in the region are largely monarchies, semi-democratic systems, or still ruled by a one-party regime.

Lebanon had a very distinct cultural characteristic that separated it from other countries in the Middle East. Beirut is a strategic gate and cosmopolitan city that is open to both the East and the West. Although it is part of the Arabic world by affiliation, culture, and language, yet it is European and Western in many ways, especially in its urban lifestyle, education, exposure, finance, and international affairs. All the other Christian communities in the whole Arabic world used to look to Lebanon for leadership, encouragement, networking, and moral support that enhanced their minority status in their own community.

While not all Arabs are Muslims, note too that not all Muslims are Arabs. Indonesia (the largest Muslim country), Iran, Pakistan, Turkey, and several African nations are legally and religiously Muslim, but culturally and ethnically they are not Arabic. In addition, large populations in the Far East, the former Soviet Union, and recently in the West are also Muslims.

Not all Middle Easterners are Arabs either. Although Iran is a Middle Eastern country, it is not Arabic but rather Persian. Cyprus is a Middle Eastern island, but half of its population is Greek, and the other half is Turkish. Cyprus is ruled by Turkey, another non-Arab nation. Algeria, Egypt, Libya, Tunisia, and Morocco are North African yet are largely Arabic nations and members of the Arabic League of Nations.

All Arabs Are Primitive People

"The first images that come to the Westerner's mind when he thinks of the Arabs are sand, desert, camels, oil wells, irrational mobs ... and the like" (Hamady, 1960, p. 229). This is a socioeconomic stereotype. "The Western world must realize that ignorance about Arabian culture and history is not 'bliss,' but a detriment to international relations" (Hamada, 1990, p. 128). That is also true of Western Christians and missionaries who are interested in investing efforts in this region. Unfortunately, many well-meaning organizations and individuals jump into the field without adequate preparation or careful consultation. The results are usually unfavorable and negative on all levels.

As is the case with other large regions, the Arabic people and nations have a wide variety of societies, subcultures, economic levels, and traditions. On one end of the spectrum, there are the oldest and most traditional lifestyles, found in villages, small towns, and among the nomads. On the other end, there are the contemporary and most complex lifestyles. Since the region is deeply rooted in land and history, many traditions and characteristics of the people are transferred through the generations and are woven into the fabric of social structure and communal living like threads of gold.

Not all Middle Eastern countries have oil, deserts, or wealth. Some are rich and well-established, while others are struggling and still developing. Lebanon, for example, was a leader in the whole region in terms of finances, education, tourism, and income per capita, although it has no oil, deserts, or camels. For decades it was called the Switzerland of the Middle East. Not anymore! Small nations often pay the price of regional conflicts and become victims of world politics. This has been the experience of Lebanon, where interference of other nations has significantly deteriorated and disintegrated the country. The Lebanese people deeply grieve the loss of their identity, their accomplishments, their uniqueness, and most probably their country. With the winds of change and unpredictable politics in the region, Lebanon may become another Cyprus or perhaps a second Palestine. It may lose its role as a leading "Christian" nation, its social and religious freedom, its historic capacity to train church leaders for the whole Middle East, and its ability to host most of the European and North American mission and parachurch organizations that serve the Near East and North Africa.

All Arabs Are Fanatics and Terrorists

In the minds of some Westerners, the term Arabic is equivalent to fanatic, radical Muslim, uncivilized, or even terrorist. This misconception could be the result, in part, of a biased media, uninformed reports, or misleading news agencies. Some Arabs, living or traveling in the West, refer to themselves as Middle Easterners rather than Arabs, because of the recent stereotypes associated with the term.

The reality is that there are different types of Muslim societies. There are the *traditional* (good and simple-hearted people, mostly rural, who enjoy a peaceful community life and a rich cultural heritage), the *secular* (mostly educated and business people, who live in fairly open and progressively complex societies), the *fundamental* (highly dedicated, zealous, and radically committed to the sociopolitical and religious causes of Islam to an extreme stand), the *moderate* (balanced in views and practices, as individuals, groups, or countries), and, finally, the *national* (who strive to establish a regime uniting the government, religion, and social life by applying the Islamic civil laws and regulations to all aspects of personal, communal, and societal affairs) (for further analysis, see Voll, 1982).

In the understanding of some "cultural" Muslims, such as Abd Al-Masih (1996), Islam is not just another religion or religious option, as many Westerners define it. "Islam is a theocentric religion" (p. 50). Real Muslims, as some of the minority "fundamentalists" explain, must aim toward a Theocratic State. Such religious states reflect the spiritual, cultural, and civil systems integrated together. According to Abd Al-Masih, there is a striking difference between Islam and Christianity regarding the view of religious wars and the use of force: Allah in the Quran commands the faithful Muslims to strive, and he promises that those who die in the holy jihad "hope to ascend directly into paradise" (p. 60). Mohammed is believed to have taken part in some raids, and his model "remains the unique ideal for all Islamic wars in the name of Allah" (p. 60).

The rise of "extremists" or "fanatics"—by far the minority—as an extreme form of resistance or, as they consider themselves, freedom fighters and carriers of supreme ideological causes in Allah's service, has reshaped the whole atmosphere in the Middle East and North Africa. Obviously, there are major reasons that so many groups are angry with the West in general and are hostile toward the United States in particular. Increasingly, they resent the West for its cultural invasion, economic exploitation, political oppression, military superiority, and imperialistic greed. They are specifically angry at the U.S. government for its unconditional and excessive support of the state of Israel. For devout Muslims, Jerusalem is an extremely important place. It is their third holiest city, after Mecca (Makkah) and Al-Madina, both in Saudi Arabia. In addition, those who "have little or nothing" can resent the level of materialism, hedonism, and affluent consumption of those who "have a lot and plenty." Also, some equate Christianity with the West and remember with bad taste the history of European Crusaders who invaded the Arabic region and the Muslim world. Furthermore, they react negatively to the corrupt lifestyles, products, items, and movies that the West constantly exports to the Middle East.

Understanding the major types of Muslim communities and the basic belief system of Islam has tremendous implications for any Christian work or workers in the Middle East. Depending on the kind of society and level of religious dedication where Christian pastors and missionaries decide to locate and serve, they must be careful in their approaches, language, and activities. The ultimate goal is to be accepted and effective in making needed contributions and, at the same time, avoiding any provocative mistakes or unnecessary offenses to the hosting community and the larger Middle Eastern society.

Historical and Religious Background

The terms Arabia and Arabah refer to the plains and wilderness. "The Arabs and Hebrews originally did not comprise either a nation or nationality. They were nomadic tribes wandering in the wilderness" (Hamada, 1990, p. 41). Most Westerners would be surprised to know that Arabs and Jews come from the same origin, "and both of them are called Semites" (p. 40). Also, the term Arab means "desert" and is probably derived from the Hebrew word Eber. "Eber literally refers to the people living 'over the other side,' or 'beyond the river [Euphrates].' Abir is the Arabic word for Eber, meaning 'to cross over'" (p. 40). In the Quran, the word Arab is also used to describe Bedouins and nomads. One of the biblical references to Arabs occurs in Jeremiah 25:24, "all the kings of Arabia and all the kings of the mixed tribes that dwell in the desert."

Although the word Islam in Arabic has the connotation of peace, fundamentally it means a total submission to the will of Allah. Islam calls for a complete surrender to God, the only One, Transcendent, and the Most High. Allah is remote and invisible, and true and faithful Muslims can only follow his laws and teachings as brought by Mohammed, who is God's closing Messenger and the Seal of God's Prophets. Mohammed appeared to be a deep thinker and a great reformer. He diligently learned about spiritual life and piety and boldly confronted paganism and social disorder of his day. His reputation quickly spread, and his message was broadly embraced. The phase of pre-Islamic Arabia, *al-jahileyya*, was referred to as a time of ignorance before Mohammed introduced "the true way." Although there were monotheist tribes around the area, which Mohammed respected and which attracted him by their faith in one God, he desired to unify Arabia and Islam.

Thus, the rise and expansion of Islam as a strong religious, cultural, and political movement resulted in the birth of a major world civilization that enjoyed significant prosperity and advances in architecture, science, and literature, while most of Europe was still struggling in dark history. That was definitely the golden age of Islam. Many Muslim groups and nations are presently trying to restore that glory. They are still hoping to recover the full power of Islam and are dreaming about its full unity and expansion. Many Muslim nations have great financial resources, mainly from the rich wells of oil, known to them as black gold. As such, they feel especially blessed by Allah and deeply obligated to preserve and spread his only true way (Youssef, 1991).

Essentially, Islam is a way of life guided by a set of beliefs, specific doctrines, spiritual rules, civil laws, and social norms. The vast interpretations of the Islamic teachings fill volumes of detailed commentaries pertaining to almost every aspect of communal life, personal behavior, and family conduct. It is important to keep in mind that Islam is like any other large, historic religion in that it contains several branches and schools of thought, as well as various traditions and cultural distinctives. Devout Muslims of all traditions strongly feel responsible to Allah to obey his laws and carry on his causes. Islam stresses the oneness of God and his unity and sovereignty. There is a great deal of overlap of stories, and there are many parallel themes between Christianity and Islam, between the Bible and the Quran.

Six Tenets of Islamic Faith

1. *Al-Shahaada*—the profession of faith. "I proclaim that there is no God but Allah (the One God), and Mohammed is the messenger (Rassooll) of Allah." This tenet is the key to becoming and remaining a true Muslim.

2. *Al-Salaatt*—prescribed prayers, five times daily, public or private, facing Makkah (Mecca), their holiest city. A prayer call is usually broadcasted from the minaret of mosques around the Muslim world. Prayers are not conversations with God, but rather tasks and repetitions of set lines, in order to obey God's demands and please him. At death, only Allah has the last word about who goes to Paradise and who goes to Fire. Moslems hope their conduct, deeds, and spiritual sincerity will weigh heavier than their sins, so that God will rule in their favor. They are free to utter personal prayers after they recite the expected ones.

3. *Al-Zakaat*—giving alms, a requirement of practicing the faith. Giving in any form and to any good cause would qualify as well (such as Islamic missions). Beggars take advantage of such practices, especially around Muslim holidays.

4. *Al-Sa'uom*—fasting, mostly limited to the holy month of Ramadan, when the Quran is believed to have been given or directly revealed to Mohammed. The Muslim year is based on 12 lunar months.

5. *Al-Hajj*—pilgrimage to Makkah. It must be made during a certain window of time of the Muslim lunar calendar and must be made at least once in a lifetime. Millions of Muslims from around the world gather in Saudi Arabia in what is known to be the largest single religious pilgrimage in history.

6. *Al-Jihad*—striving for a holy cause or serving Allah with fervent zeal and supreme effort. This term may have both a soft and a strong connotation. It can be applied on the personal level (e.g., an individual quest toward purity and piety), as well as on the communal or national level (e.g., seeking greater dedication to Islam as a country). If necessary, it can take an intense or extreme meaning like "fighting a holy war," which is believed to be the duty of every dedicated Muslim—man or woman, boy or girl—in the face of corruption, threat, or injustice. Jihad is called for in order to defend, empower, or reform the faith. Although most Muslims are friendly and compassionate people, yet inside the core of Muslim doctrine there is room for extreme views, extreme interpretations, and radical positions, which easily can lead to militant sentiments and the use of aggression or force.

It is no secret that not only organizations and groups support the multiple efforts to spread out the Islamic faith and its practice, but certain official governments send major funding to advance the cause of Islam worldwide. They are supporting a variety of intense efforts to teach the Quran and win converts in Africa, to empower Muslim communities and struggling nations in the former Soviet Union, and to build large mosques and Islamic centers throughout Europe and North America. Islamic strategists are using methods, devices, and approaches similar to those used by Christians in evangelism and missionary work. According to Wertsman (2001, p. 42), "Despite the disproportionate number of Christian Arabs, the influx of Muslim Arabs has contributed to Islam becoming one of the fastest-growing religions in the United States. It is believed that in the next few decades, Muslims will outnumber Jews in the United States."

As the Muslim message is going further West, the Christian message is going further East. However, many Muslim nations closely protect their people and their borders from any Christian influence. They are concerned about any Christian or non-Muslim penetration. They do not allow any freedom of religion besides Islam, which is to them the only religion. Such countries are known to be restrictive and operate under severe laws (reinforcing Islamic law). They tend to oppose and, at times, persecute any non-Muslim beliefs and activity. Christian workers who live in such environments must carefully watch their movements, relationships, and activities. In contrast, Western countries in general offer Muslim (and other) immigrants and strategists freedom to move, worship, teach, recruit others, and practice their faith and customs.

Challenges Facing Christian Ministry

The more active an Evangelical or Protestant ministry is, the more resistance it may face. This resistance may come not only from non-Christian religious leaders, from the state, or from the radical social and political groups, but also from some leaders of the traditional and ancient churches, who question the authenticity of such recent church and parachurch movements. The latter group can perceive Evangelicals and Protestants as not belonging to the Middle East's long history and heritage. Rather, their ministries are seen as imported forms of Christianity from the West, which lack continuity, substance, and cohesion among Middle Easterners. Other groups which are politically leftist and radical in their ideologies think that Evangelicals and Protestants have hidden political agendas and are pro-West and therefore pro-Zionist in their orientation. This belief greatly complicates ministry. Local pastors and missionaries must try to explain and demonstrate that they are truly biblical, that they are non-political, that they have nothing to do with the modern state of Israel as a Jewish nation, and that they have a lot in common with the traditional churches and historic Christian faiths in the region.

The more open and friendly pastors and missionaries are to the local spiritual and community leaders (it's better to befriend the non-Christian religious leaders as well), the more acceptable they and their ministry will be. Unfortunately, some Evangelical pastors and missionaries bring with them an individualistic and more isolated approach, which causes more harm than good. Instead of building toward cooperative efforts and working alongside the nationals and other locals, the isolated strategies normally create negative impressions, bad publicity, and increased suspicion. Most importantly, those who follow such strategies alienate themselves and those around them in the community.

I often tell my colleagues in the Middle East that we cannot afford to criticize, oppose, or fight each other because of doctrinal or practical differences. We need to unify our efforts and support each other, allowing room for unique styles and approaches within the larger Christian community. Thankfully, we see this happening more and more through the formation of "strategic partnerships" of Christians within the region, both nationals and expatriates. These groups bring together different organizations and denominations in order to pray and develop cooperative strategies for ministry together. They are a breath of fresh air and an essential encouragement in the midst of pressure and turmoil.

Pastors and missionaries often face significant emotional struggles and psychological distress in their personal, marital, and family life. In addition, they often serve a troubled population and families all around the area who need careful help and, at times, professional attention. To be effective, Christian workers need sound training and continuing education, as well as skills in problem solving, crisis intervention, and basic counseling. They also have needs for belonging and for true camaraderie, needs for personal and intellectual growth, and a need for someone to check on them, stand by them, and encourage them. They long to be nurtured, mentored, and well supported.

During the last five years, I have been spending several months in the Middle East every year, making myself available to the churches and the community at large. I have tried to help in any way possible—teaching, counseling, preaching, training, and encouraging. I have greatly enjoyed meeting with Christian workers and listening to their remarkable journeys.

Besides the chronic uncertainties and major stresses of everyday life, many Christian workers from the Middle East—just like their compatriots in other parts of the world—carry with them heavy burdens, along with profound sadness and grief. Many have been through numerous crises, have experienced major losses, and have been exposed to traumatic events. And the agonies continue. In addition, there can be severe economic hardships, which put an additional burden on pastors and nationals. Just living on the bare minimum is a challenge. Many people have to work at two jobs in order to survive. Some have been refugees and immigrants, even within their own countries. Their lives have been uprooted, family relations have been forcefully disrupted, and their loved ones have been scattered. Their hopes for even a minimum level of stability have been broken and lost. Yet, they try to keep the faith diligently and serve the Lord earnestly. They are truly heroes of the faith.

Reflections on Religious Persecution

In the second half of this article, I (Anneke) would like to share a brief chapter from my book on women in the persecuted church, *Hidden Sorrow, Lasting Joy* (Companjen, 2000). The specific focus is on some cases of persecution against Christians in Iran. These cases are a vivid example of the high price that believers and church leaders often pay. Takoosh, the main subject, gave her consent to use her name and to share her story.

Please understand that I am in no way trying to single out Iran, since persecution and discrimination are taking place in many shapes and forms in several countries—and not just in the Middle East alone—and they are affecting a number of other faiths and world religions. Nonetheless, Christians are by far the largest group who suffer as a result of their faith. In fact, over 200 million Christians lack their full human rights as described in Article 18 of the United Nations' 1948 *Universal Declaration of Human Rights*, primarily because of their religious convictions (Candelin, 2001).

Article 18 states: "Everyone has the right to freedom of thought, conscience, and religion; this right includes freedom to change his religion or belief, and freedom, either alone or in community with others and in public or private, to manifest his religion of belief in teaching, practice, worship, and observance." In 1981, the United Nations General Assembly reaffirmed the principles enunciated in this Declaration and other earlier documents via its *Declaration on the Elimination of All Forms of Intolerance and of Discrimination Based on Religion or Belief.*

Takoosh Hovsepian: In God's University

Takoosh was a lively Iranian teenager from an Armenian background with flashing dark eyes and a beautiful smile. She sometimes attended church with her grandmother, and there she heard that she could have a personal relationship with Jesus Christ. For some reason, she just couldn't get the idea out of her mind, and after several conversations she prayed with some of her friends and invited the Lord into her life.

Soon after she came to Jesus, Takoosh brought a very important request to God in prayer. "Lord, please give me a husband who loves you. I want so much to serve you, and I pray for a partner who is a Christian so that we can serve you together."

Of course she had no way of knowing that a young man named Haik Hovsepian was bringing a very similar request before God. Haik was a believer, too. He had just finished his studies and felt he was being called by God into Christian ministry.

"Lord," he prayed, "I want you to use me in your service. But I need someone to stand with me, someone to share my ministry with me. Please help me find a godly girl who wants to please you above all else. Lead me to her, Lord, and I'll ask her to be my wife."

Haik often served as a guest speaker in various churches. One Sunday morning he visited the city of Isfahan. While he was preaching there, his eyes fell on a fifteen-year-old girl sitting in the audience. There were quite a few other young women sitting in the congregation, but for some reason his eyes were drawn to that one special face. He had fasted and prayed that he would find a godly wife before making the journey. Was it his imagination, or was the Lord saying, *This is the woman you have prayed for. I have chosen her for you!*

Could it be so? Or was he simply responding to a pair of dark eyes, a quiet spirit, a lovely smile? He couldn't be sure. She seemed a little too tall and slim, but something in his spirit kept saying, *This is the one*. Well aware that he was about to make one of the most important decisions of his life, Haik fasted and prayed for three days. And by the end of his fasting, he still felt that the Lord was speaking to him in the same way.

Fighting off his doubts and fears, the young man summoned all his courage and went to talk to Takoosh. He told her about his prayer for a godly wife. "This is a little hard to explain," he began rather sheepishly, "but I think God has shown me that you're the woman he has chosen for me."

Takoosh was stunned. She wasn't sure what to say, but deep in her heart she had much the same feeling. In an unsteady voice, she answered, "Like you, I've been praying for a mate who wants to serve the Lord with me. Maybe you're the answer to my prayer, too."

Later that evening, when she tried to talk things over with her parents, they weren't at all pleased. "You don't even know this man!" they protested. "And you need to finish your education. What if you're left alone some day and you have to work? You'll have nothing to fall back on!"

But the more she talked to Haik and the more she talked to God, the more Takoosh was convinced that this man really was the one for her. After much conversation with her parents and after many private prayers, Takoosh's family eventually relented. They were, in fact, impressed with the young man, too.

"He is an exceptional boy," her father said. "I can see that for myself."

Great Joy, Deep Sorrow

So at quite a young age, Takoosh became Mrs. Hovsepian. She soon found out that being married to a pastor in Iran was not exactly an easy life. But Haik's love and his gentle, romantic ways helped her through the early adjustments. He clearly loved her, and they both deeply loved the Lord.

Those were days of increasing political upheaval in Iran, which eventually culminated in the 1979 Islamic Revolution. Before long, Takoosh's parents fled the country and moved to the United States.

"Are you wishing you could move to the States, too?" Haik asked her the day she told her parents good-bye.

"No," Takoosh told him. "There's no way I'm leaving you. I am staying here. But just remember—I'm doing it for you!"

"I'd rather you stayed for God," Haik countered.

But from that time on, perhaps because he was the only family she now had in the country, Haik began to treat his wife like a queen. He realized it was painful for Takoosh to live such a huge distance away from her loved ones. So he did everything he could to encourage her and keep her spirits up.

The two of them were genuinely well matched and content with one another, and their happiness was inexpressible when their first child, a little boy, was born. Like most new fathers, Haik was enormously proud of the baby. And the more Haik fell in love with their son, the more Takoosh fell in love with Haik. Those were the most joyful days of her life—caring for her infant son and watching his father's delight in him.

"God, you are so good to us," Takoosh sometimes prayed, feeling deep gratitude for her new family. "You've given me a wonderful husband who loves you and a beautiful baby. I'm so thankful that we're serving you together."

By then, Haik was pastoring a Christian fellowship, which was growing larger ever week. Not only was he an excellent Bible teacher, but Haik was also a gifted musician who loved to lead the congregation in praise. He had an exceptionally good voice, and the worship in their church never failed to move her to tears. "Thank you, Lord, for all you've done for us," Takoosh often prayed, feeling blessed in ways she never could have imagined.

Unfortunately, the greatest joys in life sometimes have to make room for the deepest sorrows. And so it would be for Takoosh, who would soon have to face more than her share of suffering. One night as they drove to a Christian meeting, Haik's car was struck head-on by another vehicle. The other driver was clearly at fault, but it was little comfort to anyone. Haik and Takoosh were severely injured. Their beautiful son was killed instantly.

Takoosh's physical pain was severe, but her emotional agony was indescribable.

"How could you allow this to happen to us, Lord?" Takoosh often cried out as her body slowly and painfully mended. "All we ever wanted to do was to serve you. Why didn't you protect us? Why did our baby have to die?"

There were no easy answers for Takoosh's desperate questions, and for many months it seemed that her broken spirit would never heal. It took her a very long time to stop being angry at God. Thankfully, the other Christians in their church understood her battle, and they interceded for her continually. They prayed that Takoosh would be able to forgive the other driver. They prayed that the Lord would heal her aching heart. And they helped in every practical way imaginable.

Eventually, Takoosh relinquished her bitterness into God's hands, and once she did so, the wound in her heart gradually diminished. As time went by, she learned how to keep her sorrow in its place, especially after the Lord gave her and Haik another son.

Meanwhile, Haik was a tower of strength during this terrible time. His strong faith in God made it possible for him not to waver in days of adversity. Rather than dwelling on his own loss, he went out of his way to help Takoosh. She was amazed to see that her husband would do anything to make her life easier. Her love for him knew no bounds. He was the light of her life.

"Brother Haik Is Missing"

Over the years, as their family increased, so did their persecutions. After the death of their first son, Haik and Takoosh were blessed with four more children—three sons and a daughter. And when Mehdi Dibaj, another Iranian pastor, was taken to prison and his wife was unable to care for their children, the family increased yet again. Haik became like a father to the Dibaj children as well.

By now Haik's role in the Iranian Christian community had become both more important and more visible. He was now chairman of the Council of Protestant Pastors. It was up to him in this position to issue a report about the violations of Christians' rights in Iran, a report that was published all over the world. He also refused to endorse a document produced by Iran's religious and political authorities stating that the Christian church in Iran enjoyed freedom of religion. This made him no friends in the hardcore fundamentalist regime that now ruled the country.

To make matters worse, when Haik was pressured to stop reaching out to Muslims with the gospel message, he flatly refused. He made it clear that his Tehran church would continue to welcome anyone and everyone who wanted to know more about Jesus the Messiah.

Brother Haik preached the gospel everywhere he went, to whoever would listen, no matter what their beliefs. No government could restrain him. His church was alive and active, and Haik was loved by everyone who knew him—everyone except the Iranian authorities. Living an outspoken Christian life in a militantly Muslim world was a challenge few believers would dare to face, but Haik faced it daily, along with other Christian leaders who shared his courage and faith. Haik set an example for the entire world to see by refusing to give in to intimidation and fear.

One day in January 1994, Haik kissed Takoosh good-bye and headed for the airport, where he was scheduled to meet with a friend. At first, when he didn't return, she thought the authorities might have detained him. But when she called around, every official said the same thing: "We don't know anything about him." Takoosh's best hope was that her husband was in jail.

A couple of days later, Johan, the children, and I were starting to eat dinner when the telephone interrupted our mealtime conversation. Johan took the call, and as he listened to the voice on the other end of the phone, the expression on his face told us all that something was terribly wrong.

The call was from California, from an Iranian Christian friend there. "Johan, Brother Haik has been missing for two days. Nobody knows where he is or what's happened to him. He went to the airport to meet somebody and never returned home. Please pray, and try to mobilize others to pray as well. Frankly, it doesn't look good...."

The sad news came as a shock, but it was not totally unexpected. We knew Pastor Haik had been extremely outspoken about the persecution of Iranian Christians. During the previous months, there had been a worldwide campaign to protest and pray against the imminent execution of Mehdi Dibaj, whose children Haik and Takoosh had been caring for the nine years he had been in jail. Dibaj had been unexpectedly released only a few days before.

Through Open Doors, we contacted friends and colleagues who organized a massive prayer effort. Within hours, thousands of people in dozens of countries were praying for Haik around the clock.

Finally, after more than a week of anxiously waiting for news about his whereabouts, on Sunday morning, January 30, the phone rang at the Hovsepian house. Takoosh handed the receiver to their oldest son, Joseph. "It's the police," she said quietly. "They want to talk to you."

When Joseph arrived at the police station, an officer unceremoniously thrust a grisly photograph into his hands. "Is this your father?" the policeman asked coldly. "We found this body in a small alleyway in Tehran. He was brutally murdered. Looks like he died about 10 days ago."

Joseph identified the body in the photograph as his father's.

Waves of shock rippled across the world. In fact, many Christians—even those who didn't know Haik personally—felt that they had lost a close friend. But Takoosh and her four children, ages ten to twenty-three, had lost the dearest person in all the world to them.

Takoosh wept for days. The skin beneath her eyes became inflamed and infected. She simply could not stop crying. Days later, our own eyes filled with tears as we watched a video of the memorial service in the Assembly of God church in Tehran. I could not take my eyes off Haik's widow. She was seated in the front row, surrounded by her children, all dressed in black. Her face was a study in tragedy. I wondered if she would ever smile again.

The church was filled to overflowing. A large picture of Haik was placed on the platform surrounded by dozens of floral wreaths and bouquets. We listened in silence to a recording of one of Haik's sermons on persecution and suffering. Later on, his beautiful voice filled the auditorium as one of his recorded songs was played.

The camera zoomed in on Mehdi Dibaj. "Not Haik, but I should have died!" he exclaimed when he spoke during the service. It wasn't long before his words proved prophetic.

Lessons to Be Learned

Christians everywhere prayed for Takoosh and her family, and for the believers in Iran who were going through such a difficult time. Thousands of letters and cards were sent. Their greetings were appreciated, but the wound in Takoosh's spirit seemed beyond repair. As the reality of Haik's murder sank in, she found herself in a mighty spiritual struggle.

Takoosh's heart was filled with hatred toward the murderers of her husband. She hated the Muslims who had brought this tremendous grief upon her and her family. Thoughts of vindication festered in her mind. She was afraid of her own rage, afraid that she would lose control and strike someone with her car or cause injury to an innocent person.

When friends visited Takoosh some months later, she shook her head and said, "I've been in God's University. I started out in the lowest grade, but slowly and steadily he began to work in my heart. First, I simply had to be *willing* to forgive the murderers. Forgiveness started with a decision of the will, and the emotions followed much later. One day, after giving God permission to take it away, I realized that the hatred was gone. At last I could forgive the people who killed my husband."

Takoosh had won a battle, but it was not long before she became aware of another hurdle. God was asking her to not only forgive her enemies but to *love* them.

"Lord, you're asking too much," she cried out to him. "How can I love them when they killed the love of my life?"

God gently took her by the hand and helped her. Little by little, step by step, she came to the point where she realized that she *could* love her enemies. She began to see the Muslim extremists the way God saw them—as lost sheep without a Shepherd. God asked Takoosh to love, and he enabled her to love. He helped her to pass the second test.

"But I still wasn't quite ready to graduate from God's University," she said. "The process was not over. God told me that he wanted me to praise and thank him for what had happened."

It was impossible. Forgiveness and love she could deal with dutifully, but praise required her to sing, to rejoice, to celebrate. How could anyone expect her to do that? God knew how much Haik had meant to her, how she needed him and depended on him.

"Still, I wanted to be obedient and grow in the Lord," Takoosh explained. "So again I had no other choice. With my mouth I started to thank the Lord, even though my heart was crying at the same time. My heart was not ready, but I obeyed with my mouth. And God, as before, started to work in my soul."

The Christian men and women in the Tehran church went out of their way to help the Hovsepian family. During the days Haik was missing, and after the news of his death was confirmed, church members and many local pastors took turns in comforting Takoosh and the children.

For a long time they took care of her everyday needs in the most practical ways. They shopped, they cooked, they cleaned, they served guests. There was not a day that Takoosh was left alone. Someone was always there to comfort her, to encourage her from the Scriptures, and to provide for her.

"Though I missed my family a lot, there was not a moment after Haik's death that I wished that they were with me," Takoosh shared. "I received all the love, care, and comfort I needed from the church."

The Lord himself was real to Takoosh in personal, sometimes amazingly tangible ways. God demonstrated to her that he was not only interested in providing for her big needs but was also concerned about the smallest details of her life. One of the little comforts Takoosh enjoyed was eating chocolate. One day, to her regret, she realized that she had only a little piece left. As she ate it she prayed, "Please, Lord, you know how I love chocolate. Would you send me some more?"

That same day some visitors from Canada and the United States arrived in her apartment. She gratefully unwrapped their gifts—toys and clothes for the other martyrs' families. And, then, at the very last, she joyfully opened something that had been brought especially for her—chocolate. Once again, Takoosh was reminded of her heavenly Father's unfailing care.

One of Takoosh's most difficult times was when Rebecca, their daughter, got married. Takoosh needed supernatural grace to somehow make it a joyful day for the young couple. Haik and Takoosh had been looking forward to this happy occasion together. Now she had to go through it alone. While the house was being decorated for the wedding, Takoosh quietly cried out to the Lord to help her through it.

It was a day of immense joy, because the two young Christians were starting out their lives together with God's blessing. Takoosh was thankful that her daughter had been given a godly husband, but for her, the day felt empty and bleak without Haik there to celebrate with them.

A Matter of Life and Death

Takoosh wasn't the only grieving Christian widow in Iran. In December 1990, Pastor Soodmand, a convert from Islam, was hanged near the city of Mashad. His wife, who was blind, had a very hard time coping with his death, but Takoosh was able to share with her what she was going through. Although Mrs. Soodmand was comforted to know that others, like Takoosh, have experienced grief much like her own, she continues to need our prayers.

As it turned out, Haik was not the only Christian pastor to lay down his life in Iran that year. In June, after six months of freedom, Mehdi Dibaj was murdered in a park, leaving his four children behind. He died as a martyr, too, even though the government blamed a terrorist group, the Moedjaheddin Khalq, for his sudden death.

Dibaj's body was released only two hours before his funeral, and even then the family was not allowed to open the coffin. This heroic servant of God had been willing to lay down his life from the start. His wife had left him during the years of his detention, and his four children suffered doubly—first they had lost their "adoptive" father, Haik, and now their own father was gone. But like the Hovsepian children, they followed in their father's footsteps and continued to serve the Lord.

Only a few days after Mehdi Dibaj's death, Pastor Tateos Michaelian was shot and killed, leaving his wife, Juliet, and three grown children. Another leader was gone. Pastor Michaelian had succeeded Haik as chairman of the Council of Protestant Pastors in Iran. Only five months after he took on this responsibility, he paid for it with his life. His wife now lives in California with one of her married daughters.

On September 28, 1996, the worldwide Christian community was shaken again. The body of Pastor Ravanbakhsh Yousefi was found hanging from a tree some twenty miles from his house in Ghaem-Shahr. He had left his home early that day to spend time in prayer and meditation. Still another Christian minister had laid down his life in Iran. And another widow, Akhtar, now faced life alone with her two small children.

The sudden death of her husband devastated Akhtar. Today, like Takoosh, she is walking the long road of sorrow, working through her pain step by step. Every day at three o'clock, Takoosh calls Akhtar. More than anyone else, she understands what Akhtar is going through.

Christians around the world often pray for their brothers and sisters in Iran, and well we should. These faithful believers are confronted with one of the most virulent persecutions on earth. But a pastor from that country, who visited the States recently, told us, "You pray for us, but maybe you need our prayers more. We cannot afford to wander away from Jesus. We need him so much for every small detail of our lives that we *have* to stay close to him. It's a matter of life and death for us."

That matter of life and death—faith in the Lord Jesus Christ—has been tried and tested in the hearts of Takoosh and her children. They continue to value our prayers for healing, wisdom, and guidance. They live in California now, but dealing with the past and moving courageously into the future continue to challenge them.

But one thing will never change. What Paul wrote to the Christians in Philippi, he would surely say to the Hovsepian family and all the other wives and children who have lost their loved ones in Iran: "He who began a good work in you will carry it on to completion until the day of Christ Jesus" (Phil. 1:6).

Reflection and Discussion

1. What are some of the main social and religious realities that affect Christian workers in the Middle East?

2. How might stressors be different for national pastors and expatriate workers?

3. What are some of the main stereotypes about the Middle East? How could these be changed?

4. Which aspects of the accounts in the case studies touched you the most and why?

5. List a few practical things that could be done to help Christians being persecuted for their faith in the Middle East.

References and Suggested Reading

Abi-Hashem, N. (1992). The impact of the Gulf War on the churches in the Middle East: A socio-cultural and spiritual analysis. *Pastoral Psychology*, *41*, 3-21.

———. (1999a). Cross-cultural psychology. In D. Benner & P. Hill (Eds.), *Baker encyclopedia of psychology and counseling* (2nd ed.) (pp. 294-298). Grand Rapids, MI: Baker.

———. (1999b). Grief, loss, and bereavement: An overview. *Journal of Psychology and Christianity*, *18*, 309-329.

———. (1999c). Grief therapy. In D. Benner & P. Hill (Eds.), *Baker encyclopedia of psychology and counseling* (2nd ed.) (pp. 1229-1230). Grand Rapids, MI: Baker.

Accad, F. (1997). *Building bridges: Christianity and Islam*. Colorado Springs, CO: NavPress.

Al-Masih, Abd. (1996). *The main challenges for committed Christians in serving Muslims* (English ed.). Villach, Austria: Light of Life.

Bell, R. (1968). *The origin of Islam in its Christian environment*. London, UK: Frank Cass.

Candelin, J. (2001). *A perspective on global religious freedom challenges facing the Christian community: The Geneva Report 2001*. World Evagelical Fellowship. (Available from: markalbrecht@xc.org)

Companjen, A. (2000). *Hidden sorrow, lasting joy: The forgotten women of the persecuted church*. Wheaton, IL: Tyndale House.

Coote, R., & Stott, J. (Eds.). (1980). *Down to earth: Studies in Christianity and culture*. Grand Rapids, MI: Eerdmans.

Esposito, J. (Ed.). (1995). *The Oxford encyclopedia of modern Islamic world*. New York, NY: Oxford University Press.

Hamada, L. (1990). *Understanding the Arab world*. Nashville, TN: Thomas Nelson.

Hamady, S. (1960). *Temperament and character of the Arabs*. New York, NY: Twayne.

Hitti, P. (1978). *History of the Arabs* (10th ed.). New York, NY: Saint Martin's Press.

Lapidus, I. (1990). *A history of Islamic societies*. Cambridge, UK: Cambridge University Press.

Levy, R. (1957). *The social structure of Islam*. Cambridge, UK: Cambridge University Press.

Littlefield, D. (1997). *The Islamic Near East and North Africa: An annotated guide*. Littleton, CO: Libraries Unlimited.

Marsella, A., & Pedersen, P. (Eds.). (1981). *Cross-cultural counseling and psychotherapy*. New York, NY: Pergamon.

Nasr, N. (1994). *Islamic spirituality I & II*. Lexington, NY: Crossroads.

Robinson, N. (1991). *Christ in Islam and Christianity: The representation of Jesus in the Qur'an and the classical Muslim commentaries*. Basingstoke, UK: Macmillan Education.

Voll, J. (1982). *Islam: Continuity and change in the modern world*. Boulder, CO: Westview Press.

Wertsman, V. (2001, June). Arab Americans: A comparative and critical analysis of leading reference sources. *MultiCultural Review*, 42-47.

Williams, J. (1971). *Themes of Islamic civilization*. Berkeley, CA: University of California.

Youssef, M. (1991). *America, oil, and the Islamic mind: The real crisis is the gulf between our ways of thinking*. Grand Rapids, MI: Zondervan.

Zwemer, S. (1986). *Arabia, the cradle of Islam: Studies in the geography, people, and politics of the peninsula with an account of Islam and mission-work*. London, UK: Darf.

Naji Abi-Hashem *is a Lebanese-American clinical and cultural psychologist and an ordained minister, currently based in Seattle, Washington. He received his M.Div. from Golden Gate Baptist Theological Seminary (1985) and his doctorate in psychology from Rosemead School of Psychology, Biola University (1992). Naji is also a diplomate of the American Board of Psychological Specialties (1998) and worked nine years with Minirth-Meier New Life Clinics. His international service has included missionary work, counseling, writing, editing, teaching, networking, consultation, and caring for caregivers. Special areas of interest are relating the Christian faith to clinical practice, pastoral care and counseling, Middle Eastern and cultural studies, grief and bereavement, political and peace psychology, existential philosophy, and contemplative spirituality. Email: NajiAH@worldnet.att.net.*

Photo Open Doors

Anneke Companjen *and her husband Johan are former Christian and Missionary Alliance missionaries to Vietnam. Since their return to their native country, The Netherlands, they have served the persecuted, suffering church with the ministry of Open Doors. Anneke has traveled extensively and seen firsthand the tragic toll of persecution. She gave a voice to women throughout the persecuted church in her book* **Hidden Sorrow, Lasting Joy**. *This book has been published in 10 languages and tells the stories of 20 women who have suffered because they, along with their husbands, chose to follow Christ despite opposition and danger. Through speaking engagements around the globe, Anneke brings awareness of how these individuals pay a heavy price for their faith in Jesus Christ. Email: Annekec@od.org.*

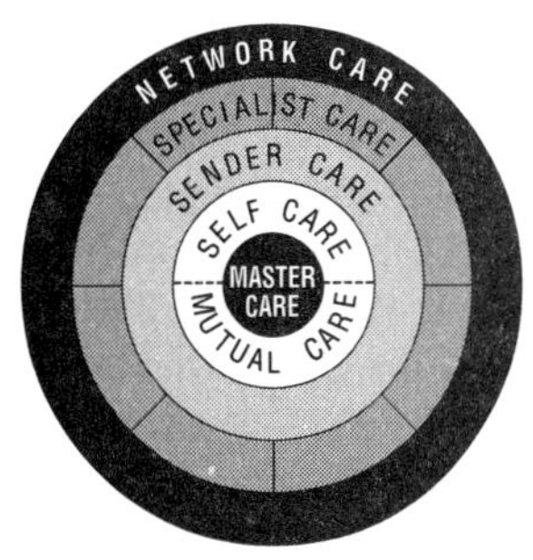

Doing Member Care In Red Zones: Examples From the Middle East

RAYMOND HICKS

Several "Red zones" exist in the Middle East and pose potential danger to the well-being of mission personnel. Red zones are specific areas marked by ethno-political tensions, instability, and potential or actual violence. The author looks at the warning signs of Red-zone stress, offers suggestions for persons living in Red zones, and provides guidelines for administrators and leaders to help their Red-zone personnel.

The term "Red zone" refers to those areas of the world where there is intense stress on a regular and sometimes daily basis, brought on by perceived or actual danger and threats to one's safety. This is true regarding many parts of our world, but it is particularly true in the Middle East, where I have served for the past 25 years. These Red zones are dangerous just by the mere fact that living and ministering in one of these locations places the individual, couple, family, and/or team at risk. Some examples of Red zones in the Middle East would include areas within Gaza and the West Bank, Lebanon, Yemen, and Syria, to name just a few.

Mission personnel who live in a cross-cultural context usually experience plenty of stress to tax their resiliency skills and reserves. It is no easy task to learn a new language, a new culture, and a new set of verbal and nonverbal cues, as well as develop a new package of living skills. In fact, it sometimes takes two or more years to acquire sufficient skills before one sees any reduction in stress. When these adjustment stressors are added to Red-zone stressors, the mix can be incapacitating, producing fear, anger, volatility, hopelessness, and helplessness even in the best trained and most dedicated of personnel. The following are some of the dangerous experiences that can cause any location to turn into a Red zone. When coupled with the normal stressors of cross-cultural living, these experiences can thrust personnel onto the quick track towards emotional, physical, or spiritual burnout:

- Potential threats of robbery, rape, or abduction.
- Death threats.
- Active repression of Christianity by governments and/or militant religious leadership.

■ Terrorism and intense anti-Western sentiment.

■ Random acts of violence, attacks, and shootings.

■ Being in close proximity to local people who have been shot, wounded, maimed, and/or killed. This stress intensifies if some of the people affected are known.

■ Political instability and political violence which create warlike/coup-like conditions.

■ Unchecked anger, hatred, and violence directed towards expatriate Westerners or towards those seen to sympathize with disavowed groups/causes.

■ Armed civilian and government warfare activities with clashes in civilian areas, increasing the potential of danger, injury, or death if a person is in the wrong place at the wrong time.

■ High unemployment, low wages, and large-scale hunger and physical needs which are accompanied by violence and political upheaval.

■ Extremely poor economic situations, which can lead to an uncharacteristic rise in theft and armed robbery, especially of Westerners or the upper class.

■ Curfews and travel restrictions.

This list could go on with increasing intensity and vividness. Any one of these characteristics by itself would not necessarily constitute a Red zone. However, when these Red-zone stressors appear in clusters of three or more in a specific location, then the area would be classified as a Red zone.

A good example of this would be the Gaza Strip in Palestine. Given the conflict between the Palestinians and the Israelis, the observable characteristics of a Red zone are clear in this location.

■ Death threats have been made on Western personnel serving with various organizations.

■ Death threats have been directed toward local Palestinians who have not followed the "prescribed group resistance."

■ Palestinian and other Christians have found themselves the target of militants who verbally abhor alcohol sale and usage of any kind. In addition, the Christian community found themselves struggling to maintain their Christian identity and at the same time participate in the activities of the Muslim majority population vis-à-vis demonstrations, violence, stone-throwing, fire-bombing, and other acts of resistance. (Christianity here often involves more of a cultural heritage than a lifestyle and relationship with God.)

■ Random acts of shooting and bombings occur on a regular basis. Israeli settlers and soldiers have wounded and killed Palestinians regularly in demonstrations, drive-by shootings, ambushes, and assassinations. Palestinians have wounded and killed Israeli soldiers and settlers who live and serve in the occupying army in the Gaza Strip. By the end of 2000, the death tally in the most recent conflict between Israelis and Palestinians was over 400, the vast majority being Palestinians.

■ Nearly every Palestinian family has been touched by the wounding and/or death of family members. Therefore, it is very common for Westerners working in the Gaza Strip to know someone who has been wounded or killed.

■ The closure of the borders between Palestine and Israel has played havoc with the local Palestinian economy. Palestinian businesses are not able to get supplies for their companies. Therefore, employees for those businesses are not able to work. Palestinians who work in Israel are not able to cross over to their jobs. As a result, the unemployment rate for Palestinians in Gaza has been reported to be approaching 50%. The average income is about $2 per day. Personnel working in such conditions find themselves extremely stressed, guilty, and saddened when they see such widespread poverty and so many unmet physical needs 24 hours a day, seven days a week.

■ Terrorism is widespread. No one knows where the next attack by the Israeli soldiers or by Palestinians will happen. But the fact is, it *will* happen, and it is very likely that it will be close. As a result, curfews and travel restrictions are commonplace.

■ In the Gaza Strip, one of the most densely populated locations on earth, political instability is a reality. Aging leadership and the more militant political youth often have a clash of ideologies. Sometimes these clashes can turn violent to various degrees, from shouting and fights to shootings and death.

■ Anger at the unquestioning support that the West gives Israel has led to hatred being directed towards Westerners and Western businesses.

Life in the Red Zone: A Case Study

The following is a family case study that illustrates what I mean by Red-zone life and the effects it has on personnel. I have changed the family information to protect their identity, but the Red-zone details are factual.

Rob and Carol are first-term international workers who have been living in a Red-zone area for three years. Both are educated to the master's level. Before overseas service, they were highly successful in their Western context and were leaders in their community and church. Both are energetic, highly motivated, and very focused on the task of reaching their unreached people group. Rob and Carol have three teenage children. As a family, they have learned the local language and fit in well with the culture.

Rob, Carol, and their children have had their share of bumps in the past three years. The children had difficulty at first adjusting to the new culture. They experienced normal adjustment problems of attending an expatriate school outside of the Red zone and at the same time living within a Red zone. The marital relationship between Rob and Carol weathered the stressors of the initial adjustment to their new location.

However, the stress that Rob, Carol, and their children have experienced in the past year and a half was compounded by the intensity of the stressors in their Red-zone location. Almost all of the Red-zone stressors above were present in their lives on a daily to weekly basis. Three examples which added to their daily stress were (1) Rob and Carol had to buy protective glass for their vehicle because they had been stoned by demonstrating youths; (2) they had to vary their travel routes daily, in order to avoid military roadblocks and demonstrations by militant crowds; and (3) several times they were not able to contact or pick their children up from school because the military had closed their travel routes.

All of these stressors are adversely affecting Rob and Carol's relationship in every area of their lives. Let us look at some of the key areas that have suffered.

■ *Relationship with God*—Rob and Carol have lost joy in their relationship with God. They have little to no time for devotional time and prayer. They are "in the desert" spiritually.

■ *Relationship with self*—Areas of "margin" (i.e., having time and energy for restoration and renewal) in their individual lives are at a minimum. There is little time for relaxation, family, or friends. There is no time for exercise. There is a marked lack of energy and initiative

■ *Relationship as a couple*—It seems that many conversations lead to a disagreement or an argument. There is not much mutual encouragement, and nagging has become a way of life in the way Rob and Carol relate to each another.

■ *Relationship with children*—There is tension between the parents and the children. Nagging has become a part of this relationship too. The children talk a lot about going back to Europe or leaving the Red zone and living closer to their friends outside the Red zone.

■ *Relationship with local people*—Barriers seem to arise more often in their relationships with nationals. As the needs of the local people increased exponentially, Rob and Carol's ability to meet their human, physical, and hunger needs decreased at the same rate. This is one of the biggest producers of stress, and it produced guilt, sadness, and frustration in Rob and Carol

- *Relationship with colleagues*—Since Rob and Carol live some distance from their colleagues, it is difficult for the colleagues to understand Rob and Carol's situation. Instead of talking more with their colleagues, Rob and Carol became more distant, making the void of discouragement wider and the voices of encouragement weaker and less frequent.

As you can see from this brief description of Rob and Carol's Red-zone experience, they are well on a "crash-and-burn trajectory" of emotional, physical, and/or spiritual burnout. I am not sure how much longer they could have handled the Red-zone pressure-cooker context without relief or intervention. In fact, the ever-present pressures had the potential to cause them to reassess their call to missions and potentially lead them away from the unreached people group to whom God had specifically called them. Rob and Carol's Red-zone scenario is all too common in the areas of the Middle East and in other Red zones of the world.

Proactive Steps

What can help Rob and Carol's scenario and similar circumstances of other personnel living in Red zones? What could they do to help themselves? What are some proactive steps that they could take to release some of the pressure from their "Red zone pressure cooker"? Two key strategies are (1) to learn to recognize the warning signs of individual Red-zone stress and (2) to develop ways to deal with that stress, especially by establishing clear personal, couple, and family margins. Dr. Kenneth Williams (2000, p. 171) defines *margin* as "a sufficient reserve of time, energy (spiritual, emotional, interpersonal, and physical), and money to provide for our needs and the needs of others." Personal development of margins allows our bodies, our emotions, and our spiritual lives to be healed, restored, and renewed from the effects of Red-zone stress.

Recognizing the Warning Signs

Over the years in the Middle East, I have noted five major warning signs of Red-zone stress, both personally and in colleagues. These are depression, suppression of feelings, lack of focus, constant fear, and spiritual dryness.

1. Depression

Some of the major symptoms of depression include sleeping too much or too little, lethargy, headaches, increased irritability and anger, lack of interest in pleasurable activities, changes in eating habits, avoiding responsibilities and relationships (e.g., watching numerous videos or spending long hours on the computer), addictive behaviors, withdrawal from others, and decreased intimacy between husband and wife. When a few of these symptoms begin to cluster together over a period of several weeks, depression might be present. It is important to consult with a health care professional.

2. Suppressed feelings

Fatigue, relationship struggles, psychosomatic problems, and psychological problems can be the result of unexpressed thoughts and feelings. The longer that these stressful experiences remain unprocessed—not shared with/discussed with confidants—the greater the possibility of further complications.

Bob is an example of what happens when someone suppresses feelings and thoughts. As the Red-zone stressors began to increase, Bob became more introverted. Instead of finding someone to talk with about his fear of death if he were kidnapped, he stuffed those thoughts and fears deep inside. When he was threatened with death at a roadblock, Bob told no one. He pushed those thoughts and feelings down deep. When he saw the injustice of the military towards civilians through unwarranted beatings on young men, he drove those thoughts and feelings deeper within. He talked less and less with his wife and colleagues about his inner life and experiences. At the same time, he found himself becoming angry more often, especially with the local people with whom he was working. Everything they did, said, or did not do infuriated him. He found himself yelling at other drivers when he was driving. He snapped at his wife when she made simple requests of him. He was short-tempered with his children, and they often asked him, "What is wrong, Daddy?" to which he responded with a quick, "Nothing!" His life slowly became more reactive than responsive to people and events around him.

Bob began dealing with his anger in very unhealthy ways. He would often state things like, "I am not angry," "It's not my fault," "You're too sensitive," or, "I don't want to talk about it." His way of dealing with differences became one of angry confrontations or silence. As Bob's personal stress and tension began to build, most of his conversations became complaint sessions. Matters of the heart ceased to be topics of conversation.

After a year like this, Bob began to have panic attacks, during which he felt extremely out of control and thought that he was going to die. These panic attacks were frightening and sometimes debilitating. Bob would exhibit one or several of the following on an increasingly frequent basis: irregular heartbeat, shortness of breath, fear of death and dying, chest discomfort, or abdominal distress. He actually thought that he was having major heart problems.

Initially, Bob kept his panic struggles from his wife and colleagues. However, after a particularly scary attack, he confided in his wife and went to his medical doctor for help. After a complete physical evaluation, it was determined that nothing was wrong physically. However, things were wrong emotionally and spiritually. Bob's physician encouraged him to see a counselor. He contacted the member care specialist in his organization and was referred to someone in his location who was qualified and available to help.

Bob's counseling initially focused on his personal relationship with God. It was difficult for Bob when he realized that the most important thing to him, his relationship with God, was one of the first relationships to be affected negatively. In addition, the counselor helped Bob look at his Red-zone stressors, his thoughts, his feelings, and his fears from a biblical perspective, as well as from a physical and psychological perspective. After a little more than two months, Bob began to return to his outgoing and energetic lifestyle. His relationship with God returned to its primary importance. His role as husband and father took on new meaning. He learned to share his thoughts and feelings more freely with his wife and with a trusted colleague. He learned to share his fears more candidly. He began to look at his Red-zone context as a place where local people could see God in his life rather than seeing it as a place where God could not be found. Bob actually became more functional than he had been in the past. He related better to family, peers, and nationals, without panic attacks plaguing him and restricting his activities.

Not all cases like Bob's can be treated on the field within a Red zone. Sometimes it is necessary to remove the person and his/her family from the area, so that intervention can take place without the active stressors of the Red zone. This kind of approach assists the person(s) by immediately reducing the stressors and allowing them to process thoughts, feelings, and fears from a distance and from a location of safety and support.

3. Lack of focus

Lack of focus is extremely hard on workers in Red zones. Personnel serving overseas usually have a high work/ministry ethic. Moreover, most are supported financially by special gifts and donations from organizations or persons in their home country who believe in them and in their work/ministry. Therefore, when a lack of focus sets in and personnel begin to realize that they are unproductive, their sense of duty, dedication, and accountability to those supporters and to their leadership causes them to feel guilty. As the lack of focus continues, the feelings of guilt, failure, and unproductiveness, when added to other Red-zone warning signs, can cause the person to sink deeper into the quicksand of despair.

4. Constant fear

This type of fear pervades life during waking moments and even during sleep. It is something that gnaws at one's heart, mind, and soul. The fear can be a personal fear of death, dying, bombing, terrorism, abduction, rape, murder, robbery, spiritual warfare attacks, or any number of other fear-producing dangers and threats. This fear can be for oneself, a family member, a friend, or a team member. It can keep us from doing the simplest of tasks and can make our behavior erratic. After being stopped and threatened at gunpoint at a roadblock by masked militants one afternoon, I found myself fearing what was around the bend on every street I traveled for the next two months. I became very edgy because of the fear that was just below the surface of my thoughts and feelings.

5. Spiritual dryness

The deserts of the Middle East have been locations of spiritual renewal and the strengthening of relationships between man and God for centuries. Jesus and Paul are two prime examples of this. Monks have gone off to these deserts to live, in order to commune with God. God calls us at times into specific desert-type experiences to woo us and develop us.

Many times, though, the spiritual lives of our personnel have become dry and barren like those deserts. I know that was the case with me. Instead of being the place that drew me closer to God, there was a period during the most intense time of Red-zone stress when I wandered farther away from God. Prayer became difficult, if not impossible. I found excuses not to read His Word. In short, I cut off the source of hope—my relationship with God—in the midst of darkness. Consider some of the reasons for such dry, spiritual conditions:

- There can be a lack of spiritual preparation for the spiritual warfare present in Red zones. Either no one told us or we did not listen to the fact that the Red-zone location in which we find ourselves is a spiritual warfare battle zone.
- There can be a lack of believers or a lack of fellowship options with other believers in the Red zone. One of the biggest mistakes which sending organizations make is to send a "unit" out to a Red zone by themselves. Sending a couple to a remote location without team members or a support base with local believers is a prescription for intense attacks of spiritual warfare. Without the spiritual support from a team, they can be defeated and disheartened quickly.
- There can be an absence of corporate and personal praise and worship time. All of us need the encouragement, strength, support, and power gained through corporate praise and worship. This is even more necessary in a Red zone.
- There can be a lack of an adequate prayer support base around the world for the specific needs and challenges of Red-zone personnel. Such a base is essential for Red-zone personnel. Without it, we face the spiritual warfare battles alone, when the Father would have us face them with the body of Christ.
- There can be a lack of a consistent and established prayer and devotional lifestyle. The spiritual disciplines are critical for all people in Red zones. Prayer, fasting, Bible reading, worship, silence, solitude, serving, stewardship, and evangelism are all disciplines which will enhance Red-zone living. In practicing these, one's relationship with God will grow and become more intimate.
- There can be an inability to prioritize life's activities. Business, work, and

ministry can begin to take on more importance than being with God.

Such spiritual dryness can lead us to wander in the wilderness of the Red zone without direction, hope, vision, and, most importantly, without the sustaining relationship of the Father.

Strategies for Red-Zone Living

A strategy is a plan for achieving a specific purpose. In the case of Red-zone living, developing strategies for living is essential. Here are 10 strategies to help personnel deal with the stress of living within a Red zone.

1. *Give others permission to speak into your life*

One of the most important things that my wife and I did when we were living in a Red zone was to give another trusted couple permission to talk freely and specifically with us about our lives. We found that living in a Red zone caused us to develop fuzzy boundaries. That means that we kept saying to ourselves, "Things aren't so bad," or, "We can handle it." Then when things got worse, such as a bomb exploding on the road just minutes before we passed by, we said, "That wasn't as bad as I thought it would be." However, when we kept moving our boundaries back, we were actually on a daily downhill slide, losing touch with our thoughts and feelings and losing the ability to cope in healthy ways. Our friends, who lived outside the Red zone, could urge us to leave the Red zone if they saw or sensed that we were beginning to minimize its realities and dangers. If they told us to get out, we trusted them enough to leave for a period of time (one to two weeks), in order to re-evaluate our situation to see if we were capable of continuing our work and ministry. Speaking into the life of another is the biblical principle found in Ephesians 4:25, where we are told, "Therefore, each of you must put off falsehood and speak truthfully to his neighbor, for we are all members of one body."

2. *Get help*

All of us feel depressed at times. All of us have fears. All of us have times of blurred focus on our tasks. All of us have times of spiritual dryness. These are normal occurrences. But when they become regular attributes, seek out help. Listen to what others are saying to you and what your body and reactions are saying. Get a physical exam to make sure that there is not something medically wrong that is causing some of your symptoms. Find a counselor or a trusted friend who can help you monitor what is going on in your life. Check in with a leader and/or member care worker in your organization, so that he/she can talk with you about your Red-zone stressors.

3. *Remember the Greatest Commandment and God's sovereignty in the midst of your troubles*

First, in Mark 12:28-31, Jesus shares with us the importance of relationships and of staying connected. Of all the commandments, He said, "The most important one is this: 'Hear, O Israel, the Lord our God, the Lord is one. Love the Lord your God with all your heart and with all your soul and with all your mind and with all your strength.' The second is this: 'Love your neighbor as yourself.' There is no commandment greater than these."

Secondly, John 17 tells us we are *never* alone, no matter what our circumstances. We are never alone in the midst of our pain and suffering. God is always present to comfort, support, and encourage, whether the suffering is happening to us or to the people whom we serve. God is always sovereign in every circumstance. He will have victory in our lives and in the Red zones. We must keep this fact of Scripture ever before us, even when we do not recognize it. The fact of His sovereignty is not dependent on our recognition or awareness. It is dependent on the truth of His Word and the reality of His presence.

Those of us living in Red zones must stay connected with God. He is our main source of strength and hope. This is not some "obligatory God comment" but an important reminder about our relationship with Him. Stay focused on God and keep yourself immersed in His Word on a daily basis. Communicate with Him in prayer, even when it is difficult. He will answer.

4. *Be prepared for spiritual warfare*

Spiritual warfare, as outlined in Ephesians 6:10-20, is perhaps the most important area to be understood and practiced in Red-zone life. Prayer for deliverance, spiritual discernment, demonic oppression, and spiritual struggles "in the heavenlies" are not just abstract concepts but realities of life. Defeat in the battles of spiritual warfare can be devastating for field personnel. It is in these battles that we lose heart, lose focus, and lose the intimate relationship with our First Love.

Many of us in the Red zone were ill-prepared for what awaited us in the arena of spiritual warfare. One striking example was a couple, Tim and Laine, who were having some marital difficulties. As it turned out, the husband was very depressed. He constantly put himself down and downplayed his ability to learn Arabic and to be an effective witness. My wife and I called in another couple so that the four of us could pray for Tim and Laine. We prayed with them for two hours. During the prayer time, Tim heard a word from the Lord that confirmed that Tim was trying to do all of this without Him. In addition, Tim realized that the language helper whom he was using was involved in Islamic curses and had called some on Tim. Immediately after our prayer time, Tim's entire countenance changed. A significant inner shift had also happened through prayer. Tim and his family returned to their Red zone, and he entered his spiritual warfare battle with renewed faith and hope. He became more intimate with the Father in his devotional time, developed a prayer strategy and support base, and initiated strategies for dealing with the curses directed at him by his language helper. Later Tim reported that his entire attitude had improved, his marital relationship was stronger, and his depression had lifted.

There are divergent views about spiritual warfare; however, there are plenty of good, balanced books on the subject. Check with your pastor or colleague to see what books would be of most benefit for you from your biblical perspective. However, remember the importance of the armor of God. George Otis, Jr. (1998, p. 187) has a helpful perspective: "Putting on the armor of God is synonymous with daily surrender to the Lordship of Jesus Christ. ... We simply dedicate our first conscious thoughts each morning to the will of the Master. Spiritual armor becomes lifestyle when, for the balance of the day, we choose to walk in the consciousness of His presence and purpose."

5. *Work at marital growth*

Spouses must not take each other for granted. It is so easy to neglect this relationship because other things seem more important at the time. Needy people, ministry demands, deadlines, and other tasks call out for our time and energy. At the end of the day, there is little left for your spouse. When you add Red-zone stress to this picture, you can end up as two individuals in a marriage who have lost the time, energy, and will to work on that relationship.

Growing apart does not occur overnight. I have worked with couples in missions who have grown so far apart that they have become two people living alone together. When this happens, the possibility of marital infidelity is just around the corner. Make time for your spouse. Maintain spiritual growth as a couple. Work at keeping the flame of romance burning. Date your spouse. Have fun and play together. Get away alone as a couple, even if it is only for a night. Be diligent to communicate clearly and regularly. Take advantage of marriage enrichment opportunities and retreats. Your relationship has the potential to sustain you in the midst of any Red-zone storm or stress.

6. *Exercise*

In the Red zone, our bodies can suffer from lack of physical exercise. It may not be safe or acceptable just to go out and exercise. Our usual exercise and eating habits can change. Consequently, our emotions and spiritual life can be affected negatively, because our heart, mind, soul, and strength are all intertwined. If one area suffers, such as the physical, the other areas are affected. A frequent question that I get from both men and women about exercise in Red zones is, "How and where do I exercise in my Red zone?" A stationary bicycle, a treadmill, step aerobics, and isometrics are all excellent ways to exercise. Videotapes can be purchased covering all aspects of exercise and can be followed in the privacy of your living room in front of a TV.

7. *Develop confidants and close friends*

Many married people would say, "My spouse is my best friend." That is great. However, at the same time, all of us would benefit greatly from having at least one same-gender confidant in our lives. This is also true, of course, for singles. One of the first things that my wife and I prayed for when we moved into a Red zone was a friend for her and a friend for me. I needed someone outside my marital relationship with whom I could relate as "guy to guy." As a rule, men usually do not cultivate a "best friend" relationship so easily. Women in Red zones usually have an easier time in finding that special friend. When you have a friendship like Ruth and Naomi or Jonathan and David, it will bless you and challenge you in your life and ministry. My Red-zone best friend was a strength and support to me, and I became that for him. It takes precious time and energy to develop such a friendship, but the benefit for both of you will be worth the effort.

8. *Give encouragement*

There are two statements in Scripture that tell us to do something daily. The first is Luke 9:23, "If anyone would come after Me, he must deny himself and take up his cross daily and follow Me." The second is Hebrews 3:13, "But encourage one another daily, as long as it is called 'today,' so that none of you may be hardened by sin's deceitfulness." Without regular encouragement, we can lose hope, vision, and focus. With it, we can do far beyond what we thought possible. Encouragement is a two-way street—it is mutual. Encouragement is both a discipline and a practice. If we are not encouraging others daily, we all run the risk of being "hardened by sin's deceitfulness." A network and ethos of encouragement for one another while in a Red zone is a good antidote for despair. It helps us see the potential good and God's power even in very difficult circumstances.

9. *Take time to talk about and process issues*

When anger, fear, hatred, and frustration begin creeping into your Red-zone life, find someone with whom you can talk about these issues. Intentionally seek out your spouse, your best friend, an accountability partner, a colleague, a member care specialist, or others. When we lived in a Red zone in the late 1980s and early 1990s, I found myself on the dangerous ground of hating the soldiers who were killing and maiming the people to whom God had called me. As that hatred began to grow, I realized that I was slipping outside of God's presence and will for my life. My wife and my best friend helped me work through many issues, helped me renew my relationship with the Lord, and helped me maintain a good perspective on life.

10. *Play and have fun*

Set apart time for relaxation, renewal, and recreation—have fun! These kinds of experiences have the potential to make our Red-zone living more bearable. Play games, go on a hike, or do other activities as a couple, family, group of couples, group of singles, team, or any other kind of grouping. It takes our minds off our Red-zone lives and allows us to step away from those ever-present worries, fears, frustrations, dangers, and stresses.

During the height of the "Intifada" (the conflict between the Palestinians and the Israelis in the late 1980s and early '90s), tensions were extremely high. We were stressed because many people we knew had been beaten, imprisoned, or shot. On top of that, we were upset by the constant roadblocks, curfews, and tense atmosphere. One weekend, about five families decided to take an all-day hike in the Judean wilderness. We hiked down canyons, forded streams, laughed, talked, and played along the way. Our minds and bodies totally disengaged from the tension of the West Bank. We returned to our homes exhausted but rejuvenated. Our physical bodies had been stretched to the maximum. Our emotions had been allowed to run free and play in the Judean hill country. Our spirits were renewed as we talked and laughed with our colleagues, who all had two things in common—our faith in God and the stress of living in a Red zone.

Guidelines for Administrators and Leaders

Sending agencies have an essential role in the lives of their personnel who live in Red zones. Mission leaders such as field directors are often the first-line, main member care providers in many situations. Here are a number of things for administrators and leaders to do, based on my experiences in living in Red zones, working as an administrator, and helping as a member care specialist.

Suggestions: Five Things to Avoid

1. Avoid overstatements

If you have never lived in a Red zone for six months or more, be careful not to overstate the phrase, "I understand what you are going through and feeling." People in Red zones are extremely sensitive. Statements like this are not received well by Red-zone personnel. This is especially true when administrators and leadership make such statements from the safety and security of their home offices in Western countries.

2. Avoid downplaying danger and stress

When talking with your personnel in Red zones, be careful not to trivialize, negate, or over-spiritualize the Red-zone dangers and stresses that they are experiencing. The best thing that you can do is speak from a caring and compassionate heart that feels the pain and the hurt of the Red-zone person and that does more listening than speaking.

3. Avoid conflict

Try not to react negatively to your personnel in Red zones, whether in person, on the telephone, or in emails. They may be quite difficult to communicate with and may not even realize it. They do not need the added stress of being in conflict with their leadership. There is a time and a place for dealing with difficult issues, but emails and telephone calls are not the right place. Save confrontations for face-to-face encounters outside their Red zone.

4. Avoid increasing personnel workloads

Try not to increase the work, ministry, or administrative loads of Red-zone personnel. Much of the time they are just trying to keep their emotional heads above the water, and any added responsibilities will only tend to increase the frustration, stress, and worry. One of the biggest workload problems that Red-zone personnel face is the "traveling spouse." I know of many organizations that have some of their personnel traveling 30-60% of the time! This is a prescription for burnout for the one traveling. Also, it is a burnout prescription for the spouse who stays behind and "tends the fort," watches the kids, and handles all the other aspects of living. Usually the one who stays behind is the wife. In addition, the tension caused by this kind of intense, husband-wife separation can play havoc with the marital relationship, particularly for those living in a Red zone. Administrators would be wise to keep the travel of their Red-zone personnel to a minimum.

5. *Avoid making decisions without personnel input*

Try not to make decisions for Red-zone personnel without their input. Always seek to value their input, and include their input in your decision-making process. Not to include them in decisions directly affecting them will set you as leader in conflict with your Red-zone personnel. Try to make decisions for these personnel with them from within the Red zone, not from the comfort and security of a Western office location.

Suggestions: Ten Things to Do

1. *Provide a range of member care support*

Never be afraid to send help to your Red-zone personnel. They will appreciate it. Crisis response workshops, spiritual life seminars/retreats, marriage enrichment, family life and education consultation, career development, debriefings, and other such opportunities will aid your personnel greatly. Member care shows them how much the organization values them and invests in them. Remember to include "member care resources" in the annual planning, budgets, and strategy development. Good member care is proactive—far more than just offering counseling when someone struggles. As I have talked with various mission personnel over the past five years, including those serving in Red zones, one key request keeps coming to the surface: "We need member care in order to make it."

2. *Keep in regular telephone contact*

Email is great. However, your personnel in Red zones need to hear your voice, and they need to know that you care, support, and encourage them. The frequency of your calls should be on a weekly basis to once per month, depending on how difficult their situation is. It would be helpful to have a set time and day on which you will call, so that your personnel are expecting to hear from you rather than being surprised by your call. Try not to mix a business call with a "checking in" call to people in the Red zone. You may think that you have checked in, but they will receive it as your doing business first and your checking in as an afterthought.

3. *Listen*

When you talk on the telephone, listen to what is being said and what is not being said. From a caring pastoral perspective, ask for their thoughts, ideas, and feelings. Listen for signs of over-rationalization, over-spiritualizing, hypersensitivity, fuzzy boundaries, or trivializing of their situation. Listen for unspoken cries for help. In addition, listen for the warning signs mentioned earlier in this chapter. Your personnel may not always realize just how in need they are. If you cannot determine what to do, you might want to set up a telephone consult with a member care specialist and your personnel, just to make sure that you are reading their situation clearly.

4. *Be an encourager*

You may be the main source of encouragement that your personnel receive, especially if they are in isolated locations by themselves. One of the major mistakes that organizational leadership makes in the placement of personnel, especially in Red zones, is the putting of one family unit in a Red-zone location by themselves. We place our personnel at great emotional and spiritual risk when we do not prepare and send out compatible families "two by two." A family unit needs the nurture, support, and encouragement of another family in difficult Red-zone locations.

5. *Provide opportunities for breaks*

Personnel living in Red zones need the opportunity to get away from the dangers of their location regularly. It is very difficult for individuals, couples, and families to stay in the "heat of battle" without hope of relief. Many organizations mandate such breaks and provide financial support at times to help personnel get away. A helpful amount of time might be two weeks every six months, but this should be determined in consultation with your Red-zone personnel, member care personnel, and other leaders. In some Red zones, these breaks would need to be out of country. In other cases, it might be somewhere away from the conflict zone but within the geographical country. Some organizations have set up "safe houses" that are available for their personnel as well as for those from other organizations.

6. *Visit your personnel whenever possible*

Visits are so important by a member care worker or leader from your organization or someone seconded from another organization. A stay for several days will provide you with much helpful information as to the difficulty and danger in that Red zone. It will allow you to walk alongside your personnel and to hear their joys, fears, difficulties, and hurts. In addition, it will allow you to minister to them. After you leave, your phone calls will take on added meaning to them and to you, because you will have a better understanding of their situation and therefore will be able to provide better support and encouragement.

7. *Provide debriefing opportunities*

Whenever any of your personnel get away from their Red zone for a break, meetings, conferences, or workshops, try to provide some kind of debriefing opportunity. For some, a regular Critical Incident Stress Debriefing (CISD) might be in order, while for others, just listening to them and then helping them clarify their thoughts/feelings/plans will be beneficial.

8. *Take directive leadership*

The time may come for you as the leader to take a more directive leadership role for personnel serving in more difficult locations. If one of your family units appears to be slowly falling apart and heading for a breakdown, be ready to act on their behalf. Talk with them, and after consulting with others such as a member care specialist, be prepared to get them out for their own safety and well-being.

9. *Monitor*

It is important to monitor your personnel during and after their Red-zone service. Use your member care specialist to check in with them by email, telephone, and personal visits. If you do not have a member care specialist, then enlist the cooperation of another organization's specialist to assist your personnel. Also, when your personnel leave the Red zone, see that they have opportunity to be involved in a Critical Incident Stress Debriefing. The CISD is a very valuable tool which can help your personnel process their Red-zone experiences and possibly keep them from having stress-related difficulties later on.

10. *Develop a Red-zone protocol and strategy*

Each organization would do well to develop a Red-zone protocol so that it can appropriately monitor Red-zone stability and appropriately respond to Red-zone crises. The protocol should be developed and communicated with personnel before they enter a Red zone, usually during pre-field orientation. Training in crisis and contingency management is also important. Some of the following things would be helpful to include in your protocol:

- Define a Red zone and have a way to monitor the degree of risk to personnel.

- Itemize work and ministry expectations of personnel.
- Provide exit strategies and clear criteria for departure.
- Provide opportunities for assistance from the organization and from a member care specialist.
- Provide resources for living in a Red zone (books on stress, exercise, spiritual growth, etc.).
- Outline an administrative strategy for dealing with Red zones (contingency plans). All administrators and leadership should be oriented to contingency management procedures.

Conclusion

Doing member care well in Red zones is the responsibility of all of us. First, member care is the responsibility of the personnel living in Red zones. Individuals, couples, and teams need to be proactive regarding their own member care. Each person needs to take steps towards developing healthy margins for living. Personnel need to be aware of Red-zone warning signs and the dangers inherent in not caring for oneself. In addition, they need to be willing to ask for help when they need it. Close friends especially provide a safety net of support and encouragement.

Secondly, member care is the responsibility of organizational and agency administrators and leadership. Good leaders do not just assume everything is OK just because they have not heard any cries for help. Rather, they regularly and sensitively check in with their Red-zone personnel. What they model and how they relate to personnel are key influences on the overall ethos and member care program of an agency. Dr. Eddie Pate, a good friend and field leader, made an excellent observation. He said, "In order to help my people make it long-term on the field (in Red zones), I need to do three things: Take care of my people, take care of my people, and take care of my people."

Thirdly, member care in Red zones is the responsibility of the member care specialists from the field team, mobile member care team, or the organization's home office. These specialists need to be available to spend quality time with personnel in order to assist them. In addition, they can apprise sending agencies about member care issues and needs. Member care specialists need to update their professional skills on a regular basis and make sure they have the breaks and support that they need as well. No one is immune from Red-zone stress! It would be helpful if member care specialists could live in a Red zone for a minimum of three to six months in order to better understand life and personnel in Red zones.

There is life in Red zones. It is possible to grow in one's relationship with God, self, and others. It is possible to find security in Him in the midst of stress and danger. Moreover, it is possible to carry out the task to which Red-zone personnel have been called. The love and support that come via good member care are keys to really making it in these difficult settings. Red zones will always be with us. May the Lord give us wisdom and hearts of compassion as we faithfully minister to needy people in these areas and as we diligently care for our workers.

Reflection and Discussion

1. What kinds of dangers and stressors describe the Red zone in which you live or in which personnel whom you know live?
2. What are some likely warning signs which you might experience to help you realize that life in a Red zone is adversely impacting you?
3. List a few ways that your organization could apply some of the suggestions made in this article.
4. Identify some personal strategies which are/were helpful to your Red-zone experience and which might be helpful to others ministering and living in Red zones.
5. What are some ways to further support national Christians who live and are "stuck" in Red zones?

References and Suggested Reading

Anderson, N., & Baumchen, H. (1999). *Finding hope again*. Ventura, CA: Regal Publishing.

Carlson, E. (1997). *Trauma assessments: A clinician's guide*. New York, NY: Guilford.

Eriksson, C., Vande Kemp, H., Gorsuch, R., Hoke, S., & Foy, D. (2001). Trauma exposure and PTSD symptoms in international relief and development personnel. *Journal of Traumatic Studies, 14*, 205-212.

Matsakis, A. (1996). *I can't get over it: A handbook for trauma survivors*. Oakland, CA: New Harbinger Publications.

Otis, G., Jr. (1998). Recognizing and defeating the powers of darkness. *International Journal of Frontier Missions, 15*, 183-192.

Welch, E. (1997). *When people are big and God is small*. Phillipsburg, NJ: P & R Publishing.

Whitney, D. (1991). *Spiritual disciplines for the Christian life*. Colorado Springs, CO: NavPress.

Williams, K. (2000). *Sharpening your interpersonal skills*. Colorado Springs, CO: Interpersonal Training Partners.

Raymond Hicks *and his wife Beverly have been involved for over 25 years in Red-zone living and ministry with the International Mission Board, SBC. Ray has assisted numerous other Christian organizations and non-governmental organizations as a member care consultant. He is currently serving as the Member Care Specialist/Consultant for the IMB in Northern Africa and the Middle East. The Hicks have lived in Israel, the West Bank, and Jordan. Ray received a Doctorate of Ministry in marriage and family from Eastern Baptist Theological Seminary in Philadelphia, Pennsylvania. He holds a Master's of Divinity with an emphasis in pastoral care from Southern Baptist Theological Seminary in Louisville, Kentucky. Ray and Beverly have been married for 31 years and have three children. Sommer and Melakee are their daughters, and Micah is their son. Email: memcare@netzero.net.*

Special thanks to the following people who reviewed this chapter: Beverly Hicks, Paul and Harriet Lawrence, Elias Moussa, Eddie and Myrla Pate, and Gerry Volkart.

Part 3
Providing and Developing Member Care

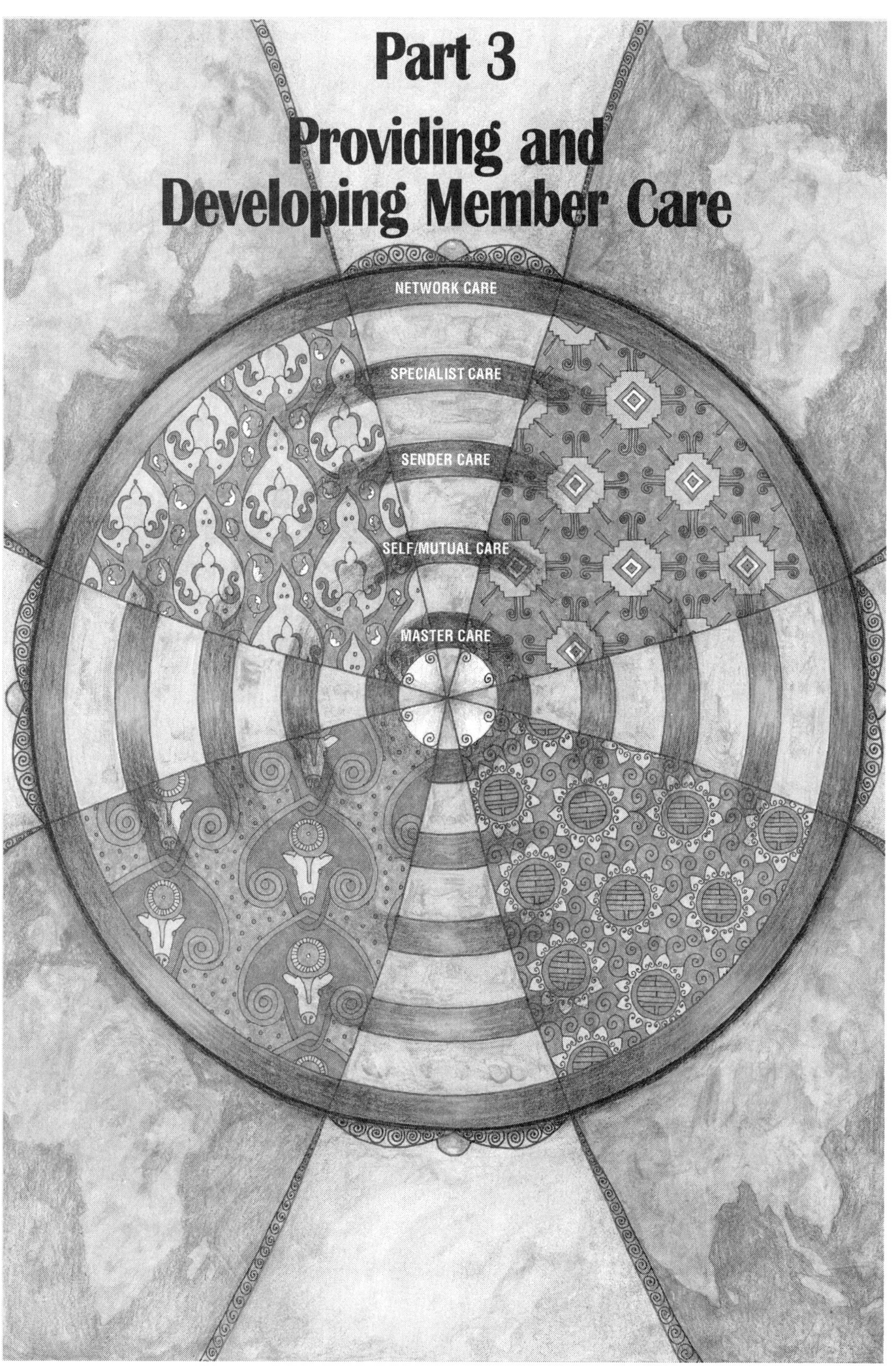

21

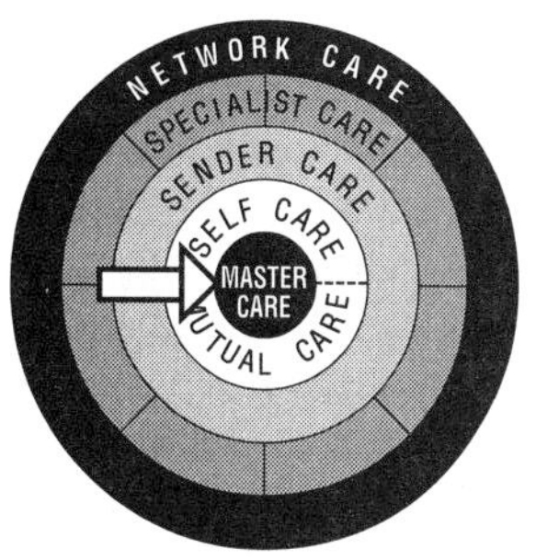

Jesus Christ: The Heart Of Member Care

DAVID HUGGETT
JOYCE HUGGETT

While here on earth, Jesus' effectiveness in ministry stemmed from the loving support given Him by God the Father and God the Holy Spirit. In turn, Jesus gave equally effective support to His disciples. He forged deep and loving relationships with each of them, modeled an alternative lifestyle to them, and showed them how life on earth can and must revolve around His Father. Jesus, the Master Carer, has much to teach member care workers and mission partners.

"What are you two intending to do with the rest of your lives?" That's the question a retired missionary put to us when we stood at one of life's crossroads in the early 1990s. For 19 years we had pastored a thriving church in England. Sensing that God was calling us out of that ministry, we handed over the leadership to others, then took sabbatical leave on the island of Cyprus—to rest, reflect, and contemplate the question, "What next?" The missionary's question, therefore, was timely.

We had been looking after a study center for missionaries for six weeks when this question was put to us. Set in a beautiful village on the island, this center provided mission partners with a place where they could come to study a variety of subjects. There was a well-stocked library with shelves packed with Bible commentaries, books on mission-related topics, books on relationships, and so on. There were teaching tapes, too, which mission partners could listen to and learn from. The missionary who was asking us about our future was aware of the work we had been doing at the center. "I feel that God might be calling you to work overseas long-term," she said. "Would you mind if I wrote to the International Director of my mission and told him about you?"

Responding to this question changed the course of our lives. A year later, we returned to Cyprus to begin an entirely new ministry. Aware that most mission partners are too tired to take time out to study, for six years we provided a place where, instead of working for examinations, they could respond to Jesus' invitation to "come with Me by yourselves to a quiet place and take some rest" (Mark 6:31). Although we have now returned to England, we continue this member care ministry in our home. "The Hiding

Place," as it is called, is a place to which mission partners delight to come: to reflect on the months or years they have been working overseas, to prepare prayerfully to go overseas for the first time, or simply to enjoy the quietness and the beauty of a place where they can meet with God without being disturbed.

Over the years, as we have been listening to such people, we have attempted to understand and apply Jesus' approach to ministry. The subject of Master care is, then, one in which we are intensely interested. By Master care, we mean the way God, having created us, puts the ongoing finishing touches to us: growing us up spiritually and emotionally, loving us, giving us the grace to love Him in return, and giving us the grace, too, to love His people and His ministry. In particular, we place the spotlight in this paper on the way Jesus trained, mentored, equipped, supported, and loved the Twelve, and we seek to relate this ministry to the ministry of mission partners and member care workers.

Rooted in Relationships

As we have studied Jesus' ministry over the years, the conviction has deepened that Master care is rooted in establishing, developing, and maintaining relationships—first the relationship between God and the caregiver and then between the caregiver and the partner being cared for. We say this because, before Jesus began His public ministry, He enjoyed a deep relationship with His Father and with the Holy Spirit. He also formed close relationships with a dozen key people, the Twelve. Indeed, one of the moving things about the method of earthly ministry Jesus models is that He called His disciples to be *with* Him before He asked them to do anything *for* Him (Mark 3:14).

We have a beautiful example of Jesus' relationships in the first chapter of John's Gospel: "The next day John was back at his post with two disciples, who were watching. He looked up, saw Jesus walking nearby, and said, 'Here he is, God's Passover Lamb.' The two disciples heard him and went after Jesus. Jesus looked over his shoulder and said to them, 'What are you after?' They said, 'Rabbi, (which means "Teacher"), where are you staying?' He replied, 'Come along and see for yourself.' They came, saw where he was living, and ended up staying with him for the day" (John 1:37-38, The Message).

Notice that, instead of simply *describing* the place where He stayed, Jesus invited them to "come and see." The result of their day together was that Jesus and Andrew became firm friends. This new relationship had such power that Andrew immediately led his brother, Simon, to the Master.

The emphasis on relationships does not end there, however. After much prayer, and from the large number of disciples who were already attracted to Him, Jesus chose just 12 men. He carefully and lovingly formed community with them *before* He sent them out on any mission. A study of the Gospels shows how deeply He loved them (John 15:9), how He called them friends (John 15:15), and how they became as family to Him. They ate together, traveled together, and in all probability bathed in the Sea of Galilee together. The Twelve watched Jesus turn water into wine, heal the sick, and cast out demons. They heard Him teach, pray, admonish, and encourage. They walked together, talked together, and went fishing together. They became one with Him in the bonds of friendship. They were open with one another. This closeness grew *before* they started to work with Jesus.

Rooted in Rhythm and Rest

Soon after Jesus involved them in His mission, however, Mark paints a picture of the group being pressured by people—so much so that "because so many people were coming and going ... they did not even have a chance to eat" (Mark 6:31).

Seeing and sensing what was happening, Jesus acted: "Come with Me by yourselves to a quiet place and get some rest"

(Mark 6:31), He insisted. He did not say *go* and take some rest. No. The invitation is to *come*: "Come with Me. Let's do it together." On another occasion, He gives them a similar invitation: "Are you tired? Worn out? Burned out on religion? Come to me. Get away with me and you'll recover your life. I'll show you how to take a real rest. Walk with me and work with me—watch how I do it. Learn the unforced rhythms of grace" (Matt. 11:28-30, The Message).

Again, notice the language: "Come. Get away *with me*. Watch how *I* do it. Learn the unforced rhythms of grace." This is the language of Jesus' heart. It is the language of Master care *par excellence.*

In her book *Jesus Man of Prayer*, Sister Margaret Magdalene (1987, p. 41) reminds us, "Jesus was rarely without a crowd around Him. His own personal space was constantly invaded—not just in terms of time but in actual physical contact. Jostled and pushed by the throng (Mark 5:31), forced to preach from a borrowed boat in order to distance Himself a little from the growing crowd on the shore (Matt. 13:2), the picture builds up of someone under incessant pressure. His compassion for the crowds meant that mothers came crashing in with their children." Jesus' need for space, then, was urgent, and He did not hesitate to make sure He had such space, even though at times this caused Him to close His ears to cries for help and to turn away from people (Matt. 5:1; Mark 1:37).

Life offers us many similar choices. In saying no to being driven and becoming too busy, Jesus was saying yes to relationships—first to His relationship with the Father and the Spirit and secondly to His relationship with His disciples. His life was rather like the ebb and flow of the sea or the rising and setting of the sun. For Him, there was a season for everything: aloneness and togetherness, busyness and rest, fruitfulness and fallowness, quality time with His Father and quality time with the disciples, with whom Jesus forged warm, loving, lasting relationships.

Rooted in a Realistic Lifestyle

The Master provided care for His disciples in three main ways: by example, through teaching, and through mentoring. In this section, we examine each of these types of care in turn.

Jesus' Example

He refuses the "tyranny of the urgent"

The example Jesus sets presents a challenge to those of us who find ourselves overwhelmed by work, overstimulated by people and ideas, living cross-culturally, and traveling often and far. Mark sums up the situation well when he recalls how, very early one morning, Jesus escaped to the hills to pray. The previous day had been hectic. Jesus had preached in the synagogue in Capernaum, healed Peter's mother-in-law, and then ministered to countless other needy people who begged for His help. Although He had gone away to meet His Father in prayer, the disciples searched Him out. "Everyone is searching for you," they said (Mark 1:37). If they were imagining that Jesus would stop His prayer time because of the needs of the crowd, they were mistaken. Jesus says, quietly but firmly, "Let's go somewhere else." They went to another part of Galilee to continue the work of evangelism, but between Capernaum where the conversation took place and the other villages lay miles of open countryside. The walk not only gave them time and space to reflect, rest, have their energy restored, and renew their relationship with God, but also gave them some much-needed time together.

Commenting on Jesus' attitude, Sister Margaret Magdalene (1987, pp. 41-42) writes: "He refused to submit to the tyranny of the urgent. He would not let the crowds or even human need dictate the priorities. He had an inner freedom to say 'No.' He could say 'No' with integrity because in His times with His Father, He clearly discerned and adopted the Father's priorities and perspectives. Not in bondage to the need to achieve, nor neurotic about the success of His mission, nor puffed up by popularity, He is free."

He ensures that output is matched by input

Jesus modeled the need to live a balanced life for the sake of our soul and our relationships. Someone has summed up this need with this piece of advice:

input=output=input=output

In other words, if we are to give out to others effectively, we must make sure that we take in as much as we give out. Output for member care workers might mean traveling to visit mission partners, relating to them, loving them, listening to their worries or pain or struggles, feeling inadequate for the task of being involved in member care, and not knowing where to turn for help. Output for mission partners might include stressful activities such as language study; adapting to a new climate, diet, and culture; coping with transition; and facing the challenge of using professional skills in an unfamiliar environment and without the tools and finances that were available in the home country.

Input for both member care workers and mission partners might include rest days and holidays, letters or emails from home, and well-planned conferences. By well-planned conferences, we mean conferences where there are spaces between sessions, with time to make and deepen relationships, time to relax, and time to enjoy periods of personal prayer, as well as informative teaching and discussions and the opportunity to talk in depth with someone qualified to listen. Input might also come in the form of a retreat where the emphasis is on one's relationship with God and/or on personal growth, rather than on listening to talks. Above all, input comes in the still, hushed place where God's voice is most clearly heard and His love most keenly felt.

He models a ministry saturated in prayer

Jesus sets us the example, not only of a balanced life, but also of a *prayerful* life. He was praying at His baptism when the heavens opened, the Spirit descended on Him, and He received the Father's affirmation (Luke 3:21-22). He was praying on that morning we mentioned earlier when, after a hectic Sabbath, long before dawn, while it was still night, His disciples found Him in a secluded spot (Mark 1:35). He was praying right through the night after He had fed the 5,000 and insisted that His disciples get into the boat and go on ahead (Mark 6:45-46).

Jesus' disciples would have been men of prayer long before their Master came on the scene. They had a prayer place—the synagogue. They had a hymnbook—the Psalms. They listened to the Old Testament being read and learned passages of it by heart. They also said prayers each morning on waking and each evening before sleeping. Certain "blessings" were also part of their vocabulary—like this early morning wake-up call: "This is the day the Lord has made; let us rejoice and be glad in it." They kept the Sabbath too. The God to whom they prayed, though, was distant, demanding, and too holy for them to come near. In fact, the name of God was considered too holy to pass a person's lips.

When Jesus came into their lives, by His own example, He taught them a new way of praying. Here was a man who obviously felt secure in the Father's love. This influenced the *way* He prayed. Intimacy, warmth, delight, and spontaneity are words that best describe His own conversations with the Father. Perhaps it is not surprising, then, that those who lived alongside Him begged Him, "Lord, teach *us* to pray" (Luke 11:1).

Did His very first suggestion surprise them? "When you pray," He suggested, "say *Abba*—daddy" (Luke 11:2). Since the Old Testament speaks often of God as Father, the Twelve would have been familiar with the *picture* of God as Father (see Ps. 103:13; Isa. 63:16; 64:8; Hos. 11:1-4). It would never have occurred to Jesus' disciples to *call* God "Father," however. As Professor Joachim Jeremias (1967) reminds us, there is not a single example of the use of "Abba" as an address to God in the whole of Jewish literature.

We are not told whether or not the disciples acted on Jesus' advice in the early days of their School of Prayer. What we are told is that Jesus tried to make sure that the disciples' image of God was accurate. His main method, in true Middle Eastern style, was to speak to their hearts by telling them stories. Take the three unforgettable stories in Luke 15, for example. Here Jesus shows that God is like a Middle Eastern shepherd who discovers that one of his sheep is lost. He searches everywhere until the sheep is safely in his arms and on its way back to the fold. When it has arrived home, the shepherd throws a party to celebrate.

God is not only like a man. Jesus also compares Him to a Middle Eastern housewife who sweeps and sweeps the floor of her home and refuses to rest until her precious coin has been found. Most moving of all, Jesus likens God to a Middle Eastern father whose two sons both wish he would drop dead. Even though they treat their father cruelly, the father offers them nothing but love.

Love is what God is. Goodness is what God is. Compassion is what God is. This is the message that Jesus wanted His disciples to believe. He wanted them to know that each of them was personally loved by His Father. Little by little, His friends accepted the good news. Brennan Manning (1994, p. 16), in *Abba's Child*, reminds us what a huge step forward this was: "It takes a profound conversion to accept that God is relentlessly tender and compassionate toward us just as we are—not in spite of our sins and faults—but with them."

Jesus not only assured His disciples that they were loved by a compassionate, tender God, He also taught them the transforming power of God's love. He did this by allowing them to see how these truths gave *Him* the power to fulfill His God-given calling, even when the way was hard. To explain what we mean, we use an adaptation of a tool the British psychiatrist Frank Lake (1966, p. 205) developed, The Dynamic Cycle of Being and Well-Being:

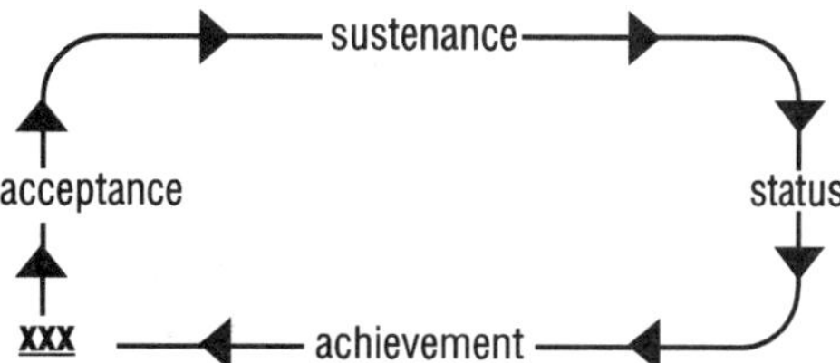

The Dynamic Cycle of Being and Well-Being

Lake used this diagram to illustrate two truths: first, to demonstrate the sense of well-being that is given to a child who experiences its mother's love and, second, to show how Jesus' sense of well-being found its roots in His Father's felt love.

Regarding the first truth, Lake reminds us how a good mother gives her child acceptance. Then, as she feeds the child, not only with milk but also with warmth and love, the child's sense of belonging in this world expands. Acceptance, welcome, and sustenance provide the child with a sense of belonging and status—so much so that it is ready to learn the achievement of relating to and giving love to others.

Jesus' relationship with His Father was not unlike the relationship a child enjoys with a good mother. While He was here on earth, He frequently retreated into His Father's presence—particularly when He was in any kind of pain, such as the bereavement He must have felt so keenly after the murder of his cousin, John the Baptist. In the silence, He poured His pain into the lap of His Father. The Father, in turn, gave Him acceptance—not in spite of the pain but *with* the grief. Jesus found Himself not only accepted, but also supported and sustained. The intimacy that bound Him to His Father reassured Him of His status. His Father had spelled this out at His baptism: "You are My Son, whom I love; with You I am well pleased"(Mark

1:11). From the fullness of acceptance, sustenance, and the status of being a beloved child, Jesus was able to return to continue the work the Father had sent Him to do: to continue to pour out redeeming love and compassion to others.

In contrast, we are reminded of an occasion when we traveled overseas to lead a prayer retreat for a group of mission partners. After the retreat, one of the partners admitted, "I love God and really want to serve Him, but I've never quite grasped that God loves *me*." Many other mission partners would echo this admission. The problem with this lack of assurance that we are loved is that we are tempted to move around the dynamic cycle in the opposite direction from Jesus:

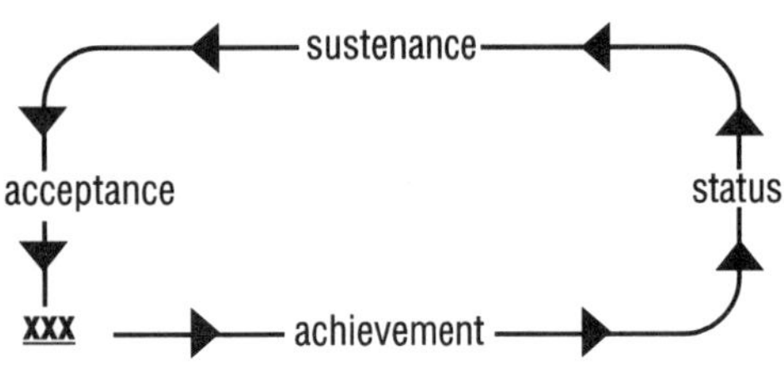

Round the Cycle
In the Opposite Direction From Jesus

Some of us who want to achieve great things for God seem to believe that our achievement brings us status. We believe that we are accepted because of what we do. We are sustained by these false ideas. We therefore try to achieve more and more to earn more and more favor with God—only to collapse from exhaustion or to suffer from burnout. "No," whispers Jesus. "The secret of fruitfulness is not work, work, work. The secret of fruitfulness is intimacy with me." "Live in me. Make your home in me, just as I do in you. In the same way that a branch can't bear grapes by itself but only by being joined to the vine, you can't bear fruit unless you are joined with me. I am the Vine, you are the branches. When you're joined with me and I with you, the relation intimate and organic, the harvest is sure to be abundant. Separated, you can't produce a thing" (John 15:4-5, The Message).

One of the saddest things that we have felt since we have been attempting to provide member care for mission partners is the reaction we frequently receive when teaching the ideas we have outlined above: "I couldn't possibly pray like this," some object. "Just look at the length of my prayer list. Life is just too busy for this kind of commitment." On the other hand, one of the greatest joys and privileges that comes our way is when someone comes to The Hiding Place and says, "I've heard about intimacy with Jesus. I've read about it. Now show me how I can experience it!"

Jesus assures us that we *can* experience such closeness anywhere and everywhere. One of the things that is so refreshing about His own relationship with the Father and the Spirit is that it grew, not only in solitude and silence, but also in the busyness of life. When Jesus was about to feed the 5,000 with five small fish and two little loaves, it was natural for Him to ask His Father to bless the meal. When He was in the Garden of Gethsemane, it was natural for Him to cry out to the Father. When He was walking in the countryside, it was natural for Him to invite His disciples to "look at the birds ... they do not sow or reap or store away in barns, and yet your Father feeds them.... See how the lilies of the field grow"(Matt. 6:26, 28).

The 17th century French monk, Brother Lawrence, called this kind of prayer "practicing the presence of God." When asked *how* we pray in this way, he said, among other things, that we should "settle ourselves firmly in God's presence by constantly talking to Him" and that we should ask for God's grace to sense His presence at odd moments of the day, reminding ourselves frequently that God loves us (Blaiklock, 1981, pp. 11-12).

Not long ago, a mission partner came to The Hiding Place for a prayer retreat. She shared many joys and sorrows. Among the sorrows was the cry that "our mission prayer meetings are so *boring*!" We understood. We have been to too many mission prayer meetings that are boring, because they start in the wrong place—with the task and not with the Master. Prayer meetings that begin with Jesus, meet with Jesus, listen to Jesus, and from that starting line focus on needy, hurting, helpless people can surely never be boring. They may be painful, because often the only prayer we can pray is one of silent grief. For those who learn to pray in the way Jesus taught, prayer meetings may be painful, even powerful, but never boring!

Jesus' Teaching

He taught the disciples before and after ministry trips

Having carefully laid the spiritual foundations and having allowed His disciples to watch Him at work and at prayer, *then* and only then Jesus sends His team out on a mission. He sends them out, not one by one, but in pairs. He sends them out with careful instructions about what to do and what not to do; what to take and what not to take; and, as far as is possible before a mission venture of this kind, He prepares them for difficulties that they might encounter. Luke paints the picture of this proactive preparation beautifully (Luke 9:1-6).

Imagine the scene. For months, these men have listened to Jesus teach and preach. They have watched Him perform miracles. Now they listen to His instructions as He prepares to send *them* into the villages to prepare people for the day when He Himself will come.

They were to preach, to heal, to cleanse, to exorcise, to trust, to bless, and to be aware of their vulnerability. They were to exercise caution and wisdom, to listen, to be prepared for difficulties, and to be like their teacher. Jesus empowered them for the task, gave them authority, and personally commissioned them. He also gave them careful instructions concerning their luggage and accommodation. They were to travel light, live simply, and be content with what they were offered. On the other hand, they were to be shrewd and, where necessary, to exercise the ministry of shaking the dust from their feet in places where they were not welcome. Mark sums up the mission in this way: "They preached with joyful urgency that life can be radically different; right and left they sent demons packing; they brought wellness to the sick, anointing their bodies and healing their spirits" (Mark 6:12-13, The Message).

They then return to Jesus. He had obviously been praying for them while they were away. As soon as they return, we see them gathering around Him, telling Him story after story. We also see Him listening to them and responding with affirmation and rejoicing. He is intimately involved in all that they have been experiencing, enjoying, and achieving. Equally, He is concerned for their welfare, so He does not just listen to them, then immediately send them out on another mission. Instead, as He hears them, He senses their need and insists that they take a break. In other words, Master care provides compassion, opportunities for ministry, passionate prayer support, vision, listening, empowering, care, and rest.

He underlined their need for mutual support

Notice that Jesus did not send His disciples out alone. He sent them out in pairs. Was this because the Old Testament stresses that "it is not good for man[kind] to be alone" (Gen. 2:18) and that the alien, the stranger, the widow, and the orphan should be protected, cared for, and placed in families? Or was it because He Himself suffered from loneliness, even though He had done everything possible to make sure that He was surrounded by those who loved Him? We are not told. What we now understand, though, is the effect that loneliness can have on people and their relationships. Ronald Rolheiser (1979), in his book *The Restless Heart*, puts it powerfully when he explains that loneliness, if not understood, can be destructive of human intimacy, can result in being overpossessive in relationships, and can prevent us from entering into any kind of creative solitude. If not faced and grappled with, loneliness can lead us to become hardened and desensitized persons. Jesus seems here to be attempting to safeguard His disciples from such subtle pressures.

He gave them a sense of vision

Jesus not only safeguarded His disciples from the scourge of loneliness by providing them with companionship and support, but also gave them a sense of vision and privilege. As He prepares to send them out, Jesus sounds like someone full of passion and vision who is inspiring His companions to share His passion and ensure that His vision is realized. He is like a teacher sending fully equipped students out into the world—or a king sending carefully schooled and *inspired* ambassadors to carry out His orders and to speak for Him. This way of preparing His team must surely have given them a sense of privilege and worth, of value and honor. They were, indeed, ambassadors *for Christ*, and they were understanding this more and more. Jesus not only commissioned and inspired them, but also empowered them. Did He breathe on them in the way He did in the Upper Room on the first Easter Sunday? We are not told. What we are told is that He did not give them a list of instructions and expect them to follow them in their own strength. He knew all too well that, if they were to achieve anything for Him, it would be by grace. The necessary grace was His free gift to them—grace for them as individuals *and* grace for them as a group.

Jesus' Mentoring

Jesus didn't just teach those who lived in community with Him. He discipled them as well. By discipling, we mean teaching through personal encounter and close relationship. Jesus did this in a variety of ways.

He showed them His glory

One way was to give the disciples the privilege of seeing His glory. So far as we are aware, the first time He revealed His glory to them was early in His earthly ministry, when He and His disciples attended the wedding at Cana. John remembers how Jesus turned gallons of water into wine and how this revelation of His glory persuaded the disciples to "put their faith in Him" (John 2:11).

He assisted them in their ministry

Another way in which Jesus discipled those whom He had called was to stay alongside them and support them while they helped Him with *His* ministry. Think, for example, of the occasion we referred to earlier, when 5,000 men plus women and children were sitting on the grassy banks that slope down to the Sea of Galilee: "'We're out in the country and it's getting late,' the disciples warned Jesus. 'Dismiss the people so they can go to the villages and get some supper.' But Jesus said, 'There is no need to dismiss them. *You* give them supper.' 'All we have are five loaves of bread and two fish,' they protested. Jesus said, 'Bring them here.'... He took the five loaves and two fish, lifted His face to heaven in prayer, blessed, broke, and *gave the bread to the disciples*. The disciples then gave the food to the congregation" (Matt. 14:13-19, The Message; emphasis added).

It is almost certain that the bread and the fish were multiplied *as the disciples gave them to the crowd.* If this is indeed what happened, imagine the impact that the nature and size of this miracle must have had on Jesus' friends. Jesus could have chosen to meet the needs of the crowd in a variety of ways. He chose to disciple His team by giving them the privilege of helping Him.

He showed them how He healed the sick

On other occasions, too, Jesus gave His disciples the privilege of watching Him heal the sick and raise the dead. He also allowed them to listen to His compassion, that is, the way He hurt in the very depths of His being for the poor. Is it any wonder, then, that in Acts 3 we find Peter making his way to the temple at the time of prayer? When he meets a crippled beggar, instead of responding to the beggar's plea for money, he responds in the way the Master would have responded had He been there in person: "Silver and gold I do not have, but what I have I give you. In the name of Jesus Christ of Nazareth, walk" (Acts 3:6).

He exposed them to His revolutionary views

While traveling with Jesus, the disciples were given the thrill of hearing His teaching on a variety of subjects: fasting, love for enemies, judging others, forgiveness, and the suffering and death He must go through. They heard Him spell out the meaning of the Beatitudes, and they were present when He gave the listening crowd a revolutionary way of ordering their priorities. Quoting Genesis 2:24, "A man will leave his father and mother and cleave to his wife, and they will become one flesh," Jesus addresses a culture that, even today, believes that men are of much greater value than women and that women are the property of their husbands in the same way that the house or the vineyard is the husband's property. Instead of agreeing with these ideas, Jesus challenges them. A wife is not a piece of property. She is a *person* loved by God. Because it is all too easy to sweep this particular piece of Jesus' teaching under the carpet and because this can cause endless damage to marriage and families, there is an urgent need in member care to tease out the implications of such practical teaching.

Marriage as God planned it, Jesus seems to insist, means that the top priority in life for a husband and wife, after their relationship with God, is that they should cleave to one another. One way of cleaving to one another is to spend quality time with each other in times of joy and to support one another in times of change or difficulty. Although an individual's relationship with God must take priority over all other relationships, married people must be given space in which to make sure that their relationship *with one another* also deepens and that they become one spiritually, emotionally, and sexually. They must therefore "leave" not only father and mother, but also many other demands to ensure that this space is always in place. The third priority for married couples—after God and the marriage relationship—is children, if God entrusts them with this precious gift. When these three priorities are safely in place, husbands and wives are then free to explore other ways of serving God and using the gifts God has given them. Sadly, many Christians—particularly mission partners and other Christian leaders—make their service for God a higher priority than their family. The family unit is then endangered and suffers unnecessarily in a way that is dishonoring to God.

For single people, too, their first priority is their relationship with God. Next, if they model themselves on the single Jesus, the priority is *not* work, work, work, but rather it is to create close relationships with friends. As Carmen Caltagirone (1983, pp. xi, 5) reminds us in *Friendship as Sacrament*, "We can look at some of our deepest relationships and find there a clue to the unfathomable love of God.... The love we share in human relationships is part of the grandness of a God who cradles us tenderly in his all-loving embrace."

He gave them privileged insights

As well as teaching His disciples while they were walking with Him or listening to Him address the crowds, Jesus frequently took them aside and gave them deep and concentrated insights that He had not shared outside of their community. Think of the time when He first told the parable of the sower, for example. He left the masses to work out the symbolism for themselves, but when He was alone with the disciples, He allowed them to ask questions. "Why do you tell stories?" they ask. "To create readiness," He replies, and He adds, "To nudge the people toward receptive insight" (Matt. 13:13, The Message). He then goes on to explain in detail the hidden meanings of this His first parable.

He prepared them for a painful transition

Most memorably of all, we recall those last few hours of Jesus' life, when, once again, we see Him engaging in proactive preparation of His disciples. He knew that they would find the transition of His death and resurrection difficult to cope with. "Love one another as I have loved you" (John 13:34), He earnestly said, underlining once again the need to serve others from the base of good relationships. During this long session with this team that was soon to take over the ministry from Him, Jesus emphasized the need to trust. "Trust in God; trust also in Me," He begged them (John 14:1). He went on to remind them where their resources were to come from. Be open to the Holy Spirit's ministry, He pleaded, knowing full well how much He personally owed to His relationship with and support from the third person of the Trinity. "He will teach you all things and will remind you of everything I have said to you.... He will testify about Me" (John 14:26; 15:26).

As well as teaching His disciples as a group, Jesus frequently addressed *crowds* of people. These Middle Eastern crowds would have consisted of individuals, couples, and whole families. Jesus gave them unforgettable, life-changing lessons in relationships and in personal and spiritual growth. From time to time, too, we see Jesus *drawing alongside* individuals and families, close friends, and couples. On the first Easter Day, for instance, He walked along the road from Jerusalem to Emmaus. On this journey, He came across two of His disciples, whom many believe to have been a married couple. After listening to their bewilderment, He gave them a thrilling account of the Jewish Scripture's teaching about Himself. Their hearts burned within them, the scales fell from their eyes, and they could scarcely bear to be parted from Him. Or again, one week later, we watch Him cooking breakfast on the beach for His bewildered disciples. After breakfast, He comes alongside Peter, the disciple who had publicly denied Him three times. The memory of the way he had failed the Master must still have been plunging Peter into despair. No condemnation comes from Jesus, however, only love and understanding, restoration, and recommissioning with all that that entailed in terms of trust. Jesus is entrusting people to Peter. He is also showing confidence that Peter will, in fact, love Him to the point of death.

If we are to follow faithfully in the footsteps of the Master Carer, we in member care will take note of Jesus' attention to detail, as well as His concern for the welfare of *individuals* (including *couples, close friends*, and *families*). We will ensure that, as well as arranging occasions when mission partners are taught in traditional Western ways—through talks and lectures and seminars and conferences—we will provide opportunity for partners to be listened to *one-to-one*, to be cared for, to be understood, and to be healed of hurts.

A Ministry Full of Mystery

The Stature of Waiting

Some of the most powerful teaching Jesus gave was lived rather than talked about. We think, for example, of the manner in which He modeled the "stature of waiting" (Vanstone, 1982). Over and over again, we find Jesus refusing to rush into ministry but rather waiting for the right moment to act. So He leaves the wonder of His Father's presence and waits in a woman's womb. For 30 years, He is content to live and learn and love, first in Egypt, then in the obscurity of Nazareth. Even when He does make His first public appearance, He insists that John the Baptist should baptize Him, and He is prepared to wait a while longer. The crowd is eager to hear, thirsting to meet their Messiah, but Jesus knows that the really *ready* moment is the right moment. So, instead of preaching or teaching or healing, He follows the Spirit's prompting and goes on a prolonged retreat in the desert. Author Sue Monk Kidd (1990, p. 14) reminds us that Jesus' earthly ministry was punctuated by such retreats: "When important times of transition came for Jesus, He entered enclosures of waiting—the wilderness, a garden, the tomb. Jesus' life was a balanced rhythm of waiting on God and expressing the fruits of waiting. There are reasons why Jesus was prepared to wait. He recognized that when you're waiting, you're *not* doing nothing. You're doing the most important something there is.... If you can't be still and wait, you can't become what God created you to be."

Mission partners, too, are frequently asked to wait. We wait for visas, we wait to learn the language, we wait to make relationships with members of our team and with our neighbors in the country to which we have been called. We wait for news from home, we wait to discover some of the reasons that God has called us to work overseas. Such waiting can seem endless. Many mission partners have not yet learned that the deep things of God do not come quickly. They are revealed in the fullness of time—God's time, not ours. Unless mission partners have grasped the value and "the stature of waiting" that the Master models, waiting may seem irksome, futile, and a waste of time and talent. It may trigger feelings of failure or a lack of self-worth. Our task in member care may therefore be to point 21st century partners programmed by secular thinking to the strange success story of the Waiting One—the Master Carer who is our model in mission and who is one in a long line of those who have discovered the rich rewards of waiting.

The Power of Powerlessness

Jesus not only endured and grew through endless waiting, He also demonstrated the power of powerlessness. We see this peculiar power at work in the Garden of Gethsemane. Having poured out His pain and dread to His Father, Jesus hands over the reins of His life to His captors. From this point on, He who had healed the sick, preached so powerfully, and master-minded the Last Supper organizes nothing. He goes where His captors lead Him. Yet John, His closest friend, helps us to see how powerful His powerlessness is. "Jesus, knowing all that was going to happen to Him, went out [to His captors] and asked them, 'Who is it you want?' 'Jesus of Nazareth,' they replied. 'I am He,' Jesus said.... When Jesus said, 'I am He,' *they drew back and fell to the ground*" (John 18:4-6, emphasis added).

Why did they fall to the ground? John provides no answer to this question. Do we find a clue, though, in what happened the following day? As Jesus hung on the cross, the penitent thief begged Him, "Jesus, remember me when you come into Your kingdom" (Luke 23:42). A little later, after Jesus had breathed His last breath, the centurion standing at the foot of the cross cried out, "Surely He was the Son of God!" (Matt. 27:54). Just as the centurion and the penitent thief saw beyond the bruised and broken body of Jesus to His glory, did His captors in the Garden similarly see His divinity shine through His human form in all its powerlessness? Possibly. Why else would they fall to the ground?

In the hours that follow, Jesus is insulted, flogged, spat upon, criticized, and crucified. But note carefully: The miracle is that He achieved more in those hours of utter powerlessness than He achieved in His three years of astonishing ministry. In these hours, He won the salvation of the world. This is Master care in action.

Many mission partners also experience powerlessness. Take the experience of being de-skilled, for example. Workers may be well qualified in their chosen profession and have proved that, in their own country, they can make good use of their qualifications. When they work overseas, though, there may be many reasons why some or all of those skills cannot be used. These individuals might then experience not just powerlessness but frustration and a creeping feeling of failure. Our role as member care workers will then involve more than identification with the frustration and feelings of the partner. We will need to unfold the mystery of a Master who has also been in this situation and is able to understand, to support, and to bring forth much fruit from this seeming powerlessness.

The Value of the Desert

We have already seen that one of the places where Jesus exercised "the stature of waiting" was in the Judean desert. It would appear that, at first, He was reluctant to go there. We say this because in his Gospel Mark uses the powerful Greek word *ekballo* ("to thrust"), when he tells us how Jesus was driven into the wilderness by the Holy Spirit.

Jesus had publicly identified Himself with John the Baptist. He had witnessed the crowds waiting to hear God's new message. He was poised to begin His public ministry. The Spirit recognizes, though, that before people act, they need space to listen—to their own hearts, to God, and even to the tempting voice of the evil one.

Jesus tuned in to the voice of God before He entered the awesome arena of the desert. The Father's message, "You are My Son, whom I love; with You I am well pleased" (Mark 1:11), must have been the food that sustained Him through His long and lonely fast. The message was particularly powerful coming at this moment in time. It reminded Jesus that, since His public ministry had not yet begun, He was loved, not for anything He had done but simply for who He was. When a person absorbs that kind of love, it elicits a response of love. In the desert, then, we hear Jesus spell out His life's motto: "*I have come to do your will, O God*." This motto must surely have been part of the armor that He wore when He engaged in spiritual warfare against the enemy.

Almost certainly, some of the questions that Jesus was thinking through as He entered the desert included, "How am I going to carry out the task My Father has given Me to do?" "How am I going to reveal the kingdom to the waiting, watching world?" Satan was quick to make persuasive suggestions: "Make yourself popular; accumulate possessions; exercise power." "Get behind Me, Satan!" With that uncompromising rebuke, Jesus rejected each of these proposals. He chose, instead, to fulfill His Father's mission in His Father's way, with the help of the Holy Spirit. He thus emerges from the howling wilderness equipped and empowered to return to the clamoring crowd and to serve the Father with authority.

Jesus was not the only one to be refined in the desert. All of the giants and giantesses of our faith were wooed into the desert by God: Abraham and Sarah, Moses and Miriam, Elijah, the Psalmists, Paul, and so on.

Mission partners may never be required to sweat it out in a physical desert, but as part of the maturing process they will almost certainly find themselves in an inner desert from time to time. The inner desert refers to any period of our life when the landscape of our heart is like the bleakness and barrenness of the actual desert. We may feel this barrenness when all of our natural, human resources have dried up or when we seem to have been tested almost beyond our ability to cope. It might be an inner place where we experience a huge emotional emptiness or loneliness or where our soul seems as dry as soil that cries out for water. It might be a feeling of helplessness, hopelessness, or fear. It might also be a feeling of wonder or awe—a place where we meet with God in a special way.

In Hannah Hurnard's (1966) delightful story ***Hinds' Feet on High Places***, the heroine, Much-Afraid, is seen serving the Chief Shepherd. Content though she is in many ways, she is nonetheless conscious that the picture of the Chief Shepherd that others gain through her is spoiled for a variety of reasons. She is a cripple, for one thing, and she has a twisted mouth. The Chief Shepherd comes for her and takes her on a long, healing journey to the "high places"—a journey that is rather like the inner journey we all have to make. At first, Much-Afraid is excited. Her excitement turns to dismay, though, when the Chief Shepherd warns her, "All My servants on their way to the High Places have had to make [a] detour through this desert.... Here they have learnt many things which otherwise they would have known nothing about" (p. 55).

Master care—the methods God uses to ensure that those who serve Him grow spiritually and emotionally—***includes*** leading His loved ones into the desert. As God said to Hosea concerning Hosea's wife, Gomer, "I am now going to allure her; I will lead her into the desert and speak tenderly to her. There I will give her back her vineyards.... There she will sing as in the days of her youth"(Hos. 2:14-15).

As member care workers and mission partners, it is our responsibility to study and grasp the meaning of the mysteries that Jesus fleshed out for us. Only then will we be able to support partners who are being required by God to learn the stature of waiting, the power of powerlessness, or the value of the desert. One way to do this is to pause, ponder, and respond to questions like the ones that follow.

- Can you think of occasions when God has asked you to wait? How did you feel? What can you learn from the way Jesus was prepared to wait? How does this help you in your work in member care—and in your own life?
- Can you remember times when you felt powerless? Looking back, how do you think God used that time to help others and to teach you? How do you feel you can best support mission partners who are feeling helpless at the moment?
- Jesus' life motto became very clear for Him while He was in the desert. What is your life motto?

Now that we have paused to ponder the mysteries Jesus modeled to us, we urge you turn to the following questions from time to time to think through the vital subject of Master care for yourself.

Reflection and Discussion

1. Reread the opening pages of this chapter, focusing on Jesus and His relationship with the Twelve. If you are the leader of a team, would people observing your group recognize that you are making Master care your model? Would it be obvious to them that you are more concerned about people than projects? Ask yourself, "How can I get to know the mission partners who are under my care?"
2. Do *you* have the courage to be like Jesus—to look for resources for yourself *before* you minister to others and after you have served them? If not, why not?
3. If you could work out a rhythm for yourself that balanced busyness with stillness, what might that rhythm look like in terms of time spent alone with God (daily, weekly, monthly, annually) and time spent serving Him?
4. Jesus gave His disciples a new understanding of prayer. As you think about the prayer patterns of Jesus, do you think your own prayer life needs to be changed in any way? If so, how might you go about making it more effective?
5. Look carefully at Jesus' priorities. Compare these with your own lifestyle, and ask yourself whether there are any changes that need to be made. How does your response relate to the way you are moving on the Dynamic Cycle of Being and Well-Being?

References

Blaiklock, E. (Trans.). (1981). *The practice of the presence of God by Brother Lawrence*. London, UK: Hodder & Stoughton.

Caltagirone, C. (1983). *Friendship as sacrament*. Bombay, India: St Paul's.

Hurnard, H. (1966). *Hinds' feet on high places*. London, UK: The Olive Press.

Jeremias, J. (1967). *The prayers of Jesus*. London, UK: SCM.

Kidd, S. Monk (1990). *When the heart waits: Spiritual direction for life's sacred questions*. San Francisco, CA: Harper & Row.

Lake, F. (1966). *Clinical theology*. London, UK: Darton, Longman, & Todd.

Magdalene, M. (1987). *Jesus man of prayer*. Guildford, UK: Eagle.

Manning, B. (1994). *Abba's child: The cry of the heart for intimate belonging*. Colorado Springs, CO: NavPress.

Rolheiser, R. (1979). *The restless heart*. London, UK: Hodder & Stoughton.

Vanstone, W. (1982). *The stature of waiting*. London, UK: Darton, Longman, & Todd.

***David Huggett** and **Joyce Huggett** were married in 1960. They have two children and four grandchildren. They became mission partners with Interserve in 1993 and for six years were based in the Middle East, traveling extensively in the region and beyond. Their role was—and still is—to provide pastoral care and spiritual resourcing for Interserve partners and other missionaries. They are now based in the UK and lead retreats for such partners from their home in Derbyshire (The Hiding Place) and elsewhere. David has a doctorate in aeronautics and space technology. After lecturing in two universities, he trained for full-time Christian ministry and was ordained as a priest in the Anglican Church in 1967. As well as various pastorates, he has trained in counseling and retreat giving. Joyce read history and theology at Southampton University, where she graduated in 1959. She later received a Manchester Certificate for teachers of the deaf. In the early 1970s, she trained in counseling with a major in marriage, as well as in spiritual direction and retreat giving. She has written 28 books, many of which have been translated into other languages. Email: 100610.427@compuserve.com.*

22

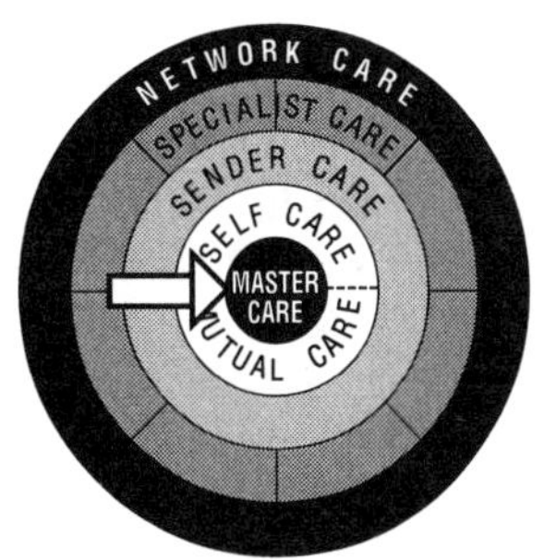

Joy and Sacrifice In the Lord

AJITH FERNANDO

Joy and suffering are intertwining threads that run through the course of our life. Both are indispensable for our growth, for our missions work, and for our relationship with Christ.

In today's world, happiness is almost considered a basic human right by many people, and it is often defined in a way that precludes suffering. This attitude has influenced the church also, and I fear that the way we train people for the ministry does not adequately prepare them for the suffering that accompanies Christian ministry. I will try to respond to this problem below. This chapter is an expanded form of something I wrote in response to the concern that some of my prayer partners expressed recently, when they knew that I was suffering from fairly severe exhaustion. This accounts for the many autobiographical sections in the article.

Commitment to Joy and to the Cross

I suppose you could call me a "Christian hedonist." I do not like this phrase, which was popularized by John Piper (1986), but it correctly describes my desire. I am a pleasure seeker, seeking the joy of the Lord as an extremely important experience in life. I resonate with George Müller, who said that the first and primary business that he ought to attend to every day was to have his soul happy in the Lord.

However, I want to have this joy coming out of a lifestyle of taking up the cross. Jesus said that He wants us to have His joy so that our joy may be complete (John 15:11). But soon after that, He commanded us to love each other, as He has loved us (v. 12). He then said, "Greater love has no one than this, that he lay down his life for his friends" (v. 13). So Christ is telling us that we must die for each other. But first there must be joy. Then the joy will issue in sacrificial service. Elsewhere, Jesus said that, unlike the hired hand, He would die for the sheep (John 10:11-15). If we are sent into the world as the Father has sent Jesus (John 20:21), then we too must die for the sheep God entrusts to us. Recently I did a careful study on Jesus as our missionary model. I made the startling discovery that when Jesus is presented as a model for Christians, most often it is as a model of suffering (John 15:12-13; Heb. 12:2; 13:12-13; 1 Pet. 2:19-24; 4:1-2, etc.).

So on the one hand, I want to pursue the joy of the Lord, and on the other hand, I also want to pursue death for the sake of the people to whom I am called to minister. Over the past few years, I have been attempting to grapple with this paradox. How can we have joy while we are dying for a cause?

Paul's life and ministry have influenced me greatly in this process. In Philippians, Paul states that the joy of the Lord is an imperative for Christians (Phil. 4:4). He wrote this while suffering in a prison. In fact, when he urged the Philippians to complete his joy by restoring unity there, he implied that he had lost his joy over their lack of unity (Phil. 2:2; cf. 4:2). He allowed himself to be hurt by and to lose a certain earthly joy over the sins of others, while he preserved his joy in the Lord. He tells the wayward Galatians that he goes through the pains of childbirth until Christ is formed in them (Gal. 4:19). He says that he faces "the daily pressure of [his] concern for all the churches." "Who is weak," he asks, "and I do not feel weak? Who is led into sin, and I do not inwardly burn?" (2 Cor. 11:28-29). He says, "Death is at work in us, but life is at work in you.... Though outwardly we are wasting away, yet inwardly we are being renewed day by day" (2 Cor. 4:12, 16). How alien these verses are to modern ministry aspirations! Today we study much more about how to avoid stress than about how to take on the type of stress that Paul is talking about here.

I feel we should do everything required for a balanced life—get adequate sleep, observe the Sabbath principle, and have times set apart for the family, for study, for exercise, and for fun. Most importantly, we must spend unhurried times with the Lord in prayer and in the Word. But while we do all these things, we must also die for those we serve. And because we are called to die, there will be struggles and strains, burdens and persecutions.

Several years ago, in a Youth for Christ (YFC) training session, I shared how I struggled with a huge burden over the weaknesses and sins of the staff workers I lead. The teachers, who were from the West, were alarmed by this confession and prayed that I would be liberated from these burdens. I have thought much about that incident, especially because those teachers were fine Christians and insightful teachers. I have come to the conclusion that it is right for me to be burdened in this way. This stress that comes from concern is a part of my dying for my people. Did not Jeremiah, Daniel, Ezra, and Nehemiah suffer depression over the problems of their people and weep over their sin (Jer. 9:1-2; Dan. 10:2-3; Ezra 9:3-6; Neh. 1:1–2:3)?

Each time I return home from a preaching assignment abroad, I experience an acute sense of frustration. I have come to recognize that this is the frustration of making the transition from being a speaker to being a leader. As a speaker, I am treated like a VIP. Much is done to make me comfortable, especially when I travel to the West. But as a biblical leader, my lifestyle should be that of a servant (Mark 10:42-45). I am (perhaps I should say, "I should be") a servant of my family and of those I lead in YFC. Unfortunately, their needs do not wait for my convenience, and sometimes they crop up at the most inappropriate times.

This was what Jesus experienced too. Mark 6:31 says, "... so many people were coming and going that [Jesus and the apostles] did not even have a chance to eat." This verse goes on to record Jesus' famous statement, "Come with Me to a quiet place by yourselves and get some rest." When we quote this statement, we often overlook the fact that Jesus and His apostles did not get the rest they desired on this occasion. In fact, Jesus went straight into teaching the crowds, who had followed Him to His supposedly quiet place. He taught the 5,000 there for a long time and then fed them. But He persevered with seeking solitude and finally found it by sending His disciples on a boat ride, while "He went up on a mountainside to pray" (Mark 6:45-46). Here Jesus demonstrates the balanced life of a servant. He served the people even when it was inconvenient, but He persevered until He found time for the other essential disciplines of life, such as the discipline of solitude.

Defining the Joy of the Lord

Perhaps at this stage I should attempt a definition of "the joy of the Lord." I believe it is an attitude toward life that emerges from reckoning certain biblical truths about our lives. I am using the verb "reckon" in the sense it is used in Romans 6:11 (KJV)—to reckon oneself dead to sin but alive to God in Christ Jesus. Some newer translations render this verb, *logizomai*, as "count" (NIV) or "consider" (NRSV, NAS). To reckon is the act of accepting that certain things are true for us. Let me mention six things that we reckon about ourselves.

First, we reckon that the burden of the guilt of sin has been removed from us because we have been forgiven (Heb. 10:22). With a cleansed conscience, we can have a great sense of freedom. If God does not reckon (*logizomenos*) our sin (2 Cor. 5:19), then we do not need to either.

Second, we reckon that God has loved us so much that He has sent his Son to die for us and for our salvation (Rom. 5:8). We know that realizing that we are loved is a great trigger of joy. Since Christ's love is the greatest possible love (John 15:13), it should trigger the greatest possible joy (John 15:11).

Third, we reckon and are amazed by the fact that God has entered into an intimate relationship with us and regards us as His beloved children (1 John 3:1). People may disappoint us, but God is our never-disappointing and constant companion (Heb. 13:5-6). He is the most important person and factor in our lives (Phil. 1:21). And sometimes in our relationship with Him, we have moments close to ecstasy: "You have made known to me the path of life; you will fill me with joy in your presence, with eternal pleasures at your right hand" (Psalm 16:11).

Fourth, we reckon that God has invested us with significance, by making us princes and princesses in the eternal kingdom of God and by giving us a vital role in the agenda of His eternal kingdom (2 Cor. 5:20). This, of course, means that we do not need to be jealous of or feel threatened by anyone else (1 Cor. 12:14-26), thus eliminating a major cause for the loss of joy in our lives.

Fifth, we reckon that the God who loves us and who is committed to our welfare (Rom. 8:32) is also sovereign. Therefore, we know that if we are obedient to Him, in all things He will work for our good (Rom. 8:28). No circumstance or person can thwart God's good plan for our lives. God will turn even the most painful incidents into something good (Gen. 50:20). This fact gives us no adequate reason to be bitter over what anyone has done to us, thus eliminating another major cause for the loss of joy.

Sixth, we reckon that we are bound for the glorious Promised Land of heaven, for which we wait with eager anticipation (Phil. 1:22-23). The frustration to which the world has been subjected and in which we participate will not be found in heaven, thus completing the redemption of which we now have only a foretaste (Rom. 8:20-24). For us, to live is Christ, a great reason for joy, and to die is gain, a greater reason for joy (Phil. 1:21).

Is it possible that reckoning these truths can indeed produce joy? It is, because this eliminates the force of those things that take away joy by reminding us of six great reasons for being joyful! And those six reasons are eternally true, in contrast to the things that take away joy, which are temporary. Joy that is founded upon such realities can co-exist with sorrow, pain, disappointment, and righteous anger. But it cannot co-exist with bitterness, selfish anger, and despair, for these are attitudes that contradict the six realities.

Joy and Feelings of Depression

I am going to dare to say that the joy of the Lord can even co-exist with our common experiences of depression, as well as be of help to clinical, major depression, which often has biochemical origins. Good and conscientious Christians, especially those who are in the so-called helping professions, often experience depression. Things like tiredness, sickness, loneliness, negative response to our work, or a sense of failure can trigger this. While we may be feeling terrible, the six realities tell us that there is a deeper reality than our feelings. Reckoning those six realities helps us bear the pain, for we are able to look at life with a positive attitude. Depression (a feeling) will then not turn into despair (an attitude). A ray of light creeps through the gloom and helps sustain us till the depression passes.

I have found that these thoughts help me a lot when I suffer from feelings of depression. As a result of the reckoning and the attitude change that results from it, we may be motivated to take steps that help us handle the depression constructively. We may decide to get some extra sleep or rest or recreation or exercise. We may decide to take off and spend some extra time with family or with friends. We may share our pain with someone else. We may go and talk to the people with whom we are upset. Of course, I am not discounting the important role that a professional physician or counselor can play in situations of extreme depression.

What I want to stress most of all here is that devout and victorious Christians may sometimes feel terrible, just as Jeremiah, Daniel, Ezra, Nehemiah, and Paul did, as expressed in the verses we quoted in the previous section. We must not forget that "laments" represent an important type of biblical literature. There are about 50 laments in the book of Psalms, making lament the largest category of Psalms. Those who are lamenting in the Bible were great people of God, not people in a backslidden state. Yet two typical features of the lament psalms show us that lament can co-exist with the joy of the Lord, as we have defined it in this article. These features are the statement of confidence in God (Psalm 22:3-5) and the vow to praise God (Psalm 22:22-26).

Sri Lanka is a land devastated by war, suffering, violence, and corruption. I have come to believe that lament must be an integral part of the life of all Christians living in Sri Lanka. Not to lament may be evidence of callous disregard for the needs of our people. For most Christians, there are reasons for lament that are closer to home than the devastation of a nation. We may groan as we see loved ones suffering or living in rebellion against God. Sometimes we may groan because of the pain that wracks our own bodies.

Paul gave a theological basis for lament when he said, "We ourselves, who have the firstfruits of the Spirit, groan inwardly as we wait eagerly for our adoption as sons, the redemption of our bodies" (Rom. 8:23). Living as we do in a world subjected to frustration (Rom. 8:20), we will groan until we get to heaven. Then a few sentences later, in verse 26, using a noun (*stenagmos*) directly related to the verb "groan" (*stenazö*) which he used in verse 23, Paul says, "the Spirit himself intercedes for us with *groans* that words cannot express" (Rom. 8:26). Even God is groaning! So I try to tell myself and others when we suffer from bad feelings, "Don't feel bad about feeling bad. This may be a necessary experience along God's joyful pathway." Thinking such thoughts takes away some of the despair that is often associated with bad feelings in the lives of Christians.

Pursuing Joy

But how could we reckon biblical truths about ourselves so as to have the joy of the Lord? Don't most Christians—happy ones and unhappy ones—accept each of these six features as essential parts of their theology? They do, but we must let these theological truths travel down from the mind (where they are stored) to the heart, so that they can challenge and influence our attitudes. This process may not be as easy as it seems. I think one of the saddest things I have seen in recent years in Sri Lanka is the phenomenon of angry Christian workers. Often they are angry at the church and its leaders because of the way they have been treated. My belief in the indispensability of joy has been greatly challenged over the years, living as I do in a land filled with corruption, lawlessness, violence, and ethnic strife. Yet I have seen people who, while having every reason to be very bitter and angry, radiantly exhibit the joy of the Lord.

One of my first conscious struggles for joy in my Christian life was when I was a university student. My heart was in the ministry, but I was studying botany, zoology, and chemistry for my degree. One-third of our grades was given for practical work done in the laboratory. But I was terribly clumsy with my hands. The result was that I never did well in my studies, even though I worked hard at them. I would often struggle with deep discouragement. During this time, I got into the habit of going for long walks. I would not turn back to return to where I was staying until I had a sense that the joy of the Lord was restored. Sometimes this did not happen for a long time, but I would persevere in grappling with the Lord until his joy returned. When that happened, I would turn to come back and then give myself to intercession during the walk back.

Since beginning "full-time" ministry, things have become a little more complex. My hurt and anger now come from people among whom I minister, and the wounds are a little deeper. But the same principle of grappling with the Lord till the joy returns has served me well. Sometimes it takes longer for the joy to return. Often an issue I thought I had settled with the Lord and buried resurfaces to torment me with bitterness. This means that I now have to be even more conscientious in my battle for the joy of the Lord. But most often the victory will not come until I can heartily affirm, without any reservation, that God is going to turn this thing that I resent into something good, and therefore I do not need to be angry or anxious.

Joy and spiritual disciplines

Over the years, I have discovered some aids to reckoning that have helped me. Prayer is the first one that comes to mind. But I will discuss this later. Next comes reading the Scriptures. The year 1989 was one of the bleakest times in our nation, and estimates of the death toll for the year from an attempted revolution went as high as 60,000. There was almost never a time when there was not a body floating on the river at the edge of our town. And most of the dead were young people, the people God has called me to serve. Schools were closed much of the time, and this meant that our children were at home. Many people left the country during this period, saying it was for the sake of their children. But we believed that God wanted our family to stay in Sri Lanka, no matter what happened.

We did have to think about the welfare of our children. My wife and I felt that the greatest legacy we could leave for them was a happy home. This was a challenge, considering that there were so many political and social things going on that we as Christians legitimately needed to be angry and upset about. Despite the surrounding national gloom, I needed to help keep the home bright. My moods were not helping with this! One day when I was in one of my bad moods, my wife told the children loudly enough for me to hear (our wives have a way of doing that!), "Thaththi (Daddy) is in a bad mood. Let's hope he will go and read his Bible." She had hit upon a very important theological principle. When we are overwhelmed by temporal circumstances, we must fix our eyes on the deeper realities of life: those unchanging truths in Scripture that enable us to look at life from the perspective of God's sovereignty. This is why the psalmist said, "If your law had not been my delight, I would have perished in my affliction" (Psalm 119:92).

I have also found that spending time with a hymnbook is a great remedy for the loss of joy. Here again, when we don't have thoughts to lift us up because of what we are experiencing, we are reminded of eternal truth by the writings of others. And those thoughts are set to music, the language of the heart. This enhances the process of truth traveling from the mind to the heart. So when Paul and Silas sang hymns to God in the jail in Philippi (Acts 16:25), they were using an effective remedy for discouragement.

Joy from counseling and community

I have, however, had to minister with some Christian workers for whom the process of the recovery of joy is much harder. This is partly because they carry wounds, often inflicted in childhood, that have not been healed. When those wounds are touched, extreme reactions often result. I am thankful for people like David Seamands (1981) who, through books like *Healing for Damaged Emotions*, have alerted us to this problem. The title of that book suggests that even these wounds can be healed. I think it is very significant that in 1 Corinthians 13:5, where we are told that love "keeps no record of wrongs," the verb used is *logizomai*, from which we get the idea of reckoning. Healing comes when we cease to reckon the hurts we have received, by letting God's love in us overcome the hurt of the wounds with which we have been inflicted.

This process of healing may be lengthy, and it may call for much patience. But I believe that it is completed only when God's love can break through with healing, so that the wounds will no longer hinder us from reckoning the six great truths that I have described. A sensitive and caring community, where hurt Christian workers can experience the acceptance that such costly, group commitment provides, can do much in bringing healing. Often trained counselors can play an important role in the healing process, by dealing with issues in a way that untrained people find difficult. However, the work of counselors is greatly enhanced through the support of a community that practices costly commitment to its members. Would that all our ministry teams were such communities!

Actually, I think that we cannot separate the joy of the Lord from the community of the Lord. All of Christianity is lived in community. While each individual is ultimately responsible for ensuring that his or her quest for the joy of the Lord is carried through conscientiously, the community can do much in mediating this joy to us. As I think of the times that I have been deeply hurt in ministry and of the struggles that I have had with bitterness over these hurts, I also think of the way God used my friends and colleagues to heal me of the pain. They listened to me; they advised my about how I should respond to the situation; and the act of verbally sharing my pain with them did much to help give me release from the burden of hurt that I was carrying.

After someone has hurt us, we could be so upset that we could extend our anger with particular people to cover all people in general. This is the attitude that says that humans cannot and must not be trusted because they always fail us. There are many such angry people around in the world today. When our friends lend a sympathetic ear and minister lovingly to us, we lose our reason for being angry at humanity. We sense that our friends are suffering with us in our pain, as Paul said they should (1 Cor. 12:26; Gal. 6:2). That takes away that lonely bitterness that destroys whatever vestiges of joy are left in us.

So God often mediates His joy through the loving concern of committed Christian friends and colleagues. Many of the biblical descriptions of joy are given in the context of the community, such as the well-known verse, "The joy of the Lord is your strength" (Neh. 8:10).

What I am going to write now seems so basic that it may look out of place in a book like this. But it is something that I have seen so often in my life and in the lives of my colleagues that it should be mentioned. One of the most common causes for the loss of joy in Christian workers is sin that has not been dealt with biblically. I have seen this so much that, when I find a colleague who has become unusually judgmental or who flies into a rage unusually quickly, one of the first questions I ask is whether he or she is burdened by some guilt that has not been cleared. Asking forgiveness from God and from those who have been affected by our sin, as well as engaging in other forms of restitution, are essential features in the processes of recovery from sin and restoration of joy (Psalm 51).

Unbiblical Stress

As I have pointed out, amid the stresses and strains of ministry, we must conscientiously pursue the joy of the Lord. Indeed, suffering is an essential ingredient of ministry, and stress and strain are two of the commonest expressions of suffering in a minister's life today. But not all the stress we face today is biblical. I have found much help from what some Western authors, especially Dr. Archibald Hart, have written about stress. I believe that there are two types of unbiblical stress commonly experienced by Christian workers: stress from wrong motives and stress from poor delegation.

Stress From Wrong Motives

This type of stress comes from sinful ambitions for success—mixed motives. We want our church or organization to grow or our book to be the best in its field. This often leads to a workaholism arising from the fact that we find our primary fulfillment in striving for earthly goals. Those with this problem do not know how to take a Sabbath rest, because they get too much fulfillment from work and success. This gives rise to a lot of stress, and failure becomes a huge burden.

I think some of us will battle with earthly ambition all our lives. Besides, it is often difficult to know when godly ambition has given way to earthly ambition. This problem is particularly acute among leaders, because often they have come to the position of leadership through sheer determination and ambition, in part by overcoming a strong sense of insecurity and inferiority. This could be a great testimony to God's grace. But it is also possible for such leaders to find too much security and identity through success.

I think God in His mercy permits us to have failures and irritations to make us aware of the problem of fleshly motivation and to purge us of its dross. A well-prepared program that we lead is ruined because of rain or because of a careless mistake that someone else makes. After working hard at a sermon, we make a mistake during its delivery, and the people seem to focus more on the mistake than on the content of the sermon. Someone we regard as our spiritual child acts in a way that is unbecoming of a Christian. I find that often after I have written a book or article on a certain topic, a problem emerges in our ministry that shows how much we fall short in this same area that I have written on!

Our response to these failures and irritations brings into focus what our inner motivations are. Our overreactions show how much selfishness and fleshly motivation are in us. The corresponding battle to deal with these situations biblically is used by God to refine us and purify our motives. The situations become the disciplines about which Hebrews 12:4-11 talks. Verse 11 brings this passage to a climax: "No discipline seems pleasant at the time, but painful. Later on, however, it produces a harvest of righteousness and peace for those who have been trained by it."

The blessing, of course, is only "for those who have been trained by it." These are those who acknowledge that they have a problem, who seek God's forgiveness, and who apologize to those who have been hurt by their excessive reactions. Some will get even angrier because of the "discipline," and that will only increase their stress. Others will thank God for the rebuke and pray for grace to have more pure motives in their service for God. They experience "a harvest of righteousness and peace." Peace, of course, is the opposite of stress.

Stress From Poor Delegation

The other type of unbiblical stress comes from an unwillingness to delegate. Jethro pointed out this problem to his son-in-law, Moses (Ex. 18). All Christians have gifts, and it is the leader's responsibility to enable others to exercise their gifts. So we will always be delegating responsibilities to others. If we do not do this, we will end up bearing unnecessary burdens. We will go to see sick people that others could see. We will speak at meetings that others should speak at. This often comes from a messiah-complex that causes us to think that we are the ones who must do all the important things in our ministries. We will end up driving ourselves to the ground.

One of the most complex challenges that we face as we mature in ministry is to learn what our priorities are and to let our schedules reflect those priorities. We must really discipline ourselves to refuse many opportunities for ministry that are outside our primary calling. Indeed, we die for those we lead, but we are not called to save the whole world. Only the eternal God can do that.

Even the biblical commands limit the scope of the people for whom we are called to lay down our lives. Jesus speaks of our friends (John 15:12-14) and Paul of our wives (Eph. 5:25). I do not think these are absolute restrictions. We can die for others too! But I do feel that it is biblical to say that we have a special responsibility to some people whom God has called us to serve. These are the people we should concentrate on. Hence, we simply cannot kill ourselves trying to solve every problem that we encounter.

This is easier said than done, of course. I believe it is so important to identify our primary callings. For me, they are to Youth for Christ, to my home church, to itinerant Bible teaching, and to writing. This means that there are many things which people expect me to do that I should not do. I hope my family and my fellow leaders in Youth for Christ and in my church understand this. But I have had to face some criticism from others about my noninvolvement in several programs and causes. I know, however, that despite my commitment to the principles outlined above, there are a lot of things that I agree to do which I should not be doing. This will probably be a battle that I will have to fight all my life.

Burnout and Prayer

While unbiblical stress must be avoided, we must affirm that stress and strain are inevitable in ministry, as in life. I demonstrated this earlier, using quotations from Paul's epistles. As a family man who is active in grassroots ministry and leadership and who also tries to do some speaking and writing, I have experienced a fair share of this stress. Some of my friends have warned me that I will get burned out soon. I listen carefully to their concern, and I consider how to make adjustments and continue on in the ministry. I believe that time spent daily *lingering* in the presence of God is a great antidote to burnout and other ill effects of stress. Let me tell you why I think this is so.

If spending a good time with God each day is a non-negotiable factor in our daily calendar, then this time could really help slow us down and heal that unhealthy restlessness and rushed attitude that could cause burnout. There are few things that help heal our restlessness as time spent lingering in the presence of God. If a fixed time has been set apart each day, then there is no point rushing through the exercise, since we are going to spend that amount of time whether we rush or not. Therefore, we are forced to change gears from stressful rush to restful lingering in the presence of God. In recent years, I have become more and more convinced of the value of this shift of gears to slow down the terrible malady of drivenness to which we leaders are susceptible. Uncontrolled activity without slowing down feeds our tendency to be driven people. Driven people could drive themselves and others to the ground, either through tiredness or through breaking Christian principles in their relentless pursuit of success.

Times alone with God (and also Sabbaths faithfully kept) help battle the natural tendency of motivated leaders to become driven people. An hour or more spent each day in the presence of the almighty and sovereign Lord of the universe does wonders to our sense of security (Psalm 46:1-11), the lack of which is another cause of burnout. With security comes "the peace of God which transcends all understanding" (Phil. 4:7), which is surely a wonderful treasure with which to live life. When we do not have security in our relationship with God, we will be restlessly running from activity to activity, subconsciously hoping that our activity would fill the void in our lives. We are, in fact, afraid to stop and be silent before God. I once heard the Singaporean church leader Dr. Robert Solomon say, "We are uncomfortable with silence because silence forces us to face God." So we go on with our busy activity till we drive ourselves to the ground!

Paul says that the peace that I just described is the result of presenting our requests to God (Phil. 4:6). When we spend time with God, we are able to "cast all [our] anxiety on Him, because He cares for [us]" (1 Pet. 5:7). It was during a time of deep crisis in our ministry that I discovered the great release that comes from consciously handing over our burdens to God. I used to have difficulty going to sleep, because I was overwhelmed by worry over the situation. I learned to confess my inability to bear these burdens alone and to place them upon God by a conscious act of release. And release was what I felt as a result.

If, during our time with God, a lot of time is spent in intercession, we have become conduits of love. When we pray for others, love is flowing out of our lives. But this is not a love that drains us of our emotional strength. We are praying, which means that we are in touch with Him who is the inexhaustible source of love. As love goes out through prayer, God's love comes in, and the regular flow of love in and out of our lives makes us glow with the joy that love alone can produce.

So our time spent with God each day becomes the most refreshing thing that we do. Such freshness attacks those triggers of burnout that often accompany the stresses and strains of costly ministry. In recent years, there has been a welcome return to emphasizing the value of corporate worship among Evangelicals. Perhaps the time is also ripe for resolutely returning to the value of one's personal time with God.

Sacrifice From Commitment to Community

Often when my Western friends hear of all the problems we face in our war-torn country, they tell me something like, "We don't realize how fortunate we are to live in the West, where we don't have all these problems." If I am able to respond to this comment, I usually say that the biggest pain I have experienced has not been in connection with the war in the land but in connection with Christian community life. And that pain is not confined to our nation. Anyone practicing true, biblical, community life in any part of the world will experience much pain. We all fall short and fail each other. Sometimes, though, this pain is avoided by inappropriately lowering one's standards of community life. I fear this has happened a lot in the church today.

If you were to make a list of all the times Paul talks about his sufferings in the epistles, you would be amazed at how often his commitment and love to those in the Christian community caused his pain. He talks about his physical sufferings and sometimes even gives a comprehensive listing of them (2 Cor. 6:4-10; 11:23-27). But it is when he describes his relationship problems with his fellow Christians that he shows his deepest feelings of pain. In 2 Corinthians 2, he expresses his inward turmoil about the opposition to him that had surfaced in Corinth. He was in Troas awaiting the arrival of Titus, whom he had sent to Corinth with a severe letter. Titus had not come yet, and he was in so much turmoil that he could not even preach the gospel, although a door of opportunity to do so had opened for him. So he went on to Macedonia (2 Cor. 2:12-13). Titus eventually brought good news of the Corinthians' remorse over the way they had hurt Paul. He was so thrilled about this that remembering it prompted his rapturous outburst on the glory of the ministry, which forms the heart of 2 Corinthians (2 Cor. 2:14–7:1). Later he explains, "But God, who comforts the downcast, comforted us by the coming of Titus" (2 Cor. 7:6). All this shows how deeply Paul was hurt and how much he was comforted by his relationships.

When we love deeply, we also hurt deeply. Many people do not want to be hurt in this way. So they stay at a safe distance from others. They do not commit themselves too deeply to others and are not very open with them, for that would make them vulnerable to hurt. Paul, on the other hand, opened himself up to others and was often deeply hurt by their rejection. He expresses his vulnerability in 2 Corinthians 6:11-12: "We have spoken freely to you, Corinthians, and opened wide our hearts to you. We are not withholding our affection from you, but you are withholding yours from us" (see also 1 Thess. 2:8).

So when we open ourselves to others and express costly commitment to them, we become vulnerable to pain. Paul expresses this pain vividly in his epistles. In 2 Corinthians 11:28-29 he says, "I face daily the pressure of my concern for all the churches. Who is weak, and I do not feel weak? Who is led into sin, and I do not inwardly burn?" In Galatians 4:19-20 he says, "My dear children, for whom I am again in the pains of childbirth until Christ is formed in you, how I wish I could be with you now and change my tone, because I am perplexed about you!" (See also 2 Cor. 2:4, 12-13; 7:5-7; 12:15; Col. 1:24; 2:1; 1 Thess. 3:5-7.)

We avoid much of the pain from community that Paul talks about by lowering our standards for what we expect from others. In the early church, "all the believers were one in heart and mind" (Acts 4:32). This must have been difficult to achieve. That is why Paul has to urge the Christians in Philippi to work hard at achieving it (Phil. 2:2; 4:2-3). In Acts we find that the members shared a oneness of mind even in the area of possessions (Acts 2:42-46; 4:32).

Many Christians consider this type of community life too difficult to achieve. It is too much of a threat to their personal independence and too time-consuming for our efficiency-oriented age. So they have settled for a model of community life that is governed by rules and tasks. Problems are dealt with in terms of conformity to the rules of the group or the tasks people have been assigned. If the crisis is fairly serious, an inquiry is held, and some action is taken based on the findings. The problem is dealt with efficiently, but is this the biblical method appropriate for Christian communities where personal relationships are so important?

I think a more biblical method is the more painful method of dealing with problems pastorally. I am not saying that rules are unimportant. What I am saying is that pastoral care is more important, even though it is much more time-consuming and perhaps much more painful. When someone breaks a rule, we talk to the person and try to find out the reason for the infraction. In solving the problem, we may choose to institute some disciplinary action against the person. But the person is comprehensively ministered to in the process. Unfortunately, we rarely adopt this approach today. Many Christian leaders think that such pastoral responses to problems are not practical, are too painful, and are too time-consuming. The person who has done something wrong may be very angry with the leader, and when we deal with him or her pastorally, this anger may surface. It may take three hours to complete the conversation. Many leaders don't have that much time and energy to give to those they lead. The great biblical leaders, like Jesus and Paul, however, spent such quality time with those they led (see John 1:39; Acts 20:7).

It may seem much more efficient and effective to adopt approaches to organizational problems which are derived from secular management practices rather than from the Bible. There is a refreshing rediscovery of the importance of commitment to people among some secular management thinkers. But I do not think that we can ever expect the world to adopt the principle that Jesus taught in John 15 that, in a community, members die for each other (vv. 12-14). In the Christian method of community life, the leader "dies" for those who have done wrong by going through a long, drawn-out process of listening to them, being exposed to their bitterness, and ministering to them in depth. The inconvenience and pain of this process are part of the suffering of Christian community life of which I am speaking.

Indeed, although the John 15 type of community life is time-consuming and painful, it also brings a depth of joy and fulfillment that few things on earth can match. In 2 Corinthians, Paul speaks a lot about his pain over his relationship with the Corinthians. But he also describes his sheer joy triggered by their positive response to him. In Philippians, Paul pleads for unity (4:2), and he says that his joy is made complete only when they are "like-minded, having the same love, being one in spirit and purpose" (2:2). But he also describes the Philippians as "my brothers, you whom I love and long for, my joy and crown" (4:1). This, then, is a life with deep pain, but it is also a life of deep fulfillment.

Yet, as in the case of the other forms of suffering that we have talked about in this article, amidst all the pain of community we must experience the joy of the Lord. Without that, we would not have the strength to take on the pain that comes with community life. We have this bedrock confidence in God, who has said that, even though a mother may forget the baby at her breast, He will not forget us (Isa. 49:15). That gives us the strength to open ourselves in deep commitment to others, which in turn makes us vulnerable to deep hurt. But we are able to handle the pain when our Christian brothers and sisters hurt us, because our strength comes from something more basic to life than human relationships, namely, the joy that comes from our relationship with God.

I think the sequence in Philippians 4:1-4 is very significant. First, Paul describes the Philippians as his joy and crown (v. 1). The Philippian Christians made him very happy. Then he pleads with two warring factions to unite (vv. 2-3). This is a description of his pain. In fact, elsewhere in Philippians he implies that the lack of unity in the church took away some of his joy (Phil. 2.2). In Philippians 4:4, Paul comes to a non-negotiable essential of the Christian life, when twice he asks his readers to rejoice in the Lord and to do so always (v. 4). That's what true Christian community life is like. There will be times of pain, and there is joy over each other, but always there must be the joy of the Lord.

Sacrificing for the Community as an Antidote to Drivenness

There is one more area related to the topic of suffering and community that needs to be addressed. I believe it is very relevant to the problem of driven leadership that we are seeing in the church today. Community, like prayer, can also act as a preventive to drivenness. Good and motivated leaders have great goals that they will somehow achieve. But they become driven leaders when they break Christian principles and drive themselves and others in an unhealthy way in achieving those goals. If, however, these motivated leaders have submitted to the body of Christ as represented by the community to which they belong, they will encounter many obstacles to their success. And attending to these will sometimes appear to be a great sacrifice.

A member of the community may not be in agreement with the plans, and trying to persuade that person may take a long time and hold up progress. The driven leader may ignore the dissenter and carry on with the program. A motivated but Christ-like leader would give the time and energy required for working toward winning the dissenter's approval.

In the heat of the battle to achieve the goal, some people are invariably going to get hurt. The motivated leader may be tense because of the pressure of the huge project, and that may express itself in a temper tantrum that leaves someone very hurt. Sometimes it may simply be a misunderstanding between two members of the team. Often tension in the leader's family comes in the middle of a project, because the leader tends to neglect or be impatient with his or her family at such a time. A driven leader may ignore those who have been hurt and pursue the goal. A motivated but Christ-like leader will take the time to minister to hurt people.

When such problems emerge, it would look like a huge sacrifice to the leader to stop the hard work towards achieving the goal in order to deal with them. But I have found that such interruptions are God's way of getting us to put first things first. So we take what seems like an enormously costly step of holding back our activities in order to minister to the community. Of course, that step is usually well worth the trouble, because as a result of it, the members of the community are united, and therefore they can work much more effectively. The end product will be so much more honoring to God, with the whole community (including our families) enjoying its fruit and, therefore, with the joy of the success being more complete. In the process, the motivated leader is saved from the trap of becoming a driven leader. He or she stopped from the busy activity to attend to something that is demanded by Christian principles. Drivenness is expressed in busy and ambitious activity that is done in a way that breaks Christian principles.

Anticipating and Accepting Suffering

It seems to me that the general approach to suffering in most churches in missionary-sending nations and the way that missions is marketed today do not adequately prepare missionaries for life on the mission field. So much is told about the excitement of missions that people are not adequately prepared for the cost. Churches in the West may teach people how to respond to suffering, but they may neglect teaching people about the indispensability of suffering—a doctrine clearly taught in the New Testament.

If missionaries are truly going to identify with and become servants of those they are called to serve, they will face severe frustration, along with what initially looks like failure and fruitlessness. If they have not been adequately prepared for this reality, the pain of suffering will be greater than it needs to be. It often results in disillusionment and deep disappointment with God. Disappointment with God is one of the hardest things to bear, for it deprives us of one of the greatest antidotes to suffering: hoping in God.

I wonder if some missionaries, in order to avoid suffering and pain, are opting not to identify fully with the people they are going to serve. Their lifestyle or their refusal to be vulnerable distances them from the people. Those who join with them may do so for wrong motives, hoping that some of the wealth of the missionary will trickle down to them. These are unscrupulous people, and missionaries may end up being deceived by them. Unfortunately, many missionaries conclude that the nationals are not to be trusted. The true picture is that the missionaries were so distant in relating to the people that many persons of integrity did not feel inclined to associate closely with them.

I think the most common expression of suffering for missionaries today is severe frustration. When faced with this, missionaries may change their work to something less troubling. Instead of persevering in the difficult experience of working with a group of believers, they may become consultants who offer their expertise to various groups without the pain of having to work closely with one group. A person called to evangelize a people group that is resistant to the gospel may shift to evangelizing a people group that is more responsive to the gospel. Some, after seeing no evangelistic results, abandon the tough work of evangelization and opt for a teaching ministry. Others return home in the middle or at the end of their first term, deeply disillusioned and perhaps even angry with the missionary mobilizers who did not adequately prepare them for the suffering they encountered.

I want to encourage as many national Christians and missionaries as I can to bear in mind constantly that suffering is an indispensable feature of discipleship. Then when it comes, they will not be surprised, and they will know how to respond to it biblically. But if I am to encourage Christians in this way, I will need to suffer as they do. Unfortunately, unlike Paul when he suffered for the church (Col. 1:24), I do not always embrace this suffering joyfully. In fact, I often give in to self-pity and start grumbling. In these circumstances, I need to spend time grappling and theologizing, so that I can learn once again to be joyful in the midst of suffering. This article is the fruit of such grappling.

Final Thought

Our fundamental call in Scripture is to have fellowship with Jesus (1 Cor. 1:9). Joy and suffering are part of this call. So we approach each day by seeking to ensure that our souls are happy in the Lord. And we also approach each day with a desire to be living sacrifices. We know, of course, that this same sacrifice will be the pathway to deeper joy and a closer relationship with Him!

Reflection and Discussion

1. Recall some examples in which joy and suffering were inseparable for you. What did you learn from these experiences?
2. The author describes six types of reckoning. Which ones are part of your life, and which ones do you need to work on?
3. Are there some examples of unbiblical stress that are affecting you? If so, what can help you change these?
4. Spending good time with the Lord is seen by the author as non-negotiable. What does this mean practically for you in your life?
5. There is joy in the Lord, even when there is pain in and from community life. To what extent is this joy part of your life?

References and Suggested Reading

Anderson, B. (1983). *Out of the depths: The Psalms speak for us today.* Philadelphia, PA: Westminster Press.

Collins, G. (1976). *How to be a people helper.* Santa Ana, CA: Vision House.

Fernando, A. (1994). *Reclaiming friendship: Relating to each other in a fallen world.* Harrisburg, PA: Herald Press.

———. (2000). Jesus: The message and model of mission. In W. Taylor (Ed.), *Global missiology for the 21st century: The Iguassu dialogue* (pp. 207-222). Grand Rapids, MI: Baker Book House.

Piper, J. (1986). *Desiring God: Meditations of a Christian hedonist.* Portland, OR: Multnomah Press.

Ryken, L. (1974). *The literature of the Bible.* Grand Rapids, MI: Zondervan Publishing House.

Seamands, D. (1981). *Healing for damaged emotions.* Wheaton, IL: Victor Books.

Ajith Fernando has led Sri Lanka Youth for Christ since 1976. His responsibilities include teaching and pastoral care of staff. Ajith and his wife Nelun are active in the leadership of a Methodist church, most of whose members are converts from other religions. He has a Master's of Theology in New Testament from Fuller Theological Seminary. His nine books have been in the area of Bible exposition, such as the ***NIV Application Commentary: Acts*** *(Zondervan, 1998), or mission theology, such as* ***The Supremacy of Christ*** *(Crossway, 1995).*

Special thanks to my wife, Nelun, and my colleague, Mayukha Perera, for their valuable input on this article.

This is an expanded version of an article entitled "Some Thoughts on Missionary Burnout," ***Evangelical Missions Quarterly*** *(1999, vol. 35, pp. 440-443), PO Box 794, Wheaton, IL 60189, USA. Used by permission.*

23

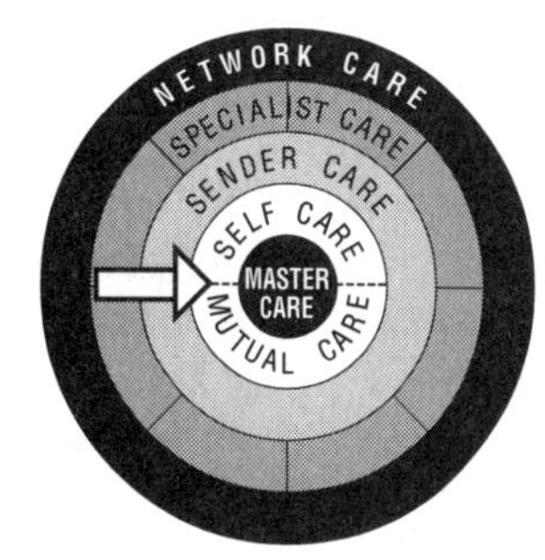

Giants, Foxes, Wolves, And Flies: Helping Ourselves and Others

Kelly O'Donnell
Michèle Lewis O'Donnell

This chapter is a collection of four short articles focusing on common areas of struggle and growth for mission personnel. Any or all of them can be used by individuals for personal reflection or by teams as part of team building sessions.

"Blessed be the Lord who trains my hands for war and my fingers for battle."
Psalm 144:1

Have you ever seen the movie, *The Wizard of Oz*? Filmed in 1939, this fantasy classic portrays the adventures of a young girl who tries to return home from a magic land lying somewhere over a rainbow. During one scene, Dorothy and her companions approach a dark forest en route to the Emerald City. Anxiously wondering what wild beasts might lie within, they begin to chant, "Lions and tigers and bears, oh my!"

For cross-cultural workers frequently beset with analogous challenges, a similar refrain can be heard: "Giants and foxes and wolves and flies!" Who are these creatures, and what do they have to do with our life and work? In brief, they are biblical metaphors representing the struggles that we often experience as we try to serve God in new ways or unfamiliar places.

Here's a quick overview:

- Giants seek to *disable* us by exploiting our vulnerabilities (2 Sam. 21:15-22).
- Foxes try to *distract* us and cause us to drift off our primary tasks (SS 2:15).
- Wolves endeavor to *distress* us, keeping our stress levels high and our lives out of balance (Matt. 10:16).
- Flies purpose to *disgrace* us by the contaminating effects of sin (Eccl. 10:1).

The enemy seeks to use all four of these creatures to sift us like wheat and ultimately destroy our life and work for the Lord. Let's take a closer look at these creatures and explore some ways to deal with them.

1.
Fighting Giants, Facing Vulnerabilities

There are some tall troublemakers lurking out there, waiting to take advantage of our vulnerabilities. How do we prepare our workers to handle these troublemakers—and their own vulnerabilities? King David's last battlefield experience highlights some strategies.

Once again, there was war with Philistia, Scripture tells us in 2 Samuel 21:15. And once again, David and the men of Israel made the familiar trek down to fight at Gob, lying on the border area between the two nations.

This time, two things were different. First, David was probably an older man, without the robust strength of his youth. Second, a Philistine giant called something like Ishbi-Benob was out to get David.

The battle commenced. In the midst of the fighting, David became exhausted. It would seem that the giant had been waiting for such a moment—when David was the most vulnerable—in order to make his move. So his assault was likely a deliberate, premeditated act. You might say that Ishbi-Benob wanted to *shish-kebab* David.

Interestingly, the text points out that Ishbi-Benob was wearing something new on his waist, perhaps a belt or a sword. The interpretation of this is not entirely clear, but its inclusion in the account is significant. One possible interpretation is that he was wearing a belt of honor, suggesting that he was a champion among the Philistines. Another possibility is that he wore a new sword, which may have been forged or dedicated for a specific task, such as killing David.

It's Abishai to the rescue, though. He comes to David's aid (surely at the risk of his own life), smites the giant, and kills him.

Now comes the important epilogue. David's valiant men gather around him and make him swear that he will never go into battle again. Why? Well, not just for David's own safety. Something even more important is at stake. It was "in order that the lamp of Israel might not go out" (2 Sam. 21:17).

What does this phrase mean? As we understand it, David, as king, was like a lamp that reflected the character and purposes of God to Israel and the surrounding peoples. To extinguish this witness would be an assault on God's redemptive purposes for the nations. Sound familiar?

Christian workers likewise are lamps to the particular people groups and ministries in which they work. We are the light of the world, the Lord tells us (Matt. 5:14). As with David, the forces of darkness seek to prey upon our vulnerabilities in order to diminish the intensity of our light—our witness—among a people group, among our neighbors, and so on. It's an age-old tactic whose only antidote is to fight the giants and face our vulnerabilities with the strength of the Lord and with the help of close friends.

Training Suggestions: Watching Over Our Hearts

We see training not only as a time to develop additional ministry skills, but also as an opportunity to reassess personal strengths and weaknesses. Indeed, the former is often the primary item on our own training agenda, while the latter can be the primary one on the Lord's! Like David and his men, we must rise to the challenge and venture down again into the border areas within our hearts, to take a closer look at our own giants and vulnerabilities. Unwanted habits such as eating struggles, a need to control others, self-hatred, depression, and many painful memories can meet us there, ready to assault us.

These struggles are to be distinguished from more serious and long-standing patterns of depression; significant marital problems; sexual identity struggles related to, for example, childhood sexual abuse; or other struggles such as addiction to pornography. These serious problems require professional help and can be identified through proper screening and selection procedures. Screening usually occurs before the training phase, but in many programs the two actually overlap.

Sharing about our struggles is risky, of course. And it is best done in training settings where there are caring people with big hearts and good helping skills, where confidentiality is honored, and where weaknesses are seen as opportunities for growth. If these are lacking, find another place!

We suggest that Christian training programs for cross-cultural ministries include the following member care components:

- Include relevant personal growth opportunities—times to look at oneself and share from one's heart up front with safe people.
- Let applicants/trainees know in advance about this emphasis on both personal and skill development.
- Use trainers and staff that model both vulnerability and strength.
- Demonstrate the overall organizational ethos (group culture) that allows for weakness, encourages appropriate self-disclosure with supportive people, and offers mutual care opportunities between staff.

These components not only help to prevent problems later on, but also reflect an important part of the body life described in the New Testament (e.g., "bear one another's burdens (giants!) and thus fulfill the law of Christ" (Gal. 6:2)).

Proverbs 4:23 instructs us to watch over our heart with all diligence, for from it flow the streams of life. Self-awareness and accountability are key for both personal growth and ministry effectiveness. We see the training phase of ministry as a critical time to encourage and model this process for our future workers. One practical way of doing this is via small-group Bible studies on this passage about David and on other passages with similar themes. Here are some questions to get you going:

Applications

Let's look at the biblical text again in 2 Samuel 21:15-17 and do some self-exploration. Read through the eight items below and answer each question. Take time to discuss your responses.

1. Like David, we all have vulnerabilities. These become even more visible for those who are in leadership positions. Sometimes we may not be aware of them until a crisis brings them to light. What are a few areas of vulnerability for you?

2. Apart from their literal meaning, what might the "giants" represent? Are they metaphors for spiritual forces, vulnerabilities, or what?

3. It was said that Ishbi-Benob had a premeditated plan for killing David. Do you think there is a similar spiritual strategy to hinder God's life in you and His work through you? If so, how?

4. David, as the leader of Israel, was a lamp reflecting the character and purposes of God. How is this true of your life? List three ways that you are doing the same practically.

5. Let's look at mutual support between workers. What does this passage imply about teamwork, our need for each other, and our willingness to let others speak into our lives?

6. David's battlefield experience began with a giant (Goliath) and ended with a giant (Ishbi-Benob). But these were not the last of the giants. Verses 18-22 of chapter 21 go on to talk about other encounters with giants. Which types of people and which types of gifts are needed to subdue the various giants? Are giants ever finally vanquished?

7. These giants did not just show up one day on the battle line in order to be promptly slain by a God-appointed warrior. Reading between the lines, we can conclude there must have been many casualties inflicted on the Jewish army by the giants. Are casualties among workers inevitable? Which personal wounds are you aware of which have come as a result

of your battles with giants? Take time to bring these areas before the Lord in prayer.

8. Can you make any other applications of this passage for your life, family, or team?

2.
Capturing the Foxes: Help for Cluttered Lives

Have you ever wanted to unclutter your desk, room, house—or even your life? You know, do a major spring cleaning? We sure have at times. If only we could just magically jettison the myriad of internal pressures that can plague us and the multitude of external demands that can distract us! Such are the yearnings of many of us involved in cross-cultural work. Let's take a closer look at some of these normal, though nonetheless unsettling sources of clutter, and let's look at a few ways to organize our lives better.

Solomon said, "Capture the foxes, the little foxes, that ruin the vineyard, while the vineyard is in blossom" (SS 2:15). What are these foxes? In the context of cross-cultural work, we would say that they are metaphors for the everyday distractions that take workers away from their primary tasks. They are the daily chores, the frequent interruptions, the legal red tape, the time needed to set up a tentmaking business, communication inefficiencies, and so on. And they are the internal preoccupations that demand our attention—concerns about family and work relationships, self-doubts from the past, loneliness, the impact of others' pain and misery, and anxieties about the future. These all eat up workers' schedules and energy, and they often interfere with the very reason they are in ministry.

We like to refer to this distracting process as "worker drift"—the natural tendency whereby life's "currents" divert one's focus (time, activities, resources, and heart direction) to areas that are peripheral to his/her objectives. In other words, workers, families, teams, and even sending agencies succumb to the inevitable trend to "major on the minors." It is not simply an issue of time management, but something far more challenging: "drift management." Let's take a closer look at seven of these distractions—foxes—to understand better what cross-cultural workers face.

■ **Doing good.** It has been aptly said that the good can become the enemy of the best. Many good things demand the attention of cross-cultural workers—like playing host or tour guide to visitors or entertaining nationals who are not members of the population one is trying to reach or serve. It is a real challenge to find the balance between involvement in such good activities (which may or may not help one connect more with the host culture) and pursuing one's primary call.

■ **Demands of living.** Basic subsistence realities are a constant energy consumer. Some wives, for example, can spend much of their day taking their children to different schools, shopping, and cooking, leaving little time for language study and other ministry-related activities. Tentmakers are frequently stretched by the need to blend their work demands with family life, social obligations, and time with nationals. The problem is there just isn't enough time!

■ **Developmental push.** This refers to the normal internal tugs that we experience during different seasons of our life. For example: the male worker in mid-life wanting to change careers and/or see something concrete established as a result of his work; the couple who meet in the host country, fall in love, and decide to return to the home country to get married and live; the push to return home to care for aging parents; the question of whether to accompany adolescent children back home as they enter into a secondary school. These and other inner yearnings must be acknowledged and prayerfully resolved.

■ **Deployment issues.** Many workers call this the "seven-year itch"—the desire to move on, try something new, seek fulfillment by working in a different way. Some may feel underemployed (the person with graduate training who teaches six hours of English each week only), underutilized (the faithful, full-time mom who wishes she had more time with nationals), or overworked (people in demanding jobs). Wrestling with the issue of personal fulfillment through one's work and embracing the need for sacrifice are an ongoing experience for many.

■ **Defaulting to the status quo.** There is a tendency in all of us to gravitate towards the familiar and the convenient. In a cross-cultural setting, this tendency can present itself as a desire to speak/learn a trade language rather than a more difficult heart language; spending extra time with expatriates rather than pursuing relationships with nationals; or planning seemingly endless work strategies on a computer rather than seeking out additional time with nationals. It takes self-discipline, intrinsic motivation, accountability, and commitment to stay focused on difficult tasks.

■ **Differences between team members.** Our individual variations reflect the creative genius of God. But these very differences in stressful situations could appear as deviance, leading to division and conflict. Differences in work expectations, lifestyle, and relationships must be discussed, understood, and harmonized as much as possible. No one wins when differences are either covered up or left unresolved.

■ **Discouragement.** Each of the previous six foxes feed into this one, making it the most menacing. Two reasons for discouragement include slow progress in one's work and having to say farewell to colleagues who move to another location. Although mourning a loss is healthy, unchecked discouragement frequently results in an inordinate self-focus that distorts one's understanding of God's perspective and decreases one's faith that God will move.

The above seven foxes (seven Ds) in and of themselves are neither wrong nor necessarily problematic. What is troublesome, though, are their unrecognized, ongoing, cumulative effects, which subtly prevent us from fulfilling our ministry (2 Tim. 4:5). Remember too that internal pressures and external distractions, although natural, can be used in unnatural ways by demonic forces. Satan is just as pleased to sabotage one's work through distracting foxes as with fearsome giants, ravenous wolves, or annoying flies.

Strategies for Capturing the Foxes

Have you ever seen a fox in the wild? We have—three of them, over a five-year period, in the woods by our house. They just seem to pop up and then vanish before you can figure out what's happening. But if you think it's hard to spot a fox, then just try catching one! In the same way, *distractions*—the little foxes from the Song of Songs 2:15—can be difficult to identify and even more difficult to apprehend. Nonetheless, there are some ways to capture these elusive creatures. Here are two proven methods: connecting with ourselves (awareness) and connecting with others (accountability).

Awareness

There is a Central Asian proverb that says, "A bitter truth is better than a sweet lie." Looking within is not always convenient or pain-free, but it certainly is far better than the alternatives: ignorance and denial. Take time to get quiet, and reflect.

Often we need a person to help us in this process—listening to the Lord, sharing with a caring friend, speaking to a counselor. We can all learn from successful "recovery" programs (e.g., dealing with unwanted habits), which emphasize a disciplined commitment to self-reflection and honesty. This is not a selfish pursuit, but rather it is an important spiritual discipline rooted in classic Christian wisdom (see Foster & Smith, 1993; Huggett, 1993).

Keeping a journal is also helpful (see Shepperson & Shepperson, 1992), especially for those working in more isolated settings. One journaling exercise that we find useful was inspired by the book *Connecting With Self and Others* (Miller et al., 1988). Find a quiet place, take a few deep breaths, and then write a current concern in the middle of a piece of paper. Draw a large circle around it. Next, respond to the five questions below, jotting down notes—that is, what you are saying to yourself—inside the circle. Pray about what you find, and consider sharing your findings with a friend.

1. What am I sensing? (physical sensations in muscles, stomach, breathing, etc.)
2. What am I feeling? (emotions)
3. What am I wanting? (changes in self, in others, in situations)
4. What am I thinking? (ideas, beliefs, themes, content)
5. What am I doing? (actions and behaviors that I do related to the concern)

Accountability

There's a Jewish proverb which says, "A true friend is the elixir of life. And those who fear the Lord make true friends." Mutual support on location is a basic necessity. Strategize together and pray through solutions to the natural drift process. Sadly, many folks do not prioritize time to build close friendships where they are. Often, it seems we are either too busy or too scared. Or sometimes the "right" persons are just not available. In the latter case, we can stay connected with confidants via letters and email. Friends help us see ourselves more clearly and support us as we set realistic limits around our work and lives (see Cloud & Townsend, 1992).

Here's an exercise that can help you build more accountability. Get together with a friend, review this article, and talk about the five items below. You can also do this with your team or family. Discuss whether and how you would want to hold each other accountable for some of your "little foxes." Using a calendar/chart is helpful to record progress daily of changes in your behaviors (e.g., praying with spouse, time with kids, use of leisure time, unwanted habits).

1. In what ways might you have drifted off your primary tasks over the past six months?
2. Which of the seven foxes previously described seem to pressure and distract you the most? Try your hand at drawing a quick picture of one of them—make it realistic, symbolic, or abstract.
3. Why do you suppose it may be hard for you to catch your foxes?
4. What helps you to stay focused on your work? List three practical steps you can take to help yourself.
5. Are there any other thoughts you have about the "little foxes"? If so, discuss your ideas.

A Final Thought

Why not do a spring cleaning and declutter some of your internal pressures and external demands? Connect with yourself more and with significant others. And as Gordon MacDonald (1989) encourages us to do, be sure to seek out "still times, safe places, and special friends" regularly.

3. Prudence in the Presence of Wolves

Mission personnel must find practical ways to be "shrewd as serpents and innocent as doves," in order not to become prey to the stress-producing wolves of ministry life.

No one would want to become "lamb chops," right? Yet that is basically what Jesus said would happen to people if they did not exercise prudence in their ministry.

Consider, for instance, His warning in Matthew 10:16, "Behold, I send you out as sheep in the midst of wolves. Therefore be wise as serpents and as innocent as doves." Notice that He did not send His disciples (or us) out as emboldened lions, but as vulnerable sheep needing the flock and needing the Shepherd. Why such a solemn warning? Because ministry life is neither easy nor always safe.

When we first started working in missions as psychologists, we understood that the main struggle for missionaries was in the area of cross-cultural adjustment. Just persevere in language and culture learning, we thought, and we will probably make it. Well, we were right—sort of.

In practically no time, though, we became painfully aware of another significant stressor for those in ministry: trying to harmonize one's background/preferences with the organizational culture of the sending agency. This stressor proved to be our own greatest struggle during our first three years overseas. Like many of our fellow workers, we soon realized the draining impact of unresolved interpersonal conflict.

Next, we became more keenly aware of spiritual warfare. And to make a long story short, as we gained even more experience on the field, we began to see a host of other "wolves"—that is, stressors—which affected us and others in cross-cultural ministry.

We soon saw the need to develop a conceptual grid to help identify and deal with the various wolves that are part of ministry life abroad. "CHOPS," as in lamb *chops*, is an acronym we gradually developed to help remember 10 general categories of stress common to those in ministry overseas. We have included this inventory below (see Figure 1 on the next page) and use it regularly as a member care tool as we work with mission personnel. It can help us deal with the stress-producing "wolves" of missionary life.

Applications

Read through the 10 categories, and then write down some of the stressors that you have experienced over the past several months. Put these in a column labeled "Struggles." In a second column, "Successes," list some of the helpful ways you have dealt with stress during the last several months. Finally, under a "Strategies" column, jot down some of your ideas for better managing stress in the future. Discuss your responses with a friend who can listen well and support you.

It is important also to identify and discuss the stressors that affect families, teams, departments, the region, and the overall agency itself. The inventory, if completed and discussed once a year, for example, is a useful means to understand and minimize stress at various levels of the ministry organization. As we deal with the stressors, we need to be reminded of Luke 12:32, "Do not fear, little flock, because your Father is pleased to give you the kingdom."

Some Questions

Stress is the response of the whole person to the internal and external demands that we experience. The following questions will help you become more familiar with how stress affects you. They will also help you look at some ways that you can deal with stress. Respond to each of the five questions below, and then discuss them as a group. What insights can you gain from one another?

1. How do you know when you are experiencing stress? What signals do you receive from your body, behavior, and emotions?

2. How does stress affect your interpersonal relationships?

3. When was the last time you went through a significant period of stress? What was it like? Briefly describe it.

4. There are at least 25 different things recorded in the Gospels that Jesus did to manage stress—to deal with the wolves and potential wolves of His ministry. How many can you identify?

5. What helps you to deal with stress, keep your life in balance, and keep the "wolves" at bay? What does not help?

Figure 1
CHOPS Inventory of Stressors

Category	Description	Struggles	Successes	Strategies
Cultural	Getting your needs met in unfamiliar ways: language learning, culture shock, reentry.			
Crises	Potentially traumatic events, often unexpected: natural disasters, wars, accidents, political instability.			
Historical	Unresolved past areas of personal struggle: family-of-origin issues, personal weaknesses.			
Human	Relationships with family members, colleagues, nationals: raising children, couple conflict, struggles with team members, social opposition.			
Occupational	Job-specific challenges and pressures: workload, travel schedule, exposure to people with problems, job satisfaction, more training, government "red tape."			
Organizational	Incongruity between one's background and the organizational ethos: differing with company policies, work style, expectations.			
Physical	Overall health and factors that affect it: nutrition, climate, illness, aging, environment.			
Psychological	Overall emotional stability and self-esteem: loneliness, frustration, depression, unwanted habits, developmental issues/ stage-of-life issues.			
Support	Resources to sustain one's work: finances, housing, clerical and technical help, donor contact.			
Spiritual	Relationship with the Lord: devotional life, subtle temptations, time with other believers, spiritual warfare.			

Answers apply to (circle): self, spouse, child, friend, department, team, company.

4. Folly From Flies

Behind many of our inner struggles are attempts to deny who we really are or to be something that we are not. Personal problems often stem from efforts to escape from legitimate suffering.

Many cross-cultural workers live in places where flies are common. So it's not too unusual, say, to find a fly in one's glass of water, which I did one hot and humid day in Thailand. Maybe the fly was just going for a swim, I told myself. Or maybe this is someone else's glass. Yet there I was, sitting with 40 expatriate leaders around several tables in a conference room, discussing work strategies and praying. This was the first time I had been invited to be part of this group, and I was feeling, well, rather special. Everything was fine, except for that wee pest in my glass.

Contamination From Flies

Quickly I flashed back to my morning devotions, pondering the verse I had meditated upon that would help me make sense out of my unsolicited visitor: "Dead flies cause the ointment of the perfumer to putrefy and send forth a vile odor; so does a little folly (in him who is valued for wisdom) outweigh wisdom and honor" (Eccl. 10:1, Amplified). The application to me was apparent.

Was I fancying myself to be just a bit too special by virtue of my inclusion now as a "leader"? You bet. And this attitude was folly. Talk about starting out on the wrong foot! Or the wrong fly! Moreover, I knew from past experience that this attitude would eventually contaminate the fragrance of Christ in my life and work (2 Cor. 2:15), just as dead flies putrefy precious perfume. This special envoy had done its job by getting my attention!

Characteristics of Flies

No one deliberately adds flies, be they dead or alive, to valuable perfume. The two are incongruous. Likewise, few of us deliberately try to pollute our own lives. Yet like flies in perfume, our folly—our sin—can alight in our souls and wreak havoc on our wisdom, honor, and work. A little leaven leavens the whole lump of dough, as Paul says (1 Cor. 5:6).

Some types of folly are more damaging than others. A few household flies, for instance, will only pester us. They are a nuisance. Think of these, analogously, as things like unwanted habits in our life and minor character weaknesses of which we are trying to rid ourselves. But lots of flies, especially those that can bite, sting, and carry diseases, could really hurt us. Think of these as serious folly: unconfessed sin, unrecognized arrogance, hidden compulsive addictions, and pervasive personality patterns that are unhealthy/unholy.

Have you ever noticed how just one public or even private manifestation of such serious folly—these wrong behaviors and attitudes—can neutralize our work effectiveness, compromise our integrity, destabilize our emotional life, and hurt others? "Wisdom is better than weapons of war, but one sinner destroys much good" (Eccl. 9:18). This is true even for Christian sinners!

Folly from flies comes in different frequencies and intensities. It can involve one-time events, in which we recognize the problem and then learn our lesson quickly. We can brush away such flies fairly easily. Folly can also take the form of intermittent events, which can be hard to predict and which seemingly just creep up on us. Additionally, folly can involve ongoing events in our lives, marked by a serious lack of self-control. These can feel like a host of flies swarming around us.

The bottom line is that folly, in whatever form, leads to disgrace. Just a bit of it is all it takes to damage our reputation—and God's—no matter how virtuous our life or noteworthy our accomplishments. Disgrace results not only from the actual content of the folly (e.g., rash words, questionable financial dealings, physical or emotional affairs). It can also come in the aftermath of our inappropriate actions. Instead of availing ourselves of God's grace, we deny or minimize our problem/sin, or we refuse to believe in God's restorative desire to forgive us and help us in our time of need (Heb. 4:16). Think of the latter as falling into "dis-grace."

Spotting Flies

It often takes an outside source, such as a close friend, the Word of God, or the Holy Spirit, to help us recognize the flies in our life. One of the biggest sources of folly is not to be in regular contact with these three "fly spotting" sources! Let's give names to some of the more common flies. Sin—as in the lust of the flesh, the lust of the eyes, and pride (1 John 2:15-16)—takes many winged forms!

- **Hidden addictions** (*mosca compulsiva*). These are closet compulsions that affect our time, judgment, and relationships. After awhile, you can smell their stench, even though they may be covered up at first. Excessive behaviors involving exercise, sun-tanning, over/undereating, preoccupation with one's appearance/body, procrastination, withdrawing, shopping, TV watching, Internet use, etc., are all part of this. We sedate and stimulate ourselves in many ways, in order to avoid seeing ourselves clearly and dealing directly with problems. Major addictions, such as pornography, gambling, and drug dependence, are even more crippling.
- **Bitterness** (*mosca vinegari*). Henri Nouwen has observed that in this life, "Love and wounds are never separated." We hurt those we love and vice versa. Working through such hurts and forgiving, though challenging, is certainly more desirable than the alternative: harboring the hurt and developing a pervasive, entrenched bitterness that can defile our souls and those of others (Heb. 12:15). Forgiveness, an act of mercy which pardons others for specific offenses, is the only sure antidote for such bitterness.
- **Improper comments** (*mosca maximus moutha*). Our mouths are sources of honor and embarrassment for us. Surely no one can tame the tongue (James 3:8). Some of our greatest verbal faux pas include making hasty, inappropriate promises, especially to God (Prov. 20:25; Eccl. 5:1-7); spewing out "brain sludge"—nonsensical things, questionable stories or jokes, or coarse jesting that does not edify (Eph. 4:3-4); gossip, which involves repeating a matter that unfairly or unnecessarily damages other people; and insensitive (poorly timed and overly harsh) criticism.
- **Arrogance** (*mosca maximus rex*). Some of us need and like to be leaders—admired, in control, taking charge, leading the way. How easy it is to be seduced by our positions of influence, and our desires to be important. Inflated pride and self-aggrandizement are two of life's greatest dangers. They are the insidious winged companions of those who believe that they are more special than they really are, and that their success has come more through their own efforts than through God's favor and anointing (Deut. 8:17).
- **Personal flies** (*mosca mia perpetua*). The list of flies that can plague us is almost endless. Can you identify any flies, dead or alive, floating in the waters of your soul?

Swatting Flies

How do we rid ourselves of such fallacious menaces? It can be tricky. And it is a process. We hit some, and we miss some. The first line of defense is to proactively attend to our personal growth: staying close to the Lord, in touch with ourselves, aware of the influence of our surroundings, and connected with confidants.

When flies do come around, they are best dealt with through honestly admitting their existence and impact (*confession*), choosing to make serious changes and amends in order to limit their influence (*repentance/restitution*), and getting ongoing supportive input from others to help us deal with them (*accountability*). Guidance from the Holy Spirit, trusted friends, Scripture meditation, counseling, and a good support group or "12 Steps" program are all important sources of help, especially for dealing with some of the more lethal varieties of flies. Confession, repentance/restitution, and accountability are like strands of the three-fold cord that is not easily broken (Eccl. 4:12). We can use this cord to knit a protective fabric which, like a mosquito net, can keep the folly out and, like a safety net, can catch us if we fall.

We often wish to experience in this life what we can only experience in heaven. We ache for something more—to be clothed with the immortal. We yearn for our personal flies to leave us permanently. Even after experiencing the best that this life has to offer, we are still left with a deep longing for wholeness and a desire to be clothed with that which will never fade. Yet as Larry Crabb (1988) tells us, the aching soul is not evidence of emotional problems, but a sign of our facing reality. It is a sign of health.

In closing, let's consider Christ's words to Peter right before Gethsemane. "Simon, Simon, behold Satan has demanded permission to sift you (plural) like wheat; but I have prayed for you (singular) that your faith may not fail; and you, when once you have turned, strengthen your brothers" (Luke 22:31-32, NASB). Note that this is a prediction primarily of Peter's faithfulness, not of his failure. I believe the Lord sees us much in the same way, as we struggle through areas of folly. He sees the potential in us. And in spite of our weaknesses, He still entrusts us, as He did Peter, to feed His sheep and to be His faithful and refreshing fragrance among the nations (John 21).

References and Resources

Cloud, H. (1992). *Changes that heal*. Grand Rapids, MI: Zondervan Publishing House.

Cloud, H., & Townsend, J. (1992). *Boundaries: When to say yes, when to say no*. Grand Rapids, MI: Zondervan Publishing House.

Crabb, L. (1988). *Inside out*. Colorado Springs, CO: NavPress.

Foster, R., & Smith, B. (1993). *Devotional classics: Selected readings for individuals and groups.* San Francisco, CA: Harper-Collins.

Hart, A. (1990). *Healing life's hidden addictions*. Ann Arbor, MI: Servant Publications.

Huggett, J. (1993). *Finding God in the fast lane*. Guilford, Surrey, UK: Eagle.

MacDonald, G. (1989). *Renewing your spiritual passion*. Nashville, TN: Thomas Nelson Publishers.

Miller, S., Wackman, D., Nunnally, E., & Miller, P. (1988). *Connecting with self and others*. Littleton, CO: Interpersonal Communications Programs.

Shepperson, V., & Shepperson, B. (1992). *Tracks in the sand: An interactive workbook* (for recovery journaling). Nashville, TN: Thomas Nelson Publishers.

Wilson, S. (1993). *Hurt people hurt people*. Nashville, TN: Thomas Nelson Publishers.

Kelly O'Donnell and Michèle Lewis O'Donnell *are psychologists, based in Europe. They work out of an interagency member care center in France called Le Rucher, located close to Geneva. They have two children, Erin, aged 12, and Ashling, aged 8. Kelly and Michèle studied clinical psychology and theology at Rosemead School of Psychology, Biola University, where they earned their Doctor of Psychology degrees. Special emphases include crisis care, team building, expatriate family life, personnel development, and developing member care affiliations. Email: 102172.170@compuserve.com.*

This is a revision of an article published in the special member care issue of the ***International Journal of Frontier Missions*** *(1995, vol. 12, pp. 185-188). The article was later expanded and published as four short articles in the journal* ***Reaching Children at Risk*** *(1998, vol. 2, no. 1, pp. 28-29; no. 2, pp. 6-10; no. 3, pp. 11-14; and 1999, vol. 3, no. 2, pp. 26-29). Used by permission.*

24

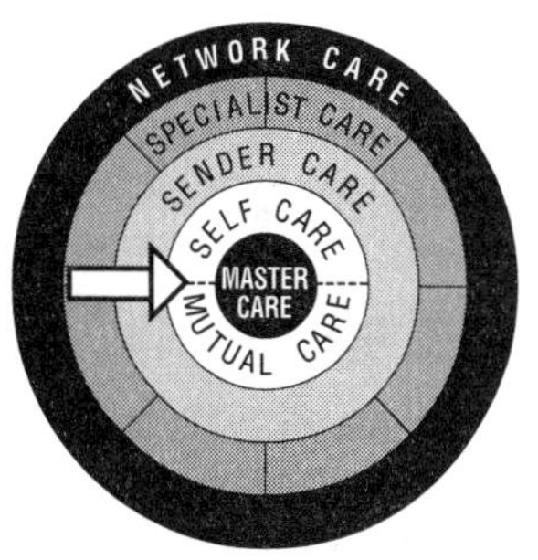

Sexual Purity In Missions

KEN WILLIAMS

Healthy sexuality is a significant issue anywhere these days. Missionaries can expect to be challenged in this area as they follow the biblical guidelines/admonitions to live sensible and holy lives (Titus 2:11-15). Here are several practical strategies and tools for remaining pure in missions and for avoiding the snares of the Evil One.

"It is God's will that you should be sanctified:
that you should avoid sexual immorality;
that each of you should learn to control his own body
in a way that is holy and honorable."
1 Thessalonians 4:3-4

We all are aware of cases of moral failure among missionaries. And how disheartening this can be for all of us, especially when it happens to close colleagues. The church in Western societies has been so inundated with sexual stimuli that what was once seen as grossly inappropriate, pornographic, and shameful is now treated as more or less "normal" and acceptable. This proliferation of distorted human sexuality is a prime tool which Satan, the enemy of our souls, is using against people in general, the church, and the missions community in particular. No longer limited to subtle temptations, he now blatantly tempts us to immorality in ways that would have been ineffective only a few years ago.

Being sexual and sane these days is no easy thing. Each of us is responsible for who we are as sexual beings. This means that at times and as Christians, we must acknowledge our sexual issues or struggles, as well as engage personally in spiritual warfare to resist Satan's sexual temptations. We are also called to help others effectively do battle in this arena.

In this chapter, I would like to remind us that as missionaries we are as vulnerable to sexual sin as anyone else. I will briefly explain the dynamics of sexual temptation and will give some ideas for developing a personal strategy for maintaining moral purity. I have also included two brief self-assessment tools on maintaining sexual purity.

Although this article does not specifically address adolescent MKs and sexuality matters, this is of course a critical issue. Missionary parents and educators may want to use this article with adolescent MKs to help them in their sexual journey into adulthood.

Be Aware of the Danger

We need to be just as concerned about understanding the normal and healthy aspects of human sexuality as we are about its potential dangers and downside. What a powerful and lovely gift we have from our Creator! An article of this nature could lead us to the false assumption that sexual feelings in themselves are evil. However, let us remember that sex was God's idea, created by Him before the fall (see Gen. 2:18-25). My perspective in this article is to focus more on safeguarding ourselves from the negative consequences of inappropriate sexual expression and temptation, especially in light of how Satan can use these things to attack us.

The first step in resisting temptation is to be aware of Satan's strategies. Paul spoke of being alert, "in order that Satan might not outwit us. For we are not unaware of his schemes" (2 Cor. 2:11). Let us be aware of Satan's schemes for trying to destroy God's work. One of his primary strategies is to convince us that we could never sink so low as to commit sexual sin.

Missionaries often face special issues that make them vulnerable to sexual temptation. Carefully consider the specific factors in your situation that may hinder your ability to resist. These may include loneliness, anonymity, unmet emotional needs, greater sexual freedom in the local culture, and loss of support systems such as family, church, and friends. Also, unrelenting stress over long periods of time can undermine our ability to resist temptation.

Sometimes missionaries are more susceptible to sexual temptation because they think that it could never happen to them. They believe the possibility is unthinkable. In counseling several missionaries who had committed adultery or fornication, I found that not one had considered himself or herself vulnerable to immorality.

You are probably well acquainted with 1 Corinthians 10:13, and you claim its precious promises: "No temptation has seized you except what is common to man. And God is faithful; He will not let you be tempted beyond what you can bear. But when you are tempted, He will also provide a way out so that you can stand up under it." But do you also know and apply the preceding verse? "So, if you think you are standing firm, be careful that you don't fall!" The Holy Spirit gave us this stern warning immediately before the promises, and both must be taken together. We cannot safely rest in God's promise of help in temptation, if we naively think we can stand without taking great care.

We need to face the facts. Each one of us is vulnerable to sexual temptation, no matter what our age, marital status, or maturity. You may be tempted to indulge in pornography. The worldwide availability of pornography on the Internet poses a relatively new and powerful temptation to missionaries, especially men. Not long ago, Focus on the Family reported that the number one reason pastors and their spouses called their hotline for help was addiction to pornography on the Internet!

Or you may find yourself tempted to "play games" with persons to whom you are attracted, without actual sexual involvement. These games can take many forms—flirting, showing special interest, touching more than is appropriate, engaging in too much eye contact, spending a lot of time together, joking about being in love, etc. While these things may not be sinful in themselves, they can put us and others in danger.

Many missionaries struggle with severe temptations to commit adultery, fornication, homosexual acts, and even incest or child molestation. Tragically, some of them succumb. What about you? Will you be one of those who end up as a lamb in Satan's slaughterhouse? Or will you walk in the power of the Holy Spirit, aware of the dangers and prepared to victoriously do battle with the forces of evil?

Understand the Dynamics of Sexual Temptation

Many missionaries do not understand the powerful dynamics of sexual temptation. As you understand these dynamics, you are able to recognize forces and processes within you and take action to resist them. Here are a few principles to keep in mind:

1. We don't fall into sin; we slide into it. When someone commits sexual sin, we tend to think of that person as suddenly falling off the cliff into an abyss. This is rarely, if ever, the case. An act of sexual sin is the ultimate and logical result of long-term habit patterns of giving in to temptations to less obvious sins. According to our Lord, sexual sin originates in the heart (Matt. 15:19). The embers of adultery may smolder in the heart for months or even years before they burst into the flame of action. See Matthew 5:8, 28; 12:35-36; Proverbs 4:23; 6:18; 23:26-28.

2. The beginnings of the slide into immorality often seem so harmless that we may not even be aware of them. We live in a sex-saturated world. Each time we are exposed to a TV program, movie, magazine, or pornography on the Internet that appeals even slightly to sexual desires that are inappropriate, a powerful, unconscious process evolves. The process is often so slow and subtle that we are rarely aware of what is happening; but as the years pass, our hatred of sexual sin is gradually lost. In fact, the process has been going on in our society long enough that many young Christians have never developed that abhorrence. And so the seeds of personal sexual sin have been sown deep in the hearts of most of us, without our even realizing it.

3. Our capacity for self-deceit is virtually limitless, according to Jeremiah 17:9. Being a missionary does not diminish this capacity! While we rejoice in God's indwelling power over sin, we must be constantly aware of the power of our hearts to deceive us. If we fail to accept this difficult truth about ourselves, we stand in great danger of sexual sin. As a counselor, I know of no area in which the power of self-deceit is stronger than in the sexual area. Most of us know of believers who tried to continue serving God while living in secret immorality and who "repented" only after getting caught. See 1 Corinthians 3:18, Galatians 6:7-8, Ephesians 5:6, James 1:22, and 1 John 1:8.

4. Close personal relationships are vital in the Christian life. God created us with legitimate needs for intimacy, and to deny these needs may make us even more vulnerable to sexual temptation. For married persons, intimacy with one's spouse must be primary, of course. But married and single persons alike need healthy, godly relationships with others. Intimacy and sexuality are not the same. A healthy, biblical view of loving intimacy allows us to relate in mutually upbuilding ways without romantic or sexual involvement. Read through the Gospels to see Jesus' model in His close friendships.

5. Intimate relationships often provide serious temptation to sin, and so they must be handled with great care and awareness of their dangers. Most missionaries slide into sexual sin through relationships that begin quite harmlessly and even out of righteous motives. The process usually develops in these stages:

- A man and woman are brought together naturally through work, common interests, or ministry.
- They begin to spend more time together, especially more time alone.
- One or both begin to have deep emotional and/or spiritual needs met in the relationship.
- At some point, they begin to touch each other, sometimes beginning with right motives. But eventually the touching, combined with the meeting of significant needs, generates romantic and/or sexual feelings.

- Powerful self-deception enables them to justify and rationalize what is happening in the relationship.

6. Once we have begun the slide, sexual temptation will probably be the strongest force we will ever experience. Its power can grow to the point that we become willing to give up everything to gratify it: relationship with Christ, spouse and children, home, ministry, reputation, friends, *everything*. And no believer is so spiritual that he or she is immune to its power.

Involvement in pornography is particularly difficult to overcome. When one has become addicted, that is, compulsively drawn to pornographic images time after time and unable to stop, he/she will need help from a colleague, a support group, or a counselor to overcome the pull. No one makes it alone in seeking to recover from addiction.

Masturbation

We Christians are very reluctant to talk about masturbation. This is such a hush-hush topic, but it is so important that I want to address it briefly. It is one of those issues with which most people, Christian or not, have struggled or are struggling. Yet convictions of its sinfulness or lack of sinfulness are held very strongly. My purpose is neither to justify it as always OK, nor condemn it as always a terrible sin. As far as I can discover, the Bible never mentions masturbation, while it does mention virtually every sexual act that is sinful.

In giving five "indisputable facts," Richard Foster (1985) summarizes the issue of masturbation in his book *Money, Sex, and Power* far better than I could: "First, masturbation is not physically harmful in any way.... Second, the Bible nowhere deals directly with masturbation.... But sexual desire also needs to be controlled, which leads us to a third affirmation: the more masturbation tends toward obsession, the more it tends toward idolatry.... A fourth affirmation: masturbation's sexual fantasies are a very real part of human life that needs to be disciplined, not eliminated.... The final thing we should say about masturbation is that, although it may electrify, it can never fully satisfy." See Foster's complete discussion for further treatment of the subject. Randy Alcorn (1985) also provides a helpful chapter on this topic in *Christians in the Wake of the Sexual Revolution*.

Build a Strategy for Ongoing Moral Purity

Here are 11 principles to help you develop a strategy for avoiding sexual sin:

1. Accept your personal vulnerability to immorality, and continue to grow in understanding your own personal responses to the dynamics of sexual temptation.

2. If married, make your relationship with your spouse a high priority. Do not let the stresses of life rob you of the rich, satisfying relationship God wants for you, according to Proverbs 5:18-20.

3. Make a list of sinful practices in which you are or have been involved. These may include thoughts, fantasies, feelings, and actions which stimulate or gratify you sexually but which you know are sinful. Then add to the list seemingly harmless practices in which you engage but which you know do not contribute to a holy life. These might include thoughts, fantasies, and feelings which are less explicit than those you first listed. They may also include TV programs and magazines which are not overtly pornographic but which you know appeal to the flesh. These activities may be permissible according to 1 Corinthians 6:12, but in time you can be enslaved to them, without even realizing it. They cause you to set your mind on the flesh rather than on the Spirit, as described in Romans 8:5.

4. Make a commitment to Jesus Christ and to your spouse, if married, to live a holy life free from sexual sin, even those sins that seem to be harmless. Write down your commitment and keep it where you will see it often. This is a commitment that must be continually reaffirmed, sometimes on a moment-by-moment basis.

5. Make a lifelong project of studying, memorizing, meditating on, and applying Scriptures which speak to this area of life. See Psalm 119:9, 11. A few key passages in this area are Proverbs 5; 6:20-35; Romans 6; 1 Corinthians 6:12-20; Ephesians 5:3-12; 1 Thessalonians 4:3-8. God's Word must be a major part of your strategy.

6. Rigorously practice Colossians 3:5. "Put to death, therefore, whatever belongs to your earthly nature: sexual immorality, impurity, lust, evil desires...." Also see Ephesians 4:22. Ask God to forgive you and to cleanse you of any practices you listed under point 3 above. Then seek to achieve freedom from those things. This process will take time, and, being human, you will probably fail at times. But don't give up in discouragement! Satan will try to convince you that it's hopeless—that you will never make significant progress.

Timing is critical. When you are first aware of being tempted, reaffirm your commitment to Christ and to putting your earthly nature to death. In this battle, even a few seconds of wavering or inaction can make the difference between victory and defeat (Eccl. 8:11).

7. Continually work on being renewed in your mind, as described in Colossians 3:10 and Ephesians 4:23-24. This involves a commitment that must be reaffirmed often, especially when you first become aware of temptation. Scripture explains the process of being renewed in our minds in different ways, so that we are able to understand it fully. Study this process in the Word, beginning with Romans 8:5-8, 12:1-3, Philippians 4:4-8, Colossians 3:1-4, and 1 Peter 1:13-17.

8. Develop a relationship of mutual accountability. We cannot hope to handle sexual temptation effectively alone. In fact, God didn't design us to survive alone in this spiritual battle. Hebrews 3:12-13 indicates that we need close personal interaction with others in order not to be "hardened by sin's deceitfulness."

It can be very difficult to "confess your sins to each other and pray for each other" (James 5:16). Yet every one of us needs to do this very thing regularly. Nothing will cause an illicit attraction or fantasy to shatter in pieces as much as sharing it with a praying friend. Specific details need not normally be shared.

9. Develop your own "early warning system" to detect the first signs of temptation. Christians often slide into sexual sin without being aware of temptation until it is too late. Romans 6:12 warns us that we can become slaves to sin and lose our freedom to obey God. If you are married, the slightest physical or emotional attraction to a person of the opposite sex should be dealt with immediately through prayer, application of God's Word, and mutual accountability.

10. Know and avoid your danger zones. The situations in which we put ourselves greatly affect our vulnerability to sexual temptation. To do battle effectively in this area, we need to know the situations that are dangerous to us. Then we must avoid them when possible. If that isn't possible, we need to plan ahead for spiritual warfare and take whatever steps are necessary to insure victory. Here are a few examples of possible danger zones:

- Traveling alone, especially overseas.
- Working alone with someone of the opposite sex.
- Counseling or praying alone with someone of the opposite sex.
- Meeting with a person of the opposite sex in a room where no one can see in.
- Getting so over-stressed that the ability to fight temptation is diminished.

11. Understand cultural cues. If you are in another culture, learn which cues signal moral looseness and which signal moral purity. Here are four questions to ask:

- What cues signal that a person is moral?
- What cues signal that a person is not interested in another person?
- What cues signal that a person is immoral?
- What cues signal that a person is interested in another person?

Be very careful to avoid immoral cues, and practice those which signal an unwillingness to become involved in illicit relationships.

Conclusion

Sexual immorality is not the unforgivable sin. Forgiveness and healing are available through the blood of Christ. If you have been or are now caught up in immorality, you can experience God's forgiveness and cleansing through confession and repentance. But to commit sexual immorality may be the most excruciatingly destructive experience that can happen in anyone's life and ministry. Begin today to build your personal strategy for a lifetime of moral purity, knowing that you will battle great temptations along the way.

Reflection and Discussion

Go through the worksheet in Appendix 1 below, "How Am I Maintaining Moral Purity?" Consider doing this exercise with a close friend (same gender), accountability group, or spouse. The second appendix is similar and is intended for use by individuals and couples.

Appendix 1
How Am I Maintaining Moral Purity?

Use the following scale to indicate your responses:

1 = Rarely; 2 = Occasionally; 3 = Sometimes; 4 = Often; 5 = Nearly always

____ 1. I am consciously aware of my vulnerability to sexual sin.

____ 2. I have definite standards as to what I watch, listen to, and read, and I am careful to live by these standards.

____ 3. I am careful about how I touch people of the opposite sex.

____ 4. I meet with an accountability partner or partners regularly.

____ 5. My actions show that I am a moral person in whatever culture I'm in.

____ 6. When tempted to lust after someone, I "take captive" those thoughts and feelings, so that they "obey Christ."

____ 7. I refrain from flirting.

____ 8. I refuse to be entertained by anything that offends God.

____ 9. If I feel attracted to someone, I am extremely careful to act in ways that will suppress emotional involvement on the part of both of us.

____ 10. If I must go into morally high-risk situations, I consciously recognize the risk before I go there, and I plan on steps to protect myself.

____ 11. When I become aware that I am on the slide toward immorality, I take immediate steps to move back toward purity.

____ 12. I dress in such a way as to demonstrate my commitment to morality, both in my culture and in other cultures.

____ 13. I do whatever I can to see that my legitimate emotional needs are met in godly, healthy ways.

____ 14. I meditate on Scriptures that encourage me and strengthen me in maintaining moral purity.

____ 15. I maintain a love relationship with Christ that is so strong that engaging in any kind of immorality is abhorred.

Appendix 2
Maintaining Moral Purity:
Opportunities for Growth

Here are some questions for prayerful reflection. Review these, and write an action plan.

Individual Issues

1. How would I describe my vulnerability to sexual temptation at this time in my life?
   a. What factors are helping me to remain pure?
   b. What factors are making it difficult for me to remain pure?
2. Am I on the slide toward immorality?
   a. Where am I now compared to five years ago? A year ago? Six months ago?
   b. What, if anything, do I need to do in order to move back toward complete purity?
3. Is there anyone with whom I am involved in the five stages toward immorality? (See point 5 under "Understand the Dynamics of Sexual Temptation.")
   a. If so, who is it?
   b. At what stage am I?
   c. What do I plan to do about it? When?
4. What does my strategy for moral purity look like right now?
   a. What aspects do I now practice?
   b. What have I stopped practicing that I used to do? What do I want to do about these things?
   c. What new things do I want to add to my strategy? When will I add them?
5. What Scriptures have I memorized in this area?
   a. How often do I review them?
   b. What new "battle passages" do I want to add to my arsenal?
   c. Memorize one of the following Scripture passages: 1 Corinthians 6:18-20, 2 Corinthians 7:1, or Ephesians 5:3-5.

Married Couple Issues

1. Talk through the individual issues with your spouse.
2. What is going on in our lives and marriage that is helping us remain morally pure?
3. What is going on right now that makes it difficult to remain pure?
4. How free are we to talk about sexual temptation and other moral issues? What do we want to do to grow in this area?

5. What can we do to make it easier for us to keep our purity?
6. In what ways can we enhance our love for each other at this time in our lives?
7. How are we doing at meeting each other's needs? Emotional needs? Physical needs? Spiritual needs? How can we do better?
8. What does our strategy for moral purity *as a couple* look like? What specifically can we do to make our strategy more effective?
9. What else do we want to say to each other or ask of each other in this area?

References

Alcorn, R. (1985). *Christians in the wake of the sexual revolution*. Portland, OR: Multnomah Press.

Foster, R. (1985). *Money, sex, and power*. San Francisco, CA: Harper & Row.

Hybels, B. (1989). *Christians in a sex-crazed culture*. Wheaton, IL: Victor Books.

Stafford, T. (1989). *The sexual Christian*. Wheaton, IL: Victor Books.

***Ken Williams** has a master's degree in psychology from Pepperdine University and a doctoral degree in human behavior from United States International University. Ken and his wife Bobbie have served with Wycliffe Bible Translators and SIL International since 1957. Ken translated the New Testament into Chuj, a language in Guatemala, then served for 22 years as a counselor, including six years as Director of Wycliffe's International Counseling Department. Since 1992, he has worked as a Wycliffe International Personnel Training Consultant, primarily serving other missions. He is Director of International Training Partners (ITP), a partnership of some 40 organizations and various host Christian leaders. ITP provides Sharpening Your Interpersonal Skills Workshops and other workshops for missionaries and host people (www.RelationshipSkills.com). Email: kenwilly@mindspring.com.*

Special thanks to Jim Holsclaw of Wycliffe Bible Translators, my mentor, encourager, and friend for many years, who spurred me on to write this article.

25

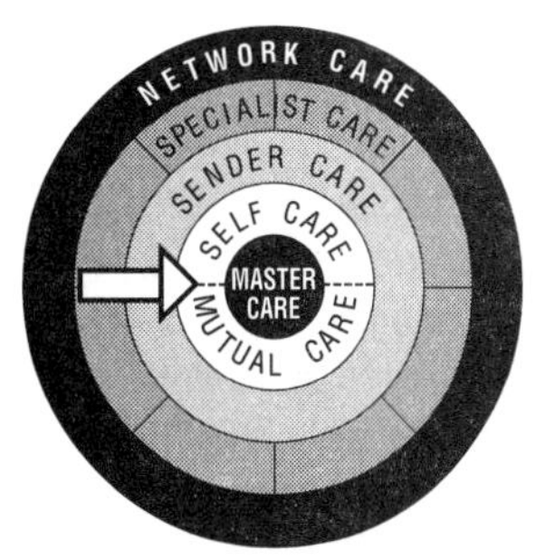

Surviving War As a Caregiver: A Personal Account

PAULA O'KEEFE

This is the story of how the author, along with several Christian friends, persevered in the midst of the horrors and privations of war. Inner struggles, especially the struggle to trust God, were as real as the external threats of loss of life. The names and places in this country have been changed for security reasons.

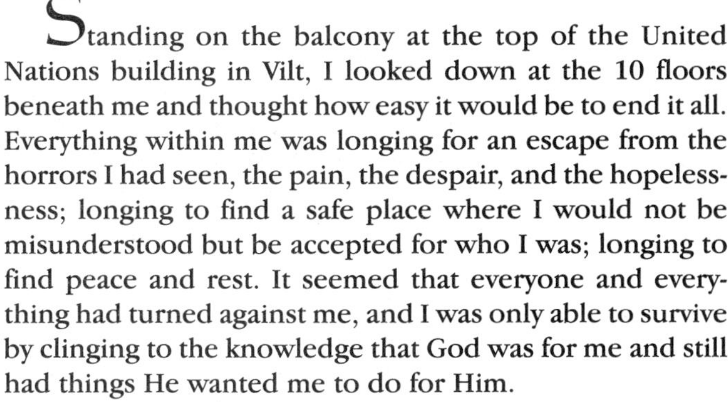

Standing on the balcony at the top of the United Nations building in Vilt, I looked down at the 10 floors beneath me and thought how easy it would be to end it all. Everything within me was longing for an escape from the horrors I had seen, the pain, the despair, and the hopelessness; longing to find a safe place where I would not be misunderstood but be accepted for who I was; longing to find peace and rest. It seemed that everyone and everything had turned against me, and I was only able to survive by clinging to the knowledge that God was for me and still had things He wanted me to do for Him.

That morning, I had awakened early from a deep sleep to the sounds of a thunderstorm reverberating through the mountains. The terror and panic that had seized my body the split second I awoke eased a little as I realized it wasn't another bombing raid. I realized how tense I was even as I slept. I tried to go back to sleep again, but the adrenaline surge that had rushed through my body made it impossible. I tried not to think about my friend, Aishad, who had been raped a few weeks previously. An armed neighbor had forced his way into the apartment I shared with her, when she had been alone one night. I also felt sick with utter helplessness as I thought of Valera, our worship leader, who had been forced off a train by armed soldiers. We hadn't had any information as to his whereabouts since he had been taken, and no one seemed interested in helping us find him: not government officials, fellow missionaries, or believers. I tried not to think about the pain of our recent church split, brought on largely because of these tragedies; nevertheless, sleep eluded me.

Later in the morning, I went to the United Nations building to receive my email from a mission organization located in that building. Receiving news from the outside world was usually an exciting occasion. I had no idea that such a blow was coming. I don't think that any of the terrible things I had been through in the past few weeks would have made me feel suicidal, had I had the support I needed. What topped it all off was the email I received from my pastor back home, suggesting that I was in some way responsible for the church split and the disappearance of Valera. Looking back, I can see how he had come to that conclusion. I had not personally been in contact with him for a few weeks. He had only heard an unfavorable report about what I was doing from another missionary in the area. This missionary not only did not know all the facts involved, but for some reason did not like what I was doing and seemed to be deliberately trying to stir trouble. But I was doing the best I knew how to at the time, in a very difficult situation, and I was on the verge of exhaustion. At that point, all I needed was someone to listen to me, encourage me, and support me.

I was in my mid-20s and had been working in a war zone for about a year when this happened. I was the only foreigner from my mission working there, although I did have a team of locals working with me. Because I was sent out by a faith mission based in my home church, I did not receive a salary or a regular income. Most of the money I received came from the gifts of friends or supporters, plus a small amount from fundraising appeals. I didn't have any set dates as to when I should be in the war zone or when to take holidays or furlough, so I was free to do what I felt was right. This freedom was good in many ways, but because of my tendency towards workaholism, it had inadvertently allowed me to work too hard and to stop looking after myself properly.

I had experienced firsthand some of the horrors of living in a 20th century war zone, although I had been fortunate enough to have missed the worst horrors of full-blown war. Each time the war had flared up, I had been out of the immediate line of combat. Sometimes I had wished that I had been there, as the agony of waiting and praying and not knowing what was happening to the people I loved at times seemed worse than actually being there with them. But it was in the Lord's hands, and He had, so far, chosen to spare me those horrors. I had, however, witnessed firsthand some of the violence and lawlessness, and I had had friends raped, beaten, robbed, and kidnapped. I had been in life-threatening situations, and while each time I had watched the deliverance of God, I had not realized the toll it had been taking on my body, soul, and spirit. The deprivations that ensued as a secondary result of war had also unwittingly worn me down. Over an extended period, things such as often having to go without electricity, gas, and running water, carrying buckets of water long distances, not getting enough sleep, not being able to get warm or have a proper bath, having no telephone lines and therefore no contact with the outside world—all these were a constant strain.

I was on the verge of breakdown, but I seemed unable to help myself. As I stood feeling so utterly desperate on the top of the United Nations building, God was very gracious to me. He prompted the missionary whose computer I had used to get my email to come out onto the balcony and ask me how I was doing. I told her about how devastated I felt, and she was so encouraging and supportive. She gave me a hug and prayed with me, and then she invited me to come to her apartment and rest for a few days. Although she and her husband lived quite basically compared to the West, it was like a luxury five-star hotel for me. They treated me like a queen, giving me a room to myself, with a TV and videos. I was able to sleep in during the mornings and just rest and have some time to myself while they were at work. In the evenings, they cooked me delicious meals, listened to me, prayed with me, and just were there for me. They even tried to help me find out some information about

Valera, our worship leader. After a few days with them, I felt able to carry on. I am so grateful to the Lord for sending them to me in my moment of need and for giving me that place of peace, safety, and rest that I was so longing for.

What Have I Learned? What Can Others Learn?

It was a combination of factors, over an extended period of time, which led me to the verge of breakdown. As I share my experiences and what I have learned from them, I hope they may outline some of the pressures that missionaries living in war zones face. I also hope to show how I think missionaries can be better supported and how they can better support themselves. Many of the things that God has taught me are very basic. I have known most of them in my head for a long time, but it was only as God showed me the truth of them in reality and spoke deep into my spirit that I have been able to put them into practice.

My Humanity

I have realized that living in a war zone is hard for anyone to deal with, but when you are a missionary, an added complication is the fact that people often expect you to be superhuman, to have no needs of your own, and always to be there for them. This expectation has often led me to do far too much, to have no regard for my own needs, and to push down my own feelings constantly for the sake of others. After all, it seems to be the Christian thing to do, since Jesus did command us to lay down our lives for our brothers and sisters. But I am not superhuman. I am a woman with emotions and needs, and I needed to have someone with whom I could share my heart.

Support From One's Pastor and Church

Why had the email I received from my pastor been so devastating to me? I think it was because it had come at such a difficult time and had made me feel misunderstood, rejected, and alone in the world. It really hurt that my church had believed what someone else had said about me, without hearing my side of the story. They seemed not to believe in me or understand how much I was struggling and needed their support. I sent my pastor a reply to his email, explaining what had been going on from my perspective, and I received a nice email back from him saying that he wanted to let me know that he was supporting me and was on my side. It was very important for me to hear that. I needed him to stand up for me and let me know that he was on my side.

Good Communication

In order to survive in a war zone, a missionary needs to have an adequate support base and good "covering." My understanding of covering is that we all need to have people who are spiritually in authority over us, to whom we are accountable. Usually these are the people who have sent us out. Their role is pastoral. Just as a shepherd cares for his sheep, so the people covering us should be strengthening and encouraging us, binding us up when we are injured, and bringing us back when we are straying (as in Ezekiel 34). They should be keeping watch over us as people who must give an account (Heb. 13:17).

Because missionaries are physically so far away from their home church or mission, they really need to know that they have this support and covering, through letters/emails and occasional phone calls. They need to know that their home church or mission is 100% behind them, praying for them and interested in their well-being. The missionary also, of course, has a responsibility to keep the people back home informed as to what is happening. I had fallen down a bit in that area, as I was spending so much time without telephone or email contact. I learned that to be accountable, I needed to really make an effort to keep in closer contact. Being a missionary can be a very lonely place, without the added pain of feeling misunderstood and unsupported.

A Good Local Team and Confidant

Another reason that I felt so desperate was that I did not feel I had anyone with whom I could really share my heart. Having a good team around you, be they locals or foreigners, is extremely important, to encourage and support one another. When you have needs, you have someone with whom you can share and ask for help and prayer. I think that in order to survive, any missionary needs to have at least one confidant. At that time, I felt that I could not share my heart with any of the locals. I had no foreigners working with me, and at times I felt the need to be able to talk to someone who could really understand what it was like to be a foreigner in this situation. The Lord knew what I needed at that moment of feeling so desperate; He blessed me with that missionary couple with whom I was able to share my heart.

Debriefing

Engaging in debriefing, where we can talk to someone about the experiences we have been through and be listened to, is essential. It is very easy to push down our emotions when we go through traumatic experiences and to think that the events have not affected us. It is true that while going through such an experience, we may need to suppress our emotions in order to survive, but as soon afterwards as possible, we need to find a safe place where we can express these emotions and give them to God. I found that I thought I had not been affected by many of the things I had been through. I assumed that since I was a Christian and since I had chosen to serve the Lord in that place and since God was with me, He had protected me. Of course, He had protected me, but as a human being I needed to deal with the emotions and the consequences of the traumatic experiences I'd had, if I was to emerge unscathed. God has helped me to do this through the help of counselors back home in the UK, who have spent many hours listening to me and praying with me.

The Invasion—and More Lessons

There were, of course, other factors leading me to the verge of breakdown. The weeks and months leading up to this incident had been stressful. The first war had officially ended the year before, when the enemy tanks had pulled out, leaving the locals to govern their own affairs. It was a time of great rejoicing, but it was followed by much heartache, which was exacerbated by the lawlessness that ensued for the next three years. About six months prior to the incident at the UN building, we had the terrible news that several aid workers had been killed in their beds in cold blood. Most aid agencies pulled out after that.

I remember that very night I was staying with Hava, a believer from our church, and we had prayed for the country until about 2:00 a.m. I have found that living in a war zone greatly improves your prayer life—hearing shooting and bombing close by causes you to fall to your knees, crying out to God for mercy for the land, in a way that nothing else can do. The next morning, we were awakened by frantic knocking at the door, as the neighbors came to tell us the terrible news. We all crowded around the TV set, and for the short time that we had electricity, we all sat and cried together—locals (both Muslims and Christians) and one English missionary. We were horrified by the futility of it all. We heard the President of the invading army declaring that if the lawlessness didn't stop, he would send in the tanks again. Then the electricity was gone, and gone also was our precious contact with the outside world.

I went about my business as usual that day, as any day, although my heart was very heavy. Hava and I went for water, which we carried up to the fourth floor, where she lived. I then went to buy some bread, tea, and sugar for our breakfast. When I had arrived at Hava's place the night before, she had absolutely nothing at all to eat or drink in the house. She said she was fasting, but I knew that she had no money and no way of getting any money. After our breakfast, we walked to the refugee camp on the outskirts of town, stopping at the market to pick up some food for the camp.

Every week I conducted a Bible study in one of the small metal huts where a family of new believers lived. Zulai had had her fair share of tragedies, but she loved Jesus. Her husband had been gunned down in front of her and their three children, and then their home and all their possessions had been burned. After studying about God's love and then praying for each of them to know God's love in the midst of the storm, we had a time of prayer for peace for their land. Afterwards, we enjoyed the tea and treats that I had brought with me, and then I went to different huts to visit other precious people whom I had come to love so dearly. As I drank tea, I listened to their stories, prayed with them, and was a shoulder for them to cry on. It was always a special time in the camp, but I often came away feeling absolutely drained.

After leaving the camp, I walked to a friend's house. She was not yet a believer but was very interested in knowing more about Jesus. She was not in when I arrived, but since I needed to see her, I waited. By the time she arrived home, it was 3:30 p.m. and was beginning to get dark. I would have had to leave then if I was to make the hour-long walk home before curfew. I decided to spend the night. We talked for hours about the Bible, Jesus, and the power of forgiveness—a totally new concept to my friend and her family. They had grown up with the idea of blood revenge being the norm.

Fellowship With God or With Fear?

Before going to bed, we watched the news, where they announced that nearly all aid agencies had pulled out, and it really looked as if full-blown war would start again at any moment. The terror of the situation hit me. I assumed that I was the only foreigner left in the country, which sent chills running down my spine. If the fighting started that night, I had many reasons to be fearful: I was staying downtown, and not only would I have been right in the center of the fighting, but I would also not have been with the people I would choose to be with during a bombing campaign, that is, my Christian friends. I went to bed, and the terror felt like a lead weight lodged in the pit of my stomach. I could not sleep.

I wrestled for a couple of hours, and I felt the Lord telling me I had a choice: I could either dwell on the fear and thus in a sense "fellowship" with it, or I could choose to fellowship with Him. It was something I had remembered hearing from a missionary in Burundi when she was talking about how God had helped her deal with fear during the war there. I knew that if God could help her, then He could help me too. I asked Him to help me to fellowship with Him, and an incredible sense of peace descended on me. I felt Him telling me that I would be okay and that He was still calling me to serve Him there, even though nearly all other agencies had pulled out. I eventually fell asleep, to the sounds of gunfire resounding not too far away, resting in the safety and security of my Savior's arms.

Time With God

I have learned how very important it is to have regular times alone with the Lord. This can be quite difficult in a war zone. Firstly, it can be hard just to find some time alone. Where I worked, it was too dangerous for a foreigner to live alone, especially a female, so I lived with locals. In every family, there is a lot of overcrowding, because of the many refugees and destroyed homes. There are no places in the town or in the countryside where it would be safe to go by myself, sit down, and enjoy some time with the Lord. Then there is the difficulty of trying to relax, when I can hear shooting in the background. So it can be a problem. But if I don't have those times with the Lord, then I would not be able to survive.

I found that I did not actually need a quiet place to spend time with God, because I could fellowship with Him wherever I was and whatever I was doing. I needed times of just being with Him, to get my focus and perspective right and to know His love and favor upon me. Every day I need to receive the new mercies that He has for me. I need to be able to come to that place of refuge and safety, where I can rest in His arms and find the peace and joy that I could not find anywhere else. Spending time with Him is the anchor I need to weather any storms I may have to go through that day.

The House Church Episode

A few days before I visited Vilt, about six months after the aid workers had been killed, we were having our weekly church meeting. We were an "underground" church and met in various homes, usually on Fridays or Saturdays. I went to the meeting via the market to pick up some food for the family in whose house we were meeting that week, as well as some tea, sugar, and cakes to enjoy after the meeting.

When I arrived, I found Nadia, the mother, in a terrible state. She was chopping an onion, and with each violent chop of the knife, she talked about killing herself or killing her son. She was a single mother who had had two alcoholic husbands. She was now on her own with her four children. Her eldest daughter was pregnant; while on a night shift during a period of heavy bombing, she had been raped by a work colleague. Often when I came, I would find that this family had hardly anything to eat. During periods of relative calm, Nadia worked at the oil refinery, although she hadn't received any wages for months. She was making soup with the two potatoes and one onion she had managed to find. That morning, she had had a fight with her son, and they weren't talking. I managed to get her to calm down before the other believers came. She eventually let me pray with her, and she put down the knife. I didn't know which was worse—the tension in the house or the tension in the country, as people waited wondering when full-blown war would start again, as once again the country was threatened by an imminent enemy invasion.

The first people to arrive at the meeting were a father and son who had been depressed for months. A few months previously, they had been forced to watch the rape of their wife and mother by armed soldiers and then had been severely beaten themselves. The woman had virtually stopped coming out of the house after that and no longer came to church. The next person to arrive at the meeting was the leader of the church, Aishad, with whom I shared an apartment when I was in the country. She seemed to be becoming more anxious and fidgety with each tragedy she experienced, including the murder of her father three years earlier and being raped only a few weeks ago. As we talked about all the terrible things that had been happening, I could feel their fear and despair beginning to come over me.

The absence of half the church, who were no longer joining us for worship, did not help. The Sunday after Aishad had been raped, Vera, a woman to whom Aishad had tearfully confided her secret, totally betrayed her trust. She stood up and accused Aishad of being involved in a sexual affair with the man who had raped her. She said that she refused to be under the leadership of an adulteress any more. Aishad ran out of the meeting crying. I was not there, so Vera took half the church with her, and they were now meeting in her house. I could hardly believe that people, who themselves had lived through war and who had also been abused in terrible ways, could be so cruel, but at that time I didn't understand quite so clearly the nature of trauma and how it can affect us.

Understanding Trauma and Self-Care

One of the hardest things I have found about living in a war zone is dealing with the pain caused in relationships, as traumatized, hurting people clash with other traumatized, hurting people. I remember one day a couple of weeks before this, when I was on the bus on my way to see Vera, the lady who had caused the church split. The bus was making its way through the center of town, where the devastation was at its worst, with piles of rubble everywhere and not one building left standing. The desolation caused by the war in that section of town was obvious everywhere I looked. I felt the Lord clearly impress upon me the fact that the people of the city had been just as devastated by what they had been through as had the buildings. It was just not so obvious at first sight. And just as it takes time and effort to bring restoration physically to the city, so it would take time and effort to bring healing to the people. This revelation gave me a new compassion for the people and particularly helped me to have compassion in that difficult church situation with which I was dealing.

The other people who had decided to stay loyal eventually arrived at our meeting on that Friday, but they all seemed to be in the same state of fear, tension, and despair. There seemed to be absolutely no good news whatsoever; life just seemed to be one complete nightmare after another. And the doom and gloom got worse and worse with each new topic of conversation. "They're going to start bombing again, and we're all going to die," said one. "And if the bombs or the bullets don't get us this time, starvation is bound to finish us off," wailed another. Changing the subject, someone starting talking about something else we were all trying not to think about: "I dread to think what terrible things are happening to Valera. Maybe they're torturing him right now." Someone helpfully added, "Unless they've killed him already." Changing the subject again to another equally depressing topic, someone grumbled, "How could the others have deserted us and gone with that awful woman?" Someone else verbalized what we were all thinking: "If that's how believers treat each other, what hope is there?" Everyone seemed to agree that it was the end; there was no hope left. I remember that sickening feeling of terror, despair, and hopelessness sticking right in the pit of my stomach. I thought to myself, "You know, they're probably right. There's no way out of this situation. It's totally hopeless, and we're all going to be killed. What's the point of going on?"

Taking a Break

I felt the Lord teaching me through this situation that I needed to take regular breaks and times away, in order not to fall into that terrible pit of despair and hopelessness that so characterized most of the people I was working with. I found that when I was actually living in the war zone itself, I needed to have a couple of days to get away every two weeks. This involved traveling about three hours to another country, which was not at war at that time. I enjoyed having contact with the outside world, being with people who were living more of a "normal" life, just relaxing and resting, and enjoying the countryside and city that had not been devastated by war.

If I did not have this break away, I found that at times I did not have the strength to rise above the despair and hopelessness that surrounded me. I needed time to be renewed in hope, to see the joy, beauty, and good things of life, and to get my perspective back on the Lord and His goodness again. I needed to have times when the Lord could make me lie down in green pastures, lead me beside quiet waters, and restore my soul (Psalm 23). Being in beautiful surroundings in the mountains in itself was restoring, and it was also really healthy from time to time just to have a break away from the devastation of war.

That morning at the house church meeting, I led the worship as best I could, and the Lord graced us with His presence and His peace. As we focused on Him, His light came in, much of the fear, despair, and hopelessness lifted, and the Lord renewed our hope and gave us the strength to go on. Even Nadia came into the meeting during the worship and sat weeping in the corner as the Lord ministered to her. Then I shared something from the Word, and we were encouraged and uplifted even more.

Worship

I have found that worship has been a lifeline in strengthening and uplifting my spirit. Sometimes when I have been so overcome with fear that I felt I could totally lose control, when I've started shaking or have been frozen to the spot, I have been able to start singing in my head and worshipping the Lord, and He has brought me through. Sometimes when I have been in dangerous situations, I have had my Walkman with me and have been able to close my eyes, listen to the music, and be caught up in worship, knowing that my life is in God's hands.

Corporate worship has also been so uplifting. Often when the despair and hopelessness are almost overwhelming, when we begin to worship together, the presence of the Lord comes. As we take our focus off the problems and focus instead on Him, He fills us with His peace and joy. Aishad and I have had times when everything seemed very bleak, and we did not feel we had the strength to go on. But as we have begun to praise the Lord, we have been filled with an amazing sense of His joy deep within our spirits, in spite of the circumstances—something that I have never experienced to that degree anywhere else. We have truly known His joy as our strength, as we have danced unashamedly before the Lord, oblivious to the sounds of gunfire in the background.

Other Episodes and Lessons

After the meeting, we prayed for all those who wanted prayer, then had tea and cakes together. We dispersed about an hour before sundown so as to make it home before curfew. Late that night, Aishad and I were praying, while her mother was in the kitchen reading. There was loud banging at the door, as soldiers shouted at us to open up. Aishad refused, telling them to go away. They told us they would break the door down, and we could hear them laughing as they beat the door with their rifle butts and kicked it with their boots. I had a tremendous sense of the peace of God and just wondered how God was going to get us out of this situation. Somehow the men decided to give up and left us, but because it was such a close call, Aishad and her mum were in a terrible state, shaking with terror. They had to take some valium to calm themselves down. I was amazed at the supernatural peace I had been given at that moment, and so I was able to pray for them and bring some comfort to them.

The following morning, exhausted from too many nights of not getting a good, undisturbed night's sleep, I walked to the bus station to begin the long journey out of the war zone to Vilt. There I was hoping to make some contact with the outside world, as well as try to find out some information about Valera, our worship leader. At the bus station, I found a seat on a rapidly overcrowding bus. I was quickly joined by a soldier who sat down next to me and placed his rifle across his lap with the barrel facing me. As we drove over and around all the bomb craters and rubble in the road, I whispered a quick prayer that the rifle would not go off. The bumps were so violent and the suspension of the rickety old bus so bad that at almost every bump, we bounced so high that our heads nearly touched the roof.

We shared a laugh together each time we landed safely back in our seats!

Humor

I realized how important it is to maintain a sense of humor in situations like that and to have times of fun and laughter. One thing I have always been able to do is laugh, and that has been a real release. Because of the high levels of despair and pain, there need to be times when I can just have fun and let out the tension. One example of this was when some friends of mine were at home, and their building was being fired at by heavy artillery. They were taking shelter under a table and were listening to their tape recorder. They decided to have some fun by recording a travel "documentary" to attract tourists to the war zone. To the sound of heavy artillery fire, the boy's voice comes on welcoming people to the sunshine state, where the grass is green and the sky is blue. This may be dark humor, but it is important to see the funny side of life and not take yourself or life too seriously. From time to time, I organize events for our church and in the camp when we can play games and just have fun together.

Hobbies

I have found that it is helpful to have a hobby or be involved in some other form of recreational activity. Creative arts such as painting, writing, and music can be an excellent way not just of relaxing, but of expressing some of those emotions which may have been pent up. God can also use this creative expression to bring healing to both soul and spirit. I enjoy painting, as well as playing the piano and guitar, and I find that taking the time to relax with these pursuits can bring release, restoration, and healing. It's also plain old fun!

Personal Growth and Healing From the Past

There were other factors that were also involved in leading me to the verge of breakdown. God wanted to do a deep work in me and purify my motives. He showed me some deep-rooted, ungodly influences that have been affecting me since early childhood, which He wanted to uproot. I had grown up in a single-parent family, without a father, and my mother had found life difficult and needed quite a lot of help and support. There was alcoholism in our extended family, which brought its own set of problems and difficulties. So as a child I had grown up with the burden of false responsibility for the lives of my family, and as an adult I realized I had the tendency to do the same thing. God gently and lovingly revealed this to me and showed me that I was subconsciously still doing it, because it made me feel good about myself and gave me a reason for living. He also showed me that because I didn't feel unconditionally loved as a child, I had been striving hard to try to please Him and earn His love, when in fact He loved me freely just the way I was. He also made me examine myself to make sure that being a missionary was not about running away in an attempt to forget my own pain. Through showing me these things, He has purified and healed me, set me back on the right track, and given me a new perspective on my life and my work.

Leading on from this, God showed me that as a missionary working with a faith mission, I had gotten caught up in the trap of "people pleasing." I grew up in a community in the South East of England where, because the Protestant work ethic was so ingrained, there was a strong sense that in order to be accepted as a person, you had to be doing something useful with your life. This was something I already struggled with because of my childhood experiences. I realized that this feeling was intensified because I was being supported and was living on the gifts of my friends and supporters. I had felt a terrible pressure to perform, to "come up with the goods," and to live up to people's expectations. This pressure to show the people who were supporting me that I was doing something useful and was not lazing around or wasting my time or their money led me to work far harder than I should have. It also sometimes pressured me to do things not because God had asked me to, but for the sake of giving a good report in my newsletter. To report that I was taking some time off or having a holiday made me feel incredibly guilty, and it seemed easier just to continue working than to take adequate rest.

Saying No

Another very important lesson I needed to learn was not to be driven by the needs of the people around me. When surrounded nearly the whole time by desperately needy people, it was very hard for me to say no or to walk away from a need. I have come to realize, however, that even if I worked tirelessly 24 hours every day, there would still be people who needed help. I was surprised one day when reading in the Gospels that Jesus sometimes said no to people in need, and He did not always heal everyone. At the Pool of Bethesda, there were many disabled people. Yet Jesus only healed one, and then He walked away, leaving the others still disabled (John 5:1-15). He also said that the poor are always with us (John 12:8).

What I am learning is that I need to do only what I see the Father doing, as Jesus used to do (John 5:19). I cannot meet the needs of all the people in the country where I work, let alone in the world. But Jesus can. I must only do what I see the Father calling me to do; the rest is His responsibility. I also needed to learn that Jesus, not I, was the Savior to these people. They were His responsibility in the end, not mine. I was no longer to take on any false burdens of responsibility.

Physical Need: Myself or Others?

Something else that I have had to come to terms with is a form of culture shock, in which I felt guilty for coming from the West and having lived a life of luxury compared to what the locals had gone through. Because they don't have any time to relax, let alone have any holidays, and they hardly ever have enough to eat, it made me feel incredibly selfish to think of taking a holiday or eating well. I felt as if they needed these things more than I did, so how could I be so selfish as to think of myself?

An example of this is that sometimes I would buy milk for myself as a special treat. Dairy products were expensive and scarce, and I hadn't had any in ages. Then I would see a child who also hadn't had any milk for a long time. After wrestling with the matter for a while, I would give the child the milk. It was lovely to watch the youngster relishing it, but I needed milk too. I also found that when people would send me vitamins for myself, I would usually take them for a couple of days and then find someone who was more needy than I was (not difficult to do in a war zone!), and I would give the vitamins away. It is difficult to find the balance here, but I am learning that I need to be strong so that I can go on helping others. If I don't learn to look after myself, I will not be around for the long haul.

Sabbath Rest

The Lord also had to teach me that I needed to take adequate rest. All of my life I have been a very hard worker, and as a child, the idea of taking a Sabbath of rest had not been modeled for me. As I have studied my Bible on the subject, I have been amazed at some of the things that God has commanded. I had read them many times before but had not really put them into practice. If the almighty, eternal God, who does not grow tired or weary, rested from all His work on the seventh day of creation, how much more should we mortal human beings take a day of rest every seventh day? Not only did He rest, He blessed this day of rest and called it holy, just because He was resting on it (Gen. 2:2-3). In the same way, our day of rest is a holy day, because we are resting on it. I was also deeply convicted when I read God's command to Moses that anyone who does *any* work on the Sabbath should be put to death (Ex. 35:2). This seems to me to be an extremely severe punishment, suitable maybe for murder or rape, but not for such a seemingly trivial crime. But God is a merciful God and does not make mistakes.

The sin of not resting was obviously as serious to God as the sin of murder or adultery. God, our creator, knows how important it is for us in body, soul, and spirit to take time out to rest and be restored. Rest is not just an afterthought; it is a command that God takes very seriously. If we don't take one day off a week, be it on a Sunday or another day if we are serving in the church on Sundays, then we are being disobedient to His commands and are opening ourselves up to the devil, to bring in sickness, depression, or exhaustion. This was a major factor in my becoming so exhausted and nearly suicidal. It is so important to learn this principle, whatever our job. How much more, when, working in a war zone, is it necessary to rest and take time to be restored.

Motives for Work

Recently God challenged me about what was motivating me in my work, and He asked if I was willing to lay my work down. This may sound like an easy thing to do (anything for an easy life!), but for me it was one of the hardest things God could have asked of me. I love my work; in fact, my life had become my work, and it had become an idol. At the time He asked me, I had many different projects running which I felt I could not just leave in the middle. I felt that I would let too many people down and that I had become indispensable.

I hadn't realized that my work had become too important to me, until the Lord tested me and showed me the state of my heart. He also showed me the pride that was in my heart. I felt good about myself, because I felt that I was not just an "ordinary" person. I was serving Him and was willing to risk my life by working in a war zone. I repented and gave all these matters up to God, and a period of refining took place. God has reconfirmed the calling on my life to serve Him where I am. He wants me to serve Him purely out of a heart of love towards Him. Now I know that it is His work, not mine, and that He can take it from me any time He chooses.

In Conclusion

There are many things that the Lord has taught me in the past few years of working in a war zone. He has taught me the importance of spending quality time with Him, of worshipping, of taking adequate rest and looking after myself, of taking breaks and having some fun. He has shown me that I can't do everything alone and that I need other people with whom I can be vulnerable and share my heart. I also need to have adequate support from my home church, along with good covering. The Lord has purified my heart of many of the ungodly motivations and influences that had been affecting me since early childhood, and He has taken away burdens of false guilt and false responsibility. He has done much healing and refining and is teaching me to enjoy just being His daughter. I am learning to get my self-worth from who I am in Him, not from what I do.

These changes have not happened overnight, and I am still in process in many areas. But I know that God is faithful to bring to completion that which He has started (Phil. 1:6). He is refining me, so that I can be a more effective minister of the gospel and so that I will be able to serve Him for the long haul. I am still working with my dear friends from this particular war zone, although I don't actually live there now. I live nearby and am in the process of setting up a Trauma Counseling Center, which will be a place of refuge, safety, and healing for them and others.

The story has some endings, not just for me, but also for my dear friends, although there are still many struggles. We found out where Valera was after three months of looking, and we were able to see him released after a short trial. God marvelously turned the situation around for His glory: while we were looking for Valera, his grandmother became a believer, one of his cell-mates became a believer, and at his trial Aishad had the opportunity to share the gospel and pray publicly for the judge and the courtroom! God also answered our prayers for his safety: not once during those three months had he been beaten or tortured. How I wish it were the same for others!

The situation involving the church split has also been resolved. About a year and a half after Vera had split the church, she repented for what she had done and asked Aishad to forgive her. The two churches were reunited again under Aishad's leadership.

At the moment of writing, the war continues to rage, and most of the people I love have lost their homes. But God is looking after them and meeting their needs; for some, including Nadia, Zulai, and their families, He has even provided the money for them to buy new homes. There does not look like much of a chance of a permanent cease-fire, but God is again turning the situation around. I do not understand all of this. Who does? Yet in the midst of war, He is bringing people to Himself, and the church is growing slowly but surely.

Reflection and Discussion

1. Under what circumstances should missionaries be sent to dangerous places? Is it different for single women and families with children?

2. When is "enough enough"? In other words, at what point should mission personnel be evacuated because the risk is too high?

3. Identify some of the main helps that enabled the author to survive in a war zone. Is there anything that you would have done differently?

4. How can missionaries be prepared to work/survive in similar settings?

5. Respond to this statement: Our loving God, who is all good, does not always protect His children against the atrocities of war.

Paula O'Keefe with Nastya, a child from a tragic background who now lives with her.

Paula O'Keefe *has been working as a missionary in this part of the world since 1993. After studying Russian, psychology, and a certificate of education in university, she went out to work as a missionary. In 1999, she returned to the United Kingdom for six months to receive further training in Christian counseling. Her field work includes leading a small house church; relief work and trauma counseling in refugee camps, orphanages, and hospitals; and a rehousing project for refugees. She is now in the process of setting up a trauma counseling center for refugees traumatized by war. Email: paulaokeefe@hotmail.com.*

26

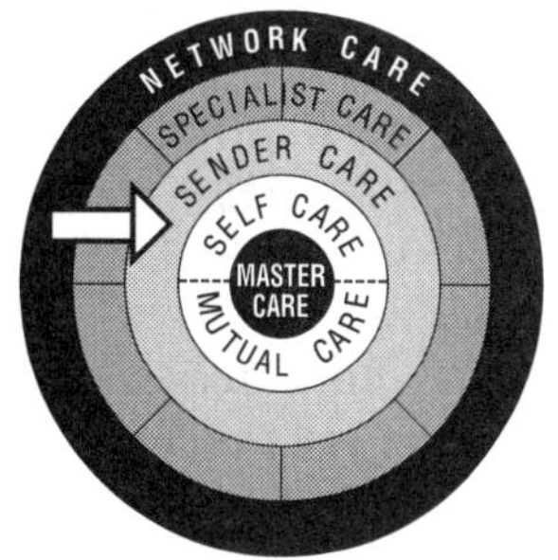

Best Practice Guidelines

Best practice codes are designed to help organizations provide quality services, manage their staff well, and remain accountable. A number of codes now exist within the Christian mission and humanitarian aid communities. Here are two examples of codes that have been carefully developed with the input of many organizations. The first is from the United Kingdom, and the second is from Canada. Both are relevant for other countries as well.

Global Connections United Kingdom

The Global Connections Code of Best Practice in Short-Term Mission is designed to apply to all visits, experiences, teams, and placements of up to two years' duration, organised by UK mission agencies, churches, and other organisations. Though formed initially with cross-cultural contexts in mind, it can apply to both UK and overseas situations, both same-culture and cross-cultural.

This Code is a code of best practice. Our motivation is based on our desire that God be glorified in all that we do. We also recognise our responsibility towards all participants and partners in our programmes, that we serve them to the highest standards possible. The Code does not necessarily indicate current achievement, but rather our aspirations towards high standards in short-term mission practice. Nonetheless, some minimum accomplishments are implied in the Code.

It is recognised that not every situation permits a literal application of every element of the Code. For example, sending local church involvement is not always a reality. Nevertheless, it *is* desirable and so must be included in a code of best practice. In the case of college placements, sending local church responsibilities belong to the college. In every case where literal application is impossible, consideration must be given to the question of who may have equivalent responsibilities.

Section 1: Aims and Objectives

1.1. A short-term mission programme will have clear aims and objectives. These will include viability and sustainability, and consideration of how the programme serves the long-term objectives of the sending organisation, the host/partner organisation or church, and other interested parties. The programme will have a clear place within Christian mission.

1.2. Attention will be given to the benefits to and responsibilities of the participant, the sending organisation, the host organisation and/or the host local church, and the sending local church.

1.3. Partnership relationships will be established, as far as possible, with host local churches and communities. Attention will be given to ownership and continuity.

1.4. Appropriate sending church involvement will be sought. An agency/participant/church partnership will be developed, as far as is reasonable.

1.5. There will be a commitment to develop the participant through the experience, including giving attention to personal Christian growth.

Section 2: Publicity, Selection, and Orientation

2.1. Publicity materials will be accurate and truthful. They will be targeted appropriately and used with integrity.

2.2. Publicity will clearly represent the ethos and vision of the sending organisation and will define the purpose of the programme in terms of service, discipleship, and vocation.

2.3. The application process, including timescale and financial responsibilities, will be clear and thorough.

2.4. A suitable selection process will be established, including selection criteria and screening. A pastoral element will be included, regardless of the outcome of selection.

2.5. Appropriate local sending church involvement in the selection process will be invited.

2.6. Orientation prior to departure and/or after arrival will be given. Team leaders, field supervisors, and field pastoral carers will be briefed.

2.7. Preparatory information (between selection and formal orientation) will be provided as early and as fully as possible.

2.8. Placement decisions will be clear and transparent, will be made with integrity, and will be communicated to all involved (including when changes are made).

Section 3: Field Management and Pastoral Care

3.1. Clear task aims and objectives and, where appropriate, a job description will be provided.

3.2. There will be clear lines of authority, supervision, communication, responsibility, and accountability. Communication and reporting will be regular.

3.3. Pastoral care and support structures will be established. The respective responsibilities of the sending church, sending organisation, host organisation/local church, and team leader/job supervisor/line manager/pastoral overseer/mentor will be made clear to all parties.

3.4. Opportunities for personal and spiritual development will be provided.

3.5. Participants will be given guidelines on behaviour and relationships.

3.6. With reference to above items 3.1–3.5, culturally appropriate ways of fulfilling these matters will be sought.

3.7. Procedures covering healthcare and insurance, medical contingencies, security and evacuation, stress management and conflict resolution, misconduct, discipline, and grievances will be established, communicated, and implemented as appropriate.

Section 4: Reentry Support, Evaluation, and Programme Development

4.1. Reentry debriefing and support will be seen as an integral part of the short-term "package" (along with orientation, task supervision, and pastoral care) and communicated as such to participants, field supervision, and the local sending church.

4.2. Reentry preparation, including placement appraisal, will begin prior to return.

4.3. The agency will have considered its role in assisting the participant through reentry, including facing unresolved personal issues, and future opportunities and directions in discipleship and service.

4.4. The sending local church will be briefed on reentry issues and any sending agency responsibilities and expectations.

4.5. An evaluation of agency procedures will be undertaken, including comment by the participant, the sending local church, and any host organisation/local church.

4.6. An evaluation of the responsibilities of the host organisation/church (where they exist) will be undertaken. An assessment of whether the host's needs and aims were fulfilled will be carried out. Culturally appropriate ways of feedback will be sought.

4.7. The results of evaluations will be communicated to relevant managers, for the improvement of future projects.

Adopting the Code

There is no suggestion that, without this Code of Best Practice, agencies and churches will not aim to develop their programmes to the highest possible level. The Code does, however, provide guidelines and a means towards excellence. The aim of any implementation procedure is not to "police" the Code, but to support its aims of continual improvement, quality, high standards, and excellence. Yet implementation must be a meaningful process, so as to avoid mere lip service, which undermines any value the Code may have.

There is a formal adoption and implementation procedure for the Global Connections Code of Best Practice in Short-Term Mission, which is as follows:

1. An agency/church decides to formally adopt the Code and advises Global Connections to this effect. We will then provide some forms for completion.

2. There will be two signatories to the Code, one being the person responsible for running the short-term programme(s), the other being an executive officer of the church/agency (e.g., chairman, CEO, senior pastor, etc.).

3. Those who adopt the Code are encouraged to indicate this on all publicity and materials relating to their programme(s) and must provide information about the Code to all participants.

4. Implementation includes the following commitments:

a. Adoptees will be represented at all biannual Global Connections Short-Term Mission Forums.

b. Before signing, active consideration will be given to how each section and element of the Code is presently being addressed by the agency/church.

c. There will be an active commitment to benchmark in every area of the Code. The Global Connections Short-Term Working Group will assist in liaison with other suitable agencies/churches and in providing training opportunities in benchmarking.

d. A brief report will be submitted annually to the Global Connections Short-Term Working Group, describing how the Code is being implemented, with submission of current operating benchmarks. A pro-forma will be provided by Global Connections for this purpose.

It is recognised that there are many different short-term programmes operated by agencies and churches. The above Code of Best Practice and implementation procedure are designed to be as flexible as possible. Benchmarking provides a means by which this variety can be taken into account, as different benchmarks are developed for different contexts.

There may be some agencies and churches for whom, for a variety of reasons, adoption of the Global Connections Code of Best Practice is not a desired outcome. Should they wish to develop instead their own internal Code of Practice, they may (if they wish) apply to the Global Connections Short-Term Working Group for approval to include the words "based on the Global Connections Code of Best Practice in Short-Term Mission" in their own Code.

For further information about the Global Connections Code of Best Practice in Short-Term Mission, please contact: Global Connections, Whitefield House, 186 Kennington Park Road, London SE11 4BT, UK; tel. 44 20 7207 2156; fax 44 20 7207 2159; email: info@globalconnections.co.uk. Used by permission.

Evangelical Fellowship of Canada

The Evangelical Fellowship of Canada Code of Best Practice in Member Care is designed as a benchmark document to guide the policies and practice of organizations regarding the care and development of cross-cultural Christian workers. Although it is written for Canadian organizations, others in the international community may find it useful. However, it must be recognized that basic resources for support may not exist or be available in many situations.

This Code does not necessarily reflect current practice but encourages aspirations toward excellence. It is not intended to establish legal standards or liability. Rather, the motivation for the development of this Code rests on the theological foundation of godly stewardship of people who are made in the image of God. Appropriate member care is a tangible reflection of Jesus' command that His disciples love one another and witness to the world that they belong to Him.

The Code was derived consensually by mission and church representatives across Canada. Discussions at a March 2000 Member Care Roundtable in Toronto, Ontario, provided the material for the initial draft, which was written by Dr. Irving Whitt and Bob Morris. This Roundtable was jointly sponsored by Missionary Health Institute, MissionPrep, The Intercultural Ministries (TIM) Centre Tyndale, and the Task Force for Global Mission of the Evangelical Fellowship of Canada. Suggestions for revision of the document were made by participants at a subsequent Roundtable in Langley, British Columbia, sponsored by the ACTS Intercultural Ministry (AIM) Centre and the Task Force for Global Mission, EFC. The Code in its present form was written by Dr. Laurel McAllister (AIM Centre), in consultation with members of the sponsoring organizations.

Core values underlying the Code include the following:

- A commitment to dependence on God for wisdom, power, and love in all aspects of member care.
- A commitment to the total well-being of cross-cultural workers—helping them minister effectively, while recognizing the hazards, stresses, and sacrifice inherent in cross-cultural life and ministry.
- A commitment to the biblical ideal of the body of Christ working together, through the church, mission organizations, and other partnerships.
- A commitment to the appropriate utilization of all available resources.
- A commitment to encourage organizations to practice care of their members with consistency, excellence, and high standards of ethical, spiritual, and moral responsibility.

Some of the main terminology in the code includes:

- **Principle**—a broad statement of purpose.
- **Key indicator**—an observable and measurable outcome related to a principle.
- **Member**—a cross-cultural Christian worker—missionary, tentmaker, or otherwise.

Section 1: Organizational Policy and Practice

Principle 1

Member care policies for all members—at home, abroad, or in transition—are effective, efficient, agreed upon, and transparent.

Key indicators

■ Leaders throughout the organization effectively model member care.

■ Human resources staff, both at home and abroad, are recruited in part for their people management skills and are adequately trained to provide member care.

■ The organization monitors how well member care policies achieve their objectives.

■ Members have clear work objectives and performance standards, know to whom they report, and know what support is provided by the organization.

■ Benefits, such as adequate health care (physical and mental) and pension plans, are provided and reviewed regularly.

Principle 2

Members participate in the development of member care policies.

Key indicators

■ Meetings of the organization's Human Resource Department (or equivalent) are regularly scheduled.

■ Policy information is distributed routinely to members, and feedback is encouraged.

■ Regular re-assessment of existing policies and practices is initiated and encouraged by the organization and its membership.

■ Mutual accountability between organization and membership is encouraged and practiced.

Principle 3

Agreed-upon personal and organizational beliefs and conduct are essential to effective member care.

Key indicators

■ The organization has clearly stated policies concerning acceptable personal and organizational belief and conduct.

■ A means of communicating these policies is in place and is utilized.

■ The policies are consistently applied.

■ Ramifications of particular unacceptable behaviors are specified.

■ The ability to accept differences in non-essentials is articulated and is in evidence.

Principle 4

The organization is committed to developing an ethos of member care that enhances kingdom ministry.

Key indicators

■ Member well-being—whether spiritual, physical, emotional, mental, moral, or social—is visibly identifiable.

■ Core values for member care are in writing and available to everyone.

■ An identifiable infrastructure exists for explicit care.

■ Sufficient financial and human resources are allocated for the care of the members.

■ Transparency, within the context of confidentiality and trust, is encouraged as part of the organizational culture of care.

■ Issues necessary to move the organization toward a culture of care have been identified.

Section 2: Selection, Training, and Career Care

Principle 5

Candidate selection is fair, thorough, and takes into consideration the anticipated role(s) of both women and men.

Key indicators

■ The organization designs and conducts a thorough, objective candidate selection process, utilizing the best available resources.

■ Issues relating to singleness, as well as to marriage and the family, are discussed.

■ The selection process includes physical and mental health screening, where possible.

■ The process is clearly written, is provided to candidates at the outset, and is periodically reviewed with them.

■ The process is undertaken in cooperation with the candidate's sending church(es).

■ Decisions throughout the selection process evidence a clear sense of God's leading to all concerned.

Principle 6

Assignments reflect the member's expertise, giftedness, developmental stage, strengths, and limitations as much as is possible—while recognizing the need for and God's call to workers in settings with limited resources and uncertain consequences.

Key indicators

■ Members are given as much information as possible regarding ministry situations, so they can give "informed consent" to the assignment from the outset.

■ In the case of married couples, assignments reflect consideration of the gifts and skills of both wife and husband.

■ Assessment tools, including effectiveness evaluations and development reviews, are implemented.

■ Team building exercises are carried out as possible and applicable.

■ Training and mentoring are provided for assignments requiring additional expertise.

Principle 7

Appropriate training and professional support for members are integral to effective member care.

Key indicators

■ The organization provides appropriate intercultural and language training before and during field assignments.

■ The organization provides opportunity for professional support, such as participation in professional conferences, professional refreshment, membership in professional societies, and opportunity for job-specific training and further studies, as appropriate.

■ The development of qualified leaders within the organization is valued and provided for.

Principle 8

Realistic work expectations, personal renewal, and endurance strategies are articulated and provided.

Key indicators

■ Job descriptions are in place and subject to annual review.

■ Discussion of strategies for long-term effectiveness are scheduled on a regular basis.

■ Resources and accountability partners are found in national churches and within the host community, when possible.

■ The specific needs of both single and married members are appropriately considered.

■ Members take an appropriate amount of time for home service (furlough) on a scheduled basis.

Principle 9

Organizational responsibilities extend beyond field service to home ministry (furlough), reentry, retirement, and to redeployment, where necessary.

Key indicators

■ Debriefing, including physical, psychological, ministry, and pastoral concerns, is required and provided.

■ Rest, renewal, and opportunity for personal and ministry assessment are considered an essential part of home service (furlough).

■ Members minister in supporting church fellowships in ways that are mutually enriching.

■ Transition opportunities/seminars, which include cultural issues and issues related to redeployment, reentry, and retirement, are provided.

■ Resources (human and financial) are allocated for follow-up care during reentry or redeployment.

Section 3: Community Life

Principle 10

Healthy Christian communities enhance personal growth and development as well as ministry effectiveness.

Key indicators

- Responsibility for self-care, in community, is modeled and encouraged by leadership.
- Mutual care is planned for, clearly defined, and its importance communicated.
- The unique needs of single members are considered and provided for.
- Members develop reciprocal relationships with a variety of people in the host community.
- Periodic personal, team, and organizational assessments are required.

Principle 11

Responsibility for member care is personal, mutual, and organizational.

Key indicators

- Trained caregivers are identified and made available to members when needed.
- Opportunity is given for member interaction and mutual caring.
- Persons responsible for each sphere of organizational care have been identified.
- Members are deemed responsible for taking an active role in managing their own care.

Section 4: Family and Missionary Children (MKs) Care

Principle 12

The effectiveness of the Christian worker is related to the holistic care of the family, appropriate and proportionate to the stages of life.

Key indicators

- There is provision for reassignment of primary homemakers as children grow through different phases of life.
- Opportunities for marital enrichment and couple retreats are provided and encouraged—both on the field and during home service (furlough).
- Financial provision and counsel are made available for families in transition, including resignation or retirement.
- The organization makes provision for follow-up care for member families at reentry, and beyond for MKs.
- Professional, personal, and spiritual assessment is provided for all members of the family.
- Care for the family may include extended family members.

Section 5: Relationships With Churches

Principle 13

The local sending church is included in the continuum of care.

Key indicators

- There is evidence of shared trust among the local sending church, the organization, and the member.
- Communication is evidenced between the local church and the organization at every stage of a member's life.
- The organization partners with the local church in a member's preparation for initial ministry assignment, reentry, redeployment, and retirement.
- Such partnerships exhibit realistic expectations and mutual benefit.
- Training of members is shared by the organization and local church where possible and mutually beneficial.

Section 6: Crisis/Contingency Care

Principle 14

Cross-cultural life and work can be uniquely stressful for individuals and families. Therefore, procedures are in place and resources provided to help members in a variety of contingencies.

Key indicators

- Members agree on what constitutes a crisis.*
- Policies governing the handling of the crisis are written and communicated to all members.
- Policies, existing to cover a variety of contingencies, have explicit information for each contingency.
- Policies exhibit flexibility and sensitivity.
- Necessary care, such as post-traumatic stress care and counseling, is available.**

Principle 15

Procedures and resources are in place to discover and deal with issues of moral lapse. A disciplinary process is defined and a process of restoration spelled out.

Key indicators

- Preventative issues and strategies are addressed in pre-field training.
- Confidentiality is respected and balanced with accountability to the organization, sending church, supporters, and other members.
- Confidentiality and all related issues are clearly defined and made known to all parties involved.
- Movement toward restoration is made whenever possible.

Reflection and Discussion

1. Is *best practice* a concept that is relevant for your setting? If so, how could it be built into the organizational culture and personnel policies? (See chapter 1.)
2. Which best practice guidelines can help us prepare and equip missionaries to care for *themselves* when overseas, particularly in isolated/difficult situations?
3. How do we prepare and equip missionaries to care for *each other*, including coaching team leaders in this area? What would be a few best practice principles to help field workers pursue mutually supportive relationships with both nationals in general and the national church in particular?
4. How can Older Sending Countries (OSCs) facilitate the emerging member care *networks* in the Newer Sending Countries (NSCs) without being patronizing or paternalistic? Which principles can enable NSCs to develop their own models of caring which will be culturally appropriate? Is there a way to "vet" member care networks—to validate them so we can safely recommend people and programs—and help them be accountable? (Refer also to chapter 47.)
5. In general, how can we *internationalize* member care more within our own settings, especially given the influence of the OSCs in this area? Should some best practice guidelines also be formulated for the global development of the member care movement?

Special thanks to Marion Knell with Global Connections/United Kingdom and with Member Care/Europe for her help with the Reflection and Discussion questions.

---

* Suggested definition of crisis: A situation which creates, or has the potential of creating, trauma for the individual or family and which needs immediate attention on the part of leadership, e.g., field issues; contingency-related issues such as disasters, political kidnapping, death, accidents; personal and family issues (including raising teens); moral issues; major medical needs; deep depression, anxiety, contemplation of suicide, etc.

** The reality of spiritual darkness and the conflict inherent in Christian ministry contexts affect workers in complex and often traumatic ways. Crises may be related to spiritual battles that workers are involved in. Caregivers need to be aware of this dimension and how to deal with it.

27

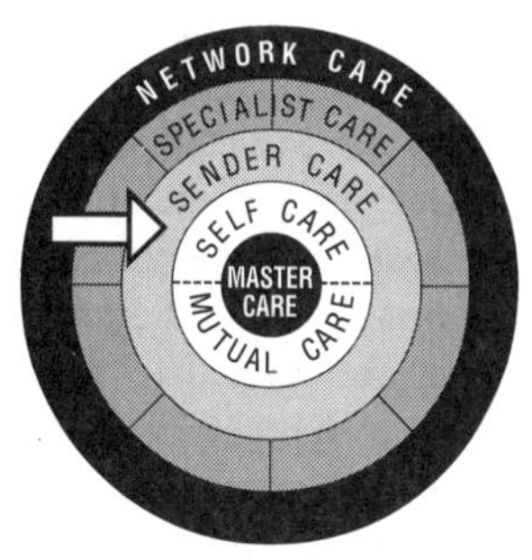

Care and Support of Local Staff in Christian Humanitarian Ministry

JOHN FAWCETT

What types of member care resources do national and local staff need? How do their needs differ from those of expatriates? What obligations do agencies have to provide locals/nationals with similar types of member care as their international and expatriate counterparts? Can we and should we do better? These questions are addressed by the author, drawing upon his experience with the humanitarian aid sector and World Vision International.

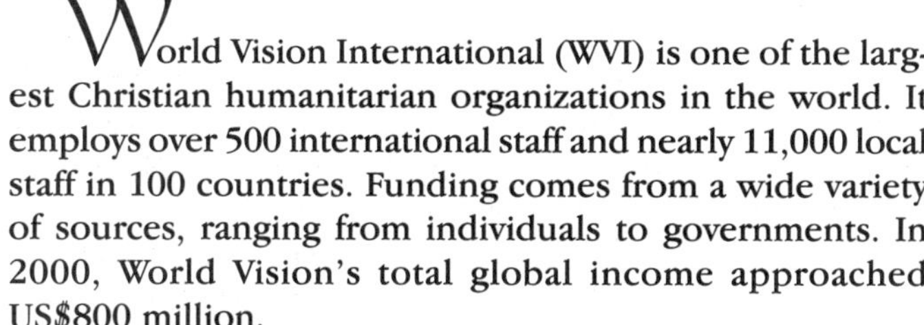

World Vision International (WVI) is one of the largest Christian humanitarian organizations in the world. It employs over 500 international staff and nearly 11,000 local staff in 100 countries. Funding comes from a wide variety of sources, ranging from individuals to governments. In 2000, World Vision's total global income approached US$800 million.

World Vision is an Evangelical Christian organization, and all expatriate staff are Christian. Many field offices, however, are located in countries where Christianity is not practiced or where there are few people with the required skills who are also Christian. Therefore, a relatively high percentage of the 11,000 local staff are not Christian. Appropriate support of these people can be a complex and challenging matter. Employment policies and practices need to ensure staff are appropriately hired, according to local and international employment law and without offending local religious or community practices. Policies and practices focused on the care and support of staff need to be inclusive and properly supportive and should not be interpreted as proselytizing.

Both the nature and complexity of international humanitarian work have changed dramatically over the past 20 years. Many organizations no longer act in ways that their founders would have predicted. World Vision began its ministry in 1950 with children orphaned as a result of the Korean War. Today, World Vision continues to work with children, but it is also involved in advocacy, community development, emergency relief, and specialist health and agriculture programs. While World Vision continues to work with local churches, it has found it equally important to maintain strong relationships with both host and home country governments. Today, no large humanitarian agency would be able to perform its mission without reference to such global entities as the United Nations, the World Health Organization, the World Bank, USAID, the European Union, and other major international bodies.

Despite these changes, one simple fact has not altered. The final connection—the point at which the assistance is actually given and received—still lies in the relationship between one human being and another. At the field level, the place where ministry is performed, one human being passes on this help to another human being who is in need. Whether in the form of food, clothing, housing, Bibles, or knowledge, the pivotal point of caring is a human relationship, birthed, in World Vision's case, in a relationship with Jesus Christ.

The Changing Face of Care and Caregivers

When World Vision began 50 years ago, the primary caregivers in the process were international missionaries, mostly from North America, who had traveled the world to assist those in need. This is no longer the case. For a variety of reasons, today almost all humanitarian activity is performed by local people, many of whom are employees. This shift has occurred for good reasons. Ideas of patronage, charity, and labeling the poor as incompetent have quite rightly been rejected as repugnant and destructive. We understand today that people are competent to care for themselves and their families, given adequate resources and freedom. Secondly, the increase in direct humanitarian assistance over the past 20 years has outstripped organizational abilities to respond adequately utilizing First World resources alone. It is no longer possible to deliver any realistic assistance without the strong partnership relationships with local communities and through local leadership. The matter of providing appropriate support to local staff in humanitarian work is therefore of increasing importance to all aid and mission organizations.

Support From "Home"

International organizations have had a tendency to view the support of staff in terms of the employees' home environment. Historically, "support" was exported with the expatriate. Organizations developed their support systems around the needs of international staff, translating point-of-origin needs into transportable versions, adapted to fit an "alien" environment. The practical needs of international employees were unconsciously defined in terms of the underlying values and cultural norms prevalent in the society from which they came. "Support" was often defined as the effort to recreate, as much as possible, conditions similar to those at "home." The extent to which this was possible depended largely on available resources rather than any ideology. Even the poorest of mission societies attempted to provide glimpses of "home" for their distant missioners, and these glimpses were always enthusiastically received. Only in rare cases did such people adopt the practices of the local people, and when they did they were often rejected by their own employers as having "gone native," or, more politely, as having lost their minds.

We can see the remnants of this mindset today in the presence of expatriate compounds, exclusive international communities, and shopping centers devoted to the importation of goods from "home." Trans-global institutions such as the United Nations and military peacekeeping forces maintain expensive and well-stocked storage facilities around the world, so that employees can always have access to the goods from their homelands. Even today, with a very diverse multinational work force, staff support systems in humanitarian and mission work tend to be biased towards First World needs.

A Move to "Local" Support

International humanitarian aid has become more complex with more expatriate staff becoming involved. International employee assistance specialists have proliferated, and organizations devoted to international support for expatriate workers have sprung up around the world. Unfortunately, while these programs offer excellent support services, they too are based on assumptions that humanitarian work is still being performed primarily by First World expatriates who are relocating to a "foreign" country. The disparity between conditions of employment for expatriate and local staff has become more apparent. The ability to transport very large items such as refrigerators, TVs, furniture, cars, and in some cases whole households around the world in "support" of expatriate staff emphasizes the myth that overseas adjustment is largely based on access to material resources. This disparity is heightened where local staff reside in conditions of poverty, and it may lead to dire consequences, including resentment, frustration, and even violence toward expatriate staff.

Organizations have responded to these challenges in different ways. Some, generally those with access to many resources, argue that a disparity in wealth between international and national staff is part of the cost of doing business. Without adequate salaries and housing, appropriately skilled expatriate staff will not be willing to move to where the work is to be performed. Other organizations, generally those with limited resources, encourage a model of "simplicity," where expatriate employees live as the locals do, residing in local accommodation and eating local foods while performing their mission. While this approach has certainly reduced obvious manifestations of financial disparity at a local level, any notion that expatriates can become locals simply by living a simple lifestyle is a fiction. Further, the expatriate always has a passport, a way to exit the stressful or even life-threatening situation, and options not always available to local staff.

Supporting Local Staff

Support of local staff in Christian humanitarian work requires attention to a number of factors:

- Integrity in employment practices.
- Treating staff as people, not producers.
- Physical and mental health.
- Skills enhancement and career planning.

The Importance of Consistent Employment Practices

Many international humanitarian and Christian missions began with the involvement of both international and local volunteers. In recent years, the practice of volunteering without pay has diminished. Although payment methods vary, most international providers of care receive some financial compensation for services rendered. The range is extreme, from the United Nations, where large salaries and considerable benefits are common, to small Christian missions making do on basic expenses and housing.

Local economies are increasingly based on industrial activities, and many people no longer have access to rural living or employment. Employment of local staff, therefore, often requires financial compensation. Increasingly, matters of labor law, policy, and practice are becoming commonplace, even in the poorest countries. It is incumbent on all aid organizations to ensure that local staff are hired legally and in accordance with both local and international labor policies and agreements.

World Vision attempts to maintain a degree of consistency between international employment and local employment. This is not to say that all staff are paid the same salary. Relatively speaking, international staff earn more than local staff. Salary levels are determined through a common process. Comparative salary surveys are conducted on a regular basis for both local and international staff, and World Vision aims to position salaries within the normal range of payment in a given labor market. International humanitarian work has a scale of salary and benefits that is relatively consistent globally, and most humanitarian agencies compare employment packages with a selected group of organizations performing similar tasks. This process can be applied by organizations at the local level as easily as internationally.

There is a need for integrity. The extent of an employment package should be consistent across all staff. For humanitarian organizations, this is extremely important; for Christians, it is essential. The recipients of assistance will measure consistency and integrity partially by how local staff are employed. If, for instance, health insurance coverage is provided for international staff, it should, if possible, be provided to locals as well. It may not be possible to provide access in all areas, but it is recommended that field managers work towards enhancing a wide range of support provisions. These should include consideration of the following:

- Leave provisions, including annual, recreation, family, medical, emergency, and bereavement leave.
- Retirement provisions.
- Unemployment compensation.
- Overtime and compensatory time.
- Employment of relatives.
- Disability insurance.
- Grievance and dispute resolution procedures.
- Internal transfers and promotions.
- Sexual and racial harassment policies.

Workers Are People Too

A major challenge is the fact that local employees are also members of local communities. While this appears at face value to be self-evident, the actual practice of many aid agencies indicates that they believe otherwise. Part of this is a result of the influence of Western concepts of "work," and part has to do with the overwhelming rate at which humanitarian aid has grown in recent years. There is a tendency to act as if humanitarian aid is a product that is somehow separated from the producers. Employees, therefore, can be hired to complete units of work, for which they are paid. This process is encouraged by the manner in which government donor funds are gained. Essentially, humanitarian organizations contract with donors to complete discrete, measurable tasks for a pre-agreed fee. This "piecework" approach to humanitarian aid encourages senior managers and field staff to view their day-to-day activities as a kind of production line. The downside of this is that workers can be viewed as separate from the product and the process. In a factory, a piece of machinery that fails to operate can be removed and replaced. Applying such concepts to humanitarian work can lead to situations in which a worker who is unable to "perform," for whatever reason, may be deemed redundant and may be replaced by another.

In international aid and missions, it is not possible to separate the worker from the work. The ministry (work) is an integral part of the person employed to perform it. In fact, there is no long-term, sustainable outcome without the worker (minister). In major relief operations, the worker may for a time be hidden behind the crates of food and medical supplies being delivered by huge cargo aircraft. But once the food has been shared out, there is no excuse for ignoring the pivotal role that the local employee will play in the full restoration of community well-being and functioning. Large organizations, therefore, need to consider carefully whether local employees are being viewed as producers or people.

Physical and Mental Health

Mission groups have long been aware of the potential health consequences of overseas work. As medical knowledge has increased, mission and humanitarian agencies have significantly improved the way in which international employees are prepared for assignments overseas. Most organizations ensure that full medical histories are taken prior to relocation overseas and that appropriate medications and immunizations are completed.

However, health care provisions for local staff have not been as comprehensive. In part, this has been due to a lack of adequate health services at field locations, but lack of attention to local needs has also added to the situation. In recent years, World Vision has acted intentionally to redress this through the development of local health insurance policies, coupled with enhancements in local medical services. Although these provisions are easier to achieve for large organizations, the most effective results have been obtained where agencies and missions jointly approach health insurers and providers with recommendations for ways to provide or enhance such services for local staff.

Organizations that have not taken steps to provide health care to staff would be well advised to do so. While there continue to be concerns over such conditions as malaria and tuberculosis, the major pandemic threatening virtually all aid and development work is HIV/AIDS. World Vision has seen a dramatic increase in the number of deaths of staff from AIDS in recent years, and the pattern is expected to grow. Partly obscured because of both intentional (the connection between AIDS and sexual behavior being unpalatable for many Evangelical Christians) and unintentional misdiagnosis, it is now apparent that AIDS will likely affect as many staff on a percentage basis as found in local populations. The potential impact on a local ministry in areas with high incidences of HIV/AIDS is significant, not only to programs but to employees and family members as well.*

The state of mental well-being has also become an important issue. In what is a relatively rapid development, mental health has become a centerpiece of international assistance. As community mental health programs have developed, particularly in relief environments, an appreciation has grown that local staff, as members of the impacted community, may also experience mental health problems.

It is difficult to identify precisely where this process began. Certainly the Rwandan experience highlighted the psychological trauma of genocide on a community. But before that, Cambodian survivors of the killing fields had drawn the attention of Western mental health experts; and prior to that, the plight of Romanian orphans, abandoned in appalling psychiatric institutions following the collapse of Communism, was noted. Certainly by the time humanitarian aid was required in the Balkans, mental health care had become a major part of the provision of assistance. While there is a significant way to go yet before it can be said with certainty what works in all environments, we do know that psychological trauma is a significant issue for survivor communities.

There is an increasing realization that front-line relief staff often experience negative psychological effects as a result of their field experiences. Although much research is still required, it is now generally accepted that exposure to extreme relief situations can result in severe psychologically disabling conditions. Recent research conducted in Kosovo by the Centers for Disease Control in Atlanta indicated that up to 17% of both international and local staff experience clinical depression, and up to 6% of local staff fall into the serious category of Post Traumatic Stress Disorder (PTSD) (Salama, 2001). In a single-country study that focused on local staff, measures of clinical depression were as high as 54%, while PTSD rates appeared to be close to 34% (World Vision, 2000).

The impact on the humanitarian aid community of this research has been considerable. It is hardly surprising that the

* World Vision International has recently implemented policies related to the health and protection of staff working in areas where HIV/AIDS is prevalent. The People In Aid Code/InterHealth contains useful guidelines as well.

mental health of international staff is today considered a serious issue. However, the research referred to above indicates that the psychological impact of disaster on local staff may be higher than that experienced by international staff.

Intuitively, this should not come as a major surprise. Yet aid agencies and missions continue to behave as if this cannot be the case. Within World Vision, as with other organizations, one of the major responses to the news has been to seek ways of limiting the incidence of psychological trauma in staff through recruiting refinements. Unfortunately, the reliability of psychological testing as a predictor of future psychological trauma is not high. While there are signs that persons with a previous psychiatric history are at higher risk than others in the development of psychological conditions, other types of personality testing do not lead to clear predictability (Salama, 2001).

For an organization the size of World Vision, the implications are wide-reaching. If the rate of clinical depression among local staff is somewhere between 17% and 50% (based on the available research), then World Vision has somewhere between 1,500 and 5,000 staff who are experiencing depressive conditions. If the real figures are nearer the lower end of the scale, there is still a significant group of people who may be in need of psychological services at a local field level.

Leaving aside the psychological discussion, the appearance of mental health issues for local staff leads inexorably back to the conclusion that despite their employment category, local staff are also survivors of whatever disaster or emergency has impacted the community. If there were no humanitarian need, there would be no need for the presence of a humanitarian organization. If there is a need and the meeting of the need requires the employment of local staff, then it is unlikely that humanitarian agencies can avoid hiring people with psychological trauma, at least to some extent.

Spirituality, Leadership, and Skills Enhancement

For a Christian organization such as World Vision, Christian spirituality is critical. The matter becomes more complex, however, where a significant percentage of World Vision's front-line staff are not Christian. Leadership in Christian ministry is intricately tied to World Vision's history. Yet local management may be in the hands of those who are not Christian. World Vision's policies preclude non-Christians from becoming senior managers, but this does not address the matter fully. The fact that World Vision actively discriminates on the basis of religious belief in certain parts of its organization creates potential problems. Yet World Vision is unashamedly Christian, and to retain this identity it needs to ensure Christian leadership.

World Vision has created a leadership training program that includes Christian maturity and experience at its core. This is a relatively new initiative and will take some years to implement fully. The overall objective is to equip leaders with the required professional skills and knowledge, while assisting them to develop Christian maturity, which will provide leaders for the future.

It remains to be seen how effective such efforts will be in retaining Christian consistency across an organization the size of World Vision. Even within the wider Christian community, there are significantly differing views as to Christian behavior, beliefs, and theology. Tensions already exist. There is also a significant number of managers who are Muslim, Hindu, or Buddhist. Many of these would expect their careers within the organization to advance. Efforts to halt this process may be problematic.

World Vision has established two working groups to seek solutions to these matters. One, focused on *Christian witness*, has the task to attempt to identify behaviors, beliefs, and lifestyles that can be defined as "Christian," in order to ensure that

World Vision is a witness to Christ, rather than to something else. The other, focused on *spiritual nurture*, is seeking to identify ways and means to help Christians grow and mature as they continue their ministry with World Vision. The major focus of both groups is local staff. While international staff are not being ignored, a core objective for World Vision is the growth and development of Christian ministry at a local level. It may not be too radical to suggest that the ongoing success of international Christian aid and missions work relies not so heavily on the presence of skilled international staff but more on the ability to attract, retain, and properly support communities of local staff and their families.

Supporting Local Staff: Case Study Honduras

In order to create an environment where the needs of local staff can be appropriately and safely addressed, World Vision has created an assessment process that fully involves local staff. Because the process is technology-free and is based on verbal conversations, it is cheap, portable, and applicable in a wide range of environments. It can be used with small or large numbers, for urban or rural programs. When applied at an organizational level, it has potential to impact individual well-being and organizational culture significantly. It can also improve productivity and help meet program goals. An example of the process as utilized in Honduras follows.

Phase 1: The Request for Assistance

Following the devastation of Hurricane Mitch in late 1998, the World Vision program in Honduras underwent significant changes. The widespread damage led to a major shift from agricultural development to relief work funded by the United States, Canadian, and European governments. The organizational demands increased proportionally, as did reported levels of staff stress. By 1999, concern among staff as to possible long-term psychological damage following Mitch led to a request that a "stress assessment" be conducted for World Vision Honduras staff. We have found that in most cases the most effective local staff support initiatives have occurred in locations where the initial request for assistance has come from local management.

Phase 2: The "Stress Assessment"

The assessment process generally takes three to five days, depending on the size of the field office. In this case, it was necessary to take the full five days. The Field Director and all the senior management staff were requested to take part in the process. (Virtually all this group are local staff.) Because the initial request had been framed in terms of stress and trauma, the first two days were spent in education on individual stress, stress management, psychological trauma, burnout, and trauma treatment alternatives. Key questions considered during these sessions were, *What is stress? What is psychological trauma? How do such things impact me?*

During day two, there was increased discussion on the importance of organizational stress factors and a clarification of the difference between organizational and individual stress. General measures of individual stress were used by the group in order for them to gain understanding of how much stress they were experiencing in the present. Measures used had been previously translated and validated for use cross-culturally. While not used in all WVI locations (some instruments require specialist guidance), measures have included the Impact of Events Scale (IES), the General Health Questionnaire (GHQ-28), the Holmes and Rahe Social Readjustment Rating Scale, the Hopkins Symptoms Checklist (HSCC), and the Harvard Trauma Questionnaire (HTQ). A general job satisfaction survey is also recommended. A key question was, *How much stress are you feeling today?*

By the beginning of day three, the discussion moved to an examination of the nature of stress in Honduran culture and how such stress is managed. Many languages do not have a word directly translatable as "stress," and the easiest way is often to take the English word and make it sound like the other language. The meaning behind the word may not have transferred, however.

Discussion continued until the participants were confident that *they* knew what they were talking about. Only when this clarification has occurred is it possible to move ahead with identifying ways to provide appropriate assistance. This process results in a culturally and linguistically relevant definition of something related to "stress" but not constricted by European concepts. Key questions during the discussion were, *What is "stress" in Honduras? What does it look like? How do you know you have "stress"?*

The ethnographic process continued into day four. This time, the focus was on how the local culture deals with or copes with stress and how, traditionally, effective interventions are undertaken. The objective here is to assist the group in beginning to identify locally available resources that may not have been accessed in order to meet identified needs. The process is two-fold and tends to move back and forth between identified needs and identified resources. The discussion of the day before will be revisited, and the training inputs on day one will be reviewed and challenged, as local culture begins to interpret and inform. A key question is, *What, traditionally, do Hondurans do to alleviate, deal with, cope with, remove, and live with "stress"?*

The objective by the end of day four is to have two clear lists. The first is a list of the factors that cause discomfort, stress, or pain (or however these are defined in the local language). The second is the list of activities, remedies, resources, or practices that traditionally lead to a reduction of the stress. It is to be expected that there will be some stress factors for which resources to ease the pain do not exist or are insufficient.

The two lists will each be subdivided into two subsections. The list of stress factors will comprise those that exist in the wider community (that is, stressors to which everyone is exposed), as well as those that exist specifically within the organization. Likewise, the resource list will be subdivided into the two categories. Key questions for this process are, *What factors cause stress (pain)? What remedies reduce stress (pain)? What are general factors? What are specific to our organization?*

Day five completed the process by determining the extent of the organization's responsibility towards stress management and the development of a plan to meet the identified needs. The World Vision Honduras team identified five major areas of need. These were human resource management, office administration, organizational culture, relationships with other World Vision offices, and the health of staff.

Each of these major topics had numerous specific items attached to them, which for reasons of space and confidentiality are not included here. However, it is interesting to note that although psychological distress was discussed, it was generally agreed that most "felt" stress was related to work factors, rather than to conditions such as poverty, community violence, or lack of educational opportunities. Nor was there any major concern over high degrees of psychological trauma, although some staff who reported significant personal losses as a result of the hurricane were identified as experiencing high stress levels. For these staff, the enhancement of access to pastoral, health, and psychological services locally was viewed as being an appropriate organizational response. Key questions here were, *What concerns or issues are those that must be addressed by the employing agency? What issues or concerns are the responsibility of the individual?*

The final part of the process is the creation and publication of a plan for implementation of the organizational response to the assessment process. This is probably the single most important component of the whole activity. At this point, senior management are asked to commit to the provision of sufficient resources of time and money so that changes can actually be implemented. Without this step, it is likely that the process will be ineffective or even viewed as negative by participants and other staff.

For World Vision Honduras, the total support of senior leadership was evident from the beginning. By the end of the last day, a fully detailed, three-year plan had been designed and agreed to for dealing with each of the issues identified throughout the week. Further, each identified task had been assigned to one or more of the management team for attention. Time frames had been determined as to how long each task would be expected to take, and each task had been assigned in the calendar to a specific quarter of one of the next three years. Preliminary estimates of costs associated with each activity had been made, and some initial potential funding sources had been identified.

The overall effect of these strategies was significant and immediate. In the first place, those who would both implement and benefit from the plan had designed the whole thing. Although external facilitation was provided, local staff had performed the work. Second, there was a clear and precise identification as to what would be addressed and when work would start. Third, senior management was clearly totally committed to the whole process.

Phase 3: Implementation and Evaluation

This phase is ongoing and is readily assessed by internal and external evaluators. Local staff support is becoming part of the overall strategy of the World Vision Honduras operational plan for the next three years and has become part of their resource assessment and acquisition. Although not all the activities have taken place in the order they were planned, and some have not occurred at all, in the overall context of a humanitarian aid and development agency working in a difficult environment, the achievements have been impressive.

Conclusions

In determining the shape, structure, and general conditions of support services for local staff, it is necessary to consider carefully how the local culture is itself structured, how support is given in that context, and how Christian service can be introduced in such a way as to be welcomed and not condemned. Appropriate care will consider the place of the family in society, the place of the individual in the group, the role of community leaders, how healing is performed, and how success is defined and recognized. In environments where poverty is extreme and nutrition may be less than balanced, it is possible that local staff needs may have more to do with what people eat than what they think and how they feel. If a staff member's family is living in a hovel, it may be that the staff person is less able to perform expected duties during the working day.

A full local staff support program will need to consider the practical conditions of life—food, housing, job security, education, health, insurance, and so on. Psychological support may be required. Counseling services, based on local cultural practices, will almost certainly be needed. Spirituality, the need for a person to meet with God, must be central, with understanding/respect being shown towards previous religious experiences. Christians occasionally diminish spiritual experience that fails to fit their own definitions, to the detriment of Christian witness. It is also important to extend an invitation to walk closer with God through the person of His Son, Jesus Christ. In sum, however, each country and each culture will need to develop its own unique form of local staff support services, if it is truly to meet the needs of all.

World Vision's program of local staff care and support is at a very early stage. At the time of writing, a few field countries have implemented comprehensive staff care. Resources for this type of initiative are limited. However, encouraging progress is being made. Most WVI field offices now employ full-time human resource (HR) managers, who have the responsibility of creating appropriate staff support services. Regional and global meetings for these managers are held at least once a year, and training opportunities are increasingly available. It is critical that partnerships with Christian missions, other NGOs, and member care professionals around the world are created to move ahead. World Vision welcomes comments on how further improvements could be made.

Reflection and Discussion

1. How might your cultural background influence your understanding of the terms for *care* and *stress*?
2. How could some of the approaches used in the Honduras case study be used by your agency in its care of staff?
3. How does your mission or agency integrate local caring resources into already-existing support services?
4. Is care of local partners an optional activity, depending on factors such as available funds? Who decides which resources will be made available?
5. How, in very practical terms, does the support provided for local partner staff compare with that provided to expatriates?

Appendix
Life for National Humanitarian Workers*

by Viola R.N. Mukasa, Uganda

Emergency and development work is a strange business, sustained by equally unusual people from within or outside a country. These are people who respond to another's cry for help and sometimes to their own cries. I choose to call them help-workers (HPWs). These people commit themselves for a time to help or even "save" a particular piece of the world. This may often cost them their security and other luxuries, including personal relationships, but they gladly pay the price, usually in the name of altruism, for the sake of a mission task that is usually defined by others who are far off.

I'm an HPW living in a location in Africa that is in prime need of help/missions. I've experienced many types of stress as I have worked in various mission programs. The most sustained tension I've experienced has been related to the urgency and the amount of work to be done in a potentially explosive social and political environment. The challenge is not only to produce expected results quickly, under tense and sometimes risky circumstances. The challenge is also to deal with the constant worry about the security and health of those within my immediate world.

There is tension from having detailed knowledge of the context and locale of the humanitarian setting. I'm often familiar with the problem, the attitude, the threats within the community, and the fickleness of certain politicians in allowing for help.

I have another line of sustained tension that comes from belonging and yet being apart. I belong to those who are helping and to those being helped, but I'm neither an expatriate nor a beneficiary.

* This section is based on a presentation given at the "Managing Stress for Humanitarian Aid Workers" conference in Amsterdam, The Netherlands, September 6-8, 2001, sponsored by the Antares Foundation and the Centers for Disease Control and Prevention.

It is as if I am being followed by a ghost which constantly reminds me that the needy person—for example, the displaced person in the transit camp—could have been me. Oh yes. And there are all kinds of other tangible reminders of my own vulnerability and mortality, as I witness the life and death experiences that link me very closely to those I'm trying to save.

The fact that emergency aid work does not directly influence conflicts, but instead responds to the devastation they cause, greatly affects national HPWs. It colors our attitude and often limits our enthusiasm. We can only do so much. The consequences of the conflict affect us strongly, because they mirror not only what could have happened but what could still happen to us and others close to us.

Further, both national and international HPWs have a difficult working environment which allows little time to process personal experiences and manage stressful situations and issues. In such situations, I'm just glad for the speed with which we must execute our work. Responding quickly to others helps keep most of my anxieties out of focus and has made me tougher. These anxieties can overwhelm an HPW, so we need to develop some emotional armor in order to last.

I often wonder if my colleagues and I, consciously or otherwise, are trying to play God. Both the helpees and the helpers can view the latter as a type of savior. The brutality of reality can obscure the closeness of the true Lord and the fact that it is not we but He who is indeed still the real Savior and Shepherd.

Since I am a committed Christian, a core part of my survival strategy is to keep in touch with God by communicating with Him and referring to His Word. We need His presence to encourage us and to remind us that we are not ultimately of this world. Yet we are called to love and help others in this world, as His co-laborers. Maintaining this perspective is so important! It is so easy to lapse into pride, anger, wrath, malice, blasphemy, and filthy language as we encounter people's pain. It's also easy to become pessimistic as we wonder why God allows wars and suffering. To keep sane, I constantly have to pray for grace and wisdom, refer to God's commands in Scripture, do my assigned duties to the best of my ability, and let God be God. I also need the support of those around me and from the organization for which I work.

Let me now share some more practical realities for national staff workers. Here is a fictitious case study of Mako, a logistician with an imaginary organization called EXACT.

The World of Mako

I'm called Mako because I'm just about the only one who can remember my long, "funny sounding" second name. It's the same for most of us local staff, though, especially as there's so little time for personal things, such as second names. I'm the logistics officer of Express Action (EXACT), and I've been working with them since the war broke out in the north over two years ago. I studied marketing and business administration, but I have now specialized in procurement, storage, and transport of aid supplies. I've learned much about EXACT on the job and, of course, from the numerous "emergency experts" regularly sent out by headquarters in Milan. Some of these experts are good. The rest are too busy to get to know. They seem always to be in a hurry and are constantly talking to Milan and the field. They've developed a brilliant evacuation plan—for themselves and non-nationals.

I like my job, and the pay is more or less adequate, given the situation in my country. But I am struck with how "cheap" life is valued up north. It's threatened by land mines, rebels, and fighter planes. Hunger, disease, and death are also present. I've been trying to trace my uncles and grandmother to see if they are safe. Their village was evacuated after the bombing last month. It's not easy to juggle work with tracing people, so I've given their names to a friend of mine at the Red Cross tracing office. My mother expects good news from me every day about the search results.

I basically enjoy the speed and urgency with which emergency operations are done. I am glad to be helping people suffering because of the war. These days, the national drivers talk more often about the risks we take, but always casually over their tea or as they pack their trucks to head out. We all worry, but we try to keep focused on our tasks. Sometimes the secretary and the cook—not many others—inquire about our journeys. They only have a vague idea of how it is for us in the field and at home.

My family worries when I travel, not convinced about the thoroughness of the security precautions that I say we take. Sometimes I really miss my family. These days, I try to avoid telling people back home that I'm going to the field. At times, I'm not sure about things myself. The politicians keep doing things more out of their own interests and not necessarily based on what is best for the people affected.

I don't share my concerns, though, with others. We all have our own share of troubles, and these risks come with the territory as an aid worker. It's enough to drink beer and joke together after a hard day. Sometimes I'm scared, and I know that the others are as well, but it's as if to acknowledge fear is to give it life. But when my anxiety becomes desperate, I try to think through my future. I stop and wonder what my family would do if I were killed or disabled by a mine, and the war moved to where we now live. I also puzzle over why we're struggling to stop the bleeding when we can't repair the artery. I've started looking for another job.

References and Suggested Reading

Danieli, Y. (2001). *Sharing the front line and the back hills: International protectors and providers, peacekeepers, humanitarian aid workers, and the media in the midst*. Amityville, NY: Baywood Publishing Company.

Danieli, Y., Rodley, N., & Weisaeth, L. (Eds.). (1996). *International responses to traumatic stress*. Amityville, NY: Baywood Publishing Company.

Janz, M., & Slead, J. (2000). *Complex humanitarian emergencies: Lessons from practitioners*. Monrovia, CA: World Vision.

Robben, C., & Suarez-Orozco, M. (Eds.). (2000). *Cultures under siege, collective violence and trauma*. Cambridge, UK: Cambridge University Press.

Salama, P. (2001, May). *Mental health outcomes among relief workers in Kosovo*. Presentation at the annual conference of the European Society for Traumatic Stress Studies, Edinburgh, Scotland.

Shepherd, B. (2001). *A war of nerves: Soldiers and psychiatrists in the 20th century*. Boston, MA: Harvard University Press.

Van Brabant, K. (2000). *Operational security management in violent environment: A field manual for aid agencies*. London, UK: Human Practice Network, Overseas Development Institute.

World Vision International. (2000). *Stress and trauma incidences among national staff in relief and development work*. Unpublished research by WVI in partnership with the Headington Program, School of Psychology, Fuller Seminary, Pasadena, CA.

***John Fawcett** is Director of Staff Support Services/Stress and Trauma Management for World Vision International. He is a New Zealander who has worked extensively in Christian and secular social services in New Zealand and other countries. Since 1990, he has worked for WVI in New Zealand, Cambodia, and presently the USA. His work regularly takes him to front-line relief situations. He also spends considerable time conducting training workshops in long-term development programs. Email: John_Fawcett@wvi.org.*

Special thanks to the local staff who comprise the Staff Stress Support Team at WVI Cambodia for leading my learning about local staff needs. Also to Dr. Michael Hegenauer (WVI Viet Nam) and Tony Culnane (Culnane Consulting, Australia) for their ongoing advice and counsel.

28

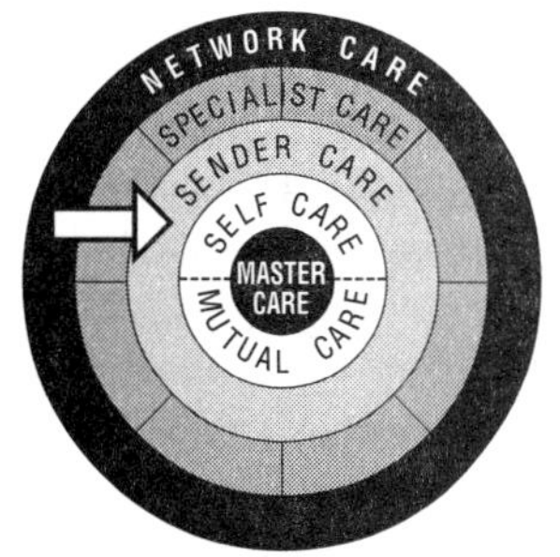

Administrative Guidelines for Remaining or Returning

Laura Mae Gardner

When a missionary family or missionary is involved in a difficult or traumatic situation, the agency administration has three choices: allow them to remain on the field, return them to the home country, or relocate them where additional resources are available. What criteria does a sending agency use to decide which of these to recommend/require?

Major decisions that affect the lives and location of mission personnel are difficult. This chapter examines an organization's decision-making process for determining the best options for struggling or traumatized personnel. I begin with five case studies, followed by some principles, resources, and procedures to consider. I finish with a discussion of the lessons to be learned.

Case Studies

Case 1

Mr. and Mrs. Lee are nearing the end of their ministry overseas. They plan to return to their home country in Asia within 15 months to obtain higher education for their three children. All of their current efforts are devoted to finishing the village program and establishing the new little church of 20 believers. Although the boarding school sends repeated reports of concern that their middle son, John, age 15, is using and distributing drugs, they seem to be oblivious to any need to respond. He is failing four of his five classes and is currently on probation.

Case 2

Jim and Lynn Smith, new in their country of assignment and deep into language and culture acquisition, are busy building relationships with the local people. Lynn has demonstrated an amazing aptitude for language learning. She is well ahead of Jim in this area, triggering in him some strong feelings of insecurity and inadequacy. Not only has he become unduly critical of Lynn and of things in general, withdrawing from spiritual and social activities, but he also has been indulging in pornography. During their application process, Jim had not mentioned a previous pornography addiction, because at that time he had been free of it for two years. He believed the desire was gone. The current increase in stress has caused it to recur, and the temptation is stronger than ever. Jim spends many evenings accessing porn sites on the computer.

Case 3

Hans and Olga spent their adult life on the field, planning to die as they had lived—among their beloved national friends. Now at ages 63 and 61, they just learned that Olga has leukemia. She has been given only two months to live. Her children and family want her to come back to their home country in Europe, but she refuses to go.

Case 4

Alfonso and Maria pioneered this region in the Sahel of Africa, making friends of nationals and hosting new mission members and visitors. But a church split at home has severely impacted their support, dropping it to subsistence level and sapping their motivation. They have no money to purchase needed supplies, such as a computer, or to pay indigenous workers. Their energy is low. They have become unproductive, bitter, and divisive. All efforts to affirm and challenge them have failed. Worse, those efforts have alienated Alfonso and Maria from their friends and from each other to the point where they seldom talk with anyone.

Case 5

Civil unrest in a Central Asian nation has reached the point where the embassies have sent directives for expatriates to return to their sending countries. Most expatriates have left the country. Not Robert and Ruth! They came, committed to lay down their lives for Jesus' sake, and they fully expect that to happen. They are determined to stay and die among their national friends. Their home church is pressuring the sending organization to "do something!" In the sending country, the couple's adult children are extremely anxious and alternate between being angry at the organization and being angry at mom and dad.

These case studies, though disguised and hypothetical, are not fictitious. They have happened in the history of mission endeavor. A prepared sending organization anticipates such occurrences by having good policies, trained managers, and on-site member care workers. However, the tendency (when the moment of decision comes) is to act based on emotion, rather than on reasoned evaluation. Even when there are counter-indications, the result is often a reluctant decision by the field administration to allow the people involved to remain on the field. How can an administrator, a superintendent, and a responsible manager make a decision that weighs all pertinent factors?

Three Principles to Follow

Principle 1: Respect

When considering options for staying or going, an administrator, leader, or member care worker must treat the members with the respect to which they are entitled, honoring their courage and commitment. Face-to-face interaction is best, if at all possible. We must keep in mind that believers who join an agency or who go out representing their church generally do so with the intention to serve in both good and bad times. Even when severe difficulty enters their lives, they cannot easily renege on their initial decision.

Principle 2: Levels of Impact

Working through location and care decisions must take into consideration the perspective of a wider community. Members must understand that the decisions they make will not only impact the national believers, but also their colleagues, their families, and their supporting partners. Awareness of the message they are sending to their adult children and other family members in the home country is vital.

Principle 3: Control

Members must be willing to yield a degree of control over their life, location, and decisions. They must be helped to understand that when they join an organization or represent a church, they give up the right to function as totally independent units. They must heed direction from their leaders, seeking and following input from experts with greater experience in crisis situations. They must be assisted to understand the liability they place on an organization when they disobey its directives.

Resources to Access

Most mission agencies have access to specialists. Such specialists should include:

- Internationally knowledgeable, Christian legal counsel.
- Crisis managers with expertise in developing contingency plans, assessing and monitoring levels of risk/danger, giving input on security and personal safety, and providing debriefings.
- Professional therapists who are missions-aware, experienced, and approachable.
- People who understand mission matters from the perspective of a leader, a manager, a pastor, and a caregiver.
- Skillful consultants who are able to evaluate danger or distress levels from a distance and who know how to coach by asking good questions.

All of the above are specialists—helpful, useful, and sometimes essential resources. It must be kept in mind, however, that in some situations, such as interacting with members who want to remain/die in the country they have called home for most of their life, the need is for basic understanding and care, not necessarily a specialist. Wise and compassionate leaders/administrators can help struggling members understand that a timely retreat can permit future return and ongoing ministry. Such leaders are key sources of encouragement during painful transitions and difficult decisions.

Some Suggested Procedures

1. Planning in Advance

What can be treated on the field? My opinion is that some situations generally should not be allowed to remain on the field. These include severe depression, behavior destructive to self or others, psychotic or suicidal behavior, major moral failure or immorality, dissociative identity disorder (multiple personality disorder), pending death, rape victims, situations of child abuse or family violence, chronic/debilitating illness requiring substantial care from others, persistent lack of production, addictions, and criminal acts (e.g., financial embezzlement, theft).

In general, the field is not the place to get treatment, especially if few or no professional resources are readily available. If the problem includes any of the above, the members usually belong back in their sending (passport) country. There they can have access to skillful professional care (true for most sending countries) and can be supervised by those who have personnel responsibility. The stress caused to this one person or family by requiring a return to the passport country must be weighed against the detrimental effects to many, should the individual or family be permitted to remain on the field.

2. Evaluating the Situation

What are the significant issues? In situations involving major problems and critical decisions, it is important for leaders/helpers to define the problem clearly and get the facts. Here are some areas to explore:

- Is the behavior appropriate, given the circumstances?
- What are the precipitating events or conditions influencing this person's behavior?

- How long has this behavior been going on? Is there a pattern?
- Is harm being caused or experienced by anyone right now?
- How pervasive is the impact of the behavior? Who is being hurt/impacted by it?
- How intrusive or restrictive is this behavior on the person's functioning?
- What is the potential for this person to harm self or others?
- Is the behavior getting worse or better?
- Is there a change in sight? Is change likely to happen? Under what circumstances?
- What are the potential benefits or liabilities of keeping this person/family on the field?
- Does the behavior threaten the organization's reputation/work in the country?
- What is the probable impact on community morale, security, and/or safety?
- Does this person's behavior disrupt the harmony and unity of the local mission group?
- What is the attitude of the member toward receiving help?
- What has already been tried? How was it received?
- If no action is taken, what are the probable/possible consequences?
- Is the situation serious enough that the home office might want to play a role?
- What are the costs (financial, emotional, administrative) to keep this person on the field?
- Are existing services able to meet the demands of this person's or this family's needs?
- Will serving this person or family stretch local services beyond their intended function?
- Will other potential users of services be excluded due to this person's or this family's needs?

3. Exploring Options

What help is available? There are a number of items to sort out regarding resources:

- What kind of local counseling care is available?
- How does the counselor's training and experience match the person's treatment needs?
- Does the counselor's schedule allow adequate time for treating this person?
- Are there more appropriate treatment opportunities available in the person's homeland?
- How will the counselor's other opportunities or responsibilities be affected?
- Will treating this person on the field prolong or shorten his/her recovery in the long run?

4. Making the Decision

Although the decision to send an individual or family home is an administrative one, in almost every situation, the person or family involved must be allowed to have input into the process as well. Many times, however, the involved individuals will not want to go home, and they are likely to minimize the extent of the difficulty, the impact they have on the local community, or the demands they are making on local resources. Therefore, the final decision is usually the responsibility of the local administrator, after appropriate consultations with home country administration, international leadership, and specific resource people.

5. Implementing the Decision

When the single/family is informed about the decision to return them home for help, fairness demands careful adherence to existing procedures and policies. These policies should require a face-to-face encounter on the field, with discussion and dialogue of issues with those involved. Permission to return to the field must be contingent on clear, written criteria for necessary changes. Good documentation is necessary. This involves a recorded history of the problem, any attempts to deal with the matter, and the overall plan to help. It is best to do all the documentation while the member is still in the country of service.

Lessons to Be Learned

Headaches and heartaches accompany moral failure, upheaval in a country, major illness, and other tragedies on the field. These can be eliminated or ameliorated by the presence of previously established policies for dealing with such problems. Here are some more items to help:

- Have members indicate through a signature upon joining the organization that they have read and are in agreement with these policies.
- Periodically review these policies with members and as an organization.
- Maintain a list of consultants and resource people for crises, therapy, and management.
- Link good management with good caring by communicating with people as individuals, discussing difficult matters early, creatively and jointly considering options, being willing to make hard and timely decisions, and accessing appropriate resources to meet people's needs.
- Affirm people. Many people have made a poor decision with good motives. Honoring the motives while helping them remake the decision can be done in a respectful way, letting people know they are wanted back (if this is so) when they have made the changes that prompted their removal from the field.
- Be accountable. In addition to organizational accountability, a leader must see himself or herself as accountable to God for how people and situations are managed. It helps people to know that their leaders look to God for help and wisdom and that the leaders themselves are under authority.
- Be aware of ripple effects. The way people are treated during their personal crisis affects their attitudes toward the Lord, the organization, and their future role. Administrative care of "Mom and Dad," for example, has an indelible impact on the children in the family.

Conclusion

People are to be valued for who they are more than for what they do. They are a trust from the Lord. How they are cared for matters to God. A sending organization that is proactive in its member care does not hesitate to speak to a situation before it escalates out of control. It has a "member friendly" stance that will encourage and promote early and honest communication with members who need help. It has an ethos that understands human weakness and the reality that "we all stumble in many ways" (James 3:2). Security comes in knowing that leaders, while not condemning individuals who fall into temptation, will neither condone harmful behavior nor allow it to continue.

Biblical authority results in building people, not bestowing punishment. The process of responsible administration may feel painful to the member at times, yet our intent is always restoration and wholeness. And so is our Lord's. As Paul says, "The authority the Master gave me is for putting people together, not taking them apart" (2 Cor. 13:10, The Message).

Reflection and Discussion

1. How much authority can an organization legitimately assume for minor children of its members? Can it insist that the parents get treatment for a child with problems? What should the administration do in cases such as the following?

   a. Parents hide a child's handicap, failing to obtain specialized educational aids.

   b. A minor teenager engages in immoral sexual behavior with a national young woman.

   c. An anorexic child is placed in a children's home and refuses to eat. Her parents have placed her there so they won't have to deal with this dilemma.

d. A child has reported sexual abuse of some kind. The parents say, "We want to deal with it ourselves."

2. What can an organization do when a charming, charismatic, productive person begins to show signs of stress and paranoia, leads an underground mutiny against the leader, and has effectively divided the group?

3. An Asian male has committed adultery with the family's maid, but to send him and his family back to their sending country would involve the highest shame and loss of face for this family, for the church, and for the sending office in that country. What other options does the agency have?

4. After considerable deliberation, an agency has asked a family to return to the passport country for counseling, due to moral lapse on the part of one of the members. The family is not in agreement and has mustered a core of supporters from among the other field members. The administration is not at liberty to divulge any details of the case to the membership because of confidentiality restrictions. How would you deal with this situation?

5. A family is in turmoil, with divorce looming and looking better to the wife all the time. After attempts to deal with the situation on the field, the husband has finally agreed to return home with his wife for marriage counseling. He insists, however, that it be a certain specialized school of counseling. He alone will be the judge as to the adequacy of the therapy and the biblical skill of the counselor. How insistent can an organization be in crafting therapy in a case like this?

Laura Mae Gardner *holds bachelor's degrees in religious education and psychology, a master's degree in missions and counseling, and a doctor of ministries degree. She is a long-time member of Wycliffe Bible Translators and SIL International. Upon completion of extensive Bible translation in Mexico, she directed the International Counseling Department, followed by the development of the function of member care in Wycliffe and SIL. All of these activities have been done in conjunction with her husband, Richard, who also works in member care. The Gardners live in Dallas, Texas. Presently, Laura Mae is Vice-President of Personnel for both Wycliffe and SIL International. She has published several articles and materials on member care and counseling. She also gives workshops and presents at conferences around the world. Email: larrie_gardner@sil.org.*

29

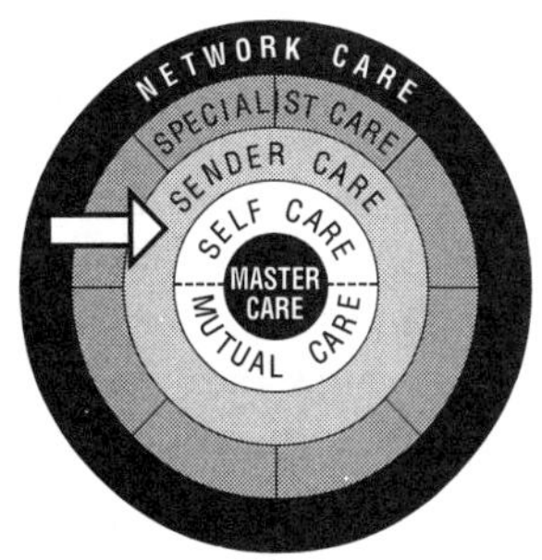

Reinventing Missionary Commitment

KATH DONOVAN
RUTH MYORS

Different generations, like cultures, make and live out commitment in different ways. For Generation X to make the rich contribution to mission of which its members are capable, mutual understanding and commitment between organization and missionary are necessary. "Systems thinking" within mission organizations could become the means of bringing about this commitment.

Generation X members, from whom most of today's Western missionary recruits come, have been brought up in a world quite unlike that of earlier generations. Consequently, they have a very different way of viewing the world. The speed with which things become obsolete, the frequency of broken marriages, and the threat of nuclear conflict with the resulting sense of a lack of future have together spawned fear and hesitancy about commitment. A survey of young Australians has found that many perceive the frequent marriage breakups of their parents' generation as the result of commitment made too early and too quickly. Therefore, they doubt their own capacity to carry through with commitment (Mackay, 1997). This explains the preference of Generation X missionary candidates to commit themselves only for short periods initially—to "see how things go."

Since this view is in sharp contrast to the traditional requirement of lifelong commitment, sight unseen, as the benchmark of the reality of a candidate's call, it has been all too easy for older generations to label this new generation "uncommitted." "What will happen to mission when they are in charge?" they anxiously ask one another. "If only they could be like us." However, being like earlier generations, even in approaches to commitment, is not what is needed in today's postmodern world. Just as the booster generation had qualities needed for their day, so today's missionaries bring to mission strengths which equip them well to be part of today's developing young churches.

The difficulty for mission agencies is that the average short term is usually inadequate for learning the host language and culture well enough for effective ministry. If we believe that Generation X is right for this day, how might this work out? We suggest that the answer lies in organizational commitment. By definition, organizational commitment is mutual commitment between employee and employer (Meyer, 1997)—in this case, between missionary and mission. Generation X members are strongly group oriented, with a high capacity for lasting attachment. This is clearly seen in the relationships they have within groups of friends with whom they typically "hang out" (Mackay, 1997). They also have the capacity for passionate commitment to an owned vision (Donovan, 2000). The challenge for mission organizations is to do what is needed to bring these strengths of Generation X to full flower in the context of mission. As a first step, a completely new look at the organization's side of organizational commitment is needed.

With this in mind, our focus in this chapter is to move towards a reinvented organizational commitment, which meets the needs and uses the strengths of both Generation X missionaries and the organization. Consideration of organizational commitment in relationship to attrition is followed by examination of generational differences in commitment, then by discussion of commitment as a two-way responsibility. The final section considers a radical paradigm shift in mission thinking, which could lead to a reinvented commitment suited to this day.

It should be noted that the research findings quoted and our own observations are based on studies from Older Sending Countries (OSCs), especially Australia. However, the suggested way forward in the final section has relevance to all sending agencies worldwide.

Organizational Commitment and Attrition

The importance of organizational commitment is underlined by its relationship to attrition. There is ample evidence of a close connection between low employee or missionary organizational commitment and attrition (Donovan & Myors, 1997a; Meyer, 1997; Wilcox, 1995). The corollary is also true: more committed people are more likely to remain with an organization (Meyer, 1997). The 1996 WEF survey of 14 nations found that "inadequate commitment" was high on the list of leaders' perceptions of causes of missionary attrition (Brierley, 1997).

Two important components of an individual's commitment to an organization are strength of attachment and identification with its values and vision (Meyer, 1997). Several studies of missionaries and Christian workers confirm that the greater the sense of belonging to an organization, the greater the likelihood of continuing with it (Donovan & Myors, 1997a; Nygren & Ukeritis, 1993; Wilcox, 1995). Since Generation X members have high capacity for both attachment and passionate pursuit of an owned vision, it seems likely that they also have high latent capacity for organizational commitment and therefore for continuing as overseas missionaries.

Three other findings are of special significance to organizations. Firstly, there is evidence that the individual's commitment is a developing process, greatly influenced by early experiences in the organization (Meyer, 1997). Secondly, older people appear to be more committed than younger ones (Donovan & Myors, 1997a; Nygren & Ukeritis, 1993). While this may partly reflect longer time to develop the organization/missionary relationship, it does underline the special need for care of younger missionaries. Thirdly, individual differences in focus of commitment may have an important influence on staying with an organization. People whose commitment is to all levels of an organization are more likely to stay than those whose commitment is mainly to one particular group, such as the team with which they work (Becker & Billings, 1993). For missions, this points to the importance of congruence between home and overseas in missionaries' experiences of their organization's commitment and to the whole concept of "systems thinking" (see the section on "Organizational Commitment as a Two-Way Responsibility" below).

Generational Differences in Views of Commitment

In this section, we will look at the influences upon each of the three generations currently working in mission, which resulted in their particular view and practice of commitment. We will identify changing patterns of commitment across generations and the ways in which these patterns match the changing needs of national churches. We see this as a vital step towards acceptance of the need for a reinvented commitment. For further details on the implications for mission of generational differences, see Donovan and Myors (1997b).

The Commitment of the Booster Generation

Born before 1946, the boosters in Western countries were primarily socialized by the modern dream of progress towards justice, wealth, and peace for all. The World Wars and the Great Depression were interpreted within that worldview. Out of those experiences came enhanced capacity to endure hardship, to persevere against any odds, to focus on a single goal, and to do whatever was needed for as long as it took to achieve.

Boosters respected and trusted leaders and were high in institutional loyalty. When the leader said, "Jump," they asked, "How high?" Thus, they brought to mission a commitment which was strong, loyal, long term, sacrificial, and focused on the task. It was exactly what was needed for the difficult work of breaking new ground for the gospel. It led boosters, sight unseen, to remote, difficult, and often dangerous situations, where they planted and nurtured churches. Their commitment was to getting the gospel to the whole world, regardless of personal cost. Everything else, whether family, career, recreation, or any other precious thing, was simply entrusted to God.

Although just right for that day, that kind of commitment became inappropriate as young churches matured, leading to "the problem of staying" (McKaughan, 1997). For example, some of these great pioneer missionaries went through the pain of rejection by the young churches they had planted, simply because they failed to see when their paternalistic leadership style was no longer wanted. Then God sent the baby boomers.

The Commitment of the Baby Boomer Generation

Born between 1946 and 1964, the baby boomers, although primarily influenced by modernism, began to ask some of the questions characteristic of postmodern thinking. The world they knew as children had experienced the meaningless devastation of World War II and the impact of blind obedience to leaders, which resulted in the Holocaust. Thus, they became questioners and protesters, discarding conformity and searching for perfection. At the same time, this was a period of unparalleled scientific advance and opportunity for education. Therefore, the baby boomers brought to mission a commitment focused on excellence in ministry—glorifying God by the best use of their training and talents wherever He led them. Quality of ministry rather than its length was the issue for them.

Boomers came to the young churches as well-trained specialists at just the right time, offering teaching and advice or technical expertise. They did not share the booster trust in leaders or the booster loyalty to institutions. When their leader said, "Jump," they asked, "Why?" since they needed to know that jumping was the most efficient and effective way of using their gifts and training. Their strong commitment to their family, especially to the educational needs of their children and their own need for professional development, often meant that their commitment was for a limited time. For them, commitment did not mean sacrifice of career or family or serving with a particular sending organization for an unlimited time.

Boomers' great strength has been the expertise and training which they have brought as brothers and sisters in Christ to the developing churches, especially in Bible teaching and theological training, management and administrative skills, and technological projects. Their weakness has been that they may leave prematurely, if an opportunity arises which they see as being a better avenue for their gifts. While modernism, with its emphasis on the rational and cognitive (Grenz, 1996), has had an important influence on the thinking of both boosters and boomers, with the coming of postmodernism, God sent Generation X.

The Commitment of Generation X

Born between 1965 and 1983, Generation X is the first generation to have been primarily socialized by postmodernism. One of the central perceptions of postmodern thought was that "the Emperor Modernism has no clothes." In other words, the more that rational man discovers about the universe, the more clearly his inability to use these discoveries for the good of mankind is seen. For example, human cleverness in splitting the atom has resulted not in global prosperity, but in the constant threat of global destruction. Thus, members of Generation X doubt whether they will have much future, and so the idea of long-term commitment becomes an absurdity.

Generation Xers are also characteristically beset by disillusionment and cynicism over the perceived hypocrisy and ineptness of world leaders. They are a generation who reject second-hand truth and who constantly search for truth and meaning that they can own. They not only have very low institutional loyalty, but they also have a deep distrust of organizations and leaders. Because many come from broken homes or have been latchkey kids, they have been primarily socialized by their peers and/or by television (Beaudoin, 1998). This is why they are so strongly group oriented. "The dethronement of reason as sole arbiter of man's destiny" (Grenz, 1996) has led to much greater emphasis on the experiential and the relational.

The members of this generation are egalitarian, assigning equal value to all people, irrespective of race, religion, gender, education, occupation, or status. They prefer participatory leadership. When the leader says, "Jump," they say, "We will, if you jump with us." Nuclear fear and the rape of the environment have produced a generation of people who are vulnerable, sensitive, and very much aware of their own, others', and the world's fragility (Beaudoin, 1998; Donovan, 2000). This sense of fragility and rejection has generated needs for pastoral care and balanced living. These needs are often misconstrued by older generations as immaturity, laziness, irresponsibility, and/or lack of commitment.

As described earlier, Generation X members bring to mission not only a tentativeness about commitment, derived from fear of not being able to see things through, but also a propensity for deep commitment in the context of a loving, trusting, tested relationship. They have a need to belong, and they yearn for a theme—an identity and vision about which they can be passionate (Beaudoin, 1998; Donovan, 2000). Because commitment is seen as risky, they usually prefer short-term ministry in order to see how everything goes. If things go well, many will renew short contracts and may continue to do so term by term.

Generation Xers are strongly relational and yet are able to "hang loose." They value people for who they are and have a preference for arriving at truth through storytelling and dialogue. Because of these qualities, they are well suited to merging into national churches in these days when missionaries are needed not to lead but to be real friends. Their strengths are their capacity for friendship with people of all cultures, an unfolding, passionate commitment to a vision that they own, and their willingness not to outstay their welcome. Their weakness is often not staying long enough to become really effective.

Summary of the Generations

In summary, moving across generations, several trends in commitment are apparent. These trends fit into the changing needs of missions, especially (but not exclusively) those of the Older Sending Countries (see Table 1). Firstly, there has been a broadening of focus beyond the task alone to include the family and then the community, along with an emphasis on improved quality of ministry through better training and more balanced living. Secondly, there has been a decline in exclusive commitment to particular sending organizations. Boosters saw service with a particular organization as an integral part of their calling. Younger generations perceive their calling as being to a particular ministry. Often, identifying a suitable mission comes later. Thirdly, the time factor has been removed from the notion of commitment. No longer is length of commitment considered to be a valid measure of its depth. As the risk of outstaying usefulness and/or welcome or of hindering growth and independence of the church is acknowledged, the value of letting go at the appropriate time is receiving far greater currency than ever before. Fourthly, there has been an increasing awareness of the need for team ministry, involving complementary gifts, mutual support, and a synergistic outcome.

Organizational Commitment as a Two-Way Responsibility

Generation X looks for commitment built on mutual attachment and trust. When leaders identify "inadequate commitment" as an important cause of missionary attrition (Brierley, 1997), it is clear that they mean the missionary's commitment. However, organizational research indicates that the level of employees' commitment to their employing organization is significantly influenced by their perception of the organization's commitment to them (Eisenger, Huntington, Hutchison, & Sowa, 1986).

Does this finding apply to missionaries? In our study of Australian missionaries, the most important influences on

Table 1
Generational Differences in Commitment

Generation	Type of Commitment	Strengths	Weaknesses
Booster	Long-term commitment to task; high commitment to organization; sacrifice; high perseverance; family entrusted to God	Planted/nurtured churches against any odds	Problem of staying
Boomer	Focus on excellence in ministry; high commitment to serving where skills are best used; high priority on family welfare; depth of commitment more important than length	Teaching/equipping growing churches; fraternalistic; use expertise for community projects	May leave prematurely
Gen X	Initial commitment tentative—short term to test; commitment with a team; low initial commitment; depth of commitment more important than length	Propensity for passionate commitment; high need to belong; accepting and relational	Field work too short to be effective; fragile; need team and need to be valued by organization to function well

Table 2
Australian Missionaries' Satisfaction With Some Organizational Support Items

Item	% Agree	% Uncertain	% Disagree
Our leaders address problems early.	30	30	40
Conflict resolution is *not* well done in this organization.	43	24	33
When there is a complaint about me, leaders discuss it with me.	39	37	24
Our organization is weak in personnel management.	40	23	37
I am satisfied with our organization's crisis management.	49	33	18
My needs for pastoral care are satisfied.	42	20	38
I am satisfied with our organization's review procedures.	38	24	38
Communication within the organization is inadequate.	42	17	41
I had adequate debriefing on home leave.	36	17	47
I need to live a more balanced life than my workload allows.	43	17	40
I am adequately consulted in areas of my expertise.	61	20	19
I am encouraged to suggest ways of improving our ministry.	61	20	19
I feel heard by the leadership here.	65	18	17

commitment to the organization were found to be a sense of being supported by the organization and a sense of satisfaction with its management procedures, including review procedures, personnel policies/practices, and debriefing on home leave (Donovan, Griffin, & Myors, 2001). The perception of being personally supported by the organization was greatest when personnel felt valued and treated fairly. It was also significantly greater when field leadership showed care for missionaries' well-being through listening, addressing problems early and honestly, and allowing them scope to develop their own ministries.

How do missionaries perceive the commitment of their mission societies to them? Results from our survey of Australian missionaries (1,398 participants—a 60% response rate—from 34 sending agencies) suggest that many perceive major deficits in care. In Table 2, some of these are highlighted. It can be seen that significant numbers were dissatisfied with personnel management in general and with things like adequacy of debriefing on home leave and conflict resolution in particular. This finding accords with anecdotal evidence from our debriefing of missionaries on home leave.

Whether or not good member care policies are in place, many missionaries perceive that their sending organizations are not serious about their commitment to them. It is a picture, as Covey (1991) reminds us, of the farmer being willing to sacrifice the well-being of the goose (production capacity) in the pursuit of more golden eggs (production).

Clearly, as McKaughan (1997) suggests, this is a systems problem rather than an individual problem. A "system" is an entity (such as a mission organization) made up of a set of units (a group of people) and the interrelationships between them (Goldenberg & Goldenberg, 1985). In a healthy system, perceived failure in one person is accepted as a systems responsibility, which may be pointing to a systems failure. It seems to us that this kind of "systems thinking" is not always evident in mission organizations.

For example, when a missionary leaves field ministry before the expected time, how do organizations respond? How much attention, in fact, is given to the possibility of failure on the part of the organization? "Often," says McKaughan (1997, p. 20), "rather than evaluate and admit our organizational guilt or ineptness, we mission leaders abdicate our responsibility and too easily write off the individual as somehow not having measured up." McKaughan goes further and suggests that organizations' misuse of missionaries (systemic abuse) is a common cause of attrition. Examples of systemic abuse include inadequate screening and training, assigning missionaries to jobs for which they have no training or experience, poor communication, failure to provide regular evaluation and mentoring, and unwillingness by leaders to deal with problem situations. Usually there will be a combination of things, as in the following example:

A baby boomer agriculturist was recruited to set up an agricultural project in a very needy area. On arrival in the host country, he found he had been assigned to a different ministry in which he had neither training nor experience. When he complained to his booster leader, he was told that he was "poor missionary material." In fact, he was never permitted to work in agriculture. The missionary returned to the home country prematurely, a very disappointed and disillusioned man. He received no support at all from the home council, having been labeled as a failure by his field leader. This was a clear systems failure resulting in the loss of a valuable worker.

So the upshot is this: In organizational commitment, the missionary and the organization have equal responsibility.

Reinventing Missionary Commitment

If the commitment of Generation X missionaries is to develop, they need to feel a sense of belonging to their organization. They need to be passionate about its vision and their own part in it. They also need a conviction that the organization is committed to their well-being, as shown by being valued, treated fairly, and empowered for ministry. Although many good member care policies have been developed, very often they are pushed aside by the busyness and/or lack of motivation in those expected to carry them out.

A first-term couple told us this story: They were asked to fill in as field administrators while others were on leave. Having discovered annual evaluation forms in a cupboard, the wife started using them to interview missionary staff as they visited the office. One senior missionary wept with appreciation and said that no one had ever sat down with her before to talk about her situation—even though annual evaluation was mission policy.

How can missions become sufficiently motivated about member care that good policies will consistently be put into action? We suggest that the answer lies in a paradigm change to systems thinking. Some key principles of systems thinking relevant to missionary commitment follow.

1. Change View of Commitment

A changing world demands a changing view of missionary commitment. The idea of personal missionary commitment needs to be broadened to include the mutuality of organizational commitment.

2. Think Systems

Organizations need to see themselves as systems and need to "think systems" in their approach to all aspects of the organization's life. This means acknowledging the interdependence and inherent value to the system of all members. Thus, when one member is having a problem, this is owned by the whole body. When the organization is sick, for whatever reason, the effects are felt by the whole body, and movement towards healing is seen as the shared responsibility of every member—that is, of the whole system. Systems thinking causes the "we/they" mentality to pass into history.

In the course of our work with missionaries, we see many systems problems causing unnecessary pain and loss of valuable personnel. One first-term horror story concerned a single man in his 20s. He was assigned by a mission agency to teach English in an indigenous university in a closed country. Regular breaks were to be taken in a nearby location which was not closed and where there were many missionaries. They included some from the young man's denomination, from whom he was assured that he could expect pastoral care. During the two years of his assignment, there was a series of stressful events, including ill health, being asked to leave his accommodation and having nowhere to go, and receiving very poor treatment from a local dentist. Insufficient orientation and language learning time heightened the missionary's lack of fellowship and extreme isolation. Whenever he went out for a break, he sought counsel and debriefing, but he found none. On one occasion, he went with a group of missionaries whom he met at a guesthouse to see the film *The Joy Luck Club*. The movie was so relevant to what he was experiencing that he sobbed all the way through it. He returned to Australia at the end of his two-year assignment depressed and disillusioned.

About the same time, we had contact with a couple who had fairly similar experiences. However, they had received regular visits from concerned superiors and competent debriefing during each break. When they returned to Australia for home leave, they had grown as people and were positive about returning.

For Generation X, systems thinking is second nature, as seen in their group/team relationships. They typically practice mutual care, accountability, and acceptance. They accept responsibility for one another when things go wrong. In projects, individuals contribute what they do best. Equal value is assigned to all members. Members work best in synergistic teams. They work things out together by dialogue and discussion.

Generation X members become disillusioned and quickly lose heart when they do not find these practices within the mission organization. On the other hand, when they find such things overseas, they thrive. One young missionary on home assignment shared that a key coping strategy for him during his first term in Africa was an accountability/fellowship group. He met one morning per week for an hour with five of his peers. They addressed topics such as their devotional life, time with family, relationships with other missionaries, relationships with national friends, and ministry. Members shared both positive and negative experiences and prayed for one another. At the next meeting, they would revisit key areas of weakness and failure and would encourage and pray for one another.

3. Maximize Use of Resources

The best use of resources will become a priority for organizations which "think systems." Here are some areas which stand out to us as urgently needing systems thinking:

Generation X newcomers often have a great deal to give

When we were young missionaries, newcomers were put in the "seen but not heard" category for at least two years. Nowadays, a healthy organization will recognize that their young missionaries have much to give. Many Generation Xers have had training in personnel management as a normal part of other training and have also experienced competent management in secular employment. The examples of the missionary who started using evaluation forms and the accountability/fellowship group (see above) speak for themselves, as does the following example:

A couple in their first term were put in charge of field services and then of a large mission guesthouse with many related ministries. While their older predecessors had returned home severely burned out, this couple completed their assignment and arrived for their home assignment debriefing interview in high spirits, enthusiastic about returning to the same job. It emerged during the interview that before going overseas, the husband had been the project coordinator of a building company. Although he was a newcomer to overseas mission, his experience in people management and in accepting responsibility led to a satisfying and fruitful ministry—and a healthy guesthouse system.

Field leaders can't do it all

Too little time and training are common reasons for field leadership failure as pastoral carers. It is disillusioning for many Generation X newcomers to find people in leadership positions with very little knowledge of basic management procedures. All too often in the past, people have been thrust into leadership because of seniority or popularity with others in the missionary team. Many have reluctantly left the ministries to which they believe themselves to have been called and have been placed in administrative/personnel care positions for which they have not been trained.

Even those who have the training and skills find themselves with workloads too great to carry. "There is a huge demand for pastoral care all over our field," one field leader, close to tears, shared with us, "and every other field leader I talk to describes the same need. Most of us are close to burnout." This baby boomer leader was not critical of people needing pastoral care. He saw it as a legitimate need. However, he also saw that it was beyond him. He was trying at least to begin to address the need by appointing a missionary to pair people off for special care for one another. For those in isolated places, this was mainly by mail, but it was better than nothing. The systemic change needed in this case was to acknowledge that the average field leader usually has his hands full with administration and cannot also be held responsible for missionary pastoral care. One solution might be to set up a department led by trained personnel with people skills. Such people would be recruited for that purpose and would head a team of others set aside for pastoral care. Management and people skills training should be mandatory for all field leaders.

Many missionaries have pastoral care needs which are not being met

In the days of the booster missionary, the cry was, "What is the world coming to? What kind of missionaries need pastoral care? Surely the Lord is enough!" Thus, those with emotional problems concealed them until there was a crisis, and even then they were often advised to get their spiritual lives into shape. Thankfully, those days are now past. We are talking about caring for a generation of missionaries who choose mission organizations "because they seem the most caring" and whose greatest fear is working in an isolated place without the support of a team.

It is no longer good enough for us to say that we do not have the resources to care properly for our staff. If we do not do it, then we can expect impoverishment in ministry and loss of valuable workers.

But again, we have evidence that Generation Xers are right for today. Not only do they openly state their need for pastoral care, but they are also excellent at providing it for their peers. Thus, they are themselves important links in the pastoral care chain. They characteristically look out for and care for one another with sensitivity and compassion. We experienced this when one of us (Ruth) was suddenly called away from an orientation course in another country because her mother was dying. One of the Generation X candidates, with tears in his eyes, presented Ruth with a big bunch of flowers as she was leaving and hugged her, assuring her of their prayers. This remains a vivid, heartwarming memory.

Many missionaries are not receiving regular evaluation and mentoring

Many Australian mission agencies currently have an accepted policy of holding an annual evaluation and an end-of-term interview for every missionary. However, the policy is only effective if field staff see that it is done and done competently. Done well, it is not only useful as a means of ministry development, but it is also a valuable form of pastoral care. A person skilled in the area can pick up signs of depression, discouragement, burnout, marital disharmony, and other issues. If such things are addressed early and competently, they can salvage missionary careers. Task-oriented, cognitive concrete thinkers are often not well suited to this ministry. It needs sensitivity to body language, the capacity to read between the lines, and the ability to reflect empathetically upon what is being said. But although listening empathetically is comforting, it is vital that the listener be in a position to bring about change or at least to give feedback about why change cannot be made. Most missionaries deplore having to fill out questionnaires and/or bare their hearts to leaders if they never see any results or receive any follow-up.

Miscasting of missionaries continues despite job descriptions

The tyranny of the urgent often seems to fly in the face of common sense in the desperate search to find someone—anyone—to fill a particular position. Probably this is a carry-over from the booster era. At the very best, posting without regard to a missionary's gifts and training may result in mediocrity; at the worst, there will be devastation all around. It is known that realistic job previews have an important influence on future commitment. Full and accurate information given prior to departure generates expectations. Where these are not fulfilled, commitment is likely to be eroded (Meyer, 1997). Thankfully, the baby boomers have taught us that Christian organizations, more than any, should be bent on excellence in every aspect of ministry. One person working in a ministry which suits his/her gifts and training is probably worth 10 who are floundering in a ministry for which they are not suited. Similarly, we should not accept people who are not trained well enough for the ministry in view.

The reality also needs to be faced that however well trained candidates may be, their performance in a cross-cultural situation cannot be predicted (McKaughan, 1997). Therefore, it is always going to be a good investment for both candidates and the mission to send them for short-term experience, so that everyone can see how it goes. We need to learn from the experience of those boosters who went sight unseen and discovered too late that they should never have gone.

Generation X teams actually work

In most missions, there are people at the grass-roots level who could take far more responsibility than they are given. Some forward-looking missions have actually given grass-roots teams major responsibility for recruitment, training, and pastoral care of personnel—and in fact for all decision making at the local level. Experienced regional supervisors visit regularly to act as consultants and mentors and, if need be, as mediators. Vital to the success of such programs are regular in-service training courses in team building and pastoral care. For missions that are doing these things, while there may be early difficulties, it seems a promising approach. The Generation X special capacity for in-depth mutual caring, already mentioned, is probably the key to success.

4. Have Open Communication

Open communication within organizations is one sign of a healthy system.

Who says why missionaries leave?

The reasons that missionaries give for leaving are often very different from those officially recorded (Brierley, 1997; Donovan & Myors, 1997b). This raises again the question of how much attention is given to the organization's part in missionaries' attrition. Where intention to resign is foreshadowed, there would be great value in giving missionaries ample opportunity to explain their reasons. Generation Xers can be relied upon to be very open and honest, and they look for the same from those with whom they're relating. The focus should be on both the person concerned and the organization's system. It may be that even at this stage, the situation can be rectified. Even if it cannot, the missionary will go away having been given an opportunity to be heard and having been treated fairly by the organization. At the same time, leaders have had opportunity to discover in the system problem areas needing to be addressed. Success in this interaction will depend on open communication and willingness to listen on both sides.

Regular review of all aspects of every missionary's life and ministry would allow problem areas, whether in the missionary or the organization's system, to be identified and addressed early.

Another way of identifying perceived deficits in care is by confidential survey of the organization's whole missionary team. Repeat surveys could then be used to assess progress when changes have been made. For example, addressing areas of dissatisfaction highlighted in Table 2, such as inadequacy of debriefing on home leave, could send a message to missionary staff that they belong to an organization that cares about their well-being. Organizational research suggests that perception that their organization is making an effort on their behalf is as important to employees as the actual help received (Meyer, 1997). Missionaries are not looking for the impossible, but they need to feel that their well-being is a matter of concern to their leaders.

What do you tell your missionaries?

In many Christian organizations, there seems to be a reluctance by some in leadership to disclose to those concerned the whole truth about perceived problem areas in their performance. This hesitancy is something affecting leaders at all levels. Some leaders have difficulty in confronting. Others seem to feel that it is kinder, more humane, or perhaps even more spiritual ("Christians should not be in conflict") to water down the truth. In fact, the opposite is the case. It is dehumanizing and deeply wounding for the people concerned. It is well known among people working with terminally ill patients that bad news is easier for most to handle than no news. Facing bad news very often helps people transcend their grief (McIntosh, 1974).

We have recently had contact with two families who were suddenly "invited to resign" by Christian organizations. In both cases, the employing organization had not been open about the reasons, and so the people concerned were angry and frustrated that they could not present their side of whatever the case was. They felt betrayed after years of ministry which they had thought was acceptable. Lack of open communication not only prevents appropriate closure, but also undermines trust in the organization. Worst of all, it leaves matters unresolved and so detracts from capacity for future ministry. These problems might be addressed, at least in part, by teaching leaders improved methods of communication and conflict resolution, along with ways of handling grief and loss.

5. Match Worldview

A healthy organization system matches the way it does mission to the worldview of Generation X. It is clear from much that has been said already that Generation X members were made for a systems approach. They are experienced in it. They understand their part in it. They are committed to it. Organizations could benefit greatly by receiving what these individuals have to offer and by changing their way of doing things to signal to them that this is an organization in which Xers would feel comfortable. Few things speak more loudly than a team approach at every stage of missionary life and an acknowledgement of the foundational need for good pastoral care, beginning with a willingness to recruit teams and train them as a group. Participative leadership and the priority given to short-term experience programs also speak of an understanding and validation of the Generation X worldview. Finally, all measures taken to build relationships and to inspire candidates with the organization's vision will resonate with today's young missionaries. All of these things are part and parcel of a systems approach to mission in a postmodern world—an approach which really works.

Conclusion

The reinvented commitment called for today involves a significant change by organizations in the way they do mission. It means a commitment by the organization to the missionary at a depth matching the missionary's commitment to the organization. For too long, organizational commitment has been assumed to be mainly the missionary's responsibility. Organizational commitment involves emotional attachment and a shared vision. Generation X members have great capacity for both. However, for maximum effectiveness and perseverance in ministry, they need to know that the organization is committed to them.

If organizations could really grasp the potential of a systems approach in their thinking about mission, remarkable changes would follow. In the first place, the quality of life of every member would be likely to improve, and better use would be made of existing resources. In the second place, there would be the unexpected bonus of the contribution of the systems-thinking Generation X individuals. For them, there would be a new freedom and empowerment for ministry, leading inevitably to a deepening trust and commitment both ways.

Reflection and Discussion

1. What characteristics of Generation Xers help them to fit into developing churches?

2. Consider the case described in this article, of the young, single, first-term missionary who was sent to teach English at a university in a closed country. In what ways did the organizational system fail him? What could have been done better on his behalf?

3. What could be done to give Generation X members a greater sense of belonging to and identifying with the vision of your organization?

4. For high-quality organizational commitment, who in general needs to accommodate most—Generation X missionaries or organizations? Why?

5. How would an organization with a healthy system support its field leaders?

References

Beaudoin, T. (1998). *Virtual faith: The irreverent spiritual quest of Generation X.* San Francisco, CA: Jossey-Bass.

Becker, T., & Billings, R. (1993). Profiles of commitment: An empirical test. *Journal of Organizational Behaviour, 14*, 177-190.

Brierley, P. (1997). Missionary attrition: The ReMAP research report. In W. Taylor (Ed.), *Too valuable to lose: Exploring the causes and cures of missionary attrition* (pp. 85-103). Pasadena, CA: William Carey Library.

Covey, S. (1991). *The seven habits of highly effective people*. New York, NY: Simon/Schuster.

Donovan, K. (2000, Winter). From separation to synergy: Receiving the richness of Generation X. *Zadok Perspective*. Paper S10.

Donovan, K., Griffin, B., & Myors, R. (2001). *Could it be the organization? Attrition in Australian missionaries*. Paper in preparation.

Donovan, K., & Myors, R. (1997a, July). *Missionary propensity to resign: Summary of survey findings*. Paper presented at Missions Interlink Forum.

———. (1997b). Reflections on attrition in career missionaries: A generational perspective into the future. In W. Taylor (Ed.), *Too valuable to lose: Exploring the causes and cures of missionary attrition* (pp. 41-73). Pasadena, CA: William Carey Library.

Eisenger, R., Huntington, R., Hutchison, S., & Sowa, D. (1986). Perceived organizational support. *Journal of Applied Psychology*, *71*, 500-507.

Goldenberg, I., & Goldenberg, H. (1985). *Family therapy: An overview*. Monterey, CA: Brooks/Cole Publishing Company.

Grenz, S. (1996). *A primer on postmodernism*. Grand Rapids, MI: Eerdmans.

Mackay, H. (1997). *Generations*. Sydney, NSW, Australia: Pan Macmillan Australia.

McIntosh, J. (1974). Processes of communication, information seeking, and control associated with cancer. *Social Science and Medicine*, *8*, 167-187.

McKaughan, P. (1997). Missionary attrition: Defining the problem. In W. Taylor (Ed.), *Too valuable to lose: Exploring the causes and cures of missionary attrition* (pp. 15-24). Pasadena, CA: William Carey Library.

Meyer, J. (1997). Organizational commitment. *International Review of Organizational Psychology*, *12*, 175-227.

Nygren, D., & Ukeritis, M. (1993). *The future of religious orders in the United States*. Westport, CO: Praeger.

Wilcox, D. (1995). Who perseveres? A discriminant analysis of missionary school personnel by intention to extend service. *Journal of Psychology and Theology*, *23*, 101-114.

Kath Donovan *(left) and* ***Ruth Myors*** *(right) are partners in the Christian Synergy Centre, an organization set up in 1986 for member care of missionaries. Both were missionaries—Kath for 17 years as a medical doctor in Papua New Guinea and Ruth for 23 years as a nurse and then a radio scriptwriter in East Africa. On her return to Australia, Ruth trained as a psychologist, specializing in assessment, debriefing, and counseling of missionaries. Together, they conduct enrichment seminars for missionaries on home assignment, reentry retreats, and day seminars. Over the years, they have been closely involved with the Evangelical Missions Association (NSW), with Missions Interlink, and with individual mission organizations on councils and in consultative and speaking/teaching capacities. They also spend time in research and writing. Kath has written* ***Growing Through Stress*** *(Aquila),* ***The Pastoral Care of Missionaries*** *(BCV), and* ***Taking the Mystery out of Malaria****. Email for both Kath and Ruth: donovank@turboweb.net.au.*

Special thanks to Barbara Griffin with WEC for her helpful review of this article.

30

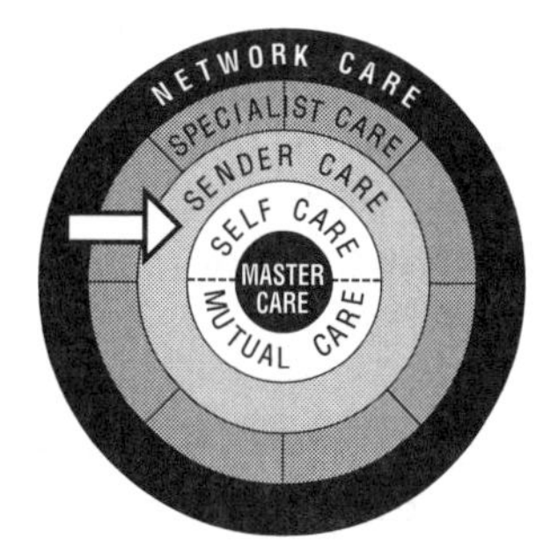

Running Well and Resting Well: Twelve Tools For Missionary Life

Kelly O'Donnell
Michèle Lewis O'Donnell

Mission personnel need a variety of supportive resources to help them grow personally and remain effective. This chapter presents 12 tools that missionaries can use during the different phases of missionary life. These tools can be adapted for your use.

There are two metaphors in the book of Hebrews which are especially relevant for mission personnel. These metaphors are the intertwining, balancing concepts of running with endurance the race set before us (Heb. 12:1-2) and being diligent to enter into God's rest (Heb. 4:9-11). Simply put, we need to "run well" and "rest well."

Running well involves staying focused on Jesus, so that we are not distracted by anything which hinders our life with and work for Him. Resting well means embracing the atoning work of Christ, so that in knowing His deep love for us, we can be at peace with and renewed in Him. Both of these concepts are foundational for our health throughout the various phases of the missionary life cycle. From recruitment through retirement, they impart a healthy balance between our "doing" and "being."

The same discipline that Paul said is needed to "run to win" (1 Cor. 9:24-27) is also needed so that we can "rest to win" (Matt. 11:25-30). Think of member care as a discipline. It is a personal, community, and specialized practice—an *intentional* practice—to help renew us and to help us remain resilient.

In this chapter, we share 12 growth tools for individuals, couples, teams, families, departments, and organizations. These tools can be used during the various stages of the missionary life cycle:

- Pre-field—recruitment, selection/candidacy, deputation, training.
- Field—first term, additional terms, change in job/location/organization.
- Reentry—furlough, home assignment, returning to the field later in life.
- Post-field—end of service, retirement.

For additional information on the missionary life cycle, as well as exercises for personal growth, see Morgan, 2001; O'Donnell, 1988, 1992; chapter 23 of this volume on helping ourselves and others, especially the CHOPS Inventory; and chapter 38 on team resiliency, including the reference section.

1. Selection Criteria: Eleven Cs for the Seven Seas

This worksheet explores 11 important factors which should be assessed before one becomes part of an organization or a team. Each criterion begins with the letter "C"—hence the name of the worksheet. The worksheet can be used for screening potential workers. Individuals who are considering becoming candidates can use the form, as well as organizations. Newly formed teams can also use this exercise as a point of departure to discuss who they are, their backgrounds, and their motivations and expectations for the team. In addition, the worksheet can be useful for teams going through a major transition period, such as a change in goals or the addition of new members.

- *Calling*—to a job/profession, to a country, to a people, to the organization, to the team, spiritual "call."
- *Character*—emotional stability, resiliency, strong and weak points.
- *Competence*—gifts and skills, training, preparation, experience.
- *Commitment*—to "calling," job, cross-cultural work, organization, team, people.
- *Christian experience*—spirituality, previous related work.
- *Cross-cultural experience*—experience living and relating with people from different cultures.
- *Compatibility*—with team goals, organizational ethos and doctrine, cultural, relational, spoken and unspoken expectations.
- *Confirmation*—from family, friends, organization, church, inner peace.
- *Corporal health*—overall physical wellness.
- *Cash*—financial assets, overall financial support system.
- *Care network*—friends and senders who will provide encouragement and support.

2. Screening for Workers: Ten Areas for Assessing Suitability for Service

This material is based on a modified clinical interview to help identify significant personal problems in potential staff. We developed this sheet in response to the requests of several field leaders who were in isolated settings and who could not easily consult with a mental health specialist. Many of these leaders were dealing with team members who had never been adequately screened and whose personal problems were disrupting team life. This material is intended to be used by mission leaders with personnel responsibility and training. Note, though, that in some countries such as the USA, there are legal requirements against discrimination in the selection process based on mental or other disabilities. Also, job-related skills are the focus of assessment, rather than personal struggles or mental disorder.

Some Suggestions

During the interview process, try to make the experience as supportive as possible. Remember, in some ways you and the candidate may be interviewing each other, as the candidate is also assessing the work setting. Be friendly, and establish rapport. Remember to ask questions in a non-threatening way, highlighting the person's strengths, though not being afraid to ask hard questions. Be sensitive to the person's cultural background and possible need for a translator. Clearly state the conditions for confidentiality, the purpose and procedure for the interview, and how the shared information will be used.

Avoid making quick judgments concerning suitability based only on first impressions. Remember that the best predictor of future behavior is past behavior, so be sure to explore previous experiences. Ask for specific examples, and do not be content with vague or general answers. Be sure to use this sheet in conjunction with references, past performance appraisals, an interview with the spouse, and a thorough application form that also includes questions about children (behavioral problems, anxiety or emotional struggles, peer relationships, developmental delays, learning difficulties). Whenever possible, seek out the advice of a mental health professional, even if it be through email. Finally, the main concern is not that a person may have struggles, but what he/she is doing to grow and help resolve such struggles.

1. Current Interests and Concerns

- How do you spend your time?
- What things do you most like to do?
- Favorite reading materials/books?
- How are you feeling these days?
- Do you have any problems sleeping or eating?
- Any medical problems?
- Are you using medication?
- How are your diet and nutrition?
- Would you like to share about any personal concerns or struggles? (Establish rapport and ease into the interview. Maybe save this question until later—see point 4 below—although if the candidate is going through a current crisis, talking about it right away may be helpful.)

2. Relationships

Evaluate how the candidate will do in a team setting and under stressful circumstances:

- Describe the quality of your relationships with others—friends, leaders, colleagues, spouse, and children.
- Any marital problems?
- What are some marital strengths?
- Describe some positive and negative past team experiences.
- Is it easy or difficult for you to forgive someone? Give examples.
- Discuss your relationship with leadership/authorities.

3. Family History

Explore what family issues/dysfunctions—both current family and family of origin—the candidate might be bringing with him/her:

- Have any family members suffered from a serious mental disorder?
- Marital instability?
- Child abuse, alcoholism, or general family dysfunction?
- What do people in your family think about your work?

4. Clinical Problems

- Is there any past or current history of any of the following?
    - Depression (significant times of feeling worthless, helpless, discouraged).
    - Anxiety (excessive concern about a person, event, situation).
    - Phobias (unusual fears of people, objects, experiences).
    - Bulimia/anorexia (problems with eating and purging or simply not eating, accompanied by weight changes).
    - Suicidal ideas/trying to hurt self or others.
    - Sexual addictions (pornography, compulsive masturbation, etc.).
    - Violence/poor anger management.
    - Substance abuse/addiction (including large doses of coffee/tea).
    - Gambling addictions/poor money management.
    - Delusions and hallucinations (significant problems in the way the candidate thinks or perceives the world—e.g., preoccupation with being persecuted or followed, exaggerated sense of importance/grandiosity).

- Learning disabilities (e.g., significant problems with reading/writing).
- Previous traumas.
- Burnout (being incapacitated physically and emotionally due to chronic levels of stress).
- Unwanted habits.
- Grief and bereavement (loss due to death, multiple moves, job change, etc.).
- Hormonal imbalance.
- Legal problems/arrests.
- Occult involvement.

■ Have you tried to get help in these areas? If so, how? (You may have to define these conditions in terms of specific symptoms, but it is very important to explore these areas in concrete ways. Some areas to probe which could uncover problems include sleep activity, interest in things one usually enjoys, guilt, energy, time with friends, fears, concentration, appetite, and sexuality.)

5. Previous Help/Treatment

Determine if the person has been under the care of medical or mental health professionals. For how long and for what reasons? Do not gloss over this area!

■ Have you had any psychiatric hospitalizations or outpatient therapy?

■ Any medical problems/surgery or head traumas?

6. Work Performance

How might the person fit into the new work setting, given past work experiences and preferences?

■ What setting will you be working in, and what types of stressors will you face?

■ How have you done in past work positions?

■ Discuss reasons for leaving previous jobs.

■ Identify the type of leadership with which you work best.

■ What types of leadership experiences and positions have you had?

■ Refer to results of previous testing, if known.

7. Spiritual Issues

Look for honest appraisal of spirituality, not getting too spiritual or overemphasizing either their importance or what God is doing through them:

■ How is your relationship with God?

■ How much time do you spend in prayer and Bible reading each day/week?

■ How much fellowship with Christians do you have?

■ Describe your involvement in a church.

■ Describe any areas in which you feel "stuck."

8. Personal Characteristics

Explore the candidate's capacity for openness and insight:

■ Identify a few personal qualities that are positive and some that are negative.

■ How might your positive characteristics help or hinder a team/setting where you might work?

9. Observations During Interview

Note the candidate's appearance, clothing, hygiene, facial expressions, behavior, unusual mannerisms, emotions displayed, speech/unusual words, thought content, eye contact, posture. How does the person relate to you? Can you connect with him/her interpersonally? What is your "gut level" feeling? (Beware of your own possible distortions/biases!)

10. Additional Comments

Make additional comments, discuss other assessment areas, and answer any questions the candidate may have for you.

3. Thirteen Survival Premises/Promises*

Have you ever had a look at your assumptions regarding what it takes to do well in missions? We all have certain assumptions about how life and missions work. Let's explore some of them. Read through the 13 statements below. Which ones make sense to you? What other assumptions would you list? Try doing this together as a group exercise with your team or department. How do these items apply to your life?

1. Life is difficult, regardless of where you are located and what you are doing. Only people trying to sell you something might say something different.
2. We are created human and are called to be mission workers, not the other way around. A human doing is not a human being.
3. Failure and casualties are inevitable in mission work.
4. The grass might be greener on the other side, but the manure is just as deep.
5. You can try to do anything in life you want; you only have to face the consequences.
6. With enough time and effort, we still cannot accomplish everything that we want.
7. The ideal team member never joins a team.
8. The healthy are usually too healthy to become frontline workers.
9. You are really someone special, but you are really not so special.
10. More people would be involved in missions if there were more unreached people groups in Switzerland and Hawaii.
11. You may never know why.
12. You probably have many other assumptions, some of which you may not be aware of.
13. These 13 premises are actually promises.

4. Some Core Challenges of Missionaries

This is a discussion tool to explore some of the core issues of missionary life. It can be used by individuals or groups. By "core" we mean those inner struggles that we wrestle with—the matters of the heart—which are often stimulated by external circumstances or problems. Try to identify how each of these issues is or has been part of your life, your family, and/or your team. What helps you work through these issues? What other areas would you include as being core challenges?

- *Lack of forgiveness*—holding on to perceived injustices which arise from conflict with colleagues, the host culture, frustration with oneself, etc.
- *Staying centered*—remaining connected with self and God in the midst of many responsibilities and the demands of living.
- *Focusing on your own interests*—self-preoccupation to the exclusion of others' needs; not checking to see how people around you are doing.
- *Drifting*—getting off the main tasks and the reason you work in missions via distractions, interruptions, avoiding responsibility, etc.
- *Transitional grief*—the pain from saying many good-byes, multiple moves, missing loved ones, unresolved relationship issues, etc.
- *Contentment*—being satisfied in knowing that you are obeying God in spite of minimal work results, pressures to perform, and limited sense of fulfillment in your work.
- *Pessimism*—losing perspective on the good things in life subsequent to the chronic exposure to human problems and misery.
- *The Midlife Club*—searching for "greener grass on the other side of the fence," often characteristic of those in mid-

* Originally published in the special member care issue of the *International Journal of Frontier Missions* (O'Donnell, 1995). Used by permission.

life and in missions for 10-plus years. Some examples:

- *Club Mediterranean*—"Yes, God, I hear you calling me to work with the affluent in the Bahamas and Beverly Hills. Please?"
- *Club Mediocrity*—"I am out of touch with my field and the work world back home. What can I do? I am out of date. I guess I have nowhere else to go except to stay in missions."
- *Club Middle Manager*—"God is calling me now to supervise others, after having worked on the field for awhile. Great, I was getting tired of it anyway. Now I'll be a consultant in a 'safer' position. I can help from afar, help from a computer screen, and help support the missions 'machine.' Hey, I can tell younger people what to do."
- *Club Midlife Bulge*—"I don't wanna do nothin'. I've earned the break and the fancy car. I've put in my time. I just wanna get fat."
- *Club Miscellaneous*—list your favorite club(s) here. Some examples:
  - *Club Martyr*—"I need to 'club' myself and feel perpetually guilty for something I did or did not do in the past."
  - *Club Martini*—"I probably won't admit it, but I am developing a compulsive habit to avoid dealing with inner areas of pain, such as the reality of aging, limited achievement, ongoing family tensions, etc., and covering up the pain by seeking out experiences that sedate or stimulate me."

5.
Personal Growth Plan*

The purpose of this exercise is to plan for, stimulate, and monitor your own growth—growth in your character, skills, and spirituality. Complete this worksheet (or something like it) once a year, and talk about it with a friend or leader.

Part 1: Personal Profile

1. List your current interests—things you do which give you personal satisfaction and pleasure (e.g., reading, sports, music).
2. List your current dislikes—things you do which you do not enjoy or which you feel you are not good at (e.g., teaching, poor habits, exercise).
3. Describe a few of your strengths.
4. Describe some of your limitations and growth areas.
5. List your current work responsibilities. Summarize your job clearly in one sentence.
6. List any other responsibilities you have (personal, professional, social, family).
7. How do your current responsibilities compare with your stated interests/strengths and limitations/dislikes?
8. What would you like to be doing in the next five years? Write a brief statement about your future roles and responsibilities—both personal and work-related.
9. What are you doing to further your spiritual life? Be specific. List areas of struggle.
10. What helps you maintain emotional stability and keeps you emotionally healthy? What do you do and how often?
11. In what ways do you continue your learning and build upon your strengths/skills?
12. Describe your relationship with your family here/back home. Any areas to improve?
13. Describe your relationship with your team/department/work/community. Any areas to improve?
14. Describe your relationship with the local community/nationals. Any areas to improve?

* This exercise is based on an initial self-assessment tool put together by the Personnel Department of the U.S. Center for World Missions in Pasadena, California. Used by permission.

Part 2: Personal and Professional Development Plan

Based on your previous answers, identify at least five specific objectives that you want to accomplish in the next 12 months. Choose objectives that are reasonably obtainable and that can be measured. Set dates for when you want to have them completed (e.g., lose five kilograms by September 1, read two books on cross-cultural relief work within the next three months, raise financial support level by 25% by the end of the year). Outline the steps you will take to accomplish each objective. Be specific. Also describe how you will evaluate your progress. Here is a short example:

Objective 1: Send newsletters to 50 friends three times a year.

Date: Mail newsletters in late April, August, and December.

Strategy: Address envelopes in advance; keep newsletter to two pages; revise it twice; include a one-page insert of interest.

Assessment: Show team leader each newsletter; ask for feedback from a few supporters on the content and style of the newsletter.

6. Job Feedback Form

This form will help you look at how your overall team/department is doing. It is intended to stimulate mutual feedback between you and your supervisor/leader and between group members when done as a joint exercise. It is also meant to complement but not to replace the use of performance appraisals. It is hoped that your assessment will lead to constructive changes for you and your work. Use a scale of 1 to 5, where 1 = strongly disagree and 5 = strongly agree, to rate the 15 areas that follow. Feel free to make additional comments for any of the items.

____ 1. The objectives of my team/department are clear to me.

____ 2. The objectives were formed with ample discussion and prayer.

____ 3. I am involved in the decision-making process in my work area.

____ 4. We meet often enough as a group.

____ 5. There is a good sense of team spirit in our work.

____ 6. The communication process is adequate within our group.

____ 7. I understand what is expected of me.

____ 8. I receive timely and sufficient feedback on my work.

____ 9. I feel respected and encouraged by my leader/supervisor.

____ 10. I feel encouraged and respected by my colleagues.

____ 11. I regularly try to encourage and support my colleagues.

____ 12. My communication with my leader/supervisor is adequate.

____ 13. I have sufficient time to fulfill my responsibilities.

____ 14. I am growing as a person as a result of my work involvement.

____ 15. Overall, I am satisfied with and enjoy my work.

■ Find your overall rating (total score divided by 15). Then find the composite score for your group (total scores divided by 15, then divided by the number of people in the group).

■ Make any additional comments on the following areas:

- Ways to improve the work we do.
- Ways to work better as a team.
- Personal areas/struggles for me that affect my work.
- Any additional concerns or suggestions.

7. Routine Debriefing Interview*

The purpose of a debriefing session is to help a worker review his/her experience on the job. This debriefing is more of a routine nature and is not intended to be used with crisis workers or those who go through a traumatic event. During routine debriefing, the worker is given the opportunity to express feelings, explore the high and low points of work, express concerns, put more closure on unresolved areas, and get a better perspective on the overall experience. The interviewer's role is to listen and help clarify, being careful to make sure the worker addresses the relevant aspects of his/her work. Debriefing does not involve counseling or performance evaluation. Keep these separate.

1. General

- What were a few rewarding aspects of your time there? Why?
- What were a few disappointing aspects of your time there? What could have prevented these or encouraged you more?

2. Work

- Summarize your job responsibilities while there.
- Was your job challenging and rewarding to you? Explain.
- How were you able to exercise your gifts and abilities?
- Are you satisfied with your contribution to your work/team?
- How was your health? How did it affect your work?
- How was your financial support level?

3. Language/Culture

- What aspects of the culture did you enjoy the most? Why?
- What aspects of the culture were the hardest for you (practices, beliefs, values)?
- What was language learning like for you? Any suggestions for improvement?
- Describe the relationships you were able to develop with nationals.
- How did the cultural and language adjustment affect your self-concept; relationship with your spouse/person with whom you live/work partner; parenting; relationship with your teammates; relationship with your team/work leader?

4. Personal

- What have you learned the most about yourself during your time there?
- Have you seen or developed any new strengths?
- Are you aware of any weaknesses that surfaced?

5. Spiritual

- In what ways have you grown spiritually—what have you learned, and how was your relationship with God?

6. Closing

- What are your plans for furlough/returning to your home?
- How could your sponsoring agency encourage/support you during this time?
- Is there anything about your next assignment that you would like to discuss?
- Is there anything else that you want to share about your time?
- Do you have any other comments or recommendations for the sponsoring organization?

Close by expressing gratitude for their work and who they are. Affirm them and their contributions.

7. Interviewer's Comments and Recommendations

Add any comments and recommendations here.

---

* This is a generic form that was developed by the organization Frontiers, which we have adapted. Used by permission.

8. Priority Time for Busy Couples

Priority time is a commitment made by a husband and wife to one another to spend a minimum of two hours a week specifically sharing their lives together.

The demands of missions sometimes place extra pressures on marriage relationships. This means we need to give the relationship special attention. Many couples find that unless they commit themselves to have a pre-arranged time of meeting together, communication gets neglected within the marriage, and their relationship declines.

The time needs to be scheduled to avoid interruption, e.g., at a time when children are asleep or at school. It should be planned together to fit with each other's schedules.

Suggestions of What to Do During Priority Time*

- Read together and discuss a book about marriage or family.
- Go out for a walk, or go out for coffee and cake or a meal. Relax together.
- Ask each other, "What pressures do you feel you have been under recently?" Pray for each other. Don't counsel each other. Listen closely and pray!
- Pray for one another's service for the Lord. Try to help each other identify your respective spiritual gifts and talents. Discuss how you can help one another be more effective in your service for the Lord.
- Discuss and pray about your financial needs and your giving to others.
- Discuss the needs of your children. Pray for them: for character growth, for their relationship with the Lord, for their relationship with their friends, for their school activities, etc.
- Ask each other the question, "Have I hurt you by anything I've said or done recently?" Resolve any of these hurts that may have occurred by asking for forgiveness and forgiving one another.
- Each write down what you think your partner's main character strengths are; then share them with each other. Encourage one another.
- Each write down what you think are your own personal character weaknesses. Ask your partner to pray for God to strengthen you in these areas of weakness.
- Play a game together.

Application

Set time aside to discuss the above suggestions with your marriage partner. Decide on a time when you could meet regularly and begin to do some of the things suggested.

Get together with the married couples on your team or in your area. Encourage each other to share some of the pressures that you feel in your marriage relationships. Help each other by sharing how you have handled these pressures.

We have found that partnering with another couple for mutual growth and accountability is key to make sure that priority times are successful.

We also like to encourage couples to start out their priority time with a tool developed by the Maces (1977) in *How to Have a Happy Marriage,* which looks at how much marital potential a couple thinks they have already developed. Each of the items below is scored on a scale from 1 to 10. The higher the score, the more potential is felt to have been fulfilled. It is the marriage that is being scored, not the individuals. This is done individually and then shared/compared with each other. A good discussion then usually ensues. Additional items can be added that are relevant to your situation.

- Common goals and values.
- Communication skills.
- Effective ways of handling conflict.

* This material is from Barry Austin's (1995) resource manual, *Personnel Development and Pastoral Care for YWAM Staff*. Used by permission.

- Commitment to growth of the marriage relationship.
- Expressions of appreciation and affection.
- Cooperation.
- Agreement on gender roles.
- Sexual fulfillment.
- Money management.
- Time management.
- Decision making.
- Interaction with children.
- Interaction with extended family.
- Issues of health—exercise, nutrition, etc.
- Involvement with work or leisure activities.
- Spiritual growth.

9. Family Scenarios

Read through the three fictitious scenarios below. Respond to the question at the end of each scenario as if you were a mission leader, a member care consultant, or a friend.

Scenario 1

An Asian family is having trouble dealing with stress while going through the orientation program of their agency. The program takes place in a North African country and requires that the participants move to a new city every two to four weeks over a three-month period. The parents are concerned that they have been moving around too much, both pre-field and now during orientation, and that their two children are suffering as a consequence. Their girl, age 8, has started wetting the bed three times a week at night. Their boy, age 2, is not eating much food.

- What could be done to help this family?

Scenario 2

A five-year-old boy from Europe does not want to go to his Portuguese-speaking primary school in Luanda, Angola, which he has been attending for two months. He is in preschool and complains that some of the other kids make fun of him by sticking out their tongues at him and saying that his drawings are ugly. For the last month, the boy has often whined and complained while getting ready for school. When he returns from school, it is hard for his parents to make contact with him, and he acts mean towards other family members.

- How would you help this boy?

Scenario 3

A couple with no children are having marital problems. They have been working on a team as agricultural tentmakers among an Asian group for the past five years. The husband is Nigerian, and the wife is from Côte d'Ivoire. The work is going well, but the long hours needed to travel and provide assistance have affected their relationship—or so they say. Both acknowledge that they have come from difficult family backgrounds, in which there was alcoholism, some spiritistic practices, and poor parental modeling of conflict resolution. They saw a counselor back in Côte d'Ivoire while on furlough, and they attended a marriage retreat on the field, but no lasting changes have occurred. The wife's relationships with the local women are significant, and she is having an impact in their lives. The husband has no close relationships outside of his work and is wondering if he is in a midlife crisis. The agency decides to let them continue on the field and to do the best they can until they can get some more help somewhere.

- How would you try to help this couple?

10. Career Consultation Cases

The two fictitious cases that follow look at some of the personal, work, and career issues facing cross-cultural workers. Read through the cases, and respond to the questions below. You are the member care consultant!

Case 1

Fred is 30 years old, married to Betty, and they have two kids—Sam, age 6, and Mary, age 4. They are Canadians. One year ago, they moved to an Asian country to provide some needed services to the people there. Fred was able to get a job as an English teacher at a university, teaching eight hours of class per week. Previously, he was an insurance salesperson. He has about 12 hours of preparation each week (correcting papers, planning lessons, and doing clerical tasks). Betty home schools Sam and basically is a house mom.

The climate is extreme—very hot in the summer and very cold in the winter. Because of this, some of the family's usual outdoor activities—such as walking together—are limited. They live in a two-bedroom apartment in a city of 100,000 people.

Fred and Betty study the local language each week, and they like practicing it with neighbors and in the market. They are not able to engage in much discussion yet, due to their language limitations. They are on email. Their financial support is adequate (they have a sponsoring agency to help support them), and they have no significant culture shock, although they miss friends and relatives.

They are part of an expatriate group of 10 that meets together for mutual support. They get along with the coordinator and other members. Twice a month, they get together for a two-hour meeting to discuss adjustment issues and exchange stories and advice. Fred enjoys helping to coordinate part of the discussion times.

Betty likes being a mom and is basically content in the new country (her first extended time overseas). Fred, though, is becoming restless, as he would really like to be doing more outside things in the host community (meeting people, talking about important matters of concern to the local people) and less time teaching English. Teaching English to internationals would probably be Fred's 20th job choice back in Canada. Fred is on a two-year contract, and it would not be possible to change jobs.

Fred sends an email message to you as his member care consultant, asking for your advice. Consider these questions in your response:

- What issues are present—what is really going on in this case?
- What materials and interventions would help?
- What additional information is needed?
- Are there any ethical, family, or organizational issues? If so, discuss these.
- How is this case similar to other situations of which you are aware?

Case 2

Dear Member Care Consultant,

I am writing to see if you could help me with some of my job-related struggles. My name is Theresa Worker, and for the past several months I have been disenchanted with my work. I would appreciate any advice and suggestions you could give me. Thanks.

Let me first give you a bit of my background and then ask you some questions. Here goes. I have worked for an international aid agency for five years. During this time, I have worked in three different settings: I helped administer two training schools, did secretarial work, and participated on a three-month relief team. I am single, Australian, aged 26, female, and am presently working at one of the agency offices in Europe while I try to sort out what I want to do. I completed two years of university prior to joining the company and am also fairly fluent in German. Do you need any additional information about me? Please let me know. Now for my questions:

- How do I know if I am effectively doing what someone in cross-cultural and humanitarian work does?
- How do I assess my strengths/weaknesses as a worker when I have worked in different settings and transitioned so much over the last five years?

- How can I set goals for the future to be more effective?
- How do I know the type of job in which I can work best?
- Do other people go through this type of frustrating experience?

In the past, I think I have been too flexible with regards to my work preferences within our company—that is, I have often worked in jobs because no one else was available to do them, and I felt it was right just to try to fill in. I would really appreciate your help as I try to assess my capabilities and involvement in this work.

Sincerely yours,
Theresa Worker

11. Crisis Intervention and Contingency Management

Workers who serve in cross-cultural settings are often subject to a variety of extreme stressors. Natural disasters, wars, sudden relocation, imprisonment, and sickness are but a few of the examples. Agencies that send their people into potentially adverse situations have an ethical responsibility to do all they can to prepare and support them. Here are four steps to help organizations better prepare for and manage crisis situations. Note that each step involves three levels of responsibility that need to be clarified: individual, organizational, and outside consultants. The four steps also overlap as you go about implementing them.

Step 1: Preparation

- *Contingency plans*—for individuals, families, teams, agencies, regions.
    - Risk assessment and management—monitoring at-risk zones.
    - Forming plans—hostage situations, natural disasters, evacuation, assault, moral failure.
    - Estate planning—writing a will, organizing and safeguarding important documents, etc.
- *Stress training*—developing coping skills via *in vivo* experiences (e.g., firearms, emergency rooms at hospitals) and simulation exercises, case studies, teaching, personal examples/reflections.
- *Pre-field and field orientation*—security guidelines, do's and don'ts, adjustment helps.

Step 2: Staying Alive

- *Using survival skills to stay alive, healthy, and sane*—to manage oneself, resources, and relationships.
- *Crisis management teams*—to monitor and make decisions during the crisis.
- *Human rights advocacy*—to use moral, legal, and political pressure.

Step 3: Crisis Intervention

- *Practical help to stabilize/protect*—ensure safety; provide food, shelter, and money.
- *Critical incident stress debriefing*—express thoughts and feelings related to the crisis.
- *Brief supportive counseling*—as needed for those affected by the critical incident(s).

Step 4: Aftercare

- *Therapy/counseling*—help with anxiety/PTSD and other adjustment problems.
- *Organizational review*—evaluate the causes, interventions, results/lessons of the crisis.
- *Follow-up*—contact those affected, implement suggested changes.

How to Use These Steps

- Use these steps as a grid—like a checklist—to consider your team/organization's readiness to handle adverse situations.
- Discuss this grid within your setting—team, organization, etc. Read through and discuss some key articles on crisis and contingency management within your respective agencies and settings. (See chapter 44 for references.)

- Take time to identify the types of crises your people are likely to face; identify some acceptable approaches to handling crises and providing care and follow-up; identify available resources to help.
- Review one or two crisis situations you have already had, discussing what was done well, what could have been done better, and the implications of each past experience for future situations.
- As a group exercise, refer to Goode (1995), and interact on the crisis intervention scenarios found at the end of his article.

12. Reentry Preparation

Returning to your home country can be an exciting and enriching experience! Whether your return is for a brief period of time, such as for furlough, or possibly permanently, adequate preparation is needed to get the most out of your life back home.

Preparation requires taking a close look at four areas:

- Who you are as a person.
- How you and your home culture may have changed.
- Your plans and goals when you are at home.
- Your strategies for adjustment.

The reentry process can be a bit like culture shock, in that you are called to meet basic needs in different and sometimes unfamiliar ways. Much of the stress experienced is brought on by returning to a setting—which includes family, friends, and work—that is presumed to be familiar. Often, the unexpected nature and the subtlety of changes in the setting are what create the greatest amount of stress.

In short, your way of thinking and doing things has changed. Sometimes it takes readjusting to your home culture to shed light on the nature of these changes.

Some common struggles during reentry include feeling disoriented and out of place, disillusionment, irritation with others and with certain aspects of the culture, a sense of loneliness or isolation, and depression. On the other hand, reentry can be a very positive experience, with minimal adjustment struggles. So do not let this list of struggles overwhelm you. Just be aware of them and prepare!

As you make preparations to return to your home country, we encourage you to reflect on a promise: "I will not in any way fail you nor give you up nor leave you without support. I will not, I will not, I will not in any degree leave you helpless, nor forsake nor let you down. Assuredly not!" (Heb. 13:15, Amplified).

Reentry Assessment

Several factors typically influence the adjustment process of workers returning to their home country. These factors involve your relationship with both the host culture and your original home culture, as well as some of your individual characteristics.

Respond to each of the 15 items on this worksheet to help you explore what reentry might be like for you. You might also want to do this exercise with/for other family members.

Host country

1. How long have you been away from your home country? Where have you lived since then?
2. In what ways have you identified with the host culture (language, customs, values, beliefs, dress, etc.)?
3. In what ways are the host culture and your home country similar and dissimilar (climate, geography, language, religion, standard of living, politics, customs, etc.)?
4. How fulfilled do you feel in your work and overall experience? What has it been like for you?
5. What do you think it will be like to be away from the host culture (saying good-bye to friends and places, stopping work)?

Worker characteristics

6. Describe your physical health, including stamina, nutrition, eating habits, medical problems, stress levels, and exercise.

7. Identify a few personal qualities that may help or hinder your adjustment back home. Discuss these with a trusted friend.

8. Have you or a friend noticed any important changes in how you think or behave since living in the host culture? List them.

9. Describe other transitions that you or family members are going through (recent marriage, childbirth, children leaving home, entering midlife or retirement, deaths).

10. How have you practically prepared for your return to your country of origin?

Home culture

11. How long will you be staying in your country of origin? List a few things that you think have changed for your family, friends, and home country. How might these impact you?

12. Describe the primary purposes/expectations for your return.

13. What have any previous reentry experiences been like? How can these past experiences help your upcoming reentry time?

14. To what extent have you stayed updated on events and changes back home (via reading, news, letters, phone calls, email, etc.)?

15. Describe the type of support groups you have back home (family, friends, work). How could they help you? With whom could you comfortably discuss your reentry experience?

References

Austin, B. (1995). *Personnel development and pastoral care for Youth With A Mission staff*. Nuneaton, UK: Author.

Goode, S. (1995). Guidelines for crisis and contingency management. *International Journal of Frontier Missions, 12*, 211-216.

Mace, D. (1977). *How to have a happy marriage*. Nashville, TN: Abingdon.

Morgan, D. (2001, May 23-27). *Spiritual formation during the missionary life cycle*. Presentation at the Third European Member Care Consultation, Budapest, Hungary. (Email: lifemetor1@msn.com)

O'Donnell, K. (1988). Developmental tasks in the life cycle of missionary families. In K. O'Donnell & M. O'Donnell (Eds.), *Helping missionaries grow: Readings in mental health and missions* (pp. 148-163). Pasadena, CA: William Carey Library.

———. (1992). Tools for team viability. In K. O'Donnell (Ed.), *Missionary care: Counting the cost for world evangelization* (pp. 184-201). Pasadena, CA: William Carey Library.

———. (1995, October). On behalf of the 10-40 window of the heart. *International Journal of Frontier Missions, 12*, 169, 223.

***Kelly O'Donnell and Michèle Lewis O'Donnell** are psychologists, based in Europe. They work out of an interagency member care center in France called Le Rucher, located close to Geneva. They have two children, Erin, aged 12, and Ashling, aged 8. Kelly and Michèle studied clinical psychology and theology at Rosemead School of Psychology, Biola University, where they earned their Doctor of Psychology degrees. Special emphases include crisis care, team building, expatriate family life, personnel development, and developing member care affiliations. Email: 102172.170@compuserve.com.*

Special thanks to Ruth Hucklesby and Liz Ippolito-Day for their helpful review of many of these tools. Thanks also to the colleagues who have used them and helped us refine them over the years.

31

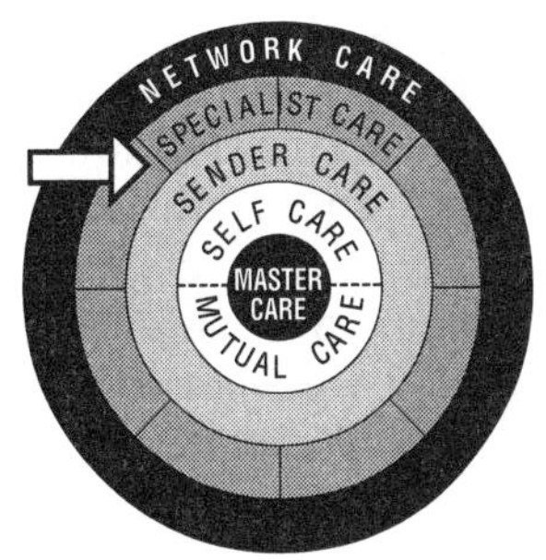

A Guest In Their World

KAREN CARR

Personal qualities and professional skills go hand in hand in working effectively in member care. Humility, cross-cultural sensitivity, a close walk with the Lord, and a commitment to be a learner are integral to the services which member care specialists provide. This is certainly true of mental health professionals working with mission personnel, as the five case studies in this chapter illustrate.

I am a clinical psychologist working full-time in the world of missions. I have discovered that there are certain values and assumptions that can serve as either bridges or roadblocks in the relationship between mental health professionals and mission administrators. Therapists or mental health consultants who want to work overseas with missionaries may need a new and different paradigm from the one they were given in their training programs, unless they have been a part of a program which is uniquely designed to equip mental health professionals for Christian service overseas.

I was trained in a secular clinical psychology program that was designed to prepare me for work in middle class America. In my program, I was taught to be an expert, but as Christians in this world, we must be servants and learners. I was taught to be non-directive and vague, but as Christian counselors, we must have something practical and tangible to offer. I was taught about confidentiality and advocacy, but not so much about their limits. I was taught about objectivity and about not having dual relationships, but then again my internship was not in a remote city of Africa. I learned secular theories regarding psychopathology that did not acknowledge the role of the soul and certainly not the healing power of the Lord. My missionary colleagues have taught me new lessons, and I'd like to share a few of them in this article.

It seems that the missions world has become much more open to the contribution and influence of the member care field and especially of mental health professionals, who are the focus of this article. Mental health professionals are needed and wanted in the missions community. Most often, they are used at the screening phase, but more are also being invited to come to the field to provide workshops, crisis intervention, or short-term counseling. These visits have the potential to encourage and build up (1 Thess. 5:11). Sometimes, however, they result in a mission administrator developing a fairly negative view of mental health professionals in general. Some of the things contributing to this negative view are the use of jargon, an absence of recognizable integration of faith and practice, a style of therapy that may not be contextually appropriate, and a misperception of the role and motives of mission administrators.

The following case studies illustrate how some of these barriers may develop. They are composites, and all names are fictitious.

Case Study 1

Dr. Tom Jenkins, a clinical psychologist, has a brother on the field and offers to provide a workshop and counseling for missionaries during the two weeks that he will be there visiting his brother. The director accepts his offer and asks him to send a brief resume for field members to read before he arrives. In his resume, Dr. Jenkins emphasizes his degree and explains that he uses a cognitive-behavioral theoretical approach. When he arrives on the field, he presents himself as an expert, describing his professional achievements in his home country.

While these credentials carry a certain weight and importance, they are not the leading quality that will bring trust or confidence from the missionary clientele. What may bring credibility on a standard resume or for a professional conference could raise more suspicion than acceptance in the missions world. While our degrees and areas of expertise and theoretical orientations are important to us (and maybe our colleagues), they will not generally impress one whose life experience may far exceed our own. Our credentials are relevant, but not as relevant as our cross-cultural understanding. Our language, whether written or verbal, needs to make a cultural shift, from an emphasis on professional expertise and clinical knowledge, to an emphasis on teachability, cultural sensitivity, and biblical understanding which reflect a genuine care for missionaries. In short, we must enter their world.

While he is on the field, Dr. Jenkins does a stress management workshop in which he gives tips on lowering stress levels. He suggests separating work from home life and maintaining firm margins and boundaries. He does not realize that there are rarely clear distinctions between work and home life in the average missionary's life. Dr. Jenkins explains the current theories on stress management, but he does not offer a scriptural basis in his teaching, nor does he promote a discussion on how spiritual resources are effective in managing stress on the field. He says little about his relationship with the Lord or any previous cross-cultural experience. As he works individually with missionaries who have been through recent losses and trauma, he discusses the impact on their job performance and their families. He does not draw out the spiritual dimensions of their grief, nor does he appreciate the depth of their struggle to give themselves permission to grieve their own losses when their national colleagues have suffered far more in their eyes.

If we are to be helpful in the culture of missions, we must have a well-grounded, deep, abiding trust in the Lord that permeates every aspect of our professional selves and naturally builds bridges, as we articulate our integration of faith and practice. This will manifest itself in a style that is genuinely humble and respectful, while also being competent and capable.

Case Study 2

Dr. Rashe Lui, a professional counselor, has been asked to come to the field for several weeks following a traumatic situation. One of the field members was raped and has left the field, but a number of her colleagues on the field are struggling with what happened and have asked to speak to a counselor. When Ms. Lui arrives, she sets up a schedule that allows individuals to sign up to see her. Several of the women she sees reveal that they were sexually abused as children, and this rape incident has stirred up troubling memories and feelings for them. Ms. Lui begins a process of intensive therapy with these women, assuming that they will continue this work with a local therapist after she leaves. Several weeks after she leaves, the administration is distressed to discover that several women in the branch can no longer perform their job duties because their functional level has so declined. Additionally, increased tension and stress have been present in their families.

Ms. Lui made several assumptions that may not be true. One assumption is that a local therapist would be available. Often, even if one is available, he or she may not speak the client's first language. Another assumption is that this kind of therapy work can be done on the field. I would propose that intensive therapy is not appropriate for the field, given the stresses and demands of field living, which require a great deal of energy. I believe that the most helpful form of therapy on the mission field is a brief, solution-oriented mode, which is educational, goal-oriented, and emphasizes strengths. Intensive work can be done in a less stressful, less demanding environment that may be available on a furlough or study leave.

Case Study 3

Nigel Smith, a qualified social worker, is asked to present at a field conference and decides to offer a workshop on grief and adjusting to loss. He makes himself available for several days after the workshop for any that want to come see him for a private counseling session. Mr. Smith emphasizes that these counseling sessions are completely confidential.

Tom and Betty have been on the field for 20 years. They have never been to see a counselor before, but both have been feeling fairly depressed and low energy, and they liked this counselor's presentation style in the workshop. As they talk with Mr. Smith, they help him understand that their new administrator has been abusive and critical. It seems that the administration has unreasonable expectations of them and does not at all understand their situation. In fact, the administration has asked them to go home to get some things taken care of, but they are convinced that this would only make things worse. They ask Mr. Smith to explain to the administration that they should stay on the field.

Although it seems obvious that Mr. Smith has only one side of the story and does not understand the system context of this situation, nevertheless he may be pulled to respond as an advocate for this couple. In fact, many counselors have fallen into this particular pitfall of advocating for the "client" missionary and becoming an adversary to the administrator. Our role, in contrast, should be to strengthen the entire system whenever possible. In this particular example, the counselor has not spoken with the administration so he does not know the circumstances of the couple being asked to leave the field. Because he has stressed absolute confidentiality, he has ruled out the possibility of a consultative, collaborative relationship with the administration. There may be possibilities he has not considered, such as moral lapse, job performance problems, interpersonal conflicts, or low financial support and debt.

Whether or not a missionary stays on the field is a complicated decision that involves a number of factors, including the person's mental health, support system, job performance, resources of the missions community, ethos of the organization, and the preferences of the family, home office, and supporting churches. As mental health professionals, we may have a contributing voice, but we do not have the right to be an authoritative or final voice in the decision. The administrator or field leader is the one who will remain on the field to care for and work with each of the missionaries there. We have the opportunity to coach and mentor administrators in the value of member care, if we take a supportive rather than an adversarial role with them.

Case Study 4

Dr. Jesse Pinto is a psychiatrist who has been interested in working with missions for many years. He has done some work with a mission agency which is based in his local area, and he eagerly accepts an invitation to travel to Africa to provide debriefing for a team of missionaries who have just been evacuated out of their country of service to another country in Africa.

As a medical doctor, Dr. Pinto is aware of the medical precautions he must take—he gets his yellow fever shot and gets started on malarial prophylaxis. Dr. Pinto has been following the international news and has some basic understanding of what has been happening politically in the country these missionaries have just left. His understanding of African politics and geography is minimal, however. He does not speak any French but will be traveling to a French-speaking country.

A combination of sleep deprivation, severe climate difference, language barriers, and general adjustment to new stimuli leads Dr. Pinto to feel much more tired than he expects. He is unable to keep the pace he had hoped to maintain. Upon arrival, he is also surprised to learn that the missionary team is a multi-national team with people from North America, the UK, Switzerland, Brazil, and Argentina. His materials are all in his first language with a lot of idioms, and as he looks over his handouts, he realizes that many of his examples are specific to his culture.

When Dr. Pinto facilitates the group and individual debriefings, he notes that some people seem uncommunicative. Some give very poor eye contact, some seem sullen, some seem despondent, and some seem angry. He interprets these behaviors within the context of what they would mean if someone were from his country. He does not appreciate or understand the cross-cultural interpersonal dynamics that he observes.

Dr. Pinto is especially uncomfortable when some of the members begin talking about the demonic aspects of what they have experienced. When some begin to talk about unexplained illnesses, curses, and demonic possession, he wonders about their grasp on reality. He does not have a spiritual framework to understand the spiritual battles and demonic activities that are commonly experienced in Africa. The missionaries served by Dr. Pinto are grateful for his availability and technical skills. They are gracious in their response to him, but privately and among themselves, they know that he is very limited in his understanding of what they have experienced.

There are several ways Dr. Pinto could increase his cross-cultural sensitivity. Before leaving his home country, he could familiarize himself with the geography, politics, religion, and culture of the country where he is going, through various news and written resources. He could also do some reading that would help him become more familiar with his own cultural values and how these are perceived by people of other cultures. He could find out in advance what nationalities he will be serving and could attempt to access resources in their mother tongue or consult with other mental health professionals from their home countries who could assist him. Upon arrival, he could spend some time with several missionaries not directly involved in the crisis, to gain a better understanding of the unique stresses and issues faced in this area. Finally, he could broaden and deepen his understanding of spiritual warfare as it is manifested in different parts of the world.

Building Relationships With Mission Personnel

Clearly, receiving training as a mental health professional (or any other health care/member care-related field) does not automatically qualify or prepare one for working with missionaries overseas. In general, however, mental health professionals have made a commitment to certain ethical principles, such as working only within their area of competence and expertise, working responsibly such that they do not harm their clients, and maintaining supervision and accountability as professionally needed. There is also an increasing commitment to cross-cultural awareness, and more training is available in this area within many of the mental health professional organizations around the world. These commitments can aid us in overcoming roadblocks and building bridges, as outlined below.

Roadblocks

- Expert mentality.
- Use of technical jargon.
- Non-directive, vague style.
- Longterm, intensive therapy model.
- Unstructured, loose use of time.
- Adversarial approach with leadership.
- Use of culturally biased materials.
- Slow response to crisis situations.
- Lack of accessibility.
- Assumptions about organizational needs.
- Inexperienced in cross-cultural counseling.
- Lack of follow-up.

Bridges

- Servant mentality.
- Humble approach.
- Integration of faith and practice.
- Biblical basis of teaching.
- Solution-focused, brief-therapy model.
- Brief, relevant workshops/devotionals.
- Knowledge of local resources.
- Knowledge of field history.
- Clear communication about confidentiality.
- Building trust and credibility through visits.
- Knowledge of demonic/spiritual warfare.
- Prayer with/for leaders.

Understanding the Mission Administrators' Perspective

Mental health professionals who take time to cultivate relationships with mission leadership will ultimately provide a better service to the missionaries on the field. Just as some psychotherapy models in the past ignored and alienated the family members of identified patients, seeing them as the source of the problem rather than pivotal to healing, so have some mental health professionals treated the mission community. Our challenge is to maintain good boundaries and competent, ethical professionalism, while also entering into relationships with missionaries and their leaders as genuine, vulnerable, co-laborers in Christ.

With these challenges in mind, we have the serious task before us of chipping away at some of the negative reputations and perceptions that have developed in the minds of many mission administrators towards mental health practitioners. Some of these perceptions are the result of actual experiences, and some based on bias or misperception. Regardless of the source, these are perceptions which can create barriers and which can perhaps be altered in the context of a genuine experience. Some examples of characteristics attributed to the "ineffective" mental health professional include evasiveness, permissiveness, promoting weakness, a touchy-feely approach, liberal theological views, and stirring up old issues which are better left alone.

Case Study 5: A Model Example

Heidi Schaeffer, a master's level counselor, is asked by a mission administrator to come to the field to do a workshop on transitions and to be available for counseling afterwards. She spends time via email and on the phone with the administrator, clarifying the expectations, needs of the community, values of the community, and recent crisis events within the community. She understands that even a crisis event that only involves one person can affect the entire community, because of the family nature of interdependence and support that is common in missionary groups. She probes further with this administrator to find out what his expectations are and who in the community might need additional attention. She clarifies before coming what will be kept confidential and what will be shared. Ms. Schaeffer talks openly with the administrator about the financial cost of her visit. They make an arrangement that covers the costs of her travel and provides for a modest honorarium. She works closely with the administrator to write a bulletin that will announce her coming and will explain her availability.

Ms. Schaeffer has been to this field before and is known by many of the missionaries there. She has developed the reputation of someone who is humble, unassuming, and available. She understands now the kinds of things that contribute to ongoing grief and stress in missionaries' lives. These are things like conflicts with others, saying good-bye to kids who will return to the home country for college, worrying about elderly parents, and severe sickness that is recurrent and life threatening in their friends and family on the field. She is aware of these things, and she prepares for her time on the field through prayer and the gathering of relevant resources.

When she meets with folks individually, she draws out their spiritual questions as well as their spiritual strengths and resources. Her work with them is brief and practical. She prays with them and commits to a follow-up plan with them. They know in advance what will and will not be communicated to their administrator. Though she is a guest in their world, they treat her as one of their own.

Conclusion

Mental health and other health care/member care specialists have a lot to contribute on the mission field. As in-house or outside service providers, we can offer workshops, consultation, assessment, and counseling. We can provide crisis intervention and debriefing. Our presence has the potential to be as Aaron and Hur were to Moses when they offered a very tangible way of providing strength, endurance, and courage in the battle (Ex. 17:12). But if we do not enter into their world with cultural sensitivity, we also have the potential to harm and do damage. Key to our effectiveness is working with mission leaders and building relationships with them. Together, we can better understand the member care needs of their people and provide the ongoing care that enhances a resilient and loving Christian community on the field. We have a lot to learn. And many from the missions community are willing and able to teach us and welcome us as guests in their world.

Reflection and Discussion

1. What are other values, assumptions, or behaviors that might be roadblocks between mental health professionals and missionaries?
2. How else can mental health professionals build bridges to missionaries and vice versa?
3. For each of the case studies, describe what you might do to improve the service being provided.
4. What could you do to become a better "guest in their world"? Or a better "host"?

5. In what ways might guests from Newer Sending Countries behave differently from guests from Older Sending Countries?

Suggested Reading

Bowers, J. (Ed.). (1998). *Raising resilient MKs*. Colorado Springs, CO: Association of Christian Schools International.

Bubeck, M. I. (1984). *Overcoming the adversary: Warfare praying against demonic activity*. Chicago, IL: Moody Bible Institute.

Dodds, L., & Dodds, L. (1997). *Collected papers on caring for cross-cultural workers*. Liverpool, PA: Heartstream Resources.

Foyle, M. (1987). *Overcoming missionary stress*. Wheaton, IL: Evangelical Missions Information Service.

Gardner, L. (1987). Proactive care of missionary personnel. *Journal of Psychology and Theology*, *15*, 308-314.

Gardner, R., & Gardner, L. (1992). Training and using member care workers. In K. O'Donnell & M. O'Donnell (Eds.), *Missionary care: Counting the cost for world evangelization* (pp. 315-331). Pasadena, CA: William Carey Library.

Johnston, L. (1988). Building relationships between mental health specialists and mission agencies. In K. O'Donnell & M. O'Donnell (Eds.), *Helping missionaries grow: Readings in mental health and missions* (pp. 449-457). Pasadena, CA: William Carey Library.

Jones, M. (1995). *Psychology of missionary adjustment*. Springfield, MO: Logion Press.

Kraft, C. (1992). *Defeating dark angels: Breaking demonic oppression in the believer's life*. Ann Arbor, MI: Servant Publications.

O'Donnell, K., & O'Donnell, M. (Eds.). (1988). *Helping missionaries grow: Readings in mental health and missions*. Pasadena, CA: William Carey Library.

———. (1992). *Missionary care: Counting the cost for world evangelization*. Pasadena, CA: William Carey Library.

Schubert, E. (1993). *What missionaries need to know about burnout and depression*. New Castle, IN: Olive Branch Publications.

Stewart, E., & Bennett, M. (1991). *American cultural patterns: A cross-cultural perspective*. Yarmouth, ME: Intercultural Press.

Wagner, C. P. (1991). *Engaging the enemy: How to fight and defeat territorial spirits*. Ventura, CA: Regal Books.

***Karen Carr** resides in Abidjan, Côte d'Ivoire, and is the Clinical Director of the Mobile Member Care Team/West Africa. She is a licensed clinical psychologist with eight years of experience as a program administrator in the Emergency Services unit of a Virginia Regional Community Mental Health Center in the USA. She has been a consultant and trainer for missions since 1993. Karen has conducted workshops in crisis response, interpersonal skills, and member care with various missions in Africa, Asia, and Latin America. Email: kfcarr@aol.com.*

Special thanks to those who gave specific input to this paper, including Darlene Jerome, John Powell, Ev Worthington, and Laura Mae Gardner.

*This is a revision of an article that first appeared in the **Christian Counseling Connection** (1999, no. 2, pp. 2-4). Used by permission.*

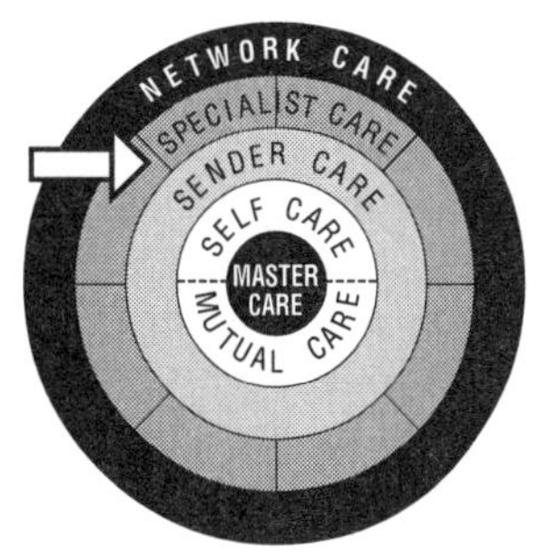

Pastoral Encouragement: Seven Letters To Christian Workers

LAREAU LINDQUIST

Scripture admonishes us to "encourage one another day after day, as long as it is called 'today,' lest any of you be hardened by the deceitfulness of sin" (Heb. 3:13). Here are seven short messages taken from the "flowing font" of letters which the author—an international champion of encouragement—regularly sends to Christian workers around the world. These letters openly address some of the main areas of struggle in cross-cultural ministry. Leaders can use such letters to provide timely, valuable support to their mission personnel.

Letter 1: Growing Through Affliction

It was one year ago today that I had my severe automobile accident. The year has been filled with the full gamut of extremes: lows and highs, difficulties and discoveries. That has been true not only physically, but also emotionally and spiritually. Now in retrospect, I more fully see that it has been a valuable year—in fact, a very valuable year. I am able to agree with the Psalmist who wrote, "It was good for me to be afflicted" (Psalm 119:71). I am careful to observe that he saw the goodness of it all after the affliction was over and not in the middle of the affliction.

Often, friends ask me if I am different now than before. I think they are asking if I see things very differently now. Any significant changes? I answer quickly and certainly, "Yes, in many ways." Let me give an illustration or two.

First, I have especially discovered the *preciousness* of the Lord. He has been and continues to be so very precious. I have focused on His specific attributes and found them to be warm and true. Like Job, I have found that everything about God has become more real, more immediate, more intimate. Job, after going through multiple losses, witnessed a new self-revelation of God. He *then* said this to God: "Once my ears had heard of you, but now my eyes have seen you" (Job 42:5). There was no longer just a third-person awareness but now a first-hand experience. I can concur with Job's personal testimonial. I, too, have discovered Him more profoundly.

Second, I have learned more about *appreciation*. After being hospitalized for 11 weeks and significantly restricted for another five months, I took my first intercontinental ministry trip to Austria and Bulgaria with Dick Anthony and Charley Warner. On the flight back to the States, I sat alone. All of a sudden, I sensed how really different things were. My life. My marriage. My ministry. My friends. I had a new sense of appreciation for everything. I no longer could take things for granted. After having almost lost everything, after having been to the brink, things were different. And things are still different.

While still thinking about all of this, I picked up a newspaper from England. I read an article about a woman who discovered that she had terminal cancer at age 25. She said that it was the darkest day of her life. Several years later, she was still living and doing very well. She wrote these words: "Eventually I discovered that my worst day had possibly become my best day *because* it became a turning point in my life. I began to celebrate each day as a special gift and each event as a special event." I also remember hearing Joni Eareckson Tada say this about her diving accident that left her permanently quadriplegic: "Outside of the day of my conversion to Christ, the greatest gift from the Lord was my accident at Chesapeake Bay."

I am not saying that all of us need an automobile wreck. Nor am I looking forward to the next wreck. Here is what I am saying: *God can be fully trusted with whatever comes into our lives.* He can bring blessings out of buffetings. He can turn tragedies into triumphs.

Earlier this afternoon, 14 of my Barnabas friends joined me at the tree, the site of the accident a year ago. A friend read from Romans chapter eight. Several of us shared what God had been teaching us through the year. We held hands as we encircled the tree. We sang to the Lord, "Great Is Thy Faithfulness." We prayed. And amazingly, there was a spirit of triumph in it all. It was a victory celebration. Only God can make that happen. Thank you, Lord.

Letter 2: Overcoming the "I Can't" Syndrome

Many of us are sometimes plagued with the *I can't* syndrome, so clearly illustrated in the life and ministry of Moses. When God called Moses to a very specific ministry assignment (Exodus 3-4), Moses repeatedly responded to God with this attitude, *I can't.* He finally submitted to the Lord, and he began to see the evidences of God's sufficiency in his life and ministry. There were times, however, when he again lapsed into his old pattern of self-dependency and its related despondency and impotency. Once, he even threatened to quit his ministry assignment (Exodus 33). He often needed to be reminded of the unlimited power of God that was promised to him when he said yes to God. We, too, need to understand the power principle that Moses and other biblical individuals discovered. Power for life, for ministry, for tough times—for everything that God puts in our paths.

Jesus told His disciples, "Without Me, you can do nothing" (John 15:5). We need to have these words deeply written on our minds and hearts. Perhaps we literally need to write them in places where we will see them frequently throughout the course of the day (e.g., at our desks, on our dashboards, above our sinks). Jesus is telling us that we are powerless without Him. *That's right, we can do nothing, nothing, nothing without Him.*

Paul, in Colossians 1:29, states it emphatically. He writes, "I labor, struggling with all His energy, which so powerfully works in me." Paul is wanting us to grasp an important truth, so he puts a lot of power words together in a single text. Let's be sure that we know what he is saying. I am emphasizing five power words here in the NIV translation: *labor, struggling, energy, powerfully, works*. Perhaps we ought to look at some other translations too:

■ "I am contending according to His energy which is energizing itself in me with power" (Rotherham's *Emphasized New Testament*).

■ "I am struggling like an athlete by His power that is working mightily in me" (William Beck's *New Testament in the Language of Today*).

As Paul loads up this verse with active, intense power words, he is *theologically* stating an important principle. Thankfully, he is also *practically* and *experientially* living out the principle in his life. In every letter, Paul speaks of God's power in us. He truly believed that God's power was available for him and us *to do* what He wants us to do, *to be* what He wants us to be, and *to become* what He wants us to become. The life stories of other biblical men and women dramatically illustrate the same truth. Too many of us have never discovered this principle, or perhaps we have simply neglected to make it a part of our lives and ministries. We needlessly live with a *power deficiency*. God's power is available to us. Yes, His power energizing you and me. Listen again: "I am struggling with all His energy, which so powerfully works in me." Paul never confused God's power with his own power. He knew that he was not the superman, but God was the Superman.

When J. B. Phillips did his first translation of the New Testament letters, he became overwhelmed with the way in which the early believers really allowed God to live in them and through them. He stated this observation in the preface to his translation: "Perhaps if we believed what they believed, we would achieve what they achieved."

Annie Johnson Flint wrote these words, which are familiar to many of us:

"His love has no limit.
His grace has no measure.
His power has no boundary known unto man.
For out of His infinite riches in Jesus,
He giveth and giveth and giveth again."

There is strength available for this day—and for the rest of the journey.

Letter 3: Perspectives on Pain

Two days ago, I spent a couple of hours with Pastor Samuel Lamb at his church in Guangzhou, China. It has been and continues to be the largest house-church in China. When I was there several years ago, I arrived late for a communion service. Hundreds of people were crowded into the second and third floors of the house. The narrow stairway was packed with people. Many others elsewhere listened by closed-circuit television or loudspeakers, some spilling out into the streets. Typically, 500 people attend these services, with a total of over 2,000 weekly. What a joy to meet these Christians, to hear them sing triumphantly to the Lord, and to share the Lord's table together.

Again this time, our team enjoyed personal time with Pastor Lamb. I asked him to share his personal story with us. What a story! Twice he has been imprisoned, once for 16 months and once for 20 years. Amazingly, he said that after the first imprisonment, there were more people in church. After the second imprisonment, there were even more people in church. They continued to see more growth. He stated and restated this observation several times: "More persecution was followed by more growth." He writes of this in his recently updated testimony: "Suffering is nothing to us. As long as we have the right attitude toward suffering (1 Peter 4), God will strengthen us. Likewise, it is not difficult to be faithful, but the difficulty is to 'be faithful, even to the point of death' (Rev. 2:10). Please continue your intercessory prayers for us. Thank you."

These words keep coming back to me: more persecution, more growth; more persecution, more growth. In Romans 8:35, Paul mentions a variety of struggles that may come to us. There can be trouble, hardship, persecution, famine, nakedness, danger, or sword, but Paul states that in all these things, we can still be more than conquerors through Christ (8:37). In 8:32, he refers to these difficulties as *grace-gifts*.

Recently, I read the book *A Grace Disguised*, by Gerald Sittser, in which the author tells of an automobile accident that he lived through. His wife, mother, and daughter were killed in the accident. Understandably, he writes of the tragic pain and loss that he suffered—incredible losses. Yet he eventually came to see that God brought some good things out of the initial horror of the event. At the time of the accident and in the early months and years following the event, he didn't see it as a *grace-gift* at all. In time , however, he recognized it as a *grace disguised*, as he entitled the book.

There seems to be a common thread in all these accounts. Samuel Lamb, the Apostle Paul, and Gerald Sittser agree that pain is real. It hurts a lot. They also agree that there is a positive side to pain and hurt. There is a potential blessing buried in the difficulty that could soon be seen as a gift from God.

The greatest illustration of this truth is focused on the weekend of Good Friday and Easter morning. The cross of Christ looked so tragic until Easter morning. Then the victory was apparent. Jesus, "for the joy set before Him," was able to endure the cross (Heb. 12:2). Beyond the cross, Jesus saw the joy of resurrection.

There is something beautiful beyond your present discomfort. The God of hope guarantees this to be true. As Otis Skillings writes, "Keep on keeping on."

Letter 4: We Have Christ

Some months ago, my brother, Lynn, and I spoke at the world headquarters for HCJB in Colorado Springs, Colorado. We spent most of one day together, which included a chapel service and several seminars. Before I spoke in chapel, I spent some quiet, personal moments alone in the office of their president, Ron Cline. I was impressed with a motto hanging on the wall, containing these five words: "For this I have Christ."

Several days ago, I talked with a Christian friend on the telephone. She shared a very distressing personal story with me. Their family is almost picture-perfect. They were a sharp couple in their mid-40s with four children, financially secure, and spiritually alive and alert. Then without any warning, speedily and unexpectedly, she was diagnosed with a potentially severe, chronic, disabling disease. Crash, bang, stop! Speaking of "a bend in the road," this was it. The Apostle Paul speaks of *troubles* and *hardships* in Romans 8:35. *Troubles* are often painful. *Hardships* are worse—more intense, more severe, perhaps more enduring. Sometimes they are very, very hard. Such was my friend's new plight.

As my friend told me of this difficulty, Ron Cline's motto came to mind, and I shared it with her. Immediately she said, "That's very good. Wait a minute as I write it down. For this I have Christ." Some time later, I talked with her husband, and he told me that she put this motto on their refrigerator door as a constant reminder of the sufficiency of Christ in their situation.

The Apostle Paul, in the context of personal affliction, wrote these words: "I eagerly expect and hope that I will in no way be ashamed, but will have sufficient courage so that now as always Christ will be exalted in my body, whether by life or by death. For to me, to live is Christ and to die is gain" (Phil. 1:20-21). J. B. Phillips translates a part of verse 21 like this: "For me, living means simply Christ." Paul's relationship with Christ was real. It was vital. It was personal. In his prison experience and in all other difficulties, he eventually learned to lean on Christ. He found that knowing Christ and trusting Him made every situation a potentially triumphant experience. He never denied the reality of trouble. He did not sweep it under the rug, pretending it wasn't there. Nor did he downplay the painfulness of pain. But he was able to see it in the larger context of the sufficiency of Jesus. Over every personal crisis, he too had this motto: "For this I have Christ." He believed it. He practiced it. It made a big difference.

As you face today and tomorrow, perhaps a trouble will visit you. It may briefly touch you. It may even linger a while. It may stay around a long time. At such a time, Jesus says to you, "Here I am." Respond with certainty, "Yes, even now, for this I have Christ."

Letter 5: Dealing With Death

Hebrews 9:27 says, "It is appointed unto man once to die and after this the judgment." Death is a certainty. It is a reality that each of us must face and accept. Although we may rarely think about it, death will eventually come to each of us. Usually we see it distantly, as in the death of a stranger. Or it may be closer, as in the death of a friend, a loved one, or even a family member. In recent days, a number of incidents have raised the awareness of death to me.

■ My wife, Evie, and I spoke at the USA headquarters of MAF in California. The remains of Nate Saint's plane were recently uncovered from the sandy beaches in Ecuador, where Nate and four colleagues were murdered in 1956 by Auca Indians. Now this plane is on display, sitting in sand, at its new home at MAF. The scene of that plane vividly reminded me of that dreadful day, so powerfully told in Elisabeth Elliot's book, *Through Gates of Splendor.*

■ Before we spoke in chapel that morning, Leon, a staff member, shared a prayer request with the congregation. He said, "By now, all of you have heard about the killing of two students by a fellow student just two days ago in a high school here in nearby Santee, California. One of those two boys, Bryan Zuckor, is my nephew by marriage. Please pray for the family."

■ Later that week, we attended a conference where four Columbine students told their story of carnage, which they observed two years ago at a high school in Colorado in the USA. They shared the details that they observed and experienced. They also told of the varied and powerful impact in their lives: drawing them closer to the Lord; having a greater appreciation for their families; developing an awareness of the brevity of life; possessing a greater alertness for ministry to hurting and lonely people; and knowing how quickly difficulties can suddenly enter our lives. One said, "I've heard people say, 'Into each life, some rain must fall.' But for us, that day brought a cloudburst of epoch proportion." He had been shot and wounded in the library where many students were killed. Another told of walking with her teacher down the hall, when one of the shooters approached them and fired. The teacher was killed. Later, while she was being escorted from the building, she stepped over the body of her dead friend, Rachel Scott. As we listened to these students tell their stories, we were again reminded that each of us encounters troubles in a variety of sizes, shapes, and severities. Some have large dosages of trouble. These four had a colossal difficulty placed into their young lives. Yet each one revealed the greatness of God in giving Himself to them in love, grace, and tenderness through the enormity of the event. Though the pain was real and severe, so were the reality and compassion of the Lord.

The Apostle Paul writes, "Who shall separate us from the love of Christ? Shall trouble or hardship or persecution or famine or nakedness or danger or sword? As it is written, 'For your sake we face death all day long; we are considered as sheep to be slaughtered.' No, in all these things we are more than conquerors through Him who loved us" (Rom. 8:35-37). The quotation in the middle of that paragraph is taken from Psalm 44:22. In spite of the *death* mentioned there, the word *victory* appears four times in the same psalm. Even as Paul writes of *death,* he speaks of being *more than conquerors.* The Old and the New Testaments are speaking of death and victory in the same phrase—in the same context. Again, Paul states that "death has been swallowed up in victory" (1 Cor. 15:54).

Even in the crescendo of severities in our lives, we Christians can draw upon the resources we have in Christ. Amazingly, we can emerge as conquerors and victors, not because of who we are but because of who He is. An unknown author has said, "God chooses *what* we go through. We choose *how* we go through it."

Letter 6: There Is No One Like Jesus

Over 600 of us Christian leaders are here together in Kuala Lumpur, Malaysia. We are delegates to the quadrennial conference of the World Evangelical Fellowship. Registrants are here from almost 100 nations around the world. Additionally, we represent over 100 Christian organizations. Understandably, there have been many moments that will indelibly stay in our hearts. One such time was this morning when 30-35 black nationals from various countries in Africa spontaneously were called to the platform to sing. They sang in a language unknown to me. Their singing, however, was made understandable by their choreography. Enthusiastically they sang these words: "There's no one like Jesus. I looked to the right, and I looked to the left, and I looked behind me, too. I still found there is no one like Jesus."

This was a part of Peter's sermon in Acts 4:12, when he said, "Salvation is found in no one else, for there is no other name under heaven given to men by which we must be saved." Other Scriptures tell us that there are many other priceless possessions that can only be found in Jesus. These come to mind, all explicitly stated as gifts from Him alone: peace, joy, fellowship, life (abundant, spiritual, and eternal), forgiveness, and heaven, to mention but a few. No matter where we look for these, we will end up agreeing with Peter that they will be found *in no one else.* You and I have found this to be true. Let's be diligent in preaching and sharing this good news with others. We are surrounded by people on dead-end streets looking for realities that will never be found outside of Jesus. Let's tell them. Maybe you, like me, need to be freely reminded to share the good news. A medical doctor/minister, serving in Africa, once said to me, "Thanks, Lareau, for helping me to get back to the basics. There is something that is even more important than their physical health. It is their spiritual well-being." So quickly we can forget the best news of all—it is Jesus.

In the Philippines, I met two young pastors who told me of their father's conversion. One of them, as a child, was very ill. Their father, a tribal chief, took him to the witch doctor. He could not help them. Then they took him to a missionary, whose prayer brought healing to the child. That day, the father decided to follow Jesus. He became an evangelist and was greatly used of God. His two sons are now preaching Christ.

As our black colleagues sang to us this morning, I immediately thought of the numerous testimonials of people I have met all over the world whose lives have been transformed by Jesus. All of them can join us in singing, "There is no one like Jesus."

Let's often rehearse for the heavenly choir, where we will surround the throne of Jesus and join others to sing of His unparalleled glory, "You are worthy to take the scroll and to open its seals, because You were slain, and with Your blood You purchased men for God from every tribe and language and people and nation.... Worthy is the Lamb, who was slain, to receive power and wealth and wisdom and strength and honor and glory and praise.... Salvation belongs to our God, who sits on the throne, and to the Lamb.... Amen! Praise and glory and wisdom and thanks and honor and power and strength be to our God for ever and ever. Amen!" (Rev. 5:9, 12; 7:10, 12).

Today's events have brought me closer to that eternal day. Indeed, we are a part of a "forever family," widely dispersed around the globe. Let's believe it and share it and sing it: there is no one like Jesus.

Letter 7: The Lord Is in Control

As Evie, my wife, and I were concluding our seminar at the WEF conference in Malaysia recently, a dear Christian brother from India, John Richard, stood to his feet and asked if he could say a word or two. He generously affirmed us and the ministries of Barnabas International around the world. He then prayed for Evie and me and for the wider ministries of Barnabas International. This phrase, in his prayer, especially caught my attention. He prayed, "Lord, we read in your Word that the steps of a good man are ordered by the Lord" (as taught in Psalm 37:23, KJV). Then he continued, "and we know that the stops along the way are also ordered by you."

Later that day and often since that day, I have pondered those truths, that the *steps* and the *stops* are ordered by the Lord. God is fully involved in our lives. His attributes are involved in our journeys every day, meaning that His wisdom, His love, His sovereignty, His grace, and His presence are at work on our behalf at all times. Let's make it personal. He is not at all detached, removed, or uninvolved in my *steps* nor in my *stops*. He is fully engaged in every detail of our lives.

The *stops* refer to our tough times, such as the delays, the detours, the afflictions, and the disappointments. Many Christians find it difficult to accept God's involvement in our dark hours. They just cannot imagine or believe that God would bring such things upon us. The authors of Scripture, however, carefully affirm this truth.

- Joseph, after the incredible abuses he suffered from his brothers, said to them, "You intended to harm me, but God meant it for good" (Gen. 50:20).
- The Psalmist wrote, "It was good for me to be afflicted.... O Lord, in faithfulness you have afflicted me" (Psalm 119:71, 75).
- Job, in his devastating afflictions, immediately said, "The Lord gave and the Lord has taken away" (Job 1:21). Throughout the book of Job, in his conversations with God, he often reaffirmed his belief that God was the Source and the Author of his tough times. In the final chapter of his book (Job 42:11), he wrote of the blessings that God gave him after all the trouble the Lord had brought upon him.

God not only *allows* tough times, He *orchestrates* them as well. We sing these words, "He's got the whole world in His hands; He's got you and me, brother, in His hands; He's got you and me, sister, in His hands." He has all creation in His hands. Listen to Isaiah's confidence in Isaiah 40:10-11: "See, the sovereign Lord comes with power, and His arm rules for Him.... He gathers the lambs in His arms and carries them close to His heart." Indeed, He is sovereign. He is powerful. And He carries us close to His heart.

Indeed, our steps and our stops are ordered by the Lord. Just weeks ago, the Christian world was shocked and saddened to read of the ABWE tragedy in Peru. The mission plane was bringing Jim and Roni Bowers to their assignment, when the plane was mistaken to be an illegal drug plane. Repeatedly, gunfire hit their plane, crippling the craft and bringing it down into the river. The pilot was severely injured. Jim's wife and infant daughter were killed. Jim, reflecting on the horrible incident, said, "It is the love of God that constrains us to go to the ends of the earth. In the will of God and providence of God, there is no such thing as an 'accident.' He plans everything that comes into our lives."

God is the Master Architect. He is in the process of creating a masterpiece out of you and me. He can be trusted to do what is best for you and me. It is not always the easiest for us to accept nor the choice we would have made. But He will do whatever He wills to do. And it will be good.

O Lord, thank you for ordering my steps and my stops. Thank you for grace to trust you in every moment. Amen.

Reflection and Discussion

1. Which of these letters are the most relevant for you right now? In what ways?
2. If you were to write an "encouragement" letter to a colleague or team, what theme would you address, and which Scriptures would you use?
3. How could similar letters (including email messages and email video clips) be incorporated into the member care program of your organization?
4. Identify some other key topics for Christian workers that could be addressed via these types of letters.
5. The seven letters in this chapter emphasize the love and closeness of Christ, and they stimulate us to persevere and not give up. Try summarizing some of these letters in one sentence, and follow each by a key verse from Scripture. Share these with some colleagues.

***Dr. Lareau Lindquist** and his wife, Evie, started Barnabas International in 1986, a ministry committed to spiritual/pastoral ministry. After 21 years in pastoral ministry and another three years as the President of the Institute of Holy Land Studies (now Jerusalem University), they sensed a call from God to begin a ministry which would exist to bless and build people involved in ministry. Lareau served as Executive Director of this ministry—Barnabas International—for 15 years, traveling to over 100 countries. Currently Lareau and Evie are spending time as Senior Associates via studying, writing, teaching, counseling, and ministering to Christian leaders worldwide. Lareau continues to write monthly letters for Christian workers called **Encouragement**. Email: Barnabas@Barnabas.org.*

Special thanks to Dottie Campbell for her help in preparing this chapter for publication.

33

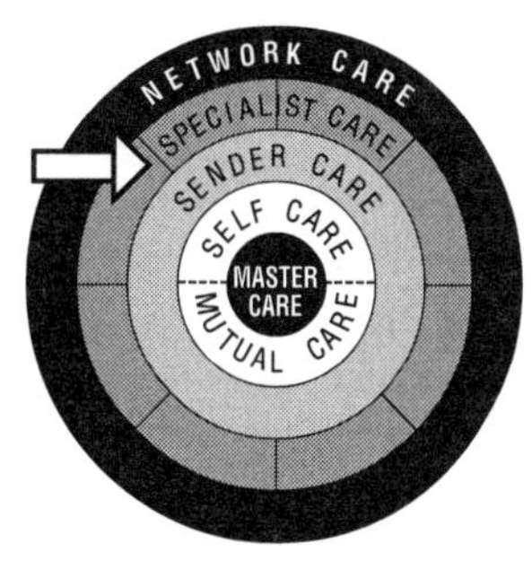

Reviewing Personal Spirituality: Reflections on Work With Overseas Personnel

ANNIE HARGRAVE

Working in overseas mission and aid is always personally challenging. People's faith, beliefs, and spirituality must be lived out in a different culture and sometimes in places of unaccustomed poverty, conflict, and difficulty. This chapter takes a look at a way of exploring what has happened for people and reflecting on what it means for them spiritually.

Everyone who works with people who are returning from an overseas assignment does so in a specific context. This context will have a bearing on how we approach the task and makes a difference in how people view us.

If you are on the staff of a mission agency and are seeing your personnel upon their return from a period of work in another country, you are likely to have some advantages. You may already know the people concerned, and as long as you have not had difficulties with each other in the past, you will probably feel reasonably comfortable with each other. You will be familiar with the particular stance of your organization, so you can use language which you believe will be welcomed and understood. For example, if you belong to an Evangelical group, you will probably use the term "pastor" or "minister." If you are part of a Roman Catholic mission, you will use the word "priest." It is possible that you will be part of the management structure. In this position, you may be able to take up a particular financial request within the organization, or you may be able to advise personnel that what they are seeking is unlikely to be well received.

If your personnel have the opportunity to review their mission with someone who is independent, there are gains for them in this arrangement as well. People usually feel a greater freedom to talk about things such as problems with field managers or doubts in their faith life, if they are able to do so in a confidential setting outside their organization. Sometimes people are less inhibited in expressing themselves, whether they feel anger, bitterness, fear, or some other emotion. This openness does not mean, however, that you can make assumptions about the language preferred for discussion, the meaning of terms, shared beliefs, or goals. Differences in these areas may slow down the review process, but they may also encourage deeper questioning. If you have to work at making yourself clear, you tend to think things through more thoroughly. Personnel are often surprised to make discoveries about what they think, believe, and do, when they have the chance to review their experiences carefully with someone outside their immediate context.

I work with an independent health care practice that is dedicated to personnel whose work takes them overseas in the charitable sector. My clients come from Christian mission agencies, as well as from emergency and relief organizations and development programs. Personnel may be working as church planters or as lorry drivers, as Bible translators or as journalists, as bishops or as prison monitors. They may serve in Uganda or New York, in Sarajevo or Sudan. They may live in a traditional mission compound or an apartment block, in a community house or a tent.

Spirituality and issues of faith are covered within an overall personal, confidential review of the time spent overseas. We use the word "review" rather than "debrief." This is because in the UK there is often a narrow definition of the word "debrief" as a technique associated with early interventions after trauma. Controversy over the meaning has made the term unhelpful for us, as we seek to work responsibly and carefully with people.

In our reviews with overseas workers, we have the advantages of being independent and of being in a position to guarantee confidentiality, unless an agreement is reached with the client to pursue a relevant issue, possibly with the sending agency or in whatever other context seems appropriate. Confidentiality is also waived in the case of a person who is deemed to be unsafe or unfit to work and who is unwilling to agree to disclose this to his/her organization. In our experience, it is almost always possible to work with someone to achieve a satisfactory agreement. In this extreme case, however, the agency concerned would be notified, although personal details would not be disclosed. The person involved would be permitted to see any written communication and would always be fully informed. In practice, this situation happens so rarely that it is discounted for the purposes of this article.

In our review sessions, we especially value the discipline of not making assumptions about people. This is particularly needful in the areas of spirituality, religious belief, and religious experience. People often feel that they are changed, that they have encountered some new and unexpected spiritual experience, that they have met God in a different way, or that they have been stretched and challenged to their limit as a result of living and working overseas. Sometimes these realities are disturbing; at other times, they are wonderful.

Principles for Reviewing Spirituality

The context I have described is the one out of which the following thoughts about reviewing people's personal spirituality arise. I suggest five basic principles as guidelines for thinking about your practice. You may be able to use them to evaluate what you do. They are applied to the brief case studies which follow. They can also enhance the clarity and policy of your organization and your own personal and professional development.

1. Purpose

It is helpful to think through, honestly and clearly, what your purpose is in reviewing personal spirituality. For example, do you see the review as an opportunity to reflect and learn from experience? Is it an organizational check to ensure that personnel remain within the bounds of the beliefs and values required? Is it a means of evaluating performance or of getting information and feedback about the workplace and task? Are you seeking material for publication and promotion? One purpose that is *not* recommended is to use the review for disciplinary measures. If a serious breach of trust should come to light during the review, the possibilities of discussing the matter in an appropriate forum can be addressed.

2. Setting

The setting in which the review takes place should be safe, and the limits and ground rules should be made clear.

The place. There should be adequate accommodation and privacy. The location should be safe.

The boundaries. The duration of the review should be explicit—whether for a set period of time or open ended. It should be clear where the responsibility for payment lies, if fees are being charged. There should be no interruptions; mobile phones should be switched off. The extent of confidentiality should be clearly understood. Is it complete? Will there be a report? Who has access to the information? Might the review appear in promotional material? Making the boundaries explicit facilitates emotional and spiritual security.

The possibilities. It is helpful, both to you and to the people returning from overseas, to have an idea of any situations which might come out of the review. For example, sometimes a follow-up appointment is possible. At other times, it is possible to offer to explore funding for a conference or for a special family visit.

Whatever you decide about your setting—whether the review will be held in a room or outside; whether you organize drinks or not; how you define the boundaries and possibilities—will be according to your ethos and needs. However, transparency and clarity about the arrangements will help you all to get the most out of the review process.

3. Your Skills and Commitment

You need to be committed to your task and as well-prepared as possible. It is helpful to be aware of both your capacities and your limitations. Knowing your capabilities allows you to be confident that what you offer is worthwhile. What you are not able to manage can be acknowledged, and further help can be sought, if appropriate.

You are there to concentrate on the workers returning from overseas. It is not appropriate to talk about your own experiences or needs—these should be addressed somewhere else.

Be as informed as possible about the overseas location where people have been serving. They will appreciate it if you have a general knowledge of the region, if you know what language is spoken there, if you are aware of any recent conflict or coup, and if you are able to recognize how different the thinking, customs, beliefs, and behavior of the local people may be from your own.

Always be willing to listen to what is actually being said, rather than what you hope or expect to hear. If the information is not clear, check it out. Reflect back what you hear, so that what is shared can be well considered and accurately understood.

Look for things that don't jibe. For example, if someone tells you about a death but continues to smile without leaving any space for sadness and loss, or if you are hearing about great achievements told in a flat tone of voice with no enthusiasm, you know something is not quite right. An attempt is being made, often without the person's realizing it, to cover over something difficult. You may not be able to understand what is occurring, but you can certainly observe that it seems to be happening.

Use your skills well, be committed to the task, and be willing to seek appropriate support and consultation for yourself. Such support will be a good safeguard in your practice and will improve your capacity to do a really good review.

4. Open Mindedness

Set aside your preconceptions, assumptions, and expectations, and cultivate an open mind. The more you can do this, the more you will learn about the people with whom you are working. You will sometimes hear things which will shock or sadden you or otherwise impact you. You must allow yourself to feel the impact without being overwhelmed. You will also be endlessly surprised and delighted by the variety and depth of experiences people will relate to you. Open mindedness is a quality which will serve you well, as you seek to accompany individuals in working through issues and as you look for a creative and appropriate way forward.

5. Not Knowing the Answers

The capacity to tolerate what is unknown, to allow a mystery, to accompany someone in distress—to *not* know the answers—has a liberating effect and increases trust. The experience is liberating, because the person who feels something to be unbearable or shameful or stupid finds that it is, in fact, tolerated and taken seriously. This opens up the event so it can be contemplated in unanticipated ways. Not knowing the answers can increase trust, because you are respecting the experience and the extent of the difficulty or struggle. You are willing to participate in the discomfort of people's pain or the awe of their discovery, without imposing an easy answer or a conventional explanation. This tends to make people feel valued, listened to, properly regarded, and respected.

Summary

When you have considered the context of your work and have thought through the opportunities and limits it offers, you can go on to think about how you actually want to conduct your reviews with people. The five principles outlined above will help you to choose appropriately how you want to proceed. They can also provide guidance for monitoring your work and for identifying areas in which you want to improve your skills and practice.

I invite you now to enter into the case studies which follow and to question and evaluate what emerges. Of course, people's experiences do not fall neatly into easily manageable categories. Their dreams, relationships, work, prayers, health, family history—everything that they are—are all woven together. We do well to bear this in mind, reminding ourselves that it is impossible to cover everything. The task of the review of personal spirituality is to discover with people what is important for them now, what they can usefully reflect on and learn from, and how they might move forward positively with the outcomes.

Case Studies

The four case studies that follow all feature Christian mission personnel, although the same approach is used with people who are working with agencies that do not claim any Christian faith or principles. The case studies are all essentially true. Identifying details and contexts have been changed to protect confidentiality.

Case 1: Community Pain

Marie was a Roman Catholic nun who was accustomed to moving, having a teaching and training role which took her from place to place. The UK was not her country of origin, and English was not her native language. She said that she was quite happy to be in London and was comfortable to be speaking English. She talked about a successful time of work and ministry in her African placement. She had collaborated well with the national priests and had felt accepted by and called to the people with whom she was working.

In spite of her apparent successes, Marie's tone of voice and expression of emotion were flat. There appeared to be little real sense of satisfaction in the achievements she was detailing. I asked if she had been able to sustain her religious observance, and she said she had maintained her disciplines... but.... The hesitations signaled that something she had found difficult was about to emerge into the discussion.

Marie had been living in a house with two other expatriate sisters. She said she was used to living with other nationalities. She did not think this should have been a problem. She took her time to tell me that the other two sisters had got on together very well. She had felt excluded, and this made her irritable, then angry, and then hostile towards them. She said she had shut herself off, hardened her heart, and acted as though she didn't care.

I commented on how terribly painful the experience was. We sat in silence for a full three minutes. I wondered what was in her mind, but she shook her head. I wondered about her sense of call.

This was the trigger for her to be able to express her central fear. She said that her whole experience of God's presence in her life was rooted in community. She had been through ups and downs before, but this time she had not been able to find a sense of belonging in the community (the mini-community of three) in which she had been placed. The exclusion she felt from the closeness between the other two sisters amounted to God's excluding her from Himself. It meant that, despite the concrete achievements she had made, her mission had been a massive failure.

Reflection

Marie was very troubled and needed to work through her pain in the context of spiritual direction within her community. She was at risk of becoming depressed. I was in a position to offer her follow-up appointments to help her make sense of her distress. However, this relief was not possible while the feeling of being excluded from God was predominating and remained unexpressed. In my view, this was the main achievement of the spiritual review. It opened up the way for Marie to address the unhappiness of her spiritual experience, and it indicated to others around her what it was that was troubling her.

In terms of the five principles described above, all of them were important in order to help Marie. The clarity of purpose, which we always explain, laid a foundation for Marie to be open enough to allow her distress to surface. The setting ensured there would be time. We would not be rushed or interrupted, so the halting silences of her emotional and spiritual struggle to express herself could be accommodated.

The third principle suggests that a genuine commitment to the task and the person you are with is important. You don't need to *tell* people that you are rushed, that you are preoccupied with something else that is "more important," or that you hope there will not be any problems to deal with. Your clients will pick such attitudes up very quickly. In response, they will almost certainly shut down on their most sensitive vulnerabilities, and you will miss your opportunity to help them with these.

In Marie's case, it was important to be informed and open regarding the priorities and language with which she would be familiar. It was even more important to be able to observe that the achievements she described did not match her flat tone of voice and her withdrawn demeanor.

Maintaining an open mind and being willing not to jump to conclusions were crucial. The reality was that I genuinely did not know how Marie would express her distress. I had to be able to tolerate that in myself, in order to enable Marie to tolerate it. In terms of the skills involved, I would point to the three-minute silence. Three minutes is such a short time in ordinary living, but it feels like a very long time indeed in the quiet, undistracted setting under discussion here!

Case 2: Surprise From Community

Sandra was a married mission partner with small children, who had been living overseas for the first time in a very densely populated urban area. She was now back in the UK for her first period of leave after three years abroad.

During our session together, I asked Sandra if she felt she had been able to nourish herself spiritually. She sighed. She said she had always enjoyed a pattern of Bible study and prayer, both privately and with others. She had tried so hard to continue this pattern in her overseas setting, but it had felt like a heavy and often impossible chore. I commented that she sounded disappointed with herself. She said she hadn't been able to find how to maintain her devotional life. Everything was so tiring. It was so hot, with so much to do. Her small children woke her early, and by evening she was too worn out. She never seemed to get enough time. It was frustrating, and she worried about how much she was really accomplishing.

As we talked, there were pauses and silences. Sandra struggled to express herself. It was halting and jerky. I then asked her how she had managed to make it so far spiritually, with so little time and so much disruption. She said she had to let go of her expectations for her devotional life. She still thought of it as valuable, but somehow she had to find other ways.

What followed next were several comments about her missing the evenings when she would sit outside with other women who were also living in her apartment complex. She smiled and reminisced about the cooler times, when people sat together, talked, played with their children, and brought cold drinks outside. She laughed and said that they talked about everything from seasonal recipes to measles, from religious constraints to opportunities in education. Some of the other women were from the church, and sometimes they talked about their faith.

Sandra then interrupted her own flow of speech. She began to notice the connection between her time with the neighbors and her time with the Lord. God had met with her in the friendships, both with other Christians and with people of other faiths. The discussion that followed explored the idea that God could meet her in unexpected ways and that these events could enrich her, her family, and her Bible study and prayer.

Reflection

Sandra was able to make good use of the atmosphere of openness, the silences, and the questioning during the review. She found a way to make sense of her experience, and she put it into a framework of meaning which connected into the narrative of her faith. The review enabled her to consider her usual and preferred devotional pattern, the frustration and disappointment she felt, and this new kind of experience of community. The experiences that she had with others could now fit better into her sense of purpose, calling, and devotional life.

Case 3: The Same Yesterday, Today, and Forever

Bernard and Joan were a mixed race, inter-cultural couple. He was a national of the country where they lived and worked, and she was an expatriate mission partner. After their marriage, they made their home overseas, but they continued to be linked with the mission agency for which Joan had originally worked. The couple had two young children.

Because of war, they had decided to relocate to Joan's passport country in order to safeguard the welfare of their children. Several members of Bernard's family, including a brother, had been murdered. Shortly after evacuating, they were informed that their house had been burned down. They were currently living with members of Joan's family.

As we met, they said they were comfortable. They had enough space and privacy but did not feel isolated, having good relations with Joan's relatives. Bernard and Joan detailed their upheavals and losses with great sadness and confusion. They said they were not angry but accepted that life was like this. Westerners, they said very emphatically, did not understand how things were. They considered Westerners to be too sentimental about human life—"people don't live forever."

I wondered about their faith in God in the midst of all the uncertainty. Both were strong in their declaration that God had "brought them through." Joan said that God was all you could rely on. Nothing else really mattered. Bernard, in a gentler tone of voice, said that he knew his brother was with God. That was what he thought about—not the way in which he had died.

I commented that what they were saying made me think of the Bible verse that says that Jesus Christ is the same yesterday, today, and forever. Both were pleased with this association, and they conveyed a sense of relief. We were able to go on to discuss what they felt they needed in their faith life at this point. Towards the end of our time, I suggested that their needs to discuss their transition and experiences might change as time went by.

Reflection

Clearly, Bernard, Joan, and their children had been through an extremely painful time which had turned their lives upside down. Their purpose, security, setting, and future were all swept from under them. The losses, including loved ones and home, could not be handled. It would take a long time to go through the processes of mourning and rebuilding their lives. They had kept the overwhelming events at bay by concentrating on the one focus which they believed would endure and survive—God.

Bernard and Joan were able to use both me and the review in various ways. One outcome was their expression of anger. They were not able, currently, to express their anger about what had happened in their country. They were, however, able to be angry with me! Their views about Westerners, directed at me, allowed me to see that their anger was indeed coming out, although not yet in appropriate ways. Being the recipient of people's hostility without taking it personally and becoming defensive sounds easy enough, but it is not!

The second outcome was the discussion that ensued by my acceptance of their declaration of faith without question. I judged that it was more helpful to accompany them exactly where they were at the time without challenge. This enabled them to relax enough to be able to talk about having needs. I also felt obliged to suggest that their needs might change over time. My hope was that the comment would be remembered and would open them up to process their experiences further at a later date.

Case 4:
Wide Open Spaces

Simon was a married man with small children. He was from a house-church background and was accustomed to taking leadership roles. In his overseas post, he exercised managerial and pastoral responsibilities in a church. He also keenly felt the burden of taking care of his family, having to adapt to life in a difficult neighborhood. They lived in a densely populated, big city.

Simon was troubled because he had been unable to find a way to live what he described as "a consistent Christian life." He longed for a desire to pray regularly and for inner strength. He had asked for help from elders both in the overseas location and from his sending church. He felt he had tried harder and harder, going "through the hoops," but he had only become more frustrated, more panicky, and more irritable.

We focused initially on the heavy responsibilities he carried, but the discussion seemed to make no impact. There were thoughtful silences, and I tried to say something about the feelings aroused by the conversation. I wondered aloud about two or three things, to which he said no. Finally, I managed to hit the nail on the head. I commented that I sensed there was something about his feeling trapped.

At this, there was an abrupt change in Simon. "Oh yes! Absolutely trapped!" he responded. He recounted how he had been brought up on an island and how he used to go for long walks on his own. He was now animated, as he reminisced about the marvels of the sea, beaches, sky, praying, singing, and enjoying life. His senses, memory, and perspectives were rekindled. There seemed no end to the enthusiasm and delight in his voice.

He stopped himself and remarked sadly that none of these things were available to him in his overseas assignment. He could only sigh as he related how impossible it felt to get out of his constraining environment.

This led to thinking about how Simon might find the external space he had always enjoyed, which would enable him to have the spiritual and emotional space to take on the demands of his calling. In considering alternatives, he was able to be flexible. He was realistically aware that he could not recreate his earlier experiences, but he was open to the possibility of finding some new equivalents.

Reflection

Simon was a very gifted and competent young man. His work practices were innovative and exciting. However, he found himself trapped, both by the environment and also by a defined way of thinking about spiritual life. Once this realization emerged, he was astonished to hear himself. It unlocked hope for him. He was full of gratitude, saying he now could see what it was all about.

In the review, I had initially focused on the heavy load of responsibilities that Simon was trying to shoulder. We addressed the idea of appraising and rethinking his workload. However, it was clear that this idea, good enough in itself, was not touching his worry about his spiritual life. The discipline of the helper remaining open minded was essential. It was not easy to locate the core of Simon's need. It was important to be alert, to continue to explore, and to keep on listening. When Simon's energy level shifted upon striking emotional "gold," we could both hear it loud and clear!

I did not see Simon again. I do not know what he did, and I had to keep myself from become preoccupied with my hope that he was able to incorporate what emerged in the review. Knowing we cannot do everything or know all the answers, we trust that people will be able to apply what is useful to them.

Final Thoughts

The approach to reviewing personal spirituality, as outlined here, is rooted in our particular context. Yours will not be the same as mine. I hope, however, that you will be able to take up whatever is useful to you.

The task is not easy. You may wish to use a checklist or ask people a number of routine questions to begin the session. Whatever you do will be worthwhile and will be appreciated, as long as you maintain respect and commitment at all times. This includes the willingness to seek help beyond yourself. Occasionally, this means more specialized consultation with a professional. It may mean a referral to a counselor or a spiritual director, or it could entail facilitating attendance at a conference or a course.

It is important that you work with others from time to time to monitor your own practice. A working partner, supervisor, or consultant with whom you have a trustworthy, confidential arrangement should be available to you.

At times, you will need to find help for yourself, care properly for yourself, and review your own stresses, conflicts, and life issues. Taking care of yourself frees you to be fully available for your task, without your personal issues getting mixed up in your work.

It is a constantly fascinating privilege to be engaged in the review of people's personal spirituality. I hope you will find the five principles outlined above to be helpful in thinking about your work with people returning from overseas and particularly as you review their spiritual experiences with them.

Reflection and Discussion

1. In what ways do you think this process of review of personal spirituality is similar to spiritual direction or pastoring? How is it different?
2. Are there other core principles that you use to guide your work with helping people? If so, what are they?
3. Review the author's comments on the advantages and disadvantages of using in-house or outside consultants. Which is more relevant for your organization and setting?
4. What is the role of prayer in doing spiritual reviews? For example, is it something to begin and/or end with? What expectations and inhibitions might you be setting up by starting with prayer? How might prayer help or interfere with the process?
5. What sort of things arising in a review of spirituality would alert you to the need for more specialized help? What resources and ideas do you have to offer, and how would you go about discussing these?

Annie Hargrave *was a youth and community worker in Birmingham, England, in the mid-1970s. She then lived in Argentina and Bolivia for 10 years, bringing up a young family there. Her work was focused on youth groups, on training and supporting Sunday school teachers, and on prison visitation and advocacy. Upon her return to the UK, she retrained as a counselor and then as an analytic psychotherapist. She currently works in London, specializing with overseas mission, relief, and development personnel, and she continues to maintain a small psychotherapy practice. Email: annieh@interhealth.org.uk.*

Special thanks to Ted Lankester, Evelyn Sharpe, Anne Yeardley, and John Steley, who reviewed and commented on this chapter for me.

34

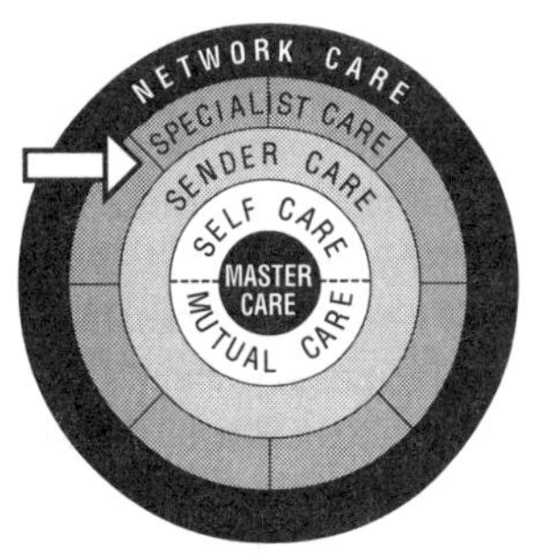

Helping Missionaries Start Healthy And Stay Healthy

MICHAEL E. JONES
KENNETH GAMBLE

In this chapter, we review ways in which physicians, acting as medical officers for mission agencies, can help ensure that candidates at selection are medically fit for their work. Physicians can also confidently reassure serving missionaries that they are fit to continue on the field. Experience and staying updated in tropical and travel medicine are essential.*

Physical Health Risks

The last 100 years have seen a radical improvement in the health risks associated with missionary service. A century ago, the health risks were high, and fatalities were common. Of the 133 missionaries sent out prior to 1915 by the Free Presbyterian Church of Scotland, 20% died (McCracken, 1973), and it was usual for missionaries to take their own coffins as they sailed away from the UK. West Africa became known as "the white man's grave," a description that ignored the fact that it was also the African's grave to the same or a greater extent. Missionaries and volunteers were exposed to the appalling health risks of a tropical climate, without the protection of vaccines or anti-malarial prophylaxis and treatment, and they paid a heavy price.

Tropical location health risks decreased after the advent of potent anti-malarial treatments and effective vaccines in the middle of the last century. The first vaccine to be used extensively was smallpox at the beginning of the 20th century, at which time 1,500 deaths occurred from this dreadful disease each year in the USA alone. Worldwide campaigns resulted in the eradication of smallpox in 1977. Typhoid vaccine was first used in British troops in the Boer war and more extensively during World War I. BCG for tuberculosis was first introduced in France in 1920, and since

* The reader is referred to two chapters in the recent *Textbook of Travel Medicine and Migrant Health*. This book includes a helpful chapter by one of the authors on "Psychological aspects of travel and the long-term expatriate" (Jones, 2000) and a chapter by Dr. Ted Lankester on "Health screening and psychological considerations in the returned traveler" (Lankester, 2000).

then 3 billion doses have been administered worldwide. Diphtheria vaccine was introduced into general use in 1938, whooping cough vaccine in 1948, polio vaccines in 1955, measles vaccine in 1968, meningococcal A and C vaccine in 1969, hepatitis B vaccine in 1981, and hepatitis A vaccines in 1992.

These advances had a marked impact on mortality risks. Between 1945 and 1970, Protestant missionaries from the USA had an overall death rate 40% lower than for a US control group, despite the fact that infectious disease risks were still about 50% higher, initially mostly due to poliomyelitis in non-vaccinated individuals and malaria (Frame, Lange, & Frankenfield, 1992). However, non-infectious disease risks have also changed, and between 1958 and 1970, American missionaries were 50% more likely to die of accidental death in Africa than if they had been in the USA.

Gaps remain in the current range of vaccines, most notably for potentially lethal and common infections such as dengue fever. The risk of acquiring TB has increased significantly (Cobelens et al., 2000) and now approaches that of hepatitis A without vaccination. BCG protects against severe forms of TB, but it is by no means an ideal vaccine, and there is no reliable way of assessing how effective it has been in stimulating cell-mediated immunity, which is important in protection against acquiring TB. Skin tests are only a partial guide.

Hepatitis B remains an under-recognized risk. In the missionary cohort, the major transmission risk is via minor contact with carriers. This may involve only tiny quantities of body fluids, i.e., not sexual and not vertical from mother to child (Van Damme et al., 1995). The risk is greatest for pre-adolescent children (Davis, Weber, & Lemon, 1989). One study of American Protestant missionaries estimated an overall hepatitis B annual attack rate of 4.2%, with overall post-service evidence of infection in 26% (Lange & Frame, 1990). Unsafe injections for those receiving health care overseas are an additional hazard. The World Health Organization (WHO) estimates that 12 billion injections are given worldwide each year, with 95% administering drugs rather than vaccines. Many of these are given without adequate sterilization of injection equipment. WHO estimates that 60% of hepatitis B prevalence in India and more than 40% in Egypt may be transmitted in this way, resulting on a global basis in 1.3 million deaths annually (WHO, 1999). All missionaries serving in areas where hepatitis B is common, including Eastern Europe, should be vaccinated, whether or not they are involved in health care work.

The advent of HIV infection two decades ago has added an entirely new risk factor, particularly for health care workers, among whom we are likely to see an increasing number of HIV infections. A tragic example was Joy Bath, an Elim Pentecostal missionary working in Zimbabwe, who contracted HIV as the result of blood splashing onto a wound on her foot in a labor ward and who died four years later in 1995 (Stokes, 1995). It is a fact of missionary life that some workers expose themselves to HIV risk through extramarital relationships, including relationships with commercial sex workers who, in both Africa and Asia, have very high rates of HIV prevalence. I have seen more than a dozen missionaries who have placed themselves at risk, and in one case HIV infection resulted.

Malaria went into decline in many developing countries as the result of colonial era mosquito control measures, but altered financial priorities after independence, a retreat from the use of DDT, and climate change have all contributed to a worldwide resurgence. These factors have unfortunately coincided with the advent of multiple-drug resistance. In Africa, chloroquine and proguanil, which for many years were the mainstays of protection for long-stay expatriates, are decreasingly effective. The current alternatives are either horrendously expensive or have infrequent but potentially serious adverse effects. It is quite possible that the future logical choice of anti-malarial medication in some areas of very high malaria transmission may cost a missionary agency £2,000 annually for a family. Malaria has returned to its former position as a potentially lethal threat to the life and health of missionaries and volunteers.

In the last quarter century, road traffic accidents (RTAs) have emerged as the leading cause of death, and frightening statistics of the deaths and injuries that occur in many developing countries were published 10 years ago (Smith & Barss, 1991). As one example, the fatality rate per 10,000 vehicles was 70 times greater in Nigeria in 1978 than in the USA. Dutch researchers have noted an increased mortality among development workers, double that of the general Dutch population, with RTAs being the leading cause of death (Schouten & Borgdorff, 1995). Murder and death during burglary now occur with disturbing and increasing frequency. A recent survey of deaths in humanitarian workers concluded that humans with weapons now pose a greater threat than motor vehicles and that both veterans and inexperienced workers are at risk (Sheik et al., 2000).

Psychological Health Risks

Even a cursory examination of the last two centuries of missionary enterprise reveals the uncomfortable fact that some eccentric individuals played a significant role in missionary endeavor. God honored their commitment and blessed their work, but a significant cost was borne by their colleagues and families, alluded to by Tucker and Andrews (1992). Those who did not make the headlines also had problems. About 90 years ago, Price (1913) analyzed over 1,000 missionaries working with the Church Missionary Society between 1890 and 1908. He found that 40% did not persevere with their assignments. In two-fifths of the cases, the problem was due to mental health issues. Much more recently, Peppiatt and Byass (1991) found an 11% risk of psychiatric disorder in a study of 212 Methodist personnel. Why is missionary service associated with detectable and sometimes significant psychological problems? It is due to a combination of the characteristics of both soil (the new environment) and seed (the character of the missionary). We now look at issues concerning the new environment.

The New Environment

Adaptation to a new culture is stressful. Culture shock, the term often still applied to the early stages of the process of cultural adaptation, was first coined by Oberg (1960), but it is only the first stage in a transitional process which may take several years to complete. Missionaries start their journey as monocultural beings and usually finish as adapted bicultural people. Oberg identified four stages. The fascination with the new country in the first few weeks gives way to hostility and aggression in the second stage, followed by a third stage of partial acceptance, during which a sense of humor re-emerges. In the final fourth stage, the immigrant operates in his/her new world without a feeling of anxiety, accepting the customs of the country as another way of living with enjoyment. Adler (1975) called the stages of cultural adaptation contact, dis-integration, re-integration, and autonomy. Hiebert (1985) in his book *Anthropological Insights for Missionaries* describes the stages as tourist, disenchantment, resolution, and adjustment.

For all who make cross-cultural transitions, the changes will be, to some extent at least, unpredictable. For most missionaries, the changes are voluntary, and there is therefore strong motivation to work through them. For some family members, however, the transition to a new culture may be involuntary. Family members with a clear sense of their own identity and a desire to make their own choices may experience considerable difficulty if they have not been party to the decision making process. This is especially true for adolescent children and spouses who are unwilling migrants, attempting to follow obediently in the steps of their parent or marriage partner. Transitions that are both involuntary and unpredictable are inherently more stressful (Hopson & Adams, 1976).

Elements of bereavement also come into the picture (Bowlby, 1984; Huntingdon, 1984; Parkes, 1972). Leaving one's home country on a longer-term basis necessarily involves varying degrees of loss, depending on personal circumstances and motivation. Where the loss is deep, a bereavement reaction will follow, which will affect functioning in the new environment.

Beyond the basic stresses of cultural adaptation, there are chronic cumulative stresses, and sadly and all too often, there are serious traumas which cannot be avoided (De Haan, 1997; Foyle, Beer, & Watson, 1998). In one study of missionary personnel, 17% of those interviewed were suffering from stress reaction (Foyle, 1991). The extent of stress reaction may vary from mild fatigue and loss of enthusiasm for work to severe exhaustion, escalation of personal conflicts, and major depressive and anxiety symptoms with suicidal ideation (Richardson, 1992).

Those working in locations with high stressor exposure and few possibilities for escape soon become ineffective helpers for those they have come to serve. In a survey of 1,300 people who had worked with the International Committee of the Red Cross (ICRC) and who were returning to their home countries, 10% were diagnosed as suffering from stress reaction. Stress was defined as *basic* (including initial culture shock, cultural adaptation, and chronic additional stressors not present in the home environment) in a quarter of the stressed cohort. It was *cumulative* (characterized by prolonged exposure to minor foreseeable traumas) in half, and it was *traumatic* (characterized by sudden, unpredictable, and involuntary psychotraumatic events) in 17%. Post-traumatic stress disorder (PTSD) was less common but was present in 7% (De Haan, 1997). The considerable frequency with which these stressors impact missionaries indicates that the wise agency will attempt to select those individuals who have the psychological resilience to cope. It is not just a question of being tough minded but of having the flexibility to rework a strategy in response to the changes which are encountered.

Candidate Selection

There is good evidence that factors which make breakdown during overseas service more likely can be identified during the screening interview of prospective missionary candidates. It is not just the stressor exposure level but also individual vulnerability which determines outcome (Harrison, 1991). On the positive side, Howes and Kealey (1979) suggest that there are characteristics which make potential expatriate workers more resilient, and Lazarus and Folkman (1984) have emphasized that the response to the stressor has important implications regarding the outcome. The following case study illustrates the interplay of the two factors:

> Ruth was a single nurse, aged 35, who worked in an isolated refugee camp, where she faced a high mortality rate and huge work pressures. She had generally coped well in the UK, but after several months working in the refugee camp, she started to react to her line manager, Susan, with frequent angry outbursts, which destabilized their relationship. It became clear that Ruth was unable to cope in the pressured environment of the camp, and the recommendation was made to terminate Ruth's contract prematurely.
>
> During a personal review, Ruth confided that Susan reminded her of her mother, who had rejected her at age five when her twin brothers were born. Soon after their birth, Ruth had become ill and had had a prolonged admission to the hospital, during which her mother did not visit. Ruth still nursed considerable resentment towards her

mother. These factors had not been identified or explored at Ruth's screening interview, and no opportunity to work through these feelings had therefore been offered.

In different circumstances, Ruth might have coped, but it was the combination of unresolved childhood issues and high stressor exposure which led to premature repatriation. Prevention is better than cure. Ideally, Ruth should have had her childhood issues identified at the initial interview. She should have been offered counseling help if she felt she could benefit from it at that stage, and she should have been assigned to a less stressful location, where adequate escapes and supportive relationships were combined.

The Candidate's Psychological Health

Candidate screening is in essence a risk assessment procedure. It aims to exclude the few individuals who will not cope with cultural adaptation, who may be harmed by expatriate life, or who may traumatize others. The screening process also identifies individuals who have attributes that prompt assessors to believe that they will be inter-culturally effective and can be considered "within normal limits," but they have some attributes that also cause some concern. The wise agency will continue to mentor their missionaries throughout their cycle of service to enhance their effectiveness.

The whole screening process, both the interview and the completion of psychometric scales, will be affected by performance bias (wanting to be seen in a favorable light). The confirmatory views of referees, particularly work colleagues, are thus vitally important. Most assessors find that a selection of psychometric scales assists understanding how the applicant functions psychologically, but scales should never be read in isolation and should be interpreted in the context of hearing the candidate's personal story first hand. Candidate strengths must also be assessed and emphasized.

Important issues to be clarified include personal and family history of mental ill health, including both first- and second-degree relatives. Childhood experiences should be explored. How does the candidate perceive the quality of parenting? Were there elements of emotional deprivation which are still functioning in adult life? Was there abuse or serious trauma? A useful and revealing question suggested by experienced missionaries is, *"Is there anything about your childhood which you would change if you had the opportunity?"* (Geoff and Dee Larcombe, personal communication).

How has the applicant coped with stressful situations in the past? Is he/she able to identify a personal style of reaction to stress? If a previous stressful situation was not handled well, what would he/she do differently next time? Sensitive areas include past sexual orientation and the likely future behavior pattern, past alcohol abuse and drug use, marital difficulties, and, for parents, reasonable solutions to the problem areas of child rearing.

"Difficult people" are a common source of stress in expatriate working groups, and in many cases the difficult person has an unhelpful personality trait or a personality disorder. Usually the person with the disorder blames everyone else for the difficulties, and the underlying cause of the conflict only emerges after interviewing a number of stressed individuals who interact with the key figure, the "problem center." It is vital that the cause of relationship stress be accurately identified if appropriate management decisions are to be made. All too often, one or two stressed individuals are repatriated because it is assumed that they are the ones who cannot cope with the pressures of expatriate life. The main or at least a contributing cause, however, can be another staff member who is allowed to continue in post and who will create problems for the next raw recruit. Organizational dysfunction may also mask the problem. The agency may not wish to confront the "problem center" and may find it more convenient to lay the blame for the relationship difficulty at the door of others.

The concept of personality disorders is well accepted in psychiatric practice, although definition is beset with difficulty. The World Health Organization (1992, pp. 198-224) defines these conditions as deeply ingrained, enduring behavior patterns manifesting with inflexible responses to a broad range of personal and social situations. Individuals with a personality disorder tend to be maladaptive, inflexible, and impaired in social and occupational functioning, and they tend to leave an indelible, negative, and often painful mark on their relationships with others. The prevalence of personality disorders in the general population ranges from 2% to 13% (Marlowe & Sugarman, 1997), so it is inevitable that individuals with these disorders will surface among people working overseas.*

John, whom I saw with a colleague a few years ago, was an example of a selection success, even though the decision was negative:

> A single male aged 40 years with a personal history of mild depression, John had lived during childhood in fear of his father, and as an adult he owned to great difficulty in sharing his feelings with others. His brother was schizophrenic, and John was socially isolated, enjoying solitary activities. His NEO Five Factor Scale (Costa & McCrae, 1990) demonstrated high neuroticism, marked introversion, and very low scores for openness, agreeableness, and conscientiousness. These results and the general impressions gained during assessment were discussed with John. After reflection, he decided he was unsuitable for the intended location and decided to withdraw his application to the missionary agency.

The Candidate's Physical Health

The candidate medical examination aims to answer the question, *"Is this individual physically fit for work in the environment to which he/she intends to go?"* Physical health screening should be performed, at least in part, by physicians with personal experience of working in developing countries or with specific training in travel medicine. Nurses trained in travel and tropical medicine have an important role in advising on anti-malarial prophylaxis and vaccinations. However, because they are not trained in a sufficient breadth of symptom interpretation, they need the help of medical colleagues for the physical examination of candidates. All candidate assessment is about risk assessment, and agencies need to be aware that no matter how detailed a candidate medical review may be, some unexpected problems are bound to occur.

Over the last couple of years, I (Michael) have seen two medical repatriations. The first one looks as though it may prevent the family from ever returning to the field. A male missionary with very minor palpitations developed serious instability of heart rhythm that has only been partially solved by catheter treatment. The other case is a young mother with a heart condition that caused a serious complication but that remains completely silent on examination by a cardiologist and was only diagnosed after very sophisticated diagnostic procedures.

At least 45 minutes should be allowed for the medical examination of candidates. Some physicians use written symptom questionnaires completed by the candidate prior to history taking, but these may actually increase the length of time it takes to do the assessment. Some feel that questionnaires give focus to an exchange that has to cover a lot of material in a short period of time. There may be a danger, if

---

* For further reading, see Esther Schubert's (1991) excellent article, in which she applies a three-cluster classification to personality disorders and their impact in expatriate groups.

questionnaires are used to shorten the process, that some issues may be glossed over by time-pressured assessors. Some candidates attempt to cloak important aspects of medical history to enhance the possibility of passing the medical review, and the non-verbal responses to questions may provide vital clues. A medical history should be detailed, covering volunteered current symptoms and a full systematic inquiry. Symptoms should be assessed in the context of the intended destination. The foothills of the Himalayas may not be the best destination for someone with osteoarthritis or significant back problems, but the same person may function well in a less physically demanding location.

Clear contraindications would include conditions like ulcerative colitis with a relapsing remitting course, and unstable angina. Relative contraindications include chronic medical disorders, poorly controlled diabetes or epilepsy, coronary artery heart disease, and abnormality of the heart valves. Some conditions, for instance epilepsy or psoriasis, may worsen if particular anti-malarial prophylactic drugs are used. Seizure control may deteriorate with chloroquine or mefloquine, and alternatives may be prohibitively expensive, much less effective, or unsuitable for long-term use. Asthma, which is well-controlled and has not resulted in hospital admission in the last few years, is not a cause for concern, since in most instances asthma will improve in a different environment with a different pattern of allergens. An important part of the medical review is the detection of previously undiagnosed problems that might become serious and pose a danger to health during service. For instance, anemia and biochemical evidence of iron deficiency suggest chronic blood loss; in post-menopausal women and men over 50 years, a hidden large bowel cancer may be the cause.

Physicians will vary in their choice of screening investigations, and here there are some differences between the UK and North America. A full blood count would be considered normal on both sides of the Atlantic, whereas an erythrocyte sedimentation rate (ESR) is now frowned on in North America. Renal and liver function tests should be performed. The necessity of doing blood lipids can be determined on the basis of family history and age. The storage of serum for later tests is wise. We would add thyroid function, prostate specific antigen, ECG/EKG for heart problems, and mammography for breast cancer, dependent on history, age, and physical examination findings. Some agencies require HIV antibody tests, although we take the view that a careful history and examination, plus the storage of serum which can be tested later, are generally adequate.

In North America and the UK, routine chest radiography is not considered to be necessary. North American physicians will probably wish to perform Mantoux tests (skin tests for TB) in most candidates, whereas in the UK, chest physicians regard a good scar at the site of BCG vaccination as adequate evidence of immunity. Further Mantoux tests are considered unnecessary, unless a candidate is scheduled to perform health care work in a highly TB endemic area. In North America, missionaries will not usually have BCG before travel abroad, but they will have a Mantoux performed prior to departure and on each subsequent home leave. Similarly, in the US mammography will be requested on women over the age of 40 years, in Canada over the age of 50 years, and less often in UK (Mittra, Baum, Thornton, & Houghton, 2000). Assessors on both sides of the Atlantic should be aware that medical fashions differ, and there is no right or wrong approach. All candidates heading for the developing world should have their blood groups ascertained, irrespective of age.

Do healthy children need blood tests prior to travel? Different opinions are held, but there are solid grounds for determining blood groups for all ages. In the event of an accident in a highly HIV endemic country, knowing the blood group will speed up the process of identifying a safe donor, either a parent or other members of a safe donor pool. The blood groups of children are not normally determined by maternity hospitals, unless there are complications at birth. We find that the "trauma" of blood tests can be minimized by using local anesthetic cream and slender butterfly-type infusion needles for all children up to 10 years and older children who wish it. While taking the sample for a blood group, it makes sense to do a full blood count and any other tests that examination or history suggests are important, since a slightly larger volume in the syringe makes little difference to the trauma of the procedure. The presence of an experienced nurse is a huge advantage, since some parents manage to communicate high levels of anxiety even if they appear calm, and most are not used to holding their children firmly. It should be noted that these children are, in any case, going to countries where blood tests to detect malaria may need to be performed when they are ill and in strange surroundings, and all children will face several episodes of needle contact with pre-travel vaccinations. In this context, a venupuncture, competently performed, does not constitute unacceptable extra trauma.

Physical Health Screening for Returning Missionaries

Normally one hour should be allowed for the medical examination of adults returning from the mission field and 30 minutes for children, although frequently adults need somewhat longer. They may come with a list of problems which they have allowed to accumulate because local medical facilities are poor, producing what amounts to a shopping list of minor or major problems which need attention. A medical history should include asking all missionaries about sexual relationships. It is very unwise to make assumptions at any age. Missionaries are human and make mistakes, sometimes with tragic consequences. It is entirely normal for doctors to experience reservation or feel awkward about inquiring into personal and private areas when taking a medical history. However, the implications of HIV for current and future health and relationships are so important that it is vital that all expatriates be asked about aspects of behavior which may have placed them at risk of infection. As an absolute minimum, we suggest that all returning expatriates be asked, *"Do you have any concerns about HIV transmission?"* In addition to asking about potential non-sexual routes of transmission, most patients should also be asked, *"Have you had any sexual contacts other than your regular partner/wife/husband while you have been abroad?"* *

Some missionaries work in areas of very high HIV prevalence. Even if not involved in health care work, they may have given assistance to the victims of road traffic accidents, or they may have received health care in medical facilities where sterilization procedures are less stringent than in their home country. Pretest discussion and performing an HIV antibody test may remove a huge burden of anxiety. Several years ago, a young woman attended my clinic in the UK for tropical screening following a two-year assignment with an aid agency. When asked whether she had had any sexual partners while in Africa, she hesitantly said, "No," then tearfully related that she had been raped on a train in Central Africa. A man in the restaurant car had misinterpreted their friendly conversation over the dinner table as a sexual invitation and had raped her in the sleeping compartment. An HIV antibody test was fortunately negative. This woman would have remained worried and untested if the question had not been asked.

Our strong preference is to conduct the medical examination prior to a personal review session with another staff member who has counseling skills and who is able to conduct this aspect of the leave medi-

* For a detailed review of the issues surrounding HIV infection and missionaries, see Jones (1999).

cal review in a relaxed and comfortable environment. Important functions of the leave medical examination are:

- To reassure both the sending agency and the missionary that the missionary is well enough to return to the field of service (a few extra investigations buy a significant increment of reassurance).
- To safeguard the financial investment of the sending agency in the missionary.
- As an expression of the value of the missionary to the agency.
- To detect pre-symptomatic chronic medical conditions, which otherwise might precipitate urgent repatriation during the next tour.
- To ensure that any vaccine boosters are given.
- To review anti-malarial prophylaxis.
- To modify medical risk behavior (e.g., swimming in African lakes) or sexual activity that places the missionary at risk.
- To identify significant stressors and advise assistance for stress management and the handling of problematic relationships.

Laboratory Tests

For the benefit of doctors and nurses who may read this chapter, we suggest a wider range of tests is indicated in returning expatriates and should include the following:

- *On all*, do ESR, FBC including eosinophil count, renal function, and hepatic enzymes.
- Add microscopy on a single stool specimen for asymptomatic travelers from developing countries. For those with symptoms, a culture should be reserved, and in such travelers three stool specimens should be sent.
- Add schistosomal serology for any missionaries who have been in direct contact with lake or slow-moving river water in Africa, China, or the Philippines.
- Add strongyloides serology if an eosinophil count is raised.
- Add a filaria ELISA for West and Central Africa.

Divergent views have been expressed regarding the value of screening expatriates returning to their sending countries after periods of service abroad. A large study of over 1,000 people without symptoms seen at the London Hospital for Tropical Diseases (Carroll et al., 1993) found abnormal laboratory results in 25%, about one-fifth with other evidence of parasitic infection, and abnormalities on physical examination in one-third. Many of the parasitic infections would have cleared spontaneously. The authors felt that physical examination added little to practical management, concluding that screening for tropical disease can be carried out by an informed health care worker using structured history taking and relevant lab tests, including HIV test discussion and antibody tests for schistosomiasis (bilharzia) for African lake swimmers.

We take a different view for several reasons. Firstly, in this study, some patients who were classified at the outset as not having symptoms were later found to have significant symptoms and were then excluded from the analysis (C. Dow, personal communication). Second, some patients who appear healthy because they do not volunteer symptoms still have important underlying health issues, which will emerge during a medical consultation. Selective screening of expatriates implies strong background knowledge of geographic aspects of disease. Without this background knowledge, selective screening may erroneously exclude some from more extensive assessment who definitely need it (MacPherson & Kozarsky, 2000). The study also does not address those medical disorders which are age related. Young children are more prone to acquire parasites and other infections than adults. Those who pass the age of 50 years will also be more prone to age related health problems. We agree with Ellis and others that travel should not be over-medicalized (Conlon & Peto, 1993; Ellis, 1993). However, the missionary cohort tend to spend longer overseas than other expatriate groups, tend to integrate more deeply with the host culture, and often work in areas with higher health risks than the average expatriate. Extra care is therefore appropriate.

A physician's chosen model of medical practice will also influence his/her attitude to routine screening by infectious disease physicians. We know that the *raison d'être* of such specialists is the identification of infectious disease, and most of us in this specialty are a little disappointed when patients are referred with potentially infectious disorders and we fail to find a cunning microbe. However, while identification and diagnostic skills are invaluable for those who screen expatriates, the use of a broader, occupational health model is crucial.

Problem Areas in the Medical Examination of Missionaries

In light of the points identified above, the likelihood of being able to complete an examination in 60 minutes may appear small. For the doctor, there are significant problem areas. Whether or not the examining physician is the family doctor for the missionary family, he/she may only have one look at each family member. We term this challenge "snapshot medicine." Frequently the clues are to be found in "soft" signs that can be easily dismissed as being of no consequence or missed by those who do not know what to look for. For example, seborrheic dermatitis, a mild skin fungal infection, and oral thrush under a denture may indicate underlying HIV infection. Glandular fever virus infection in someone with HIV infection may produce filmy vertical white streaks on the edges of the tongue (oral hairy leucoplakia), which is almost always a reliable sign of HIV infection. It may be missed unless the tongue is not only protruded but also wagged from side to side.

Some years ago, I (Michael) saw a returning missionary who at examination had two abnormal physical signs: a mildly raised pulse rate and a cardiac murmur. She did not have sweaty palms, a fine finger tremor, or the eye signs of an overactive thyroid gland. Because I was concerned about the presence of the murmur, I asked her family doctor to refer her to a cardiologist. By the time this had been arranged several months later, the physical signs were much more obviously those of an overactive thyroid. Thyroid function tests confirmed this and provided a more-than-adequate explanation for the murmur and the raised resting pulse rate. With the benefit of hindsight, I would now order thyroid function tests in any patient with these minimal signs. It was an important diagnosis to make, and the woman would almost certainly have been repatriated from the field in a much worse state of health, if she had returned overseas without this condition being identified.

Problems in this pre-symptomatic phase at medical review that are missed or underestimated may cause major difficulty after return to the field, as the following story illustrates:

> David was a 43-year-old missionary working in West Africa. At detailed review in the UK, it emerged that fresh water contact made the possibility of the bowel form of schistosomiasis (bilharzia) likely. He was mildly anemic and had traces of blood in his feces. These results were sent to his family doctor, who later referred him to a surgical clinic after David also developed intermittent abdominal pain. The surgeons performed an ultrasound examination of his abdomen, which was normal. They also performed a colonoscopy, but the instrument could not be advanced through the entire colon.
>
> David was considered clear of serious causes for his chronic blood loss and returned to West Africa, but three months later he was repatriated with severe anemia. At laparotomy, a colonic cancer was found in the segment which the surgeons had not been able to visualize. This was resected, and despite its relatively advanced stage, David thank-

fully remains well with no signs of recurrence 10 years later.

Fatigue in Returning Missionaries

Fatigue may be difficult to interpret. Missionaries may simply be travel weary or jet lagged if seen within a few days of arrival in their home country, or they may be depressed. Debbie Lovell (1997) found that 40% of aid workers reported "depression" occurring either during or after service. In missionaries making their final return to their home country, tiredness may be a symptom of bereavement, although usually there will be other clear features, as illustrated below:

A 60-year-old missionary returned after a lifetime of service in an African country, where she had also grown up as a missionary kid. She was unwisely advised to make a clean break with the past and arrived in the UK with a couple of suitcases and little to remind her of her life's work. She had only a few aging relatives and found that being in the UK carried no sense of being at home at all. At medical review, she was generally fatigued but was also disturbed to find herself bursting into tears for no apparent reason. She found it difficult to speak at public meetings, because she was not sure that she could retain emotional control.

At interview, it was clear that she was experiencing classical bereavement symptoms, having lost a great part of her personal identity in leaving her adopted country. We advised that she be exempted from the public speaking commitments with which she did not feel able to cope, encouraged her to enlarge photographs she had taken in Africa to decorate her new flat, and encouraged her to talk about the life that she had left behind in an environment where she felt safe and accepted. The opportunity developed for her to return to work for another year in the same country. During this additional tour, she was able to adjust to her final departure with much greater ease, this time returning with important physical reminders of her life's work.

Chronic fatigue syndrome (CFS) is not uncommon in the missionary cohort. The old term of myalgic encephalomyelitis (ME) is no longer used and is misleading, since it implies an inflammation of the nervous system, of which exhaustive research has failed to find any evidence. Nor is there any reliable evidence of chronic viral infection. While some patients become ill with CFS after viral illnesses, it may follow bereavement or trauma, suggesting a variety of precipitating factors. CFS tends to attract strongly polarized views, and a balanced attitude will include the possibility that some patients have unidentified physical causes, while psychosocial factors predominate in others. At the turn of the 20th century, 20% of missionaries were repatriated with symptoms that now sound very similar to modern definitions of CFS. Repatriation was more frequent among those working in Japan than those working in China, India, or Africa.

More recent research suggests that CFS is quite common in expatriates (Lovell, 1999). I (Michael) have the impression, unsupported by clear data, that CFS clusters in certain types of missionary activity, and this may reflect the personality structures of those attracted to this kind of work. When physicians have seen large numbers of such patients, they become aware that the invalid or disabled role is one that may have positive benefits and may even achieve a strong degree of control over others or over the working environment. It may prevent posting to a less desirable location, or it may act as a magnet for the support of others with whom the patient relates closely. I have gained the impression that personal insight among missionary patients with CFS is sometimes limited, and the gains from illness, which may be apparent to an outside observer, are often denied by the sufferer (Jones, 1996). Lovell (1999) found an open attitude towards causation among her patients, and she noted that expatriates with CFS tend to be hard working, to have an overactive pre-morbid lifestyle, and to have experienced stressful life events in the period leading up to the onset of CFS.

Several medical conditions may present with fatigue as a symptom, including anemia, hepatitis, intestinal infections with single-cell organisms such as amoebiasis, giardiasis, bacterial infections such as brucellosis, and worm infections such as schistosomiasis. These should be excluded before the label of CFS is applied, but most of these may also act as trigger factors for CFS. A recent study by workers at the London Hospital for Tropical Diseases demonstrated that tiredness is the most common symptom in schistosomiasis, occurring in 50% of those with confirmed infection with this fluke (Whitty et al., 2000).

Trauma

Personal violence is more likely in the developing world than in the developed West, due to both war and criminal activity. Some organizations like ICRC have seen a transition over the last decade from their workers being relatively protected from personal violence to being deliberate targets. Sometimes those who have been quite seriously traumatized will volunteer nothing about what has happened, but they may disclose more on direct, sensitive questioning, as the following case history demonstrates:

> A 30-year-old man was sent by his family doctor to my tropical clinic for screening for schistosomiasis. Due to a cancellation, I had more time available and ascertained during history taking that all had not gone well on his last trip. He had been the leader and truck driver of an overland safari. The convoy was held up by bandits, wholesale robbery ensued, and young women were raped in front of their companions, while all were threatened with death by machete. The trauma extended beyond the initial incident, as the man subsequently arranged for the hospitalization of the rape victims and post-exposure anti-HIV drugs to be flown from another country. He was still disabled by deep anger and accepted the offer of time with a staff counselor.

Mixed Pictures

Sometimes it is very difficult to sort out the relative contributions of contributory factors. In the following case history, there were personnel management deficits in the expatriate community, anti-malarial prophylaxis was not being wisely handled, and post-traumatic stress disorder intermingled with a serious tropical virus infection to cause repatriation.

> Sam was a 50-year-old pilot working in Asia. He had operated a light aircraft service in a developed country, but after arrival in Asia he experienced difficulty integrating with other expatriates, who treated him as an inexperienced junior missionary despite his wealth of flying experience. The first traumatic incident was the serious illness of his wife, who developed cerebral malaria. Sam attempted to fly her to the hospital, but as he was taking off, a tire burst and he slowed to a halt, narrowly avoiding crashing. He had a further near-fatal aircraft incident a few months later. While flying over difficult terrain, he heard a loud explosion from his engine. His passengers were church leaders who realized that the situation was serious, and they began praying fervently. Sam was certain he would crash, but the engine kept running despite oil pressure registering zero. The engine continued to run until he reached an airstrip,

where he landed safely. When he inspected the engine, he found that a cylinder head had blown off.

Some months later, Sam had an illness with fever and crippling joint pains that persisted for months afterwards. He also started to have disturbing dreams with flashbacks reliving the trauma. The clear primary diagnosis was PTSD, and primary management comprised counseling. The joint pains still needed further assessment. A rheumatologist diagnosed early seronegative rheumatoid arthritis, but viral serology subsequently identified an uncommon tropical virus as the cause. Other issues that needed attention included revision of antimalarial prophylaxis for both Sam and his wife.

Is All This Effort by Medical Doctors Worth It?

What is the evidence that thorough medical examination of returning missionaries is not a waste of time? As indicated above, medical review is not just about detection of medical disorder. It also functions to identify psychological health issues and has an eye to protection in the future with vaccines and altered antimalarial prophylaxis. A medical student, Kirsteen Wintour, and one of the authors (Michael) are assessing the results of over 600 routine medical examinations done between 1990 and 2000. The examinations were performed under the auspices of Care for Mission (CFM) at a clinic in the Scottish Borders and after its relocation at the Elphinstone International Health Centre (EIHC) near Edinburgh. The data mentioned below are not yet finalized but are largely reliable.

The age range of the patient group varied widely, between one year and 74 years, and the mean duration of overseas service was longer than among most expatriate groups, at nine years. Of the group, 290 worked in Africa, 72 in South America, 25 in Europe, and one was reviewed after completing a world tour on behalf of his agency. The patients were examined according to a standard protocol, including history, examination, and a battery of laboratory tests, as described above.

Abnormal results were found in 16% of samples sent to both a hematology and biochemical laboratory, and microbiologists found parasites or abnormal bacteria in 9% of stool samples. Examination of the urine was abnormal in 14%, and chemical tests detected blood in 2.3% of stool samples. Antibody tests on blood detected schistosomiasis in 15% of the 100 missionaries who reported exposure to suspect fresh water.

Important first-time diagnoses included HIV infection, pulmonary TB, malaria, strongyloides infection, schistosomiasis, inadequately treated onchocerciasis, pernicious anemia, adult coeliac disease, chronic hepatitis C, primary biliary cirrhosis, chronic proliferative glomerulonephritis, transitional cell bladder carcinoma, prostatic carcinoma, renal calculus with non-functioning kidney, diabetes mellitus, inadequately treated subthyroidism, and hyperthyroidism. Two referrals to CFM/EIHC resulted in nullification of diagnoses made abroad of heart valve disorder and chronic inflammation of the liver, respectively.

In over 200 patients, referral to a specialist hospital service was recommended, and for one-fifth referral to more than one hospital department was recommended. In 13, the family doctor had already commenced referral following a patient consultation prior to review at EIHC, one of these for suspected (and later confirmed) breast cancer. The family doctor refused to make the referral recommended by CFM/EIHC in three cases, on the mistaken grounds that the patients were not eligible for free treatment in the National Health Service, and these patients returned to overseas service without specialist review. The most common destination hospital specialties for referrals were gastroenterology, cardiology, and renal medicine/urology. The results of hospital review were only available in 70 of the 215 referred patients, but in 52/70 (75%) referral resulted in a change in management.

To summarize, careful medical evaluation of returning missionaries, working predominantly in the developing world, yields abnormalities on clinical examination or laboratory tests, and it indicates the need for referral to specialist services in about one-third. In those for whom a hospital report was available, management was changed in three-quarters.

Conclusion

Medically speaking, missionary service is far safer in the early 21st century than in the early 20th century. Some physical health risks are becoming more common, and deaths from RTAs or violence appear to be increasing. Candidate assessment needs to identify those with the physical and psychological stamina to cope in demanding environments. Such assessment should be carried out by physicians and other health care professionals with understanding, experience, and requisite skills. The evaluation of missionaries on leave needs adequate time, knowledge of tropical and travel medicine, and good clinical skills. Known problems accumulated during overseas service need attention, and the medical examination should be thorough enough to detect serious problems that are not yet causing symptoms. Personal review sessions should help to detect those with important emotional health issues. Limited research data suggest that the effort is worthwhile, and there is a significant yield of important medical problems. Those who risk much in the service of their Risen Lord deserve appropriately thorough medical care.

Reflection and Discussion

1. How thorough are the pre-field screening and furlough evaluation for medical problems in your organization? How could the screening and examination processes be improved?

2. What are the main illnesses that affect workers in your setting/region? Are there some ways to better prevent these problems?

3. Road traffic accidents (RTAs) are a leading cause of injury and impairment for expatriates. Discuss how your organization can help prevent RTAs and other types of accidents (see chapter 35).

4. What are some of the main health care books, websites, medical centers, and medical specialists that are/could be used for workers in your organization?

5. How could an organization with limited funds still provide adequate medical coverage for its personnel?

References

Adler, P. (1975). The transitional experience: An alternative view of culture shock. *Journal of Humanistic Psychology, 15*, 13-23.

Bowlby, J. (1984). *Attachment and loss* (Vol. 3). Middlesex, UK: Penguin Books.

Carroll, B., Dow, C., Snashall, D., et al. (1993). Post-tropical screening: Is it necessary? *British Medical Journal, 307*, 541.

Cobelens, F., van Duetekom, H., Draayer-Jansen, I., et al. (2000). Risk of infection with mycobacterium tuberculosis in travellers to areas of high tuberculosis endemnicity. *Lancet, 356*, 461.

Conlon, C., & Peto, T. (1993). Post-tropical screening is of little value. *British Medical Journal, 307*, 1008.

Costa, P., & McCrae, R. (1990). Personality disorders and the five factor model of personality. *Journal of Personality Disorders, 4*, 362-371.

Davis, L., Weber, D., & Lemon, S. (1989). Horizontal transmission of hepatitis B virus. *Lancet, 333*, 889-893.

De Haan, B. (1997). *Stress and psychological issues in humanitarian activities: The experience of the International Committee of the Red Cross*. Paper presented at the Fifth International Conference on Travel Medicine, Geneva, Switzerland. Program and Abstracts, No. 110, p. 126.

Ellis, C. (1993). Post-tropical screening is of little value unless the traveller feels unwell. *British Medical Journal, 307*, 1008.

Foyle, M. (1991, June). Missionary stress. *Voluntary Agency Medical Advisors Newsletter*, 2-14. (Available from Elphinstone International Health Centre, Elphinstone Wing, Carberry, UK)

Foyle, M., Beer, M., & Watson, J. (1998). Expatriate mental health. *Acta Psychiatrica Scandinavia*, *97*, 278-283.

Frame, J., Lange, W., & Frankenfield, D. (1992). Mortality trends in USA missionaries in Africa 1945-1985. *American Journal of Tropical Medicine and Hygiene*, *46*, 686-689.

Harrison, G. (1991). Migration and mental disorder. *Medicine International*, 3978-3980.

Hiebert, P. (1985). *Anthropological insights for missionaries*. Grand Rapids, MI: Baker Book House.

Hopson, B., & Adams, J. (1976). Towards an understanding of transition: Defining some boundaries of transition dynamics. In J. Adams, J. Hayes, & B. Hopson (Eds.), *Transition: Understanding and managing personal change* (pp. 3-25). London, UK: Martin Robertson.

Houweling, H., & Coutinho, R. (1991). Risk of HIV infection among Dutch expatriates in sub-Saharan Africa. *International Journal of Sexually Transmitted Diseases and AIDS*, *2*, 252-257.

Howes, F., & Kealey, D. (1979). *Canadians in development*. Ottawa, ON, Canada: Canadian International Development Agency.

Huntingdon, J. (1984). *Migration as bereavement*. Paper presented at the Second Annual Symposium on Expatriate Stress and Breakdown, Royal College of Physicians, London, UK.

Jones, M. (1996). Understanding and managing chronic fatigue syndrome in missionaries. In M. Jones & E. Jones (Eds.), *Caring for the missionary into the 21st century* (pp. 36-43). (Available from Elphinstone International Health Centre, Elphinstone Wing, Carberry, UK)

———. (1999). HIV and the returning expatriate. *Journal of Travel Medicine*, *6*, 99-106.

———. (2000). Psychological aspects of travel and protracted visits. In C. Lockie, L. Calvert, J. Cossar, R. Knill Jones, F. Raeside, & E. Walker (Eds.), *Textbook of travel medicine and migrant health* (pp. 115-141). London, UK: Churchill Livingstone.

Lange, W., & Frame, J. (1990). High incidence of viral hepatitis among American missionaries in Africa. *American Journal of Tropical Medicine and Hygiene*, *43*, 527-533.

Lankester, T. (2000). Health screening and psychological considerations in the returned traveller. In C. Lockie, L. Calvert, J. Cossar, R. Knill Jones, F. Raeside, & E. Walker (Eds.), *Textbook of travel medicine and migrant health* (pp. 443-453). London, UK: Churchill Livingstone.

Lazarus, R., & Folkman, S. (1984). *Stress appraisal and coping*. New York, NY: Springer.

Lovell, D. (1997). *Psychological adjustment among returned overseas aid workers*. Unpublished doctoral thesis. University of Wales, Bangor.

———. (1999). Chronic fatigue syndrome amongst overseas development workers. *Journal of Travel Medicine*, *6*, 16-23.

MacPherson, D., & Kozarsky, P. (2000). Screening the long-term traveller. In G. Strickland (Ed.), *Hunter's tropical medicine and emerging diseases* (8th ed.) (pp. 1044-1045). Philadelphia, PA: W. B. Saunders.

Marlowe, M., & Sugarman, P. (1997). Disorders of personality. *British Medical Journal*, *315*, 176-179.

McCracken, K. (1973). Scottish medical missions in Africa. *Medical History*, *17*, 188-191.

Mittra, I., Baum, M., Thornton, H., & Houghton, J. (2000). Is clinical breast examination an acceptable alternative to mammographic screening? *British Medical Journal*, *321*, 1071-1073.

Oberg, K. (1960). Cultural shock: Adjustment to new cultural environments. *Practical Anthropology*, 7, 177-182.

Parkes, C. (1972). *Bereavement: Studies of grief in adult life*. London, UK: Tavistock.

Peppiatt, R., & Byass, P. (1991). A survey of the health of British missionaries. *British Journal of General Practice*, *41*, 159-162.

Price, G. (1913). Discussion on the cause of invaliding from the tropics. *British Medical Journal*, *2*, 1290-1297.

Richardson, J. (1992). Psychopathology in mission personnel. In K. O'Donnell (Ed.), *Missionary care: Counting the cost for world evangelization* (pp. 89-109). Pasadena, CA: William Carey Library.

Schouten, E., & Borgdorff, M. (1995). Increased mortality among Dutch development workers. *British Medical Journal, 311*, 1343-1344.

Schubert E. (1991). Personality disorders and the selection process for overseas missionaries. *International Bulletin of Missionary Research, 15*, 33-36.

Sheik, M., Gutierrez, D., Bolton, P., et al. (2000). Deaths amongst humanitarian workers. *British Medical Journal, 321*, 166-168.

Smith, G., & Barss, P. (1991). Unintentional injuries in developing countries: The epidemiology of a neglected problem. *Epidemiologic Reviews, 13*, 228-266.

Stokes, P. (1995, April 18). Nurse who caught AIDS in African mission is dead. *Daily Telegraph* (p. 5).

Tucker, R., & Andrews, L. (1992). Historical notes on missionary care. In K. O'Donnell (Ed.), *Missionary care: Counting the cost for world evangelization* (pp. 24-36). Pasadena, CA: William Carey Library.

Van Damme, P., Cramm, M., Van Der Auwera, J., et al. (1995). Horizontal transmission of hepatitis B virus. *Lancet, 345*, 27-29.

Whitty, M., Mabey, D., Armstrong, M., et al. (2000). Presentation and outcome of 1107 cases of schistosomiasis from Africa diagnosed in a non-endemic country. *Transactions of the Royal Society of Tropical Medicine and Hygiene, 94*, 531-534.

World Health Organization (WHO). (1992). *The ICD-10 classification of mental and behavioral disorders: Clinical descriptions and diagnostic guidelines*. Geneva, Switzerland: Author.

———. (1999, October). *Safety of injections*. Fact sheet No. 232. Geneva, Switzerland: Author.

***Michael E. Jones**, MB, ChB, FRCP Edin, Dip PC, completed undergraduate medical studies at Aberdeen, Scotland, where he also trained in internal medicine. In 1976, he went to Tanzania to work as Medical Specialist at Kilimanjaro Christian Medical Centre, a teaching hospital. When he and his wife Elizabeth (now a qualified counselor) returned in 1982 to the UK, they founded Care for Mission (CFM), a charity providing health care services for the missionary community located in the Scottish Borders. Mike also commenced a part-time appointment as Associate Specialist at the Infectious Diseases Unit in Edinburgh. In 1999, CFM relocated closer to Edinburgh and now operates as the Elphinstone International Health Centre, where Mike is Director and Senior Physician, and Elizabeth is Director and Counsellor. They have two children, both married, and one grandson. Email: mejones@eihc.org.*

***Kenneth Gamble** completed his medical training at the University of Saskatchewan, Canada, anticipating a lifelong career as a missionary physician. His initial posting was at Mosvold Hospital in the Northern Kwa Zulu district of Natal, South Africa. There he served with TEAM from 1978 through 1982 as Medical Superintendent. In 1982 he accepted an appointment as Executive Director of the Missionary Health Institute, Toronto, Ontario, Canada, and part-time Staff Physician at the Center for Travel and Tropical Medicine at the University of Toronto. Ken and his wife Linda have two sons, Nathan and Joel. Email: Ken.Gamble@attglobal.net.*

Special thanks to Ted Lankester, Director of InterHealth in London, and Philip Welsby, Consultant Physician at Western General Hospital in Edinburgh, for their helpful review of this chapter.

35

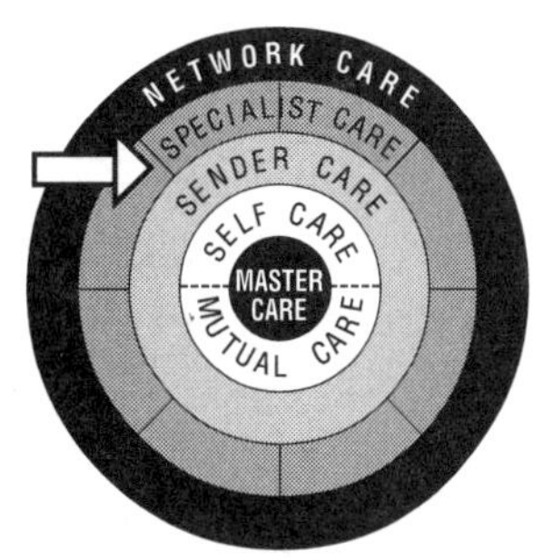

Health and Safety Guidelines For Preventing Accidents

INTERHEALTH
PEOPLE IN AID

This chapter outlines principles for giving advice to field staff and for drawing up accident guidelines. It will be particularly useful for personnel or human resource managers and field or programme managers. Employers have a duty of care to all field staff, but everyone has a role in ensuring safety!

An aid worker had been killed in a motorbike accident the week before I hopped on a moped after work without a helmet. I was tired and didn't want to wait for a lift home by car. I hit the only cement-lined drainage ditch in Burundi head first. It needn't have happened—I just didn't think.

As this story shows, many accidents result from human error—in other words, they are avoidable and can be prevented. Accidents are the most common cause of death, serious injury, and emergency repatriation among travellers abroad (World Health Organization, 1998). The most common of these are road accidents, swimming accidents, and household accidents.

Accident prevention guidelines are the single most important set of guidelines your agency can use to protect staff from avoidable injury or death. Field staff and their families must be aware of the importance of preventing accidents before they happen. They need to be given clear advice on accident prevention and response. They also need to understand the agency's accident guidelines and should agree to adhere to them.

Giving Advice

We were driving to Ruhengeri in Rwanda, four of us. I was in the front and noticed that the others in the back weren't wearing their seat belts. "Shouldn't you put those seat belts on?" I said. "Yes," they said, but they didn't put them on. These two were doctors!

Getting the message across requires persistence and patience! As one staff health officer said, "First timers are interested, but the old timers think they know it all."

The advice you give to staff will be based on information from *local risk assessments*. These should be carried out by appropriately qualified and experienced managers, and they should be regularly updated. Advice will, of course, vary according to the person, the job, and the circumstances in the region or country. Here are some suggestions for giving advice:

- Find out what staff and their families already know and what they need and want to know.
- Give people advice face-to-face, not just in writing. Talk through with them scenarios that have actually happened.
- Make sure that staff have read, understand, and agree to adhere to your agency's accident guidelines.
- Train staff in the use of First Aid procedures, where appropriate.
- Make sure field managers include accident prevention in team meetings. Ask them to report back to you on this! Staff could give presentations on accident prevention. This is a sure way to remember and promote key principles!

Accident Prevention Guidelines

Accident prevention guidelines are an important part of the advice you give. They tell staff:

- How to minimise accident risk.
- How to respond if an accident occurs.

Don't assume that experience is transferable between different countries. An appropriate response in one country may be dangerous or offensive in another.

Get field staff involved when developing or reviewing guidelines—this way they're more likely to remember and use them! Your guidelines should cover prevention of road, household, and swimming accidents. These areas follow next.

Safe Road Travel

From the moment's inattention that risks tragedy, to the driver deliberately flouting speed and drinking laws, traffic accidents are both an everyday part of life and a worsening global disaster.... By 1990, traffic accidents were assessed to be the world's ninth biggest cause of death, killing at least 500,000 people a year, though some put the fatality figure as high as a million, and injuring around 15 million (World Disasters Report, 1998).

Agencies must actively prepare field staff to travel safely by road or to drive or ride motor vehicles. Consider these top priorities:

Top Priorities

- Keep vehicles in good repair through regular, competent servicing and regular inspection of brakes, tyres, steering, and lights. Train staff who use or drive/ride vehicles in the essentials of maintenance. Keep records of vehicle maintenance and staff training.
- Fit seat belts to both front and rear seats in passenger and goods vehicles, and provide helmets and protective clothing for motor cycle users. Using seat belts is the single most important way of saving lives—ensure they are used by all, even for the shortest journey. Even if seat belts or helmets are not required by law, they should still be used.
- Choose passenger and goods vehicles that have air conditioning, if possible, and good seats. These are not luxuries; they help prevent heat exhaustion, discomfort, and distraction.
- Assume incompetence in motorcycle, four-wheel, HGV, off-road, defensive, and safe driving/riding until you are proved wrong. Ensure drivers are licensed and competent to use programme vehicles.
- Ensure motor cyclists wear crash helmets, even for the shortest journeys. They also need heavy-duty footwear, gloves, and jackets. Sandals and t-shirts give no protection.
- Never allow drivers or riders to use vehicles when under the influence of drugs or alcohol.
- Plan journeys and allow enough time to avoid having to travel at unsafe speeds or at night. Except in emergencies, avoid driving when excessively tired or for prolonged periods without a break.

■ Except in emergencies, avoid using two-way radios while driving.

■ Avoid driving without a co-driver on long journeys.

■ Ensure all vehicles carry a First Aid kit, a working torch, and leather gloves. Ensure staff understand how to apply First Aid procedures.

■ Set up a "Trusted Donor List" or other safe blood donor scheme and procedure, in case blood transfusion is needed after serious accidents.

Household Safety

One day my cat caught a squirrel. I rescued the squirrel but got bitten in the process. I needed a course of rabies jabs, but Sri Lanka had no serum stocks—all the doctors had run out. In the end, another agency in Colombo managed to find me some. But if I had been cut off from the capital because of the war, it could have been a different story.

In Britain, we know that accidents in the home account for more injuries and deaths than road accidents. They are described as the "hidden epidemic" by the Royal Society for the Prevention of Accidents. Children and those over 65 are particularly vulnerable to accidents in the home. But human error, stress, change of routine, and unsafe practices all contribute to an environment in which *anyone* can be at risk in a new or temporary home. Families with children can be particularly vulnerable.

Top Priorities

■ Carry out a risk assessment of housing or temporary accommodation, including hotels and their surroundings, before signing agreements or on first arrival. Take into account the needs of families with young children and other family members with special needs. Think about your responsibilities towards domestic staff too.

■ When assessing risks, consider the most common causes of household injuries and deaths in the home. These will include electric shocks and unsafe wiring (e.g., in showers); burns and scalding (e.g., from house/cooking fires and kitchen equipment); slips, trips, and falls, inside or from stairs, windows, or balconies; cuts, including from glass in doors and windows; being bitten or stung by animals or insects; drowning (a child can drown in as little as three inches of water); and poisoning (e.g., by medicines or household chemicals).

■ Assessments should consider the extent to which local factors might increase these common risks. For example: climate; construction, including layout, emergency exits, and wiring; culture shock, change of routine, change of accommodation, stress; access to clean water; access to alcohol; presence of rabies or malaria; isolation of posting and/or lack of access to transport.

■ Wherever possible, ensure provision of fire extinguishers, fire blankets, and smoke alarms.

■ Ensure individuals and/or households have a First Aid kit.

Safe Swimming

I had a day off and took a minibus out of Accra to the coast. I was on my own and planned to spend a couple of hours on the beach. The waves didn't look too high, and I am a strong swimmer, but I wasn't prepared for what happened. I was dragged down by the undertow and rolled like a ball inside the wave. To this day, I'm not sure how I got out. Afterwards, I realised I should have found out about that particular stretch of coast and shouldn't have gone alone.

Top Priorities

Advise staff to:

■ Find out how safe local beaches, lakes, rivers, or swimming pools are.

■ Swim only in waters free from dangerous currents, severe pollution, and the presence of dangerous fauna.

■ Swim within their depth.

■ Swim with a companion rather than alone; supervise children at all times.

- Avoid swimming after consumption of alcohol or a heavy meal. Alcohol can create a false sense of security and can induce people to swim alone or stay too long in cold water.
- Avoid running along the edge of hotel or public swimming pools, diving into cloudy pools, or diving into any pool without first checking the water depth.

In Case of Accident or Near Misses

Top Priorities

- Apply local guidelines on safe response to accidents. Remember that a safe, appropriate response can differ from country to country.
- Apply safe blood donor scheme procedures. Do not use locally available blood from unknown sources, except in extreme circumstances.
- Follow insurance and agency procedures to enable removal to specialist hospitals in-country or abroad, if necessary.
- See that all accidents are reported to the local and head offices, and record details in writing.
- Investigate accidents that result in serious injury or death.
- Keep an accident book in field offices. In line with the People In Aid Code, keep records of injuries, accidents, and fatalities, and use them to help assess and reduce further risk to field staff and their families.
- Use records to compare your agency's performance with that of others.

Reflection and Discussion

1. What did you find most useful about the information in these guidelines?
2. How could these guidelines be improved?
3. Which accidents are most common in your organization?
4. What policies have helped contribute to accident prevention in your agency?
5. How do you use or plan to use these guidelines in your agency?

References and Additional Resources

Alcohol Concern. (1994). *Alcohol and accidents. Factsheet 20*. London, UK: Author.

Department of Trade and Industry. (1998). *Home accident surveillance system*. (Available from: DTI, 1 Victoria Street, London SW1H OET, UK; tel. 44 171 215 5000)

Lankester, T. (1998, April). Just don't do it. *The Health Exchange*. (Available from: info@ihe.org.uk)

———. (1999). *The traveller's good health guide*. London, UK: Hodder & Stoughton.

Overseas Development Institute. (1997). *People In Aid code of best practice in the management and support of aid personnel*. London, UK: ODI. (Also available in French and Spanish from: Aidpeople@aol.com)

Royal Society for the Prevention of Accidents. *Home safety fact sheet HS274*.

World disasters report. (1998). Geneva, Switzerland: International Federation of Red Cross and Red Crescent Societies.

World Health Organization. (1998). *International travel and health*. Geneva, Switzerland: Author.

This article was written by ***Dr. Ted Lankester*** *with InterHealth and* ***Sara Davidson*** *with People In Aid. Special thanks to Isobel McConnan for her help with editing. Thanks also to Barry Coleman (Riders for Health), Gay Harper (Save the Children Fund UK), Karen Howell (Travel Health Ltd), Annie Macarthy (InterHealth), Rachel Roberts (MAF Europe), and the aid workers who shared their field experiences. Suggestions for further developing these guidelines are welcome.*

InterHealth *provides medical and psychological services for overseas mission personnel and aid workers. 157 Waterloo Road, London SE1 8US, UK. Tel: 44 (0)207 902 9000. Fax: 44 (0)207 928 0927. Email: doctors@interhealth.org.uk.*

People In Aid *has developed a variety of best practice guidelines for aid workers, in conjunction with other organizations. 9 Grosvenor Crescent, London SW1X 7EF, UK. Tel/fax: 44 (0)207 235 0895. Email: Aidpeople@aol.com.*

36

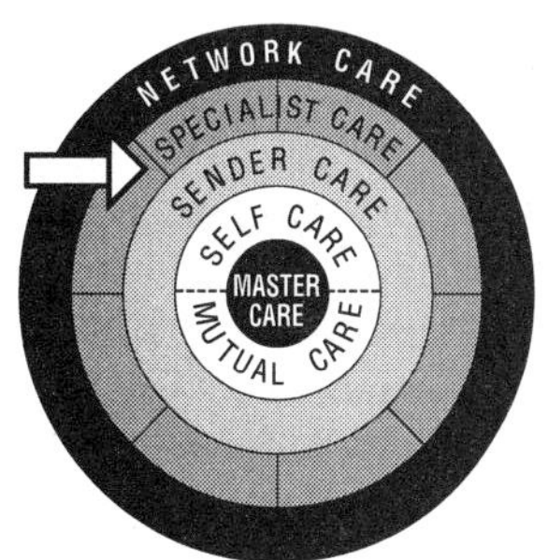

Career Development For Mission Personnel

GORDON JONES
ROSEMARY JONES

A good job fit, serving with one's gifts/strengths, ongoing training, and willingness to sacrifice all blend together to form resilient, effective, and satisfied mission personnel. "As each one has received a special gift, so use it to serve one another, as good stewards of the manifold grace of God" (1 Peter 4:10).

"I thought missionaries are expected to do the things they like least and for which they are least gifted." This comment was made to us as we were sitting in the student lounge at a seminary in Switzerland, chatting with a couple of students about member care. We had told them that we found career counseling a helpful tool in working with colleagues in Africa. By now, the interest was obvious, and the number of students around us increased from two or three to about a dozen. All agreed that the concept that we could use our natural gifts in mission work and find enjoyment and satisfaction in such work was a new thought!

On the field, we sometimes have to perform tasks that we do not like, stepping in to do whatever is necessary to help the group. However, if God has uniquely gifted each of us, then surely our normal expectation is that He wants to anoint and use those gifts in His service. "Everyone has different gifts, and these differences create a broad spectrum of Christian usefulness. As a general rule, God plans to put square pegs into square holes" (Foyle, 2001, p. 44).

Some Current Realities

Few mission members have any career development plan. Indeed, the idea of using the word "career" and the concept of career development in mission work almost seem oxymoronic. At a time when the number of people wanting to make a long-term commitment to missions is dropping and the number of short-termers is increasing, we need to attract long-term career people more than ever. All mission personnel need opportunities to develop their skills. Yet much money can be used for recruitment and mobilization, with little invested in the further development of mission personnel, especially long-term workers and potential future leaders.

"One of the basic challenges of a mission agency is to find a balance between its commitment to accomplishing evangelistic tasks and its commitment to care for and develop staff. Too frequently, the emphasis falls more on the side of the task, to the near exclusion of the people who are needed to work on the task. Organizational practices which place task attainment over staff development are considered a non-acceptable operating procedure in today's business world, and rightfully so. This should be especially true within the mission agency, considering the biblical exhortations to care for and honor one another" (Shedlosky, 1992, p. 247).

The cross-cultural adjustments for those coming from the Newer Sending Countries (NSCs) are just as enormous as those faced by Western missionaries going to the developing world. However, sometimes their preparation is less extensive, and the sending agencies have less corporate experience. There is a danger of their repeating our mistakes. Those of us from the traditional sending countries may have more opportunities for career development, change, and growth. We must recognize that people coming into mission service from the NSCs may also need help and encouragement in career development and change.

Multinational companies recruiting from universities are now also emphasizing opportunities for in-house training and development, along with the salary and benefits package. Today's young adults rate personal growth opportunities and opportunities to develop their career potential as very important values. Some multinational professional service providers have an in-house career management service. Such a service is totally confidential to the client and gives help with career development both within and outside the company.

At the other end of the career path, there is an increasing trend for people to take early retirement in order to serve in missions as a second career—"the Finishers." Other people volunteer for missions following normal retirement. Many of those who join missions in later life bring with them many years of experience shaped by personal development and training opportunities. This may leave the long-term missionaries feeling woefully lacking in skills, in contrast to the specialties that these "later arrivals" are bringing.

Natural Gifts

Does finding a place in missions for career development mean that we are buying into the latest "trend," reinforcing a "give me this, I deserve it" mentality, and bypassing the values of service and sacrifice? Not at all! There are enough frustrations, plenty of opportunities to die to self, illnesses, refusal of visas, and general stress, without having to add to them the pressure of having to work consistently in areas in which we are not naturally gifted. In describing the relationship between stress and natural gifts, we can think of a continuum ranging from those tasks that we do easily and well (natural gifts) to those that we will always do poorly (see Figure 1). The latter are the ones in which we are all "fingers and thumbs." We can all do tasks that are outside our areas of gifting for short periods of time. However, if we have to function really outside our natural gift range for long periods of time, then this will drain our energy, increase our stress, and cause many of us to begin to malfunction.

Figure 1

Relationship Between Natural Gifts and Stress*

Natural Gifts	Learned Skills	Unskilled
Gifted	Non-gifted	
(energizers)	(energy drainers)	(stressors)

* Adapted from work done by J. Warkentin with SIL Intl.

"Ducks swim easily in water, but they still have to walk on land—and they do that poorly. Such waddling is a normal and inevitable cause of frustration. But although ducks can't eliminate land excursions, they don't make backpacking a major part of their activity. You can't eliminate your waddling, nor should you attempt to do so. Just don't make it a primary activity. We suggest the 60/40 rule: Spend at least 60% of your time in your areas of strength, as indicated by your natural talents, and no more than 40% of your time in areas of non-strength" (Bradley & Carty, 1991, p. 37).

Obviously, there is a potential clash for the "willing servant" who tends to respond to perceived need and does not pay sufficient attention to God's gifting and His plan to use our gifts. The same is true for willing teams, departments, and organizations that sometimes go after areas of service that are beyond them.

Under-Performers

People working in the wrong role are sometimes judged to be poor at coping and/or cultural adjustment. Relationships may be fraught with tension. Yet when we are in the wrong job, it is normal for our coping mechanisms to be affected, and so we do not cope well with all the other pressures of cross-cultural living.

"The incompetence we see everywhere is not because people lack gifts, but because they are not in the right place for their gifts. They are not being stewards of what God has given them. There are plenty of gifts to do all the work that needs to be done everywhere and to do all of it gloriously well—so well, in fact, that people would go rejoicing from day to day over how much was accomplished and how well it was accomplished" (Miller & Mattson, 1982, p. 41).

Some personality types fare better than others. For example, some highly creative people who value authenticity and personal growth are particularly vulnerable to high stress when doing work for which they are ill suited. They feel they are not being true to themselves and can begin to malfunction more quickly than some other personality types. People with personalities who need to be needed, however, are energized by serving and meeting needs in others, and this motivation may enable them to function outside of their natural gifting. Others are "company workers," who love to support the organization, and they can sometimes work outside their strength area if "the company" needs help. They often feel very virtuous about doing this, which is a reward in itself.

In their book, *The Truth About You*, Miller and Mattson (1977, p. 43) stress the importance of identifying what it is that provides motivation. They suggest a method of looking back over life and identifying the motivating factor in each accomplishment. They write, "Every time you accomplished what you enjoyed and believed you did well, you achieved a result of great importance to you. You got something out of what you did. That 'something' is always the same."

Career Development and Counseling

Career development for Christians is a lifelong process of determining how we can most effectively use our gifts in forwarding the work of the Lord. It includes managing our own development, growing in our understanding of our gifts, and adjusting to the changing needs and opportunities in God's kingdom.

Career counseling may be best defined as a set of services designed to assist a person in the career development process. The counselor can guide the client to a greater self-awareness through an assessment process aimed at defining those intrinsic motivators which ignite one's passion and guide one's choices. These motivators will determine, within the limits of one's freedom to choose, what the person chooses to work on and the natural abilities he/she brings to work.

Often, people receiving career counseling in the missions context are aware of themselves—their interests, motivations, and gifts. However, the tasks to which they are called may be difficult to "know" or define. An independent person, who has the time to listen and with whom workers can talk things over and share their misgivings, may be what is really needed. Our experience has been that we are rarely called on to help people move out of mission, just to help them understand their job circumstances better and maybe how to change things a little to obtain a better match between gifts and job.

The constraints of life as it really is on the field make the above an ideal that is difficult to achieve. Those on the overseas field may be far away from access to a career counselor, or indeed from anyone with whom they can freely discuss such issues. To address this need, we wrote a self-help career counseling book, *Naturally Gifted* (1991), which enables users to produce a personal profile of their gifts, motivators, values, etc., in a work situation. The book has been successfully used by many missionaries on the field, especially in Africa.

Benefits From Career Counseling

People who are new to missions

Many people, such as doctors, nurses, pilots, and teachers, come into missions to work in their area of training and expertise. Others come because of a call to overseas service, without a clear job role. The latter will benefit from some career counseling input, possibly even before leaving for overseas. This should help to obviate the stress of the "square pegs in round holes" syndrome.

A young man, who had been working for a local government office for seven years, came on a training course in linguistics, with a view to doing Bible translation or literacy work. His gifts did not make him a natural language worker. The course tutors suggested he could function in such work in a restricted role. He was uneasy about this and came to us for some career counseling help, to see if there was not a better fit for him elsewhere. He wrote recently: "After talking to the career people in the personnel department, I discovered that the thousand and one things that I seemed interested in (people, maintenance, managing, even cooking) fit well with the role of center manager of one of our overseas mission bases. They listened, and I can now look back on 15 years and say I have been a very happy round peg in a round hole."

People who seek a change in role

Circumstances change. People change and grow. Many go to the field to fulfill one role and end up doing another. Most of us are not content to fill one role or job for the whole of our working life. These days, people are looking for lifelong learning and growth opportunities. All of these factors mean that career development is a lifelong process, with particular points at which career counseling may help the process.

In the middle of their career path, many in their 30s and 40s are stopping to ask, "I've done this and achieved that, but I feel God has more for me. What does He have for me now?" This is a normal adult developmental stage at mid-life, looking back at what has been achieved and looking forward and planning for the future. We have seen this process happening to many career missionaries. Without help to develop their mission careers in a satisfying and fulfilling way, many of them will leave and go back into more fulfilling secular employment. Surely there is nothing unspiritual or unbiblical in admitting that Christians also follow the normal adult developmental stages. Perhaps the Lord used Abraham's mid-life quest to call him to leave Ur and move on.

In the course of normal working life or even in an annual review, it is not always possible for one's supervisor to cover adequately future job options, further training possibilities, etc., since such options could well impinge negatively on the person's program in the short term. A personnel officer or even a counselor or consultant can usually be more objective. It is sometimes possible to receive some help by email these days, if it is not feasible to meet face to face.

A missionary mother based in an African city was trying to find her role, now that her children were at school and she had more time. Should she go back to her pre-mission career of teaching? Where would her natural skills best fit in mission work? This is what she said:

"At the time I went for career help, I was wondering whether I should resign from the mission and go back into teaching or pursue the member care role I had been offered. Teaching part time at a local school showed me I loved the contact with children, but I didn't enjoy all the extra stress and paperwork that would be involved. I thought the teaching role would also hinder the time I would have available to be with my own children. At that point, though, I wasn't sure if I was ready for a complete change of job. Going into the new area of member care was a bit scary.

"Having the career counseling confirmed my thinking that in taking the member care role, I wasn't starting a track I would hate or for which I would be totally unsuitable. It was nice to talk things over with someone with mission experience but no vested interest in my decision. I saw that the gifts and skills I used in teaching were transferable gifts that I could use in member care. I think the counseling gave me the confidence to give it a go. Since then, I have been thrilled at how good a match this kind of job is for my skills and abilities."

People who are "square pegs in round holes"

Jennifer was a lively, happy, fun, and extroverted young adult in missions. She had made a great contribution in interesting young people to consider missions. She was asked to lead a team, when she hated leading others, in a task in which she had little experience, to a country where she had not yet worked. Even before the team went overseas, the tensions of the training course began to sap her emotional energy. The lively, happy person disappeared. She began to question her call to missions and started exploring other options for service. The project was canceled.

How can we take such gifted people and misuse them so? Is it our task orientation that drives us to try to squeeze square pegs into round holes? We Evangelicals seem to have a strong tendency to consider the task of evangelism so important that we can be, as Pamela Evans (1999) entitles her book, driven beyond the call of God. Consider Alister McGrath's (1994) sobering words: "The price paid for Evangelical activism is all too often Evangelical burnout. Evangelicalism has had its great successes; it also seems to produce more than its fair share of walking wounded."

People who struggle with aspects of their role

A Bible translator living in a rural African village appeared not to be making much progress. The family had been in this assignment for nearly a decade, and their administrator wanted more reports, more visible written results. Some career counseling help was given to this couple, and as a result a short-term member was added to the team to write up the linguistic data and satisfy the administrator's requirements. The short-termer used his natural gifts to do this work, allowing the missionary family to concentrate on their strength areas. This is an example of the fact that career counseling doesn't always mean career change, but it may result in job enrichment and/or redesign. Sometimes help is necessary to get people "over the hump." One member of SIL International wrote:

"Arriving in Africa at age 30, I had assumed that this new career in Bible translation would be as successful as my previous one in industry. But I found that

I was mismatched entirely for the context. My training was good, the vision was valid, but what I actually had to do in the daily life of the project was very, very far from my personality and gifts. I came to the conclusion that, at the least, I needed to leave my organization. In addition, I had to question whether I knew the least bit about how to listen to God.

"The counseling I received from trained colleagues showed me that I had not followed the wrong vision but the wrong avenue of service. Some of us are so taken by the need that we can only see one way to answer it. I found that God did indeed make me for Bible translation, and for the last 10 years I've been doing so in technical support and training, and now in management and in funding administration. I'm certainly doing more for the Bibleless peoples of Africa than I would have if I had been able to stay in my first assignment, and I'm certainly enjoying it more. Should this sort of evaluation have been available at our mission training school? Yes, certainly. And it is now. I'm very happy that the Lord made it available to me when I needed it."

Those called to leadership

A frequently encountered scenario in missions is that of someone who is already functioning well in a particular role being asked to take on a leadership role. Maybe the person is interacting with local people, evangelizing and planting churches, when the field leader is called back to the home country for family reasons. Almost all missions are desperately in need of competent and experienced leaders, and a member of the team who is inexperienced in management is asked to take over the administrator/leader's role.

But the administrator's role, involving such things as corresponding with sending countries, working on field finances, and trying to guide strong-minded subordinates, uses very different gifts and skills from the ones used in relating to local people. Some career counseling help, given before the switch is made, can sometimes prevent a disaster. If there is no other option for the position of leader/administrator, some help can be given to identify ways and means of coping, given the constraints of the individual's own personality, and maybe ways of using the gifts of the others on the team.

In teamwork and relationship building

When two families were assigned to a project in a remote part of Africa, colleagues commented on how very different they were from each other. One family was comprised of organized, forward planners, while the other family had a casual, "go with the flow" style. One family came from a Reformed theological background; the other, from a Pentecostal tradition. One husband was an introverted, analytic academic; the other used a relational, people-oriented approach. We spent a week doing some team building with these two couples. Over the years, a gradually deepening understanding of one another emerged. This developed into a strong partnership in which each person could be appreciated for his/her different personality, skills, and abilities.

Team building can include the use of career counseling tools, such as the Interest Test (included in our book, *Naturally Gifted*), in order to help each team member identify his/her natural gifts and styles of working. We usually include the Self-Perception Inventory (also in *Naturally Gifted*), which enables team members to identify their natural team role or roles. In addition, we almost always allow time for a considerable amount of open-ended discussion with the team, using such questions as, "What have you appreciated about being on this team so far?" and, "What would you like to see change in the future?" At the end of each chapter in our book *Teamwork* (1995), there are activities that a team can do to help themselves become a better functioning team.

Conclusion

Mission service tends to have a poor image, not only with the secular world, but in some cases within the Christian church as well. Career development is a tool that can help reverse that negative image. Each person is a unique creation of God, called to manifest the values of God's kingdom, not just to accomplish certain mission tasks. If we ignore these truths, we miss something of God's purpose for us in our working together with Him.

Reflection and Discussion

1. Continue to look at the relationship between career development and the place of sacrifice in missions. How do you integrate these two areas?
2. How realistic is it to talk about career development for personnel from sending groups/nations having limited resources, such as those from the NSCs?
3. List a few things you are doing to further develop yourself and your work. What else could you do?
4. What are some of the main ways that your organization is providing career development for its personnel?
5. Which of the approaches/tools listed in the article seem the most useful for you in your setting?

References

Bradley, J., & Carty, J. (1991). *Unlocking your sixth suitcase: How to love what you do and do what you love*. Colorado Springs, CO: NavPress.

Evans, P. (1999). *Driven beyond the call of God: Discovering the rhythms of grace*. Oxford, UK: The Bible Reading Fellowship.

Foyle, M. (2001). *Honourably wounded: Stress among Christian workers*. London, UK: Monarch.

Jones, G., & Jones, R. (1991). *Naturally gifted: A Christian perspective on personality, gifts, and abilities*. London, UK: Scripture Union. (Available from: Hatters Lane Publications, 196 Hatters Lane, High Wycombe, Bucks HP13 7LY, UK)

———. (1995). *Teamwork*. London, UK: Scripture Union. (Available from: Hatters Lane Publications, 196 Hatters Lane, High Wycombe, Bucks HP13 7LY, UK)

McGrath, A. (1994). *Evangelicalism and the future of Christianity*. London, UK: Hodder & Stoughton.

Miller, A., & Mattson, R. (1977). *The truth about you: Discover what you should be doing with your life*. Old Tappan, NJ: Fleming H. Revell.

———. (1982). *Finding a job you can love*. Nashville, TN: Thomas Nelson.

Shedlosky, P. (1992). Career development and the mission agency. In K. O'Donnell (Ed.), *Missionary care: Counting the cost for world evangelization* (pp. 247-259). Pasadena, CA: William Carey Library.

__Gordon Jones__ and __Rosemary Jones__ have worked for 36 years with Wycliffe Bible Translators/SIL International. The last 13 years, they have been Personnel Development Coordinators for Africa. They have traveled extensively in Africa, doing career counseling, short-term pastoral counseling, team building, and retreat leading. Before that, Gordon was Personnel Director for British Wycliffe. Gordon has a bachelor's degree in metallurgy (Aston University, Birmingham, UK) and a diploma in theology (London University). Rosemary has a bachelor's degree in psychology (Open University, UK) and a diploma in pastoral counseling (Nottingham University, UK). Both trained as career counselors at Dallas, Texas, within SIL. They have written two books, __Naturally Gifted__ (1991) and __Teamwork__ (1995). Email for both Gordon and Rosemary: G.R.Jones@Libertysurf.co.uk.

37

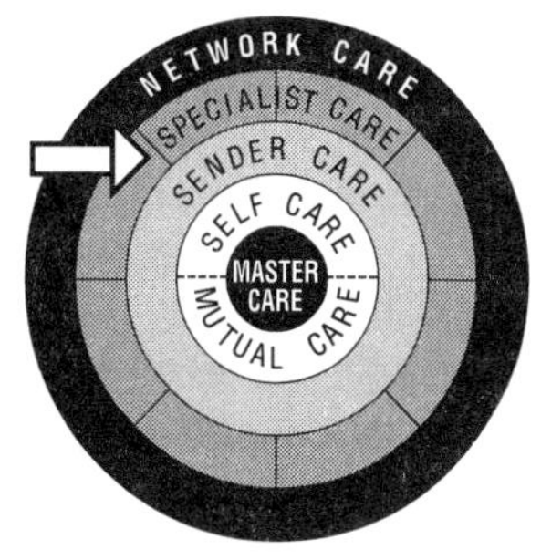

Training Asian Counselors For Missionary Care

RON NOLL
BARBARA ROHNERT-NOLL

Called one of the "Little Tigers" of Asian commerce, Singapore is imbued with an ancient Chinese Confucian culture that readily absorbs Western commerce and technology, yet subtly prevents many Christian values from taking root any deeper than its shiny, commercial veneer. We wondered what God had in mind by sending us to Singapore. Our vision for missionary care evolved into a 10-year strategic plan of development, contextualization, and application. In the first year, we came to realize that bringing the modern Christian counseling movement together with the burgeoning Asian mission movement was, in fact, our major task. It would continue to be so for many additional years, but for now we would begin by seeking to train counselors in a Singapore seminary and help prepare them for ministry with sending churches and mission organizations of Asia. In addition, we were endeavoring to provide emergency care for missionaries in crisis, as a model and practical example of our central goal of missionary care. The process proved a challenging one, and numerous obstacles had to be overcome, as we detail below.

Singapore, previously the tropical gem of the British Empire's colonial system, is located right on the equator. On my first mission survey visit to Singapore in 1988, it looked like any other world mega-city, but even more modern and most certainly cleaner than most Western cities. What a strategic and inviting place to launch a member care ministry on behalf of Asians! But when we finally settled there in 1992, we found the modern appearance, along with the hopes for a relatively smooth ministry, extremely deceptive.

The Preliminary Platforms for Start-Up

The first strategic planning step involved our specific commitment to God's call. In retrospect, like many things in our lives, we now see the actual timing and purpose of His hand behind it all. In 1987, I (Ron) finally accepted as real the "word" I had received from God: "Go develop a Singapore-based triage and missionary care program, connected with an email network support system, for missionary families at risk in Asia." God saw the future and gave direction. Our 10-year plan was completed in almost exactly 10 years from the time I first wrote it and committed it to the Lord in 1987. Below are the basic moves God put us through to reach the goal. They are now listed in neat, linear order, even though at times in reality they overlapped. We often found ourselves asking, "Which project via which platform is most urgent?"

A Platform for Strategic Location in Asia

In the 1950s, after returning from a difficult stint on the field in Guatemala, I tried to evangelize Asians on campuses with InterVarsity Christian Fellowship. I had no success, and I told God, "Send me back to the field—anywhere but to Asia!" In 1987, I received a call to return to my first love, the mission field. It was to Asia! But Barbara wanted to return to her first love, Africa, where she had served before we were married. God confirmed Singapore to me, and it seemed logical, since we needed to settle where the largest number of Asian missions and sending centers were located. Looking back, God's choice of Singapore was perfect. Today, Singapore is even more strategic to missionary training and sending, since Hong Kong has now gone under Chinese Communist rule.

Platforms for Promoting Holistic Member Care in Asia

In order to anchor new concepts in a culture like Singapore, we believed we had to find platforms in formal, tertiary education settings that granted degrees that were accepted by the strict Singapore government. We also needed practical experience platforms in which to do hands-on training in our new model of holistic mission and church member care. From these platforms, we could teach the basics of cross-cultural counseling and modern pastoral care and better prepare mission candidates. We felt that this training could work preventively to help reduce the attrition rate among Christian workers. So Barbara and I accepted positions in the Pastoral Counseling Department of a Singapore seminary. These positions provided the government-certified, formal, academic platform we needed.

Practical Experience Platforms via the Church

Just as in medical training, where students gain experience at a teaching hospital, we needed a platform where our students could practice what we were teaching. Some of the new churches in Singapore provided this platform for showing how our holistic member care model worked in action. We did lots of basic training on listening, feeling focus, and critical incident debriefing, plus tracking and recording behaviorally observable growth of the client. Fortunately, the Singaporean Chinese churches in which we worked, being very communal, found a place for nearly everyone to fit into the body and feel a sense of belonging. This was something we saw lacking in many Western churches in which we worked. In the Chinese churches, membership meant being an active member of a small group. The result was that there were few isolated folks in the church. In spite of attempts at covering problems to save face, at the first sign of physical or emotional disorder or marital disharmony, these caring churches took responsibility for early identification and initiation of the healing process at the cell group level. They did not wait until the problem got worse and then send members out of the church to secular specialists. However, some of the care they gave made things worse, so we were invited to help. Thus, these churches became our second platform for exposing Singaporeans to a holistic model of member caregiving.

A Cross-Cultural Training Platform for Asians

The third platform that we needed for people bound for foreign service was an agency or institution that offered a cross-cultural counseling experience, especially outside the Asian, Confucian culture. Internships in Asia were not well monitored, so we sponsored our students' internships at the Good Samaritan Ministry International (GSM) training center near Portland, Oregon, in the United States. This gave us the cross-cultural counselor training needed for missionary counselor candidates who had never been out of Asia. The free scholarships, including board and room, were and still are extended to those we trained. This meant that these Asian students had to pay only for their air tickets. This training opened a whole new door of understanding in Singapore as to what holistic member care really meant. Here is a humorous anecdote from the debriefing of one of our Chinese students returning from GSM's three-month cross-cultural counseling internship:

"I got my first client at GSM and was overwhelmed. I am just 5 foot, 1 inch tall. The huge 300-pound black man that entered the counseling room almost filled it with his 6 foot, 4 inch frame and shoulders like an American football player. He sat down and addressed me this way: 'Whass happenin', baby?' I did not know what to say. I had no idea what to do. I latched onto the only word I understood, 'baby.' So I asked him to tell me about his baby."

A Platform for Reaching Professionals in the Community

A fourth platform was for introducing our model and our witness to Asian professionals in the general public. We developed this public platform with a Singaporean social worker, Mrs. Esther Zer-Wong. Esther helped us found the Church Recovery Network, which soon became the Community Recovery Network (CRN). This organization continues today as Singapore's central clearinghouse for "recovery training" (recovery in the sense of healing from various types of addictive behavior, including workaholism, eating disorders, sexual addictions, substance abuse, etc.). Today, under the direction of Esther, CRN connects and trains both nonprofessional and professional care workers, including government drug and prison counselors, Muslim and Hindu social workers, and Christian church and mission staff.

CRN's initial focus was on introducing the holistic, developmental recovery and member care model, in contrast to Singapore's traditional medical model. This strategy gradually gained acceptance among the governmental, church, mission, and secular communities. For example, we were eventually invited to do a weekly radio program, "Ask the Counselors." This program drew telephone call-in questions, which we were allowed to answer from a member care counseling point of view, as long as we did not mention church, missions, or religion in general. Eventually, using CRN as a local, grass-roots launching pad, we were ready for the next step of our strategy. With the encouragement of some international and local member care colleagues, such as Sam Kuna with Singapore Teen Challenge, we established a regional interagency affiliation called Member Care Associates Asia (MCAA).

A Favorite Training Approach

The two CRN training topics that gained the most favor among Asians in the public sector were the workshops on grieving and addiction. The two training methods most favored were our adaptation of a "fishbowl" exercise and our model of small recovery groups. The fishbowl used real live volunteer cases from the audience. The lively interaction during this exercise compared favorably with what Singaporeans usually received. Normal fare ran from the so-called "hit and run" international counseling speakers, who were highly cognitive and theoretical, to the other extreme, in which the conferences were highly ritualized political rallies for government programs.

The fishbowl exercise was focused on building "processing" competence. The first learning objective of the training was to reduce resistance, so as to reprogram the "passive student" or "uninvolved observer" behavior, common even among trained professionals. Once we had established participants' trust through a sense of safety and clinical competence, the exercise seemed to cut right through the secrecy of their face-saving, cultural shame and fear of exposure to ridicule.

The fishbowl exercise began with one hour of teaching on a counseling topic, followed by questions and a coffee break. During the break, the trainees were given an assignment to discuss what was just presented with another trainee whom they knew the least. Then the presenter, a skilled therapist, would sit facing a volunteer client, with both individuals sitting in the middle of two concentric circles of trainees. The trainees in circle 1, the inner circle around the therapist and the focus person, were chosen because they had experienced a problem similar to that of the focus person. These individuals remained quiet observers for the first hour. Then, after an hour of intensive process between the therapist and the focus person, the trainees in circle 1 of the fishbowl could ask questions of the focus person and the therapist. After another tea and coffee break, those seated in the outer circle 2, could volunteer to exchange places with those in circle 1 and ask questions. This gave the more apprehensive trainees a chance to find their comfort level and test the safety level of the process. Later in the day, the plenary group broke up into small groups led by facilitators whom we had trained and who gave us feedback as to how learning was progressing.

The fishbowl was actually part of week-long seminars that we offered. We started by having everyone introduce themselves and tell why they were there and what they wanted to learn. Then content-oriented presentations were made. Each morning, the seminar themes were progressively explained a bit deeper. But these content lectures were never more than an hour long and were followed by a time for questions and answers. Then there was a coffee break for social exchange and for our local facilitators to interact and get a sense of how far into the process the trainees were. We held the time schedules and basic structure as constants for all our training, so the participants came to know what to expect from our training group from year to year. Yet the content often changed from day to day and from event to event, to target the audience's needs better. Changes depended on our local facilitators' feedback and assessment of how the trainees were progressing. The constancy and predictability of the basic structure provided security to these Asian trainees. For us, it provided a reference point against which we could measure other variables over time. We found that this structure released high group energy and interest, and it resulted in a steeper learning curve.

We followed up on the process with free monthly CRN meetings, where our local facilitators and trainees could report on how they were using what they had learned. There they could also network with others to learn new applications and to gain support to continue, even against resistance from "traditionalists." The key to training success was the constant feedback system from local facilitators, whom we trained during the seminars. The facilitators were trainees who, after attending one of our seminars, returned and volunteered to lead the small groups and give us feedback. During a seminar, we met them for training and feedback three times daily: in the morning at breakfast, at lunch, and at dinner in the evening. Once they were trained in our small-group format, many CRN facilitators went on to run groups in their own home communities or agencies. We had 14 CRN small groups for support/recovery running in Singapore at one time, some even in prisons. For those facilitators who wanted to continue on, we offered an ongoing member care Training Of Trainers (TOTs) program. These were the people who kept our training practical and kept it hitting the felt needs of Asians. One director of a government counseling agency responded to a questionnaire by saying, "We have never experienced such deep, live-action, process training in all the years of training as government-employed counselors."

This response of a government official brought a breath of relief. We had gambled that our strategy of staying flexible, with no budget and bypassing the government's formal registration of CRN as a "formal organization," would pay off. We did this by building a network of equal, independent, volunteer associates. We thus avoided legal fees and avoided becoming a professional, traditional, static, structured organization in which we would have to spend most of our time filling out government application and permission forms. Thus, with the network model, CRN survived and had more flexibility to respond to immediate felt needs of the local trainees.

Issues in Planting New Models for Helping and Member Care

In making the transition from the United States/Europe to Asia, we encountered a number of obstacles. Among these were the need to develop personal credibility, the need to reconsider the models in which we had been trained, cultural obstacles, institutional and personal limitations, and compassion fatigue. In this section, we will examine these challenges and some of the ways we were able to resolve them.

Training Levels in Asian Seminaries and Churches

At our jobs in the seminary, we soon encountered some problems that we had not anticipated. It is said that getting into higher education in Asia is difficult. But once you are in, you will graduate almost no matter what. We had to decide what kind of counselors we could realistically train and still ethically call it a Master of Arts program in pastoral counseling. We wanted to provide entry-level counselor education for Asians, without the depth of psychological training of American or European programs. But we did not want simply to be a "diploma paper mill" to get them certified. Could we do it?

The upshot was that we had to decide what levels of training we could offer both inside and outside the seminary's structure. Based on the work of Richard and Laura Mae Gardner (1992) of Wycliffe, we considered four levels of training:

- *Level 1* includes people involved in people-related tasks, needing only workshops to get training, discussion, and some practice of core interpersonal skills.
- *Level 2* involves the "skilled people helpers" or "peer counselors." Training is now available around the globe for those interested in learning peer-level helping skills. The Stephens Ministry program is excellent for those starting out in this area.
- *Level 3* is for those more serious about counseling but with no time or resources available to go into a full-time training program. They may take courses piece-meal and eventually enter a formal degree program, but at the present they may receive training in the field through mentoring and email. Examples of such programs include Wycliffe's training (based in Texas, USA) and the mentoring program of Western Seminary (Oregon, USA), with which we are affiliated.
- *Level 4* is addressed to people pursuing graduate degrees, who desire to provide a full scope of therapeutic, preventive, growth and enrichment, consultative, and educative services, as well as crisis intervention and referrals.

We decided that we could handle levels 1 and 2 in CRN and levels 3 and 4 at the seminary where we were teaching, but of course there was much overlap. Our original target in Singapore was to develop a cross-cultural, member care counselor-training program. Graduates would function both in missions and in churches. While we were more focused on training competent Christian peer-counselors for the sending churches, the seminary focused more on turning out pastoral counselors with master's degrees, who would function as encouragers, giving a Bible verse, a prayer, and a pep talk about looking to God for the answer. The seminary leadership criticized our approach, expressing that they were afraid that our technical and psychological counseling training, even if Christian, would cause too much dependency on man and not enough on God.

From a "Counseling Only" to a "Whole Person" Ministry

At our first arrival, we were seen and used only as academicians, teaching pastoral counseling inside the seminary walls. Local leaders needed us as instructors in order to get accreditation, but they resisted counseling as non-Christian and missionary care as primarily for those who are mentally ill and weak. Then one day, six months later, there was a potential staff suicide. The director did not want anyone outside the organization to find out about it, so we were called on for our crisis intervention skills. Now we realized we were being seen somewhat like firemen, called only after the fire starts. We were not used for our prevention-oriented, member care skills or vision. But at least our roles were expanding from being classroom-bound academicians to being useful practitioners on the field.

We had the definite sense that our mission leadership had not yet embraced member care. Yet trusting relationships with individuals opened the door for us to do member care for the staff, at our home and after official work hours. The needs were real, but there was a reluctance to have anyone know about them. Progress in selling member care as a biblical, holistic approach was still in question. This was a lesson in patience for us, since we saw the pain and need every day in churches and missions.

After three years, we were allowed to form a member care committee at mission headquarters with the personnel director. After about four years, Barbara was permitted by the seminary to write curriculum and teach the first formal education-level member care class in Asia. Then we were invited to write a proposal for a member care program patterned after Employee Assistance Programs (EAPs), which I had previously developed in the international corporate community and military.

Understanding of member care in many missions and seminaries was moving slowly, so we focused our energies on building the community network we had established (CRN) as a member care launching platform. Then we moved to establish Member Care Associates Asia (MCAA) as independent from any one mission or church affiliation, making it open to all denominations, missions, and missionaries needing help. Within the next year, MCAA was openly serving individual missionaries from many Asian missions stationed in Singapore. Next, we were invited to teach the member care model in several East and Central Asian nations. Locally, as members of the Singapore Association of Counseling, we were asked to write the first legislation draft for national certification of counselors. We developed a licensing program with an entry ladder that started with counseling students as "associates" and led all the way up to full doctoral-level licensing. This program was designed to encourage beginning Asian counselors to continue their training, seek qualified supervision, and become competent licensed practitioners.

These developments brought us right up to the end of our 10-year plan, at which time we intended to turn over the programs we had established to locals. Then God, through a series of painful events ending in our visas being cancelled, moved us to Germany, where we had done some previous member care work. Since Europe already had many trained counselors, we were freed from much direct contact with counseling, and we focused on developing primary prevention member care courses for young missionary leaders. We called these courses Character Development for Christian Leaders (CD1). Our email consultation for member care workers helped see us through the time of grieving over the loss of contact with Asian friends, many of whom were Asian missionary counselors with whom we had worked and trained. This need for personal continuity of our global friendships has motivated us to continue our work by linking with other similar resource agencies.

A Clash of Cultures

To return to our time in Singapore, we found a distinct difference in the ease and issues of training church members versus training educated (bachelor's level) Asians. When training seminary students in counseling, especially in the member care model, we soon found ourselves caught in a clash between Chinese racial and social classes, as well as a clash with other Asian cultures. Multiculturalism was legislated by the authoritarian government of Singapore. However, it had not seeped all the way down to the grass-roots level, even though Christianity had facilitated the process more in Singapore than in Indonesia and Malaysia.

One hindrance was our own overly rational, Western approach and linear view of reality and Christianity. Our previous cross-cultural training had done little to equip us for the magnitude of the conflict. We were not prepared for Asian circular thinking, for other uniquely Asian cultural complexities, or for the satanic forces that were openly hostile to missionaries in non-Western cultures. Despite all the assurance that we were invited by Singaporeans to help them in the area of education, we still faced tremendous periods of doubt and depression. There were days that we needed counseling more than our clients and students. We clung to our belief that God had called us there to do a specific job. But it certainly was not easy or straightforward, as we Westerners expected it to be.

At the end of the first year, we realized that many Asian cultural values were almost diametrically opposed to those by which modern, Western counseling and education operate. With more experience, we came to believe that this clash of values is not really a conflict between Asian and Western values. Western values and traditional educational practice, along with some leading Evangelicals, conflict with these counseling values too. We had to learn how to understand the conflict before we could appreciate the challenge that we faced. So as not to impugn the Chinese culture, we wish to state that having worked on three continents, we realize what we have said here of the Chinese culture can be said of all traditional cultures regarding resistance to change. Below are several issues that arose as we explored the contrast between Asian and Western values affecting cross-cultural counselor training and education in general.

The Asian model of personal interaction

Such practices as "saving face," a dictatorial level of authority, emotional passivity, and practical ownership of family members by elders struck us as simply not "Christian" when we first arrived. But we soon came to see not only the downside but also the upside of our host culture—the high value placed on honor, respect, and care for elders as they aged, a moral code that in many ways seemed superior to that of Western Evangelicals. As Christian "agents of change," we continually had to ask ourselves where the line was between teaching new changes and respecting old cultural traditions and customs that seemed "non-Christian" to us Westerners.

The new therapeutic models

New therapeutic models include discovering inward truth, wearing one's true face, taking more personal responsibility, emotional awareness, authority which empowers others, etc.

The new education models

In this category are adult-oriented, self-motivated education, with the non-hierarchical teacher as a co-equal learning facilitator, versus traditional pedagogy, in which the superior teacher lectures to the inferior student; experiential, guided, self-directed, discovery learning rather than authoritative indoctrination; holistic, growth-centered learning; empowering of students to their full, God-given potential (i.e., focusing on enhancement of students' development to full functioning, rather than on institutional and social/political correctness); and interaction as colleagues versus a hierarchical system.

It was features of the new educational model that we sought to implement which placed us in the most conflict with more traditional educators. Basically, we attempted a non-formal approach to education, based on the thinking of Ted Ward and others, while assuming that as adults the students were self-motivated and were attempting a change from the traditional Asian model under which they had grown up. In our minds, the motivation and responsibility for learning shifted from the teachers to the local Asians themselves. This approach appeared extremely radical, even to some of the older American missionaries. But as we will explain later, we came to see that it worked well, once we got the students out of the classrooms and into "simulation training" in the field.

Seminarians at the Cross or at Cross-Purposes

After the honeymoon period of entry to the new culture was over, we realized that only a few seminary students were working at their own personal growth or Christian character development. The mission leaders said that in practice character development is a private matter, not the responsibility of the mission or academic organization. Yet we had made it a part of the training requirement. There was an especially noticeable class-based arrogance in university-educated Asians. We could not get them to give up their biased, class elitism and "bring it to the cross." For example, we worked with hand workers from the churches. The seminary students looked down on these hand workers and even more so on the people in our addiction programs. We gave grade points to the students for helping each other, but this offended their pride. Competition was rife, while needing help seemed to be only for weak, uneducated persons. We wanted to model that the member care approach stressed equality and acting more like a family, in which the members take care of each other. But cultural conflict continually entered the scene. We found one solution was to invite students to CRN meetings and to run the meetings more like Alcoholics Anonymous and less like church or seminary.

Another example of culture clash involved a group of Korean students. These students appreciated our making a student lounge outside our office, where they could meet more like family. A Chinese student leader came and tried to tear the lounge apart. He told us a seminary should be run like a business office, where one comes to do academic paper work, not with this family-like informality. Against his wishes, the Koreans continued to meet in the lounge to support one another anyway. Of course, this forced a wedge between the two largest groups of students in the seminary. A final resolution came when a Korean replaced an American as director of the seminary; then there was no question which way the seminary would go.

Critical Thinking vs. Critical Spirit

We sought to prepare cross-cultural counselors to counsel with appropriate respect for other cultures, yet to confront evil and dysfunction wherever they saw it. We wanted to teach them "reflective thinking" versus their tendency to do "all or nothing" or to engage in "black and white thinking." Our dilemma came when we attempted to teach the students to see and think in categories of delicate, subtle, cultural shades of gray. We were then accused by other American missionaries of teaching "unbiblical, psychological, and moral relativism." This hurt us tremendously and drove us even deeper into community work and more and more involvement with the many Charismatic churches of Singapore.

More cultural differences surfaced when we tried to teach the difference between criticism and critical thinking. Instead of scolding the students as they were used to, we asked them to evaluate their behavior and reflect on the consequences. We used lectures, written explanations, and question and answer sessions. We attempted to be very collegial. We also invited them to critique our style and not merely criticize it. However, we were told that this just would not work between teachers and students in this culture. Nonetheless, we continued to teach what we thought was culturally appropriate to Christians, with openness and friendliness, yet maintaining appropriate boundaries between our students and ourselves. We wanted to make both our students and our clients feel relaxed and ready to open up and express themselves freely. But for the first few years, the friendly interactions between teacher and student and even non-directive counseling sessions were often seen as a weakness and were met with suspicion. The students often thought in "all or nothing" terms, believing that what we wanted was intimate friendship or else that we ourselves were weak, needy individuals.

Invisible Curriculum Development

It was around this time that we began to realize that we had an enormous challenge of curriculum development ahead of us. The seminary had been modeled after a conservative seminary in the United States, without a sense of the "non-content" oriented, invisible curriculum that cross-cultural psychologists and educators had been developing over the last decades. The situation prompted us to seek out other pioneer cross-cultural counseling educators, such as Gary Sweeten and Gary Collins. These men were open-minded supporters who went beyond merely teaching an American ethnocentric psychology and theology from American texts. The new curriculum would have to consider not only the cognitive domain, but also the affective domain (or emotional intelligence), and it would have to be understandable in the cultural context. We had some local support on this emphasis, since the Prime Minister said Singaporeans must open up and learn emotional intelligence in order to survive in the new century. Thus we found ourselves thrust into the role of being more than just teachers, but also social change agents.

"Hit and Run" vs. "Staying and Caring"

Gary Collins, in a video interview with us, used the term "hit and run" counseling to describe the random, one-time speakers that inundate Singapore (usually to sell their books). He noted that this approach was in contrast to the hard follow-through process we were doing in Singapore after the hit-and-run speakers had left. We felt supported by Gary and his comments. The challenge for us was creating safety and openness over time, so that trainees could dig beneath protecting their social image and say what was hurting them. We believe that this is necessary in order to develop deeper internal self-knowledge in our relationship to God. Psychologically, the Confucian culture's practice of face-saving is based on the appearance of honor. But in today's world, these practices are diametrically opposed to deeper self-knowledge and independent critical thinking. The most vivid example is seen in Asia's various religious cults, marked by "group think" and herd instincts to follow the leader into personally destructive practices.

Our Christian counseling methods were based on a notion of ongoing Christian development and progressive sanctification of the inner man. For the first few years, we wondered whether we were even scratching the surface. However, the practice of caring for one another (outside one's family) was opened up to some degree by the Charismatic movement that is still impacting Singapore. Charismatic pastors taught members of their churches healing techniques that they could easily practice with each other. The first of these was prayer for healing and for deliverance from the demonic. By the early 1990s, many churches were practicing all-night deliverance on everyone for everything. As is typical in such movements, the pendulum swung to extremes before reaching a balance. Eventually, I was called in to consult about diagnoses, since some pastors were getting burned out. Excessive diagnosis of demonization was gradually tempered in most cases. By the mid-1990s, the pastor of a large Singapore church led the way by commending counseling as an alternative, when appropriate. We were then able to introduce peer helper training to some 100 pastors.

Breaking Through Destructive Taboos

Though talk of sex is a taboo in this Confucian culture, we were given permission to teach a course on Christian sexuality at the seminary, which was open to the general public. We dealt with a wide spectrum of sexual behavior, using the book *Sex for Christians* by Lewis Smedes (1994). One of our guest speakers was a Christian recovered homosexual, Cy Rogers of Exodus International. His presentation broke down some barriers to discussion. This was needed, since many Singaporeans were in the midst of rapid change. They were facing challenges they never had imagined in their homes, with rigid traditional values and unwillingness to allow discussion about problems. Thus, many young people were defenseless when confronted with new issues, especially in the area of sexuality.

This class did not work very well at first, until we found that Asians could become openly emotional while viewing films dealing with their core issues. So we used films as a springboard to discussion of the most taboo topics. These topics included freedom of thought and individual action, filial piety, sex, divorce, cross-ethnic marriage, and growth away from the old, traditional Asian values. If our students were to operate as missionaries and cross-cultural counselors outside the walls of the Christian compound, they had to have experience in dealing with these issues.

The first film we used was from the book of a noted Chinese author, Amy Tan, called *The Joy Luck Club*. This story is about a Chinese family facing the above-named taboo issues and coming out from under traditional society into modern society. However, this excellent film challenged Chinese traditional values and thus was described by the Singapore newspaper as being too Western or American.

The other side of the coin is the case of a denominational leader who was overseer for 40 Singaporean churches. Speaking about the member care team we trained in his home church, he said, "Your methods of handling things are not ours. They do not match our traditional culture. But ours didn't work, and yours do. So I think when the other churches taste of this approach, they will want more."

Re-education in a Hierarchical System

Teaching compassionate, empathic understanding was most difficult with many of our Asian seminary students who had a "higher education." They acted and seemed to think of themselves like rich ladies trying to do charity work for the lower class without getting their hands dirty. They spoke as if people who needed counseling were either morally inferior or, at the other extreme, having a spiritual problem and needing deliverance. The most humbling and most resisted experience for these students was the requirement to attend and pay for 20 sessions of personal psychological counseling with a qualified Christian Singaporean counselor. The resistance to this requirement even came from the older American leadership, who tried to do away with it.

We had to start most Asian bachelor-level students in the program at a level equal to a United States high school general psychology class. We attempted to work them up slowly to the level of a graduate student. Generally, Asian students could memorize easily and quickly, but application was a mystery to them. To assist in this area, we rewrote our entire curriculum, contextualizing it to our students' felt needs as Asians and following tips from *The Seven Laws of the Learner* by Bruce Wilkinson (1997). We introduced skits, role-plays, and psychodrama to bring lessons alive. Our lesson plans were prepared fresh for each day, depending on where the majority of the class was in their understanding and personal experience. And finally, we wrote plays and made our own videos with students in them, in order to contextualize accurately the examples we used.

A Breakthrough via Role Playing

Once the students saw videos featuring their peers, a real breakthrough came through the use of role playing and later through psychodrama. The latter was used as a way of safely dramatizing one's life span, stages, and mistakes which block character development. The entire progression was done in a few hours, rather than taking sometimes months to see these patterns. This strategy, ironically, had its chief effect on the part-time students, community church counselors, social workers, pastors, and missionaries we worked with. All of these people were interested primarily in practical problem solving and counseling competence, not just grades. For them, these counseling skills were the new-found doorway to dealing with sticky congregational, family, and mission team problems. They loved to role-play and learned application well from skits. The skits had to be written to contain the elements of the subject, topic, and problem all woven into favorite Asian themes. Those with sad endings were very popular. So we often wrote short skits, rehearsed parts with students before class, and then directed them into deeper process as they did their skit in class. We then divided up into small groups of no more than five. The ones that spoke the best English and a mother tongue would moderate the discussion group in other languages.

Useful Tools in Cross-Cultural Member Care Training

We have already mentioned the fishbowl and role-playing exercises. In addition, "simulation training" outside of the classroom for missionary candidates from the churches as well as for our seminary students became an exciting new learning tool. If we did not challenge the old way of doing things, our students would just put the new content into the compartmentalized boxes of the "old school." No application would come from that. We found that once we got the students out of the classroom, they performed differently. They gradually seemed to awaken and switched from their passive student role of "learned helplessness" to a more flexible, "adult, self-motivated mode." They were then more ready to face the member care helping process and reality.

To help students identify their internal "negative self-talk" without diagnosing it as something horrible or demonic, we jokingly introduced a new internal observation practice to them. We told them that they had a little inner "Babbler," whose voice one could learn to hear and distinguish from the voice of God. William Backus (1980), in *Telling Yourself the Truth*, calls it the "inner *homunculus*." If students could learn to hear their personal Babbler, they could make a conscious decision whether they wanted to consider the voice or not. We explained to them that we were not training them to sear their native consciences, but to become aware of the subtleties of the enemy and the biases of their home culture. We explained this in the framework of our Christian Character Development class, using Henry Cloud's (1992) book, *Changes That Heal*, as a text. We saw this as stress prevention, enabling the students to think and discern instead of just reacting under field stressors.

Holding the Line on Competence Requirements

The seminary context

As time went on at the seminary, the issue of face-saving and its heavy effect on academic requirements made student evaluation a political time bomb. Face-saving exists in all cultures, but it has reached a high degree of importance in Asia. This was evident in the difficulty we had teaching cross-cultural issues such as non-judgmental acceptance of a client's race, cultural habits, etc. We found issues of boundaries, competency, counseling ethics, and policy definition all enmeshed and very difficult to deal with. Our educational ethics felt strained by administrative pressure to get the students through school. This not only affected grades and graduation, at which proud parents attended, but it also affected field readiness.

Much academic/political pressure was placed on us to help students not be shamed by their own misbehavior—to help them avoid consequences from which they could learn. In the United States, we would have called this "enabling"—reinforcing and encouraging another's unhealthy behavior by not confronting it. Of course, the phenomenon exists elsewhere too and not just in Asian schools.

The final competence evaluation requirements that we designed for the seminary master's degree stated that students would turn in video recordings of three clients they had counseled. Professional persons from outside the system would judge the counseling student. To save face, however, this requirement was replaced by the traditional written exam.

The church context

Similarly, in the church settings, we taught that getting to the mission field sooner meant showing a willingness to get involved in the counseling process. We had more influence in the churches than in the seminary. They wanted quality over tranquility and face-saving. Candidates were required to sign up and attend a small group for at least one round of seven meetings. If they missed one session without a valid excuse, they were assigned to a second and third round until they got honest and stopped playing the face-saving game. This was "face-breaking" or admitting one's brokenness before the Lord and others in a safe place. It sought to help candidates in becoming more open and vulnerable, promoting vulnerability and self-awareness of their unfinished character development issues. These were not encounter groups. No confrontation or advice-giving was allowed in the group, only sharing what was giving one trouble or blocking one's character development and spiritual growth. In this way, we believed that the Holy Spirit was allowed to convict. This conviction opened proactively what otherwise might be opened under stressful pressures of the foreign field.

Following the missionary candidate's application period, the individual was assigned to a work supervisor and a character development trainer who kept independent records of the person's behavior and placed him/her on a developmental scale called the "Ramp." The trainer marked a candidate's score in several areas and then during evaluation would take an average between them before discussing the candidate. No one had the authority to change the cut-off for an individual's score. That had to be agreed to beforehand and recorded with a sign-off similar to the military. To the candidate or trainee, we described the Ramp as an evaluation instrument and as a "take-off ramp" to the mission field or to the new, desired position. When a candidate was failing, the approach taken was not scolding but asking, "How can I help you get over your next growth hurdle on the Ramp?" Below are some of the items observed during the Ramp assessment process.

- *Character development scores*. A willingness to laugh at self; escape through recreation when appropriate; read and do assignments, making application of content to their own lives; deal with blocks, addictions, habits, friends, and family members that hindered their progress toward their goal in spite of social pressure to conform to the cultural expectation. The Christian version of the FIRO-B, an interpersonal style inventory, provides some interpersonal and temperament data supporting this assessment area.

■ *Marriage or other intimate relationship scores*. Willingness to go through the seven small-group sessions required, without resistance in terms of absenteeism, tardiness for sessions, and other disruptions; willingness to deal with family issues or time scheduling flexibly and openly. The various assessment areas are similar to those from the Prepare and Enrich inventories for premarital, marital, and team relationships, respectively.

■ *Integrity and interpersonal caring scores*. In practice sessions, we expected to see students relating to others in an empowering way. They were given peer helper projects that their supervisors could observe and record for use in weekly evaluation sessions during the trial period. Our goal was not to make them feel good, but to empower them toward their capacity to understand and grow to Christian maturity. The real problems usually lay hidden under fear of failure (cultural perfectionism), the taboo against losing face, and the potential of dishonoring their family. This area was also rated by the above-described supervisors as part of the Ramp score. This system which was taught to Asians in the churches gave leaders something more objective than their own cultural criterion by which to judge, since these candidates were being prepared for overseas duty.

Some Conclusions: Learning to Modify Ourselves and Our Models

As we look back, we see that we have had to work the hardest with the types of issues that affected our sense of comfort and belonging. Our adaptation for crossing cultures with new ideas first had to start with our affective response, before we could get down to serious cognitive and planning issues. First, we had to handle basic and obvious cross-cultural issues, such as anti-foreigner attitudes, non-confrontive politeness (saving face and making peace at any price), and heavy restrictions and superstitions constricting emotional expression, so that a newcomer could not tell what an Asian co-worker really thought about issues.

Then there were our own attitudes that were brought to the surface in response to the new situation and that needed immediate pruning before they alienated us from locals. The advice we were given during the time we were reacting to the strictures of the culture was, "Missionary sojourners in Asia must have the attitude of a humble and interested learner." We wanted to handle our own personal struggles authentically, so as to model and teach others, first of all, to do the same and, second, to be more tolerant of different cultural values and ways of dealing with problems. This was a real problem, when we were having difficulty dealing with the situation ourselves. At times, it was difficult trying simultaneously to be both "an agent of change" and "a humble learner." As with effective cross-cultural counselors, we had to be constant students of our own culture and of the host culture. We needed to be open to the feedback (including criticism) from others too. We had to give extra concern to the delicate difference between "critical thinking" and "critical spirit"—and not just for our students, but for ourselves too. That really stretched whatever holiness we thought we had previously acquired.

The opportunity to establish counselor training and member care in Asia presented us with numerous challenges to our existing training models and strategies. Cultural resistance around saving face and a hierarchical social system, especially in educational settings, also presented challenges. What proved most effective was to focus on experiential learning in less formal educational structures. It was also essential to develop personal credibility and to be willing to work opportunistically with the situations that presented themselves. Gradually, an effective model for training and member care emerged. In the process of developing this model, a cooperative member care movement became established, which operates across both denominational and organizational lines. Our time in Singapore was so enriching and challenging. We miss this country, but even more our Singaporean friends!

Reflection and Discussion

1. How does a member care worker find the balance between being a Christian caregiver, being a change agent, and respecting a traditional host culture?
2. When member care help is considered inappropriate by a mission organization, how can one proceed to give care to hurting missionaries without threatening leadership?
3. Review the authors' recollections about what worked well for them, as well as their struggles. Would you have done things differently?
4. What are some ways to include member care courses as part of the curriculum of missionary training institutions?
5. The authors see character development as being key for Christian counselors and other member care workers. How does one go about changing character? What are a few areas that you would like to change in your own character?

References

Backus, W. (1980). *Telling yourself the truth*. Minneapolis, MN: Bethany Press.

Cloud, H. (1992). *Changes that heal*. Grand Rapids, MI: Zondervan.

Gardner, R., & Gardner, L. (1992). Training and using member care workers. In K. O'Donnell (Ed.), *Missionary care: Counting the cost for world evangelization* (pp. 315-331). Pasadena, CA: William Carey Library.

Smedes, L. (1994). *Sex for Christians*. Grand Rapids, MI: Eerdmans Publishers.

Wilkinson, B. (1997). *The seven laws of the learner*. Portland, OR: Multnomah Press.

Ron Noll *is a licensed clinical psychologist from the United States and a member care consultant for Campus Crusade for Christ in Germany. He also coordinates Member Care Network International, a missionary counselor and consultation network. Ron's Ph.D. is in education, curriculum, and instruction from the University of Oregon. Since 1961, he has counseled and taught in several colleges, seminaries, and universities in the United States, Europe, and Asia. He is the founder of Affective Communication Training Seminars (ACTS), a personal development program, as well as co-author for Member Character Development (CD1), a one-week growth and prevention program which he and his wife Barbara give three times a year in Europe. Email: 73422.3170@compuserve.com.*

Barbara Rohnert-Noll*, R.N., M.A., M.A., a German citizen, has been a missionary with Campus Crusade for Christ (CCC) for 21 years, having served five years in Africa as a bush nurse. She has published in German psychiatric journals, taught seminary, and started the first foreign mission office in CCC Germany before going to teach at the International School of Theology, Singapore, with her husband, Ron. She is presently pursuing a Ph.D. in missions in the area of missionary care. Barbara is currently the Director of the Character Development Program under the CCC training department in Giessen, Germany. Email: brnoll@aol.com.*

Special thanks to Roger Burford, Joe Cooke, and Tom Lee for their input and review of this article.

38

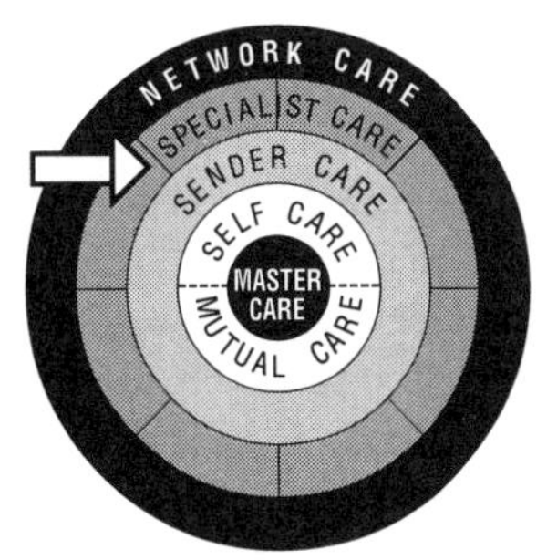

Building Resilient Teams: The CACTUS Kit

Kelly O'Donnell

There are three sure ways to undermine a team—or a family. In a phrase—don't talk, don't share feelings, and don't trust. Teams, like families, need intentional care to be healthy.

Every struggling team that I have worked with has had the three "don'ts" listed at the right in common. In each case, there was the clear absence of a regular, acceptable forum for dealing with concerns about team relationships and tasks. This observation fits well with the research on missionary adjustment too—where one of the greatest stressors is confronting one another when necessary (Gish, 1983). It just seems so challenging to work through our differences!

Dealing With Differences

Everyone wins when we practice biblical reconciliation (Matt. 5:22-26; 18:15-22). For me, the essence of sorting out our differences involves "care-fronting": "We care about our relationship and about the issues, so we honestly confront each other to work it out" (Augsburger, 1981; Palmer, 1991). In certain cross-cultural situations, however, more indirect approaches to conflict resolution are appropriate, such as using a mediator to talk on your behalf (Augsburger, 1992; Elmer, 1993).

Working through differences can stir up an uncomfortable feeling of being "all bad" or "all wrong"—sometimes a reminder of similar feelings from our childhood. Differences can also evoke an underlying struggle for control and power within the relationship. When coupled with our basic human insecurity, the result can be a steady regression of distancing ourselves from each other. First, we label "differentness" as deviance; then we experience relational discord, followed by destructive comments and behaviors, personal and group despair, and eventually team dissolution (Johnson & Royer, 2001). Hearts break, groups split, and a multitude of sins covers love (Livingstone, 1993,

p. 115). No doubt this process has influenced the emergence of more than 20,000 separate Christian denominations and churches over the last two millennia (Barrett, 1982, p. 34)!

What else can undermine a team? Katzenbach and Smith (1993) say that a major contributor is a reluctance to think precisely about the nature of a "true" team. Just like teams in the business world, not every mission "team" is actually a team. For these researchers, true teams involve certain basics: "a small number of people with complementary skills who are committed to a common purpose, performance goals, and approach for which they hold themselves mutually accountable" (p. 45). The most successful teams are committed to developing these team basics. In addition, they have a high commitment to one another's success, and they embrace a "demanding performance challenge" that inspires team members. In what way is your team life characterized by the above?

Help From the Cactus

During my youth, I used to roam the hills around our home in Southern California with our dog, a black Great Dane. One of my favorite imaginary games was to fight the masses of entrenched cacti, using a stick as my saber. Yet no matter how many jabs I made or pieces I cut off, I could not defeat this plant. It was just too well-suited for the dry, desert-like environment, with its protective, waxy coating to keep precious fluids inside and its annoying, sharp prickles to keep predators out. It was, in fact, very resilient.

Missionary teams can learn from the cactus. This is especially true for teams that live in harsh environments—e.g., with limited supportive resources, political instability, poverty, or social opposition. Like the cactus, they must find ways to become resilient—to maintain the life of the team within (relationships), while maintaining their focus in the midst of challenges from without (tasks). Resiliency, though, is neither automatic nor quickly obtained. Rather, we "grow into" resiliency through the various stages of team life (Love, 1996).

The Core and Care of Cactus

I routinely advise teams to have a special team building time, in addition to their usual meetings, about once every two months. The focus is on strengthening one or more of four basic team dimensions: relationships (connecting with and seeing each other in new ways), task (discussing and planning work-related strategies), spiritual life (worshiping and praying together), and ethos (looking at *how* the team members relate and work together—e.g., work styles and expectations for intimacy). Team building works best when four "Ps" are in place:

- A *point of focus* that is clear and consensually derived.
- *Participation* by all from the heart.
- A *person* with good facilitating skills.
- A sense of the Lord's *presence*.

I like to supplement the more familiar "SET" tools ("Standard Evangelical Team" tools—like discussions and prayer times) with some more novel ones. Several examples are described in this chapter, such as creative drawing, trust walks, and role playing (see also Jones & Jones, 1995; O'Donnell, 1992). Self-disclosure, active listening, and cooperation are required. Most team members appreciate the opportunity to learn more from each other and to grow together.

Let's look now at eight core characteristics of resilient teams (summarized by the acronym CCACTUSS), along with some tools for team care. These characteristics/tools are derived from research on strong families and healthy teams, along with my consultation experience. Hence, the material can apply as much to family life as it does to team life. Shelby Harrison's (1990) article, "Healthy Families and Missions," was especially helpful in my initial development of the "CACTUS Kit."

Characteristics of Resilient Teams

The eight characteristics that I now describe are as follows:

- Coping ability
- Commitment
- Appreciation
- Communication
- Time together
- Understanding
- Structure
- Spiritual wellness

Coping Ability

Perseverance and inner strength mark the resilient team. Challenges are seen as opportunities to grow. Members believe the best in each other in spite of weaknesses, and they recall the many examples of endurance and success in the past. They work through communication impasses and try alternative approaches to work when necessary. They also minimize distractions in order to stay focused on their work, and they regularly use resources outside of the team for ongoing training and coaching (Lewis & Lewis, 1992; Harrison, 1997).

Care Tools

- *Successes*. Successful team performance breeds team cohesion. Review two work challenges your team faced and overcame during the last few months. Try using the CHOPS Inventory—a brief stress assessment tool—to identify struggles and coping strategies (see chapter 23 and also O'Donnell & O'Donnell, 1995). In addition, define ongoing/upcoming challenges in manageable ways so as to see your progress (e.g., learning 20 new phrases this week vs. becoming fluent).
- *Strengths/weaknesses*. Draw a picture of your perception of the team's greatest coping strength and another picture of its greatest weakness. Write a title and a caption for each, and then discuss the drawings as a group.

Commitment

Aim at everything and you'll hit nothing. Resilient teams have specific goals, clear ministry strategies, and defined relationships into which they invest themselves. Members are resolutely dedicated to each other's well-being and to accomplishing the team's purpose. Members feel that they belong to and can influence their group. The goals of the team are highly valued and prioritized, yet with due regard for members' responsibilities to family, friends, the local community, and other groups.

Care Tools

- *Good team / bad team*. Identify a team you were on that was successful and one that was not successful. Describe each team in terms of the four team dimensions mentioned above—relationships, task, spiritual life, and ethos. How does your previous experience influence the type of team that you are part of now?
- *Mutual accountability*. Do you have a written team agreement or set of guidelines? (See Appendix 1 for a discussion of Memos of Understanding.) Are there planned feedback/performance appraisals? Review these as a group, and have team members give some input about their content. This can help to build mutual accountability, which is so important for encouragement and better performance.

Appreciation

Team members should have both planned and spontaneous times when they express their appreciation for each other. Thanking one another and acknowledging each other's contributions add much to group cohesion. Like the other team characteristics in this kit, appreciation is both an attitude and a behavior. So cultivate both! Children are part of teams too, so be sure to include them when handing out encouragement.

Care Tools

■ *Surprises*. Surprise team members by sending a "get well" card to someone who is sick, or invite someone over for a beverage or a meal. Celebrate the anniversary of someone's arrival on the field or of joining the organization, or acknowledge a recent accomplishment. Appreciation is also expressed by offering comfort and a listening ear during hard times.

■ *Service*. Following Richard Foster's (1978, p. 122) suggestion, choose a simple way that you can help someone each day, and encourage that person with your service. Maybe even do it anonymously. This can be more challenging than you think!

Communication

Members of strong teams have good communication skills, including conflict resolution. They listen well and can empathize by reflecting back what they hear and by validating others' feelings. They value self-awareness—taking time to step back and reflect in order to step forward and connect with others. Genuine efforts are made to explore and relate together in culturally sensitive ways. There are also clear written and verbal channels for exchanging information and updates about life and work.

Care Tools

■ *Listening skills*. Divide into pairs, and spend five minutes listening to your partner describe something important to him/her. Briefly summarize what you heard. Then change roles. Conclude by asking each other a few questions about what was shared.

■ *Communication check*. Identify the main sources of communication within your group. Who are the information brokers? Who communicates the most/least? What languages are used? What content areas of communication are needed? Identify a situation in which communication did not flow well. How could you improve the communication links? Try drawing a communication flow chart.

Time Together

Teams need quality time together—a great quantity of it. This is especially true during significant transitions, such as when teams regroup with new members, during crisis situations, or during the early stages of team life. Two complementary adages are: know God and make Him known, and know and be known by others. Intimacy with a few members but congeniality with all is a reasonable goal. Resiliency also results from periodically having "fun" times together, simply enjoying one another's company, as well as from building mutually supportive friendships with nationals.

Care Tools

■ *Building trust*. Trust is deepened by shared experiences over time. It is earned, not assumed. Identify those on your team with whom you spend the most/least time. Try doing a "trust walk" with someone you do not know too well—one person is blindfolded and is led around for five minutes, the roles are reversed, and then the experience is discussed.

■ *Team relationships*. Becky Lewis with Frontiers describes four types of relationships on teams: kindred spirits (like Ruth/Naomi, David/Jonathan), colleagues (friendly/compatible yet not so intimate), enigmas (mysterious people you do not understand), and irritants (people you frankly do not like). Discuss these four categories in light of some stimulating comments on friendship, such as from Ecclesiasticus chapter 6 (apocryphal Jewish wisdom literature emphasizing that trust takes time, that one should not trust anyone too readily, and that a true friend is the elixir of life—see Appendix 2). Try doing something mutually enjoyable with the enigma and irritant. We can change relationship categories—hopefully for the better—and it's easier than we think!

Understanding

Henri Nouwen observed that one of life's hardest realities is that "love and wounds are never separated." Healthy teams will experience tensions and hurts. There are times when our darker sides will emerge. And there are times when just being different from each other will create friction. To lessen the impact, team members can look at their different "styles" and preferences: personality, leadership, decision making, learning, work, communication, and spirituality. The focus is more on "fitting together" than on identifying someone's weaknesses. Team members thus genuinely try to understand and accept one another's "way of being," while also being free to speak into each other's lives. Rounding things off is the practice of receiving and offering forgiveness—for me, the *sine qua non* of team relational health.

Care Tools

■ *Relationship principles*. Look at the book of Proverbs as a group, and identify 10-20 proverbs to guide your team interactions and conflict resolution. Write these down. Are they transcultural principles? How might they be applied by team members from different cultures? Also helpful is identifying several of the "one another" verses in the New Testament (such as encouraging one another each day, Heb. 3:13).

■ *Cross-cultural preferences*. Discuss Sandra Mackin's (1992) article, "Multinational Teams," relating what she says to the types of leadership, structures, decision making, relationships, etc., that you have or want on your team. Make sure everyone has a chance to talk, and explain how one's background influences practices and preferences. Relate these to norms in the host culture.

Structure

Resiliency requires regimen. It's important to have clear roles for leaders and other members, well-defined methods for decision making, agreed-upon guidelines for accountability and conflict resolution, and in many cases a written agreement or Memo of Understanding. Everyone has designated and chosen responsibilities, so people know how they fit and where they belong. Structure thus brings a sense of security. Structural issues are especially important for multinational teams, where different expectations—spoken and unspoken—must be clarified and harmonized over time (see Cho & Greenlee, 1995; Roembke, 2000).

Care Tools

■ *Team trees*. Draw a picture of a tree which represents your team. It may be abstract, realistic, or impressionistic. Place the team members in and around the tree. Afterwards, discuss your drawings. What do the drawings say about perceptions of the team structure and function? Who are the closest? The most influential? What roles are represented? Ask each other a few questions; then hang your trees on the wall for a few days to create a "team orchard." This is also a good way of exploring the team "ethos."

■ *Conflict protocols*. What guidelines are in place for resolving differences and conflict? Review or possibly even role-play how the team handled a recent conflict. List a few things you did right and a few things you could have improved. Were the conflict guidelines followed? Do they need to be adjusted?

Spiritual Wellness

Human doings are not human beings. God calls us for relationship with Himself (1 Cor. 1:9), in addition to creating us for specific tasks (Eph. 2:10). Spiritual health is the foundation for team resiliency. It develops during the ups and downs of team life, as members "clothe themselves in humility" (1 Peter 5:5) and seek God together through "PACTS"—proclamation of His character, adoration, confession of faults, thanksgiving, and supplication for needs.

Care Tools

■ *Reading together*. Read a devotional book together, such as a book on developing character through difficult circumstances. A good example is Joyce Huggett's (1997) *Formed by the Desert*.

■ *Bearing burdens*. There is an Uzbek proverb which says, "A bitter truth is better than a sweet lie." And Proverbs 14:8 states,"The way of the prudent is to understand one's way, but the folly of fools is deceit." On a scale of 1 to 10, how open can you be with each other? Talk about how you want to share, and pray about individual and team burdens (Gal. 6:1).

Final Thoughts

Developing resilient teams is much like developing resilient families. It takes lots of wisdom, attention, perseverance, and often "seasons of sacrifice" to make them work (Prov. 24:3-4). Every team gets stuck at times and requires care to get back on track. This CACTUS Kit can help. Review it periodically, using some of the suggested tools to strengthen your team. Elton Trueblood is right: "What is most rewarding is doing something that really matters with congenial colleagues who share with us the firm conviction that it needs to be done."

Reflection and Discussion

1. In what ways do mission personnel need to be like cactus?

2. Refer to the summary comments of Katzenbach and Smith's research on high-performance teams. How does your team line up with the characteristics of such teams?

3. Which tools described in this chapter would be most useful for improving the resiliency of your team? Which would be most useful for your family?

4. List some of the possible benefits and liabilities of using these tools on a multinational team.

5. Recall a few examples of "seasons of sacrifice" which you experienced in your team or family. How did they strengthen you or weaken you as a group?

Appendix 1
Memos of Understanding*

Putting together a viable team is a challenge. One important initial step is to develop a team agreement, or Memo of Understanding (MOU). Here are some suggestions for team leaders to draw up this document. The MOU is intended to help clarify and adjust expectations between all the team members.

1. People follow someone who leads. So share your dream in such a way that it enhances others' confidence that it can be done.

2. Do as much as you can to enable the other team members to picture what it would be like coming on this team and how they would spend their time.

3. What's your style of leadership? How can team members participate? Give them a scenario for the group's interpersonal relationships.

4. Team members want security that they will get both help and leadership, along with freedom to try a lot of things their own way. Do not expect human beings to be consistent. At times, they may want you to have all the answers and to make sure things don't go wrong, and at other times, they may resist your way of doing things.

5. People want to go with a winner. Give them some ideas on how and why you believe this team is able to be effective and accomplish its tasks.

6. You may want to get some ideas from some other MOUs, but be careful not to include something that you really don't intend to provide or do on your team.

7. You may want to let the potential team leaders know your strengths and weaknesses and how you can see them complementing your gifts. Why do you need a team in the first place? People need to be needed.

---

* Based on a worksheet developed by Tim Lewis. Used by permission.

8. Specific questions an MOU should address include the following: Where are we going? What type of work are we going to do and with whom? How are we going to get resident visas? What's our living standard going to be? How much money are we going to need for our share of things? Do we pool funds or share them in some other way, or is there a team work fund to which we all contribute? How do we resolve conflict? If we don't like it there, how soon can we leave, or how long does our commitment need to be? What recourse do we have if we don't get on with the team leader? How am I going to learn a language? What are the expectations for mothers? Who makes my lifestyle decisions, what do I have to agree on before I go, and what can we decide over there? What skills am I expected to have before I leave for overseas? What kind of religious backgrounds would fit best on this team? What do we want to see happen, how soon, what's our part, and what roles will we have? What provisions are made for sickness or emergencies? To whom is the team leader accountable? How do our sending organizations fit into our team's effort? What kind of coaching are we going to get from the outside? How often can we come home?

Appendix 2
Ecclesiasticus 6:5-17*

A kindly turn of speech multiplies a man's friends,
and a courteous way of speaking invites many a friendly reply.
Let your acquaintances be many,
but your advisors one in a thousand.

If you want to make a friend, take him on trial,
and be in no hurry to trust him;
for one kind of friend is only so when it suits him
but will not stand by you in your day of trouble.
Another kind of friend will fall out with you
and to your dismay make your quarrel public,
and a third kind of friend will share your table,
but not stand by you in your day of trouble:
when you are doing well he will be your second self,
ordering your servants about;
but if ever you are brought low he will turn against you
and will hide himself from you.
Keep well clear of your enemies,
and be wary of your friends.

A faithful friend is a sure shelter,
whoever finds one has found a rare treasure.
A faithful friend is something beyond price,
there is no measuring his worth.
A faithful friend is the elixir of life
and those who fear the Lord will find one.
Whoever fears the Lord makes true friends,
for as a man is, so is his friend.

---

* *The Jerusalem Bible*. (1966). pp. 1042-1043. Garden City, NY: Doubleday & Company.

References

Augsburger, D. (1981). *Caring enough to confront*. Ventura, CA: Regal Books.

———. (1992). *Conflict mediation across cultures: Pathways and patterns*. Louisville, KY: Westminster/John Knox Press.

Barrett, D. (Ed.). (1982). *World Christian encyclopedia*. Nairobi, Kenya: Oxford University Press.

Cho, Y., & Greenlee, D. (1995). Avoiding pitfalls on multi-cultural teams. *International Journal of Frontier Missions, 12*, 179-183.

Elmer, D. (1993). *Cross-cultural conflict: Building relationships for effective ministry*. Downers Grove, IL: InterVarsity Press.

Foster, R. (1978). *Celebration of discipline*. San Francisco, CA: Harper & Row.

Gish, D. (1983). Sources of worker stress. *Journal of Psychology and Theology, 15*, 238-242.

Harrison, M. (1997). On-field training and supervision: Perspective of the old sending countries. In W. Taylor (Ed.), *Too valuable to lose: Exploring the causes and cures of missionary attrition* (pp. 265-275). Pasadena, CA: William Carey Library.

Harrison, S. (1990, February). Healthy families and missions. *World Christian Magazine*, pp. 25-27.

Huggett, J. (1997). *Formed by the desert*. Guilford, Surrey, UK: Eagle Press.

Katzenbach, J., & Smith, D. (1993). *The wisdom of teams: Creating the high performance organization*. Boston, MA: Harvard Business School Press.

Johnson, D., & Royer, K. (2001). *Team re-building*. Unpublished paper. Available from: KenRoyer@aol.com.

Jones, G., & Jones, R. (1995). *Teamwork*. London, UK: Scripture Union.

Lewis, T., & Lewis, B. (1992). Coaching missionary teams. In K. O'Donnell (Ed.), *Missionary care: Counting the cost for world evangelization* (pp. 163-170). Pasadena, CA: William Carey Library.

Livingstone, G. (1993). *Planting churches in Muslim cities: A team approach*. Grand Rapids, MI: Baker Book House.

Love, R. (1996). Four stages of team development. *Evangelical Missions Quarterly, 32*, 312-316.

Mackin, S. (1992). Multinational teams. In K. O'Donnell (Ed.), *Missionary care: Counting the cost for world evangelization* (pp. 155-162). Pasadena, CA: William Carey Library.

O'Donnell, K. (1992). Tools for team viability. In K. O'Donnell (Ed.), *Missionary care: Counting the cost for world evangelization* (pp. 184-201). Pasadena, CA: William Carey Library.

O'Donnell, K., & O'Donnell, M. (1995). Foxes, giants, and wolves. *International Journal of Frontier Missions, 12*, 185-188.

Palmer, D. (1991). *Managing conflict creatively: A guide for missionaries and Christian workers*. Pasadena, CA: William Carey Library.

Roembke, L. (2000). *Building credible multicultural teams*. Pasadena, CA: William Carey Library.

__Kelly O'Donnell__ is a psychologist working with Youth With A Mission and Mercy Ministries International, based in Europe. He co chairs with Dave Pollock the Member Care Task Force (MemCa), part of the World Evangelical Alliance's Missions Commission. Kelly studied clinical psychology and theology at Rosemead School of Psychology, Biola University, in the United States. Specialties include personnel development, setting up member care affiliations, team building, and crisis care. Together with his wife, Michèle, he has published several articles in the member care field, along with editing __Helping Missionaries Grow__ (1988) and __Missionary Care__ (1992). They have two daughters: Erin, aged 12, and Ashling, aged 8. Email: 102172.170@compuserve.com.

This is a revision of an article that first appeared in __Evangelical Missions Quarterly__ (1999, vol. 35, pp. 72-78); PO Box 794, Wheaton, IL 60189, USA. Used by permission.

39

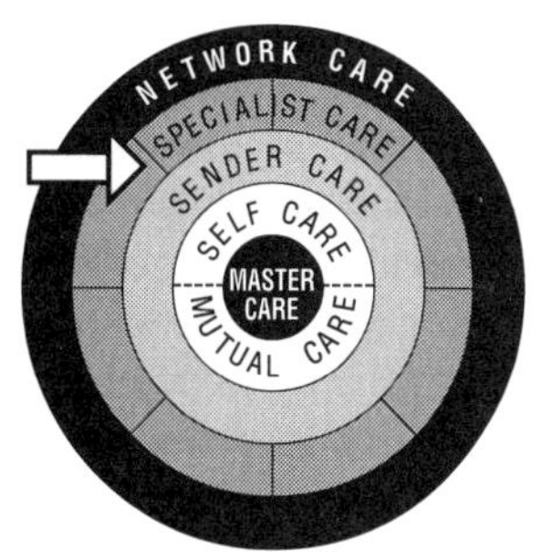

The Potential and Pitfalls of Multicultural Mission Teams

David Greenlee
Yong Joong Cho
Abraham Thulare

With the globalization of missions, multicultural mission teams have become increasingly common. Along with their advantages, potential conflicts exist which may destroy the team's sense of community and its fruitful ministry. This chapter explores the possible strengths of multicultural teams. We then discuss potential weaknesses of an imaginary team comprised of Koreans, Brazilians, black South Africans, and Americans. We conclude with a few brief case studies.

Our focus in this chapter is on understanding how teams can be impacted by different underlying values—the long-enduring judgments appraising the worth of an idea, object, person, place, or practice (Dodd, 1991, p. 85). We also attempt to understand the observed behavior of missionaries from Brazil, Korea, black South Africa, and the USA. We know that all missionaries from these countries will not act precisely in the ways we suggest. In fact, descriptions of normal behavior for a given culture tend to apply only in a general way to the group, not specifically to any individual. Yet it is our hope that both the cultural tendencies we discuss and the process of discussion itself will stimulate useful dialogue involving these and other nationality mixes on mission teams.

A Sense of Community

Key to the survival of multinational teams in missions is fostering what community psychologists over the last 25 years have called a "sense of community." This can be defined as "the perception of similarity to others, an acknowledged interdependence with others, a willingness to maintain this interdependence by giving or doing for others what one expects from them, [and] the feeling that one is part of a larger dependable and stable structure" (Sarasson, 1974, p. 157).

McMillan and Chavis (1986, cited in Stoner, 1993) define four elements necessary for a high sense of community within a particular reference group:

- *The element of membership*—the feeling of belonging or sharing a sense of personal relatedness.
- *The element of influence*—the sense of having influence over a group and being influenced by that group.

■ *The element of fulfillment of needs*—the belief that one's needs can be and are being met through the collective resources of the group.

■ *The element of shared emotional connection*—the commitment and cohesion that grows out of the experience of shared history.

It can be quite a challenging and time-consuming process for multicultural teams, or any teams, to develop this sense of community. However, when team members commit themselves to grow together through this process, the benefits can be great.

Strengths of Multicultural Teams

Multicultural teams can model the diversity of the body of Christ in microcosm better than monocultural teams. A monocultural team does not readily demonstrate the international nature of Christianity. For example, an African Minister of Education once told the crew of Operation Mobilization's ship *Logos*, "You are like the United Nations, except for one thing—you really are united!"

Multicultural teams can be a demonstration of God's transforming power in intercultural relations. People notice God's healing power for the nations when workers from powerful nations joyfully serve under a leader from a less powerful country. Unity among erstwhile enemies—such as prayer together among Argentine and British missionary co-workers during the 1982 South Atlantic conflict or among Serbian and Western European Christians during the 1999 Balkans crisis—is a credit to the gospel and makes a great impact on outsiders.

Multicultural teams have a built-in, heightened sensitivity as to what is biblical and what is cultural about themselves. They help their members see themselves and the host culture from outside their individual cultures. Diverse cultural backgrounds provide perspective and help the team, as a unit, to respond appropriately, reducing the risk of unnecessarily giving or taking offense.

Multicultural teams, because of their diverse mix, may be less likely confused by others as having "political agents" and so be less likely to be perceived as subversive by the host country. Americans are not the only ones who may face such suspicions!

Although all humans are unique within their own culture, each national group tends to have certain typical characteristics which can enrich the team. Brazilian vibrancy, Korean zeal, South African commitment, and American organization can complement each other to make the combined unit much stronger than the individual parts.

Finally, the home churches benefit, enriched through the multinational team experience of those they send. If these churches stay in close contact with their missionaries, they will gain a heightened understanding of the body of Christ and the nature of God's mission.

Problems in Multicultural Teams

Although the blend of cultures brings great benefits, it is not without potential pitfalls. Proper orientation and an ongoing attitude of learning and servanthood are necessary to resolve these problems. Mackin (1992, pp. 156-157) states that one of the ongoing challenges is for the team to distinguish things that are clearly condemned and clearly approved by Scripture from things that are either neutral or else subject to varying interpretation, such as drinking alcoholic beverages.

The examples of potential problems that we describe below stem principally from the neutral and gray areas. As Mackin reminds her readers, love, unity, and wholesomeness must be emphasized as the team works through the various issues at hand.

Leadership-Related Problems

Starting with communication style, an American team leader may cause offense by using an open, direct style both in giving direction and in correcting problems. A leader who is most comfortable with an "open" style of communication may expect a similar style of openness and frankness from the team members in expressing their needs. Further, the American may presume that authority is based primarily on a job description, rather than on strong relationships and age-based respect.

On a team, failure to spend time developing relationships with team members could diminish the team's perception of the American leader's authority. To be in touch with all the team members, the American must develop a network of listeners to help him understand other team members. An example would be finding out the needs of a single Korean woman on a team through a Korean couple who are aware of her particular situation.

A Korean leader may find egalitarian-minded Americans too direct in expressing disagreement with his views. The informal style of language and body posture of Americans and Brazilians may not convey to him the respect he desires. On the other hand, his directive style may well offend Americans and, to some extent, Brazilians.

Listening carefully in a group meeting, an African leader might not overtly express his own opinions until the end, when he summarizes what has been said in his own words. The lack of outward direction could leave some Americans or Koreans wondering if the leader is leading or just following the rest. Meanwhile, Koreans will resonate with African deference to elders, something youth-oriented Americans and Brazilians may struggle with.

Female leaders may be accepted by Americans and perhaps by Brazilians. Korean men, however, would find it hard to submit to a woman unless she has significant experience to set her above the men. African women, although given certain authority in society, are not often given leadership roles in church structures. American women who are open to assuming leadership positions may feel stifled by Koreans and to a certain extent by Brazilians, who may not want them to move above a middle-level managerial position.

Finally, leaders often become engaged in informal counseling with team members. The Korean educational system molds Koreans to assume that the expert does the talking, and the learner does the listening. Thus, a Korean leader may be more inclined to tell his team members what to do, rather than to listen to their needs. The American or Brazilian who does not give clearly defined guidelines in counseling may be perceived by Korean team members to be a weak leader.

Lifestyle Issues

Some of the most emotionally charged pitfalls of multicultural teams lie in the area of lifestyle. These issues move beyond one's job to questions of one's personal and deeply held values and feelings.

Language and truth

The team leaders will likely need to speak English. Brazilians and Koreans will be hampered by this. In particular, Koreans will find it difficult to express deep feelings, the language gap being complicated by a generally reserved nature as compared to their colleagues. Personal frustrations and superficial relationships may result. A danger exists of forming exclusive national cliques centered on language differences.

Africans on the team may speak excellent English, but although they may mix easily with other cultures, they may struggle with expressing their deep feelings in a way the others understand. Relationships may be valued by Africans not for any benefit they bring but simply for the intrinsic value of relationship itself.

Regarding truth-telling, traditional Korean values perceive lying in terms of causing intentional harm, more than as a failure to give a literal account of the facts. It is not seen as a black and white issue but a continuum. If a Korean man is unavailable to speak to someone on the telephone, he may in good conscience tell his child to say that he is not at home. An American would consider this to be lying, even if it is a "white lie." Such underlying values related to indirect speech and not desiring to hurt the feelings of others, versus a value of direct honesty, may cause division on the team. In this area, as well as in other conflicts, the African concern both for truth and for the feelings of others may be helpful, with inappropriate behavior being dealt with in a non-confrontational manner.

Families

Americans, in contrast with others, tend to delineate sharply between family and ministry, between personal time and ministry or work time. Conflict may arise when Americans are considered to be too protective of their time or, on the other hand, when Americans think their colleagues are not caring properly for their families. Africans may have the most holistic view on family issues, making little distinction between private and public time or allocation of resources for family, work, and ministry.

The values and feelings of wives on the team, raised in different cultures and thus with differing values and expectations, must be taken into account. The same is true for the values and feelings of the children being raised together in a multicultural setting. Korean parents may find it difficult when their children, who may be studying at an American-controlled school, begin to expect their parents to treat them in an American way and not a Korean way.

Americans may be offended by child-rearing practices in what they perceive to be spoiled, undisciplined Korean children, and they may consider the children's parents to be failing in their role. This applies even to very young children, such as three- and four-year-olds, whom Korean parents do not yet discipline. However, elementary-age and older Korean children may chafe at the strictures on their time, as compared to their MK playmates from other cultures. Koreans, Brazilians, and black South Africans may not understand how an American mother can let a baby cry, for example when the baby wakes at night. Team members, therefore, must respect the culturally conditioned child-raising styles of each set of parents, but parents must also be sensitive to the impact their children's behavior has on the team. Although the other families might benefit by moving toward Korean disciplines, such as in study and music lessons, Korean parents should be prepared for the inevitable influences toward less structured use of children's time.

Education of children is a major concern for missionary parents. Families from the USA and the UK tend to have more options linked to their homelands than missionaries from other lands. Koreans, South Africans, and Brazilians will likely not find schooling compatible with the system in their home countries. Attendance at an American or British school will contribute to a loss of national identity on the part of the children. This leads to a tendency of Korean families not to return to Korea for furlough, since their children do not fit into the educational structure.

Time

The dimensions of "time orientation" versus "event orientation" (Lingenfelter & Mayers, 1986) can be especially troublesome. Africans focus on the present, not sacrificing the relationship or the process for the goal. Americans, frustrated when others are not "on time" for team meetings and appointments, need to learn the importance of focusing on the people who are present, not on those who are absent. Meanwhile, the others may benefit from the Americans' concern for those who are absent. Koreans seem to have combined the strengths of being group-oriented while also succeeding in "getting things done." Perhaps all could learn from the adage, "There is no rush in Africa, but when it's harvest time, everybody gets busy except a fool."

Unity

Africans and Koreans tend to be more group-oriented than Americans and Brazilians. Americans and Brazilians may feel that their Korean team mates over-protect one another from criticism. The Koreans, however, will likely feel that their actions display love and unity. Americans and Brazilians can learn from the Koreans' and Africans' emphasis on unity, so that it positively affects the entire team. Koreans can learn from the others the value of a broader sense of team that is not centered on an ethnic cluster.

Space

Use of space must also be considered: personal, intimate, and social space, as well as clean and holy areas. The removal of shoes in homes or on entering a church pulpit is characteristic of Koreans. Mutual respect should be shown in each other's homes on this issue. The comfort zones involving physical distance vary. American men tend to keep their distance from each other, while Korean men may walk together arm in arm. Americans, despite their typical openness to others, are more likely than Africans, Brazilians, or Koreans to try to prevent intrusions on their "personal" space, possessions, and time.

Food

Food may be another area of conflict, as well as a source of good-natured humor. Korean food is quite distinct from American, African, and Brazilian food. American and Brazilian singles living with Koreans, or families living next to Koreans, may find the distinctive smells offensive, while Africans may adapt more readily. Common meals based on the host country diet may provide a solution to this problem.

Romance

Finally, multicultural teams involving singles increase the likelihood of intercultural romance and marriage. Agreement should be reached in advance on how romance will be handled on the team and, in particular, whether intercultural relationships will be permitted. Normal friendliness in one culture may be perceived as romantic attention in another. Team leaders may need outside counsel to help couples who are developing a relationship. Koreans may find intercultural romance a particular difficulty, since marrying a non-Korean will likely cause a disruption in the ability to fit into Korean culture. The challenges of intercultural marriages are high, but for Africans, Brazilians, and Americans, such marriages tend to be more readily accepted in the home country than in Korea.

Patterns of Ministry

The question of personal spirituality is important in defining the team's ministry. Again, team members from differing cultures must learn from each other. Presumption that one's view of spirituality is normative for all—be it an emphasis on daily devotional times alone or as a group, getting a specific "word of the Lord," practicing rigorous spiritual disciplines, and so on—may cause division and lack of mutual respect.

Styles of worship are likely to vary. A Brazilian Baptist may be more effusive than an American Pentecostal. Koreans may display a vocal style in their prayer times that Brazilians and Americans find dominating. Africans are likely to be accommodating to a wide variety of styles. On joining the team, new members should be oriented to these differences and asked to be more observant than demonstrative in public worship, until they have a sense of the team's corporate style. This style will develop over time, having the potential of becoming a beautiful display of the diverse worship traditions represented.

Finally, there is potential conflict over the way to go about evangelism and church planting. The Americans will tend to want to research the area with social science tools and conduct outreach according to a logically derived plan. Brazilians will more likely emphasize the importance of building relationships in the community. To the Koreans, zeal will be a dominant characteristic, with preaching and other direct evangelism emphasized if language is not a barrier. Prayer will also be a vital element of Korean strategy, along with total personal devotion to church planting activities. A black South African may have the most holistic overall approach that is relational and spontaneous, zealous to preach but also concerned to share resources with the poor, and in it all acutely aware of the need for prayerful dependence on God.

Conclusion

Multicultural teams are an important part of missions strategy. In fact, they may well be the main workhorses that God will use to help plow, cultivate, and harvest frontier fields. We have outlined some concrete areas that these teams need to consider as they seek to establish a sense of community among themselves, as well as ministry viability. Strong multinational teams take time to develop. This strength comes from understanding each other's cultural values, along with practicing the biblical values of serving one another, giving preference to each other, and being willing to change for the sake of mutual edification.

Intercultural relations expert Geert Hofstede (1997, p. 237) states, "The principle of surviving in a multicultural world is that one does not need to think, feel, and act in the same way in order to agree on practical issues and to cooperate." If this is viable in the business world, how much more should we, united in Christ and operating in the Spirit's grace and power, be able to join together in fruitful service of our Lord!

Case Studies

Case 1

David Wilson, the American field director for Central Asia, is visiting one of his multinational teams. He knows that some of the Koreans on the team do not yet speak English very well, although they are making a heroic effort to learn. During his individual interviews with all the team members, he asks if there are any personal problems of which he should be aware. He is particularly impressed with how cheerful and pleasant Soo Jung, a newcomer, is, and he comments on this to the team leader. Later, the team leader writes to David. As it turns out, Soo had smiled but actually had hardly understood a word that David had said. In reality, she was facing a personal crisis related to the illness of her non-Christian father back home in Korea. "But how was I to know?" protests David to himself. "I asked her, and she did not tell me anything!" What could David do differently in the future? Any advice for Soo Jung or the team leader?

Case 2

Jeremias Silva has worked for nearly 10 years in Africa, far from his native São Paulo home. Sometimes, he wonders if he would prefer to go back to earlier years, when he and his wife worked alone rather than on a team. The Smiths (Americans) and the Kims (Koreans), each with school-age children, joined the Silvas two years ago. Both couples were highly committed when they came, but now disunity has settled into the team. Dave Smith believes strongly that community development work—drilling water wells and conducting primary health care classes—should play an equal role with direct witness in the team's ministry. Won Ho Kim, though, considers such development activities to be second best. Both men use arguments from Scripture to support their position. Jeremias wonders if there are not underlying cultural issues involved that are separating his co-workers. What might some of these issues be? How could Jeremias help resolve any issues?

Case 3

A mission agency's executive committee faces a perplexing situation. One of their team leaders living in a male-dominated land has had to step down. A replacement must be named soon. There is one clear choice to succeed him in terms of gifts, skills, and experience: Elisabete, a single Brazilian woman. The problem is that she is a woman and single. The issues for many are her gender and marital status, not her abilities. If nominated, doubtless she would humbly decline, but the committee believes she would accept if they encouraged her to take on the responsibility. However, even if she did accept, the committee wonders if her multicultural team would accept her as leader. How would she relate to the handful of leaders, all men, from the fledgling national church? How do you think the executive committee should proceed? Assuming they appoint Elisabete, how can they help her to succeed?

Case 4

It has been a real struggle to accomplish much during the last three weekly meetings of a multinational team in Asia. One of the single Brazilian men has fallen in love with a Korean team member, and this has led to some division. The Korean team leader and his wife believe it is better not to encourage this relationship. The other three members of the team, an American couple and their 20-year-old son, see no serious problem with it, providing they go slowly and remain accountable. The leader tries to instruct the Brazilian man privately, but they end up arguing. The oldest American tries to act as mediator between both parties, as this issue is brought up during the team meetings. The Korean woman is confused, the team leader feels his authority is being overlooked, the Americans want to move on and focus on ministry issues, and the Brazilian is afraid that he will lose a potential wife. Take the part of one of the seven team members, and describe what you might do to help resolve this situation.

Case 5

There are four couples, along with several singles, working together in a North African city. Tension between the wives seems to be ready to break out into open criticism. Jane, from America, is disappointed that her efforts to organize a support group for team wives have failed. Hae Sook, from Korea, seems to be content to quietly cook, clean house, and serve her husband—or is it that it just seems that way? They both feel rejected by Silvina, from Brazil, whose physical features and good language skills help her to fit in with local women. Meanwhile, Esther, from South Africa, is reminded of earlier days in her homeland by some negative, race-related experiences she has had while going about the town. How would you help these women understand and support each other?

Reflection and Discussion

Go through the five case studies above, and respond to the items at the end of each case. Use the material presented in this article, your own experience, and other sources to interact with these cases. Discussing these cases is a great tool for team building!

References and Suggested Reading

Allen, F. (1991). Your church planting team can be booby-trapped. *Evangelical Missions Quarterly*, *27*, 294-297.

Dodd, C. (1991). *Dynamics of intercultural communication* (3rd ed.). Dubuque, IA: William C. Brown Publishers.

Elmer, D. (1993). *Cross-cultural conflict: Building relationships for effective ministry*. Downers Grove, IL: InterVarsity Press.

Fraser-Smith, J. (1993). *Love across latitudes: A pre-marital workbook for cross-cultural relationships*. (Available from AWM, Worthing, UK, and Upper Darby, PA, USA; ISBN 0-904971-03-1)

Hofstede, G. (1997). *Cultures and organizations: Software of the mind*. New York, NY: McGraw Hill.

Jones, G., & Jones, R. (1995). *Teamwork*. London, UK: Scripture Union.

Lingenfelter, S., & Mayers, M. (1986). *Ministering cross-culturally: An incarnational model for personal relationships*. Grand Rapids, MI: Baker.

Mackin, S. (1992). Multinational teams. In K. O'Donnell (Ed.), *Missionary care: Counting the cost for world evangelization* (pp. 155-162). Pasadena, CA: William Carey Library.

McMillan, D., & Chavis, D. (1986). Sense of community: A definition and theory. *American Journal of Community Psychology, 14*, 3-5.

Roembke, L. (2000). *Building credible multicultural teams*. Pasadena, CA: William Carey Library.

Sarasson, S. (1974). *The psychological sense of community: Prospects for a community psychology*. San Francisco, CA: Jossey-Bass.

Stoner, D. (1993). *Sense of community: A review of precedent life*. Unpublished manuscript. Trinity Evangelical Divinity School, Deerfield, IL.

David Greenlee *spent many of his formative years in Colombia and Ecuador as part of a missionary family. After training in electrical engineering, he joined Operation Mobilization. He served with OM's ship ministry for 14 years in both technical and leadership roles. David later had oversight of a region of the 10/40 window for OM and then worked as International Research and Strategy Associate. He is married to Vreni, from Switzerland, and they have three children: Rebekka, Jonathan, and Sarah. He holds a Doctor of Philosophy degree in intercultural studies from Trinity Evangelical Divinity School. Email: research@om.org.*

Yong Joong Cho *received his Master of Divinity, Master of Theology, and Doctor of Philosophy from Trinity Evangelical Divinity School. He is actively involved in the missions movement in Third World churches, serving as General Coordinator of Third World Missions Association. He is also serving as the National Director of Global Partners USA, an organization with 120 missionaries serving in 17 countries. Email: yongjcho@pacbell.net.*

Abraham Thulare *has been with Operation Mobilization since 1997 and has taught part time at Tshwane Theological College in South Africa. Previously, he worked with WEC in Japan. He is from the Northern Sotho tribe in South Africa and is married to Meselle, living in Pretoria. Abraham received his Bachelor of Arts degree from Hatfield School of Theology, a Bachelor of Theology with honors from the University of South Africa, and is currently working on a Master of Theology degree from the University of South Africa. Email: wilheminah.thulare@satrim.co.za.*

This is an expanded article, which was first published in the special member care issue of the ***International Journal of Frontier Missions*** *(1995, vol. 12, pp. 179-183). Used by permission.*

40

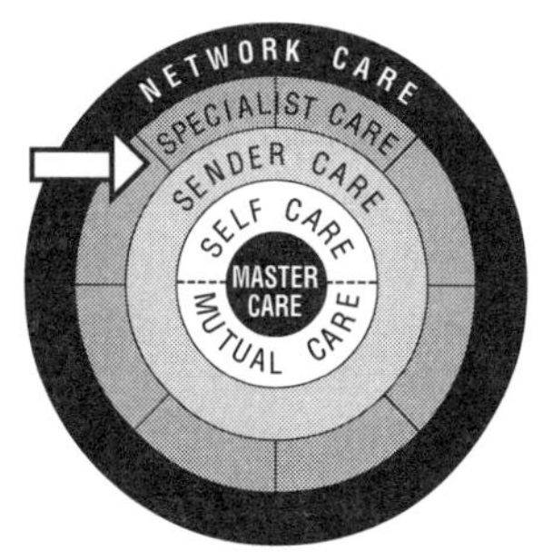

Caring for Missionary Families: Applications From the Military

Hans V. Ritschard

There are valuable lessons from military life that might make Christian missions more effective. This chapter outlines some of the member care structures and practices used by the United States Air Force to care for its families. Two aspects of Air Force family care are discussed and applied to mission families: spiritual member care and physical/emotional member care.

The Apostle Paul had many things to say about being a soldier of Christ Jesus. To Timothy he wrote, "No one serving as a soldier gets involved in civilian affairs—he wants to please his commanding officer" (2 Tim. 2:4). Paul certainly understood the context for these remarks. They were the same difficulties encountered by all armies everywhere: how best to prepare for, sustain, and win a military campaign. Whether contending for the faith or fighting for one's country, there are many similar challenges, including challenges for proper personnel care. Indeed, modern Western armies have discovered that outstanding member care (which involves physical and logistical support) is a key to success. In the military, healthy, rested soldiers are the best soldiers. Soldiers distracted by personal problems, family problems, health problems, or financial problems cannot perform their duties as ready, focused soldiers. The best way to handle "civilian affairs," such as housing, family needs, educational concerns, and so on, is to anticipate them and meet them head on as they arise. The best way to ensure military failure is to pretend there are no "civilian" demands and to ignore them when they occur. Member care is a crucial military function.

Spiritual Member Care

All United States Air Force (USAF) members have access to a chapel system, which is staffed by ordained priests and ministers from most religious denominations. All Air Force families have access to the full range of chapel services. Chapel resources vary, depending on the size of the military population and the base community it serves. Worship, education, outreach, and community service are all aspects of the Air Force chapel system. Chaplains play a central role in knitting together the military community. It is the chaplain who is called when spiritual wisdom is needed.

Chaplains, as with their counterparts in the practice of law, enjoy full legal privilege with their counselees. Chaplains are one of the few sources of completely confidential counseling within the military community. This provides an extremely important aspect of care to military members, since other professional counselors in the medical setting are required to wear two hats, that of a counselor and that of a government representative. Licensed counseling providers are required by Air Force regulation to pass on information to commanders that may be important to preserve the mission of the Air Force. Chaplains, however, maintain full confidentiality with their clients. Understandably, because of ensured confidentiality, many Air Force members prefer to get help and support through the chapel system.

The role of the chaplain is specifically protected in another major way. By regulation, chaplains are never permitted to serve in command roles. This means that even though a chaplain may outrank all other members of a deployed unit, the chaplain may not serve as the unit leader. The Air Force has learned that putting chaplains in command of others compromises their primary role as spiritual advisor.

Physical and Emotional Member Care

The emotional member care in the Air Force may be divided into two broad categories. The first of these is the Air Force health care system, including medical personnel, licensed social workers, clinical psychologists, and psychiatrists, who are available through the hospital or clinic to provide medical care, counseling, and/or psychotherapy services. The second category may be called family support services, which include educational programs, relocation and housing assistance, and child care services.

Health Care

The health care system available to Air Force families includes resources for both the physical and mental health needs of service members and their families. Downsizing efforts in the early 1990s have reduced the number of active-duty medical providers, but services are still available through the Department of Defense Tricare system. In general, military clinics are the starting point for obtaining health care. If specialty care is not available there, beneficiaries are directed to civilian care providers.

All airmen receive an initial medical evaluation prior to joining the Air Force. Minimal medical standards for service must be met. Airmen then meet with a medical provider to determine whether there are any special needs among family members. Any special needs are documented in the medical record (maintained by the local Air Force clinic or hospital). This information is then forwarded to the Exceptional Family Member Program (EFMP) officer for review. Families with a special need are required by Air Force regulations to enroll in the EFMP.

The EFMP program is worth considering in some detail, since a similar system might be readily adapted in both small and large mission organizations. Most importantly, the EFMP is a Department of Defense directive, meaning that all branches of the service must implement the policy. Since it was first developed in the late 1980s, it has developed into a comprehensive system of tracking the needs of families with special needs.

Enrollment is the key to the success of the EFMP program. Families with possible special needs (as identified by health care providers or parents) are required by the Air Force to make an appointment with the EFMP officer, who conducts an initial family interview. Part of the interview is a review of paperwork completed by health care specialists, documenting the nature of the special needs in the family. See Table 1 for a representative list of possible

Table 1
Possible Qualifying Conditions for the Exceptional Family Member Program

Medical Conditions

- Active management two or more times a year by a medical sub-specialist (e.g., occupational or physical therapy, mental health specialists, specialty dental care).
- Repeated hospitalization for the same medical condition.
- Physical disability requiring adaptive equipment (e.g., hearing aids, wheelchairs, home or environmental modifications).
- One or more children requiring intensive treatment for Attention Deficit Hyperactivity Disorder and additional management by a sub-specialist (developmental pediatrician, child psychiatrist, child psychologist).
- Severe asthma.
- Chronic physical disability (e.g., cerebral palsy, multiple sclerosis, etc.).
- Chronic mental health impairment (e.g., psychiatric hospitalization, chronic emotional disorders, substance abuse, etc.).

Educational Conditions (for family members under age 21)

- Children with an Individualized Education Program who receive more than 20% of educational programming in special education.
- Children who receive occupational or physical therapy as part of their special education program.
- Children receiving Early Intervention Services (i.e., for children aged birth to three years).
- Children with developmental delays as identified by parent, physician, or child care provider.

qualifying conditions for enrollment. There is some variation in the implementation of the program, since the EFMP officer may decide whether a condition is serious enough for enrollment. Once a service member is enrolled in the program (i.e., once a family member has a qualifying condition), an "identifier" is placed in the personnel record of the service member. The identifier placed in the records is the same, regardless of how the family qualified for the program.

Personnel with EFMP identifiers receive special consideration when duty assignments are made. Potential duty locations are selected for EFMP enrollees as for the rest of the Air Force; however, once a potential duty location is picked, the EFMP officer obtains a packet of information detailing the special needs of the family member(s). This information is generally gathered from educators and health care providers on standardized forms. These forms are then sent to the potential place of assignment, and another EFMP officer reviews and distributes the forms. Health care providers and educators at the new location then review the information, determine whether the needs of the family can be met, and send their decision back to the originating EFMP office. In this way, families in the EFMP are "cleared," through a detailed information-based process, for all the assignments they receive while enrolled in the program. *The goal of the program is to ensure that families with special needs go only to locations where support is available.* Thus, a parent of an autistic child would only be stationed at a location where the necessary educational and medical services were available. The EFMP is designed to meet the special needs of families, in an effort to deal directly with the "civilian affairs" of the military member and to keep the military mission intact.

The integrity of the EFMP is ensured in two ways. First, the EFMP officer has primary responsibility for the program. At most Air Force installations, the program is located in an office in or near the mental health clinic and is usually administered by a social worker. Every installation has an EFMP officer who is responsible to enroll eligible families and to help in the process of finding appropriate assignments and locations for moving families. Airmen are not eligible for an assignment unless there are sufficient resources in the area to support the family. For example, the special education needs of children must be met before a family is allowed to move to a new area. All assignment officers and commanders have access to the EFMP enrollment database when recommending assignments.

Second, whenever families move within the Air Force, a medical clearance, granted by a senior medical officer, is required for all family members. This maintains the accuracy and completeness of the EFMP database. The medical officer conducts a formal interview to review family medical records and to report any qualifying EFMP conditions that were not previously known. These interviews are done as part of the first step of a move and usually consist of an interview of the airman, which is done with all family medical records available. A service member with no special family needs is considered "worldwide qualified" and is then free to move to a mission-required duty location.

Special family needs identified during these interviews result in enrollment in the EFMP, followed by the special process outlined above, resulting in a tailored assignment. Again, the EFMP code works in two ways. On the one hand, it prevents airmen from taking assignments where necessary services are unavailable. On the other hand, it guarantees that the special needs of family members will be met, thus preserving the military mission. The EFMP also provides mutual accountability. Families are accountable to Air Force requirements, and the Air Force is accountable to provide duty locations that are appropriate in the light of family needs.

Although some members may view the EFMP program as a hindrance to their career, because it may prevent members from taking certain assignments that may enhance a career, most appreciate the benefits that the program offers. Families are never sent to areas where needs cannot be met. The program formalizes the spirit of family care that is part of the Air Force ethos. Most importantly, it allows for quick reassignment when a new need is identified, if services are not available in the immediate area.

Family Support Services

As reported by Paden and Pezor (1993), military family support centers have been around since about 1965, with a consistent network since the early 1980s. These centers arose out of recognition that military members were most often married, and in order to provide adequate support for the military mission, such centers were necessary to help families cope with the demands of military service. In the Air Force, these centers are called Family Support Centers (FSCs). They are staffed by full-time, part-time, and volunteer staff and generally offer a wide range of educational, counseling, and supportive services.

Educational topics vary depending on center resources and staff, but they almost always include programs specifically tailored to the military experience. Classes on moving, transitions, acculturation, budgeting and financial planning, retirement, parenting, career planning, and family stresses are quite common. Informal counseling is usually also available, as are support groups offered by various community groups. Services often include computer terminals for Internet searches, a small lending library on topics important to family life in the military, videotapes of other military installations to help with planning a move, and a staff who are regularly and readily available for advice and support. In addition to its supportive functions, most FSCs provide meeting space for community groups and lectures.

Applications to Family Care in Missions

Member care in the Evangelical missions community has mushroomed in the last 25 years. Landmark papers in the 1970s outlined the problems of missions devoid of member care. Burned-out missionaries, disproportionate attrition after the first "tour of duty," and ineffective and inadequate pastoral guidance were just a few of the problems cited as possible causes for missionary turnover. Fortunately, our understanding of these problems has also grown.

We now know that character problems, health problems, and family problems account for about 38% of missionary attrition (Brierley, 1997). Although there is some variation in this figure, depending on whether Newer or Older Sending Countries are considered, these issues are clearly part of the "civilian affairs" of which Paul wrote. Ignoring these potential problem areas does nothing to avoid entanglement. The US military has learned that specific structures to head off specific problems are the best ways to keep the mission intact.

Spiritual Care

Let's return to the discussion of family care in the US Air Force, in the light of research on the needs of missionary families. First, consider the need for spiritual member care. Giron (1997), in his integrated model of missions, recognizes what the USAF practices: spiritual (pastoral) care ought to be distinct from supervisory (task-oriented) care. It seems clear that confidential spiritual counsel is a vital aspect of member care. While team leaders who are "qualified in a variety of helping and interpersonal skills" might be desirable (Kang, 1997), it is important to recognize that there will inevitably be problems that must be shared outside the "chain of command." This is difficult in missions, since the chain of command may be assumed to be implicitly spiritual—the missionary reports to his/her field leader, who reports to the mission leader, who reports to God. Therefore, the argument goes, why should not spiritual issues be taken up with spiritual leaders, that is, mission leaders?

Clearly, many spiritual problems are deeply personal and private, so much so that much trust must exist before they can be shared with another person. The USAF recognizes that these deeply personal problems require privacy and privilege. Even if they could be shared with task supervisors, these problems would undoubtedly cloud the relationship between supervisor and subordinate. Evangelical missions would do well to provide confidential counseling, either in-house or by using consultants. None of the results of this counseling would be shared with the mission without the consent of the counselee. Whenever an airman turns to a chaplain, he is guaranteed that his privileged communication will not be shared, ***even when the integrity of the mission is threatened***. Chaplains encourage Air Force members to share vital information with commanders, but privacy is taken very seriously in the chaplain community.

There may be some lessons here for missionary member care. Spiritual counsel and guidance are often provided directly by senior mission personnel, who not only have spiritual wisdom and authority, but who are also "commanders" of the mission organization. While they usually offer extensive missions experience, combined with a deep spirituality, the lack of confidentiality for the missionary may make it difficult for missionaries to get the true spiritual support they need.

Physical and Emotional Care

It is true that the resources of the US Air Force far surpass those available to most mission agencies. It is unrealistic to think that all of the resources available to the Air Force be provided by each mission. At the same time, however, the model might be more easily adapted than is first apparent.

First, consider the health needs of missionary families. According to the Reducing Missionary Attrition Project (ReMAP, Taylor, 1997, pp. 92-94), these needs are a major source of unwanted attrition among missionaries. Health reasons are also a major threat to the US military mission, and the USAF takes the health of its member families very seriously. As outlined above, the EFMP provides a formal system for tracking the physical and emotional needs of its members. Physical health care for missionaries requires careful planning and realistic assessment of likely needs before missionary families are sent to their assignments.

Elkins (1997) offers helpful insight on how certain missions keep their attrition numbers exceptionally low. He outlines a model used by the Christian and Missionary Alliance, which uses a tracking system employing an annual and tri-annual review system to assess each missionary's progress. This is quite similar to the concepts underlying the EFMP and could be readily applied in most mission agencies.

Combining Elkins' (1997) ideas with current practice in the Air Force, mission families could be screened for health and emotional needs during the initial selection and training process. Families with special needs could be given an identifying code that would place them in a "Special Family Program," so that their needs would be considered during the assignment process. They would also be tracked throughout their service to the mission. The checklist presented in Table 1 could be readily adapted to most mission agencies. If coded families felt called to certain locations where services were not available, explicit discussions could be held about whether (1) such a calling was strong enough to disregard obvious future needs and (2) if it were, how such likely needs would be met in the future. Ideally, families with special needs would only serve in locations where necessary services were accessible.

After initial coding (enrollment) in the Special Family Program, missionary families could be followed annually, tri-annually, or at whatever frequency the mission leadership found helpful. As noted by Elkins (1997), this sort of regular "check-up" seems to keep missionary attrition as low as 2% annually. Successful mission agencies appear to provide a very high degree of accountability to their member families. Again, the EFMP keeps both the Air Force and its families accountable to the terms of its mission.

Curiously, the term "accountability" almost never occurs in Taylor's (1997) outstanding review of the ReMAP project, an edited volume covering all aspects of missionary attrition. Not only does it not appear in the index, but almost none of the chapters speak in terms of keeping missionaries accountable. Certainly, most authors implicitly recognize the need for accountability; but why do most authors choose other terms?

Perhaps today's boomer and buster missionaries (Donovon & Myors, 1997), along with wanting more mutuality and teamwork in missions, also want less accountability to the mission, vision, direction, and leadership of their organizations. "Participatory management" seems to mean that employees and their leadership are involved in a continuous dialectic in defining an organizational purpose. Despite the evolving nature of Air Force doctrine and structure, however, most families (and all Air Force members) know what the Air Force will demand of them. The EFMP holds families to those demands. A program for enrolling special needs families would provide mission agencies with a way to meet the needs of its members and to hold them accountable to the unique vision and purpose of the organization.

Interestingly, in their analysis of the ReMAP data, Bloecher and Lewis (1997, p. 111) found that "good communication with the missionary may be the single most significant support item in helping lower preventable attrition." This suggests that initial clear communication about organizational expectations, vision, and structure, along with regular contact thereafter, are essential. Enrollment in a special needs family program would clearly facilitate such regular communication.

Family Check-Ups and Research

The EFMP program provides for regular "family check-ups." How might these "check-ups" be provided to missionary families? Many authors have written about the stresses and strains placed on people living overseas. A study by Bowen (1989) found that the best predictor of positive Army family adaptation to living overseas was the extent to which family expectations meshed with their actual experience. Another strong predictor in this study was the level of community support families received. A related study found that separation of family members is the most serious threat to adaptation and that, for military families, relocation is the most frequent stressor encountered (Schumm, Bell, & Tran, 1994).

Figley (1989a, 1989b) characterized positive and negative coping styles in military families during the Gulf War. His findings are outlined in Table 2 and are relevant for mission families as well. Similarly, Bartone (1999) reported that the personality trait of "hardiness," defined as a strong sense of life and work commitment, combined with a greater feeling of control and an openness to change and to face the challenges in life, leads to better adjustment. Hardy persons tend to interpret stressful and painful experiences as a normal part of life and see them as things that make life interesting and worthwhile.

A variety of studies have found that hardiness is a significant moderator or buffer of stress. A closely related term, "resiliency," has been used to describe successful adjustment and adaptation. Various inventories have been developed to assess both individual and family resiliency (McCubbin & McCubbin, 1996). Similarly, several studies have elucidated factors

Table 2
Healthy vs. Unhealthy Family Coping Styles*

Functional Family Coping	Dysfunctional Family Coping
■ Clear acceptance of the stressor.	■ Denial or misinterpretation of the stressor.
■ Family-centered locus of the problem.	■ Individual-centered locus of the problem.
■ Solution-oriented problem solving.	■ Blame-oriented problem solving.
■ High tolerance of other family members.	■ Low tolerance for other family members.
■ Clear/direct expression of commitment.	■ Indirect/missing expressions of commitment.
■ Clear/direct expression of affections.	■ Indirect/missing expressions of affections.
■ Open and effective communication.	■ Closed or ineffective communication.
■ High family cohesion.	■ Low or poor family cohesion.
■ Flexible family roles.	■ Rigid family roles.
■ Efficient resource utilization.	■ Inefficient resource utilization.
■ Absence of violence.	■ Utilization of violence.
■ Infrequency of substance abuse.	■ Abuse or frequent use of habit-forming substances.

* Figley, 1989a, 1989b.

important in understanding the stressors and "protective factors" for missionary life. Allen (1986) gave an excellent overview of areas of concern for missionary families. O'Donnell and O'Donnell (1992) and O'Donnell (1997a) have described what they call the CHOPS model of missionary stress, outlining 10 categories of stress and stress reduction that can affect missionaries and missionary families (see chapter 23).

Finally, several studies have sought to determine what helps children to adjust most readily to moving frequently. In a comprehensive review of the available literature, Vernberg and Field (1990) concluded that a variety of factors influence a child's adjustment to a new environment. Some of these include the developmental and personal characteristics of the child, the circumstances (amount of support) surrounding the transition, and the unique features of the old and new settings. A survey completed by 1,036 US Army soldiers and their spouses found that families with preschool and school-age children require the most support to adapt and cope (McCubbin & Lavee, 1986). In a study of gifted students, Plucker and Yecke (1999) reported that, although some children experienced social difficulties related to frequent relocation, overall these relocations had little impact on parent and student perceptions of the gifted child's long-term social, emotional, and academic development.

The Air Force EFMP program seeks to identify families with special needs to maximize family adjustment to the military lifestyle. An expanded interview form, based on the initial EFMP enrollment data, is used for family members to provide updates on how special needs are being met and what needs are likely to arise in the future. This form is used each time a family prepares to move to a new assignment. If special needs continue within the family, the family remains enrolled; otherwise, if needs no longer exist, the family is removed from the EFMP, and the special EFMP code is removed from the personnel file. Combining the approach of the Air Force with some of the findings in the literature might lead to a family interview based on the questions outlined in Table 3. A positive answer to any of the questions could lead to enrollment in the mission's Special Family Program, described above.

Family Support Services

The Air Force has over 86 Family Support Centers worldwide that provide remarkable support services to families. Clearly this is unrealistic for most Evangelical mission agencies, so how might this concept be applied to missions?

Sharing resources is the key to effective worldwide missions. As member care services have expanded, so have centers and agencies sprung up to provide these services. In fact, O'Donnell (1997b) has compiled a list of over 100 organizations worldwide that actively provide various support services to missionaries (updated in chapter 49). These organizations include health clinics, counseling centers, and fully developed missionary development, recovery, and renewal centers. As more and more member care groups are strategically placed around the globe, more and more missionaries will enjoy the same support enjoyed by their secular military counterparts.

Conclusion

The US Air Force is firmly committed to caring for the needs of its members. Most Air Force families are generally aware of the resources available to them and how to access them. All families are screened for enrollment in the EFMP, both to keep them accountable to Air Force requirements and to formalize the care the Air Force provides for special needs families. Regular EFMP interviews hold everyone accountable. Caring for families in these ways ensures a fit fighting force.

Keeping a fit, effective missionary force requires no less. Past research and newer insights into missionary attrition have re-

Table 3
Suggested Questions for Use During an Annual Missionary Family "Check-Up"

Medical Conditions

Does anyone in the family: [a]

- Require management two or more times a year by a medical sub-specialist?
- Expect repeated hospitalization for the same medical condition?
- Have a known or new physical disability requiring adaptive equipment?
- Require intensive treatment for Attention Deficit Hyperactivity Disorder, including additional management by a sub-specialist?
- Have severe asthma?
- Have a chronic mental health impairment or a physical disability?

Spiritual and Support Concerns

Do family members:

- Lack a clear and common call to missionary service? [b]
- Exhibit dysfunctional family coping (as defined in Table 2)? [c]
- Individually and corporately lack a healthy spirituality, as defined by the mission? [b]
- Lack a sense that cultural adaptation has been progressive and positive? [b]
- Lack good relationships with other missionary families? [b]
- Feel that they do not receive adequate pastoral care? [b]
- Have serious concerns about their financial support? [b]
- Report job-related or organizational stresses? [d]
- Lack hardiness and see stress and pain as abnormal and something to be avoided in life? [e]
- Feel that their expectations for service have not been met? [g]

Educational Conditions (for family members under age 21) [a]

Do any of the children:

- Require special education classes that comprise more than 20% of educational programming? [a]
- Receive occupational or physical therapy as part of their special education program? [a]
- Receive Early Intervention Services (i.e., for children aged birth to three years)? [a]
- Have developmental delays as identified by parent, physician, or child care provider? [a]
- Have a history of being negatively affected by frequent relocations? [f]

[a] USAF EFMP questions; [b] Brierley, 1997; [c] Figley, 1989a, 1989b; [d] O'Donnell, 1997a; [e] Bartone, 1999; [f] Plucker & Yecke, 1999; [g] Bowen, 1989.

vealed the nature of the "civilian affairs" that can so easily entangle and distract missionaries. A system of comprehensive care, including spiritual, physical, and emotional care, is absolutely vital to maintaining our missionary force. This requires a way to track special family needs, to provide regular family "check-ups," and to make general support services available worldwide. The USAF has a well-established system to do all these things. In most cases, the military approach to member care can be replicated to further world evangelization.

Reflection and Discussion

1. Why does the USAF choose to extend special privilege (confidentiality) to chaplains? How might this be possible in the missions community?

2. What is the purpose of the Exceptional Family Member Program in the USAF? How are the enrollment criteria from Table 1 relevant to missionary families?

3. Look again at Table 2. Do the characteristics of functional vs. dysfunctional families seem to apply to Christian missionaries? Are there any basic differences in the types of characteristics used to describe functional/dysfunctional families from the Newer and Older Sending Countries?

4. How might a "special needs program" be set up for families in your mission agency? Would it be feasible to "code" these families in some way? Who in the mission agency would be responsible for such a program? How would it be possible to "code" in a clear way to help without families feeling singled out as "unfit"?

5. Review Table 3. How could the suggested interview be adapted to fit the needs of your family or organization? How often should such an interview be conducted, and who should conduct it? Who would review the information? How would the information be protected?

References

Allen, F. (1986). Why do they leave? Reflections on attrition. *Evangelical Missions Quarterly, 22*, 118-129.

Bartone, P. (1999). Hardiness protects against war-related stress in Army Reserve forces. *Consulting Psychology Journal: Practice and Research, 51*(2), 72-81.

Bloecher, D., & Lewis, J. (1997). Further findings in the research data. In W. Taylor (Ed.), *Too valuable to lose: Exploring the causes and cures of missionary attrition* (pp. 105-125). Pasadena, CA: William Carey Library.

Bowen, G. (1989). *Family adaptation to relocation: An empirical analysis of family stressors, adaptive resources, and sense of coherence (Tech. Rep. 856)*. Alexandria, VA: U.S. Army Research Institute for the Behavioral and Social Sciences.

Brierley, P. (1997). Missionary attrition: The ReMAP research report. In W. Taylor (Ed.), *Too valuable to lose: Exploring the causes and cures of missionary attrition* (pp. 85-104). Pasadena, CA: William Carey Library.

Donovan, K., & Myors, R. (1997). Reflections on attrition in career missionaries: A generational perspective into the future. In W. Taylor (Ed.), *Too valuable to lose: Exploring the causes and cures of missionary attrition* (pp. 41-73). Pasadena, CA: William Carey Library.

Elkins, P. (1997). Attrition in the USA and Canada. In W. Taylor (Ed.), *Too valuable to lose: Exploring the causes and cures of missionary attrition* (pp. 371-376). Pasadena, CA: William Carey Library.

Figley, C. (1989a). *Helping traumatized families*. San Francisco, CA: Jossey-Bass.

———. (1989b). *Treating stress in families*. New York, NY: Brunner/Mazel.

Giron, R. (1997). An integrated model of missions. In W. Taylor (Ed.), *Too valuable to lose: Exploring the causes and cures of missionary attrition* (pp. 25-40). Pasadena, CA: William Carey Library.

Kang, S. (1997). Missionary attrition issues: Supervision. In W. Taylor (Ed.), *Too valuable to lose: Exploring the causes and cures of missionary attrition* (pp. 251-264). Pasadena, CA: William Carey Library.

McCubbin, H., & Lavee, Y. (1986). Strengthening Army families: A family life cycle stage perspective. *Evaluation and Program Planning, 9*, 221-231.

McCubbin, M., & McCubbin, H. (1996). Resiliency in families: A conceptual model of family adjustment and adaptation in response to stress and crisis. In H. McCubbin, I. Thompson, & M. McCubbin (Eds.), *Family assessment: Resiliency, coping, and adaptation—inventories for research and practice* (pp. 1-64). Madison, WI: University of Wisconsin System.

O'Donnell, K. (1997a). Member care in missions: Global perspectives and future directions. *Journal of Psychology and Theology*, *25*, 143-154.

———. (1997b). An international guide for member care resources. In W. Taylor (Ed.), *Too valuable to lose: Exploring the causes and cures of missionary attrition* (pp. 325-338). Pasadena, CA: William Carey Library.

O'Donnell, K., & O'Donnell, M. (1992). Understanding and managing stress. In K. O'Donnell (Ed.), *Missionary care: Counting the cost for world evangelization* (pp. 110-122). Pasadena, CA: William Carey Library.

Paden, L., & Pezor, L. (1993). Uniforms and youth: The military child and his or her family. In F. Kaslow (Ed.), *The military family in peace and war* (pp. 3-24). New York, NY: Springer.

Plucker, J., & Yecke, C. (1999). The effect of relocation on gifted students. *Gifted Child Quarterly, 43*(2), 95-106.

Schumm, W., Bell, D., & Tran, G. (1994). *Family adaptation to the demands of Army life: A review of findings (ARI Research Report 1658)*. Alexandria, VA: U.S. Army Research Institute for the Behavioral and Social Sciences.

Taylor, W. (Ed.). (1997). *Too valuable to lose: Exploring the causes and cures of missionary attrition*. Pasadena, CA: William Carey Library.

Vernberg, E., & Field, T. (1990). Transitional stress in children and young adolescents moving to new environments. In S. Fisher & C. Cooper (Eds.), *On the move: The psychology of change and transition* (pp. 127-151). New York, NY: John Wiley & Sons.

Hans V. Ritschard *is a Major and a child/pediatric clinical psychologist in the United States Air Force. He currently works at RAF Lakenheath in England. He has served the USAF overseas for six of the past eight years and has special expertise in the areas of cross-cultural adjustment, military and missionary children, and organizational and team consulting. He has been actively involved in international member care since 1989. He provides frequent pro bono consultation to missionary families and organizations. Email: ritschard@yahoo.com.*

Special thanks to Gay Galleher, Ph.D., and Bryan Vyverberg, M.D., for their very thoughtful and thorough review of earlier drafts of this article. As always, my wife Carolyn provided tremendous support during this writing project.

The views expressed in this article are those of the author and do not necessarily reflect the official policy or position of the United States Air Force, the Department of Defense, or the United States Government.

41

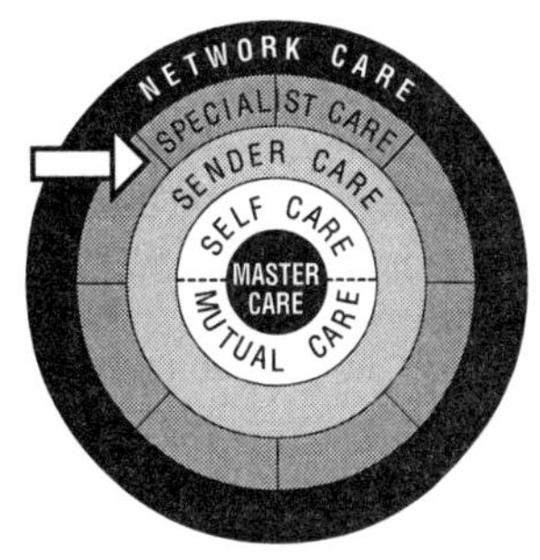

Supporting Expatriate Women In Difficult Settings

ANNEMIE GROSSHAUSER

Going through the marketplace in a male-dominated country, being single in a family-centered society, working in the context of very different and sometimes hostile cultural and religious settings, educating children without proper school systems, trying to show compassion to people in need, serving together in a multicultural team—these are some of the challenges confronting expatriate women. This chapter addresses these issues and takes a closer look at their causes and remedies.

As a psychologist and a Christian, I have been privileged to minister over the last 18 years to both local women and expatriate women, supporting them with counseling, debriefing, and crisis intervention. Living and working in restricted countries in East Africa and Central Asia, I have experienced and witnessed the stresses of living in the Developing World. It can be a hard and dark environment, even if one enters it prepared and with ongoing emotional and relational support. My experience and struggles are not unique. Yet I felt it important to write them down concisely, so that other Christian women can be better equipped not only to survive, but to run the race in such a way as to get the prize (1 Cor. 9:24).

In this chapter, I will look at the coping challenges and strategies of expatriate Christian women who live in Muslim countries. I will focus on five areas:

- *Islam*—the role of women in Islam and in the West; the difference in expectations for personal rights; issues such as submission, fulfillment, and job satisfaction, which are frequent causes of stress and psychological problems.
- *Past personal issues*—emotional struggles from one's past. This area is especially important, since the spiritual realities and cultural restrictions in Islam seem to trigger stronger, more dramatic reactions to unresolved problems than would be experienced back home.
- *Spiritual dimensions*—spiritual preparation for service and an ongoing walk with God in a difficult environment; the quality of one's own maturity; one's call; familiarity with spiritual resources.
- *Team viability*—the need for a supportive and caring team, in which the members look out for each other,

especially for the female co-workers; some of the obstacles and potential for international teams.

■ *New roles, identity, and lifestyle*—a look at how transitions and cross-cultural living test our stability, beliefs, and sense of who we are; differences in the way singles, couples, and families are affected.

Islam

One-fourth of the world's three billion women are Muslim. While holding key positions of influence within their own families, these women usually have only limited access to education, health care facilities, and basic human rights. Due to the cultural and religious separation between men and women in many Muslim countries, the gospel is primarily communicated to Muslim women by other women. What a challenge—and opportunity—this presents for female Christian workers to spend time with Muslim women and to model Christ through their lives.

Muslim countries embrace "one faith," but the way that faith is practiced varies from country to country. For example, there are many factors contributing to the determination of the role and rights of women in Muslim communities, including level of education, economic status, urban or rural setting, impact of Western influence, and degree of fundamentalism. Consequently, there is no unified concept of women's rights or their role in society. In some countries, women are in political leadership positions, while in others, they might never see the outside of their own home.

Teachings in the Quran give a basic understanding of the expressed (though often not literally adhered to) position of women in Islam. For example, Surah 4,34 states, "Men are in charge of women, because Allah hath made the one of them to excel the other, and because they spend of their property (for the support of women). So good women are the obedient, guarding in secret that which Allah hath guarded. As for those from whom ye fear rebellion, admonish them and banish them to beds apart, and scourge them. Then if they obey you, seek not a way against them" (Pickthall, 1988).

Mohammed, in his time, instituted new laws for women and children which protected them—especially the widows and orphans. In general, though, men's superiority over women is taught in Islam.*

The result of Islamic teaching is that Muslim women, in comparison to non-Muslim women, are generally more restricted and less visible publicly, and they live in submission to males. Under Islam, men are clearly the superior gender in the created order. This position affects their attitudes towards women and produces a tendency to take a lot of liberties. The result is that both local and expatriate women often feel abused just from the way they are looked at or when they are treated condescendingly. On the other hand, Muslim men generally feel very protective of women, especially those of their own family. It must be kept in mind that many of the restrictions for women are exacerbated by cultural habits quite apart from Islamic teaching per se. Still, women in most non-Muslim nations have more equal opportunities to work and study, they are equal partners in society, and they expect to reach a certain level of fulfillment and job satisfaction. When going into a Muslim environment, expatriate women often underestimate the potential effects of religious and cultural restrictions and of limited job opportunities.

There are many areas where women can serve with their expertise and gifts, such as physical and mental health care, administration, teaching, hospitality, caring, and prayer. Compared with what they left back home or compared with their ini-

* An extensive discourse on this subject would exceed the content and purpose of this chapter; see bibliography for further study.

tial expectations, their current job may seem to lack prestige, but at the same time it can be intensely fulfilling and satisfying to see their impact on local women's lives.

Women going into Muslim settings must understand and expect a certain amount of gender discrimination. Actually, the battle is not primarily a gender one, but spiritual. The reality is often very painful for expatriate women, when they are inappropriately touched or are the target of shouted obscenities. These are not exceptions! When women experience this kind of treatment, they get hurt deep down, and they feel abused, unworthy, even "undressed." Expatriate women are viewed as unbelievers and therefore are even more vulnerable. Essentially, they are equal to prostitutes in the eyes of the local men. Of course, the Western films portraying sexual freedom support this thinking. Women therefore need to be aware of these issues, guard themselves, and deal with the issues constructively. Condemnation and anger not only inhibit witness, but also affect peace of mind.

Past Personal Issues

"If I had known this 50 years ago, my life could have been so different!" This lament was voiced to me following a service in which I spoke on inner healing, wholeness, and dealing with our past "baggage." Although much has been written about these topics, the need to address them in our own lives is often not recognized or dealt with until we face a crisis or other major challenge—an almost inevitable occurrence when serving overseas.

Inner healing deals with our deep past hurts—those memories of actions, abuse, and sins (things/events that were imposed on us, that we imposed on others, or that just happened to us) which had a crippling effect on our development, our health, our ability to cope and work, or our ability to accept and love ourselves and others. These hurts can manifest themselves in many ways, including low self-esteem, insecurity, authority problems, addictions, self-rejection, anger, negative attitudes, depression, and psychosomatic disorders.

Often we are not aware of this baggage. When we find ourselves struggling with issues such as trust toward God and others, interpersonal relationships, guilt, authority, etc., we tend to blame our parents, circumstances, and other people, failing to see where the roots really lie. Inner healing helps us to untie the knots of the past and requires a willingness to:

- Recognize and accept (vs. denial).
- Confess, forgive, and let go.
- Allow God to heal and restore.
- Be delivered of any occult roots or bondage.

We are all special and precious—unique in our upbringing, worldview, attitudes, values, feelings, and memories. Our own uniqueness is our greatest gift, but it is also our biggest challenge. What we model in our lives and ministries depends, in part, on our willingness to look at our own past and to allow God to deal with our hurts and pains.

The roots of many of our struggles can be found in four major areas: pre-birth, childhood, adolescence/adulthood, and spiritual bondage. I will just touch on each area here, giving key words of problematic conditions and adding a few illustrations. There are many good books dealing with these issues for further study (see bibliography).

Pre-Birth

Conditions that develop at this stage include being unwanted, surviving an attempted abortion, being illegitimate, having parents with deep needs, difficult pregnancy for the mother, illness of the mother, and instability through major conflicts or war.

In my counseling, I encountered a woman who vividly illustrates this pre-birth struggle. After serving on the field for many years, she felt an increasing heaviness, both in her spiritual life and in raising her family. As we talked, she admitted having an ongoing, difficult relationship with her mother, which made her feel guilty. We asked the Holy Spirit to reveal the roots of this conflict, and she began to remember some of her mother's remarks about her unwanted pregnancy and the possibility of abortion. God's Spirit also revealed how the enemy had taken advantage of this rejection, keeping the woman from being joyful or feeling secure. Taking authority over these crippling messages, she experienced a tremendous freedom and was able to forgive her mother and accept her with a new love. In return, she was enabled to love the Lord and her family with a new joy.

While this woman may have experienced the same crippling feelings in her home country, it is a fact that we are more vulnerable when we are out of our comfort and security zone (home). Those who live in spiritually hostile environments, especially those with unhealed wounds, are an easier target for enemy attacks.

Childhood

Conditions that may cause problems at this stage of life include being unwanted, poor sibling relationships, parental conflicts/divorce, feelings of being a failure or unworthy, lack of self-acceptance over personal appearance, being handicapped, being adopted, being orphaned, under-achievement, struggles in school, being belittled by teachers and friends, fears and feelings of rejection and resentment, emotional abuse, physical abuse, and sexual abuse.

I counseled a lady struggling with a depression that was affecting her marriage and seriously impacting the team. In one session, she poured out her anger and bitterness at having grown up with a very outgoing and gifted twin. She had felt second best all her life, never having been able to measure up. She needed healing, forgiveness, deliverance, and a fresh understanding that she is fearfully and wonderfully made by her Creator God (Psalm 139, a wonderful psalm for inner healing and reassurance). As she was able to unravel her past and accept herself the way she was, her depression improved, as well as her working relationships.

An area of crucial importance in our ministry as women serving in a Muslim context is that of our relationship to our fathers. If a girl has been physically, emotionally, or sexually abused or has been raised in an atmosphere of orders and punishments rather than one of love, acceptance, and affection, she will find it difficult to trust anyone, including our heavenly Father. This deep wounding can produce a generalized mistrust, fear, and hatred of men, which is exacerbated by living in a male-dominated society. It may take years of counseling and healing before the ability to trust God is restored and the woman is able to relate to men without resentment.

I have often prayed with women serving in Muslim societies who found themselves emotionally reliving a childhood trauma that they thought they had already completely resolved. But when they experienced disrespect from Muslim men—being stared at or impurely touched in the bazaar—the wounds opened again, filling them with great anger and bitterness. Life in a "macho" culture is difficult for any woman, even more so for one who is scarred. I have observed this to be one of the major stress points for women. If it is not healed from the roots, it may lead to deep resentment and even attrition.

Adolescence/Adulthood

In adolescence and adulthood, there may be relationship problems with family/friends/colleagues, peer pressures, sexual problems, marriage problems, difficulties with in-laws, struggles with singleness, job pressures, guilt and anxiety, loss of belongings, war, injuries, and death of loved ones.

Life, of course, is a mixture of ups and downs, joys and sorrows. When areas of pain and anger are bottled up and denied, they can cause great insecurity and instability in our personality. Our development (physical, spiritual, emotional, cognitive, relational) may be hindered, and our relationship with others and with the Lord may be deeply affected.

I counseled a young woman who served with her husband in a restricted area. When she became pregnant, she got quite ill. Although she wanted the baby, she was apprehensive in looking ahead to motherhood. Her lack of wellness, apart from normal pregnancy sickness, had deeper psychological roots. Becoming a mother made her face her anger and hate towards her own mother, who, in her memory, lacked so much in love and care. Her rejection went so far that she did not want her mother ever to be involved with the baby. Asking the Lord to heal the wounds of neglect enabled this woman to see her mother's failings in a new light. By releasing bitterness and grudges and by forgiving others, we set people free from being indebted to us. This is a very important step in the process of moving toward emotional freedom and spiritual maturity.

A beautiful example of inner healing is found in Luke 7, where a sinful woman pours out her shame and pain through tears while anointing Jesus with perfume and kissing His feet. Jesus restores her, forgiving her sins and releasing her from her past. She leaves joyfully—healed, forgiven, and restored.

Spiritual Bondage

Satan is the father of all lies (John 8:44). His goal is to destroy God's creation, seeking entry points to make us and our ministry ineffective. It is therefore of utmost importance to maintain our relationship with the Lord and with other believers and to be on our guard (1 Peter 5:8).

Bondage can come into our lives in many ways, including ancestral involvement in the occult (Eastern religions, cults, Freemasonry, New Age), the tragedy of a family suicide, sins such as murder or sexual abuse, involvement with or interest in the demonic through pornography, "party" games that invoke spirits, reading horoscopes, or other superstitious beliefs. All of these provide footholds to demonic forces, allowing them to harass and oppress not only the people involved, but also their families.

It is perhaps not surprising that the effect of Freemasonry on people's lives is not as widely known as it should be, because it is a secret society and people often do not know of their ancestors' involvement in it. One young couple were disturbed by night noises in their home. A ministry team came together, and after prayer, the Holy Spirit revealed that both sets of parents had been involved in Freemasonry. The astonishing thing was that both spouses had known of this but had forgotten, and neither was aware of its oppressive effects. We took authority over the spirit of Freemasonry in their lives and cleansed their home through prayer. They were never bothered again. We are serving a God of power who wants us to be alert and to use the authority He has delegated to us.

In the Islamic world, as in others, we have to deal with the effects of magical practices. Curses, amulets, shrines of deceased "holy" men, etc., play a dominant part in folk-Islam and have a spiritual effect on the Christian community as well. These practices, often overlooked or underestimated, can cause responses like lethargy, depression, marital conflict, and team disunity. As Christians serving in cultures where oppressive spirits operate, we must be alert and do what we can to deal with our own past. We need to be honest and willing to let the Lord heal and restore us. How else can we be a light in the darkness?

Spiritual Dimensions

In the ReMAP Research Report on missionary attrition (Brierley, 1997), healthy spirituality was ranked third among the factors impacting our survival and effectiveness on the field. It was preceded in importance by a clear call and the backing of a supportive family. Christian workers must ask themselves time and again, "Am I centered in Christ? Who is in control of my life—myself, others, the work itself, or the Lord?" I encourage all missionaries to examine their current lives and past areas of struggle honestly, preferably with a faithful friend, and to anchor themselves as securely as possible in Christ. This is a process that needs regular attention both on the field and at home.

Spiritual Health

There is a wealth of good books available on the subject of spiritual growth, and many of us read them. What we often lack is the application of the information gained. A healthy spiritual diet consists of a daily time with the Lord, Scripture reading, worship (in song or listening to music), and an open heart ready to be a vessel for the Lord—for our own family, our team, or anyone who needs a listening ear, as well as through hospitality, sharing our faith, and attending to the needs of others. I still remember how much I struggled with my quiet time when our children were small (and even since they are bigger!). When there was time, I was too tired, and I often struggled with feelings of guilt. Then I realized that I could enjoy God's presence and pray while I was nursing, while listening to teaching and worship tapes, while walking with a friend, or while on a shopping trip. We need to learn to be creative about how we feed ourselves our daily spiritual food. An accountability/prayer partner can be of great support through encouragement and by asking honest questions.

Our Call

Spiritual growth is a lifelong process. Elisabeth Elliot (1999, p. 21), a pioneer missionary to South America, knows of the cost, saying, "I think it takes a deep, spiritual encounter with the cross before we're really qualified to call ourselves missionaries." We need to accept our own need for forgiveness and salvation, as well as our need for growth through discipleship. Missionaries are not made; rather, they grow out of a deep relationship with the Lord and the desire to serve Him, whatever the cost. Therefore, it is of utmost importance to be sure of our calling. Other motives, such as adventure, improvement of our resume and professional skills, employment, or running away from difficult circumstances and relationships, can lead to frustration and defeat, because the focus and force of the spiritual battle are misunderstood.

It cannot be stressed enough that the husband and the wife must each have a calling to ministry abroad. A wife who follows her husband into the Muslim world purely out of support or obedience is at high risk. Missionary life in itself is a huge challenge involving much loss and change. With the added strain of separation from family and friends, loneliness, adjusting to a new culture and possibly a difficult climate, learning a new language, coping with previously unknown illnesses, arranging for or doing schooling, etc., it would be unwise to venture out without a personal call on the part of each person. If the wife has not chosen this step out of her own conviction and calling, and unless she is extremely adaptable and easy-going, she will struggle with resentment towards the people and culture, as well as toward her husband. She may subconsciously blame him for her ill-feelings. Women struggling in this area tend either to internalize their conflict and suffer from various psychosomatic disorders or depression, or they get very angry and confrontational. It is to everyone's advantage for sending agencies to be sure that each partner has a calling.

Spiritual Warfare

"Mission work is not a game but a war. The spiritual battle is a reality, while at the same time all sorts of tensions occur in daily life. A missionary needs perseverance and the ability to cope with stressful situations, sometimes without external help" (Ekström, 1997, p. 188). Added to the challenge of loss and change is spiritual warfare on the field—a battleground for which many workers are unprepared. In the international workshop on attrition held at All Nations Christian College, UK, in April 1996, a discussion group on pre-field training formulated a statement concerning the spiritual qualities of prospective missionaries. It reads, in part: "We also believe that candidates should be prepared and trained for spiritual warfare with regard to demonic oppression in all its manifestations" (Adiwardana, 1997, p. 210).

An example of demonic oppression was reported to me by two single women on their return from a survey trip in a neighboring war-torn country. While spending the night in a local home in a remote village, they were awakened, sensing a strange presence in the room. Looking up, they saw the spirit of a woman crouching in a corner. As she moved, her spirit passed through solid items in the room. She was obviously busy with something, taking no notice of the women. The workers knew enough about spiritual realities to understand that this was the spirit of the lady who had lived there before. The next night, having just begun to work through the first shock, the women heard an explosion beneath the wooden house (a possible attack on their lives), which shook the foundation. On their return from the village, I took them through the helpful steps of debriefing. We prayed for deliverance as well, not just from the recent experience, but also from spirits of fear and death which can take hold of a person who has been made vulnerable through exposure to traumatic experiences. The workers came through this trauma extremely well and continued their ministry.

Many workers are confronted with the cruelties of war, either in the lives of their local friends or in personal experiences of intimidation, evacuation, robbery, assault, and rape. Because we are invading enemy territory, one of our most important pre-field tasks is to set up an extensive prayer shield at home, consisting of committed friends who pray for us daily and with discernment. Likewise, it is essential for workers to listen to each other, pray together, and support one another on the field.

When my family first came to East Africa in 1982, we knew little about spiritual warfare or about deliverance ministry. But spiritual battles constantly confronted us—local people being tormented by demonic forces and people involved in magic and occult practices based on folk-Islam. Motivated by our desires to help those living under oppression and to avoid defeat ourselves, we learned the importance of understanding the powers of Islam/folk-Islam. We also saw the need of getting training in spiritual warfare and of having a balanced understanding of power encounters when ministering in the Muslim world.

The best teacher in spiritual warfare is the Word of God. Ephesians 6 states:

- "Finally (from now on) be strong in the Lord and in His mighty power." First of all, we need to know who we are in Christ, and we need to know that on the cross He won the victory over Satan. He has all power and authority, and He has delegated it to us.
- "Put on the full armor of God so that you can take your stand against the devil's schemes." Secondly, we need to know our weapons, which are for both attack and defense.
- "For our struggle is not against flesh and blood, but against the rulers, against the authorities, against the powers of this dark world, and against the spiritual forces of evil in the heavenly realms." Thirdly, we should not be ignorant about the enemy, who and where he is. We need to know how to battle effectively.

We are all involved in three major areas of warfare, whether we realize it or not. There is a battle within ourselves, a battle within the Christian community, and a battle against strongholds in the unreached. How we deal with these areas of warfare can greatly impact our ministry.

Battle within ourselves

The enemy knows our weaknesses and vulnerable places (entry points). He attacks these at times when we have let down our guard because of exhaustion, sickness, or sin, challenging our spiritual disciplines and our commitment to walk in holiness. Often when difficulties arise, our time with the Lord gets lost, and we struggle with self-pity, criticism, resentment, and bitterness, as well as with anger against the culture, the people, and the leadership.

Battle within the Christian community

Satan's goal is to destroy unity, whether in marriage, family, team, or fellowship. He uses criticism, egotism, negative thoughts and words, lack of supportive attitudes toward each other, envy, sexual temptation, nationalism, unforgiveness, colonial attitudes, and struggles with authority and accountability. The result is damage to our spiritual wholeness as a community, which makes our personal and corporate ministry ineffective (Rom. 15:5-6; Col. 3:12-14). Strained relationships are often an indication that the enemy is at work. We begin to feel joyless and heavy, tired and depressed. These feelings lead to a lack of interest in prayer and outreach, resulting in a withdrawal from our cross-cultural ministry and retreat to selected friends in the expatriate community.

Battle against strongholds (sin) in the unreached

There are many good books on folk-Islam, which help us understand its spiritual implications (see bibliography). For example, many Muslims fear the evil eye or fear receiving a curse in the form of a *Jadu*—a small, wrapped-up paper containing Quranic and magic verses written by so-called holy men or religious leaders, which are thought to bring sickness, disaster, and mental illness upon the intended victim. Jealousy, a very dominant spirit in these cultures, is a common motive for wishing others evil. Many young women, struggling with barrenness, try to undo a suspected curse by paying religious men to destroy the power of the *Jadu*. They also pray for fertility at the graves of deceased holy men (shrines).

It is very important that we are aware of these practices, both to pray effectively for those who are struggling with the effects of curses, as well as for our own protection. I have seen many instances of God's powerful intervention in these cases. One example from my personal experience occurred after our first years abroad, when I reached a point of total emotional, spiritual, and physical exhaustion. I developed a suicidal depression. After a year of struggle, with lots of prayer and support by others, I finally sought deliverance ministry. A pastor, experienced in this field, identified many areas of demonic intimidation and prayed for deliverance, which I received. I was completely set free from my heaviness.

Our best spiritual safeguard is to cultivate our relationship with God. This means we focus on prayer, learn more about the power of the Holy Spirit, remain accountable and transparent, live in a spirit of forgiveness, and embrace challenges, making them into opportunities for our own growth.

Ministry Tools

I now discuss four major areas to develop for ministry among Muslims. They are personal spiritual maturity, language and friendships, host culture and religion, and God-given authority.

Personal spiritual maturity

Christ-likeness—God's character and conduct reflected through us—is our most powerful ministry tool. As His ambassadors and servants, the more we are willing to live out of the Word of God and be molded by it, the more it shows in our lives and actions. As commendable as professional training and language skills are, our character is what counts.

Spiritual maturity is also displayed in the ability to "live in the opposite spirit." Jesus is our best teacher in this lifestyle: He stayed calm when there was turmoil

(Luke 8:22-25), He showed compassion when there was condemnation (John 8:1-11), and He exercised authority when there was demonic confrontation and chaos (Luke 4:31-37).

When we live in a negative atmosphere, we are easily drawn into it if we are not on our guard. The best weapon and testimony is to live in the opposite spirit to negative attitudes which we encounter, e.g., to give and be hospitable where there is greed, to be humble where there is pride, to live out of God's peace where there is fear, to convey confidence where there is insecurity. But we can only display God's character if we know who our Lord is.

Language and friendships

For cross-cultural workers, facility in the target language and culture is a very important requirement for ministry. Language acquisition serves as a pathway to the heart, enabling us to build friendships—a crucial foundation for sharing the good news. The interest evidenced by our effort in language learning is greatly appreciated. I have witnessed the excited response of local women when I was able to listen to and understand their worries. Such understanding builds trust, which is something that women living in countries of strife and war seldom experience. It also opens opportunities to pray with these religious and devout women about sickness and the worries of daily life. In this way, we can introduce them to the Healer and Prince of Peace.

As we seek to relate to the local people, a subtle danger may arise. Because we inevitably compare their painful lives with the blessings that we have, we may find ourselves overwhelmed with guilt, and we may unnecessarily deny ourselves and our families. An expatriate mother of two, living in a war-torn country, shared with me about her increasing lack of joy. Her neighbors' constant struggle to feed their many children and keep their houses warm, their pleas for help and her efforts to respond affected her enjoyment of her own little home. She began to question her family's right to eat well in the face of poverty. We talked about God's perfect plan of creation and the fact that His desire is for peace and well-being, not war and poverty. It helped to discuss with her some basic issues about suffering and spiritual warfare. If Satan gets a foothold in a country through evil, such as the shedding of innocent blood, it can result in consequences such as poverty and starvation. The enemy tries to replace God's blessings with calamities. We must resist the spirit of guilt and condemnation and must not allow Satan to rob us of the peace and energy we need in order to face the challenges of suffering and poverty around us. If, through neglect of our own basic needs, we allow ourselves to get sick and drained, we are of little use in God's kingdom.

Host culture and religion

In the Islamic world, culture and religion are intertwined. A good understanding of cultural practices and beliefs can save us from many embarrassing encounters and can help us "make the most of every opportunity" (Eph. 5:16).

Befriending women during pregnancy and being with them during and after childbirth has given me many opportunities to share God's love and compassion. However, in Muslim society, superstition and fear of the evil eye are an integral part of this natural process. One must know what is permissible to say and do, and when.

For example, I once visited a friend from a very religious background who had just had her second child. After congratulating her, I went over to admire the sweet little girl, wanting to pick her up. This caused great distress to my friend and the other women in the room. A grim-faced woman immediately entered the room with strong-smelling incense. She waved the incense around the baby, clearly indicating that I should stay away. According to their beliefs, the child had to be cleansed and protected from the evil eye, which I, as an unbeliever in their religion, had evoked through my behavior.

Cultural understanding is therefore a must. A reference from the online magazine *Women of the Harvest* (September 2000) sums it up concisely: "Cultural sensitivity means understanding why people behave the way they do and actually embracing their lifestyles. Cultural sensitivity means loosening our staunch grip on the social landscape that defines us and embracing instead the territory of a people without Christ, for the sake of the gospel."

God-given authority

It is easy to feel overwhelmed and intimidated by all the challenges that surround us overseas—dust and dirt, noise, crowded streets, male domination, poverty, sickness, the presence of weapons and violence, etc. The flooding images of injustice stir up feelings of helplessness, distress, and even aggression. The force of these impressions relegates us to a "grasshopper" perspective of powerlessness and spiritual defeat. Jesus, Himself living in a similar atmosphere, overcame evil with good as He appropriated His Father's delegated authority. This high calling is ours as well. We too have this power and authority delegated to us for our own protection and for the healing and deliverance of others (Luke 10:19; Eph. 3:14-21).

A Muslim mother once brought me her five-year-old daughter, who had been suffering from nightly suffocation attacks for weeks. Many doctors had checked the child thoroughly, pumping her full of antibiotics and painkillers, but without any improvement. The mother related to me the sad story of her life and pregnancy and of the little girl's childhood. When she was three months pregnant, her husband was killed by a missile while he was waiting for a bus. She lost all hope and considered terminating her pregnancy but eventually decided against having an abortion. When the baby was born, the child was well received and loved by all.

Muslims are well aware of demons in their daily lives, so it was not difficult to convince the mother of demonic interference. It did take some time, though, for her to understand that Satan tries to impoverish life even before birth. After some hesitation, reaffirming that she was a practicing Muslim, she accepted my offer to pray for the girl in the name of Jesus. I bound the forces of death and fear over the child's life, which had already taken root in the womb and apparently were expressing themselves in the current suffocation attacks. We prayed for healing of the girl's past and for the Lord's touch on her life. She never suffered under the attacks again.

Jesus came to set the captives free. This is not just some cliché that makes us feel good. He wants us to step out boldly in faith and in His authority. We can learn from others by sitting in when they minister to the oppressed, and we can pray for more courage and anointing to do God's will. It is important to pray for protection for ourselves and for our loved ones before we minister. We also need to pray for cleansing afterwards to avoid unnecessary backlashes from the enemy. Such prayer is also advisable whenever we visit or have visitors of other convictions in our home. No one but the Holy Spirit should reign in our lives and homes.

Team Viability

"The essence of a team is common commitment to a mutually agreed goal for which it holds itself responsible" (Jones & Jones, 1995, p. 18). Clearly defined goals stemming from a clear purpose statement provide direction and motivation for ministry overseas. However, they do not lessen the challenges of living and working with Christians from different cultures and denominations, as illustrated by the frequently-heard statement, "Culture shock is nothing compared with the challenge of working together in an international Christian team." Or even a mono-national team! From my experience, there are three main reasons for this interpersonal tension: expectations, past experience, and disunity.

Expectations

We are prepared to encounter a new culture that will be different. However, we often do not anticipate the need to adjust to our Christian teammates, and we find ourselves surprised, if not annoyed, by the way they live and work. Working relationships need to be developed, and they require both grace and tolerance in their formation. Pre-field training to develop cross-cultural awareness among team members, as well as regular team-building exercises on the field, can ease the friction.

Past Experience

"Team life, at both the conscious and unconscious levels, stirs up many associations with one's family of origin" (O'Donnell, 1992, p. 188). Unresolved traumas and hurts from the past (see above) can cause us to transfer bad feelings toward individuals in our pasts to our current co-workers who resemble them in some way. This can greatly affect our ability to build relationships and be gracious to those who think and act differently, and it can lead to unpleasant conflicts.

Disunity

Satan is the main opponent of any Christian work. He defends his territory by any means he can, preventing those in darkness from hearing the good news. What better way than by disarming the Lord's spiritual messengers? He does this through the sowing of disunity, which destroys their testimony and makes their witness ineffective. Satan's divisive work finds expression in pride, conflict, slander, cultural intolerance, and dissatisfaction with the team and with leadership. He also finds his way into team life through competition and through disagreement concerning forms of worship and strategies for evangelism. Unfortunately, our humanity falls prey again and again to this deception. We forget that our battle is not against people, whether Christians or Muslims, but against the spiritual forces of evil in the heavenly realms. Nonbelievers watch us, wondering just how real and how powerful this new life about which we talk is. We must remember how the Lord Himself urged us to love one another and to live in unity, so that the world will know that we are His disciples (John 13:35; 17:23).

A vital aspect of teamwork is preventive member care. Those who are gifted listeners, empathetic and hospitable, have an important ministry role within the team. Corporate worship and prayer are also crucial parts of preventive member care in which all can participate. These are powerful weapons against friction, discouragement, and culture shock, putting the Lord and the issues around us into proper perspective. Praying as a group focuses us heavenwards, not on our problems. It releases a special anointing from which new strength, direction, unity, and equipping flow.

Our team began each working day as a group with an hour of worship, which included prayer, music, a short devotional thought, and ample time for intercession for our staff and projects, local friends, team, personal issues, and current world affairs. This time helped us stay focused on our purpose and sensitive to one another. We prayed for urgent needs and formed a prayer cover for those who were struggling with issues like fatigue, illness, culture, family problems, etc. This very effective tool for team unity provides both preventive and practical member care.

Covering for Female Workers

There is a particular team responsibility to cover female co-workers in prayer. In the Muslim world, women, more often than men, are a target in terms of isolation, loneliness, abuse, and spiritual heaviness (van Dalen, 2000). In the same way that Christ is the head of the church and the husband is the head of the wife (Eph. 5:23), we felt an obligation for the men in the team to be a shield for the women (both married and single). Occasionally, the men would symbolically form a circle around the women and cover them with prayer and blessings. At other times, when one of the women had been sexually offended by touch or word, provided she was willing, I would debrief her and would pray for cleansing and deliverance, in order to prevent roots of bitterness from growing.

Single women, without a spouse to share joys and frustrations, need special support from the team. It is helpful if singles live together, but there is also a deep need to be part of a family, especially in the Muslim culture, which is totally family defined. A vivid example of team support occurred when one of our single teachers was struggling with a difficult situation at an international school. Strained relationships between parents and teachers added to an already tense atmosphere, due to incidences of student injury and parental complaints. Some of our team went one evening and worshiped in every classroom of the school building, praying for each child and teacher by name and binding every force that was not of God. The subsequent change of atmosphere was obvious, inspiring unsolicited comments on the positive and joyful spirit around school. There is a tremendous potential in team ministry, but unfortunately it is often under-utilized. When we are unaware of reasons for tensions in our teams, we tend to invest our energies in the wrong places, thus missing out on the blessings the Lord has for our team and its ministry.

New Roles, Identity, and Lifestyle

People and Events

The Muslim world generally is focused on people and events, not time or work. People visit whenever they have time, and they are very hospitable. Even the very poor share from the little they have, sometimes running into debt in order to entertain their guests. Things happen when they happen, not according to a planned schedule. This may require a significant adjustment in one's attitude toward work. It took me some time to learn to accept this cultural way of being. At the end of the day, nothing was done from my to-do list, but I had served many cups of tea, fed beggars, given medicine to the sick, listened to painful life-stories, and been able to pray for those without hope. I needed to adjust my cultural value system to accommodate that of the country in which I served, in order to grow into a new role and identity.

Whereas men tend to continue work in their professional fields overseas, women often do not, which affects their sense of worth and value. Women, married or unmarried, with or without children, all need to adapt to a new set of expectations, which have their own challenges and pressures. Feelings of loneliness and isolation are often the result of the restricted lifestyle women have to lead. Courage and energy are needed to leave the safe home, to overcome language barriers, and to cope with intimidation.

Physical Exercise

One common problem for female workers is lack of physical exercise. Both the culture and the pollution in the cities restrict outside sports, even going for walks. Because exercise plays a vital part in our psychological well-being, as well as helping us stay in shape, we need to be creative in finding avenues for exercise, such as aerobics at home. Other options, such as tennis or swimming, can be very limited, except where there is an international hotel close by.

Mothers With Small Children

Mothers with small children are even more confined to their homes. Since children are very prestigious and are greatly loved in Muslim cultures, though, they can be great bridge-builders as mothers seek to reach out to their neighbors. Children also generally have fewer inhibitions than adults in adapting to new surroundings and a new language.

Schooling

An area of great concern for parents can be the schooling of their children. If local schooling is not possible, home schooling or boarding school are the only alternatives. Separation can be very difficult for both parents and children, necessitating lots of support from both the field and the home base.

Married Couples

Married couples need to know how to maintain a healthy and loving partnership in a culture where the sexes are separated and where showing affection in public is unacceptable. It is therefore of great importance to have a comfortable home where couples can feel secure and enjoy total privacy. Regular dates with each other, away from guests and work, should be scheduled.

Expatriate Men

There is a tendency for some expatriate men to begin unconsciously to identify with the Muslim cultural idea of manhood. They may exhibit more macho behavior, such as walking in front of their wives, helping less around the house or with the children, and being predominantly in male company. This behavior can be quite annoying, especially for wives. It needs to be addressed and brought to their awareness before it causes conflict.

Single Women

Single women feel the restrictions of the culture even more than married women do. Additionally, they are under constant pressure from well-meaning local friends who question their singleness and make them feel incomplete. (Married women without children are under the same type of scrutiny.) On the other hand, if singles are sure of their calling and have a resilient personality, their ministry can be very rewarding, since they are independent and enjoy more freedom in sharing their lives with local families. A developing courtship can be difficult to handle because of the cultural restrictions. Families need to open their homes to courting couples, so that they can date without harming their reputations.

Women Who Work

Women who work outside the home may not battle with loneliness so much as with frustrations and limitations due to culture, bureaucracy, or corruption. For example, a doctor or a nurse will find it difficult, when treating a local newborn, to persuade the mother to refrain from applying charcoal to the baby's eyelids (the traditional way to protect the child from the evil eye). It can be difficult to persuade the parent of a child with diarrhea to give her lots of fluids rather than high doses of antibiotics. Or the office work might suffer, because the manager left without notice to attend to family matters.

Adjusting to Transitions

In our new place of ministry, we are exposed to many cultural differences—changes in professional roles, tasks, and social networks. The series of reactions and feelings triggered by change has the potential to undermine our sense of identity and security. A diagram that helps us understand this process is the Transition Curve, developed by Adams, Hayes, and Hopson (1977). The curve is divided into two phases, a *reactive phase*, where we grieve the past, and a *proactive phase*, where we create the future (see Figure 1). The following is my adaptation and application of this diagram to the situation of missionaries going abroad for ministry.

Initially, we go through a time of fascination (tourist-type experience), during which we are excited about the new challenges. This phase lasts until we enter culture shock, when the transition really begins. A move out of the known and into the unknown means leaving home, fam-

Figure 1
Transition Curve

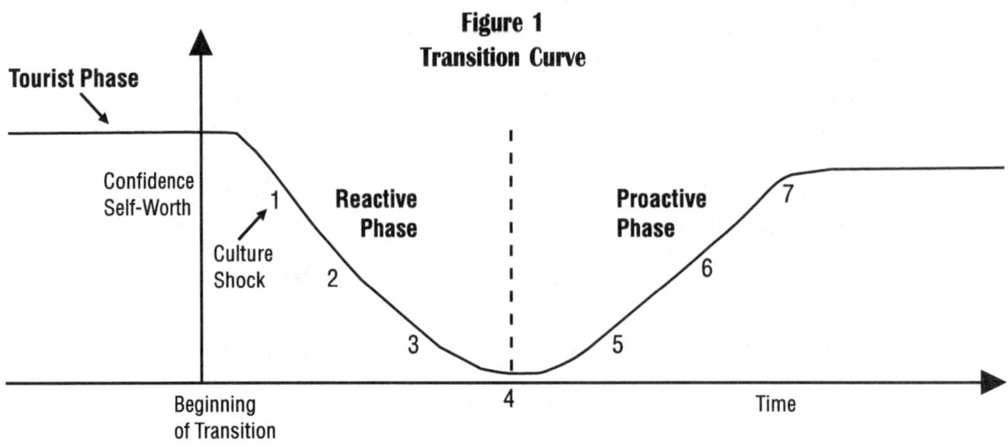

ily, friends, and job and entering into a new country, a new culture, and new responsibilities. Culture shock can stretch us to the point of immobilization, as we struggle with language acquisition, dress code, isolation, loneliness for family and friends, and coping with negative aspects of the culture. It can shake our confidence and cause us to question our self-worth. In this *reactive phase*, we move from a sense of being overwhelmed (1), to denial (2), where we minimize the change through a kind of temporary retreat.

The next step is marked by feelings of frustration and being out of control (3). We question everything and feel trapped and angry. We finally hit bottom, where we start to let go and accept reality (4). This step involves the process of disengaging from what we left behind. People in the reactive phase are intensely affected by their physical and social environment and are driven by feelings.

Then begins the slow process of *proactive* adaptation, where we become more involved and try out new things (5). We begin to make progress in learning the language, build friendships, put some roots down, and cut ourselves loose from home ties. At the next step, we start to conceptualize, reflect, and evaluate the change (6). Finally, we internalize and more freely accept the process of change, and stability returns (7). During this process, we take more initiative and regain our ability to respond as a result of values rather than as a result of feelings/reactions.

A typical example of the adjustment process is a mother with young children. She leaves not only her own family and friends behind, but also her children's friends, which she has to replace in the beginning. The many new challenges of learning the language, adjusting to a new diet and climate, sicknesses, and trying to make new friends can totally overwhelm and immobilize her. If not helped, she will withdraw to focus on her own home, repressing feelings of anger and frustration. Everything seems to be threatening, too much, too difficult. After a good look at the situation, encouraging letters from friends, support from team members on the field, and some time of adaptation and routine, things start to improve. There are little successes in using the language, she can recognize the positive side of the host culture, she starts making friends, and she engages more and more in responsibilities outside the home and in the spiritual battle. Once she is able to engage herself and call this new place "home," she has taken a big step in the adjustment process. Unfortunately, some people return home prematurely, without pressing on and experiencing the rewarding breakthrough, when we come out of the dark valley and start putting roots down.

In our individual uniqueness and complexity, we seldom move neatly from phase to phase, but it helps to understand that what we experience is not uncommon and that it can take a year and often longer to adjust fully. It is important to stress that any change has the potential for growth. By embracing the challenges and making them into our opportunities, we are strengthened rather than defeated.

Conclusion

Women missionaries play a vital role in bringing the good news to the female population in Muslim nations. Exercising that ambassadorship poses formidable challenges that require careful preparation and circumspect living. Half the battle is won when we are willing to examine ourselves thoroughly and with absolute honesty, scrutinizing our motives; acquire training in field-related subjects such as Islam, local culture, and spiritual warfare; and submit to any needed counseling before departing from the home country. A good support system, a personal desire for spiritual growth, team-mindedness, servant-heartedness, alertness to specific cultural and spiritual realities, and a committed walk in the Lord's authority and love determine effectiveness and long-term survival in a challenging ministry situation. Transition is not easy, but it is manageable and enriching for our identity and growth, and it helps to make ministry overseas a rewarding experience and a wonderful testimony to others.

Reflection and Discussion

1. What are the main stress areas that affect female Christian workers in the Muslim world? How can you relate to them from your own experience?

2. Why and how do women need special "covering" and support in a team?

3. What can sending organizations do to better prepare and care for their female personnel who are working in Muslim settings? List at least three practical suggestions.

4. How have you worked through past unresolved areas in your own life? How could you get help for any areas that continue to bother you?

5. What role do you see for spiritual warfare and using the authority of Christ in your ministry? What are your experiences?

References

Adams, J., Hayes, J., & Hopson, B. (1977). *Transition: Understanding and managing personal change*. Leeds, UK: University of Leeds.

Adiwardana, M. (1997). Formal and non-formal pre-field training: Perspective of the new sending countries. In W. Taylor (Ed.), *Too valuable to lose: Exploring the causes and cures of missionary attrition* (pp. 207-215). Pasadena, CA: William Carey Library.

Brierley, P. (1997). Missionary attrition: The ReMAP research project. In W. Taylor (Ed.), *Too valuable to lose: Exploring the causes and cures of missionary attrition* (pp. 85-103). Pasadena, CA: William Carey Library.

Ekström, B. (1997). The selection process and the issue of attrition: Perspective of the new sending countries. In W. Taylor (Ed.), *Too valuable to lose: Exploring the causes and cures of missionary attrition* (pp. 183-193). Pasadena, CA: William Carey Library.

Elliot, E. (1999, August). Interview with R. G. Shubin: Strength in the face of adversity. *Mission Frontiers*, pp. 20-22.

Jones, G., & Jones, R. (1995). *Teamwork*. London, UK: Scripture Union.

O'Donnell, K. (1992). Tools for team viability. In K. O'Donnell (Ed.), *Missionary care: Counting the cost for world evangelization*. Pasadena, CA: William Carey Library.

Pickthall, M. (1988). *Holy Quran* (English Translation). Karachi, Pakistan: Taj Company Ltd.

van Dalen, E. (2000, October). Raising radiant daughters in dark places. *Interact*, *9*, 6-13.

Women of the Harvest. (2000, September). Earning your mastering adjustment degree. Online magazine article. (Available from: www.womenoftheharvest.com)

Recommendations for Further Reading

Islam

Geisler, L., & Saleeb, A. (1993). *Answering Islam: The crescent in the light of the cross*. Grand Rapids, MI: Baker Books.

Glaser, I., & John, N. (1998). *Partners or prisoners? Christians thinking about women and Islam*. Cumbria, UK: Solway.

Love, F., & Eckheart, J. (Eds.). (2000). *Ministry to Muslim women: Longing to call them sisters*. Pasadena, CA: William Carey Library.

Mallouhi, C. (1994). *Miniskirts, mothers, and Muslims*. Carlisle, UK: Spear Publications.

Musk, B. (1989). *The unseen face of Islam: Sharing the gospel with ordinary Muslims*. Eastbourne, UK: MARC.

———. (1992). *Passionate believing: The "fundamentalist" face of Islam*. Harpenden, UK: MARC.

———. (1995). *Touching the soul of Islam: Sharing the gospel in Muslim cultures*. Crowborough, UK: MARC.

Otis, G., Jr. (1991). *The last of the giants: Lifting the veil on Islam and the end times*. Tarrytown, NY: Chosen Books.

Stacey, V. (1995). *Women in Islam*. London, UK: Interserve.

Help and Inner Healing

Anderson, N. (1990). *The bondage breaker*. Harpenden, UK: Monarch Publications.

Foyle, M. (2001). *Honourably wounded: Stress among Christian workers*. London, UK: Monarch Books.

O'Donnell, K., & O'Donnell, M. (Eds.). (1988). *Helping missionaries grow*. Pasadena, CA: William Carey Library.

Roembke, L. (2000). *Building credible multicultural teams*. Pasadena, CA: William Carey Library.

Sandford, J., & Sandford, P. (1982). *The transformation of the inner man*. Tulsa, OK: Victory House.

———. (1985). *Healing the wounded spirit*. South Plainfield, NJ: Bridge Publishing.

Prayer

Jacobs, C. (1993). *Possessing the gates of the enemy: An intercessionary prayer manual*. London, UK: Marshall Pickering.

Sheets, D. (1996). *Intercessory prayer: How God can use your prayers to move heaven and earth*. Ventura, CA: Regal Books.

Wagner, C. P. (1992). *Warfare prayer*. Tunbridge Wells, UK: Monarch Publications.

Annemie Grossbauser *is German and trained as a psychologist. She is married to Toni, a medical doctor and the International Director of ORA International. Together, they have been running Christian humanitarian aid and refugee work in East Africa and Central Asia for the last 18 years. During this time, Annemie has worked as a counselor ministering to expatriate women and teams, as well as to traumatized local people. Currently based back in Germany, Annemie travels to teach and consult within the international missions/member care community. She and Toni have four children, ages 18-23. Email: agrosshauser@yahoo.com.*

Special thanks to Adalee Lewis from Wycliffe for her revision of this article and her helpful suggestions.

42

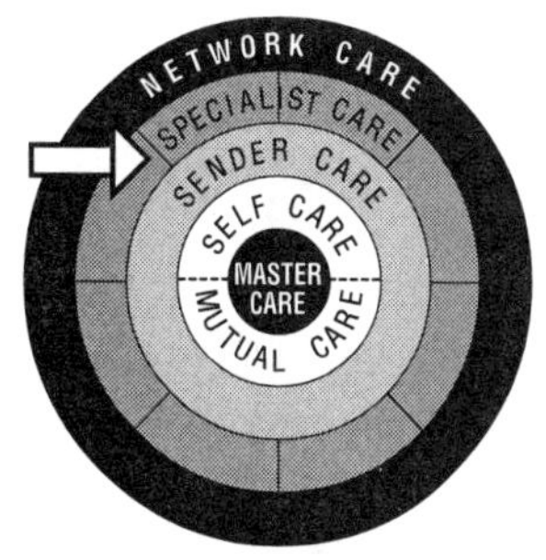

A Mindset And Department For Member Care

BRUCE SWANSON

Member care is a core value that we build into our hearts and into our organizations. It is a way of thinking and a way of being. This chapter offers many practical suggestions for cultivating the type of attitudes (mindset) and programs (departments) necessary to support our mission personnel adequately.

I oversee a member care department for a large North American mission organization, and I can dedicate most of my working time to personnel issues. What a blessing! But how can I write about member care and missions and make it helpful to the vast majority of mission situations around the world? Most agencies operate with fewer resources than my organization and I have available. In addition, many churches worldwide send workers directly, without using mission agencies. Very few churches are large enough or wealthy enough to feel that they have adequate resources to designate a person or department solely for member care.

The solution to my dilemma will be to focus on developing a "member care mindset," rather than focusing solely on how to form a member care department. A member care mindset, when it exists, permeates the whole organization. It shapes the policies, structures, and working style of the agency or church. Member care must be woven into the very fabric of day-to-day operations rather than "departmentalized." Cross-cultural workers are not just sent; they are also prepared and preserved for effective service, and when necessary, they are restored.

In this chapter, I will examine some member care principles and dynamics that I believe are relevant for most sending organizations. I will apply them to situations where member care departments are a possibility, as well as to situations where such departments remain a distant dream. In truth, the goal of a "member care mindset" must captivate every church or agency, no matter how big or resource-rich it is. Member care must be part of everyone's thinking. It must not be relegated to one or two full-time people in a department on the fringe of day-to-day operations. Nor must it be considered a nice option to include, if one can afford it. A member care mindset will help member care take its proper place as a core component of doing missions.

Why Is Member Care So Important?

Understood in this full sense, member care, or preferably for me, "personnel development," is important for both theological and pragmatic reasons.

Theological Basis

Doing member care reflects God's heart and kingdom values. All through the Bible, God challenged and stretched His people. He keenly desired their development into all they could be, to His honor and glory. Abraham, Joseph, Moses, David, and Jesus' disciples were never allowed to settle into their comfort zones. They were always being challenged to grow and mature.

At the same time, God provided rest, encouragement, and restoration for His people. A few examples are the principle of Sabbath rest, His care of Elijah in the wilderness (1 Kings 19:1-9), Jesus pulling His disciples out of their hectic pace for rest (Mark 6:30-32), and John Mark's restoration to mission service through Barnabas. In every New Testament epistle, Jesus' followers are commanded to encourage and build each other up.

It follows that as leaders of God's kingdom workers, we should treat them as God does. We must not coddle them—that usually is not a problem! We must also be zealous for their growth, for their preservation, and for their restoration when wounded or fallen. How can we do kingdom work without reflecting kingdom values and ethos? Jesus' Great Commission should be carried out in the spirit of his Great Commandment—by loving one another.

Kingdom workers are not just pieces on a cosmic chessboard. They are individuals created in God's image, highly valued, and loved by God Himself. Mission leaders must treat workers as God's creation—as His children and as His servants, not theirs.

Pragmatic Considerations

If we are to accomplish the task Christ left for us to do, we must be good stewards of the resources God has chosen to work through—people! The business world in Europe, North America, and beyond has many examples that show how caring for employees is important for the company's survival and success. Those of us in missions can learn from their experience.

The cost of not doing member care is revealed when a worker "crashes and burns." There is the human suffering of the worker, his/her family, and colleagues. Lower morale sets in when workers perceive they are valued only for their work, not for their person. There is lost credibility with people of the host country and with donors back home. Huge amounts of money are expended in salary, start-up costs, training, and repatriation. The quiet cost of not doing member care is revealed when a worker limps along, joyless, powerless, and ineffective.

In sum, a member care mindset should be at the core of doing missions, because it mirrors God's values and because it helps us accomplish the task.

Why Is Member Care Such a Challenge?

If member care is so crucial to missions, why does it often seem to be an afterthought? What are the barriers to developing a member care mindset? Let's look at three obstacles that strike me as significant.

Task Over People

First, I believe the Western church has been subverted, in part, by its culture. The Western world is materialistic and task oriented. People tend to be ignored. What matters is that the job gets done. Western churches and mission organizations have tended to do missions the same way. The task must be accomplished—all the more because it is a divinely ordered task. Unfortunately, the people doing the task have not always been a priority. Those of us who are mission and church leaders would never affirm such a thing consciously, but our decisions, policies, and structures too often reveal such a mindset.

It appears that this mindset has been too effectively modeled to the churches of Newer Sending Countries (NSCs) and that they are beginning to repeat the same mistakes. For example, workers all over the world are sent out without adequate contingency funds and without provisions for regular or yearly Sabbath rest. They are allowed to neglect their families and their own spiritual and physical health, to do what sometimes amounts to three full-time jobs. These few examples could be multiplied many times over.

Lack of Information and Understanding

A second barrier has simply been a lack of information and understanding. I grew up immersed in the post-World War II missions emphasis in Evangelical churches of North America. My home church lived and breathed cross-cultural missions. I heard the stories and read the books. What a heritage! Upon reflection, I now realize that we all considered missions to be something hard and demanding, and we believed that the workers just had to tough it out. The hardy, good workers hung in there; the weaker ones did not. That is just the way it was, and there was not much to do about it.

Those perceptions I absorbed as a child contain a lot of truth. Mission work *is* hard, extremely hard at times. To a large degree, workers need to hang on and tough it out, honoring their duty to the Lord's call. However—and this is a huge however—the vast majority of good, hardy workers *will* wear out if they are not developed and cared for, not just the "weak" ones. We now have the information to understand how much leaders in missions *can* "do about it." The very existence of this book and the growing movement in member care bear witness to the fact that the "critical mass" of knowledge has been accumulated. Now, the issue is putting knowledge into practice.

Great Need and Limited Resources

A third barrier comes from a combination of infinite need and limited resources. The physical and spiritual needs of the world are so great and the resources so limited that we can feel compelled to pour all our money and person-power into accomplishing the task, neglecting the workers.

We could liken the situation to that of a rural evangelist who uses an old scooter to get from village to village to preach the gospel and treat the sick. If he has only enough money either to buy gas and medicines or to replace a worn, crumbling tire, how can he not get the gas and medicines? People are dying without the Lord, and the tire can always be stretched a bit further ... and a bit further, until one day the tire ruptures when the worker tries to go down a steep path. Then the tire must be attended to—as well as the evangelist's leg, broken in the crash. In the long run, the work suffers much more, and so does the worker. But in the press of the day-to-day need, it can be very hard to discipline oneself to look beyond immediate needs.

In missions, the choices can be hard ones. Is money spent on training workers or on feeding orphans? Do workers receive enough salary to take breaks away from the work, or is their support stripped to the bare minimum so the association of churches can send out another family? The ongoing needs and compelling task lure us to "keep putting gas into the scooter," thereby putting the welfare of the workers and the work itself at risk.

It's fairly easy for me, a member of an Older Sending Country (OSC), to point out the danger of focusing on immediate ministry needs and neglecting the worker. My country is so rich! It's easier to put resources into both gas and medicine and new tires for the scooter. How much greater is the pressure for many in the NSCs, where resources are more scarce! Organizations and churches in OSCs and NSCs can both pursue creative sources of funds and exhort believers to sacrifice. But eventually, the infinite need will put all of us in the same tension of having to choose between "more gas and medicine or a new tire."

Jesus provides the example we need to escape the dilemma. In the early chapters of Mark, we see Him resisting being swallowed up by the insatiable, legitimate needs of the masses. Make no mistake about it—Jesus kept quite busy preaching the gospel, healing the sick, and delivering the demonized. But He refused to let the unending need keep Him from following His Father's agenda. He left behind needy folk to go to other villages to heal and preach. He took breaks in order to refresh Himself spiritually and physically. He followed the divine blueprint for His ministry. Jesus also shows us how to keep the need around us from robbing us of peace or joy. Jesus radiated life and joy. He regularly went to social events and "parties"—He was even accused of being a glutton and a drunkard (Matt. 11:19). Jesus was motivated to do the Father's will, not to meet every need and opportunity for ministry around Him (John 4:34; Mark 1:28-38).

Kingdom workers today need to follow the example of Jesus, and their leaders must pave the way for them. In my visits with workers around the world, I have noticed that those who are most effective have learned how to relax in and enjoy good things about their local culture. They work hard for the kingdom, but they also take time to enjoy life and the people God has put around them. Effective workers have also come to peace with the fact that they will never be able to meet all the needs around them. They are content "simply" to serve the Father with their best effort, pacing themselves for many years of service.

How Does One Begin?

Let us assume that you are already convinced that member care should be a central part of your church's, association's, or agency's strategy for doing missions. Let us also assume that you are in the minority—that most of the decision makers in your organization either do not see or do not prioritize the importance of developing and caring for their personnel on the field or in the home office. How can you begin to influence your organization with a member care mindset? (If your church or agency already is committed to member care, these same principles can be followed. It will just be easier to use them.)

- Pray and study the Scriptures to better appreciate God's heart for the development and care of His servants. Let the certainty grow in your own heart that this is a core issue for missions.
- Dialogue with your colleagues and with the leaders of your church, association, or agency. Your convictions, biblical rationale, and pragmatic arguments can be compelling and can help others rethink the Great Commission in the light of the Great Commandment. On the other hand, hearing your leaders' hearts and the weighty issues they face can help you understand the dilemmas they struggle with and keep a balanced view of the issues. Let them know of your heart for the lost and the ministry too!
- In partnership with your leaders, seek to educate your church or association of churches about the need to make member care a part of missions. The task of developing and caring for workers requires additional resources, and the churches which actually send the workers need to be willing to spend the time, energy, and money that will be needed.
- Preserve your relationship with anyone with whom you disagree. The Holy

Spirit will better steer you all to God's will if you are united rather than divided. Leadership in missions is a spiritual endeavor and must be treated as such.

Foundational Issues

Here are some of the basic issues that your church, association, or agency should think through in order to develop a coherent strategy. They should help you make the development and care of kingdom workers a central part of doing missions, whether it be through a department or "simply" in day-to-day operations.

What Are We Trying to Accomplish?

Many times, it can be helpful to write out a vision statement that describes the results of personnel development/member care. My own vision statement for my department reads: "The Missionary Development Department envisions a corps of well-prepared, hardy, CBInternational workers who evidence personal growth and increasing kingdom impact, being energized by spiritual power; balanced living; organizational structures; and growing relationships with God, family, colleagues, and supporters." A clear picture of the goal is the first step to reaching it. During all subsequent steps, you must always evaluate your options and decisions in the light of your vision statement.

Exactly what is personnel development or member care?

There are no limits to what can be done in this arena; one can always do more. A clear definition of member care helps a member care department or an organization draw the needed boundaries. My own definition of member care involves the "formal and informal efforts to develop, preserve, and restore kingdom workers for effective service."

- "Formal efforts" can include workshops, medical check-ups, study leave, regular ministry reviews, pastoral visits on the field, etc.
- "Informal efforts" can include body life principles from the New Testament, a church sending a tape of a service or the Brazilian football championship, a worker watching another's children for an evening, taking a regular day off, etc.
- "Developing" can involve training, mentoring, helping someone learn to cook with new ingredients, personal growth through difficulties, etc.
- "Preserving" can involve vacation policy, health insurance, coaching on stress management, evacuation for medical reasons or civil unrest, etc.
- "Restoring" can involve counseling, church internships, rest at a home church or retreat center, a church setting up a furlough apartment for a returning worker, etc.
- "Effective service" is the goal of developing and caring for workers. Member care must be the servant of the church's, association's, or agency's goal to extend the kingdom. Of course, accomplishing the task must be done in accordance with kingdom values.

A clear definition of personnel development/member care will help an association or church weave such care into the fabric of its day-to-day operations. It will also help a member care department, if created, to focus its efforts and integrate them into the rest of the organization's activities.

Seek to organize your efforts through conceptual models

The needs and possibilities in doing member care can seem limitless. Helpful models can make it easier to organize one's approach and avoid chaos. Again, let me offer what my department does as an illustration.

The flow of a worker's life can be understood in terms of developmental phases of a personal or family life cycle, with common challenges or developmental tasks (McGoldrick & Carter, 1982). For example, a married person's life cycle can be organized into single young adult, newly married, young children, launching children, etc. Each phase presents the individual with fairly common tasks to master: adapting to a partner, adapting to children, learning to relate to your children as adults, etc. Member care can anticipate these challenges and help a worker meet them, including the unique complications generated by experiencing the life cycle in cross-cultural ministry.

The flow of a worker's career can be broken down into a similar life cycle and phases—for example, being set apart for service, raising support, first-term language learning and cultural adaptation, returning to the home country, etc. (O'Donnell, 1987). Each phase has its fairly common tasks to accomplish. Member care can anticipate those tasks, as well as prepare the worker for them.

Member care can also anticipate the unique challenges presented by the intersection of these two life cycles (Swanson, 1993). Here are two examples: The challenges of language learning will be different for a couple with young children and for an older couple with no children at home. Also, being overseas accentuates the pressures a middle-aged couple can feel as their parents grow older and as their children enter adult life back in their passport country.

In my department, we seek to organize our efforts according to the diagram below. Based on research (Kayser, 1994; Sikkema & Niyekawa, 1987), we target our efforts at five arenas of an individual's life. The lower arenas are the most important, and each subsequent arena builds on the previous ones. This model helps us prioritize initiatives and helps us avoid ignoring foundational matters such as spiritual formation.

Figure 1
Arenas of Missionary Life

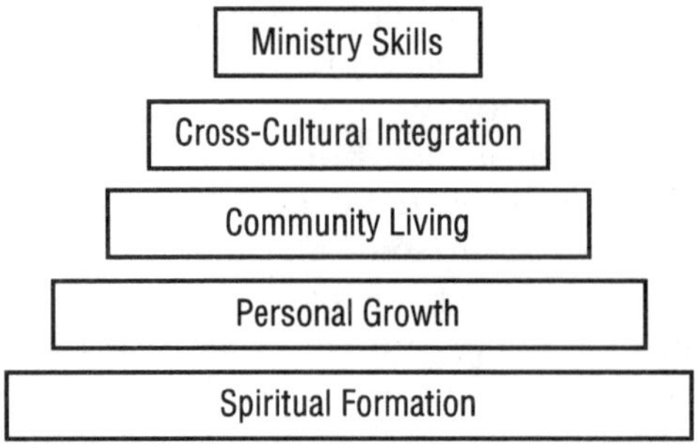

Ministry Skills
Cross-Cultural Integration
Community Living
Personal Growth
Spiritual Formation

To illustrate the relationship between these areas, consider a worker who is a great preacher in his passport country. That important ministry skill will be of limited impact if the preacher does not learn the new language and know how to connect at a heart level in the new culture. His ministry skill depends on integrating cross-culturally. If the preacher integrates well and preaches effectively in the new culture, his impact will be limited if he continually offends mission colleagues and nationals. His ability to live in community ends up being more foundational than both skills and cross-cultural integration. But, like this preacher, all workers cross cultures with blind spots and weaknesses. So, even more important is the worker's willingness to be humble, to recognize his need to learn, and to pursue personal growth. Otherwise, he will be stuck in weaknesses that will limit his impact. Finally, even if the preacher successfully adapts culturally, graciously lives in community, and grows as a person, if he neglects his relationship with God, he will be attempting to do everything in his own power. He will not last, nor will his heroic efforts have the spiritual impact they could have if he was keeping fresh spiritually. Thus, spiritual formation forms the foundation for all else.

Developing Member Care Well

Whether a member care mindset is woven into the existing structures of your church or organization or whether it is promoted through a distinct member care department, some basic principles can help you do member care well.

Anticipate What It Will Take to Succeed

Here are some personal observations regarding what is needed to succeed in member care, gleaned from my own experience and from talking with colleagues in member care.

Personal characteristics of the member care advocate/facilitator

■ Conscious dependence on God and a commitment to personal spiritual health.

■ Humility and a servant attitude. Someone with a member care mindset seeks to help others succeed. She/he is happy to see her/his fruit produced on others' trees. This attitude mirrors that of Christ—He places His fruit on our branches as we abide in Him (John 15).

■ Willingness to try new initiatives and take risks.

Mutual trust and cooperation between organizational leaders or departments

■ If a member care department exists, to be effective it must build relationships and trust with the other parts of the organization. Only then will it be allowed to influence decisions and gain access to needed resources to accomplish the goals of member care.

■ If member care is to be woven into a church's or smaller organization's existing structures, each decision maker must be willing to share information and be a team player with the others. For example, if someone in an organization wants to send a pastor out to encourage the workers, schedules must be coordinated, funds raised and disbursed, and permission granted for workers and the pastor to take "time off" for the visit.

Credibility with field personnel

■ All entities that send workers far away face the constant erosion of trust due to the distance that separates leaders from field personnel. Not having face-to-face contact can make it easy for all parties to misunderstand each other's decisions and motives, jump to conclusions, and begin to second-guess each other. Acknowledge this dynamic, and plan for it.

■ Seek to model and teach a healthy strategy for dealing with a disagreement. For example, suspend judgment, assume there is information you do not know, and ask a couple more questions to get clarification.

■ Keep in touch through regular communication and encouragement, *not* just when there is "business" to take care of.

■ Do everything possible to increase face-to-face contact between leadership and field personnel.

Active networking with others devoted to member care

■ Compare notes with others who are involved in member care, exchange ideas, and encourage each other in the process. Do this with others both within and outside your organization, region, and discipline.

Establish Ground Rules for Promoting Member Care

Wise principles are like a good road map to guide us as we develop member care in our churches or organizations. Here are some of the principles to which I hold:

1. Scripture must be foundational for all that you seek to build into the life of the organization and into the lives of its workers (2 Tim. 3:16).

2. Make member care developmental, not just for "putting out fires." Even a crisis can be an opportunity to draw individuals, teams, and the whole organization or church to greater growth. For example, if national church leadership communicates to the mission leadership that it can no longer cooperate with a certain worker, two approaches can be taken. A "firefighter" approach would merely try to solve the problem, perhaps by convincing

the worker to apologize to the leaders. A developmental approach will dig deeper into the situation and take the time to isolate the attitudes and behaviors (habitual, situational, cultural, or sinful) that generated the breakdown in relationship. Such an approach will help the worker understand those factors and seek to do his or her part to grow past them. It will, on the basis of that growth, seek reconciliation between the worker and national leadership and, hopefully, will see a stronger partnership established. A developmental approach requires a lot more effort, but it yields deeper results for the worker and for the kingdom.

3. Understand that obedience to God and service for His kingdom bring hardship and suffering, without exception (2 Cor. 4:11-12). The goal of member care is not that workers will experience minimal difficulties. The goal is that they will be continually molded into the likeness of Christ and will serve effectively as they face a manageable amount of difficulties.

4. Godly character and living are more important than being busy for God. Note that the New Testament qualifications for church leadership focus almost exclusively on character qualities, not ministry skills (1 Tim. 3; Titus 1).

5. Decentralize member care. Do not make it all begin with or flow through one department or through the home structures. That will only stifle it. The "holy grail" of member care is workers meeting their needs through each other (Rom. 12; 1 Cor. 12), through their adopted communities, and through their supporters, with help from their mission leaders.

6. Think in terms of systems; do not focus only on one person or facet of a problem. For example, if a worker is burning out through overwork, don't just focus on the worker and convince him/her to take Sabbath rests or relax. Consider the team with whom the person works. Does it promote a culture of overwork? Consider the host culture. Does it reward workaholics? Consider church or agency policies and subtle attitudes. Do they give permission to be human and rest? Consider the person's family of origin. Did the parents show love only when the children met their standards?

7. Preserve the dignity and responsibility of the worker.

- The worker's well-being, ultimately, is his or her own responsibility. The church or agency should help the worker fulfill that responsibility and certainly should not get in the way. Neither should the mission leadership take that responsibility from the worker and make him/her dependent.
- Confidentiality needs to be carefully defined. How will personal or negative information about a worker be handled? How is such information stored in the personnel or member care department? Who will be told, and who has access? How will trust and a sense of emotional safety be preserved?
- Normally, do not let issues slide by. If danger signs surface in a worker's life or family, lovingly bring the matter up. Not to do so shirks a biblical responsibility and plays "Russian roulette" with the well-being of the worker, his/her family, and ministry. For example, let's suppose that, when staying with a worker's family, a visiting pastor notices that the husband and wife argue a lot and seem distant from each other. It would be easy not to ask about how they are doing and avoid what might be a difficult discussion. But the danger sign should not be ignored. For the sake of the couple, their family, and their kingdom work, they need to be lovingly led to explore and work on the matter.

Involve the Workers' Sending Churches

Mission thinkers are recognizing that the local church is a key arena where a kingdom worker is shaped for service (Girón, 1997). Mission agencies and associations of churches need to give the sending church a central place in the process of development and care. Hopefully, the church is ready to assume its key role. If not, leaders of the mission enterprise will do well to help educate the churches they serve about the churches' role in member care. Here are some principles to help mission leaders partner with churches:

■ Screen for a candidate's spiritual grounding and maturity in his/her sending church. If the candidate does not have such a church community, beware!

■ Partner with the church to continue the worker's growth during the pre-field process and on-field ministry. For example, at CBInternational, we direct new workers to link up with mentors in their sending churches, and we coach them about how to do that.

■ Encourage a church and worker to build a deep, safe relationship so that as the worker encounters struggles and crises, he/she has a safe place to debrief and to seek prayer and emotional support.

■ Encourage the church to give active encouragement to their worker via letters, emails, phone calls, visits, acts of kindness, etc., according to the church's resources.

■ Partner with the sending church as the primary arena of healing and restoration for a traumatized, wounded, or fallen worker.

■ Seek to involve the sending church in key decisions affecting the worker—for example, deployment, repatriation, engagement in high-risk ministries, and decisions to evacuate or not.

From Mindset to Action

Sooner or later, one must move past theory to action, whether those action steps involve creating a member care department or starting to shape day-to-day actions and policies of a church, church association, or mission agency. Here are some practical suggestions that should help you get off to a good start when you step out in faith and try the first initiative:

■ Mobilize some intercessors to pray on behalf of you and the member care mindset you desire to develop and translate into action.

■ Take time to build trust and relationships with the key people whose support you need. Ideas new to your organization cannot stand on their own merit, because they are untested in your context. They will need to stand on the strength of others' trust in you—in your integrity and competence.

■ Consider the scope of issues that member care can influence, and choose an area that will meet a keenly felt need among your church's, association's, or agency's workers and leaders. There are many possibilities: training in language learning; teaching about culture; education of children; orientation to the organization; training in raising support; influencing policies about vacation, salary, insurance, and emergencies; restoration strategies for the tired or wounded; retirement planning, and so on. You must carefully choose an initiative that will meet a felt need, be fairly easy to do, and will yield results fairly quickly. An early success will generate confidence in the concept of doing member care.

■ Help workers and leadership understand the value of the initiative you are proposing. Cite examples of other churches or organizations that are already doing it and the positive results they are experiencing. In short, sell your idea. Remember, workers and leaders are not against caring for personal needs. However, the pressure of ministry needs and the weight of tradition will force any new way of doing things to compete for attention and resources.

■ Start small and let the new member care initiatives grow slowly and naturally. Do not begin by creating notebooks full of complicated structures and procedures. Begin with simple, concrete actions, and let new structures evolve to support and solidify member care that is already happening. Let form follow function.

■ Seek to evaluate the effectiveness of your initiatives. Simple pre- and post-intervention testing, follow-up interviews, or opportunities for feedback can help fine-tune your efforts and help demonstrate the value of doing member care.

Concluding Thoughts

Doing member care is like Italian grandmothers making spaghetti sauce or Indian women making curry; everyone has a unique way of doing it. The practice of doing member care will vary from church to church, from organization to organization, and from culture to culture. It must be that way to be effective. However, just as spaghetti sauce always involves tomatoes, member care always involves certain elements and principles. I trust that this brief review of some of those elements and principles will help us all nurture and put into practice a member care mindset and possibly develop a member care department in the settings in which we serve.

Reflection and Discussion

1. What is your motivation for promoting member care in your church or organization? Negative experiences of your own? Biblical convictions? A sense that others are doing it so you should too? How might your motivation impact your ability to bring about change in your sphere of influence?

2. Who are some key people in your church or organization that need to support any attempt to create a member care mindset or department and put it into action? How can you best gain a hearing and build trust with them?

3. What is your own vision of what member care will accomplish for your workers and church or organization? For the kingdom?

4. How will you organize member care efforts? How will you establish priorities as you apply limited resources to an overwhelming array of possible initiatives?

5. What will be your first initiative/project? What steps will you take to launch it and evaluate its effectiveness?

References

Girón, R. (1997). An integrated model of missions. In W. Taylor (Ed.), *Too valuable to lose: Exploring the causes and cures of missionary attrition* (pp. 25-40). Pasadena, CA: William Carey Library.

Kayser, J. (1994). *Criteria and predictors of missionary cross-cultural competence in selected North American Evangelical missions*. Doctoral dissertation, University of Edinburgh, Scotland.

McGoldrick, M., & Carter, E. (1982). The stages of the family life cycle. In F. Walsh (Ed.), *Normal family processes*. New York, NY: Guilford.

O'Donnell, K. (1987). Developmental tasks in the life cycle of mission families. *Journal of Psychology and Theology*, *15*, 281-290.

Sikkema, M., & Niyekawa, A. (1987). *Design for cross-cultural learning*. Yarmouth, ME: Intercultural Press.

Swanson, B. (1993). *Whirling teacups: A bi-cycle analysis of missionary growth*. Presentation given at the Mental Health and Missions Conference, Angola, IN.

Bruce Swanson *served with CBInternational in Portugal for 10 years in church planting, leadership development, and compassion efforts. In 1992, he transferred to the home office in order to direct CBI's Missionary Development Department. Bruce has master's degrees in New Testament studies and counseling. He spends time biking in the mountains with Laurie, his wife, and three children. He also enjoys running, working with his hands, and eating his way through cultures around the world as he visits CBI's field personnel. Email: bruce@cbi.org.*

Special thanks to Laura Mae and Richard Gardner for reviewing this article.

43

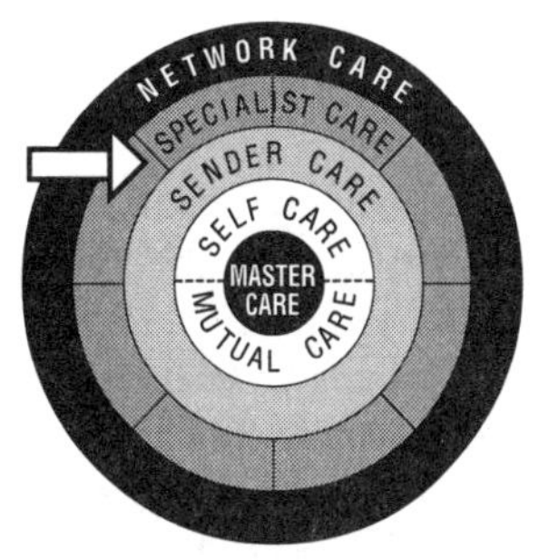

The Perils of Pioneering: Responsible Logistics For Hostile Places

STEVE HOLLOWAY
KITTY HOLLOWAY

Doing logistics well in potentially dangerous and antagonistic settings: that is quite a task! This chapter explores this subject via a team which went through sudden expulsion from their host country. There is much to learn as the authors discuss the salient factors which affect outcomes: good preparation, group cohesion, contingency plans, debriefing, organizational support, and concern for persecuted national believers.

"And this gospel of the kingdom shall be preached in the whole world for a witness to all the nations, and then the end will come."
Matthew 24:14

We watch and wait, eager for the day of the Lord's return. Yet Matthew 24:14 is quite clear that this will happen only after all nations have had an opportunity to hear the good news of reconciliation through the cross and have responded one way or another to the revelation of God. The word translated as "nations" in this verse comes from the Greek *ethne,* from which we get "ethnic." *Ethne* refers to people who are grouped together by their common language, tribal, or cultural identity, rather than the political groupings we term as "nations" in English today. Although there are some 200 political countries in the world now, these contain an estimated 24,000 ethnic or people groups.

The best research estimates that of these approximately 24,000 people groups, two-thirds have access to the gospel. That is, the members of some 16,000 people groups currently have opportunity to understand and evaluate the claims of Christ and to respond to His invitation to enter His kingdom. For these people, there is a fellowship of followers of Christ who speak their language and who are able to communicate with them. In addition, there may be portions of the Bible available to them in their language. But one-third of the world's distinct people groups—the *ethne*—are as yet without any access to the gospel. They still wait to hear.

Many of these remaining people groups are still unreached for obvious reasons. Some have been inaccessible (e.g., isolated due to geography or political climate) or overlooked (e.g., hidden among larger surrounding cultural groups or denied a voice by political powers). The worldwide church is just now marshaling resources to reach out to these groups. Other people groups are still unreached because they have historically demonstrated resistance or hostility to the gospel. Encountering this resistance, Christians have often chosen a path of less resistance, focusing instead on people groups that seem more open to hear the gospel message.

Obviously, the more resistant people groups are included in the Great Commission of Jesus (Matt. 28:18-20). In recent years, the church has become alert to their existence and has increasingly focused its mission efforts on them, sending bearers of the good news to many environments which are inhospitable—physically, emotionally, mentally, and spiritually.

Of these remaining unreached groups, the largest bloc by far consists of peoples who are identified with or live under the influence of Islam. They comprise almost half of the people in the unreached people groups today. The case study that follows describes an effort by the mission agency Frontiers to reach one such unreached Muslim group, along with the cost required. Before we launch into the case study itself, it will be helpful first to give an overview of Frontiers and its approach.

Frontiers: The Nature of Our Ministry and Work

Frontiers is a relatively young mission agency, born out of the strategic emphases of "unreached peoples" in the late 1970s and early 1980s. Founded in 1983 by Dr. Greg Livingstone, Frontiers accepted a mandate to focus solely on unreached Muslim people groups. This mandate grew out of the then-current reality that only a small number of missionaries and few resources of the church were focused on Muslim peoples, due primarily to their perceived hostility towards and resistance to the gospel. An early slogan of Frontiers reflected these statistics: "Missionaries to Muslims are one in a million. Literally."

Today, Frontiers is comprised of more than 600 missionaries serving on more than 100 teams throughout the Muslim world. These teams draw candidates and resources from 20 Frontiers "sending bases" in North and South America, Europe, Asia, and Africa. A small international office in England coordinates both the teams and the sending bases.

Frontiers is a mission agency that has adapted to the realities of communicating the gospel in harsh and often hostile environments. The agency is relatively decentralized, allowing teams and sending bases wide latitude in making decisions which affect the pursuit of their objectives in their respective cultural contexts. Frontiers has adopted a "flat" organizational structure, with a minimum of hierarchy between teams or sending bases and the international office.

With such a loose structure, an organization like Frontiers needs a clear, common vision and ethos in order to maintain cohesion and fulfill its mandate. The glue holding Frontiers together is a set of six core principles to which all members of the mission agree:

- **We only work among Muslim peoples.** As mentioned above, this focus seeks to redress the historical under-representation of mission effort among Muslim peoples.
- **We work in teams.** Frontiers defines a team as at least six adults working together in the same geographical area and among the same Muslim people group. A healthy team residing among the people to whom they have been called provides a powerful redemptive testimony through community and provides continuity of effort over time.
- **We plant churches.** We are not content to see a few individuals enter the kingdom but are called to see viable fellowships of Muslim-background believers (MBBs) established and multiplying within their culture. We have a theology of "closure," in which the missionary team re-

duces its influence as the church matures. Eventually, the team moves to a partnering or participation stage with the MBB church or even withdraws completely.

■ **We are eager for coaching and accountability.** Each team requires some pre-field training, and each sending base provides a candidate school. Most of the training in Frontiers, however, is done in the field through on-site coaching by individuals with skills relevant to that field and that team's phase of church planting. Ongoing mentoring structures for accountability, encouragement, and leadership development are provided as well.

■ **We are "grace oriented."** We are unified under what we consider essentials: our statement of faith, core principles, and the ethos of Frontiers. Beyond these essentials, we are an interdenominational agency that allows significant diversity of Evangelical doctrine and theology, lifestyle, and strategy for each team and field, defined primarily by the team leaders.

■ **We are "field governed."** The highest governing body in Frontiers is an International Council made up of all team leaders, the International Director, and the International Field Director of Frontiers. The rationale behind this structure is that those actually engaged in church planting on Muslim soil should have the final decision on how the organization is shaped to serve this mandate.

In addition to these core principles, there is a significant amount of shared ethos in the Frontiers organizational culture. For example, only a handful of field workers have "missionary visas." Most gain residency among the people to whom they are called through their professional skills, a business, or other activity. Frontiers teams also practice an incarnational approach to communicating the gospel, by adapting the message to the local language and culture in ways that reduce any foreign element, without compromising the scriptural integrity of the message God has sent for all peoples.

Because of the oppressive and sometimes hostile nature of the environments in which we work, we have had to develop a practical theology of sacrifice and suffering. Not only is there spiritual and often political resistance to the gospel on Muslim fields, but also our team members must balance the responsibilities of their residency role (often a full-time job), language and culture learning, ministry to nationals, team life, family, and, for leaders, a leadership role. In the midst of all these stresses, the missionaries are motivated by a deep calling to minister to the people to whom God has brought them. We have had to ensure that our philosophy of member care, along with our crisis and contingency management approach, respect what God asks of our workers, even though they sometimes go against the prevailing attitude of "safety, security, and reduction of stress levels at all costs" that is characteristic of many Western cultures. Although no Frontiers worker morbidly seeks or desires others to go through pain, sacrifice, or suffering, we have come to realize that such experiences, according to Scripture and history, normally accompany the spread of God's kingdom.

The gospel confronts all cultures in some way, and it is often threatening to people's vested interests, beliefs, values, and traditions. This conflict often triggers persecution of those wanting to embrace the gospel truth. For many who put their faith in Jesus, the Lord becomes the pearl of such great value to them that they are willing to withstand the fires of persecution.

Our field workers relate amazing testimonies from their frontline experiences. God walks with them at the cutting edge of His kingdom. As they are willing to follow His leading, no matter the cost, He demonstrates His sovereignty and faithfulness at depths they experienced less frequently while back in their home cultures, where deep dependency on God might seem unnatural, unnecessary, or even frightening to complacent Christians.

The Momboc Case Study

This case study is part of living history, a story that is continuing to unfold and develop even at the time of this writing. Due to reasons that will become clear below, names and details that identify the actual area have been changed to protect believers and the ongoing outreach.

We want to share this story to encourage other Christians who are obeying a calling to plant churches where Christ is not yet known. We also want to encourage those who support such workers by holding the "lifelines." Good logistical support, like good crisis logistics, is so important!

This story is a testimony, among many in the world today, of the power of the gospel breaking into the darkness of one people group—the Momboc. We also share this story in hope that it may help those who find it difficult to imagine the gospel being a reason for anyone to go through suffering or persecution. We trust that by reading this testimony, such people would be prompted to pray for their brothers and sisters in Christ who suffer for their faith. We also hope that they would be able to test their own faith by putting themselves in the shoes of their brothers and sisters in Momboc.

We want thc tcstimony of God's faithfulness to shine clearly. God is faithful to fulfill His Word in calling out individuals from the Momboc culture to become part of His kingdom. He is also faithful to walk with His beloved children through the dark valley. We count it as joy that it has been granted to us not only to believe in Jesus, but also to suffer for Him (Phil. 1:27-30). There will be members of the church of Momboc among the throngs gathered before the throne worshiping the Lamb (Rev. 7:9-17). We now know some of their names, and we have had the privilege of personally hearing some of their first expressions of worship.

Some Background

Momboc is a small area of the Muslim world which prides itself on being 100% Muslim. In fact, the government of the Momboc province requires that all citizens conform to the Islamic beliefs approved and promoted by the civil government. There is no freedom of religious expression in this province, and the government has demonstrated that it has no tolerance for dissension. It will utilize the full force of the state to ensure compliance with the government-sanctioned form of Islam. The government specifically opposes other forms of Islam as well as Christianity.

In spite of this environment of hostility to the Christian faith, there had been a quiet missions effort in the area for at least 13 years prior to the crisis. Frontiers workers and other Christians from many nations, employed in a variety of professions, were attempting to bless the nation with the contribution of their skills and love, befriending many Mombocs and communicating the gospel to them.

This communication involved dedicated efforts to learn the local language without the aid of traditional language courses or grammar helps, alertness to learn the local culture and worldview, and the many "lessons" necessary to learn how to build sincere trust relationships with Mombocs. This was very hard work. It was often frustrating and thankless, although at times it was sweetened by the reward of reciprocated trust and friendship. Each team family and individual had a network of Christians behind them in their home countries, supporting them in prayer, encouragement, accountability, and many practical ways. Without this support, the workers would not have been able to persevere for the initial, seemingly fruitless years.

Before moving to the Momboc province, each Frontiers team member had signed an agreement with their team leader that set out the expectations, goals, and methods of the team and ministry. Each had gone through pre-field training, which included learning about Islam and folk-Islam, learning how to acquire a new language without the benefit of language schools, and basic principles of cross-cultural awareness and church planting. In addition, most attended a Frontiers candidate program for orientation.

The team leader interviewed candidates applying to the field and made the final decision whether to accept the individual or couple onto the team. Candidates joining the Momboc team were encouraged to establish their residence visa in Momboc independent of other team members. Team members offered advice about whom to contact, but new team members entering the province were required to negotiate their own residency.

By 1998, the Frontiers effort in Momboc had grown from one team to three teams, each with a leader who was responsible for helping them focus on their main goal of church planting, encouraging all the team members' spiritual gifts and roles to mesh together, and ensuring accountability between all members. The three teams, though administratively distinct, worked together as one community. They were interdependent and sought to encourage one another. The three leaders worked closely together, like elders, for the church planting effort.

Each team met at least weekly for worship, prayer, and continuing discussion of team building and church planting issues. The leaders took part in annual meetings outside the country that enabled them to interact with leaders from other Muslim fields. Team leaders established regular accountability (both written and face-to-face) for team members. They themselves were also accountable monthly to their overseer, who was based outside the country. This person had begun the church planting work among the Mombocs and continued his involvement by mentoring the team leaders and supporting them in their roles.

The Lord used these efforts to bring a small number of Momboc people into the kingdom of God. Those who had chosen to be baptized were meeting weekly to worship and study portions of the Bible together, and their family and friends were being attracted to Jesus. In close cooperation with these followers of *Isa al Masih* (Jesus the Messiah), Frontiers missionaries completed the first translations of Bible portions, wrote and produced indigenous worship songs, and organized a radio broadcast in the Momboc language.

Those involved in discipling the MBBs (Muslim-background believers) were careful to discuss often the potential persecution that would come as their faith became more apparent to their families, friends, and political leaders. The MBBs were well aware of the dangers, even more than the expatriates, as they all personally knew fellow Mombocs who had been arrested and mistreated for other reasons. They knew that in the past, and very recently, Momboc citizens who had openly begun to follow Jesus had been interrogated mercilessly, had been exiled to distant parts of the province, and had reputedly recanted their faith. For some of those persecuted believers, this treatment resulted in long-term mental problems.

Surprisingly, government officials in the province were well aware of the missionary intentions of many foreigners working in their area, but they were willing to "look the other way." Apparently, these missionaries enjoyed a good reputation and were perceived as having a positive influence among the people. One government minister also mentioned in a conversation with a Frontiers team member, "... and of course [the Christian workers] could not be successful anyway."

The teams discussed and agreed upon a contingency plan in the case of a believer being arrested and subjected to governmental persecution, or in the case of a team member being arrested and accused of anti-government activity. The team members had all been vigilant over the years to maintain a certain level of security, primarily ensuring that their ministry was not explicitly described in printed publications.

In 1998, the government became aware that portions of Scripture had been published in the language of the Momboc. In addition, a weekly radio program in the Momboc language, which looked at scriptural principles applied to everyday Momboc life, began being broadcast into the province, outside of governmental control. These incidents sparked a heated political debate, since it was an election year. A small minority of Muslim fundamentalists in the province, who were trying to build a local power base of their own, accused the incumbent official of allowing Christianity to enter the province during his term of office. Apparently to demonstrate his Islamic credentials, the government official who was running for reelection quietly organized a crackdown on perceived Christian activity throughout the area. At that time, a relative of one of the Momboc believers, angered by a recent family conflict, went to government police headquarters and personally identified all the Momboc believers and foreign missionaries he knew.

Search, Seizure, Interrogation, Expulsion

Over a two-day period in June 1998, Momboc government police raided the homes of more than a dozen foreign families (some with Frontiers, some not). Government police arrived unannounced at the homes and systematically searched the premises without any warrants, confiscating all literature, music, files, computers, photographs, and other media suspected of being linked to Christianity. They were especially interested in any materials in the local language.

The government brought in specialists to break into even secure files on the computers, including personal diaries and church-planting training materials. In the months that followed, various parts of this confidential information were published in the local paper or spread by word of mouth from the police officials to others involved in the crisis. Photographs were used to identify Momboc people who had been friends with the team members and believers and who thus were under suspicion of being favorable to Christianity themselves.

During the next several days, all the foreigners whose homes had been searched were brought to police headquarters in the capital city. Their passports were taken, and they were subjected to questioning. After hours of interrogation, they were coerced into signing statements that often did not reflect their views or that included statements or confessions that they had neither made nor agreed with. They were also asked to review the lists of confiscated items, although they were told that none would be returned any time soon.

While these events were happening, the government police also rounded up at least 60 Momboc citizens on the charge of "being Christian" and jailed them. Many of these citizens were, in fact, followers of Jesus (some were not related to the Frontiers team) or sympathetic to the gospel, though some were not.

While the foreigners waited for hours in the police headquarters, their Momboc friends were brought in, possibly to allow the police to gauge the reaction between them—whether they recognized or acknowledged each other. These meetings seemed to be carefully staged to give the Momboc believers the impression that their foreign friends were choosing to betray them and then leave the province painlessly. Both the foreigners and the Momboc believers agonized over how to respond during these unexpected meetings, as well as how to answer during the interrogations. Most of the foreigners felt high levels of guilt and regret, no matter whether they acknowledged the MBBs or not in these staged meetings and no matter how they answered the questions.

All foreign families were informed of their imminent deportation from the province, and they quickly began to pack and prepare for leaving. The expulsion order applied to all members of all three Frontiers teams. Within the highly charged environment, there were understandably high levels of stress for all of the families preparing to be deported. Stresses included concern for the local believers, concern for what might be happening to other team members, repeated trips to the police station for questioning, unexpected visits by police at any hour of the day, the inability to go out to communicate with employers and their friends, and the injunction to stay in their homes. Many felt sick and nauseous, had trouble sleeping, and lost their appetites. Some at times even forgot simple tasks like feeding their children regularly.

Within 10 days of the initial raids, almost all foreigners under investigation had been deported from the province and forced to sign a statement that they had broken local laws (though no law was specified) and were "expelled for life." Government police escorted those expelled to the plane, even accompanying some of them on the flight to a nearby country. Expelled team members were from several countries, and personnel from their respective embassies met them at the airport when they disembarked from the Momboc flight.

After the foreigners were expelled, most of the Momboc believers were imprisoned, along with the other Momboc people being accused as sympathetic to Christians. The believers were kept in prison for several months, with repeated interrogations and teachings designed to force them to return to Islamic beliefs. One Momboc citizen was singled out as the ringleader and was subjected to torture, beatings, and solitary confinement for five months.

The Momboc citizens who were arrested were all taken without warning—simply a knock on the door by uniformed men, followed by confinement at the police station. Their families were at first given no contact with them, although as the months progressed, some husbands were allowed a 10-minute visit once a week with their wives. The families faced strong community disapproval. However, not one of the unbelieving spouses sought divorce from their imprisoned believing spouse during this time or even later. This is significant, as the Momboc area is infamous for its very high divorce rate and lack of commitment in marriage relationships.

Frontiers' Response to the Crisis

The Frontiers teams in Momboc had prepared a contingency plan with protocols for handling a variety of field crises. Within hours of the raids by the government police, they began to put this plan into effect.

As part of this plan, the leaders of the three teams carefully managed the flow of information about the crisis, meeting frequently to assess the situation. Team members kept in touch with each other through visits, and they communicated updates to their leaders as the situation developed. Rumors about the crisis were controlled by ensuring that the facts were checked and verified. The team members agreed on a common response before they communicated with contacts outside the country.

All information was channeled to the team leaders' overseer outside the country via email and phone through one designated spokesperson. Team members agreed not to speak with the local or international press without permission. They shared information with family and close friends, but only what had been agreed to by the leaders and other team members. Meanwhile, the overseer for the team leaders was watching closely, evaluating how best to support the teams through the crisis and which information to share with outsiders for prayer and action.

The contingency plan stipulated that if team members were expelled, they would gather to be debriefed in a neutral country before returning to their home countries. It was important that they be given a chance to process their experience before facing family, friends, and churches. They managed to assemble at the agreed-upon meeting point at a specific hotel in a nearby country, after first making contact with the embassies of their home countries to report what had happened to them and to file a report asking for the return of their personal items.

Meanwhile, the Frontiers international office quickly pulled together a crisis debriefing team, comprised of a psychologist who had been in contact with several team members over the past years, the Momboc team overseer-mentors, and a representative from a Frontiers sending base. This debriefing team quickly disengaged from their other responsibilities and flew out at short notice to be at the team assembly point as the first team members began to arrive.

A pool of funds managed by the International Headquarters covered the costs of this trip for them. The psychologist brought special treats for the children of the teams, to encourage them during the debriefing. He also brought basic medications and a water filter, to ensure that no one became more ill during this high-stress time in an area with poor standards of cleanliness.

In the first meeting, the debriefing team was introduced, and the basic plan for the debriefing was discussed. The debriefing team sketched out an introduction to the different phases that individuals and groups go through when facing a serious crisis or "critical incident":

- *Alarm phase*—individuals are shocked and stunned; they try to adjust and make sense of what is happening; they wonder if it will mean prison, torture, nothing significant, etc.
- *Mobilization phase*—those affected recover from the initial shock and begin to develop plans, or they try to remember contingency plans.
- *Action phase*—a high level of activity takes place; constructive work and cooperation occur during this diligent and heroic phase; the phase also produces high levels of stress and possibly frustration.
- *Let-down phase*—transition from the crisis experience back to normal routine occurs; this is often the most intense period, as feelings that were suppressed, denied, or put on hold during the crisis now surface.
- *Letting-go phase*—this phase is marked by sadness, depression, restlessness, inability to get involved with regular work responsibilities, and annoyance at work; it often involves coming out of "emotional armor"; feelings of estrangement or alienation from those who didn't go through the trauma may be present.

All the team families were essentially still in the *action phase* as they arrived at the hotel. The first deported team members noticed that government police had followed them to the hotel that their country's embassy had arranged for their initial arrival. They were still feeling on "high alert" as they later arrived at the assembly point. In fact, it took several days for the group to make a successful transition from the action phase to the let-down phase, because team members who arrived later, still full of adrenaline from their experience with the government police, reactivated the action-phase feelings of those who had arrived earlier.

As the group settled, the team members were encouraged to tell their stories—relating the facts of what happened to them—and also to hear the stories of other team members, which they had not had the chance either to hear or to fully understand on the field. The story telling was done as a large group, with the psychologist moderating and helping the stories to be told in an orderly manner. Many discussed tough decisions they faced and vivid thoughts or sensory memories (sounds, smells, sights) from their experience. Many relived step by step all the people they had interacted with during the last days. The debriefing staff encouraged the team members to stay with just the facts at this point and to reserve the emotional responses for a later stage of the debriefing. Those with children had to take turns being in this meeting, as there was no ready system of childcare available. The psychologist used a similar approach (age-appropriate) to work with the children of the families, helping them to process, come to terms with, and begin to understand what they and their parents had been through. There were eight children at the debriefing, all under age eight.

The debriefing took several days and helped everyone get a much better understanding of the full picture of the crisis. Many were encouraged by the instances of God's intervention and the positive accounts/perspectives of others, especially instances involving Momboc friends. Many Momboc friends cared for them during the days of crisis in Momboc, at great risk to themselves, by providing meals for the families on their own initiative, helping care for the children while the parents went through interrogations, helping families pack and close up their houses, and taking the risk to pass on last messages to other close friends.

The debriefing team encouraged all team members to write up their stories during the next few days, both to help them process their experiences and to provide a record of their part in the incident. Within a month after the debriefing sessions, these stories had been gathered into one document that all could read, so that they could see the overall picture of what they had been through.

Once the missionaries had told their personal stories, the debriefing staff encouraged the team members to answer the question: "What did this mean to me personally?" Many then talked about their anger, fear, frustration, sense of having betrayed the Momboc believers, sense of having been betrayed, stress, confusion, guilt, grief, etc. As they listened to each other, empathized, and identified, many began to gain more emotional distance from the experience and a lessening of the pain and intensity. They felt a great relief in being able to address these issues in a safe and controlled environment with trusted team members.

In the next stage of debriefing, team members were encouraged to interact with each other—to discuss any conflicts or other relational issues that needed resolution. They had an opportunity to say the things they felt they needed to say to others on the team and to express appreciation or encouragement.

The focus then shifted to the next steps. Many on the team were quite concerned about the national believers who had been left behind, especially those in prison for their faith. They drafted plans to start an international prayer and letter writing campaign built around the lack of freedom of religious expression in the Momboc province.

The representatives from the international office also agreed that expelled team members would continue to be recognized as members of the three teams and as field missionaries by Frontiers for the next six months. This promise of continued identity with Frontiers gave the missionaries a sense of security in the midst of so many abrupt changes—changes of home, country, job, role, ministry, friends, daily routine, neighbors, language, essential lifestyle, "team family," and so on. It would also give them time to reflect on what they should do next. Plans were made to hold a small team conference at the end of the six-month period, at which time the team would be officially dissolved. Individuals would then be released to pursue the Lord's directions for them—namely, whether to continue work with Momboc people, to join a team on another Muslim field, to work with another agency, or to leave missions work altogether.

The follow-up team conference was subsequently held in January 1999 in Europe, and all of the expelled team members attended. The conference provided an excellent opportunity for the team members to interact with each other and with other invitees who had a vital interest in the Momboc effort. Also attending were those who had earlier been part of the teams, who had left Momboc before the expulsion occurred, as well as new candidates who felt they were being called to minister in the future to Momboc people. The participants discussed their insights and the lessons learned in many aspects of their lives and ministry among the Momboc people. They prayed together often. The conference helped the group to bring closure to the efforts of the three teams thus far and to commission the teams of the future.

The Next Two Years

As a result of international pressure applied through the efforts of the expelled team members, all Momboc believers were released from prison within six months. They returned to their family and community context and have remained there. This presence in Momboc is very important. Those who have believed have not been "extracted" or exiled from their culture; instead, their testimony remains.

Of the Frontiers missionaries expelled from or prevented from returning to Momboc, 16 have chosen to continue in a church planting effort among Momboc people, eight have pursued or are planning to pursue ministry to other mission fields, and three have left missions to pursue other work. Several of the expelled team members have been able to make face-to-face contact with the Momboc believers who went through the torture and imprisonment, have debriefed them, and have helped them work through the crisis in ways similar to those used by the debriefing team.

Although we have no way of hearing direct news about all the believers, we have received second-hand reports from Momboc friends in the area. There are indications that a few Momboc believers are continuing on in their faith, seeking teaching and fellowship whenever they are able to travel outside of the province. As yet, there is no sign that they are daring to fellowship with each other while inside the province. They have been threatened with yet worse punishment if they are accused of or found to be praying to Jesus, talking about Him, or using any literature about Him.

There are also indications that interest in the gospel has significantly increased in the province, due to sympathy for those imprisoned and expelled during the crisis. In addition, the earlier church planting strategies continue via the ongoing efforts in translation, radio broadcasts, and development of indigenous worship songs. This interest continues despite a climate of extreme tension and fear. There are still frequent government warnings against Christianity and threats of punishment to those who spread news about Jesus, openly follow Him, or neglect to report others who do these things. The general population continues to be warned about the methods that may be used by missionaries, including friendliness, helpfulness, and desire to learn the local language.

Recently, some team members who had been expelled have settled in provinces near the Momboc province to reestablish ministry among the Momboc people. All of these team members who have resumed ministry with the Momboc people have had to work through difficult emotions and fears as they return to proximity to the province. In their new locations, they find they can minister in very different ways from their previous methods. Free from the influence of the Momboc government, they have liberty in communicating the gospel, and they can openly discuss the crisis they went through with their Momboc friends. Even so, many still fight off irrational fears of being expelled suddenly from their new location. In addition, they, along with those who have not returned to face-to-face Momboc ministry, continue to experience the normal grief involved in such an abrupt change of life which entailed so many losses. Even the supportive response to the crisis described in this article cannot erase the trauma of the event.

News of the Momboc experience sparked interest in a variety of mission agencies in how to provide effective assistance to MBBs experiencing persecution in hostile environments. Early in 1999, a multi-agency steering committee was formed in Europe from Elam, Frontiers, Tear Fund, Oxford Centre for Mission Studies, People International, and YWAM to hold a consultation exploring social, cultural, economic, legal, and human rights factors that MBBs must address as they respond to the gospel.

This consultation was held in February 2001, and two-thirds of the attendees were MBB leaders. Participants prepared case studies from the specific cultural contexts and perspectives of MBBs, reflecting on principles and lessons learned from their personal experiences. These case studies were reviewed, and common patterns and principles were identified. The principles were then used as a basis for in-depth discussions at the consultation, which resulted in an initial list of best practice principles compiled by MBB leaders. This list will soon be published to stimulate a wider discussion and refinement of these principles among those involved in Muslim ministry.

The story of the Momboc field is, of course, not finished, and this case study is only one small chapter of a book that covers hundreds of years of God's redemptive work. Even so, it is clear that in this case, what the enemy of human souls intended for evil, God is using for good, in ways we would never have imagined. Member care that recognizes the role of sacrifice and suffering has been critical to the process. Such member care helped to bridge the crisis effectively and ensure that the effort to bring good news to the Momboc people continues—and that captives are being set free.

Reflection and Discussion

1. What were the logistical factors that helped this team evacuate and work through the trauma of expulsion?

2. Based on the information in this case study, identify three things that stand out as being done well and three areas that could have been improved.

3. Has your mission agency/sending church developed a "theology of suffering" to help it evaluate how to respond proactively (rather than reactively) to persecution on its fields, both for missionaries and national believers? If so, what are the basic points?

4. In your organization, what are some of the main logistics needed to prepare missionaries and teams for crises? For example, what contingency plans are in place to anticipate the 3-5 most likely crises for individual mission fields? Has a secure, safe, and neutral "assembly site" been identified where an adequate debriefing can be held? Has a debriefing team been identified, trained in critical incident debriefing techniques, and made available to respond to such situations?

5. Is preparation for persecution part of the discipling program for national believers? What plans and/or protocols have been made for national believers left behind?

Some Suggested Readings

Brabant, K. (2001, March). *Mainstreaming safety and security management in aid agencies*. London, UK: Humanitarian Policy Group Briefing. (Available from: hpgadmin@odi.org.uk)

Carr, K. (1997). Crisis intervention for missionaries. *Evangelical Missions Quarterly, 33*, 450-458.

Companjen, A. (2000). *Hidden sorrow, lasting joy: The forgotten women of the persecuted church*. London, UK: Hodder & Stoughton.

Fink, S. (1986). *Crisis management: Planning for the inevitable*. New York, NY: American Management Association.

Gardner, L. (1992). Crisis intervention in the mission community. In K. O'Donnell (Ed.), *Missionary care: Counting the cost for world evangelization* (pp. 136-150). Pasadena, CA: William Carey Library,

Goode, S. (1995). Guidelines for crisis and contingency management. *International Journal of Frontier Missions, 12*, 211-216.

Grose, V. (1987). *Managing risk*. Englewood, NJ: Prentice-Hall.

Janz, M., Rogers, C., Slead, J., & Abifarin, A. (2000). Risk and security essentials for humanitarian operations: Liberia. In M. Janz & J. Slead (Eds.), *Complex humanitarian emergencies: Lessons from practitioners* (pp. 66-91). Monrovia, CA: World Vision.

Mitchell, J., & Everly, G. (1996). *Critical incident stress debriefing: An operations manual for the prevention of traumatic stress among emergency services and disaster personnel* (2nd ed., revised). Elliot City, MD: Chevron Publishing Corporation.

***Steve Holloway** and **Kitty Holloway** pioneered the effort to the Momboc people, and as the teams multiplied, they became and continue to be mentors and overseers of the effort. Kitty remains actively involved in Bible translation efforts for the Momboc people and assists in the development of tracts and radio programs. Steve is active in leadership development at the International Headquarters of Frontiers. He also mentors other teams and helps develop partnerships with national leaders to establish church planting teams in South Asia. Email: scealh@myrealbox.com.*

Special thanks to Jeleta Eckheart for her helpful review of this article.

44

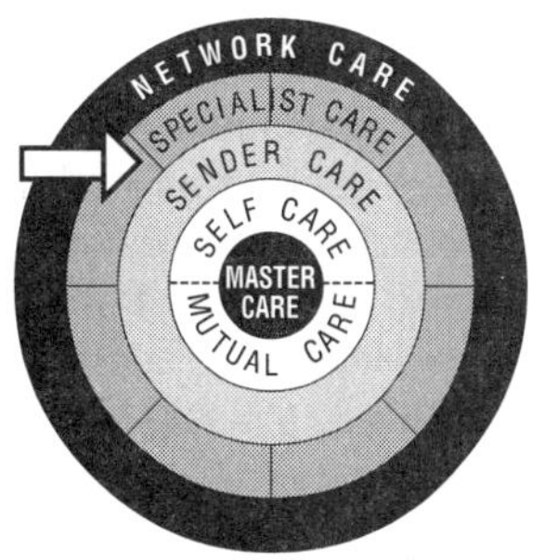

Guidelines for Crisis And Routine Debriefing

Debbie Lovell Hawker

There is much discussion about debriefing these days at conferences, within organizations, and in the literature. Debriefing, in terms of current best practice thinking, is an essential service to provide for mission personnel. But what exactly is it? What types of debriefing are available? Which skills are needed to do it well? And how does it work? The author looks at these and other questions in light of the literature and research on the subject, sharing from her extensive experience on both crisis and routine debriefing.

The young woman sitting in front of me had been working with a missionary organization during a time of "ethnic cleansing." She told me about a woman who had been forced to cook her dead child's body in a pot; about a whole classroom of children who had been massacred; and about villages where it was said that the men had been captured and injected in an attempt to make them HIV positive, so that they (and their wives) would die slowly and painfully from AIDS. She said she had been unable to tell anyone about the dreadful things which she had encountered. I asked how she had managed to cope with so much horror. She replied, "The thing that kept me going was knowing that I would be able to talk about it during this Critical Incident Debriefing. That saved me from going under."

A few weeks later, a man from a different organization came to be debriefed. He had just returned after being overseas for five years. He said that he had generally enjoyed his time overseas and had not experienced anything which he would describe as "traumatic." However, he had found the time stressful, as there had been difficulties within his team, and he had worked long hours each day. He was feeling rather burned out and exhausted and was wondering what he should do next. At the end of the debriefing session, he said it had been very helpful to talk with someone outside the organization, and he was relieved to hear that his feelings were normal, given the circumstances. He added that he now realized that there was no reason to feel guilty about taking some time off work to rest. He decided that he would try to use the stress management strategies which had been discussed during the session.

What Is Debriefing?

"Debriefing" is a general term that refers to talking through an experience after it has taken place. Various types of debriefing may be offered to mission partners. They can be defined as follows:

- *Operational debriefing* – Asking for information about work performed and about what was achieved. The aim is to gain more information about the project.
- *Personal debriefing* – Asking how the experience was for the individual and how it has affected him/her. The aims are to offer any support that might be needed and to help the individual with the readjustment process.
- *Critical Incident Debriefing (CID)* – A highly structured form of personal debriefing, which can take place after a traumatic experience (such as a natural disaster, a violent incident, or a traffic accident). The aims are to help accelerate recovery and to prevent post-traumatic stress reactions from developing.

It is normal practice to give operational debriefing to all returned mission partners. The organization can then learn how projects are going and can implement changes where necessary. This chapter will focus on debriefing which is person-centered rather than task-centered. In particular, the chapter will describe the use of Critical Incident Debriefing (CID). The CID structure will first be discussed in relation to its use following traumatic incidents. Then an adapted version of CID will be outlined. This can be used to provide routine debriefing at the end of assignments, even when there have not been any traumatic incidents.

Why Offer Personal Debriefing to Missionaries?

Mission partners are often at increased risk of experiencing traumatic incidents due to the places where they are based. For example, there may be risks related to traffic accidents, illness epidemics, natural disasters, riots, robbery, sexual harassment, war, terrorist activities, evacuation, or land mines. In some areas, expatriates are targeted for hostage taking or assassination. Mission partners may be imprisoned or attacked by those opposed to their religious practices or because they are willing to help "the other side" in a conflict situation. People who have experienced such stressors tend to appreciate an opportunity to reflect on their experiences with a debriefer (Lovell, 1999).

The occurrence of traumatic incidents is not the only reason to offer debriefing. Personal debriefing can also provide an opportunity to discuss longer-term difficulties. In one study (Lovell, 1997), 145 mission partners and aid workers who had completed their assignments were asked what the worst part of their overseas experience had been. Only 8% reported that traumatic events had been the worst part (although many had experienced traumatic incidents). The factors which were most commonly reported as the worst part of the experience were relationship problems (18%), cultural difficulties and frustrations (21%), and dissatisfaction with the organization or the work (17%). Ongoing frustrations may be psychologically more harmful than short-lived traumatic events. Even though the experience as a whole was generally perceived as a positive one, more than 92% of the respondents reported that there were stressful aspects. Personal debriefing can help people who have experienced such stress.

It is not surprising that most mission partners experience stress. Change is stressful. Missionaries experience the change involved in moving between cultures. They often move house several times while preparing to go overseas and during their time abroad. The American Academy of Child and Adolescent Psychiatry (1999, p. 1) reports, "Moving to a new community may be one of the most stress-producing experiences a family faces.... Studies show children who move frequently are more likely to have problems at school." Many missionaries return "home" earlier than they expected, for one reason or another (Taylor, 1997). Even those who return at the time they had expected may have some difficulty readjusting to life back "home." At least 60% report such difficulties (Lovell, 1997).

Because of the stress associated with living in a different culture and readjusting to the "home" culture on return, it has been recommended that all mission partners and aid workers should routinely be offered personal debriefing after they have completed their period of service, to provide support and help during the time of transition (Davidson, 1997; Global Connections, 1997). Mission partners generally appreciate such debriefing (Lovell, 1999). McConnan (1992) found that 73% of aid workers reported feeling inadequately debriefed and supported on their return. Those who were not offered personal debriefing may think that their efforts were not valued, and they may feel unsupported as they readjust to life at home (Lovell, 1997). They may be less likely to remain in contact with the organization or to apply for a further period of service with them.

It is common for expatriates who have recently returned to their country of origin to feel isolated. Personal debriefing can help to reduce such isolation, by providing at least one person who is interested in what they have to say. If they are experiencing difficulties with "reverse culture shock," they can be reassured that this is very common. Such symptoms tend to disappear more quickly among people who realize that they are normal and who do not worry about them. A debriefer can help individuals identify what can be done to relax and deal with stress. The debriefer can also give information about sources of help which are available if symptoms persist or if people want to receive counseling or any other help. Practical information (e.g., about accommodation or financial matters) can be provided, and questions can be answered. Debriefing also provides an opportunity to identify those who are in need of psychiatric help (a very small percentage of mission partners, but a group who should not be overlooked).

Personal debriefing aims to help mission partners integrate their experiences into their life as a whole and perceive the mission experience in a more meaningful way. Debriefing can help bring a sense of closure, so that they are ready to move on to new areas of life.

Structured or Unstructured Debriefing?

Personal debriefing may be offered either in an unstructured manner or using a more structured format. Some debriefers invite participants to talk about any aspects of their overseas experience which they choose, without structuring the process. Others use a more structured approach. Some advantages of a structured approach are listed below. The structure which is recommended is based on Critical Incident Debriefing (summarized below; see also Dyregrov, 1989; Mitchell, 1983), because this is the only form of debriefing which has been widely used, documented, and researched.

Advantages of using the CID structure for debriefing are that it:

- Provides a starting place, so that people don't say, "I've got nothing to talk about."
- Ensures that the most important aspects are discussed.
- Prevents deeper issues (from the past) from becoming the main focus.
- Stops the session from becoming a counseling session.
- Provides people with a sense of security, as the clear structure is explained at the outset, so they know what to expect.
- Allows two debriefers to work together, knowing that they are going in the same direction.
- Works for groups as well as individuals.
- Can be conducted by mental health professionals and those who are not.

- Helps debriefers feel confident, because this is an approach which they understand and use effectively.
- Makes it less likely that debriefers will feel lost or out of their depth or think that they said "the wrong thing," because there is a clear structure to follow.

Now that some of the reasons for choosing the CID format for debriefings have been presented, let us examine this approach in more detail. The CID approach will first be described as it was originally used with *groups of people following a traumatic incident*. This will be followed by a description of how the process can be modified for one-to-one use and for routine debriefing at the end of an assignment when there has not been a particular "critical" (or traumatic) incident.

Theoretical Framework for Critical Incident Debriefing

Most people believe that the world is basically a good and meaningful place and that they are worthwhile as individuals. A traumatic event can shatter these basic assumptions (Janoff-Bulman, 1992). For example, after surviving a disaster, one may think, "I'm not safe," "The world is meaningless and random," or, "I'm a terrible person." Such conclusions produce a sense of ongoing threat. This is associated with increased risk of post-traumatic stress disorder (PTSD) (Ehlers & Clark, 2000). The symptoms of PTSD include trying to avoid reminders of the traumatic event, persistently re-experiencing the event (e.g., in nightmares or in recurrent intrusive images or thoughts about the event), and experiencing increased arousal (e.g., being irritable or "jumpy" or having problems with concentration or sleep).

One theory (see Horowitz, 1975; Janoff-Bulman, 1992) suggests that it is difficult to store a traumatic event in long-term memory, because it does not fit in with pre-existing beliefs about the world. The brain cannot make sense of what has happened, and so the traumatic experience is kept in the "active memory" instead of being stored away. Some people try to avoid thinking about what happened, but because the brain is still trying to process the information, intrusive thoughts and images keep coming to mind.

The CID process encourages individuals to talk about the incident, instead of avoiding thinking about it. This helps them process the event and store it in long-term memory. If you have told your story to someone, your brain no longer needs to keep holding it in active memory, waiting for the information to be "sorted through and filed." (An analogy might be a librarian cataloguing new books. Before the information is catalogued, it sits in a messy pile on the desk, getting in the way when the librarian tries to do other work. Once catalogued, it can be retrieved when you want to retrieve it, but the rest of the time it is out of the way so you can get on with other things. Telling your story helps to organize the information, give it meaning, and "catalogue" it in your mind.)

When a person describes everything that happened, the brain begins to make some sense of the events. This promotes a more rapid recovery. Once the story has been told in detail, the symptoms of avoidance and re-experiencing are likely to decrease. The incident can be placed in the context of the rest of the person's life, instead of taking over his/her whole life. Thoughts such as, "The world is not safe," or, "I am bad," can be re-appraised within this context—for example, "Usually I am safe, but accidents occasionally happen."

Ehlers and Clark (2000, p. 320) report, "It is assumed that, unlike individuals who recover naturally, individuals with persistent PTSD are unable to see the trauma as a time-limited event that does not have global negative implications for their future." A CID can provide a sense of "closure," which may help prevent the development of PTSD. The event is over, the person is no longer under threat, and he/she can start to move on.

Describing details of the traumatic experience may also help the person to make connections and be aware of things which might trigger memories of the trauma in the future. For example, if a woman was raped while looking at a ceiling with a distinctive crack in it, seeing similar cracks in the future might trigger a flashback of the rape (i.e., a feeling that she is experiencing it again). If she does not know why the memory has been triggered, she may feel that she is still in danger. However, if she has spoken about the crack and has thus brought it to conscious awareness, when she next sees a similar crack, it is likely to lead to a memory in context ("that's like the crack I was looking at as I was raped"), rather than an automatic flashback. As she understands the trigger and knows that she is no longer in danger, the memory is less likely to cause distress. A CID does not aim to take away the memory of the event, but it can stop the flashbacks—and flashbacks tend to be perceived as much more distressing than normal memories, because people do not know what has triggered them.

When people try to avoid thinking about a traumatic event or only focus on certain aspects rather than the whole context of the event, they may be more prone to persistent PTSD. Describing the whole experience from start to finish, so that it is all linked together in an autobiographical memory base, appears to reduce the likelihood that isolated stimuli which are associated with the memory (such as a crack or a distinct sound or smell) will trigger a recollection of the event. Thus, putting the memory in context may reduce the likelihood of developing persistent PTSD (see Ehlers & Clark, 2000).

Research has indicated that writing or speaking about personally stressful events can have physical benefits (in terms of improving immune response), as well as psychological benefits. Disclosing both the facts and one's feelings about a stressful event appears to have more physical and psychological health benefits than disclosing just the facts or just the feelings (Pennebaker & Beall, 1986). Although it is beneficial to write about one's reactions to stressful events, it appears to be even more beneficial to talk about them (Esterling, Antoni, Fletcher, Margulies, & Schneiderman, 1994).

After stressful experiences, some people talk freely with friends and family members. However, many people do not feel able to do this. Mission partners who have been under stress often report that they feel unable to tell anyone about it because they are expected to be able to cope with difficulties themselves, and people only want to hear their positive stories. Some feel isolated and do not have anyone they can confide in who would understand their feelings. Some of those who have experienced significant trauma (e.g., acts of gross cruelty) do not want to tell even their spouse or closest friend. They are afraid that the people they tell might be traumatized or worried about their safety. Some long to talk to someone who is outside the situation and who can bring another perspective and yet understand, but they do not know where to find such a person. Some mission partners worry about whether they are "going crazy." They want to talk confidentially to someone who can tell them whether their symptoms of stress are normal. Who is there to talk to? A CID can fill this need.

The Critical Incident Debriefing (CID) Procedure

Mitchell (1983) and Dyregrov (1989) originally described the structure of CID. It was initially designed to be used with a group of people who had experienced a traumatic incident together. It was devised to help prevent difficulties such as PTSD from developing and to help speed up normal recovery. Thus, it is not a "treatment" for people who have already developed difficulties, but rather a preventative measure from which everyone might benefit. The CID process has been used with innumerable different groups of people worldwide.

Mitchell (1983) recommended that debriefing should ideally take place 24–72 hours after the traumatic event. During the first 24 hours, people may be in too much shock to benefit from a CID. However, waiting more than 72 hours is not good either. It is useful to provide CID before people draw firm conclusions such as, "I should have done more." A typical CID lasts between two and three hours, although the timing will vary depending on the size of the group and the amount that people want to say. The process should not be rushed.

Characteristics of the Debriefer

Before describing the process further, we should say a little about the debriefer. Debriefers do not need to be mental health professionals. What is important is that they have been trained in the skills of debriefing (a minimum would be a good two-day training course), have good listening skills, and are non-judgmental, affirming, and able to empathize. Debriefers need to recognize their own limitations and should be willing to refer people for further help if necessary. They should receive supervision. Debriefers can suffer from "secondary traumatization" (i.e., they may feel traumatized by the things they are hearing), if they are not adequately debriefed and supported themselves.

Some people prefer to be debriefed by someone within their organization who understands the way the organization works. Others prefer an external debriefer, who can be told matters which the person does not wish to disclose to anyone in the organization. If possible, it is best to ask the people who are going to be debriefed whether they have a preference for an internal or external debriefer and whether they mind whether the debriefer is male or female. In some cases, no choice can be offered, as only one debriefer is available. That need not be a problem. Issues of gender and organization are much less important than the fact that the debriefer is trained and experienced and demonstrates skill and understanding. Sometimes two debriefers work together. This is especially helpful when debriefing a couple or group or when one debriefer has limited experience. Debriefers should be aware of any potential role conflicts (e.g., if they also know the people they are debriefing in another capacity or if they may be involved in assessing them for a future post).

The credibility of the debriefer may also be important. Fawcett (1999) recommends that debriefers should demonstrate that they understand what is being talked about, ideally through having experienced something similar. For instance, when debriefing someone who is struggling with adjusting to life back "home," it is helpful if the debriefer has had experience living in a different culture. It also helps if the debriefer has some knowledge of the culture in which the participant was based. Mission partners often have a preference to be debriefed by Christian debriefers, who are likely to share their values and biblical framework.

The Seven Steps of Critical Incident Debriefing

The CID process involves seven steps, as outlined below. These steps are designed to allow for a gentle "step down" into discussion of the more emotional aspects, followed by "climbing back up" so that the session ends positively by thinking about support and the future. Those who wish to use this method of debriefing are strongly advised to attend a training course in this procedure, as space does not permit full discussion of it here. The guidelines below are for debriefing following a traumatic incident. Later in the chapter, we will look at how these steps can be adapted for routine end-of-assignment debriefing.

Step 1: Introductions

Introduce yourself. To help establish credibility, it can be helpful to refer to your experience as a debriefer and (when working with mission personnel) any experience you have of working overseas. Ask the others who are present to introduce themselves. *Explain the purpose* of the

CID. *Discuss confidentiality* (e.g., promise that everything they say will be confidential, unless you think there is a risk that they will seriously harm themselves or someone else, or if they disclose that a child is being abused, in which case you are legally or morally required to tell someone). Check that any mobile phones have been turned off. Discuss how much time there is available (e.g., "It's hard to say how long this debriefing will last. Usually we take about two or three hours, but we can be flexible. I don't have anything else booked today. Is there a time that you will have to leave by?")

Explain that you will be using a structure which has been proven to be useful. If debriefing more than one person, say that everyone will be asked the same questions in turn. Point out that it's not an interrogation, and if they don't want to answer a question, that's fine. Ask if there are any questions at this point.

Step 2: The Facts About the Experience

Rather than beginning with an emotional description of the events, participants are eased in gently. Explain that you will ask about their feelings later, but first you would like to hear the facts about what happened. This is especially useful with people who find it difficult to talk about their feelings. It also encourages people to tell the full story, which helps them to process their experiences. *Ask them to describe what happened*, from beginning to end. Prompt them with questions, if necessary: "Where were you? What were you doing? How did you first know something was wrong? What happened next?"

Step 3: The Thoughts During and After the Experience

Ask questions such as, "What was your first thought when you realized something was wrong? What did you expect? *What were your thoughts* during the incident? Was there any point at which you thought you (or a family member or friend) were going to die? What were your thoughts and impressions afterwards?" People often begin to reinterpret their experience simply by talking in this way, and they may start to get rid of negative beliefs.

Step 4: The Sensory Impressions and Emotions

Only now, when people feel more comfortable, are they asked about any particularly memorable sensations from the experience and about their feelings. The purpose is not to make them recall the incident so vividly that they re-experience it during the debriefing. In fact, there is some research that suggests that asking people to keep going over a traumatic event in great detail may have a negative effect, especially if this happens very soon after the event. It may cause them to encode the memory in such vivid detail that it will keep coming back to their mind in a distressing manner. Therefore, it is best not to probe for lots of details. Rather, *ask general questions such as, "Were there any sights, sounds, or smells that were especially vivid or memorable?"* Verbalizing anything which stands out may help them make connections which will prevent flashbacks later. If individuals choose to talk about lots of details, they should be allowed to do so, as that indicates that the memories are already very vivid. Otherwise, keep the questions more general.

Next, *ask about the feelings* they had during the event. If they need prompting, pick up on any emotions which they have already mentioned, or choose a few which you think they might have experienced and ask about those, e.g., "Did you feel any anger, guilt, fear, or helplessness?" Ask, "*What was the worst part* for you?" When they have answered this, add, "What were your feelings then?" You might also ask whether they cried at any point and how they have been feeling about the incident since it happened.

Step 5: Teaching About Normal Symptoms

After step 4, people are helped to move forward. By this time, they may have mentioned some symptoms of stress which they experienced during the incident or shortly afterwards, and perhaps some of these still remain. These might be physical symptoms, emotions, behaviors, thoughts, or beliefs. In step 5, *provide information about normal symptoms of stress*. This is important, because people who think that the symptoms which they are experiencing are a sign of inadequacy are more likely to develop further problems. Those who think, "I must be going mad," or, "I will never get over it," when they have intrusive memories of a traumatic event are more likely to have symptoms of PTSD one year after the event (Ehlers, Mayou, & Bryant, 1998). Among mission partners, one of the best ways of predicting who will go on to develop problems is to find out which people tend to think that they are "overreacting"—these are the people who are likely to develop difficulties (Lovell, 1997). In contrast, people who know that it is "normal" to feel tearful or to have sleeping problems or to get very tired after a period of stress are likely to be kinder to themselves and adjust well.

Step 5 involves explaining that symptoms of stress are normal after a major change or a traumatic event. It may be useful to *provide a list of common symptoms of stress*, such as the one in the appendix to this chapter, and ask whether the participants have experienced any of these symptoms (either during the incident or since then). Point out that some people do not experience any of these, and that's OK, but many people experience at least a few symptoms after a time of stress. These symptoms are normal, and usually they disappear by themselves as time passes. If individuals have intrusive recollections about an experience, they do not need to try to push such thoughts out of their mind (as that tends to cause more intrusive thoughts). It is better just to let the thoughts come and go, without worrying about them or trying to fight them.

In some cases, it is useful to ask general questions to help people talk about changes which they have noticed in their lives. For example, you might ask, "How do you think the experience has affected you?" If their partner or family were also involved in the incident, it may be appropriate to ask how they have been affected.

Sometimes it becomes apparent that the persons being debriefed feel guilty about the way they behaved. For example, they may have run away from a crisis instead of helping other people, or they might feel that their mistake caused other people to suffer. It can be appropriate during this teaching stage to point out that in times of stress, people often respond automatically and in ways that are out of character. In a crisis, we are unable to think as we usually would. Trying to save oneself can be an automatic instinct, and people often make mistakes when under stress. You may be able to reassure them that what they did is completely understandable. If there are major issues of guilt, it may be appropriate to recommend that they receive counseling.

Step 6: Discussing Coping Strategies and Future Planning

After discussing symptoms of stress, the next step is to *discuss strategies for coping*. Ask participants what usually helps them to relax, and encourage them to do things which help reduce stress reactions. For people who are under constant stress or who have very busy lifestyles with little time for relaxation built in, it may be useful to work through the material in some of the other chapters in this book (especially the section on Self and Mutual Care) to identify the underlying causes of stress or busyness and to help individuals deal with these appropriately. This step is also the place to *discuss the support which is available* to them. Ask about their personal support. Whom can they talk to, especially about their feelings?

Some people find it hard to move on after a stressful experience. They may stop going out. They may avoid meeting people or getting involved in activities, because they feel they do not have the energy. If this behavior persists for a number of weeks, the individuals are at risk of becoming depressed. It can be helpful to encourage them gently to start doing some of the things which they enjoy and to build up more social contacts. This can be done gradually, as rest time will also be needed, but some progress should be encouraged so that people feel they are moving on. Moderate activity (such as walking or swimming) may help to reduce tension, depression, and fatigue.

People should be asked about *their plans for the future*. Although it is unwise to make important decisions immediately after a stressful experience, it is still useful to ask about future plans. After a traumatic experience, some people lack hope and fulfillment. Asking what they would like to do in the future may help to dismantle this sense of hopelessness and prompt them to set new goals. If they don't feel hopeless, they may still appreciate having someone help them think about their plans.

You should also *describe how they can obtain counseling or other professional support*, should they want to receive further help. Stress-related symptoms usually subside over a period of a few weeks. Individuals should be advised to seek professional help if significant symptoms persist beyond this or become worse or significantly interfere with their life, work, or relationships. Tell them whom they can contact (e.g., a specific person at the organization or their physician). If they appear to require immediate help (e.g., if they are contemplating suicide), arrange professional help.

Step 7: Ending the Session

The debriefing has focused on the negative aspects of the experience, but there are sometimes also positive aspects. It is good to give an opportunity to reflect on these, *by asking if anything positive has come out of this incident*, or if they have learned anything from it. For example, some people state that surviving a difficult experience has given them a stronger sense of gratitude or a greater determination to enjoy every day. Some people report a deeper appreciation of their family or a sense of achievement and self-confidence.

Ask if they have *any other comments or questions*. If you have planned a follow-up session, mention the details at this point. (It can be helpful to follow people up after a few weeks, either in person or by phone or email.)

To close, *summarize the debriefing* (perhaps by reminding them that symptoms of stress are normal and encouraging them to try out strategies for dealing with their stress). Ask how they are feeling now. If appropriate, say that it's not unusual for some people to feel worse at the end of a debriefing, since memories of the trauma will have been brought to mind. This is helpful in the long term and is part of the recovery process. Thank them for sharing their experiences, and end the session (in prayer, if appropriate).

After everyone has left, *evaluate* the session and think about any lessons you have learned. Then *receive some debriefing* yourself, because it is not easy to listen to difficult experiences. Find someone whom you can talk with about any emotions the session evoked for you. Be sure to maintain confidentiality as you talk.

Debriefing Groups and Individuals

The CID procedure was originally designed to be used with groups. After the introductions, each person in turn is asked to describe what happened to him/her. After each person has spoken about the facts, the debriefer asks each person in turn about his/her thoughts, and so on.

An advantage of the group format is that group members have the opportunity to discover that other people are experiencing similar reactions. This helps people realize that they are not "weak," but merely experiencing normal symptoms following an abnormal event. Groups of people with shared experience of trauma can be very supportive. Each person learns that he/she is not alone, and this realization can facilitate recovery.

A group debriefing can also help people piece together what has happened, as they gain extra information from others who were present. This may help to dismantle negative beliefs such as, "The problems were all my fault." In addition, group debriefing is much less time-consuming for the debriefer than conducting a separate debriefing with each individual.*

However, there are also many situations when it is preferable to debrief an individual, a couple, or a family, rather than a larger group. Sometimes the traumatic event was only experienced by one person. A mission partner on furlough might want to receive debriefing related to an incident which took place overseas, and this might only be possible as an individual debriefing. Some people feel uncomfortable speaking about personal matters in a group setting. During an individual debriefing, there is more time available to identify coping strategies for that one person, without pressuring the person to speed up responses to allow time for everyone else to speak. The CID structure can be used with individuals as well as with groups.

What Is the Evidence for the Effectiveness of CID?

Many papers have been published showing that participants *report* finding the CID process very helpful. It is more difficult, though, to assess whether people who received a CID are likely to have less severe symptoms of stress afterwards. A review identified eight studies in which people who had experienced a trauma had been randomly assigned to receive either individual debriefing or no debriefing. Taking the eight studies together, the reviewers concluded that there was no evidence that debriefing was useful for the prevention of mental health problems, but they added that the "quality of these studies was generally poor" (Wessely, Rose, & Bisson, 2000). The debriefing generally lasted for only 20-60 minutes, which was probably too short to be of great benefit. In at least two studies, the debriefing also occurred too soon, within the first 24 hours after an injury. Relatively inexperienced debriefers were often used, and there were several other research difficulties. Therefore, it would be wrong to conclude from these findings that debriefing is not beneficial.

One study conducted specifically on the debriefing of mission partners indicates that debriefing may in fact have significant health benefits (Lovell, 1999). In this study, 33 missionaries who had received a routine CID following their return home completed anonymous questionnaires evaluating the debriefing. None of the respondents described the debriefing as a negative experience, although six felt that it was unnecessary for them. The remaining 27 (82%) reported that they found the debriefing helpful or very helpful. Forty percent of the respondents reported that there had been a significant positive change after they had received debriefing. For example, they had experienced fewer flashbacks afterwards or felt, "It gave me permission to feel the way I was feeling—a sense of release and relief."

The respondents also completed a widely used questionnaire, the Impact of Event Scale (Horowitz, Wilner, & Alvarez, 1979). This measures symptoms associated with PTSD. The scores were compared with responses from a group of 145 returned overseas workers who had not been offered a CID. The results showed that 24% of the non-debriefed group were experiencing a clinically serious level of unpleasant intrusive memories about their experience overseas, compared with only 7% of the debriefed group. Likewise, 25% of the non-debriefed group reported clini-

* See Fawcett (1999) for further insights concerning group debriefing.

cally significant levels of avoidance, compared with only 7% of those who had been debriefed. These differences could not be explained by differences such as age, gender, or different experiences within the two groups.

Debriefing Individuals After Their Return "Home"

It is possible to consider the whole overseas experience as a "critical incident" and to use a modification of the CID structure for routine debriefing of returned mission partners.* The focus should not be just on traumatic episodes. Day-to-day stresses should also be considered. A number of mission partners have said that they found it a great relief to learn that their whole experience overseas could be considered as a critical incident. This helped them to understand why they developed stress-related symptoms, although they had not experienced any particular "traumatic incident." I recommend adapting the CID structure as follows for routine debriefing:

1. Introductions

At the end of the "introductions" stage, ask for some basic details about the work overseas, if you don't already know—e.g., where they were, how long they were away, what they were doing, and when they returned "home." Then invite them to give an overview of their time overseas, by describing their experiences (in brief).

2. Identifying What Was Most Troubling

If critical incidents or difficulties were mentioned during the overview, list these and say that you would like to spend time talking about each one. Ask if there was anything else that was troubling or stressful which they would like to talk about in more detail as well. If no particular difficulties emerged during the overview, say something like, "As you look back on the whole experience, what was worst or most stressful or troubling for you—either specific events or stressful parts of the experience?" Encourage them to choose about three issues.

3. Facts, Thoughts, Feelings

Say that you would like to talk through each of the stressful/troubling factors which have been identified. Ask them which one they would like to start with. Take this issue, and ask about the facts, thoughts, then feelings, as you would in the traditional CID procedure. Then do the same with each of the other issues. Don't rush!

4. Any Other Aspect You Want to Talk About?

After discussing all of the identified topics, ask whether there is anything else that the individual would like to speak about. Give an opportunity to talk about issues which might not fit into the CID structure so well—e.g., problems with the organization, unmet expectations, the fact that they were bereaved while overseas, spiritual issues, or any other factor.

5. Symptoms

Ask whether they experienced any stress-related symptoms at any point while overseas or since returning home (see appendix).

6. Normalizing and Teaching

As in a standard CID, state that symptoms are normal and that having them does not mean that they are overreacting. Talk about coping strategies and ways to help reduce stress. Where there have been multiple stressors, processing all of them might not be finished during the debriefing. Encourage individuals to continue to process their experiences afterwards, and talk about how they can do this. Ask what support is available to them.

---

* See Armstrong (2000) on multiple stressor debriefing.

7. Positive or Meaningful Aspects

Ask whether there was anything positive about their time overseas. Positives may already have emerged during the overview, in which case you could ask more about them and ask what was best. Was anything learned? Were friendships formed? Were there ways (however small) in which they feel they helped someone or made a difference? Are they glad they went?

If they appear to think that their time overseas was meaningless (which is rare), try to explore whether there were any positive or meaningful aspects at all (e.g., anything that the organization has learned or recommendations that could be made to help people in the future). Helping them to reframe the experience as a meaningful one may assist in preventing future depression. It may be useful to suggest that they might want to write down anything positive or meaningful which has come out of their experience. If they remain entirely negative, professional help should be recommended.

8. Returning "Home"

Ask how the return "home" has been. If they have not had many previous experiences of reentry, discuss "reverse culture shock" and the readjustment process. Prepare them for the fact that some people might not be interested in their experiences. A handout or relevant book (e.g., Jordan, 1992) may be helpful. You may also be able to direct them to other resources and useful information (e.g., in areas of finance and employment). Ask about any worries.

9. The Future

Ask about future plans. Some mission partners greatly value discussing their plans with someone who can bring an outside perspective. For example, they may feel under pressure from their organization to return overseas very quickly, and they might value reassurance that they need time to rest before taking on further demands or making big decisions. Those who feel guilty about having some time off should be told that rest is strongly recommended after working overseas. Failure to rest adequately can lead to significant health problems.

If it seems appropriate, a follow-up session can be offered. Also tell them how they can obtain further help (e.g., counseling) if they want it. Point out that although they might not want more help now, they might decide later that they would like assistance. Ask whether they have any questions or anything else they want to say. Occasionally people may ask if you would provide some general feedback to the organization based on their experiences or if you would make a concern known. If this is requested, it can be very helpful, although you should be careful about issues of confidentiality.

10. Close

Summarize some of the important things which have arisen from the session. Ask individuals how they are feeling now.

Some Issues to Consider

1. Who Should Be Offered Personal Debriefing?

Many people say that they did not realize that they would benefit from debriefing until after they had received it (Lovell, 1999). Nearly everyone can benefit from having a skilled listener to help them explore their experiences and reactions. Ideally, personal debriefing should be offered to every returned mission partner. There are two reasons that it should not be offered just to those who are known to have experienced a "traumatic incident." Firstly, the organization is often not aware when there has been an incident which the individual regards as traumatic. Secondly, the whole overseas experience and return "home" can be regarded as a "critical incident" which involves change and stress. Nearly all mission partners who have been overseas for more than six months report that there were some stressful parts of the experience, and the majority also report some difficulties readjusting on their return "home" (Lovell, 1997).

If personal debriefing is available only to those who request it, most people will not request it, either because they think that they do not "need" it, or because they do not want people to think they "have problems." It is better to arrange debriefing for everyone, allowing people to "opt out" rather than "opt in." Some organizations require those who opt out to sign a disclaimer form, stating that they were offered debriefing but refused. This illustrates how seriously they take debriefing.

When debriefing a team, it is best if everybody in the team attends. If a team went through a difficult incident and two members were elsewhere at the time, it is wise to invite the members who were absent to join the rest of the group for debriefing. It will be helpful for them to hear about what happened. They may have felt guilty about not being there to help, or they may have experienced other strong feelings which they can share with the group. This will help keep the team from dividing into separate groups (those who were there and those who were not). It is preferable that no other observers be present during a debriefing. People tend to feel inhibited if someone has been invited to "come and observe."

2. Debriefing for Children

It is common to attempt to shelter children from distress by trying not to mention concerns in front of them. However, when a family has been involved in a traumatic or stressful experience, even young children can pick up that something is wrong. It is much more frightening for them to know that something is the matter but not know what (allowing their imagination to run riot), than for them to hear about what is happening and share their own thoughts and feelings. Therefore, it is best to include children in discussions about difficulties or changes and to allow them to ask questions. This does not have to be in a formal debriefing setting. Very young children can be given an opportunity to draw what has happened, or act it out with toys, and to share their feelings. They should receive reassurance.

Older children and adolescents may benefit from sharing in a family debriefing, and they may also appreciate a separate debriefing away from their parents. (The parents may also receive a separate debriefing if there are especially sensitive details which the children do not need to hear.) Yule (1992) found that children who had received debriefing reported fewer fears, less avoidance, and fewer intrusive memories five months after a disaster than children who were not debriefed.

If children appear to be experiencing significant problems following a traumatic event, it is important to refer them on for further help. The family physician may be able to refer them to a psychiatrist or a clinical psychologist. For information about how to help children cope with trauma and death, see Goodall (1995) and Kilbourn (1995).

When a family has returned home after a pleasant period of overseas service with no traumatic incidents, it can still be helpful to include the children in a family debriefing. They can be helped to explore the similarities and differences between the cultures they have lived in; their feelings of loss at leaving friends (and perhaps places and possessions they have loved); and their attempts to adjust to life in a new culture and make new friends. They may have strong feelings (perhaps of anger or grief). Foyle (2001) and Pollock and Van Reken (1999) provide some useful guidance on helping children and adolescents with such transitions. Pollock and Van Reken also list organizations which provide support for children in this position. It should be remembered that the place which is considered "home" by the parents might not be perceived as "home" by the children. For older children, it can be a source of great frustration when other people constantly refer to them as having "come home," when in fact they are now in a foreign country.

3. Venue and Timing

Debriefing should take place in a comfortable, well-lit room where there will be no interruptions. If there has been a traumatic incident, it can be helpful to offer debriefing near the site (as long as it is safe), rather than evacuating people for debriefing. The ideal time to debrief mission partners appears to be a few days after a traumatic incident, or between one and three weeks after their return "home" (when they have had time to overcome jetlag, visit family and friends, and begin to readjust).

4. Cross-Cultural Issues

Interventions which are offered in the Western world may be inappropriate in other settings (Bracken & Petty, 1998; Ober, Peeters, Archer, & Kelly, 2000; Summerfield, 1999). The definition of what is "traumatic" may vary from one society to another. For example, the death of a relative in the war front may be experienced as a triumph and not a tragedy if the war is seen as a matter of religious significance (De Silva, 1993). In some cultures, rape victims and their families are considered shameful, and the victim may even be put to death if the rape is disclosed. To offer the victim an opportunity to talk about the rape might be terrifying. Even if the issue is not sexual assault, there may be a reluctance to disclose intimate material outside a close family setting. Alternatively, people may reject offers of psychological help because their main concerns are for food, housing, safety, and education or employment. They may feel angry that resources are being "wasted" in offering psychological support when they need help with more practical matters first.

When "specialists" are brought in to "help" people after a disaster, local methods of coping are sometimes swept aside. This can leave people feeling devalued. In subsequent occasions of distress, they may feel less able to take initiative and support each other. In contrast, when local people are encouraged to believe that they can do something for themselves, and their ways of coping are validated, they are likely to feel empowered, enthusiastic, and more hopeful about the future. As long as the practices are not anti-biblical or harmful (physically, psychologically, or spiritually), it may be beneficial to encourage people to use the resources which are already available to them, offering any additional resources to supplement these rather than replace them.

Although CID has been used in a variety of cultures, empirical research on its effectiveness in non-Western cultures is sparse. If it is decided that debriefing should be offered in addition to local means of support, one should discuss its appropriateness first with people from that culture. It is important to consider whether the process should be modified in order to make it culturally appropriate. It is helpful if one of the debriefers is familiar with the culture of the person who is being debriefed. If the debriefer is not from the relevant culture, he/she should at least try to gain an understanding of the culture in advance—including finding out about such issues as the use of eye contact and humor, and whether decisions (e.g., concerning further help) tend to be made by individuals or by a group.

In some traditions, people will not cry in front of others or discuss their feelings openly, as this is perceived as a criticism of God's will and is believed to weaken the family in their struggle to survive. When debriefing someone who holds such a belief, it would not be helpful to say, "Crying is useful and normal," as the person may conclude that the debriefer is either foolish or a liar. The individual may, however, find it helpful during the "teaching" stage to consider the health benefits of crying and to look at the place of crying in the Bible. This should occur as a discussion, rather than a monologue from the debriefer. The debriefer should make every effort to understand the views expressed and not cause offense.

In certain cultures, vengeance is routinely sought after a perceived "wrong," and forgiveness is regarded as a weakness. Again, when working within a Christian framework, it might be possible to explore these ideas during the teaching stage.

It is useful to be aware of any relevant rituals which may be observed in a culture, such as rituals concerning bereavement. Such rituals may be very helpful (Lovell, Hemmings, & Hill, 1993). Some communities use story-telling, plays, dance, or music to express emotions (Blomquist, 1995). One should also be aware of the normal stress symptoms in the particular culture. For instance, people might talk about headaches, abdominal pain, and feeling weak rather than discussing emotional pain. Some cultures do not even have a word for "depression." In others, exhibiting anxiety means loss of face, so emotional distress is translated into physical pain. It is helpful to try to understand what people perceive as the cause of different symptoms. For example, Blomquist (1995) discovered that some Liberians who experienced flashbacks or other intrusive thoughts believed that their enemies were using supernatural forces to cause them to feel as if they were re-experiencing a painful event. It helps if the debriefer is aware of such beliefs.

If a translator is to be used, that person should be selected very carefully. Translators need the ability to translate sensitively, listen patiently, and be able to cope with hearing and repeating distressing information. This process has the potential to cause them to feel traumatized themselves, and so they need to be debriefed afterwards. It should also be remembered that debriefing through a translator doubles the amount of time needed for the debriefing.

Debriefers should always try to find out in advance what sources of follow-up support and professional help are available in the area. It is unethical to raise expectations of further help when no such assistance is available. If there really is no possibility of ongoing support, one should question whether debriefing should be offered at all. Even if there is a possibility of professional help, one should realize that it may be considered unacceptable if it is based on a worldview which is not in harmony with the beliefs of the individual.

Evaluation is especially important after debriefing in a new context. One should aim to reflect and learn from each new experience.

5. Providing Answers

A debriefer does not need to provide answers. The purpose is to walk with those being debriefed until they feel heard and until they have begun to integrate the stressful experience into their life and feel ready to move on.

A debriefing is usually not the best place to try to respond to spiritual doubts. The person being debriefed may ask questions such as, "Did God put us there?" or, "Why did God allow this to happen?" A quick, easy answer will probably not help—that would be like putting a little tissue on a deep wound. The person may be trying to express a feeling (e.g., anger or confusion) rather than seeking a response. Spiritual insights generally are not absorbed while individuals are in a stage of shock or anger. They may need to go through a time of questioning in order to find their own answers and come out stronger. The debriefer can help simply by listening and by stating that difficult experiences often do bring up this sort of question, which takes time to be worked through. If the ones being debriefed say that they really want to discuss this matter further, the debriefer can suggest someone who might be able to help. The debriefer should try to be aware of his/her own issues and emotions. For instance, some people find it difficult to cope with spiritual doubts and want to feel that they have "fixed it." They should remember that they do not need to "make everything all right." They should aim to create an atmosphere where people feel able to raise questions and doubts without feeling guilty.

6. What About Other Forms of Debriefing?

The debriefing structure described above is not the only effective form of debriefing. Other forms such as unstructured debriefing or group debriefing may also be effective, although they have not been subject to rigorous research.

7. A Biblical Framework for Debriefing

We are called to care for each other (e.g., Isa. 61:1-2; John 13:35; 21:16; 2 Cor. 1:3-4; Gal. 6:2). Debriefing is a way of showing we care. Listening is central to debriefing, and the Bible teaches us to listen (Prov. 18:13; James 1:19). In modern society, it can be difficult to find someone willing to make time to really listen. Mission partners often feel isolated. Listening breaks down this isolation. The Bible affirms that there is a place for both reviewing the past together (Isa. 43:26) and moving on to new things (Isa. 43:19). Both occur during debriefing.

Debriefing involves teaching that emotions are normal and valid. The Bible also teaches this. Ecclesiastes 3:4 reminds us that there is "a time to weep and a time to laugh." The Bible contains plenty of anger, fear, and tears (e.g., in the Psalms). Jesus did not condemn a man who admitted unbelief, but allowed him to express this (Mark 9:24). He taught by example that it was all right to cry (Luke 19:41; John 11:35; Heb. 5:7). He expressed anguish in the Garden of Gethsemane and said that His soul was "overwhelmed with sorrow" (Matt. 26:38). In past times and different cultures, people have *known* that it is normal to feel certain emotions after trauma. Today, some people need to be told this explicitly.

Here are some biblical examples of components of debriefing (or telling one's story):

- After the crucifixion, two disciples were walking down the Emmaus Road (Luke 24:13-24). Jesus joined them and asked what had happened. That was not for His benefit—He already knew what had taken place. His question gave them the opportunity to tell their story—both the facts and their feelings of disappointment. Jesus then helped them put things into context.
- Elijah experienced a death threat (1 Kings 19:2) and fled for his life. He was afraid, and he prayed that he might die. Later, after Elijah's physical needs had been met, God asked what was going on. Elijah told God his story—twice (vv. 10, 14). Then God moved Elijah to think about the future and told him that he would not be alone because there were 7,000 other believers (v. 18). Moreover, God directed Elijah to Elisha (v. 16ff), who would give him more support.
- A woman who had been bleeding for 12 years (possibly following trauma) touched Jesus (Luke 8:43-48). He asked, "Who touched Me?" Why did He ask? Not to embarrass her, but to allow her to tell her story, so that she would gain emotional healing as well as physical healing.

8. The Context

Finally, it is vital that we realize that debriefing alone is not enough to ensure that mission partners are receiving adequate care. Debriefing should be just one component of a package of care (Gamble, Lovell, Lankester, & Keystone, 2001), including:

- Careful selection and placement.
- Adequate training (about the relevant culture, culture shock, conflict resolution, negotiation skills, problem solving, working in teams, etc.) and medical preparation (vaccinations, etc.).
- Security briefing, including teaching on do's and don'ts to increase safety, and written contingency plans to be followed in the case of evacuation, hostage taking, or other crises (see Goode, 1995); also a briefing on dealing with stress and critical incidents.
- Ongoing support while on assignment.
- CID following any traumatic incident.

■ Preparation for return "home"; debriefing one to three weeks after returning home.

■ Follow-up; continuing care/referral for further help if required.

Reflection and Discussion

1. How much responsibility do mission organizations have to provide debriefing for their mission partners?

2. When and how should people be offered routine debriefing—e.g., individual or group, before or after they return home?

3. What scriptural passages support some of the components of Critical Incident Debriefing?

4. How might the Critical Incident Debriefing model be adapted for different cultures in which you or your organization work?

5. When might debriefers need to take a break from debriefing?

Appendix Common Symptoms of Stress

Physical

- Tiredness
- Difficulty sleeping
- Nightmares
- Headaches
- Back pain
- Inability to relax
- Dry mouth and throat
- Feeling sick or dizzy
- Sweating and trembling
- Stomachache and diarrhea
- Loss of appetite or overeating
- Feeling very hot or cold
- Pounding heart
- Shortness of breath
- Shallow, fast breathing
- Hypervigilance
- Frequent need to urinate
- Missed menstruation
- Increased risk of ulcers, high blood pressure, coronary heart disease

Emotional

- Depression
- Tearfulness or feeling a desire to cry but being unable to
- Mood swings
- Anger (at self or others)
- Agitation
- Impatience
- Guilt and shame
- Feeling helpless and inadequate
- Feeling different or isolated from others
- Feeling shocked
- Feeling overwhelmed or unable to cope
- Feeling rushed all the time
- Anxiety (feeling fearful, tense, nervous)
- Panics and phobias
- Loss of sense of humor
- Boredom
- Lowered self-esteem
- Loss of confidence
- Unrealistic expectations (of self and others)
- Self-centeredness
- Insecurity
- Feeling that life is a waste of time and there is no point bothering
- Feeling vulnerable
- Feeling worthless

Behavioral

- Withdrawal from others or becoming dependent on them
- Irritability and cynicism
- Critical attitude
- Lack of self-care
- Nail biting
- Picking at spots
- Speaking in slow, monotonous voice or fast, agitated speech
- Taking unnecessary risks
- Trying to do several things at once
- Lack of initiative
- Working long hours
- Poor productivity
- Loss of job satisfaction
- Carelessness
- Absenteeism
- Increased smoking or use of alcohol or drugs
- Promiscuity or loss of interest in sex
- Excessive spending or engagement in other activities to try not to think about the stress

- Sitting doing nothing or spending a lot of time in bed
- Self-harm or suicidal behavior

Thoughts

- Difficulty concentrating and remembering
- Difficulty making decisions
- Putting things off
- Thinking in "all or nothing" terms
- Extreme sensitivity to criticism
- Self-critical thoughts
- Doubting own ability and that of others
- Inflexibility
- Loss of interest in previously enjoyed activities
- Pessimism
- Preoccupation with health
- Expecting to die young
- Trying to avoid thinking about problems
- Intrusive thoughts about difficulties
- Confusion and disorientation
- Feeling that time has slowed down or speeded up
- Hindsight thinking ("Why didn't I…")
- Hopelessness
- Suicidal thoughts

Spiritual

- Spiritual dryness—no excitement
- Lack of thanksgiving
- Unforgiveness
- Bitterness
- Feeling far from God
- Difficulty reading Bible or praying
- Changes in beliefs
- Legalistic, ritualistic
- Anger at God
- Doubts
- Questioning the meaning of life
- Loss of purpose
- Giving up faith
- Despair

References

American Academy of Child and Adolescent Psychiatry (1999). *Children and family moves* (Handout 14). Washington, DC: AACAP. www.aacap.org/publications/factsfam/fmlymove.htm.

Armstrong, K. (2000). Multiple stressor debriefing as a model for intervention. In B. Raphael & J. Wilson (Eds.), *Psychological debriefing: Theory, practice and evidence* (pp. 290-301). Cambridge, UK: Cambridge University Press.

Blomquist, C. (1995). A community of care: Ministry to children in war. In P. Kilbourn (Ed.), *Healing the children of war* (pp. 215-224). Monrovia, CA: MARC.

Bracken, P., & Petty, C. (Eds.). (1998). *Rethinking the trauma of war*. London, UK: Save the Children/Free Association Books.

Davidson, S. (1997). *People in Aid: Code of best practice*. London, UK: Overseas Development Institute.

De Silva, P. (1993). Post-traumatic stress disorders: Cross-cultural aspects. *International Review of Psychiatry, 5*, 217-229.

Dyregrov, A. (1989). Caring for helpers in disaster situations: Psychological debriefing. *Disaster Management, 2*, 25-30.

Ehlers, A., & Clark, D. (2000). A cognitive model of posttraumatic stress disorder. *Behaviour Research and Therapy, 38*, 319-345.

Ehlers, A., Mayou, R., & Bryant, B. (1998). Psychological predictors of chronic posttraumatic stress disorder after motor vehicle accidents. *Journal of Abnormal Psychology, 107*, 508-519.

Esterling, B., Antoni, M., Fletcher, M., Margulies, S., & Schneiderman, N. (1994). Emotional disclosure through writing or speaking modulates latent Epstein-Barr virus antibody titers. *Journal of Consulting and Clinical Psychology, 62*, 130-140.

Fawcett, G. (1999). *Ad-Mission: The briefing and debriefing of teams of missionaries and aid workers*. Harpenden, UK: Author.

Foyle, M. (2001). *Honourably wounded: Stress among Christian workers*. London, UK: Monarch Books.

Gamble, K., Lovell, D., Lankester, T., & Keystone, J. (2001). Aid workers, expatriates and travel. In J. Zukerman & A. Zukerman (Eds.), *Principles and practice of travel medicine*. Chichester, UK: John Wiley & Sons.

Global Connections (1997). *Code of best practice in short-term mission*. London, UK: Global Connections. www.globalconnections.co.uk.

Goodall, J. (1995). *Children and grieving*. London, UK: Scripture Union.

Goode, G. (1995). Guidelines for crisis and contingency management. *International Journal of Frontier Missions, 14*, 211-216.

Horowitz, M. (1975). Intrusive and repetitive thoughts after experimental stress. *Archives of General Psychiatry, 32*, 1457-1463.

Horowitz, M., Wilner, N., & Alvarez, W. (1979). Impact of event scale: A measure of subjective distress. *Psychosomatic Medicine, 41*, 209-218.

Janoff-Bulman, R. (1992). *Shattered assumptions: Towards a new psychology of trauma.* New York, NY: The Free Press.

Jordan, P. (1992). *Re-entry*. Seattle, WA: YWAM.

Kilbourn, P. (Ed.). (1995). *Healing the children of war*. Monrovia, CA: MARC.

Lovell, D. (1997). *Psychological adjustment among returned overseas aid workers.* Unpublished doctoral dissertation, University of Wales, Bangor, UK.

———. (1999). *Evaluation of Tearfund's critical incident debriefing process.* Internal paper produced for Tearfund, Teddington, UK.

Lovell, D., Hemmings, G., & Hill, A. (1993). Bereavement reactions of female Scots and Swazis. *British Journal of Medical Psychology, 66*, 259-274.

McConnan, I. (1992). *Recruiting health workers for emergencies and disaster relief in developing countries.* London, UK: International Health Exchange.

Mitchell, J. (1983). When disaster strikes: The critical incident debriefing process. *Journal of the Emergency Medical Services, 8*, 36-39.

Ober, C., Peeters, L., Archer, R., & Kelly, K. (2000). Debriefing in different cultural frameworks: Responding to acute trauma in Australian Aboriginal contexts. In B. Raphael & J. Wilson (Eds.), *Psychological debriefing: Theory, practice and evidence* (pp. 241-253). Cambridge, UK: Cambridge University Press.

Pennebaker, J., & Beall, S. (1986). Confronting a traumatic event: Toward an understanding of inhibition and disease. *Journal of Abnormal Psychology, 95*, 274-281.

Pollock, D., & Van Reken, R. (1999). *The third culture kid experience.* Yarmouth, ME: Intercultural Press.

Summerfield, D. (1999). A critique of seven assumptions behind psychological trauma programmes in war-affected areas. *Social Science and Medicine, 48*, 1449-1462.

Taylor, W. (Ed.). (1997). *Too valuable to lose: Exploring the causes and cures of missionary attrition.* Pasadena, CA: William Carey Library.

Wessely, S., Rose, S., & Bisson, J. (2000). Brief psychological interventions ("debriefing") for trauma-related symptoms and the prevention of post traumatic stress disorder (Cochrane Review). In *The Cochrane Library,* Issue 3. Oxford, UK: Update Software.

Yule, W. (1992). Post-traumatic stress disorder in child survivors of shipping disasters: The sinking of the "Jupiter." *Journal of Psychotherapy and Psychosomatics, 57*, 200-205.

Debbie Lovell Hawker *is a clinical psychologist working for the University of Oxford, England. She spends part of her time working with mission partners, providing psychological assessments, individual and group debriefing, and longer-term treatment. She provides supervision for a number of mission and development organizations and also makes short overseas trips each year to provide member care on the field. Qualifications: B.A., Ph.D., D.Clin.Psy., C.Psychol. Email: debbie.lovell@psychiatry.oxford.ac.uk.*

Many thanks to Marjory Foyle and Graham Fawcett for their helpful comments on the first draft of this chapter.

45

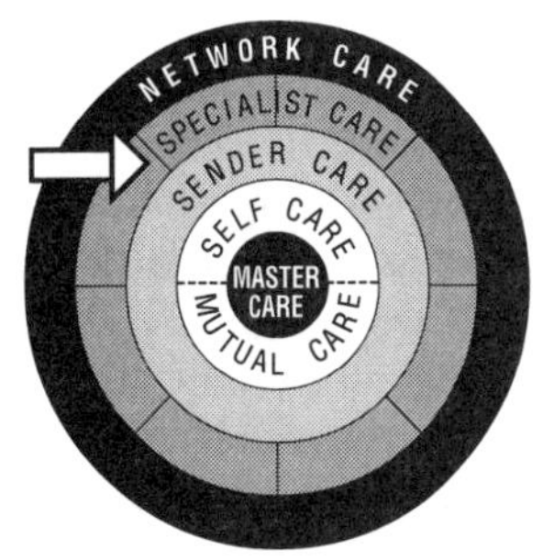

Human Rights Advocacy in Missions

Wilfred Wong

Mission personnel can play a key role in supporting the persecuted church. The seven guidelines for advocacy in this chapter, along with the case study, illustrate how to provide practical help to those who are suffering because of their religious faith.

"I just returned from Sulawesi yesterday, where I met with leaders who oversee about 2,000 church planters, pastors, and evangelists in the Maluku islands, Indonesia. They have lost about 100 workers in the last several months. Some were burnt alive and others cut to pieces. One evangelist had his head cut off and placed in a public place with his genitals in his mouth. One pastor lost his children and grandchildren. Another pastor was forcibly circumcised along with his children, including his five-year-old girl. I am just so overwhelmed with pain in my heart. As I sat with them, I couldn't bear to listen. But even more painful is what one pastor asked me: 'Why doesn't anyone care for us?'" *

There is nothing new about the persecution of Christians. Such actions have taken place since the birth of the church 2,000 years ago. More Christians have been imprisoned, tortured, and killed for their faith in the 20th and 21st centuries than at any other time in the church's history. The intensity of anti-Christian persecution during the 20th century gave rise to various organizations working to assist the suffering church in different ways, including the smuggling of Bibles and other Christian literature, the supply of humanitarian aid, and human rights advocacy.

To engage in human rights advocacy is basically to raise concerns about human rights violations and to call on the responsible government to rectify this injustice. It also involves getting parliamentarians, governments, and members of the public in other countries to put pressure on the responsible government to end the human rights violations.

---

* Report from Beram Kumar, Member Care Network/Malaysia, February, 2001. Used by permission.

Human rights advocacy can be done at different levels, ranging from very public and strong pressure to quiet negotiations, to persuade a government to stop the human rights abuses. Some examples of human rights advocacy organizations are Jubilee Campaign, Christian Solidarity Worldwide, and Amnesty International.

I work with the Jubilee Campaign, a non-profit organization that was set up in 1986 to campaign for persecuted Christians around the world. We started during the Cold War, and inevitably many of the cases we took on during this period originated in the Communist world. Much has changed since the break-up of the Soviet Union and the fall of Communist governments in Eastern Europe. For a while, it was thought that perhaps there would be much less anti-Christian persecution in the world, but today we see just the opposite with the rise of Islamic militancy (as in the horrific cases mentioned above), Hindu extremism, and die-hard Communist regimes in Asia continuing to oppress Christians.

It's not all doom and gloom, though. One reason that there is persecution in so many different countries today is that the church is expanding its frontiers throughout the world. More than at any other time in the history of Christianity, we can truly regard the church as a global community. It is because the church is growing in places traditionally hostile to the gospel that the backlash of persecution occurs in many of these locations. Governments or religious extremists feel threatened by the spread of Christianity and try all sorts of methods to stop its growth. Tactics range from murder and genocide, as in Sudan, to more subtle measures, such as the introduction of restrictive laws on church registration, which is common in a number of Central Asian countries.

Today, the list of countries where Jubilee Campaign is advocating for persecuted Christians is long. It includes Sudan, Pakistan, Uzbekistan, Turkmenistan, Saudi Arabia, China, Laos, Vietnam, Indonesia, Sri Lanka, India, Nepal, and Egypt. Missionaries often find that the growth of the church in their mission field invites the escalation of religious persecution. This is not surprising, given that there are both demonic and earthly forces deeply opposed to the spread of the gospel.

Solidarity With Christians

As Christians, I believe we must show solidarity with other believers who are facing persecution. Failing to do what we can to try to help them in their time of need is akin to failure to help the wounded stranger on the road. I desire to behave like the Good Samaritan, rather than like the "religious" people who simply walked by and ignored the stranger's—their neighbor's—plight. If in God's eyes we owe a fraternal duty of care to strangers who do not even share our faith, we owe an even stronger duty to fellow members of the body of Christ. In 1 Corinthians 12:25-27, we read: "so that there should be no division in the body, but that its parts should have equal concern for each other. If one part suffers, every part suffers with it; if one part is honored, every part rejoices with it. Now you are the body of Christ, and each one of you is a part of it."

We are called to identify with the suffering of other Christians to the point that we suffer along with them. Now that's real empathy! These words were not high-flown ideals written from the perspective of an armchair observer, but they arose out of the crucible of the Apostle Paul's own immense suffering in the face of persecution. It seems to me that Paul's identification of believers with Christ's body may have stemmed from his dramatic conversion experience on the road to Damascus, where Jesus clearly identified Himself as being *one* with His suffering followers. "Saul, Saul, why do you persecute me? … I am Jesus, whom you are persecuting" (Acts 9:4-5). Jesus could have said that Saul was persecuting His followers, but instead He said that Saul was persecuting Him. Jesus identifies Himself as one with His suffering church.

In Galatians 6:9-10, Paul offers these instructions: "Let us not become weary in doing good, for at the proper time we will reap a harvest if we do not give up. Therefore, as we have opportunity, let us do good to all people, especially to those who belong to the family of believers." Certainly we must do good to all, but we are especially called to do good to other Christians. Galatians 6:2 states, "Carry each other's burdens, and in this way you will fulfill the law of Christ." This letter was written to believers, enjoining them to bear one another's burdens.

When Christians are persecuted, the body of Christ, Jesus Himself, is also being assaulted. We should not stand idly by when Christ is under attack. We are called to identify closely with the suffering of our fellow believers and to be especially mindful of doing good to them.

It is not right to assume that persecution is always good for the church. If that were the case, the devil would have stopped using persecution as a weapon a long time ago. The devil is evil, but he is not stupid. Although God sometimes brings good results out of persecution, there are also many cases in which such attacks weaken the growth of the church. Take, for instance, Egypt, Turkey, and North Africa, where more than a millennium ago there were large numbers of Christians. After the Islamic invasion and occupation of these lands, there has been a long period of persecution and discrimination. Although today there are still Christian communities in these countries, they are not of the size that they once were.

I believe that in the end only God knows whether a particular situation of persecution will weaken or strengthen the church. It is not for us to try to guess the outcome. The Scriptures do call on us, however, to assist our fellow believers in whatever way we can, bearing their burdens and standing together with them in their time of need. The three ways in which we can help are through prayer, advocacy, and giving. In this chapter, I will concentrate on human rights advocacy in missions settings.

Advocacy for Christians

Human rights advocacy is not just about human rights; it is also a key form of mission support. It involves speaking out against injustices and trying to have such situations rectified. We believe in a God of justice (Isa. 30:18), whose prophets, like Amos, uncompromisingly called for justice (Amos 5:24). It thus amazes me when Christians think that closing one's eyes to injustice is somehow the more "spiritual" thing to do. Human rights advocacy is not about seeking political power; it is about seeking justice. It should not be considered any more political than the prophetic utterances of Amos, Elijah, Isaiah, or any of the other prophets of the Bible.

In my 10 years of advocacy work for the persecuted church, I have seen many situations of persecution resolved and Christian mission strengthened. Prisoners have been released, Bibles were allowed to be delivered, Christian organizations have been registered, and killings were reduced or stopped altogether. As with most things, we cannot claim that human rights advocacy is always successful, and we must always combine advocacy with prayer, but it works more often than most missionaries seem to realize. In the end, I believe God wants us at least to try to help our fellow believers in their time of need, even if we fail to achieve any results.

Missionaries have a key role to play in human rights advocacy by carefully and accurately communicating relevant information about anti-Christian persecution and discrimination to the outside world. Groups like Jubilee Campaign will do the overt advocacy work, communicating with parliamentarians and governments. Missionaries must usually stay in the background, quietly supplying information about religious persecution or discrimination to human rights advocacy groups, so as not to jeopardize their own safety or permission to stay in the country. There is no need for missionaries to take on an overt advocacy role; their main and very crucial contribution to the process of securing justice is to supply the relevant information.

Guidelines to Help With Advocacy

I now present seven guidelines about how one can prepare for and respond to crises on the mission field. This is not an exhaustive list covering every conceivable contingency. I will emphasize how best to gather, verify, and communicate information and how best to be prepared for advocacy situations.

Overview of the Seven Guidelines

1. **Pray for God's guidance.** If possible, get others to pray and fast about the situation and for you while you take action.

2. **Identify possible sources of information.** Verify the information by getting independent corroboration of the facts. When a problem is starting to arise, start to gather the relevant facts, in case advocacy needs to be used and for the purposes of informing others so they can pray.

3. **Discuss** with the appropriate person **the issue of authorization** for advocacy or whatever course of action needs to be taken. The best people to give authorization are, first, the person/victim, then the closest immediate family of the person, and then the leader of the church/fellowship group to which the person belongs.

4. **Communicate the information** and a request for prayer and action (if authorization has been given) to the relevant contacts in as speedy and secure a manner as possible. Follow this initial contact with further updates as more information is obtained and as the situation develops.

5. **Consider contacting a lawyer** if a person is being detained—someone who may already be known to the person, sympathetic to the case, and able to help.

6. **Consider approaching any locally based people** (such as sympathetic diplomats in the foreign embassies or local human rights groups) for assistance. But be sure that these people are trustworthy, and bear in mind the implications that their involvement may have for your own security.

7. **Consider** whether the person has any **dependents who may need assistance** as a result of the crisis; e.g., the person may be in prison and unable to provide for the family's needs. It is usually better for funds to be channeled through the local church/fellowship, via the approval of the leader, unless there are exceptional circumstances.

Typical Scenarios and Information Needed

There are many types of situations in which persecution or discrimination occurs: imprisonment, sectarian violence, harassment, extra-judicial execution, psychiatric detention, and laws restricting religious freedom. Here is the type of information that is needed for each of these situations.

1. Imprisonment

- Full name of the prisoner.
- Age and sex of the prisoner.
- Identity card number and/or passport number of the prisoner.
- Reason for imprisonment—both the real reason and the officially given reason.
- Location of the place of detention.
- Whether any torture or other form of mistreatment is taking place.
- Whether the prisoner has any serious physical or mental health problems.
- Whether the prisoner has been allowed any legal advice and representation.
- If a court appearance is scheduled, when and where it is to take place.

■ Whether the prisoner has been persecuted by the authorities in the past and, if so, how.

■ Whether a sentence has already been passed; what the sentence is.

■ Whether the prisoner is under pressure to give up his/her faith.

■ Photograph of the prisoner.

■ Any other information you think may be relevant. There is never too much information!

It is rare that you will be able to obtain all of the above information in a short time. The important thing is to get the essential minimum of information out first for advocacy, if that is what is needed. The following are the minimum items needed for effective advocacy:

■ Name of the prisoner.

■ Real reason for detention—e.g., because of religious activities—in order to show that the person is not being detained on any reasonable grounds.

■ Location where the prisoner is being held. If the specific location is not available, then at least the general location should be given. Even in the complete absence of knowledge of the prisoner's location, the case can still be raised with the government, if it can be shown that the authorities are responsible for the detention. If not, pressure could be put on the government to locate the detainee as a matter of urgency.

■ Clear authorization for advocacy (this will be dealt with in more detail below).

2. *Sectarian violence against Christians*

■ Casualty figures—including names of the casualties unless too numerous.

■ Nature and extent of property damage.

■ Date and time of the incident.

■ Response of the police/security forces to the outbreak of violence. This includes how long they took to react, any reasonable justification for a slow response, what they did, and what they failed to do to help.

Complaints that the security forces were slow to protect Christians facing sectarian violence are common. But for such claims to be credible, there needs to be some clear evidence that the authorities failed to respond as they should have.

3. *Harassment of Christians*

Harassment can take many forms, from repeated interrogation and beatings to sexual assault.

■ Name of the person facing harassment.

■ Age and sex of the victim.

■ Physical and mental health of the victim.

■ Nature of the harassment—including its frequency, dates, and location.

■ Name and rank of the officers carrying out the harassment.

■ Name and location of the station where the officers involved are based.

■ Reason for the harassment.

4. *Extra-judicial execution*

■ Nature of the killing and the circumstances surrounding it. Include where it took place, the method used, and the date of the killing.

■ Full name and occupation of the victim.

■ Age and sex of the victim.

■ Likely reason that the authorities may have wanted to kill the victim, e.g., evangelism.

■ Whether there was a past history of persecution against the victim, what the nature of the persecution was, and when it happened. Whether any threats were made against the person, the date when any such threats were made, and the nature of the threats.

■ Where/with whom the victim was last seen alive and what he/she was doing at the time.

■ Any evidence whatsoever which throws suspicion on the authorities as having been responsible for the killing, e.g., the authorities refuse to allow an independent autopsy on the victim and insist on a quick burial, or the victim was last seen alive with members of the security forces. If the authorities are not suspects, then is there any evidence which sheds any light on who might have carried out the killing?

■ Whether there has been a past pattern of extra-judicial executions against Christians in that country.

■ Whether there are any other Christians in particular who might be in danger of being killed next. If this is the case, measures should be taken to try to enhance their security. These could include:

- Getting others to pray for them.
- Ensuring they are not left unaccompanied.
- Considering whether to get an advocacy group like Jubilee to raise concerns about their safety with the government of that country. (By doing this, we might put pressure on the government to ensure that nothing happens to the Christians, since the government would be held directly responsible if anything happens.)
- Varying their patterns of movement and being discreet about what their program is.

5. *Psychiatric detention*

In such cases, governments often try to disguise their imprisonment of a person by putting him/her in a psychiatric ward. The dangers involved in such detention include the possible harm the victim may suffer at the hands of other mental patients and how the forced infusion of drugs into the victim might harm his/her mental and physical health.

In cases of psychiatric detention, Jubilee usually challenges the authorities' assessment of the patient and requests that an independent psychiatrist be able to access the patient. This approach tends to put the government in a corner. They should have no reasonable grounds for objection to such a medical check-up, since the patient has normally not been technically charged with any offense. The following information is useful:

■ Past history of the victim's health record, both mental and physical.

■ Full name of the victim.

■ Sex and date of birth of the victim.

■ Date of admission to the psychiatric ward and the name and location of the hospital.

■ Official reasons given for the psychiatric detention and how long they intend to detain the person. (Copies of medical certificates and the order to commit the person to a mental institution would be helpful.)

■ The real reason for the psychiatric detention. This has to be deduced from the circumstances.

■ Whether anyone independent of the authorities has had a chance to check the victim and, if so, what his/her qualifications and assessment of the victim are. (Likewise here, the written observations of the health care professional would be useful.)

■ Conditions in the ward where the person is kept and what sort of drugs are being administered. (If possible, name the drugs, size of doses, and regularity of intake.) Try to assess the threat to the victim's physical and mental health.

6. *Laws restricting religious freedom*

It is common that those who wish to stem the activities of Christian mission work would introduce laws to that effect. Unfortunately, what often happens is that the laws are passed or are close to being passed before the Christians in the country are fully aware of the implications or take action on the matter. One is likely to end up with a situation of "too little, too late."

In practice, it is much harder (though certainly not impossible) to have a law amended or repealed when it has already been passed, rather than when it is still going through the legislative process. For this reason, it is essential to get lobbying action going as soon as possible when a problem is perceived. As soon as you are aware of a law being proposed to curb religious activities, it is normally wise to try immediately to find out as much as possible about such proposed legislation. This includes getting a copy of the bill and any discussion paper that may have been written about it. If you find that the authorities are, without reasonable cause, unwilling to let you see the bill or to consult with the church on the proposed laws, this can often be taken as a sign that something detrimental to religious freedom is contained in the proposals.

In such a case, you should seriously consider requesting advocacy on the issue of the government's reluctance to be open about the laws they are proposing. This might place some pressure on them to ensure that they do not introduce unreasonably restrictive laws, since they will be aware that parts of the international community are watching developments closely. The following information is useful to have with regard to possible restrictive laws:

- The impact that the law would have on a whole range of religious activities, such as:
  - evangelism
  - printing Christian literature
  - distributing Christian literature
  - obtaining a meeting place for Christian worship
  - setting up a church or other type of Christian organization
  - training Christian clergy
  - inviting foreign Christians to come and assist the local church
  - conducting a Christian meeting in one's own home
- Whether there has been any consultation with Christian leaders about the proposed laws.
- The government's intentions behind introducing such laws.
- The laws' stage in the legislative process and when they are expected to be passed. It would also be very useful to give a general description of the stages that a bill goes through before it becomes law.
- The provisions in the constitution that exist for safeguarding religious freedom.
- The legal process available in the country for challenging laws which violate human rights—e.g., challenging a law as unconstitutional because it contravenes the safeguards in the constitution dealing with religious freedom.

Please note that it is wise to have information about the constitution and legislative procedures even before any attempts are made to pass restrictive laws, just in case such action does happen. It is also prudent to monitor as best as one can the national and local government's attitude to religious freedom, so as to identify quickly in the early stages any attempts to curb religious liberty.

Verification of Information

Insofar as you are able, verify the information you have received. One way of doing this is by getting corroboration of the facts regarding the persecution. Corroboration should come from a source that is separate from the source from which you first got the information. If the sources did not get the information by witnessing it firsthand, then check that they did not both get it from the same source, because if that common source was tainted, then both sources will be reporting inaccurate information.

Before making inquiries, bear in mind that you must be cautious about questioning people who might not be at all sympathetic with your ministry and who may be suspicious about your interest in the case. Once you have verified the information and ascertained that advocacy might be needed, the next step is to obtain authorization.

If the authorities announce that a prisoner has been released or that a situation of persecution has been resolved, do not simply take their message at face value but seek independent verification. Jubilee Campaign's experience has indicated to us that governments sometimes falsely announce prisoner releases in order to stop the human rights campaign that has been taking place for the prisoner.

Wherever possible, consider getting photos or films which may be useful in communicating the issue to the outside world. For example, where sectarian violence has taken place, a video or photos of the damage done may be useful. Documentation may also be helpful as evidence of persecution, such as court papers, letters from the police, and summons to the victim to report to the authorities.

Authorization

Advocacy is not necessarily appropriate for every situation, but at the least, it should be seriously examined and should not be dismissed without being given proper consideration. Ideally, authorization should be sought from the victim of the persecution. However, this is often difficult, because the victim is likely to be in detention. In such a case, authorization can be sought from the immediate family of the victim. This would be the spouse or, in the absence of a spouse, the parents of the victim. If neither parent is alive, anyone who would be considered "next of kin" can be contacted. However, this effort should be done within reason, and only immediate family would normally be approached. It is important to note that in some circumstances, the family members might not have the best interests of the victim at heart. An example may be if the victim is a convert to Christianity from Islam, and the family members are Muslim with an antagonistic attitude towards the victim. If none of the immediate family is suitable for giving authorization, then the leader of the church/fellowship group of which the victim was a member should be asked for authorization.

Although mission workers may not be the appropriate ones to give authorization for advocacy, they may have to advise on the factors determining whether advocacy should be sought. Some of these factors are as follows:

- The gravity of the persecution and whether it is life-threatening. For instance, if a person is frail and elderly and has been imprisoned in very harsh conditions, there is a danger that he/she may die as a result of the imprisonment. Such circumstances usually lean in favor of a need for urgent advocacy. Similarly, a victim who has a heart problem or who is in need of medication which is denied in prison would be a likely candidate for urgent advocacy.
- The nature of the government of the country where the persecution is taking place. How has the government responded in the past to being lobbied over human rights cases? How sensitive are they about their reputation in the West?
- The chances that advocacy over this case may worsen the situation for the victim or jeopardize anybody else. (Note that the standard practice of Jubilee Campaign is not to cite sources, in order to protect them.)

Communication of Information

Communicate the information and authorization to the necessary contact(s) in as speedy and secure a manner as possible. The paramount consideration in all communications is security, if the person communicating the information is in the country where the persecution has taken place. It is usually much better to communicate in writing, for the sake of clarity and in order to prevent any misunderstandings from occurring.

Unfortunately, mail, fax, and email can all be intercepted, and phone lines can be tapped. Even couriers can be searched. Encrypted email is not foolproof, and it might arouse suspicion by the fact that it is encrypted. The communicant must decide which is the safest means of sharing the information under the circumstances. Such means of communication should be considered *before* an emergency arises, both to save time and because clear thinking may be difficult once one is under pressure to communicate the message as quickly as possible.

If we have received authorization from the relevant persons, the information is then communicated to parliamentarians with whom we work. They will raise these issues with the British government and with the government of the country of concern. In major cases, we will attempt to get the British government to lobby their colleagues in Europe so as to have the European Union raise the case with the relevant government as well. The information will also be communicated to Jubilee's branches in the United States and Holland, who will do similar campaigning in these countries. The information may also be shared with our supporters to get them to pray and write to their Member of Parliament about the persecution case. Where the case is not too sensitive and publicity may help by increasing pressure on the authorities, the information will be shared with the media in an attempt to get them to cover the issue. It is a fact of life that governments generally tend to take issues more seriously when they see them covered in the media.

Some Further Points to Consider

Contraindications for help

In some cases, visits by foreigners to local Christians being persecuted for their faith may actually worsen their situation, because of the perception that they are colluding with foreigners. It is important to consider the local situation and consult with trusted locals before any such move is made. In some cases, it may be wiser to ask sympathetic family members to do the necessary visiting instead, since a visit from one family member to another is rarely likely to cause suspicion. Likewise, getting Christians to write to a Christian in detention might give the people detaining the prisoner the impression that the detainee has many concerned supporters around the world. This could either enhance the person's protection, or it might lead to further persecution, because of the perception of consorting with foreigners. The effect will vary from one local situation to another.

Financial assistance

Jubilee has given financial assistance to persecuted Christians in the past, through our charitable organization, Jubilee Action. Factors which determine whether to give such help include:

- The amount involved.
- The reputation of the person who would receive the assistance.
- Whether authorization has been given by the leader of the local church or Christian fellowship to which the recipient belongs (in some cases, this may be a tentmaker). Unlike the situations described above, the ideal person to give authorization for financial assistance is not the person in need but the leader of the local church, unless there are circumstances to indicate that this person may not be able to deal with the issue objectively or unless security reasons are involved. Of course, whatever the recipient says will be taken into account as well. Where possible and appropriate, we prefer to give the money through the local church or fellowship.
- The circumstances of the need which the person has.
- How the gift of money might affect the recipient's position, including his/her security. (In some countries, to receive money from foreigners can provoke the authorities.)

Legal assistance

Where legal assistance is needed, it is normally better for the aid-giving organization to pay the lawyer directly, rather than to give the money to the victim to pay to the lawyer. This normally makes the transaction simpler and ensures that the lawyer promptly receives the money set aside for legal expenses. Likewise, if a large amount of money needs to be paid to a third party by the victim for services rendered, it is better for the funds to be paid directly to the creditor by the aid-giving organization. If it is appropriate, this should be done through the local church. All the above are simply guidelines, and account has to be taken of security considerations and the best way of transferring money, since in some countries the banking systems are very slow in handling the transfer of money from overseas.

Be Prepared

More thought and preparation should be given to dealing with emergencies in the mission field. In the event of a crisis, speed is usually crucial, and lack of preparation can lead to unnecessary delays or terrible mistakes. A day in prison may seem like a year for someone undergoing persecution, so there needs to be a sense of urgency in responding. Preparation for possible crises in the mission field can include:

- Training of mission workers in crisis management, especially with simulations and role playing.
- Setting up secure and efficient communications networks for relaying information about crises and about requests for assistance. These networks would be established for the purposes of communicating information for prayer and, where appropriate, advocacy or other forms of assistance.
- Familiarizing trusted local believers with the action that can be taken in the event of a crisis and how they can assist through activity such as information gathering.
- Identifying local lawyers, local human rights groups, diplomats stationed locally who may be sympathetic, and anyone else who may be of assistance in the event of a crisis. Of course, one will have to assess how helpful and trustworthy they may be. It is important to have a local network of support that may be able to assist in the event of a crisis.
- Researching the legal and constitutional position of the country with regard to religious freedom. This would mean understanding the position on operating churches, engaging in evangelism, undergoing conversion, distributing Christian literature, etc. The research should include finding out whether there are any processes for redress—e.g., challenging unjust laws in the constitutional court or complaining to the human rights ministry.
- Collating information about names, addresses, email addresses, fax numbers, and telephone numbers of key political leaders who may need to be lobbied in the event of a crisis. Obviously, if the crisis is very urgent, then it is far better for letters to be sent by fax rather than by mail. These key leaders would normally include the following:
  - President or equivalent head of state
  - Prime Minister
  - Foreign Minister
  - Minister of the Interior
  - Minister of Justice
  - Minister of Human Rights (some countries have Human Rights ministries)

  It is too late to start searching for these details only after a crisis has erupted and advocacy is requested.
- Identifying the best means of transferring money quickly from abroad in case this service is needed.
- Identifying the best way to get someone out of the country quickly, in case this is urgently needed, and identifying the most likely country to give assistance to such a person (e.g., whether a visa is required, how sympathetic the country might be to granting asylum, how long visitors are permitted to stay, etc.).

A Composite Case Study

Susan is a tentmaker in an Islamic country. One day, she hears from a friend that Mohammed, a convert from Islam to Christianity, has not been seen since he went to the local police station for questioning.

Susan goes to make inquiries with Mohammed's wife, Farida, who is also a convert from Islam to Christianity. Farida confirms that Mohammed has not returned home for the last 48 hours. She says that she went to the police station to ask them where he was. The police refused to tell her and would not let her see her husband. Neither would the police reveal why they were holding Mohammed.

Farida is very concerned for her husband's safety and is worried that he might be tortured at the hands of the police. Susan explains to Farida that there are ways to put pressure on the government to have Mohammed released from detention and that the general expressions of concern about Mohammed's case by parliamentarians and governments in other countries are likely at least to reduce the chances that Mohammed might continue to be badly mistreated while he is in detention. This is because the local authorities will then be aware that there is international concern and awareness about Mohammed's case and that the case is being closely monitored from the outside.

Susan points out that nothing can be guaranteed in this kind of situation, including the behavior of the local authorities, but it seems that, even at worst, no difference will be made to Mohammed's case by human rights advocacy. Based on Susan's knowledge of the government and its past responses to human rights advocacy, she says to Farida that it is unlikely that the authorities will be so hard-line and indifferent to international opinion as to increase the persecution against Mohammed in response to human rights advocacy from the outside.

Susan and Farida pray together, and Susan then asks Farida if she would agree to authorize such advocacy for her husband. Farida agrees to do so, and Susan then records whatever Farida knows about Mohammed's case, including Mohammed's full name, age, state of health, identity card number, reason that he was summoned to the police station, the name of the police station, the names of the officers involved, and details of previous occasions when Mohammed was detained by the police, including the reason for each detention. With some of this information, Susan is able to put together a strong case for saying that Mohammed's interrogation and detention are linked to his conversion to Christianity and his Christian activities.

Susan asks Farida if she would also like to engage a lawyer to make an application to the courts to have Mohammed released. Farida agrees to this, but she points out that she has no money to pay for a lawyer and has three young children to support. Their financial situation is dire, now that the breadwinner, Mohammed, is in detention and unable to go to work.

Susan gives some money to Farida for her and her children and promises to get more support if Mohammed's detention turns out to be a lengthy one. She then goes back home and sends an encrypted email to a human rights organization abroad, whose work she has some familiarity with and that she feels she can trust. In her encrypted message, she gives the details of Mohammed's case and states that his family had asked for human rights advocacy on his behalf. Upon receiving this information, the human rights organization starts to mobilize parliamentarians and Western governments to raise concerns about Mohammed with the government of his country.

After sending out the message, Susan goes to a trusted lawyer with whom she had previously established contact (because she knew that one day the Muslim-background believers in the area might need legal assistance), to ask him if he would take up Mohammed's case. He agrees to do so, and Susan raises the funds to pay the lawyer from her own resources, from other tentmakers, and from the local fellowship of which Mohammed is a member. However, Susan is careful to ensure that the payment of the lawyer is done in Farida's name so that she is in no way officially linked with the case.

As Mohammed's case develops and new information is obtained, Susan is very careful to update the human rights organization which is working for him. After a few weeks of intense prayer and international pressure, together with local pressure by Mohammed's lawyer taking the case through the courts, the government decides to instruct the police to release Mohammed, to prevent any further embarrassment arising out of his case.

Reflection and Discussion

1. Review the seven guidelines for advocacy. Are these feasible for you to follow in your setting?

2. A Christian is imprisoned for his faith and is held without any contact with outsiders. His wife wants human rights advocacy on his behalf, but his local church leader is opposed to it because he is very frightened of any actions that may potentially cause problems for his church. Whose view should have priority in deciding whether to authorize human rights advocacy?

3. In general, what do you think God expects Christians who are not facing persecution to do for those who are facing persecution?

4. Imagine you are investigating a case of anti-Christian persecution, with a view to getting a human rights organization to act on it. Is it good to interview as many people as possible who have information about this case? Why or why not?

5. Imagine you are a tentmaker in a restricted country. Anti-Christian persecution by the government has not yet started, but with the growing number of converts it's likely to happen in the near future. What sort of preparations for such persecution can you, other tentmakers, and the local believers make now, in advance?

Some Human Rights Advocacy Groups

Amnesty International
International Secretariat
1 Easton Street
London WC1X 8DJ, UK
Tel: +44-207-413 5500
Fax: +44-207-956 1157

Christian Solidarity Worldwide
PO Box 99
New Malden
Surrey KT3 3YF, UK
Tel: +44-208-942 8810

Jubilee Campaign
Wilfred Wong
c/o Ian Bruce
MP, Room LG6
Norman Shaw North
Victoria Embankment
London SW1A 2HZ, UK
Tel/Fax: +44-207-219 5129
Email: 100675.670@compuserve.com

***Wilfred Wong** is an Evangelical Christian lawyer who has been campaigning for persecuted Christians since 1989. He has been doing full-time research and parliamentary lobbying on this issue for Jubilee Campaign United Kingdom since 1993. For the last eight years, Wilfred has also been regularly lobbying at the United Nations Human Rights Commission on behalf of persecuted Christians. As part of his research for Jubilee Campaign into the plight of the suffering church, he has undertaken fact-finding missions to several countries in different parts of the world. Email: 100675.670@compuserve.com.*

46

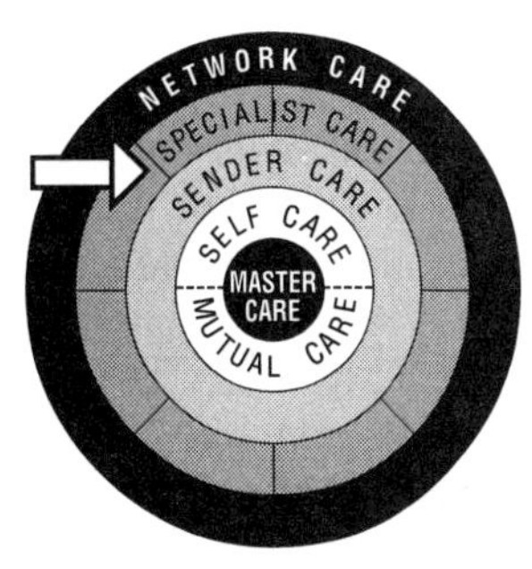

Field Counseling: Sifting the Wheat From the Chaff

LEONARD J. CERNY II
DAVID S. SMITH

Providing good member care can be a tricky enterprise, even for seasoned mental health professionals. This chapter describes eight member care errors, followed by specific suggestions for improving practice. The disguised examples are based on true field experiences encountered by the authors during their eight years of work with mission personnel.

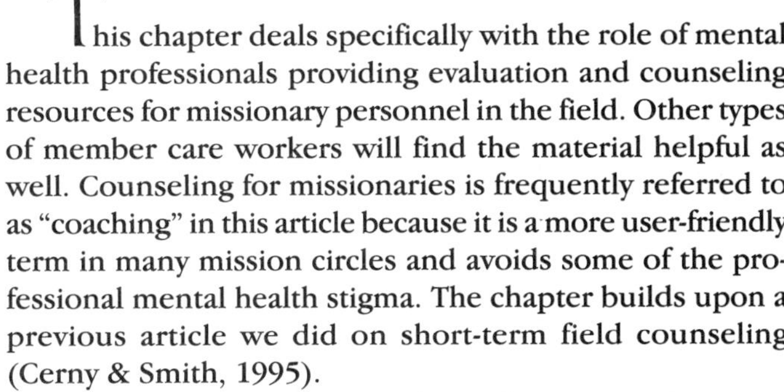

This chapter deals specifically with the role of mental health professionals providing evaluation and counseling resources for missionary personnel in the field. Other types of member care workers will find the material helpful as well. Counseling for missionaries is frequently referred to as "coaching" in this article because it is a more user-friendly term in many mission circles and avoids some of the professional mental health stigma. The chapter builds upon a previous article we did on short-term field counseling (Cerny & Smith, 1995).

The authors' perspectives derive from our experiences as clinical psychologists providing short-term coaching services for international missionary teams primarily composed of Westerners working in emerging nations. Our services commonly include crisis intervention, critical incident debriefing, team building, educational workshops, and short-term individual, marital, and family coaching. Of the many problem areas that we have seen, the main ones would be depression, anxiety, destructive anger, unwanted habits, addictions (most frequently sexual), attention problems, relational conflict, and various types of abuse.

Ethical and Professional Practice Guidelines

Most Christian mental health professionals approach working with missionaries from the perspective of professional education and training oriented towards hospital, clinic, agency, or private practice work. The ethical and professional practice guidelines that they use are oriented towards those professional practice settings (e.g., Austin, 1990). These guidelines, when combined with experience and good clinical judgment, provide a helpful professional foundation for working with missionary groups. However, to provide appropriate care for missionaries in the field, we must also consider some additional practical principles. Here are five principles that help to guide our work with mission personnel:

1. Reaching Out

Typically, clients seek out or are referred to mental health professionals for help. They enter into the helping relationship with an anticipation of trust and benefit due to the provider's professional skills and reputation. Clients normally make an investment in treatment by paying for professional services. They come to the therapist's professional setting to receive the treatment.

In contrast, in order to help missionaries and mission organizations, mental health professionals must usually first seek out and develop relationships with them. This often involves overcoming issues of distrust regarding psychology or psychiatry and questions about the compatibility of professional mental health services with spirituality. Often the mental health professional provides services at either no cost or minimal cost and sometimes at his/her own expense.

2. Multiple Cross-Cultural Issues

At least three levels of challenging cross-cultural issues exist in providing member care support for missionaries and mission organizations. The first such issue is the *organizational ethos* of the mission agency. Each agency has its own unique style of theological, missiological, organizational, personal, and relational values and practices. Usually these values have developed from the educational tradition, experience, and preferences of the founder or founding organization. Especially in a team-led organization, each team is also likely to have a memorandum of understanding (MOU), which reflects the ethos of the team. Desire and openness to learn and respect organizational culture are essential to providing mental health services within that culture.

The second level involves developing awareness and respect for the *cultural backgrounds of the individual members and families*. It is becoming increasingly common to see North American, European, Latin American, African, and Asian team members laboring side by side on international teams. Member care workers can provide valuable support in helping build effective team relationships in which individual differences and preferences are understood, appreciated, and utilized, with the goals of building unity and maximizing ministry effectiveness. Additionally, understanding and respecting cross-cultural issues are essential to effective individual and family coaching. Many missionary teams also have workers who are the children of missionaries themselves. These MKs have their own cultural uniqueness, as many researchers point out (e.g., Pollock & van Reken, 1999).

While humility is an essential element in the first two levels, it is especially necessary in the third level, the cross-cultural bridging with *the host culture* in which the team and/or individuals are working. Frequently this is the most foreign culture for the member care worker, and the professional is highly reliant on the missionaries for assistance in understanding, appreciating, and functioning minimally within the host culture. Treatment of individual missionaries and families should always be oriented towards encouraging and supporting their adaptive functioning within the host culture. Sometimes member care workers are asked to stretch their capacities in providing consultation for friends and new believers within the host culture, but most frequently language barriers preclude significant involvement.

3. Managing "Dual Relationships"

In the mental health professional's traditional work, "dual relationships," such as forming a friendship or business relationship with a patient outside the counseling office, are ethically and often legally forbidden. This ethical and professional practice principle is relaxed somewhat for mental health professionals who function in small communities, where practical and social necessities require patient contact in contexts beyond the counseling office. Flexibility with external boundaries always requires good awareness of one's internal boundaries and personal needs, as well as what is in the client's best interest.

While professionals are working with missionaries in the field, dual relationships are very common (Hall & Barber, 1996). In fact, they are frequently necessary in order to develop trusting relationships. There is a less formal nature to the coaching/counseling relationships. One can give professional input while walking or driving together or while sipping tea at a cafe. The coach may also be lodged at the client's house, with plenty of opportunity to get to know each other during and after the meeting times. Coach-counselors need to be attentive to the nuances of maintaining healthy boundaries, to the need to adjust therapeutic techniques, and to possible feelings and memories that get stirred up during their different types of involvement with the missionary clients (transference and counter-transference).

4. Responsibilities to Both Counselee and Organization

For mental health professionals, the question, "Who is the client?" is an important one, especially in the area of maintaining confidentiality. Confidentiality is an issue for the counselee, as he/she considers what to reveal and how much privacy is guaranteed in the counseling relationship. The concern for the organization usually is that it be made aware of significant problems that go beyond the counseling relationship and may require organizational intervention, support, or accountability. "Confidentiality procedures must be clarified for in-house consultants and counselors who are responsible to protect the interests of the organization in addition to the individual" (O'Donnell & O'Donnell, 1992, p. 264).

Two principles from professional ethical and legal guidelines commonly found in the United States help address this issue. The first is that responsibility and confidentiality issues should always be spelled out in advance, so that people and organizations can make informed choices. The second principle is that confidentiality for the counselee is mandated, with as few exceptions as possible. Exceptions commonly include suicidal risk to self, homicidal risk to others, and abuse (sexual, physical, or emotional) of someone weaker, such as a child, spouse, or elder.

The Sample Member Care Confidentiality Policy shown in Table 1 on the next page was developed from collaboration between member care professionals and a mission agency. It presents a balanced approach to addressing both individual and organizational concerns and has been field tested for about five years. In contrast to this guideline, however, it should be noted that some organizations encourage but do not require their staff and consultants to report significant struggles when such reporting is not legally mandated. It is important that there is a common understanding of the member care worker's role and responsibilities, in order to give proper service to both field teams and mission agency leadership.

5. Therapeutic Use of Email

For most missionaries and agencies, email has become the primary means of communication. It is fast, informal, and inexpensive. However, it has questionable confidentiality and is vulnerable to miscommunication. Our experience is that mental health professionals should never try to conduct counseling by email. Yet,

Table 1
Sample Member Care Confidentiality Policy

All information shared with members of the member care team by email or during counseling is kept confidential with two exceptions. The first is where disclosure is mandated by law (e.g., in the USA for child/elder abuse, suicidal/homicidal threat). The second is when personal struggles significantly interfere with one's work role (e.g., major depression, abusive leadership, moral failure, or serious marital conflict).

We see these struggles as being larger than the counseling relationship and thus necessitating the help of others within the organization. So, in such cases, the mission organization requires that organizational leadership be informed by both the person (counselee) and the counselor. For field workers, this leadership would include the team leader, appropriate team leader overseer, or the field director. For support staff, this leadership would include the supervisor or the sending base director.

email can be very helpful for providing limited evaluation and/or consultation. It is also very helpful for providing follow-up accountability after face-to-face work. Sometimes email provides the only immediate means for responding to urgent needs, when direct contact is not possible and professional on-site resources are not available. Long-distance phone calls, while more expensive, are usually more effective. Many current issues concerning email consultation and counseling are summarized in the excellent article by Rosik and Brown (2000).

Vignettes and Commentary

The following vignettes highlight some of the mistakes that we have observed in providing member care. Our goal is that others can learn from these mistakes and improve the quality of their services. We begin by presenting two of our own errors.

Case 1: Cross-Cultural Insensitivity

Responding to a family's request for help, Len and David were excited about finally landing at Iskurt, the capital of a country with a culture very unfamiliar to them. The flight was difficult. Not only was the plane's toilet out of order, but the engines were unusually loud, and sleep was not possible. As soon as the plane had landed and taxied to the gate, loud, discordant music suddenly burst out over the plane's speakers. Very tired, the typically sensitive David yelled to Len over the music, "I hope I don't have to listen to this the whole time I'm here!" Len became embarrassed and quickly informed him that the music was the national anthem of the country in which they were arriving as guests.

Discussion

We are guests in the cultures in which we work or visit. What may be experienced as funny or inert in one's own culture may likely be perceived as insensitive in a foreign setting. It is always important to err on the side of humility and respect. This vignette also demonstrates the importance of being aware of the increase in stress that occurs while traveling to new countries. Being tired, irritable, and stressed can lead to a lower threshold of tolerance. Member care workers have to exercise good self-care and manage their stress appropriately. Another lesson from this vignette is the importance of traveling in pairs. Frances White (1992) mentions this strategy in her guidelines for short-term service. With the help of an observing partner, tension can be lessened with humor, and insensitivity can quickly be confronted, before one makes major cross-cultural blunders.

Foreign visitors are often under observation by the locals. So get coached on what it means to be courteous and on how to show respect. Step outside familiar cultural tastes. Be curious, flexible, and willing to develop new tastes. Immediately begin looking for aspects of value and meaning within the host culture. Adopt the position of a learner, and explore/inquire about the culture of the host country whenever possible.

Case 2: Coaching Reports

Len, a clinical psychologist, made a coaching visit to a large mission team in Africa and found that the team was experiencing major conflict between the team leader and the elders of the church that the team helped start. It was an extremely busy week of mediation. Then the team leader delayed the final meeting to the day of Len's departure. This meant that Len was not able to finish his coaching report and recommendations. Usually he would process his report with the local leadership, to make certain there was mutual agreement about the accuracy and wisdom of conclusions and recommendations, before leaving the field and submitting the report to the overseeing agency.

During the following week of email interaction, Len allowed the team leader to cause further delay in the submission of the report, because the team leader alleged that certain contents were inaccurate and offensive. A mutually agreed-upon report was submitted but at the cost of three weeks' delay. The field director, previously unaware of the seriousness of the conflict, was rightfully upset at not being informed sooner about the team situation. Later, additional facts came out which revealed serious character issues on the part of the team leader.

Discussion

There are three main issues in this vignette. The first is the value of writing a coaching report before leaving the field. It is generally a good policy to write, discuss, and adjust the report as the final stage of a field visit. Processing the summary report with field leadership to produce wording that all agree upon builds trust with both field and agency leaders. A report is also important because a mutually agreed-upon record of the visit, including treatment goals and follow-up accountability, is established. Over time, people forget details of past events, and the things agreed upon can become fuzzy. The risk of misunderstandings or misinterpretations is greater when the report is not written and discussed on the field.

The second issue in this vignette is that, in his desire to build trust by working in a mutually agreeable way, Len allowed himself to be manipulated by the team leader. First, the team leader changed the meeting schedule at the last minute, eliminating the final evening and day needed for processing the report and relaxing together after having completed the work. Second, Len allowed himself to be delayed three weeks in submitting the report, trying to process differences with the team leader by email. If problems can't be resolved in person, they will not likely be resolved by email. The team leader was avoiding his role in the problems and projecting blame onto others. It is not surprising that later developments revealed major character issues. When there are significant impasses in agreeing to the content of a report, it would be wiser for the member care worker to suggest that separate reports be written giving different perspectives of the problem.

The third lesson learned from this vignette is that organizational leaders need to be informed of problems in a timely manner. The authority structure must be honored and leaders informed of progress and impasses. Trust develops when communication is clear and timely reports are made to the leaders of the organization. If the coaching report was going to be delayed, Len should have called the field director to alert him regarding the team situation.

Case 3: Confidentiality Issues

John, a licensed counselor, received permission from a team leader to provide a week of family therapy to a family from the Balkans that requested help. Eager to help the family feel safe, John informed the family that everything they discussed would be held in total confidence. Within a short time, what were initially straightforward family issues became complex and confused. As more information was revealed by the parents, issues of suitability for the job and personal safety on the field were raised. Because of John's commitment to total confidentiality, the family said they would feel betrayed if John talked with their team leader about information they had revealed. They also expressed their distrust in the team leader.

Honoring his commitment, John did not discuss the family's needs with the team leader. Nor did he write a coaching report, because the family would not give him permission to release information. Because the family was desperate for more help, John agreed to return six months later to provide more family therapy. In the meantime, the family reported to the team leader that the visit had been helpful and that all was well. John was unable to return in six months because of an unforeseen illness. Within the next year, the family had to leave the field permanently on an emergency basis, because of a family crisis that could have been dangerous to their children.

Discussion

John made an unprofessional promise when he guaranteed total confidentiality. In most countries, the confidential relationship between a licensed professional and his/her client has ethical and legal limitations. These relationship guidelines are spelled out by the overseeing professional organization (e.g., the American Psychological Association in the USA) and local laws. Professional counselors are also required to inform clients in advance that confidentiality is protected except for endangerment to themselves or to someone else. Also, reporting is mandatory for child abuse, elder abuse, and, in some cases, spousal abuse.

If John had used the approach previously outlined in the Member Care Confidentiality Policy, he would have protected himself, the family, and the team leader from unrealistic expectations. The family would have known what the realistic consequences were regarding what they chose to reveal. The team leader would have been notified when issues needed organizational awareness and support. John could have worked with the family in notifying the team leader about the concerns of safety and suitability. He could also have helped them develop better communication, trust, and mutual support.

Case 4: Treating Minors

Jan, a licensed marriage and family counselor, was part of a pastoral care team providing a week of teaching and renewal for a church planting team in India. During her visit, she observed a team meeting and was alarmed by the social behavior of a female adolescent named Diane. Jan was so troubled that she mentioned these concerns during dinner to her expatriate host family with whom she was staying. Her hosts were supportive and offered their own observations regarding Diane. In the rush of saying good-byes while leaving the country the next morning, Jan never discussed her concerns with Diane's parents, nor did she initiate any future email contact with the family. After returning to her busy private practice in New York City, Jan quickly became occupied with current pressing events and forgot about her concerns regarding Diane.

A month later, when Diane's parents were informed of Jan's expressed concerns by Jan's host family, Diane's family felt confused and betrayed by Jan. In an email, they informed Jan that they felt betrayed for two reasons: first, that she had been alarmed by something she had observed about their daughter and had not contacted them, and second, that she had discussed her concerns with another family rather than speaking to them directly.

Discussion

The intensity of field visits and the apparent casualness of the setting and relationships can lead member care workers to lower their professional sensitivity. Informal relationships, added with constantly changing circumstances and/or unfamiliar settings, require that professionals maintain especially good boundaries. In this case, an important principle is that any child concern should always be discussed with the parents first. To discuss these concerns with a host is gossip and leaves the host in a difficult position. Traveling with a colleague is a real asset. In this situation, Jan might have consulted with another professional on the member care team regarding her concerns and benefited from a more objective opinion on the best way to address her concerns.

Case 5: Child Abuse

During a field visit to a church planting team in Estonia, Jeff, a licensed clinical social worker from Canada, was staying with the Jones family, who were the newest members of the team. During a counseling session on the last day of Jeff's visit, both Mr. and Mrs. Jones revealed that they had been abused as children. Mr. Jones also reported that about six months earlier he had observed their team leader's son Fred, age 13, having inappropriate sexual contact with the Jones' daughter Amy, age 8. Mr. Jones said he immediately confronted and talked with the children. Because Fred appeared so repentant, Mr. Jones said he promised not to say anything to Fred's parents if Fred would promise never to do anything like that again. Since then, Mr. and Mrs. Jones have protected Amy from being alone with Fred.

When Jeff encouraged the Jones to speak with their team leader about the incident, Mr. Jones refused, because of his promise to Fred. Mrs. Jones said she could not, because of fear of how the team leader might respond, since they were new on the team and did not know the team leader and his wife very well. Jeff did not know what to do, especially because he was leaving the next day. He decided to wait until he could consult with a mentor upon his return to Canada. Jeff's mentor encouraged him to attend an upcoming conference attended by both families the next month and there inform the team leader that an anonymous family had reported observing inappropriate sexual behavior on Fred's part with a younger child. Jeff followed the mentor's advice.

Discussion

The decision for Jeff to consult with a mentor was a good one. In this case, however, both Jeff and his mentor made poor decisions. If Jeff had previously informed the Jones of the Member Care Confidentiality Policy, it would have been of no surprise for him to encourage them to speak with their team leader and for him to support them in the process. If they refused this advice, it would then be Jeff's responsibility to inform the team leader. The second error was in waiting further for a more convenient time and circumstance in order to inform Fred's parents and confront the issue. When suspected child abuse is the issue, immediate response is required.

There are two key principles here. The first is that the member care worker should always encourage direct communication between families regarding the needs of their children. It is easy to get caught up in the passivity of others, especially when confronting leaders. Talking directly with team leaders allows for difficult yet critical concerns to be aired. Then Jeff could also support the team leader's family, help evaluate their child's needs, and obtain further assistance and professional help.

The second principle is that immediate priority should always be given to the protection of children from harm. Just because the Jones family protected their

Table 2
Suspected Child Abuse: Response Priorities for Member Care Workers

- Consider the safety and welfare of children who are vulnerable to injury. Protect as needed.
- Notify the team leader and parents of vulnerable children.
- Educate all parties regarding child abuse issues.
- Support the team leader in providing for team welfare.
- Identify the perpetrator, if possible.
- Establish safe boundaries, and provide for ongoing therapeutic support as needed.
- Be aware of and consult concerning abuse laws and regulations in both the home country and the host county. For example, citizens of the USA should be aware that child abuse outside the United States is generally not reportable in the United States.

daughter does not mean other children on the team were safe. When inappropriate sexual behavior between children is alleged, the parents of both children should be immediately informed, and all parents of children at potential risk should also be informed in a timely manner. Table 2 presents a list of suspected child abuse response priorities that can be helpful in responding to similar situations.

Case 6: Trauma Caused by Treatment

Monica, a social worker with many years of experience working for a public child protection agency, was leading the member care team that was providing services at a large regional conference in Thailand for church planting teams from Southeast Asia. Circumstantial evidence from a team member led Monica to believe that Jennifer, age 8, might have been sexually abused on the field, possibly by her father, Robert. Robert was the leader of a large and successful church planting team, and Jennifer was his youngest daughter. Attending the conference was his last responsibility before visiting supporters in Europe for a month and then returning to his native Scotland for a year of furlough.

Monica confronted Robert and his wife, Ann, with her concerns about Jennifer and intimated that Robert might be an abuser. Monica instructed them not to discuss the matter with their team, because she feared that this would influence any possible evidence that could come from the team. Monica also informed Robert's assistant team leader of her suspicions and the actions she had taken. She asked the assistant not to discuss the matter with the team, until the team had returned to the field from the Thailand conference and a member care professional could be present. Finally, she wrote a report to agency leaders of her concerns, her process of evaluation, and the actions she had taken.

Robert and Ann, extremely concerned for their daughter, asked if Monica could evaluate Jennifer professionally during the conference to determine if she had actually been abused. Monica said she was unable to do so, because of limited time and the lack of her professional equipment for interviewing, such as her tape recorder. She was concerned that the interview would not be useful as court evidence if Jennifer had been abused. Monica rather recommended that a professional in Scotland evaluate Jennifer, when they arrived after a month of traveling and visiting supporters in European countries.

Robert and Ann were very disturbed by Monica's unwillingness to evaluate Jennifer at the conference and about not being allowed to process this issue with their team before leaving on furlough. At the same time, they were afraid of appearing defensive or uncooperative with the member care professional's recommendations, because they had been questioned and felt that they were under suspicion of child abuse. At significant expense, they consulted with an expert in Scotland, who evaluated their daughter and family. The expert reported to agency leaders that there was no evidence that Jennifer had ever been sexually abused and that their family system appeared to be quite healthy.

Discussion

Possibly because of her background in a public child protective agency, Monica was overly concerned about gathering legal evidence and overly pessimistic that if Jennifer had been abused, it was likely by her parents. Her professional background in dealing with hardened sex offenders may have affected her lack of sensitivity to the trauma created for Robert and Ann in this situation. Monica cut them off from their normal avenue of understanding and support, which was to process important issues with their team.

It was an error for her not to evaluate Jennifer immediately. She was an expert trained in doing child abuse evaluations. Even if she had not been an expert, she should have done the best professional evaluation she could do under the circumstances, to gather more concrete information and to support Jennifer and her family. Her concern for strict procedures sacrificed practicality. When she refused to evaluate Jennifer after expressing her concerns, it was confusing to the family. Sending them out for a month of unsupervised family traveling before getting a professional evaluation was not protecting Jennifer or her parents.

If a leader is suspected of having committed child abuse, it is best to support him/her in fulfilling family and organizational responsibilities for the good of the others, while maintaining child safety. Support the family and organization in practical ways that encourage direct communication about concerns. Investigate potential culpability as soon as possible in a professional manner. If the person in leadership is found to be guilty, then support his/her superior and the individual in providing for an orderly transfer of responsibilities within the organization. In working with Western teams, direct, open communication of problems should be encouraged, while secrets and indirect communication should be avoided.

Case 7: The Too-Busy Expert Lacking Common Sense

After a major escalation in danger, the decision was made to evacuate a team in Western Africa from its war-torn host country to a neighboring stable country. The team was filled with both situational stress and relational conflict. Bert, a Dutch psychiatrist who had written a book on crisis intervention and debriefing, was asked to debrief the team, but his heavy speaking schedule did not allow him to break free for two weeks. The agency was concerned about the time delay, but they did not have another member care volunteer to call upon. They considered sending a mature pastoral care couple with no professional training but good relational skills and some field experience. Bert objected because of the strong empirical evidence supporting his debriefing technique and his concern that nonprofessional involvement might escalate the relationship conflict. He also instructed the team just to rest and not talk about any critical incidents until he arrived to help them.

Discussion

Bert provides an example of how a member care worker can be too narrow in his/her view and too untrusting of others. It would have been much more helpful for Bert to support the pastoral care couple through consultation and encouragement as they supported and ministered to the team. Their coming immediately would have been a needed expression of care by the organization. Bert could have consulted with them in stabilizing the team and could have been available by phone or email during the two-week period before his arrival. It is wise for member care professionals to support and develop existing organizational resources rather than try to work outside of the organization. Also, if Bert could have modeled his skills with this couple, then they could have multiplied his efforts in their daily pastoral care work.

It was also unhelpful and unrealistic for Bert to ask the team not to discuss their trauma. Teams need to struggle and learn to process issues constructively. A member care worker or leader with just some basic training could have helped by letting each person share, one at a time, and by allowing for uninterrupted communication. In critical incidents, it is important to help the individuals communicate as soon as possible after they are safe and have had a day or two of rest.

Case 8: Follow-Up and Homework

Jason, a counseling psychologist, traveled from his native Australia to Southern Africa to participate in a five-day member care coaching visit with an international team. Although initially resistant, Kevin, a South African missionary on the team, showed significant progress in working on his anger management issues with his family and the team. Before leaving, Jason taught Kevin how to chart his anger by rating it every day, and he encouraged him to have his team leader be an accountability partner. Kevin agreed to read and complete a workbook on anger provided by Jason. Jason recommended that Kevin also discuss the workbook with his team leader in order to follow up on their work. Jason then left the field feeling good about the changes he saw taking place in Kevin's life. For the next two days, Kevin charted his anger and then lost his chart. He did not meet with his team leader to discuss his anger or accountability.

Discussion

Homework can be an excellent tool to further one's growth, but it needs to be structured. And accountability needs to be put in place for it to work. This was not done very thoroughly in the vignette. As the saying goes, it is not the expected but the inspected that gets done! A monthly brief email contact for the next six months will often suffice. Commitments to follow up are easy to de-prioritize, especially when one returns to a busy schedule back home.

A small goal completed is much more powerful than a large unfinished goal. Well-organized assignments that are specific and that make sense to everyone are the most helpful. As in this vignette, merely suggesting that someone read a book is too general and almost a guarantee for failure. There are many good workbooks, and helping clients obtain them may be necessary. Workbooks offer structured exercises that can be completed and then discussed with another person, such as the member care worker via email or a trusted colleague on location. The debriefing time with a team leader at the end of a coaching visit and the coaching report should include all follow-up and homework arrangements.

Reflection and Discussion

1. How may "dual relationship" issues need to be managed differently when counseling with a missionary family in the field, compared to the way they are managed in a professional counseling office or agency setting?

2. If invited to provide a workshop and counseling services at a missions conference, what factors might you consider in preparing to address confidentiality issues?

3. What cross-cultural factors might you consider when asked by a mission agency to travel to Nigeria and help a missionary team that is in distress?

4. Why are coaching reports important?

5. You have just received a phone call from a team leader in Central Asia who says he doesn't know what to do regarding a situation of alleged child abuse on his team. How would you approach advising him?

References and Suggested Reading

Austin, K. (1990). *Confronting malpractice: Legal and ethical dilemmas in psychotherapy*. Newbury Park, CA: Sage Publications.

Bergin, A., & Garfield, S. (1994). *Handbook of psychotherapy and behavior change* (4th ed.). New York, NY: John Wiley & Sons.

Cerny, L., & Smith, D. (1995). Short-term counseling on the frontiers: A case study. *International Journal of Frontier Missions, 12*, 189-194.

Dinger, T. (1999). Ethical codes, decision making, and Christian faith. *Journal of Psychology and Christianity, 18*, 270-274.

Gardner, L. (1992). Crisis intervention in the missions community. In K. O'Donnell (Ed.), *Missionary care: Counting the cost for world evangelization* (pp. 136-150). Pasadena, CA: William Carey Library.

Hall, E., & Barber, B. (1996). The therapist in a missions context: Avoiding dual role conflicts. *Journal of Psychology and Theology, 24*, 212-219.

Lewis, T., & Lewis, B. (1992). Coaching missionary teams. In K. O'Donnell (Ed.), *Missionary care: Counting the cost for world evangelization* (pp. 163-170). Pasadena, CA: William Carey Library.

O'Donnell, K. (1988). Some suggested ethical guidelines for the delivery of mental health services in mission settings. In K. O'Donnell & M. O'Donnell (Eds.), *Helping missionaries grow: Readings in mental health and missions* (pp. 466-479). Pasadena, CA: William Carey Library.

O'Donnell, K., & O'Donnell, M. (1992). Ethical concerns in providing member care services. In K. O'Donnell (Ed.), *Missionary care: Counting the cost for world evangelization* (pp. 260-268). Pasadena, CA: William Carey Library.

Pollock, D., & van Reken, R. (1999). *The third culture kid experience: Growing up among worlds*. Yarmouth, ME: Intercultural Press.

Powell, J. (1992). Short-term missionary counseling. In K. O'Donnell (Ed.), *Missionary care: Counting the cost for world evangelization* (pp. 123-135). Pasadena, CA: William Carey Library.

Rosik, C., & Brown, R. (2000). *Professional use of the Internet: Legal and ethical issues*. Presentation given at the Mental Health and Missions Conference, Angola, IN.

White, F. (1992). Guidelines for short-term field consultants. In K. O'Donnell (Ed.), *Missionary care: Counting the cost for world evangelization* (pp. 202-216). Pasadena, CA: William Carey Library.

Leonard J. Cerny II is General Director of Missionary Care International, a non-profit missions support agency that specializes in providing pastoral care and coaching for missionary teams in the field. Len is a clinical psychologist and pastoral counselor with 25 years of experience in ministry, private practice, and hospital settings. He is married to Patricia Cerny, Psy.D., and is a co-author of ***Learning to Love: A Recovery Primer*** *and the* ***Bible Memory Verse Handbook****. Email: memcare@pacbell.net.*

David S. Smith *is a clinical psychologist in California. He is also the President of Missionary Care International, a non-profit missions support agency that specializes in providing pastoral care and coaching for missionary teams in the field. Dave is a graduate of Taylor University, Denver Seminary, and The Professional School for Psychological Studies. He has been married to his wife Karen for over 20 years and has two teenage children, Aaron and Lauren. He has also co-authored various books and articles with his good friend and business partner, Len Cerny. Email: membercare@mediaone.net.*

47

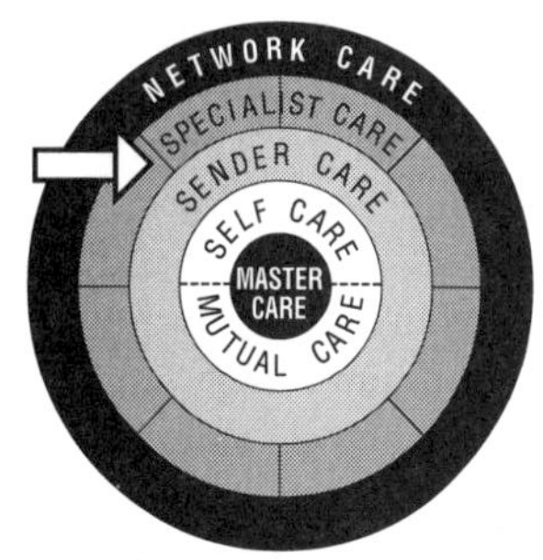

The Cross of Christ In Debriefing and Ethnic Reconciliation

Erik Spruyt
Rhiannon Lloyd
Renée Schudel

Jesus Christ took not only our sin, but also our pain upon Himself when He died on the cross. This truth is a core part of the ministry that the authors have for healing emotional wounds. Erik works with missionaries via debriefing, Rhiannon works with ethnic groups that have been in conflict, while Renée follows up their work with further equipping in the area of community development. Their innovative work reflects how member care is expanding into new areas.

Healing Missionary Wounds

For many years, my wife and I (Erik) had a dream to care for missionary personnel. We witnessed missionaries going into places in the world where no one really wants to go. They would come face to face with poverty, violence, and situations very hard to digest emotionally and spiritually. We consider these missionaries our heroes. The establishment of Le Rucher in 1994/95 is our dream come true, a place where missionaries can be refreshed in their calling in God and remain effective to serve in those difficult places.

Nestled at the foot of the Jura Mountains with a view of Mount Blanc and the Alps, Le Rucher is located in the beautiful French countryside, just over the Swiss border from Geneva. At Le Rucher, we provide debriefing, trauma care, and brief counseling for missionaries and Christian aid workers. We also offer training and international consulting in member care, community development, and ethnic reconciliation. Our desire is to actively integrate these various ministries for mutual support and greater effectiveness. We are committed to developing and providing resources on behalf of personnel working with those who are least evangelized, least developed, and/or highly traumatized. We also serve those involved in complex humanitarian emergencies. As we work with people, we endeavor to develop their competencies and character to help them respond to suffering and poverty and to lift human dignity in their communities.

Some Background

At any given moment during the past decade, there were about 50 armed conflicts going on simultaneously throughout the world. From the mid-1980s to the mid-1990s, 2 million children died in war, 4-5 million were wounded or disabled, 12 million were made homeless, and 1 million were orphaned or separated from their parents. Ninety percent of all war refugees are in developing countries, and 2½–5 million of the 40-50 million refugees are unaccompanied children. All of these statistics point out the shift that has taken place in who becomes a casualty in war. In World War I, for example, 5% of the casualties were civilians. During World War II, that figure went up to 50%. The Vietnam War saw an 80% civilian casualty rate. Currently, the rate is 90% around the world (UNICEF, 1996).

A shift has also taken place from nation fighting nation to so-called internal militia warfare, in which factions within one country fight each other and/or their government. This shift has changed the nature of armed conflict. Violence and torture are no longer used only for extracting information, but as a means of social control by terrorizing a civilian population. Militias create a state of terror that affects the total fabric of social structures and relationships, as well as the mental health of a population. To advance their political goals or aspirations of greed and power (e.g., Liberia, Sierra Leone, Angola, Afghanistan, etc.), militias can target the way of life of a whole population. These strategies seem very effective, especially when the professions in a society that sustain the infrastructure are targeted. Often, these are the roles that aid and community workers—including missionaries—have fulfilled through time: teachers, nurses, primary health care workers, doctors, agriculturists, orphanage workers, and pastors. The militias will try to destabilize the population to prove that the government cannot protect them, and so the militia gains control (Summerfield, 1998).

Mission personnel often serve in nations where the basic unit for society is not the individual, but the community. Individual thoughts, priorities, or feelings are subject to the communal priorities. Identity, success, pain, and suffering are validated primarily within a communal context. People derive their value and significance from being part of and functioning in that people or ethnic group. When the basic structure of the community is destroyed through armed conflict, the majority of the people can lose their pathway for validating what they have gone through. Whether the individual is victimized or not, he or she also suffers and feels pain because the community/ethnic group was targeted. A state of "shalom" in the Old Testament was much more than an individual being blessed. Shalom involves prospering in all relationships—with God, self, neighbor, community, even livestock and the land and peoples around them. (Both trauma care and reconciliation as they relate to the inner fabric of a community are further discussed later in this chapter.)

In debriefing missionaries during the past five years, we have seen many people who are serving in the various unstable and potentially traumatizing settings mentioned above. Many had been exposed to violence and injustices or had lived for months or years under the threat of violence. Missionaries often do not have the luxury of regular debriefings. They frequently show symptoms from cumulated stressful events spread out over several years. Although there is an increasing interest in finding new ways to care, many of the caregivers have limited firsthand understanding of what life is like in Africa, Asia, or Eastern Europe. Nor do they really understand the concept of the "communal soul" and not just the individual being injured and needing healing. Both of these areas—getting more field experience and including social/community perspectives for healing—are growing edges for the member care field. I greatly respect a psychologist who moved his family to Africa and has lived there for the past four years. This family has been through an enormous adaptation process. Because of this field experience, the missionaries that my friend counsels feel understood from the beginning.

The Place of the Cross in Care

A crucial element in missionary care (of both expatriate and indigenous missionaries) is the place of the cross of Jesus Christ. We use two principal "testimonies" about Jesus and His work on the cross as a central part of the two to five days of debriefing that we do with missionaries.

The testimony of John the Baptist

Jesus is "the Lamb of God that takes away the sins of the world" (John 1:29). This is probably the best-known testimony of Jesus and the motivation of missions to bring this message to the ends of the world. As Christians, we are familiar with the incredible power of Jesus in dealing with sin: through the cross we are set free from sin and guilt in a guilt-ridden world! We all have a testimony, and we have heard the testimony of others regarding the enormous changes that meeting and then walking with Jesus bring to a human life. This is also the core of missions: a personal relationship with Jesus Christ and a lifestyle that lines up with that relationship. Jesus invites us to let our sin fall on Him, and He becomes sin for us. In this way, He dies in our place.

The testimony of Jesus about Himself

After His baptism and the 40 days in the desert, we find Jesus in Luke 4:18-19 quoting from Isaiah 61:1-3. This Old Testament passage tells why Jesus came: "to bind up the broken hearted," "to comfort all who mourn," "to provide for those who grieve," and "to bestow on them a crown of beauty instead of ashes" and "the oil of gladness instead of mourning." Jesus did all these things at the beginning of His ministry, but we also find Him teaching the same principles at the very end of His ministry, in Luke 18:31-34. At this time, He is going up to Jerusalem to die, but His disciples do not understand this. Jesus teaches that "everything that is written by the prophets about the Son of Man will be fulfilled." In verse 32, we read a very graphic description of what Jesus is to go through and ultimately the types of pain in others with which He can identify. The prophet Isaiah says similar things, as he describes the Messiah as "despised and rejected by men, a man of sorrows, and familiar with sufering" (Isa. 53:3).

We try to help missionaries understand this second element of the cross: *Jesus takes upon Himself our suffering and pain*. We want people as part of their debriefing to connect fully with the Lord and to hear Him validate their cross-cultural experience: He says our struggles, trauma, and pain really have happened, and now He invites us to let our pain fall on Him and let Him become pain for us. In this way, Jesus is not only the "sin bearer" but also the "pain bearer." It is interesting that Isaiah 53 and 61 talk about sorrow and grief repeatedly. Often, these verses are quoted as a basis for praying for physical healing for others or as a basis for us to go into the world and tell others about this ministry of Jesus. Unfortunately, we have missed the point. *These verses are actually for us.*

The Gospels are quite direct when they state that no one can come to the Father except through Jesus. No one can be set free of sin except through the Son. I also see in Scripture a directive about where to go with our emotional pain, grief, loss, and failure (Matt. 11:28; Col. 1:19-24). In the debriefing process, we find that the missionary is often struggling with issues very similar to a grieving process, such as having to overcome personal, organizational, and often traumatic losses. Similarly, in trauma care, we deal mostly with grief and loss. As the cross and the resurrection were the pivotal events in Jesus' life, we as caregivers can bring missionaries who are in need back to that cross and to the person of the living Lord—especially in situations of grief, loss, pain, and failure.

Jesus is so capable of binding up the brokenhearted. In our debriefing times, we often listen for hours, sometimes for several days, as missionaries journal, draw, cry, and express all kinds of emotions. After a few days, we start to reflect gently together on the verses mentioned above, and we start to bring to the cross all that the missionaries have said, written down, and drawn, in order to give the pain to Jesus. There is Someone to whom we can bring our pain—Someone who validates our pain and who can handle our pain.

Africa Case

John was a missionary in Africa with over 10 years of experience. He had all the symptoms of secondary traumatization—vicarious trauma from being around those who had themselves experienced trauma. He wanted to leave and could no longer tolerate the accounts of others and the unstable environment. He was exhausted and found himself mulling over the stories he had heard day and night, to the point of not being able to work. We met with John and his team for several hours per day over a four-day period for debriefing, initially in a neutral African country, followed by sessions with the team in their own land. John shared many specific things that were bothering him and details of what he had experienced. During the teaching phase of the debriefing, we shared from Isaiah 61and 53, as well as Luke 4 and 18. After the fourth day, John had a powerful experience. As he put it, "I felt my heart being bound up [that is, bandaged and comforted to bring healing]." This was not simply catharsis, but a deep emotional change and revelation of Jesus.

John came to Le Rucher for more debriefing six months later. We found sustained emotional and mental stability in him, although he had gone back to serve in the aftermath of incredible atrocities and had heard and seen much more during those six months. He was learning to bring his pain to the Lord and was finding that Jesus is incredibly powerful to meet us and take the pain on Himself. It is part of the "exchange" that took place at the cross and that continues today: peace in place of pain, righteousness in place of sin, blessing in place of curse, acceptance in place of rejection, glory in place of shame, etc. (see Prince, 2000). We have to remember our pain and then forgive—not forgive and forget. In this process, Jesus becomes the pain bearer, and the burdens become much lighter.

More on the Debriefing Process

Field personnel from many "hot spots" have come to Le Rucher for care and rest. We frequently help them deal with issues such as suffering, injustice, personal and organizational loss, pain, and failure. For those wanting routine debriefing appointments (people who are going through forms of transition in their work, family, or career), we have an application and advance screening procedure. For emergency and/or traumatic situations, we take people in immediately.

Our debriefing process at Le Rucher involves a short-term, intensive, residential care package in a Critical Incidents Debriefing framework. Our process is very similar to Mitchell and Everly's (1993) model of phases: introduction, facts, thought, reaction/feeling, symptoms, teaching, and reentry phase. Specific counseling may follow this process. The process is offered both to groups and to individuals, usually with a team of two debriefers/counselors. Generally, this means we spend from two to four hours per day with each client during a five-day stay at Le Rucher. We encourage the use of journaling, meditation, worship, prayer, and other means with which clients may be comfortable, to express their experiences and enhance the debriefing process.

We invite clients to find new meaning in their relationship with God in the face of their suffering and loss. The cross can be a very powerful connector with Christ and His identification with our suffering. Thus, we particularly focus on the meaning of the cross for those who desire to do so. We have found that at the end of a careful debriefing process, bringing one's suffering/losses to the cross can be the beginning of a powerful time of healing and restoration.

For those who appreciate symbolism, we may give them the opportunity to write their losses and pains down on a small slip of paper and then physically nail the paper to a small cross we have available. Following prayer, those papers are then taken from the cross and burned as a symbol of giving those hurts to Jesus for Him to carry for them. For most, a sense of release is experienced through this exercise.

We see people receive deep healing experiences that are sustained and that keep growing as we follow up after three or six months. Some people stay in touch and tell us how even after a year, they feel strengthened and still see positive emotional and spiritual growth in their lives. Workers coming from such troubled areas as Sierra Leone, Sudan, Rwanda, Congo, South Africa, Chechnya, Kosovo, and Afghanistan have testified of sustained change in their lives through the debriefing process and through taking their suffering to the cross. One worker who came to us had to handle the dead bodies of friends unexpectedly, another had lost all her belongings, another had been taken hostage, and most had experienced armed robbery or the ongoing threat of violence. Some come back later and ask for further help on new issues. Others have been referred for longer-term counseling for personal and family issues that have come to the surface as part of their field and/or traumatic stress experience.

Summary

Debriefing, counseling, and the cross can go well together. The usual approach is to keep counseling separate from debriefing and to see Christ as our sin bearer more than as our pain bearer. We have combined these approaches in our work. Using the model that I have described, we have seen several people who had little intention of ever returning to the field being helped and then returning to the field after all, strengthened in their calling and understanding. Key to the healing is our understanding and experience of Christ coming alongside us in our pain, based upon what He has done on the cross. We encourage missionaries to bring their pain to Jesus not only during the debriefing, but also as often as necessary afterwards. Often they do this on their own, with a supportive friend or as part of a supportive group.

Healing the Wounds of Ethnic Conflict

Ethnic conflict is running rampant all over the world today. Individual people groups cry out for autonomy and individuality. People who have suffered injustice quietly for generations do so no longer. They now demand justice. Powerful nations react defensively, trying to hold onto supposed superiority and territorial rights. In other parts of the world, power struggles erupt between ethnic groups, sometimes resulting in attempts at ethnic cleansing. Today, about two-thirds of contemporary wars are being fought over issues of religious, ethnic, or national identity (Appleby, 2000, p. 17).

Is there any hope for our sinful, hurting world? The following material suggests strongly that there is hope, because there is a "God of hope" (Rom. 15:13). This is not some simplistic wish or assertion. Hope is part of God's character. God has a strategy to use His church to be the agents of healing and reconciliation in different nations, but first, the church must be healed!

Some Background

I (Rhiannon) began developing material on healing from ethnic conflict while in the wake of the terrible Rwanda genocide of 1994. During an initial visit shortly after the genocide, I met with Christian leaders from different denominations and ethnic groups. They were discussing the failure of the church and existing needs. They were wondering how this atrocity could have occurred in a nation where 85% of the population attends church, and they were wondering what the role of the church would be in healing the nation.

From these initial meetings, a vision was born to gather church leaders from every denomination to see how the church could help bring healing, forgiveness, and reconciliation. I was at a loss as to the best way to approach this difficult subject, and I was uncertain how the Lord could use me, as a European outsider. The first "trial" sessions I taught were met with much enthusiasm from the church leaders, along with an expression of their desire for the teaching to be heard in every town of Rwanda.

The seminars were offered initially to pastors and key church leaders as potential change agents in their local communities. It is important to take participants away from other distractions, so they can concentrate fully and receive healing from God. Thus, each seminar was offered as a three-day residential workshop, complete with lodging and meals.

God's Heart: Foundational for the Seminars

I believe that understanding and experiencing God's heart are at the foundation of all healing, and we had to begin there. From that starting point, we could move on to find healing through the cross for our inner wounds. By reading from Isaiah 61 at the start of His ministry, Jesus made it clear that healing wounds was a priority for Him. It is very difficult to forgive while the heart is full of pain, but once we begin to experience healing, our hearts are free to forgive and then to begin to think about reconciliation. To talk about forgiveness and reconciliation before discussing healing is like trying to put a roof on a house before building the walls.

Overcoming Cultural Barriers in Expressing Emotion

I was surprised to find that in Rwandan culture there is little expression of emotion, and there is no word for "emotion" in their language. Shedding tears is seen as a sign of weakness, and from an early age, the people are taught always to appear strong. Public expression of grief is unacceptable, especially for men. There is a saying that a man's tears should flow into his stomach. The Rwandese also believe that talking about traumatic experiences traumatizes them even more. This was obviously a major obstacle to helping people towards healing! I wondered how to overcome this cultural barrier without in any way implying that my culture was superior.

I found two acceptable ways. The first was presenting medical evidence from my training and experience as a psychiatrist (e.g., the place of grieving in dealing with bereavement and the pathological consequences of repressing emotions). The second and even more helpful approach was to focus on Jesus as the transcultural model of perfect humanity, from whom all cultures could learn. Jesus expressed many emotions during the course of His ministry. Starting from this foundation, we could have lively discussions examining our self-protective coping mechanisms. This resulted in taking steps toward giving each other permission to have feelings.

Finding God in the Midst of Suffering

I usually began my seminars by asking the questions that were pounding in most people's hearts: "Where was God in April 1994? Did He send these troubles? Why did He allow the genocide? Has God abandoned us?" I wanted to create a safe place where participants could own their doubts and voice their inner questions without fear of being condemned.

Storytelling is a well-received form of teaching in Rwanda, so I often made use of personal testimony. I would tell them of my struggles and my own pilgrimage to find a God of love in the midst of my family's sufferings, as well as in the historical injustices that the Welsh (my people group) have suffered at the hands of the English. We tried to grapple honestly with the problem of human suffering, the devastating consequences of the fall, the will of God versus man's freedom of choice, etc. I encouraged the participants, as church leaders, to allow people to ask their questions and to be merciful to those who doubt, seeking a deeper understanding of God's ways and a new revelation of His heart. We focused on God's pain when His will is not done on earth (Gen. 6:5-6; Luke 13:34; 19:41-44) and how He suffers with us (Isa. 63:9).

Discovering Jesus as the Pain Bearer

It is only when we are reassured of God's intentions and feelings towards us that we can risk coming to Him with our pain. Something that has transformed my own life and my counseling is discovering Jesus as pain bearer as well as sin bearer. Isaiah 53:4 tells us that He bore our griefs and sorrows. Not only our sins were taken to the cross, but all the consequences of sin as well. The whole tragic human condition is there. The cross deals with our woundedness and our sinfulness. In our seminars, we looked at the Lamb who is inviting us to off-load our grief onto Him, saying, "Let Me do the hurting instead of you." They were able to grasp this concept, resulting in great pain being expressed, often in loud wails, as they brought their sorrow to Him.

This time of bringing their pain to the cross usually needs a full three-hour session within the seminar. It is done as a group experience, because individual counseling is not culturally understood or even feasible, given the scale of the trauma. The whole community is traumatized! To make the transfer of pain to Jesus more real, we used the symbolism of nailing their terrible stories to a large wooden cross that we transported around Rwanda. We would then take the cross outside and burn the papers. Afterwards, I heard many encouraging testimonies. "I've been to many seminars, but this was different because I was able to leave my pain at the cross." "My heart is so healed! Everyone in Rwanda needs to do this." Sometimes, though, people need further help after this session on the cross. They may need someone to accompany them to a site associated with some atrocity or to a graveside, to help them express their grief and receive God's love right at that point.

Ideally, the "cross workshop" should be done as part of the three-day seminar, so that all the teaching is given on either side of it. However, it can also be conducted on its own, with some preliminary teaching on "Jesus the Pain Bearer." We have done this in some orphanages and for widows' groups. I have even conducted this part of the seminar as a separate module for groups where only one or two were committed Christians, with very positive results. The message of the cross is for everyone, and we have seen people led into salvation through their participation.

The seminar was conducted successfully just eight weeks after the genocide had ended, with unburied bodies still lying around. Recently, I met pastors who were in that original workshop in September 1994, and it was amazing to me to hear them say how the seminar healed them and gave them the courage to go on serving God to this day.

The Need to Hear and Be Heard

Before pouring out their pain to the Lord, seminar participants also needed to listen to each other's hearts. We put people from different ethnic groups and different denominations into small groups together and asked them to share their stories. They were not only to listen to the facts, but also to listen to the pain in each other's hearts. Often there was resistance to doing this exercise, but usually the vast majority agreed to try it. We found that the dividing walls began to be demolished at this point. This willingness to listen to each other with compassion was especially important after the refugees returned to Rwanda from the camps in Zaire and Tanzania, when much fear, suspicion, and hostility were present in the country.

Understanding Real Forgiveness

We talked about the transfer of pain to Jesus as being a prerequisite to being able to forgive from the heart, as Scripture requires of us. All too often, I heard people say, "I've forgiven—it's all past," as a means of avoiding facing the pain. Others opposed the preaching of forgiveness by the church, thinking it meant condoning the wrong that had been committed. We needed to understand biblical forgiveness and its cost. I believe that forgiving others requires the atoning sacrifice of the Lamb, just as much as our receiving God's forgiveness. There has to be Someone who can carry the sin sinned against us, bear our pain for us, and take responsibility for ministering to our wounded hearts, before we can truly forgive. It was only after the participants had brought their pain to the cross that we would begin to teach on forgiveness, usually to discover that a miracle had already taken place in their hearts. Many testified of having left their hatred behind at the cross and now being ready to forgive.

What if there is no evidence of repentance on the part of the offender? Can there be forgiveness then? I believe the key is found in 1 Peter 2:23. Jesus could forgive the unrepentant by committing His case into the hands of a Just Judge. There will be a day of judgment, and the unrepentant will be judged, but those who repent will find mercy. We can safely entrust our case into the hands of this Judge and refuse to be the judge ourselves. Our hearts will then be set free.

Discovering Jesus as Redeemer

Another key was to discover Jesus as the redeemer, not only of our sins, but also of all our lives' tragedies. As we discover and experience His heart in the place of greatest darkness, He can then "turn our trials into gold," as in Keith Green's song. Instead of working against us, the worst tragedies of life can be transformed by God to work for us, so that we can continue living, having been enriched within. John 10:10 tells of the thief who robs us of so many things. However, Jesus came to give us life and to restore to our spirits what Satan robbed from us. What's more, He does so *abundantly,* causing us to end up with more spiritually than we lost in the first place. Holding on to the bigger picture of God being able to redeem everything gives us hope to face the future.

Exploring God's Ways of Dealing With Ethnic Conflict

We spent quite a lot of time looking at the roots of ethnic conflict. Because our ethnicity gives us so much of our identity, ethnic conflict is an attack on the core of our being. Here again, I used my own testimony of growing up feeling like a second-class citizen because I was Welsh. We focused on two ways of coming to a place of reconciliation: discovering a new identity in God's holy nation and standing in the gap with identificational repentance.

Discovering a new identity in God's holy nation

We needed to discover our new identity as fellow citizens of God's holy nation (1 Pet. 2:9). This was a life-changing concept for me, to hear for myself God's call to every child of Abraham: "Leave your country, your people, and your father's household, and go to the land I will show you" (Gen. 12:1). It was thrilling to see light dawn as people began to understand God's call to be clothed with a higher identity than their tribal (national) identity. They could then take their place as members of His nation, where equality, mutual respect for each other's cultures, and joy in one another are found. I heard people say, "We Christians are no longer Hutu or Tutsi—we are all members of God's holy nation!"

Standing in the gap with identificational repentance

I shared how God had disarmed my heart of resentment and prejudice against the English through the repentance of some English Christians on behalf of their forefathers. I have found that identificational repentance is a very powerful key to healing woundedness (i.e., taking on the priestly role of repenting on behalf of our nation, people group, forefathers, men, women, fathers, mothers, etc.). This identificational repentance cannot absolve the guilt of the past, but it can release grace in the present for the offended to be able to forgive.

Each time I taught on this subject, God said to me, "You start." And time after time, God gave me a gift of repentance as a white European in Africa. I confessed the sins of my forefathers, asked for forgiveness, and prayed for the healing of the African people. This often became the catalyst for heart change in my listeners, opening a whole new dimension in working towards reconciliation. Though it was not the cultural norm for them, both Hutu and Tutsi began to stand in the gap, asking forgiveness on behalf of their people group, as well as confessing their own sinful attitudes. In seminar after seminar, we saw them weeping in each other's arms as God did a deep, reconciling work among us.

South Africa

On the invitation of local South African Christians, I began similar seminars in South Africa. At first, I wondered if the same basic format would also be anointed in a more sophisticated South Africa, but I am finding that the message of the cross is just as powerful in bringing healing and reconciliation there.

There are, however, some differences in emphasis when ministering in South Africa. In Rwanda, the pain and division are uppermost in people's thinking, so it is possible to move straight in and look for solutions. In South Africa, however, things are supposed to be all right now. Many think that since the end of apartheid in 1994, they are now reconciled, so there is little enthusiasm for attending a seminar on reconciliation. One does not have to look far beneath the surface, however, to discover that reconciliation is needed now more than ever. Despair, fear, and judgmental attitudes abound, and (apart from some noteworthy exceptions) the various ethnic groups are retreating to their own ghettos. Sadly, the church appears to be particularly slow in discovering their brothers and sisters in the other ethnic groups. Because of the cultural differences, additional principles have been added, which I discuss below.

Different Ethnic Groups: A Blessing or a Curse?

We look at how God views the various ethnic groups, and many have testified that their perspectives were radically changed at this point. The God who loves infinite variety has made His divine nature clearly visible in creation (Rom. 1:20). From one man, He made all the different nations (Acts 17:26) for His pleasure and for the display of His glory. He delights in mankind (Prov. 8:30-31). He desires all the ethnic groups to bring their own glory and splendor into the New Jerusalem (Psalm 86:9; Rev. 7:9; 21:26). God's intention was that we would enrich and bless one another through the variety of our cultural expressions. His glory is so vast that no one people group could adequately express His image. Rather, we all help to form a multifaceted diamond.

Following this discussion, we then explore God's pain, as His plan from the beginning was destroyed and as ethnicity became a reason for wounding, rejection, injustice, pride, and even massacres to take place. This concept is clearly a new revelation for most participants!

Cultural Redemption in the Holy Nation

As the members of each ethnic group rediscover their value and significance as fellow citizens in God's holy nation (1 Pet. 2:9), it is possible for them to treat each other as equals and to honor and enjoy one another. When cultures are viewed through the prism of God's Word, we can discern between the special treasures that God placed in every culture and that which is a sinful. We can have new faith for the redeeming of our culture, *in order that the culture can take its rightful place in and enhance the holy nation*. I believe it is crucial to keep this perspective. Redeeming culture should never become an end in itself, for then it leads to idolatry.

The Thief: Robbing Us of Seeing God's Character

We look specifically at how the history of South Africa has distorted the truth about God's character for each of the different ethnic groups. The responses have always been profoundly disturbing. The Zulus say, "He is the God of the oppressor, and He favors whites. The churches had a notice, 'No dogs or blacks here.'" The Coloreds (i.e., mixed race) ask, "Did He want us to exist, or are we a mistake?" The Indians assert, "God doesn't like Indians—we have to become Westernized to be acceptable to Him." The Afrikaners maintain, "He's the God of the Old Covenant, and we are His chosen people. We obey Him, but He's harsh and distant from us." The English claim, "God is an Englishman!" It is helpful to see that the thief of John 10:10 has been at work in all sections of the community, robbing everyone of the true character of God. There are no winners in this situation. We all need to rebuild the foundation by having a revelation of God's heart.

Understanding the Wounded Spirit

We examine the graphic imagery of the "bruised reed" and the "dimly burning wick" (Isa. 42:3) to understand the meaning of the wounded spirit. God wants to lift up those who are bowed down (Psalm 145:14), and He revives the spirit of the lowly (Isa. 57:15). He is particularly close to those who are crushed in spirit (Psalm 34:18). We look at various different behavior patterns demonstrated by people who have a wounded spirit, and then we spend some time looking at the fruits of passing judgments. I find that each ethnic group had judged the other ethnic groups, and these judgments have to be renounced in order for people to be set free of the "sowing and reaping" principle (Gal. 6:7). We note, somberly, that the oppressed often become the oppressors, unless the grace of God intervenes. The response to this discussion has been very positive, as participants gain insight into each other's woundedness and the judgments each has made.

Rediscovering Each Other at the "King's Table"

In Rwanda, we ended the seminar with the repentance time, with both personal and vicarious identification. In South Africa, however, I felt the need to add something else. During the last break, we quickly and secretly set up a lavish table of bread, wine, exotic fruits, nuts, candies, candles, and flowers. After reminding ourselves of the story of Mephibosheth in 2 Samuel 9 and the kingdom feast in Matthew 8:11, we would invite the participants to eat at the "King's table." Each was asked to take a golden (paper) crown, place it on the head of someone from a different ethnic group, and say, "Welcome to the King's table, fellow citizen of God's holy nation!" After serving one another and praying for each other, we finish by inviting each ethnic group in turn into the center. The rest of us would then affirm the members of that group and would say what we particularly appreciated about the group. We then pronounced blessings on them, sharing any encouraging and prophetic words we felt God was giving us. Each "feast" has been an amazing time of healing and celebration! Participants kept saying, "I'm *so happy!* I'll *never* forget this day!"

Results of the Seminars

For the first two years in Rwanda, I worked with church leaders of all denominations and both ethnic groups. God wonderfully answered the prayers of our many prayer partners, as people left the seminars testifying that they had been healed and were now ready to forgive and be reconciled. Skeptics said, "You don't know the Rwandese people. They can play games. How do you know it wasn't just an emotional experience?"

We decided to go back for a follow-up seminar three months later. At that time, we asked, "Did anything change as a result of the seminar in you, your church, and your neighborhood?" The testimonies started pouring in of hearts set free to forgive and love their enemies, of churches that had been divided by ethnicity now finding a new unity, of local initiatives taking place to reach out to bring healing and reconciliation to their communities. We heard so often, "The workshop with the cross changed everything for me! I've been healed ever since!"

Skeptics still said, "Wait until the refugees come back. It's easy to say you forgive when your enemies are in a different country." However, the follow-up seminars after the refugees returned were still more encouraging! (By God's sovereign grace, we had just completed taking the seminar to each town in Rwanda three weeks before the refugees started returning.) We heard of Christian leaders who had gone out to welcome those returning and of wonderful stories of reconciliation that had taken place (e.g., a woman who had lost 200 out of 250 of her extended family invited those involved in the killings to a meal at her home).

We began to hold new seminars, with Christian leaders from the refugee camps joining with those from inside the country. This time it was much harder. The atmosphere was often charged with fear, suspicion, and sometimes hostility. However, the workshop with the cross repeatedly led to a breakthrough, as they listened to the pain in each other's hearts and then knelt side by side at the cross. Although the seminars were much tougher on the first day, the work of the Spirit by the third day was deeper. We saw both ethnic groups singing and dancing together, often until the early hours of the morning. The repentance time at the end brought more tears than the time at the cross. Again and again, we heard people say, "For the first time, I now believe that reconciliation is possible!"

The testimonies we are now receiving from South Africa are similarly dramatic. People often report that they left the seminar looking at the other ethnic groups with new eyes. "I've been transformed deep inside. Life can never be the same again!" In spite of being aware of the intense spiritual opposition to this ministry, those who have attended the seminars are on fire to put the principles into practice. Participants have started taking the initiative to spread the message of reconciliation. They have led multi-ethnic meetings and camps, where they are seeing the same results. To God be all the glory!

Current Ministry and Future Directions

The ministry in Rwanda has now been handed over to Rwandese brothers from both ethnic groups ministering together, and God is greatly using them. Even local government officials are recognizing their powerful message and are inviting their help in local initiatives. The area in the north, where hostilities and killings continue, has been the place where we have seen the greatest work of the Holy Spirit. There is much work still to do. At first, only Protestant leaders responded to the invitations to the seminars, but now, after much prayer, the doors are opening to share the same message with Catholic leaders. I am thrilled to report that there are now interdenominational, inter-ethnic teams forming in most of the prefectures to take the message of healing and reconciliation through the cross down to the grassroots. Our core team is visiting them to advise and encourage them in their local initiatives.

We are expanding the work in South Africa and are hoping to see multi-ethnic teams released in different parts of the country to carry the good news of reconciliation through the cross across the land. We especially desire to see reconciliation lived out in practical ways in the local society. Consequently, we have teamed up with community development workers to equip the reconciled churches to work together in serving the poorest of their communities, so their societies may give expression to the reality of reconciled relationships.

We have also received many invitations to expand into the Balkan region. A divisive spirit runs deep in the Balkans, not only between ethnic Muslims and Christians, but also within the Christian community itself. Even many of the agencies working in the Balkans are dealing with strong divisive elements within their own teams, and there is a high need for reconciliation even between those trying to reach out within the Balkans. We are prayerfully seeking partner organizations with whom we can work and who can help us contextualize the ministry for this region.

Final Thoughts

Reconciliation work is not a type of work one can do for months on end without breaks, especially with the pressures inherent in ministering ethnic reconciliation in places that are often still violent. Those who think about launching out in this type of ministry should keep in mind that there is a real price to pay in physical, emotional, mental, and spiritual terms. The strain can be intense. Good member care for such workers requires proper accountability to insure that breaks are taken and that care and support are being utilized.

This chapter has focused on member care via debriefing and ethnic reconciliation, emphasizing the place of Christ's cross for both. Debriefing and reconciliation, however, are not an end in themselves. They are part of the larger process of demonstrating the kingdom of God, by holistically transforming communities that are the least evangelized, the least developed, and highly traumatized.

Reflection and Discussion

1. Identify a few ways that even "normal" cross-cultural experiences can be painful.

2. What are some of the "curative factors" for wounds that the authors describe?

3. How can you apply what the authors have said about Christ as the sin bearer and the pain bearer?

4. Reflect on the notion that as citizens of the kingdom of God, our true ethnicity is celestial and transnational. How can this identity help prevent and resolve ethnic conflicts?

5. What are some of the steps needed to develop networks for debriefing and ethnic reconciliation ministries?

References and Suggested Reading

Appleby, R. (2000). *The ambivalence of the sacred: Religion, violence, and reconciliation*. Lanham, MD: Rowman & Littlefield Publishers.

Baum, G., & Wells, H. (1997). *The reconciliation of peoples: Challenge to the churches*. Maryknoll, NY: Orbis Books.

Fawcett, G. (1999). *Ad-mission: The briefing and debriefing of teams of missionaries and aid workers*. Harpenden, UK: Author.

Lampman, L. (Ed.). (1999). *God and the victim: Theological reflections on evil, victimization, justice, and forgiveness*. Grand Rapids, MI: Eerdmans.

Lederach, J. (1997). *Building peace: Sustainable reconciliation in divided societies*. Washington, DC: United States Institute of Peace.

———. (1999). *Journey toward reconciliation*. Scottdale, PA: Herald Press.

Lloyd, R. (1998, rev. 2001). *Healing the wounds of ethnic conflict: The role of the church in healing, forgiveness, and ethnic reconciliation*. Geneva, Switzerland: Mercy Ministries International.

Mitchell, J., & Everly, G. (1993). *Critical incident stress debriefing: An operations manual for the prevention of traumatic stress among emergency services and disaster workers*. Ellicott City, MD: Chevron Publishing.

Prince, D. (2000). *Atonement: Your appointment with God*. Baldock, UK: Derek Prince Ministries.

Rogers, C. (1998, January–March). The changing shape of security for NGO field workers (special issue). *Together*. Monrovia, CA: World Vision International.

Robb, J., & Hill, J. (2000). *The peacemaking power of prayer*. Nashville, TN: Broadman & Holman Publishers.

Samuel, V., & Sugden, C. (Eds.). (1999). *Mission as transformation: A theology of the whole gospel*. Oxford, UK: Regnum Books.

Shriver, D. (1995). *An ethic for enemies: Forgiveness in politics*. New York, NY: Oxford University Press.

Summerfield, D. (1998). The social experience of war and some issues for the humanitarian field. In P. Bracken & C. Petty (Eds.), *Rethinking the trauma of war*. London, UK: Save the Children.

UNICEF. (1996). *The state of the world's children*. Oxford, UK: Oxford University Press.

***Erik Spruyt** is a second-career mission worker. He and his wife, Jeltje, are both Dutch and are the founders/directors of Le Rucher. They have been involved with missions since 1980. They have two children who are currently finishing post-graduate courses. Erik holds a bachelor's degree in physical therapy and a master's degree in orthopedic manipulative therapy. He further specialized in leadership development, counseling, and trauma care. He is a resource lecturer for the University of the Nations, College of Counseling and Health Care, for which he developed several accredited courses. Apart from the residential work at Le Rucher, Erik has conducted trauma care seminars in South Africa, Sierra Leone, Liberia, Guinea, Albania, and Kosovo for both expatriate and indigenous workers, pastors, and police officers. Email: mercyministries@lerucher.org.*

***Rhiannon Lloyd**, a former doctor of medicine and psychiatry, has been in full-time Christian work since 1985, ministering extensively in cross-cultural situations. Before starting the work in Rwanda, she spent many years teaching courses for Christian workers and counseling people with deep emotional needs. Rhiannon and her ministry are endorsed by African Enterprise, Operation Mobilization, World Vision, Tear Fund, Youth With A Mission, and Christians in Caring Professions. Rhiannon is also an associate member of the International Reconciliation Coalition. Email: rhiannonlloyd@compuserve.com.*

***Renée Schudel** is the Assistant Director at Le Rucher/Mercy Ministries International, where she has served for the past five years, primarily doing consulting and training in community development work. She has worked in missions since 1988, including seven years in war-torn Liberia, facilitating and training churches in local community development initiatives. Prior to her missions career, she worked for Boeing Aerospace Company for several years as a computer consultant. Email: mercyministries@lerucher.org.*

48

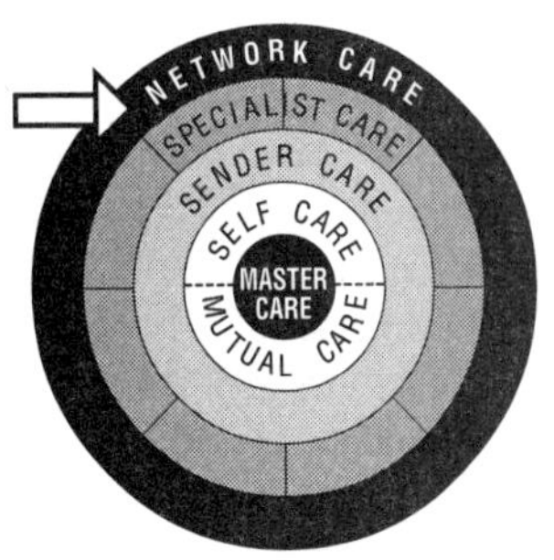

Developing Member Care Affiliations

KELLY O'DONNELL

Regional interagency member care affiliations (RIMAs) help to identify and develop needed resources to support mission personnel in a specific geographic location. They reflect the growing cooperative efforts within both the international health care and mission communities. This chapter explores several characteristics of these strategic new affiliations, interspersing the discussion with some personal reflections from the author, along with suggestions for the formation and maintenance of RIMAs.

It is encouraging to observe the continuous expansion of the global missions movement, with current estimates of over 400,000 personnel in cross-cultural ministries (Barrett, 1997). A majority of these come from the Older Sending Countries (e.g., United States, United Kingdom, Australia, Canada), with the movement growing rapidly in the Newer Sending Countries (e.g., Nigeria, India, Brazil, Korea). Interfacing with this growing movement is the maturing domain of member care, an interdisciplinary field whose overall purpose is to nurture and develop mission personnel, from their recruitment through their retirement (O'Donnell & O'Donnell, 1992). The need to sustain missionaries over the long haul is seen in the recent figures on missionary attrition, in which each year an estimated 3.1% (possibly 12,000 people) depart prematurely, permanently, and for preventable reasons (Brierley, 1997). Such undesirable attrition also spills over onto others, as its ripple effects negatively impact thousands of family members and friends in the home and host communities.

How can mission organizations, sending churches, and member care groups work together to help provide the necessary "flow of care" (Pollock, 1997) for the increasing numbers of mission personnel? One important way is to form affiliations of experienced member care practitioners, who are familiar with missions and who band together for the purpose of developing important member care resources within a specific geographic region (e.g., North Africa), people group (e.g., tribal groups in North India), or type of ministry (e.g., trauma management). These affiliations, when set up and maintained properly, help complement the supportive resources that sending agencies are already providing (e.g., team building, crisis care, and pastoral field visits). In many cases, they also fill in significant member care gaps.

This chapter takes a closer look at a specific type of affiliation referred to by the acronym *RIMA*—regional interagency member care affiliation. I have had the good and challenging fortune of being involved with seven RIMAs over the past several years. Some are functioning well, while others are still getting off the ground. My background in community psychology has been especially helpful for me, as several core principles from this field have shaped my involvement with these affiliations.

The main thrust of this chapter is to explore some of the characteristics of RIMAs, relating these to community psychology principles. Community psychology's relevance is found in the similarity and compatibility of many of its concepts with those of the member care field (O'Donnell, 1986). Examples include the emphasis on working with at-risk groups (e.g., focusing on missionaries in isolated, unstable settings), assessing felt needs in order to develop supportive resources (e.g., doing a needs assessment for Latin American field personnel), and empowering missionary personnel with additional skills for personal adjustment and work effectiveness (e.g., offering workshops on stress management and contingency planning).

Interspersed with the discussion that follows are some personal comments about my involvement with RIMAs, along with suggestions for the formation and maintenance of these affiliations. The following questions are addressed: What types of personnel are needed? What types of projects are prioritized? What are some of the pitfalls? In short, how can these affiliations become relevant for the missions community? I also report on the work of some current member care affiliations, and I review similar cooperative efforts which have been occurring within the international health care and the global missions communities.

Some Historical Perspectives

In the early 1990s, I began to explore the viability of developing more coordinated member care efforts at both international and interagency levels. I became convinced that the time had come for deliberate pursuit of a consensually derived "macro model" of member care, in order to provide further support for the church's mission efforts, especially among unreached people groups. My initial ideas were published in the article, "An Agenda for Member Care," in which I encouraged leaders in the member care field to "step forward and help steer this field in response to the Lord's direction" (O'Donnell, 1992, p. 112).

These aspirations for a more global and coordinated member care approach were neither unrealistic nor without precedent. Cooperative endeavors were being seen in the rise of national and international missionary associations, as well as in the formation of partnerships of ministries/organizations focusing on specific unreached people groups (Taylor, 1995). Likewise, in the area of missionary care, there had been some encouraging cooperative developments via three International Conferences on Missionary Kids (ICMK, in 1984, 1987, and 1989). These historic gatherings, in retrospect, served as the main interagency, international forums for member care workers (not just MK care personnel) to come together. ICMK eventually evolved into three regional groups for the Americas, Asia, and Europe/Africa, along with several local chapters (Wilcox, 1998).

Member care, like missions, was rapidly growing in the 1980s, and by the early 1990s, it had developed into its own specialized field (O'Donnell, 1997). The next step was to see various streams of this field come together (psychologists, residential care centers, crisis care specialists, mission pastors, etc.), not just for mutual support and additional training, but to provide and develop additional resources on behalf of the mission community in a more systematic way (e.g., counseling, training, crisis care, screening tools, MK reentry programs).

Several joint member care projects were launched in the 1990s. Examples include the MK-CART/CORE group's research on missionary kids and school personnel; the 1992 book, *Missionary Care*, which was the collaborative effort of six consulting editors and 23 authors; the 1997 WEF book on missionary attrition, *Too Valuable to Lose,* which was a landmark book in that it included authors from all over the world; special gatherings that have brought together member care workers, such as the three European Member Care Consultations held in 1997, 1999, and 2001; smaller, informal, day consultations in Singapore to address member care topics via case studies; and, as this article describes, the formation of separate interagency member care groups for the regions of the Middle East (1993), North Africa (1994), Europe (1997), Asia (1998), and Latin America (1999).

Similar developments were making and continue to make their mark on the health sciences—that is, there is a growing recognition of the need for international, interdisciplinary cooperation to tackle human problems. Currently, for example, there are over 60 international psychological associations and related organizations (APA Office of International Affairs, 1998). International psychology, seen as both a vast network and a social movement, is actively involved as a health care partner around the globe. Pawlik and d'Ydewalle (1996, p. 489) comment:

"The role of international cooperation and exchange (of persons, knowledge, and experience) may seem all too obvious in the interest of developing cross-national understanding and goodwill among people of different nationality, ethnic, or other background. Psychology has been opening up to and has become a partner in many such initiatives, too numerous to be cited in detail.... A more re-

Table 1
People In Aid: Principles for the Care/Management of Aid Personnel

Principle 1:	The people who work for us are integral to our effectiveness and success.... Human resource issues are integral to our strategic plans.
Principle 2:	Our human resource policies aim for best practice.... We do not aim to respond solely to minimum legal, professional, or donor requirements.
Principle 3:	Our human resource policies aim to be effective, efficient, fair, and transparent.... Our policies must enable us to achieve both effectiveness in our work and good quality of working life for our staff ... and to promote equal opportunity.
Principle 4:	We consult our field staff when we develop human resource policy. We recognize that we must implement, monitor, and continuously develop our human resource policies in consultation with the people who work for us.
Principle 5:	Plans and budgets reflect our responsibilities towards our field staff ... for staff management, support, development, security, and well-being.
Principle 6:	We provide appropriate training, ... professional support, and development before, during, and after [staff] field assignments.
Principle 7:	We take all reasonable steps to ensure staff security and well-being. We recognize that the work of relief and development agencies often places great demands on staff in conditions of complexity and risk.

cent example is the initiative (through the [International Union of Psychological Science] Committee for the Psychological Study of Peace...) to help mitigate postwar stress disorders in war-stricken Rwanda and Burundi. Other examples are psychology's contributions to international educational programs ... or to worldwide health education initiatives under the aegis of the World Health Organization (WHO)."

Another example of coordinated efforts is seen in People In Aid's (1997) *Code of Best Practice*. This document, formulated by several humanitarian aid organizations from the United Kingdom and Ireland, discusses seven core principles for the management and support of aid personnel. Recognizing the draining realities of this labor-intensive profession, guidelines were drawn up to help ensure the security and well-being of staff (see Table 1). Organizations, both religious and nonreligious, as well as those outside the United Kingdom/Ireland, have been encouraged to discuss these principles, weave them into their ethos, and hold themselves accountable for their implementation. Outside funding for projects will likely be increasingly contingent on the degree to which aid and mission organizations are putting a code such as this into practice.

Characteristics of RIMAs

RIMA Personnel

RIMAs, in community psychology terms, are strategies for meeting a community's felt needs by creating new or alternative "settings" (Sarason, 1972). These settings can be health care task forces, support groups, and so on. At times, such settings are birthed out of a sense of frustration that the existing health service structures and social programs are inadequately serving groups within their catchment areas. At other times, the settings are created as an amicable way of complementing existing resources. For RIMAs, the latter is by far the case. Nonetheless, there is a motivating conviction among most RIMA members that much more needs to be done. A prime example of this is seen in the organization of various regional and national member care consultations, whereby member care practitioners (e.g., mental health professionals, physicians specializing in tropical medicine, personnel directors, pastors) and church/mission leaders have met each other, have exchanged information/updates, and in many instances have decided to work more closely together (Ritschard, 1992).

Most RIMAs are inclusive in their membership. They have a good representation of people from different organizations and nations, who have diverse mission and member care experience. Such diversity is welcomed and encouraged among community and organizational psychologists working in international contexts, as it helps assure that various groups' needs are understood and that culturally relevant approaches to meeting such needs are developed (Adler, 1991). Initially, though, North Americans have often been in the majority. An example of some criteria that have been used to invite colleagues to participate in RIMAs is presented in Table 2, taken from the Member Care Task Force of the World Evangelical Alliance's Missions Commission.

Not surprisingly, I have found that RIMAs work best when a number of their members have had a prior trusting relationship. In fact, group diversity without group trust is quite difficult to manage. It often seems that *function* (working on strategic joint tasks) usually brings friends and colleagues together, but *friendship* and Christian *fellowship* keep them together. From this foundation of function and friendship eventually emerges a more definite *form* (structure) to help support the affiliation's efforts. With time, many other colleagues usually connect with this core group, forming a broad network of affiliates who relate to the group for information, joint projects, and encouragement.

Table 2
Guidelines for RIMA Members: Selection and Ongoing Involvement

- Is spiritually and emotionally mature, with good family life, if married, and a support group for personal growth and accountability.
- Is actively involved in member care, has specific member care skills, and works with different missions/member care networks.
- Has growing or broad international experience and is a respected leader (via position and/or sphere of influence).
- Has a call/desire to further develop member care in broader arenas than one's usual work setting.
- Involvement in this Task Force is supported by one's organization—it is part of the job description in many cases.
- Has access to electronic mail to communicate regularly with other members; meets with other members at least once every two years.
- Term of service is three years; works on at least one Task Force project at any given time.
- Has adequate clerical and financial support to participate.
- Is a team player, committed to work in unity of purpose and objectives.
- Understands and agrees with these guidelines and with the WEA Statement of Faith.

RIMA members need to cultivate several different roles within their group. The challenge is similar to that of community psychologists and others involved in community work, where the issue is not just what one can do or what one is good at, but also what really needs to be done. In other words, how do members adjust their usual roles, in order to meet the felt needs of under-served groups? For RIMAs, this means that members must be willing to stretch their role parameters at times on behalf of the mission communities they serve. Moderating an email forum for member care workers within a given region is a good example. The task may be tedious, but it is quite valuable.

I see four types of roles as being basic to those who want to develop member care in general and RIMAs in particular:

- *Scouts*—to monitor what is happening (trends, events, needs) and report back to others in the affiliation and in the mission/member care community.
- *Scribes*—to make accurate notes and write/disseminate material about what is happening.
- *Bards*—to inspire others, point out future directions, and eloquently retell what is happening via discussions, presentations, and training.
- *Brokers*—to connect the right information about regional needs with the right resources (especially people) that can help.

RIMA Projects

Member care affiliations, whether they focus on regions (e.g., South Asia), people groups (e.g., unreached groups in Indonesia, China), or specific ministries (e.g., trauma care), identify a number of projects in keeping with the group's goals. Each joint project usually has a coordinator, a written plan with an estimate of costs and funding sources, and an evaluation at the end. None of the RIMAs I have worked on have offered remuneration for our efforts. We work as volunteers; however, funds have periodically been available to cover many expenses, made possible through contributions from one's organization and from outside sources.

At the heart of RIMA projects is the goal to make a significant difference on behalf of mission personnel. At the task level, this means developing relevant resources that fill in significant regional member care gaps. At the relationship level, this means demonstrating the love Christians have for one another, as described in John 13-17, by supporting missionaries with member care resources and by encouraging them to support each other (Pollock, 1997). RIMAs can benefit from community psychology's emphasis on working with groups whose well-being is "at risk" due to inadequate development or distribution of available and potentially available resources (e.g., immunization programs, transportation to schools, single-parent support groups). In the member care context, at-risk groups would include missionaries serving in isolated, potentially traumatic, and/or politically unstable areas, with limited access to important supportive resources (e.g., fellowship, recreation opportunities, safe and consistent sources for food, desirable educational options for missionary children).

For Collins and Porras (1994), organizational consultants who write about the successful practices of visionary companies, going after large and at times audacious goals is a necessary means to stay on the cutting edge in the marketplace, provided that such goals stem from the company's core vision—its *raison d'être*. In terms of RIMAs, this means that members must not be content with just discussing issues, sharing updates, providing mutual support, and helping each other with their organizational-related work. Rather, members must deliberately and ambitiously desire to pursue larger-scale projects that will strategically impact the mission community.

Here are three broad categories of projects—member care gaps—which RIMAs can address. Each gap heading represents a major community psychology principle and practice. Getting missionaries themselves and other member care colleagues involved in these projects, which is not unlike the community psychology practice of "citizen participation" (Heller, 1990), is key to creating a sense of ownership in the projects and making sure that they are relevant. Using electronic mail to create "virtual offices/teams" is a promising way to accomplish many of these projects (Koster, 1994).

Gap 1: Going into the community to provide acceptable/accessible services

- Develop an interagency team/network/center of caregivers within the region (e.g., Southeast Asia, West Africa, Commonwealth of Independent States).
- Provide services via short-term field visits and also for the participants at strategic conferences (e.g., workshops, counseling, team building, consultation).
- Consult with regional and national mission associations concerning member care; maintain close working relationships with mission leaders.
- Set up regional consultations where people actively involved in member care can meet each other, pray together, exchange information/updates, and receive additional training.

Gap 2: Developing a "sense of community" via communication and writing

- Oversee an email forum for people within the region to communicate about member care issues, needs, and news.
- Send out an email newsletter and hard copy twice a year, with updates about past and future member care-related events, together with commentaries/perspectives.
- Set up web sites for sharing and disseminating member care-related materials—an electronic "clearinghouse" for information, current events, referral listing, and useful publications.
- Translate and write member care materials in different languages, not just in English. Submit articles to regional journals and magazines (e.g., *Asian Mission*, *Africa Journal of Evangelical Theology*, *Ellos Y Nosotros* in Latin America).

Gap 3: Empower mission personnel and member care workers

■ Organize a network of trainers that can give workshops for national Christians, member care workers, missionaries, and mission leaders at key locations, such as at graduate/Bible schools, training centers, special regional gatherings, and field settings. Important topics include:

- Crisis and contingency management.
- Interpersonal skills/peer counseling.
- Team building skills.
- Spiritual life/retreats.
- Family life/MK seminars; child safety.
- Member care overview course.
- Grief/depression/transition.
- Addictions/unwanted habits.
- MK personnel orientation.
- Stress management.

■ Develop practicum and training opportunities in missionary care for graduate students and other member care workers (e.g., inviting colleagues to work at an overseas mission conference or to do a field visit; offering a three-month practicum for graduate students).

■ Train missionaries and national Christian workers with member care skills, in order to provide needed services to nationals (e.g., training for counseling, debriefing, and running support and recovery groups).

RIMAs in the Broader Context

RIMAs do not exist on their own. They are part of and dependent upon the missions and member care communities. RIMAs are not merely special interest groups, lobbying for some cause. Rather, they are fundamentally *mission* groups, specializing in member care but intricately woven into the missions movement. In most cases, RIMAs would not exist without the backing and involvement of concerned mission leaders who function as "gatekeepers" to help member care workers access mission communities. In some ways, RIMAs may embody the vibrant spirit of the grass-roots groups and movements which have historically been part of the community psychology landscape. At the same time, though, RIMAs are relationally linked to leadership structures in missions, along with other related member care groups.

Metaphorically, RIMAs function like a thumb on the member care hand, in that they are able to touch, influence, and complement the movements of the four fingers—i.e., other member care resources. Members of the European RIMA called Member Care/Europe, for instance, have helped organize two interagency teams of mental health and education specialists to provide consultation services to missionaries in Central Asia. They have also sponsored two intensive member care courses in Germany to provide further training for European mission personnel who have member care responsibilities.

RIMAs also represent a key component envisioned in PACTS, a further development of the macro model of member care mentioned previously (O'Donnell, 1997). This model summarizes five future directions for this field, with the "A" standing for affiliations. Again, if PACTS were a hand, the "A" would function like the thumb, inasmuch as it works alongside to help support the work of the other four appendages, or member care directions:

■ Pioneering member care for at-risk groups who have limited access to supportive resources.

■ Affiliating together for mutual support and joint work, such as via RIMAs.

■ Continuing education/personal growth for member care workers.

■ Training others in member care via key workshops and courses.

■ Specializing in strategic projects to provide and develop important member care resources.

Pulling It Together

In summary, RIMAs need three things to be relevant. First, they need the *right platform* which they can use as a solid base for themselves. For many, this means being part of (and often emerging from) an existing mission structure, such as the Association of Evangelicals in Africa, the World Evangelical Alliance, or COMIBAM (Iberoamerican Missions Cooperation), plus having connections with mission leaders. Such relationships provide more credibility and access to resources. Second, RIMAs require the *right personnel*: members who have good relationships with health care/mission networks, who are respected (for godly character, competence, contributions), and who can provide resources (time, skills, funding). Third, RIMAs must pursue the *right projects* on behalf of different groups or "levels" of mission personnel: agencies, nations, regions, and also globally. Table 3 summarizes these factors via a member care "relevance grid" and includes relevant concepts from community psychology.

Table 3
RIMA Relevance Grid for Developing Member Care

1. PLATFORM: The Right Organizational Backing

Working with mission associations/influential leaders to create new "settings"

2. PERSONNEL: The Right Relationships, Respect, Resources

Encouraging diversity/new roles for RIMA members and "citizen participation"

3. PROJECTS: The Right Tasks

Developing resources for groups of mission personnel, especially those "at risk"

- Coordinating groups (task forces, member care affiliations)
- Consultations (training, joint projects, sense of community)
- Centers (facilities, geographic service hubs, groups providing member care)
- Compilation of resources (written materials, service organizations, referrals)
- Courses/workshops (prevention of problems, empowerment for ministry)
- Comprehensive study and information (research, web sites)
- Coalitions/networks (tropical medicine, MK ministries, crisis care teams)

4. LEVEL OF FOCUS

Agency / National / Regional / Global

RIMAS: Practicalities and Pitfalls

It takes a lot of work for RIMAs to reach a point of viability. In my experience, it is a three- to five-year process to "knit the net"—to help organize a network of basic resources within a region. The process is similar to that of building a house, described in Proverbs 24:3-4, in which wisdom, knowledge, and skill are needed to establish the house and fill it with precious goods.

Some people and projects start off with much enthusiasm but then eventually fade, largely due to time constraints. At times, there can be relational differences and cultural misunderstandings which drain energy from projects. Different agendas and personalities can clash. There can also be different commitments to look at or go after "the bigger regional picture." A coordinator may not keep the communication flowing over time and over large geographic distances—functions which are essential when people live in different countries and their work is done in cyberspace via electronic mail. Sometimes the coordinator gets stuck with most of the work, or there is no true accountability for the timely completion of projects, or funds are not available to do projects. The possible hindrances to RIMA viability, frankly, are legion.

The potential gains, however, are worth the trouble. The things that have helped me persevere are the support and involvement of close friends, plus a basic road map to help guide my involvement in affiliations. With regards to the latter, I am indebted to the work of Phill Butler and the staff of Interdev, and I have mingled several of his ideas regarding forming ministry partnerships with my own thoughts for member care affiliations (summarized in Table 4 on the next page).

Current Examples of RIMAs

The 1990s were a decade for member care affiliations, especially RIMAs. Most RIMAs were established as a result of an international mission conference (e.g., Asia Mission Congress II and COMIBAM in 1997) or an international member care consultation (e.g., Middle East Member Care Consultation in 1993, European Member Care Consultation in 1997). Participants got together, identified needs and resources, and then formed the beginning of some type of group, which then developed into a RIMA.

In 1992, I became involved in my first two RIMAs. One was for mission personnel in the Middle East; the other, for personnel in North Africa. These groups came into being as member care workers and mission leaders within these regions met to discuss regional needs and resources. For the Middle East, the group took shape following a three-day workshop which overviewed member care. For North Africa, a group emerged at the end of an 18-month process of discussion with leaders and member care workers involved in this region. In both cases, there was uncertainty as to what would materialize practically as a result of our efforts to talk with people from such diverse backgrounds.

Several other RIMAs now exist and are continuing to be developed. On one end of the task continuum, some groups tend to function more like discussion groups, with occasional joint projects. On the other end of the continuum are those that want to be more like cohesive teams and that intentionally go after "demanding performance challenges" (Katzenbach & Smith, 1993) to develop member care, while prioritizing mutual accountability/ support.

Table 4
Guidelines for Effective Member Care Affiliations*

1. Affiliations are built on friendship, trust, and mutual concerns. Function (tasks) usually brings people together, but friendship keeps them together. Affiliations are spiritual entities as well as working groups, so both dimensions require attention. Prayer, worship, and sharing from Scripture are encouraged.
2. Affiliations need at least one coordinator who functions by consensus to bring the affiliation together and keep the fires burning. Coordinators are like roving ambassadors that can articulate the purposes of the affiliation, while helping to bring people and resources together. They champion the group's cause.
3. Affiliations exist in order to accomplish a specific vision and tasks. Partnership for partnership's sake is a sure recipe for failure. Consensus is always involved in identifying tasks. Working together successfully on demanding performance challenges also helps to rally the group and hold it together.
4. Affiliations have limited, achievable objectives in the beginning and become more expansive with time. They start by identifying the most important needs and member care gaps among the people/region being served. Members endeavor to get behind, not in front of, the mission community in a given region (emphasizing felt needs rather than individual agendas).
5. Affiliations are a process, not an event. They may be birthed via a conference/special gathering, but they take time to form and reach viability. Lots of behind-the-scenes relationship building, exploratory meetings, and trust development occur before the groups are launched. They are even more challenging to maintain than to start. Making sure the vision stays alive, the focus remains clear, communications are good, and outcomes are relevant takes effort and long-term commitment—and not just from the coordinator!
6. Affiliations are made up of members with different backgrounds and skills. These members have relationships with mission leaders and networks, are respected, and have access to important resources. Inclusion, interdependency, and cooperation are core values; hence, other groups and individuals are invited to participate on projects.
7. Affiliations acknowledge, even celebrate, the differences in their members' backgrounds. They focus on a common vision and values to help fulfill the group's objectives. Members feel that they truly belong and can influence the group. People and groups participate because they want to be there and want to work together—there is a high level of ownership and participation.
8. Affiliations remain focused on their ultimate goals or vision and are not overly distracted by day-to-day operational demands. Practical jobs need to be done, and members often function in clerical roles. Nonetheless, the end product is kept in mind to guide and inspire. Mutual accountability is essential to make sure that plans are carried out in a timely fashion.
9. Affiliations do not come free. Personal finances at first may be needed, as well as funds from one's mission organization/church. Ultimately, outside funding, especially for larger projects, is needed.
10. Affiliations expect problems, and they plan ahead for them. They have an agreed-upon protocol for handling differing expectations, disappointments, and friction.

* Adapted from Butler (as cited in Taylor, 1995, pp. 409-410).

Following is a brief description of the main RIMAs.

World Evangelical Alliance Missions Commission Member Care Task Force (MemCa)

Following the International Attrition/ Pastoral Care Consultation in England in 1996, plans were made to develop a Member Care Task Force that would help stimulate missionary care around the world. After much planning and interaction, 11 individuals met in England in September 1998 to refine and launch this strategic coordinating body. MemCa functions like a global interagency affiliation. It could potentially be a good structure to help catalyze and pull together several RIMAs around the world. The focus is on developing resources on behalf of mission personnel from the "Triple A" (Asia, Africa, and América-latina) and on behalf of those working among unreached people groups. MemCa also maintains a web site (www.membercare.org), which includes an updated, global list of member care resources (books, counselors, events, training, important articles, etc.). MemCa regrouped during a special consultation in Malaysia in May 2001, and it now has 25 members.

Evangelical Fellowship of Asia Missions Commission Member Care/Asia Task Force

This RIMA is the joint effort of MK and other member care specialists. It was discussed at the Asia Missions Congress II in Thailand in October 1997. It was then birthed in May 1998, as its 10 members met for the first time. Asia is an incredibly diverse continent, and so the strategy is to help develop member care resources at the national level. Prime examples of this effort are encouraging missions and member care workers to convene national member care consultations, increasing awareness of the needs of Asian MKs, and publishing materials in both English and Asian languages.

Iberoamerican Missionary Cooperation (COMIBAM) Pastoral Care Working Group

This group continues to develop and is part of the COMIBAM structure for Latin America, Spain, and Portugal. It officially was set up at COMIBAM II in Acapulco, Mexico, in November 1997. It never really materialized at that time and was reorganized in the summer of 1998 and then again in November 2001 during a small, continental, pastoral care consultation held in Lima, Peru. Some of the goals are to publish member care materials in Spanish/Portuguese, develop a network of Christian mental health professionals who can provide consultation services (e.g., screening, assessment, counseling), maintain an email forum for member care, and organize Latin American member care consultations in different regions.

Middle East Member Care Team

Based in Europe, this interagency group was set up in 1992 to help care for Christian workers and their families in the Middle East. A special focus is resourcing support personnel based in Cyprus. Some members travel to the field to provide services. They also sponsor retreats and member care workshops at various locations. A main goal is to set up a member care center in proximity to the Middle East.

North Africa Member Care Group

Based in Europe, this is one of the working groups of a larger regional partnership. It meets four to six times a year to help coordinate and provide member care services in North Africa and Spain, including retreats for MKs, workshops, and some field visits.

Member Care/Europe

This group of 20 people developed as a result of the First European Member Care Consultation, held near Geneva in 1997. Two other successful member care consultations have been held since then, in France (1999) and in Hungary (2001). Examples of projects include organizing the bi-annual European consultation; linking more extensively with member care personnel from Eastern Europe; providing field services together; maintaining an email forum; teaching in seminaries and institutions; and encouraging the formation of other national member care affiliations. The overall goal is to help develop member care within and from Europe.

Central Asia Member Care Working Group

This group is currently re-forming with five active members and is pursuing these goals: helping to place and resource member care workers in Central Asia, helping to monitor and exchange member care-related information with mission leaders working in this area, supporting a daily radio program being broadcast into the region to encourage workers, and providing referrals for professional care.

Other Types of Member Care Affiliations

- *Mobile Member Care Team*—This is an interagency group of member care specialists. The team is developing a network of consultants who can provide crisis response training and crisis intervention on the field. The first team is located in West Africa and is described in chapter 12 of this book.
- *YWAM Frontier Missions Member Care Group*—This group is an affiliation of consultants in Youth With A Mission (YWAM—an agency with over 15,000 staff) which provides and develops member care resources to frontier mission personnel in YWAM. The main function is to provide professional consultation to each other via email and to provide counseling/workshops at regional YWAM conferences.
- *National affiliations*—Other regional/national member care affiliations continue to emerge, such as for Malaysia, the Philippines, and Brazil. The national member care group for the Netherlands is focusing on such items as the medical, material, career, and counseling needs of Dutch missionaries. The one for Germany is focusing on training and network building.
- *Additional groups*—There are other groupings of member care personnel, such as national gatherings of personnel directors, regional meetings of MK personnel and cross-cultural trainers, research groups, health care/tropical medicine groups, and Internet member care forums.

For Everything There Is a Season—and a Summons

The reality of living in a global society calls each of us to take a serious look beyond our own national, organizational, and disciplinary borders. As Ray Fowler (1998, p. 3), the CEO of the American Psychological Association, puts it, "To limit our information to developments in the United States now makes no more sense for psychologists than it does for economists, chemists, or political scientists. More than ever, we are citizens of the world." The same charge holds true for mental health professionals from other countries.

Member care likewise continues to mature and internationalize. We in this field have the dual responsibility of providing for those in our own cultures/organizations, as well as promoting cross-cultural understanding and cross-cultural cooperation to help fill in important member care gaps. This is no small task. People from other countries can see things very differently, whether it be how best to conceptualize and resolve human problems (e.g., Zaman, 1998) or how best to form and maintain member care affiliations.

Member care workers, be they mission pastors, psychologists, or personnel directors, are encouraged to "capitalize on those aspects of their current professional life which are their greatest strengths, and to find some ways to translate those strengths into an effective contribution to the missionary endeavor" (Richardson, 1988, p. 6). For some, these contributions will take the form of working as part of RIMAs and other strategic member care groups, stretching themselves to develop additional strengths, in order to provide further support for missions.

I have sometimes wondered if RIMAs will become a passing trend, slated to go the way of many well-intentioned aspirations. But I really do not think so. It would seem that the season for member care affiliations is just beginning. If the way forward to reach the unreached is to work cooperatively across organizational, cultural, and disciplinary lines, pulling our strengths, skills, and prayers together, then RIMAs are right on target. RIMAs, when carefully formed and maintained, have already played and will continue to play an important role in world evangelization.

Reflection and Discussion

1. How could a RIMA be developed for your region? Who could be involved? How could you share about the need for these affiliations?

2. Review the 10 summary principles in Table 4. Which ones seem to be the most important for RIMA cohesion and effectiveness?

3. What are some of the main hindrances that can prevent RIMAs from achieving viability?

4. Comment on the author's optimistic perspective on the role and future of RIMAs.

5. Some member care people are better gifted for providing services within a specific setting, and others are more oriented towards developing resources at broader, regional levels. What are some ways that these two types of people could work together to provide better care for mission personnel?

References

Adler, N. (1991). *International dimensions of organizational behavior* (2nd ed.). Boston, MA: PWS-Kent.

APA Office of International Affairs. (1998). International snapshots. *Psychology International, 9*(3), 10.

Barrett, D. (1997). Annual statistical table on global mission: 1997. *International Bulletin of Missionary Research, 21*, 24-25.

Brierley, P. (1997). Missionary attrition: The ReMAP research report. In W. Taylor (Ed.), *Too valuable to lose: Exploring the causes and cures of missionary attrition* (pp. 85-104). Pasadena, CA: William Carey Library.

Collins, J., & Porras, J. (1994). *Built to last: Successful habits of visionary companies*. New York, NY: Harper Business.

Fowler, R. (1998, May). Sample psychology's international flavor. *APA Monitor*, p. 3.

Heller, K. (1990). Limitations and barriers to citizen participation. *Community Psychologist, 2*, 11-12.

Katzenbach, J., & Smith, D. (1993). *The wisdom of teams: Creating the high-performance organization*. Boston, MA: Harvard Business School Press.

Koster, J. (1994). *Knights of the tele-round table: Third millennium leadership*. New York, NY: Warner Books.

O'Donnell, K. (1986). Community psychology and unreached peoples: Applications to needs and resource assessment. *Journal of Psychology and Theology, 14*, 213-224.

———. (1992). An agenda for member care in frontier missions. *International Journal of Frontier Missions, 9*, 107-112.

———. (1997). Member care in missions: Global perspectives and future directions. *Journal of Psychology and Theology, 25*, 143-154.

O'Donnell, K., & O'Donnell, M. (1992). Perspectives on member care in missions. In K. O'Donnell (Ed.), *Missionary care: Counting the cost for world evangelization* (pp. 10-23). Pasadena, CA: William Carey Library.

Pawlik, K., & d'Ydewalle, G. (1996). Psychology and the global commons: Perspectives of international psychology. *American Psychologist, 51*, 488-495.

People In Aid. (1997). *Code of best practice in the management and support of aid personnel*. London, UK: Overseas Development Institute.

Pollock, D. (1997). Developing a flow of care. *Interact*, *7*, 1-6.

Richardson, J. (1988). *Teaching Nigerian psychiatry in Nigeria*. Presentation at the annual Mental Health and Missions Conference, Angola, IN.

Ritschard, H. (1992). The member care consultation. In K. O'Donnell (Ed.), *Missionary care: Counting the cost for world evangelization* (pp. 345-356). Pasadena, CA: William Carey Library.

Sarason, S. (1972). *The creation of settings and the future societies*. San Francisco, CA: Josey-Bass.

Taylor, W. (1995). Lessons from partnerships. *Evangelical Missions Quarterly*, *31*, 406-415.

Wilcox, D. (1998). Development of regional networks. In J. Bowers (Ed.), *Raising resilient MKs: Resources for caregivers, parents, and teachers* (pp. 456-464). Colorado Springs, CO: ACSI.

Zaman, R. (1998). The adaptation of Western psychotherapeutic methods to Muslim societies: The case of Pakistan. *World Psychology*, *3*, 65-88.

Kelly O'Donnell *is a psychologist working with Youth With A Mission and Mercy Ministries International, based in Europe. He co-chairs with Dave Pollock the Member Care Task Force (MemCa), part of the World Evangelical Alliance's Missions Commission. Kelly studied clinical psychology and theology at Rosemead School of Psychology, Biola University, in the United States. Specialties include personnel development, setting up member care affiliations, team building, and crisis care. Together with his wife, Michèle, he has published several articles in the member care field, along with editing* ***Helping Missionaries Grow*** *(1988) and* ***Missionary Care*** *(1992). They have two daughters: Erin, aged 12, and Ashling, aged 8. Email: 102172.170@compuserve.com.*

This is an update of an article that was first published in the ***Journal of Psychology and Theology*** *(1999, vol. 27, pp. 119-129). Used by permission.*

49

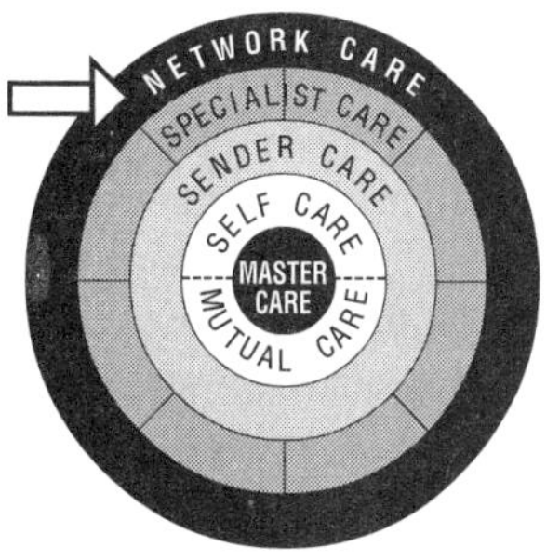

Global Member Care Resource List

Harry Hoffmann
Kelly O'Donnell

Member Care services are not just for those who are struggling. Everyone needs them! This Global Member Care Resource List is a reference tool that you or your group can use to take advantage of the many member care resources that exist and are being developed.

This listing updates the "International Guide for Member Care Resources" in *Too Valuable to Lose* (1997). The listing is not exhaustive. Rather, it includes a good sampling of some 200 service organizations around the globe. These are primarily Christian groups and individuals, plus some sending agencies that provide interagency resources. Most of these organizations are actively involved in the care and development of mission personnel.

In general, the main services emphasized are pastoral care, psychological consultation, training, counseling, and medical advice. These member care services are meant to complement the various ones that mission agencies are already providing their own people. They are an important part of the overall member care strategy needed for healthy personnel.

To use this guide, look up the geographic area in which you are interested and then read the brief description of the services that are offered under each listing. Contact one or more of the listings for more specific information about services (types, fee structure, languages spoken, background experience, or referrals).

In case you need more specific information and help, you can also contact one of the Regional Member Care Groups or send an email to one of the Member Care Forums (see the Publications section of this listing), which can send out your request to a broader group of people who might be able to help. You can also contact regional Evangelical missions associations for possible referrals.

Several agencies also provide services outside the country where they are located via field visits and email communication. Remember to talk openly with and interview the potential counselor/consultant in order to ensure a good fit between your needs and the types of services that are offered. Finding member care resources for missionaries in creative access countries is done discreetly and by word of mouth, rather than via a "public" listing like this one. Be sensitive of security issues as you communicate with people in these countries.

Note that there are several other excellent service agencies that were not included here, due to space limitations or lack of information. A group/person's inclusion in this listing does not mean we are "certifying" or "vetting" them. Further, certain geographic areas are deliberately not listed for security reasons and/or because few service agencies are actually located within these regions.

This listing will be updated on a regular basis. If there are other organizations and people to include in future updates, or if there are any changes in other entries, please contact the authors via email at <member-care-resource@gmx.net>. You can find an updated version of this list on the WEA Member Care web site at <www.membercare.org>.

Contents

Part 1: Continents

AFRICA

Côte d'Ivoire

Mobile Member Care Team West Africa
Dr. Karen Carr, Clinical Director
25 B.P. 498, 25 Abidjan
Fax: +1-360-838 8826
Email: Kfcarr@aol.com
Email: Darlene_Jerome@sil.org

An inter-mission multidisciplinary group of counselors and trainers focusing on trauma care. Also provides crisis response training, critical incident stress debriefing, crisis management consulting, interpersonal skills workshops, brief counseling, referral and training, and mentoring of peer response teams.

Ghana

Africa Christian Mission
Seth Anyomi, Director
Box 2632, Accra
Tel: +233-21-775268
Fax: +233-21-775268
Email: skanyomi@ncs.com.gh

Provides reentry help, debriefing for crisis and trauma, medical evaluation and care, and referrals.

Kenya

Oasis Counselling Centre
Gladys K. Mwiti, Chief Executive & Founder
P.O. Box 76117, Nairobi
Tel: +254-2-715 023
Fax: +254-2-721 157
Email: glmwiti@fuller.edu

Pan-African organization that provides Christian counseling and training. Languages: English, Kiswahili.

Tumaini Counselling Centre
Dr. Roger Brown
P.O. Box 21141, Nairobi
Tel: +254-2-716 441
Fax: +254-2-724 725
Email: supervisor_aim-care@aimint.org

Serves missionaries working in 26 African nations from over 100 mission organizations. Provides care following trauma and evacuations, marriage/family counseling, short-term individual counseling, consulting with MK schools and organizations, and preventive care seminars.

Nigeria

AEA/Evanglism & Missions Commission
Naomi Famonure
Messiah College, Barkin Ladi, Plateau State
Tel: +234-735-43110
Email: bayo@rcl.nig.com

Helps missionaries realize their potential in missions. Special emphasis on families and MKs. Languages: English, French.

North Africa

Member Care North Africa
See Europe/Spain for more details.

Senegal

United World Mission
Scott Hicks, Counselor
B.P. 3189, 497 Dakar
Tel: +221-832-0682 / Fax: +221-832-1721
Email: scotth@telecomplus.sn

Resource for member care in Senegal.

South Africa

Member Care Southern Africa
Marina Prins
8 Eben Olivier Street, 7560 Brackenfell
Tel: +27-21-981 2973
Fax: +27-21-981 0000
Email: mprins@proteahoogte.co.za

Helps equip local churches in member care, on-field care, reentry, assessment, and research. Languages: Afrikaans, English.

Zimbabwe

YWAM South Central Africa
Laurie Crull, Pastoral Coordinator
YWAM P.O. Box A 420 Avondale, Harrare
Tel: +263-4-300069
Email: ywam.reg.office.@ic.co.zw
Web site: www.ywamsca.com

Provides training in pastoral care. Languages: Portuguese, English.

ASIA

Hong Kong

Dr. Ben Wat
Hong Kong
Email: ben_wat@yahoo.com

Works as a therapist with pastors and missionaries in Hong Kong.

Bethany Ministries Ltd.
17a The Peak, Cheung Chau Island
Tel: +852-2981 7114
Fax: +852-2981 5047
Email: bethany@pacific.net.hk

Provides a "home away from home" for Christians of all denominations working in Hong Kong and Asia. Provides informal pastoral care and encouragement to workers in the field.

Child and Family Centre
Caleb Knight, Psychologist
15F The Strand
49 Bonham Strand East, Sheung Wan
Tel: +852-2543 0993
Fax: +852-2543 0996
Email: cknight@asiaonline.net

Secular resource: Provides psychological services for children and families.

Hong Kong Assoc. of Christian Missions
Dr. Terina Khoo, Psychologist
340 Portland Street, Unit 2, 6F
Mongkok, Kowloon
Tel: +852-2392-8223
Fax: +852-2899-0773
Email: hkacmktl@hkacm.org.hk

Provides assessment, counseling, field visits, and a contact for Hong Kong member care.

India

India Missions Association
Pramila Rajendran
48, first Main Road
East Shenoy Nagar, 600030 Chennai
Tel: +91-44-6258896
Fax: +91-44-6255092
Email: rajpramila@eth.net

Contact/resource person for member care.

Missionary Upholders Trust
John Ratnakumar, Coordinator
2/91 551 JI Bethel Bharathidasan Street
632 002 Vellore
Tel: +91-416-265187
Fax: +91-416-265187
Email: mutu@giasmd01.vsnl.net.in
Web site: www.careandserve.org

Serves Indian missionaries through prayer, emergency funds for medical services, and planning for pension and rest houses.

Wycliffe Bible Translators
Jacob George C., Coordinator for South Asia
P.O. Box 376, Andhra University
P.O., AP_530003, Vizag
Tel: +91-891-530641 / 538101
Fax: +91-891-701732
Email: jacob_george@wycliffe.org

Supports the church, missions, and missionaries by informing, motivating, and equipping.

Japan

Family Focus Japan
Tsuneo Maejima, Committee member
831 Takada, 381-0034
Nagano-Shi, Nagano-Ken
Tel/Fax: +81-26-227 4632
Tel/Fax: +81-45-972 3971
Email: familyfj@po.cnet-na.ne.jp
Email: info@familyfocus.gr.jp
Web site: www.familyfocus.gr.jp

Provides books, tapes, magazines, and seminars to help families. Counseling is offered through mail and email only. Languages: Japanese, English.

Member Care Working Group
Faith de la Cour
Email: faithdlc@aol.com

Discusses/plans for the member care needs of expatriate missionaries in Japan; part of JEMA.

MK Care WBT (Wycliffe) Japan
Toshio Nagai
4-31-7 Hamadayama
Suginamiku, 168-0065 Tokyo
Tel: +81-3-3313-5029
Fax: +81-3-3313-5048
Email: toshio_nagai@sil.org

Contact for member care in Japan. Specializes in MKs. Languages: Japanese, English.

Korea

Global Missionary Fellowship
Moon-Gap Doh, Executive Director
Ansan P.O. Box 131
Kyung-Ghee Province, Ansan City
Tel: +82-31-419 6192
Fax: +82-31-401 3940
Email: mgdoh@netsgo.com
Web site: www.gmpkorea.org

Member care contact for Korean missionaries.

Global Missionary Training Center
David Tai-Woong Lee, Director
231-188 Mok 2-Dong
Yangchun-Gu, 158-052 Seoul
Tel: +82-2-2649 3197
Email: gmtc@chollian.net
Web site: www.gmtc.or.kr

Provides training for Korean missionaries.

Hanse Clinic
Dr. Eun-sup Son, Director
16-7 Dangsan-dong 5-ga
Youngdeungpo-gu, 150-045 Seoul
Tel: +82-2-2635 8668
Fax: +82-2-2634 0239
Email: sones@eland.co.kr
Web site: www.hanse.pe.kr

Provides holistic care for missionaries: at present, physical checkups and medical advice.

Missionary Counselling Care Centre
Lee Man-Hong, Director
Dept. of Psychiatry, Yonsei Medical Centre
CPO Box 8044, Seoul
Tel/Fax: +82-2-364 6134
Email: mcckor@yumc.yonsei.ac.kr
Web site: www.nownuri.net/-k541/mcc.html

Provides aptitude tests, job ability tests, and counseling for home assignees and candidates.

MK Care and Development (IMB)
Phala Echols, Coordinator
Youido P.O. Box 45, 150-601 Seoul
Tel: +82-2-761 1337
Fax: +82-2-761 1338
Email: echolspb@iname.com

Provides care for MKs in the Philippines, Korea, and Japan.

MK Nest
Ruth Insook Baek
Mok 2-dong, Yangchun-Ku, 231-163 Seoul
Tel: +82-2-653 3519
Fax: +82-2-652 3870
Email: ruthbaek@chollian.net
Web site: www.mknest.org

Helps Korean MKs through networking, education, support, and training. Provides counseling, educational information, training of MK teachers, parents seminars, etc. Languages: Korean, English.

Malaysia

Intercare Berhad
P.O. Box 13002, 50769 Kuala Lumpur
Tel: +60-3-7784 8430
Fax: +60-3-7784 8403
Email: icare@tm.net.my

Provides debriefing and full medical checkups for partners on furlough. Helps in reentry process, including rest/relaxation and holiday/retreat.

Member Care Malaysia
Beram Kumar, Contact
P.O. Box 8036, Pejabat Pos Kelana Jaya
46780 Petaling Jaya, Lelangor Darul Ehsan
Email: sbks@pc.jaring.my

Contact for resources and referrals; editor of a member care handbook, Malaysian missions.

Philippines

Alliance Biblical Seminary
Heather and Fred Gingrich, Counselors
P.O. Box 1095, 1099 Manila
Email: frether@pacific.net.ph
Web site: www.abs.edu.ph

Offers counseling, marriage and family ministry programs, and referrals.

EIRENE Psychological Services
Naome G. Basilio, Psychotherapist
Corner Francisco University Avenue
Juna Subd., Matina, 8000 Davao City
Tel: +63-82-298 2820
Email: eirene@skyinet.net

Offers individual, marital, and family counseling and testing in English and Tagalog.

Philippine Member Care Group
Eric Miole, Coordinator
Email: eric.miole@cbnasia.org

An interagency group developing member care resources for Filipino missionaries.

Wholeness Ministries
Virmi G.Nery, Chairperson
148 Soliven-Alvendia Street
S. Green Heights Village, 1770 Muntinlupa
Tel: +63-2-8070 117
Fax: +63-2-9131 675
Email: virmi@uplink.com.ph
Email: pcec@amanet.net

Part of the Philippine Council of Evangelical Churches. Offers prayer counseling, training, and seminars in English, Tagalog, and Cebuano.

Youth With A Mission
Brenda Bosch
P.O. Box 196, 1900 Cainta
Tel: +63-2-646 7359
Fax: +63-2-646 7368
Email: brendab@pacific.net.ph

Provides consultation in personnel development, debriefing, staff orientation, and training of potential member care workers from all churches and agencies in Asia and Africa.

Singapore

Counselling and Care Centre
Gracia Wiarda, Therapist
Block 536 Upper Cross Street
050536 Singapore
Tel: +65-536 6366
Fax: +65-536 6356
Email: wiarda@mbox2.singnet.com.sg

Provides counseling, debriefing, psychological assessments, training and supervision in counseling, field visits, and workshops.

Member Care Associates – Asia
Esther Tzer Wong, Coordinator
Email: esther@lifestreams.org.sg

Interagency group that organizes workshops and helps to coordinate member care resources in/from Singapore.

Resources for Living
Thomas Hock-Seng Lee, Clinical Psychologist
Marine Parade P.O. Box 667
914406 Singapore
Tel: +65-4408862
Fax: +65-3466552
Email: leereliv@mbox4.singnet.com.sg

Supports and facilitates cross-cultural sojourners in their personal growth and effectiveness. Offers candidate screening/assessment, individual and family therapy, and missions agency consulting/training. Languages: English, Mandarin.

St. Andrew's Lifestreams
250 Tangjong Pagar, 088541
#02-01 St. Andrew's Centre, Singapore
Tel: +65-323-2902
Email: esther@lifestreams.org.sg

A training and resource center for those in the caring and counseling profession. A community project of St. Andrew's Mission Hospital for holistic care in the community through training, consultation, and networking.

Taiwan

Chang-I Bonnie Chen, Professor
Dep. of Psychology, National Chengchi U.
116 Taipei
Tel: +886-2-29387398
Fax: +886-2-86618099
Email: cychen@psy.nccu.edu.tw
Email: cychen2@cc.nccu.edu.tw

Provides personality and aptitude testing for missionaries and potential missionaries.

Center for Counseling and Growth
Steve Spinella, Director
Ta Yi Street, Lane 29, #18, 2F-1
Taichung 404
Tel: +886-4-236 6145
Fax: +886-4-236 2109
Email: spinella@alumni.rice.edu
Web site: www.team.org.tw/spinella

Serves the international community with counseling for adults, children, couples, and families; seminars, retreats, focus groups, clinical supervision, psychological testing, and career counseling. Languages: English, Mandarin, Taiwanese, Spanish, German.

Thailand

Cara Flanders, Marriage/Family Therapist
95/78 Moo Baan Nantawan
Nimmanhemin Rd Tambol
Amphur Muang
50200 Chiang Mai
Tel: +66-53-215787
Mobile: +66-1-7653595
Email: chrisf@chmai2.loxinfo.co.th

Marriage/family therapist in private practice.

Dr. Esther Wakeman, Psychologist
Payap University
50000 Chiang Mai
Tel: +66-53-243 645
Fax: +66-53-241 983
Email: rainrctr@loxinfo.co.th

Provides short-term consultations and 2-3 crisis sessions, then refers to competent lay prayer ministry counselors in Chiang Mai. Languages: English, Thai.

Asia Center for World Missions
Dr. Danny Martin
5/28 Fisherman Way, Vises Road
Rawai, 83130 Phuket
Tel: +66-76-280208
Fax: +66-76-280523
Email: info@asiacenter.ac
Web site: www.AsiaCenter.ac

Provides counseling service and mentoring for Christian workers needing encouragement and direction. Also offers training, conferences, and relaxing vacations in southern Thailand. Languages: English, Mandarin, Cantonese.

Juniper Tree
Hua Hin
Tel: +66-32-511139
Email: junitree@cscoms.com
Web site: www.j3-16.com/junipertree

Rest and relaxation place for Christian workers at the seaside of southern Thailand.

Juniper Tree 2
Chiang Mai
Tel: +66-53-277104
Fax: +66-53-279913
Email: juniper2@loxinfo.co.th
Web site: www.j3-16.com/junipertree

Rest and relaxation place for Christian workers.

Member Care Network Chiang Mai
Harry Hoffmann, Coordinator
P.O. Box 290 CMU
50202 Chiang Mai
Tel: +66-1-9982954
Fax: +66-53-357886
Email: HoffmannHT@compuserve.com

An affiliation of international colleagues to develop member care for Christian workers in Chiang Mai and surrounding regions via mutual support/encouragement, facilitating workshops, networking, and referrals. Developing an interagency member care office and a resource/counseling center for the region.

Raintree Resource Centre
3 Charoen Muang Road, P.O. Box 18
50000 Chiang Mai
Tel: +66-53-262 660
Email: rainrctr@loxinfo.co.th
Web site: www.raintreecenter.org

Provides orientation material, database, and library for expatriates in Chiang Mai.

AUSTRALASIA

Australia

Christian Synergy Centre
Dr. Kathleen Donovan
204 Wommara Avenue
2280 Belmont NSW
Tel: +61-2-49458484
Fax: +61-2-49455413
Email: donovank@turboweb.net.au

Provides member care training/resources, involvement in inter-mission conferences and councils to promote member care, assessment, debriefing, and counseling. Contact for Australia.

Communication Care Network Asia/Pacific
John and Tima Bakker, Directors
P.O. Box 7, ACT 2911, Mitchell
Tel: +61-2-6241 5500
Fax: +61-2-6241 6098
Email: comcarenet@crosswinds.net

Provides training and resources for workers in the Asia/Pacific regions. Contact for Australia.

Listening Ear
Lindsay Sutherland, Counsellor
24 Efron Street, VIC 3131, Nunawading
Tel/Fax: +61-3-9894 3761
Email: lcsutho@chessnet.com.au
Web site: www.chessnet.com.au

A counseling service to church members, missionaries, missionary kids, and their families.

New Zealand

Arahura Center
Murray Winn
406 Barrington St.
8002 Spreydon, Christchurch
Tel: +64-3-338 1080
Fax: +64-3-338 6654
Email: m.winn@clear.net.nz

Provides a supportive Christian community producing quality, innovative healthcare within a holistic framework for clinical, educational, social/community, research, and advocacy needs. Offers assessment and psychological services.

Living Stones Consultancy
Don Smith, Psychologist
14 Arizona Grova
Brooklyn, Wellington
Tel: +64-4-384 2361
Fax: +64-21-524 843
Email: living.stones@clear.net.nz

Contact person for NZ. Clinical psychologist, consults with mission boards and churches providing psychological assessments for candidates and returning missionaries.

Third Culture People's Network
Stephen and Raewyn Pattemore
12 Colin Wild Place
1310 Auckland
Tel/Fax: +64-649-441 9298
Email: swp@ww.co.nz

A peer support group for MKs and other TCKs returning to NZ and dealing with transition. Runs social programs and camps to link newly returned MKs with those who have been back some time.

CENTRAL ASIA

Member Care by Radio
Trans World Radio – Europe
Postfach 141
1235 Vienna, Austria
Email: mcbr@twr-europe.at
Web site: www.twr.org

Provides a daily radio program in English directed to workers living in Central Asia, transmitted by Trans World Radio. Broadcasts daily at 16:25-16:40 o'clock UTC on 864 kHz (MW) and 49 mb (SW).

EUROPE

Austria

Judith Davids, Counselor
Kohlstattgasse 3/30
6021 Innsbruck
Tel: +43-664-243 4684
Fax: +43-512-560 527
Email: pjdavids@compuserve.com
www.myworld.privateweb.at/pjdavids/default

Provides counseling for missionaries/pastors in Europe.

Barnabas Zentrum
Steven Williams, Ph.D., Director
Stall 35, 9832 Stall/Moeltal
Tel: +43-4823-315 (ext. 2 or 5)
Fax: +43-4823-315
Email: Bzentrum@compuserve.com
www.netlifemin.org/ministries/bzentrum/index

Focuses on families of missionaries who are serving in Europe, North Africa, and the Middle East. The facility is an interdenominational personal and marital retreat center providing a 12-day retreat counseling program to address issues such as marital crises, stress, burnout, interpersonal relations, sexual problems, depression, vocational conflicts, etc.

Missionswerk "Leben in Jesus Christus"
Postfach 197, 6460 Imst
Tel: +43-5412-65684
Fax: +43-5412-61401

Provides seminars and retreats for spiritual renewal, counseling, and marriage/family enrichment.

Pro Family Counseling Center
Art and Ursula Spooner, Counselors
Frauengasse 4/2
1170 Vienna
Tel: +43-699-19564238
Email: Uspooner@usa.net

Provides consultation/counseling to Austrians, missionaries, and expatriates in Vienna.

Belgium

Centrum voor Pastorale Counselling
Jef De Vriese, Director
St. Jansbergsesteenweg 97, 3001 Haverlee
Tel: +32-16-200927
Email: cpc@pastoralecounseling.org
Web site: www.pastoralecounseling.org

Offers pastoral counseling for adults and children; training in Belgium and the Netherlands.

Denmark

John Rosenstock, Psychologist
Katrinevej 31, 2900 Hellerup
Tel: +45-3962-0848

Consultant for mission boards; offers psychological counseling for missionaries. Languages: Danish, English.

Jorgen and Anette Due Madsen, Psychiatrist and Psychologist
Alkershvilevej 59, 2880 Bagsvaerd
Tel: +45-4498-1737
Email: duemadsen@dadlnet.dk

Consultants for mission boards; offer psychological counseling for missionaries. Languages: Danish, English.

Danish Mission Council
Mogens S. Mogensen, General Secretary
Skt. Lukas Vej 13, 2900 Hellerup
Tel: +45-3961-2777
Fax: +45-3940-1954
Email: dmr@dmr.org
Web site: www.dmr.org

Network of groups and individuals that provide member care services to Danish missionaries in Denmark, including pre-field training, psychiatric consultation, counseling, debriefing, and graduate level training.

DUO
Jacob Hoeg Jenson
Evanstonevej 4a, 1.tv, 2900 Hellerup
Tel: +45-3918-4535
Email: krfjahj@folketinget.dk
Web site: www.duopage.dk

Provides seminars and consultation on third-culture children. Languages: Danish, English.

Institute for Diakoni og Sjaelesorg
Lene Oestergaard
Kolonien Filadelfia, 4293 Dianalund
Tel: +45-5826-4200
Fax: +45-5826-4239
Email: institut@vestamt.dk

Provides debriefing, individual counseling, and retreats. Languages: Danish, English.

Missionary Fellowship
Ove Bro Henriksen, Coordinator
Gyvelvej 22, 761 Ejstrupholm
Tel: +45-75772904

Provides seminars and retreats for former missionaries.

France

Entrepierres
Jonathan Ward, Director
Le Vieux Village
04200 Entrepierres
Tel/Fax: +33-492-612509
Jonathan_Rachel_Ward@compuserve.com
Web site: www.famillejetaime.com

Offers Christ-centered rest, refreshment, and restoration via pastoral care, counseling, and consultation for Christian workers and their families in French-speaking Europe.

Famille et Jeunesse en Action
Claude and Ginette Gaasch, Directors
17 avenue Marechal Foch
68500 Guebwiller
Tel: +33-389-621011
Fax: +33-389-621100
Email: fja@famillejetaime.com
Web site: www.famillejetaime.com

Offers training in counseling, men's ministry/groups, family camps, conferences, counseling, and counseling supervision.

Inter. Family and Church Growth Institute
Dr. Walter Stuart, Director
13b rue Principale
68610 Lautenbach
Tel: +33-389-763159
Fax: +33-389-763979
Email: Waltstuart@compuserve.com

Offers pastoral/family counseling; crisis and trauma debriefing; consultations and medication for missionaries, MKs, and mission organizations.

Le Rucher
Erik and Jeltje Spruyt, Directors
2067 Rte de Tutegny
01170 Cessy
Tel: +33-450-283379
Fax: +33-450-283385
Email: lerucher@compuserve.com
Web site: www.lerucher.org

An interagency mission center developing and providing member care resources in/from Europe. Focus is on personnel serving in relief, development, and frontier settings. Offers debriefing and trauma counseling in English, French, German, and Dutch.

One Another Member Care Services
Dr. Robert Lugar, Director
150 Chemin des Colombiers
34820 Assas
Tel: +33-4-6755 6690
Email: Lugar@compuserve.com
Web site: www.OneAnother.com

Provides crisis intervention, conflict mediation, counseling, consulting, and training for missionaries and pastors.

Germany

Annemie Grosshauser, Psychologist
ORA International
Lindenstr. 16, 21521 Aumuehle
Tel: +49-4104-7571
Fax: +49-4104-692896
Email: agrosshauser@aol.com

Offers debriefing, crisis intervention, and counseling (inner healing, deliverance). Special emphasis: Muslim world. Languages: German, English, Farsi.

Dr. Lianne Roembke
Otto-von-Guericke-Str. 106
39104 Magdeburg
Tel/Fax: +49-391-561 9737
Email: Roembke@Campus-D.de

Consultant for multicultural teams, speaker and consultant for missionary staff conferences in English and German.

Columbia International Univ. – Germany
Hindenburgstr. 36
70825 Korntal-Munchingen
Tel: +49-711-8396533
Fax: +49-711-8380545
Email: cbsinfo@aem.de
Web site: www.aem.de

Offers seminars in the German language and context for missionaries on furlough and people preparing for cross-cultural ministry. Emphasis is on Christian maturity, instruction in biblical and theological curricula, and training in the skills needed for effective cross-cultural ministry.

El Shalom E.V.
Irmgard Ott
Uhlandstr. 2
71120 Grafenau
Tel: +49-7033-130747
Fax: +49-7033-130748
Email: elshalom@t-online.de

Offers counseling, consulting, and retreats.

IGNIS Academy for Christian Psychology
Kanzler-Stuertzel-Str. 2
97318 Kitzingen
Tel: +49-9321-13300
Fax: +49-9321-133041
Email: info@ignis.de
Web site: www.ignis.de

Counseling center, Christian graduate program in psychology, referral source for counselors in the German-speaking world. Also runs an inpatient psychiatric facility.

Janz Team Ministries
Bryan Sweet
European Personnel Supervisor
Im Kaeppele 8, 79400 Kandern
Tel: +49-7626-916080
Fax: +49-7626-916009
Email: bsweet@janzteam.com
Web site: www.janzteam.com

Contact for developing a missionary care program from recruitment to retirement.

Klinik Hohe Mark
Friedlaenderstr. 2, 61440 Oberursel
Tel: +49-6171-204 0
Fax: +49-6171-204 8000
Email: klinik@hohemark.de
Web site: www.hohemark.de

Christian psychiatric facility with residential and outpatient services. Treatment for trauma and mental disorders.

Member Care Network International
Ron and Barbara Noll, Coordinators
Email: brNoll@aol.com

Provides counseling, crisis care, courses in character development/member care, mentoring of missionary counselors, and training for small group leaders. Languages: English, German, Spanish.

Member Care Partners Germany
Friedhilde and Helmut Stricker
Coordinators
Kirchberg 2, 74243 Langenbrettach
Tel: +49-7946-91 51 31
Fax: +49-7946-91 51 51
Email: Friedhilde.Stricker@stricker-it.de

Contact for member care in Germany. Provides networking with Evangelical mission agencies, consulting missionaries, and referrals. Aim is to build a partnership of counselors, mission leaders, and missionaries and to encourage local churches in member care.

MK-Care
Priscilla Elsaesser, Contact
Aberlin-Joerg-Str. 20, 70372 Stuttgart
Tel: +49-711-5594770

Maintains a network for MK care in Germany.

Neue Hoffnung E.V.
Gisela Stuebner
Frankfurter Str. 4, 35091 Coelbe
Tel: +49-6427-931519
Email: giselastuebner@gmx.de

Offers seminars and counseling for missionaries and full-time Christian workers.

Renew Counseling Services
Dr. Roni Pruitt, Psychotherapist
Willmann Damm 10, 10827 Berlin
Tel: +49-30-781 8091
Email: Rhondapruitt@compuserve.com

Provides therapy, seminars, and member care courses by trained professionals who have served as career missionaries. Also provides field resources to support mission personnel.

Hungary

Dr. Evan Parks
Menyecske u. 1, VI-40, 1112 Budapest
Tel: +36-1-310 1321
Email: Eparks@attglobal.net

Developing a care center for individuals and couples seeking spiritual/emotional renewal.

Ministry Essentials
David Shepherd, President
Nadudvar ut.6/A, 1116 Budapest
Tel: +36-1-226 5391
Email: dave@mei.org.hu

Offers leadership development through spiritual formation/direction, retreats, and therapy.

SHARE Educational Services
Dr. David Brooks, President
Ifjusag u. 11, 2049 Diosd
Tel: +36-23-381 951
Fax: +36-23-381 208
Email: sharenet@compuserve.com
Web site: www.share-ed-services.org

Provides information, counsel, materials, and human resource support to missionary families in Europe and the former Soviet Union in meeting the educational needs of their children.

Norway

RoB, Instituut for Sjelesorg
Solveig and Bjoern Lande, Psychiatrists
Hoenskollen 7, 1384 Asker
Tel: +66-78-2897
Fax: +66-78-4217
Email: solveig.lande@start.no

Practicing general psychiatry including crisis intervention; family therapy; psychotherapy for children, adults, and groups; counseling in conflict situations; debriefing; reentry; lecturing; and supervising counselors and missionary leaders. The pastoral members of RoB provide counseling, debriefing, retreats, shorter courses, and more extensive education in counseling.

Poland

Life and Mission Ministry
Henrik and Alina Wieja
Ul. 3 - go Maja 3, 45-450 Ustron
Tel: +48-33-54 29 95
Email: awieja@misja.org.pl
Email: hwieja@misja.org.pl
Web site: www.silesia.pik-net.pl/forum/misja

Offers Christian counseling and promotion of biblical concepts and apologetics in Polish society.

Russia

Moscow Center of Psychology
Alexander Makhnach, Director
13 Yaroslavskaya Street
129366 Moscow
Tel/Fax: +7-95-283 5150
Email: a.makhnach@psychol.ras.ru
Email: wmah@ipras.msk.su

Psychological support for couples, families, and children in Russia. Languages: Russian, English.

Spain

Carolyn Kerr, Ph.D.
C/Montelirio 8
41908 Castilleja de Guzman
Tel/Fax: +34-95-572 0503
EdwinAndCarolynKerr@compuserve.com

Offers consultation and emergency psychological evaluation; short-term individual, marital, and family counseling; conflict resolution; seminars on burnout; and training in counseling. Languages: English, Spanish.

Centro de Neuropsiquiatría y Psicología
Raúl García, Psychiatrist
Mateo Inurria, 13, 1º B,
28036 Madrid
Tel: +34-91-3598600 / 3598609
Fax: +34-91-3503651
Email: rgarciap@teleline.es

Offers individual and family therapy, counseling.

De Familia a Familia; FamilyLife
Victor and Cesca Miron, Coordinators
37 Malats bajos
08030 Barcelona
Tel: +34-93-2740642
Fax: +34-93-4530915
Email: dfamilia@arrakis.es
Web site: www.defamilia.org

Focuses on prevention in the areas of marriage and family, with marriage conferences, small group material, premarital seminars, parenting seminars, and basic counseling.

El Faro
Calle Plata 16 primero
41014 Seville
Tel: +34-546-93398
Email: 101334.21@compuserve.com

A Christian pastoral counseling and retreat center ministering to the brokenness of persons through a process of biblical counseling and healing prayer in a safe atmosphere.

Member Care North Africa
Anke Tissingh, Chairperson
Apdo. 109, 29620 Torremolinos
Tel/Fax: +34-952-3822 33
Email: 100767.527@compuserve.com

Develops and provides member care resources and networking for North Africa. Languages: English, French, German, Spanish, Dutch.

Switzerland

Centre Chretien de Psychologie
Daniel and Denise Bouvier, Directors
31 rue de la Colmbiere
1260 Nyon
Tel: +41-22-361 6505
Fax: +41-22-361 6507
Email: paloma.psy@bluewin.ch

Offers counseling in French and English; referrals.

Fed. de Missiones Evangel. Francophones
Stefan Schmid, M.Th.
Case Postale 68
1806 Saint-Legier
Tel: +41-21-943 18 91
Fax: +41-21-943 43 65
Email: iem.fmef@bluewin.ch
Web site: www.temanet.org/iem

Offers annual conferences on member care and referrals to French-speaking counselors.

Psychiatric Clinic Sonnenhalde
Samuel Pfeifer, M.D.
Ganshaldenweg 22-32
4125 Riehen
Tel: +41-61-645 46 46
Fax: +41-61-645 46 00
Email: pfeifer@sonnenhalde.ch
Web site: www.sonnenhalde.ch

Christian psychiatric clinic with 59 inpatient beds and three doctors working in the outpatient department. Offers psychotherapeutic counseling and treatment of organic aspects of depression, anxiety, and psychosis as well as the common mental problems.

The Netherlands

Foundation ZON
Teo van der Weele, M.A.
Korhoelaan 1/19
3847LL, Harderwijk
Tel: +31-341-410341
Fax: +31-341-410007
Email: tjvdweele@uni-one.nl

Offers counseling/therapy and a 10-day summer program in Denmark. Languages: Dutch, German, English, Thai.

Hands to Serve
Steve Simmons, Director
Postbus 5740, 3290 AA, Strijen
Tel: +31-78-6571509
Fax: +31-78-6742293
Email: 100105.3214@compuserve.com

Serves missionaries while they are in Holland with loan cars, computer repairs, etc.

Ins. for Transcultural Mis. and Psychology
Margrete Bac-Fahner, Psychologist
Royaars van den Hamkade 44a
3552 CN, Utrecht
Tel: +31-30-2437673 / 30-2542208
Email: bac.fahner@hetnet.nl

Offers psychological help to missionaries and other expatriates, providing preventative and curative care, by means of testing, assessment, training courses, lectures, publications, counseling, therapy, and debriefing. Languages: Dutch, English.

Member Care Nederland
Rita van Netten
Egelantierstraat 88
1171 JR, Badhoevedorp
Tel/Fax: +31-20-6599833
Email: rvnetten@daxis.nl

Member care network for Dutch missionaries, providing a network and referrals for medical care, counseling, practical resources, etc.

Tabitha
Dr. Jurg
Anerweg Noord 86, 7775 AV, Lutten
Tel: +31-523-683275
Fax: +31-523-683475
Email: hulpverlening@tabitha.nl

Offers pastoral counseling, individual consultation, group therapy, art therapy, recreation.

United Kingdom

Campus Crusade for Christ International
Don R. Myers, Director
24 Birchwood Grove
TW123DU, Hampton
Tel: +44-208-941 7463
Fax: +44-208-979 7842
Email: donrmyers@compuserve.com

Conducts family life, marriage, and parenting conferences in Europe, Africa, Asia, and the Middle East.

Care for Mission
Dr. Michael Jones
Elphinstone Wing, Carberry
EH21 9DR, Musselburgh
Tel: +44-131-653 6767
Fax: +44-131-653 3646
Email: mejones@eihc.org

Provides health care services including full medical assessment, personal review assessment of candidates, counseling, and supervision.

COMET – Families on the Move
Marion Knell, Chairperson
11 Victoria Road
LE12 8RF, Woodhouse Eaves
Tel: +44-1509-890268
Email: bryan.knell@ukgateway.net

Provides resources and networking for MK care and training. Conducts day conferences and MK holidays.

Conway House Training Centre – OM
115 Russell Road
LL18 3NR, Rhyl
Tel: +44-1745-343085
Fax: +44-1745-330790
Email: leaderm@rhyl.om.org

Offers training and pastoral care courses to equip leaders and missionaries.

Equip
Tony Horsfall, Manager
Bawtry Hall, Bawtry
DN10 6JH, Doncaster
Tel: +44-1302-710020
Fax: +44-1302-710027
Email: equip@bawtryhall.co.uk

Prepares and equips Christians for service both at home and abroad. Courses include preparing for change, handling missionary stress, serving as senders, etc.

Healing for the Nations
24 Scotforth Road
LA1 4ST, Lancaster
Tel/Fax: +44-1524-843977

Offers retreats and spiritual formation.

Hiding Place
David and Joyce Huggett, Directors
Email: 100610.427@compuserve.com

Provides brief retreats and spiritual direction to mission partners in a restful setting.

InterHealth
Dr. Ted Lankester
157 Waterloo Road
SE1 8US, London
Tel: +44-207-902 9000
Fax: +44-207-928 0927
Email: info@interhealth.org.uk

Provides a full range of medical and psychological care for missionaries, aid workers, volunteers, and their sending agencies, including counseling, debriefing, medical screening, travel clinic, travel health shop, tropical and occupational medicine, research, and publications. Languages: English, Portuguese, Spanish, German.

King's Centre
High Street, Aldershot
GU11 1DJ, Hampshire
Tel: +44-1252-333233
Fax: +44-1252-310814
Email: info@kingscare.org
www.kingscare.org/Caucasus/trauma.htm

Trauma counseling center in Chechnya. "Zhivaya Voda" (Living Waters) provides a safe place for traumatized refugees from Chechnya to receive healing in body, soul, and spirit.

Member Care Associates – UK
Marion Knell, Coordinator
Email: Marion@Knell.net

Support group based in the UK, meets four times a year to provide personal and professional support, discuss issues, and exchange updates.

Mission Encouragement Trust
Janice Rowland, Director
P.O. Box 3016, BN12 6RL, Worthing
Tel/Fax: +44-1903-603405
Email: officeMET@cs.com

Provides encouragement and support for long-term missionaries via visits primarily in Western Europe, Poland, Hungary, and Romania. Languages: English, French, Afrikaans, Hebrew.

Missionary Training Service
Ian Benson, Coordinator
18 Aston Way
SY11 2XY, Oswestry, Shropshire
Tel: +44-1691-653 619
Email: coordmts@xc.org

Provides training for missionaries, develops missionary training materials, and facilitates a network of missionary trainers.

Network of Christians in Psychology
Email: info@necip.org.uk
Web site: www.necip.org.uk

A network of over 200 members representing professional clinical, occupational, educational, counseling, and academic psychologists in the UK. Aim is to support psychologists and students studying psychology as Christians.

Palmer Fry Counselling Services
Michael and Dot Palmer Fry
58 Hanover Gardens
SE11 5TN, London
Tel/Fax: +44-207-582 4130
Email: Mikendot@aol.com

Offers professional Christian counseling to those who are struggling emotionally, are in crisis, or are in habitual sin. Languages: English, Spanish.

Penhurst Retreat Centre
Penhurst Charitable Trust
44 St. Mary's Road
CV31 1JP, Leamington Spa
Tel: +44-1926-425403
Fax: +44-870-734 5436
Email: Mmyers4544@aol.com

A place of physical, mental, and spiritual renewal for individuals or small groups preparing to work overseas or returning from working in stressful environments abroad or at home. Also offers guided/unguided retreats.

Waverley Christian Training
Waverley Abbey House, Waverley Lane
GU9 8EP, Farnham
Tel: +44-1252-784731
Fax: +44-1252-784734
Web site: www.christiancounselling.com

Provides training in Christian counseling.

Wellsprings
Marjorie Salmon, Coordinator
Bawtry Hall, Bawtry
DN10 6JH, Doncater
Tel: +44-1302-710020
Fax: +44-1302-710027
Email: 106341.2266@compuserve.com

Residential service for missionary personnel needing time to recover, relax, and be renewed.

MIDDLE EAST

Cyprus

Middle East Member Care Group
Tim Rigdon, Coordinator
7 Evagoras Palikarides
4712 Alassa
Tel: +357-5-434 115
Email: tim@memct.org
Web site: www.memct.org

An interagency group that helps coordinate member care and referrals for the Middle East region. Has an extensive compilation of written resources related to cross-cultural life and work in the Middle East.

NORTH AMERICA

Canada

International Medical Services
Dr. Duncan Westwood, Ph.D.
4000 Leslie Street
North York, Ontario M2K 2R9
Tel. +1-416-494 7512
Fax: +1-416-492 3740
Email: expatriatecare@sympatico.ca

Provides medical and mental health assessment, screening, and interventions. Languages: English, Mandarin Chinese.

Missionary Health Institute
Dr. Kenneth Gamble, Executive Director
4000 Leslie Street
North York, Ontario M2K 2R9
Tel: +1-416-494 7512
Fax: +1-416-492 3740
Email: mhiims@attglobal.net

Specializes in expatriate care and tropical medicine, medical assessment, and screening.

MissionPrep
Robert Cousins, Director
36 Goldberry Square
Scarborough, Ontario MIC 3H5
Tel/Fax: +1-416-284 5645
Email: micanada@interlog.com
www.tyndale-canada.edu/tim/missionprep

Specializes in personal assessment, interpersonal skills, health matters, cross-cultural training, and language counseling.

USA

Alongside, Inc.
Steve Maybee, M.A., Coordinator
870 Sunrise Boulevard
Mount Bethel, PA 18343
Tel: +1-570-897 5115
Fax: +1-570-897 0144
Email: stevem@alongsidecares.org
Web site: www.alongsidecares.org

Formerly Tuscarora Resource Center. Provides professional spiritual, mental, and emotional caregiving services to people in vocational Christian ministry by offering three-week intense outpatient counseling programs.

Assoc. of Christian Schools International
David K. Wilcox, Assistant Vice President
P.O. Box 35097
Colorado Springs, CO 80935
Tel: +1-719-594 4612
Email: International_Ministries@acsi.org

Serves as a resource for MK boarding schools worldwide, MK educators, and boarding home parents.

Barnabas International
Dr. Lareau Lindquist, President
P.O. Box 11211
Rockford, IL 61126
Tel: +1-815-395 1335
Fax: +1-815-395 1385
Email: Barnabas@barnabas.org
Web site: www.barnabas.org

Offers a worldwide ministry of encouragement to strengthen Christian workers through personal, small group, and conference ministries. Targets missionaries, pastors, and national church leaders overseas, together with their families. Maintains a list of retreat centers for Christian workers. Sponsors an annual conference, "Pastors to Missionaries."

Bethesda Foundation
James Schlottman, Director
4596 East Cliff Avenue
Denver, CO 80222
Tel: +1-303-639 9066
Email: Foundation@BethesdaCares.org
Web site: www.BethesdaCares.org

Offers educational retreats for missionaries, pastors, and their families.

Cedar Ridge Ministries
David and Susan Black, Directors
R.R.3, P.O. Box 340
Gosport, IN 47433
Tel: +1-812-879 4361
Email: cedridgmin@smithville.net
www.home.bluemarble.net/~cedridgmin

Provides professional care for missionaries for personal growth, relational healing, and renewal of one's vision of God.

Christian Counseling Center
3355 Eagle Park Drive NE, Suite 106
Grand Rapids, MI 49525
Tel: +1-616-956 1122
Fax: +1-616-956 8033
Email: counsel@gospelcom.net
Web site: www.gospelcom.net/counsel

Offers pre-field screening, counseling, and crisis intervention. Project Stephanas provides on-field educational, consultation/counseling services to missionaries. Michigan Member Care Network is for mental health professionals interested in offering field services for missionaries.

Christian Training Center International
Larry Pons, Director
234 Watchman Lane
Franklin, NC 28734
Tel: +1-828-524 5741
Fax: +1-828-369 2019
Email: innlastresortctci@juno.com

Provides retreats, seminars, and training for Christian families.

Crisis Consulting International
Robert Klamser, Director
9452 Telephone Road, #223
Ventura, CA 93004
Tel: +1-805-642 2549
Fax: +1-805-642 1748
Email: info@hostagerescue.org
Web site: www.hostagerescue.org

Serves the Christian missionary and NGO communities with security/crisis management training, risk assessment and contingency planning, emergency assistance, and hostage negotiation.

Elijah Company, Inc.
Norman Przybylski, Executive Director
P.O. Box 64016
Virginia Beach, VA 23467
Tel: +1-757-474 2054
Email: normprzy@aol.com
Web site: www.elijahcompany.org

Offers training camps, overseas trips, and seminars with a special emphasis on personality profiles and development, team building, reconciliation, and mentoring. Languages: English, Spanish.

Elim Retreat Ministries
Henry and Diane Stewart
2803 Apple Tree Court
Waukesha, WI 53188
Tel: +1-262-524 0167
Email: hstewart5@juno.com
Web site: www.barnabas.org

Provides retreats for missionaries free of charge.

Emerge Ministries, Inc.
Richard Dobbins, Ph.D., President
900 Mull Avenue
Akron, OH 44313
Tel: +1-303-867 5603
Fax: +1-330-873 3439
Email: emerge@emerge.org
Web site: www.emerge.org

Christian mental health center providing biblically based counseling and missionary screening.

Godspeed Missionary Care
Barney M. Davis, Jr., Executive Director
19 Federal Street, Suite 2a
Easton, MD 21601
Tel: +1-410-819 0497
Fax: +1-410-819 0498
Email: Godspeed@MAF.org
Web site: www.missionarycare.org

Assists missionaries struggling with emotional stress, conflict situations, or physical illness.

Grace Ministries International
Derryck McLuhan, Executive Director
131 Village Parkway NE, Bldg. 4
Marietta, GA 30067
Tel: +1-770-690 0433
Fax: +1-770-850 9304
Email: GMI@gmint.org
Web site: www.gmint.org

Provides leadership development, restoration, counseling, discipleship, and training.

Greenwood Counseling Associates
Richard Ruegg, Psychologist
948 Fry Road
Greenwood, IN 46254
Tel: +1-317-885 1150
Fax: +1-317-885 1070
Email: gca@indy.net

Assists individuals and families of international organizations via counseling, reentry programs, and critical incident management.

Heartstream Resources
Dr. Larry and Dr. Lois Dodds
101 Herman Lee Circle
Liverpool, PA 17045
Tel: +1-717-444 2374
Fax: +1-717-444 2474
Email: heartstream@compuserve.com
Web site: www.membercare.org

Offers restoration of cross-cultural workers, prevention programs, consultation with mission agencies/church mission committees, and research.

Hope International, Inc.
1605 Elizabeth Street
Pasadena, CA 91104
Tel/Fax: +1-323-753 5741

Provides training, research, assistance, and networking for traumatized people.

Interaction, Inc.
David C. Pollock, Executive Director
P.O. Box 158
Houghton, NY 14744
Tel: +1-716-567 8774
Fax: +1-716-567 4598
Email: Interaction@compuserve.com
Web site: www.tckinteract.net

Serves as a catalyst and resource for third culture kids and families through seminars, conferences, and resources.

Letters
Ruth E. van Reken, Author/Publisher
8124 N. Lincoln Blvd., P.O. Box 90084
Indianapolis, IN 49240
Tel/Fax: +1-317-251 4933
Email: Rdvanreken@aol.com
Web site: http://members.aol.com/Rdvanreken/

Offers annual "Families in Global Transition" conference. Focus is on adult MKs/TCKs.

Link Care Center
Brent Lindquist, Ph.D., President
1734 West Shaw Avenue
Fresno, CA 93711
Tel: +1-559-439 5920
Fax: +1-559-439 2214
Email: info@linkcare.org
Web site: www.LinkCare.org

Counseling and pastoral care center for missionaries. Offers seminars on candidate assessment, restoration, personal growth, and reentry.

Makahiki Ministries
Billie Hair, Director
P.O. Box 415
Mariposa, CA 95338
Tel/Fax: +1-209-966 2988
Email: makahiki@sierratel.com
Web site: www.pastorsnet.org/caregiver_ministries/members/makahiki_ministries.html

A network of over 100 homes around the world, offering Christian workers a place to rest and be refreshed.

Marble Retreat
Dr. Louis and Melissa McBurney
139 Bannockburn
Marble, CO 81623
Tel: +1-970-963 2499
Fax: +1-970-963 0217
Email: mretreat@compuserve.com
Web site: www.marbleretreat.org

A Christian psychotherapy center for missionaries and Christian ministers. Offers retreat program with group and intensive counseling.

Ministry Essentials
P.O. Box 822224
Dallas, TX 75382
Tel/Fax: +1-214-341 3749
Email: MinEssentials@compuserve.com

Offers spiritual formation groups, personal spiritual retreats, team building, and training. See also Europe/Hungary.

Minnesota Renewal Center
Patrick Repp, Executive Director
1075 West County Road E, Suite 209
Shoreview, MN 55126
Tel: +1-651-486 4828
Fax: +1-651-482 9119
Email: mail@minnesotarenewal.com
Web site: www.minnesotarenewal.com

Offers assessment, counseling, leadership training, consultation, mediation, reconciliation.

Mission Nannys
Betty Sullins, Director
P.O. Box 609
Edgewater, MD 21037
Tel: +1-410-956 3142
Fax: +1-410-956 2807
Email: bettysullins@juno.com

Helps missionary families in unusual situations by sending women over 50 years old to serve younger families.

Missionary Care Services
Doug Feil, MA LPC, Director
141 West Davies Avenue
Littleton, CO 80120
Tel: +1-303-730 1717
Fax: +1-303-730 1531
Email: SouthwestCA@viafamily.com
Web site: www.SCA-solutions.org

Offers missionary assessment, wellness checkups, crisis intervention, intensive counseling, prevention, training, and field visits.

Missionary Training International
Paul Nelson, President
5245 Centennial Blvd., Suite 202
Colorado Springs, CO 80919
Tel: +1-719-262 0329
Fax: +1-719-594 4682
Email: mintern@aol.com
Email: info@mti.org
Web site: www.mti.org

Works with churches and mission agencies to prepare and nurture Christians for effective intercultural life and ministry. Facilitates debriefing and renewal programs and runs an annual conference, "Mental Health and Missions" (www.mti.org/mhm.htm).

Missionary Kids Ministry
Rick and Margaret Rineer, Coordinators
2801 Cowpath Road
Hatfield, PA 19440
Tel: +1-215-368 0485
Fax: +1-215-368 9021
Email: mkm-hatfield@aimint.org

A "home away from home" for older MKs and college age MKs while their parents are overseas. A ministry of Africa Inland Mission.

Missionary Retreat Fellowship
R.R. 4, Box 303
Lake Ariel, PA 18436
Tel/Fax: +1-570-689 2984
Email: mrf65@juno.com
Web site: www.missionary-retreat.org

A place that missionaries can call home while on home assignment and where missionary appointees can stay during pre-field ministry.

Mobility International USA
Email: exchange@miusa.org
www.miusa.org/general/miusaexchange.html

Secular resource: Offers leadership training community service, cross-cultural experiential learning, and advocacy for the rights and inclusion of persons with disabilities.

Mountain Top Retreat
Rev. Charley Blom
13705 Cottonwood Canyon Drive
Bozeman, MT 59718
Tel: +1-406-763 4566
Fax: +1-406-763 3034
Email: mountaintopmin@mcn.net
Web site: www.mcn.net/~mountaintopmin

Offers rest and renewal through quiet surroundings. Counseling is available on request.

Narramore Christian Foundation
Dr. Bruce Narramore, President
250 West Colorado Blvd., Suite 200
Arcadia, CA 91007
Tel: +1-626-821 8400
Fax: +1-626-821 8409
Email: ncf@ncfliving.org
Web site: www.ncfliving.org

A Christian mental health organization serving missionaries via two annual reentry programs, online services, radio, literature, training, consulting, on-field counseling, and correspondence. Free magazine, *Psychology for Living*.

New Hope International Ministries
Ronald Koteskey, Professor of Psychology
1 Macklem Drive
Wilmore, CA 91390
Tel: +1-859-858 3436
Fax: +1-859-858 3921
Email: ronald.koteskey@asbury.edu
www.asbury.edu/academ/psych/mis_care

Works with individuals, couples, or larger groups with an emphasis on prevention. Web site offers many member care materials.

Operation Impact
Grace Barnes, Director
Azusa University, P.O. Box 7000
Azusa, CA 91702
Tel: +1-818-815 3848
Fax: +1-818-815 3868
Email: gbarnes@apu.edu

Offers courses and a master's degree program at different locations around the world on leadership training, for missionaries and others.

Pebble Creek Counseling
Elizabeth A. Olson, Psychologist
710 North Mead Street
St. Johns, MI 48879
Tel: +1-517-224 6624
Fax: +1-517-224 8797
Email: PebbleCreek@voyager.net

Offers marriage and family therapy for missionaries, their families, and adult MKs.

Pilgrims Rest
2511 Tower Drive North
Brainerd, MN 56401
Tel: +1-218-764 2869
Fax: +1-218-825 9551
Email: 74724.244@compuserve.com
Web site: www.membercare.org/pilgrims.htm

Offers counseling and residential services for missionaries.

Remuda Ranch
One East Apache
Wickenburg, AZ 85390
Tel: +1-800-445 1900
Web site: www.remuda-ranch.com

Offers programs for anorexia and bulimia, designed exclusively for women and adolescent girls.

Servant Care International
Rick Ryding, Executive Director
rickryding@servantcareinternational.org
Web site: www.servantcareinternational.org

Provides care for missionaries.

Sharpening Your Interpersonal Skills
Dr. Ken Williams, Wycliffe
8805 Bloombury Court
Colorado Springs, CO 80920
Tel: +1-719-532 1956
Fax: +1-719-532 1447
Email: ken@RelationshipSkills.com
Web site: www.RelationshipSkills.com

Provides five-day workshops on interpersonal skills, focusing on missionaries. Also offers training for workshop facilitators.

Third Culture Family Services
Elsie Purnell, Director
2685 Meguiar Drive
Pasadena, CA 91107
Tel: +1-626-794 9406
Email: empurn@aol.com

Provides MK consultation services, including educational options, reentry, and adult MK issues/groups.

Timber Bay Camp and Retreat Center
Mark Ritchie, Camp Director
18955 Woodland Road
Onamia, MN 56359
Tel: +1-320-532 3200
Fax: +1-320-532 3199
Email: tbcamp@timberbay.org
Web site: www.timberbay.org

A "getaway" for singles, couples, and families.

Transition Dynamics
2448 NW 63rd Street
Seattle, WA 98107
Tel: +1-206-789 3290
Fax: +1-206-781 2439
Web site: www.transition-dynamics.com

Secular resource: A consultancy group serving the international expatriate community.

Trinity Bible College (EFCM)
Dr. Dennis and Lydia Bowen, Teachers
c/o IPS, Box 169
New York, NY 10103
Email: dlbowen@xc.org

Involved in educating students in Russia and other regions about the basics of Christian counseling and family ministry.

Walking in Their Shoes
Lee and Carolyn Baas
PMB 261, 101 Washington Street
Grand Haven, MI 49417
Tel: +1-616-844 3360
Email: witsministry@juno.com

A volunteer service to mission organizations and missionaries providing pastoral care.

SOUTH AMERICA

Brazil

COMIBAM Pastoral Care Working Group
Marcia Tostes, Coordinator
Email: mrast10@uol.com.br

Regional contact person for member care in Latin America. The group seeks to develop member care resources in/from Latin America.

Pastoral Care Commission, Brazil Churches
Antonia van der Meer
Caixa Postal 53
36 570 000 Vicosa
Tel: +55-31-3892 7960
Fax: +55-31-3891 3030
Email: tonica@homenet.com.br

Provides pre-field orientation, on-field care, and retreats for missionaries during furlough or when they return. Languages: Portuguese, Spanish.

Part 2: Other Resources

REGIONAL MEMBER CARE GROUPS

These are interagency member care affiliations which seek to further develop member care resources within their region (see chapter 48). Each group has strong relational links with the WEA Member Care Task Force (MemCa).

Member Care Africa
Naomi Famonure, Coordinator
Email: naomi_messiah@hotmail.com

Member Care Asia
Polly Chan, Coordinator
Email: ChanPolly@omf.net

Member Care Central Asia
Annemie Grosshauser, Coordinator
Email: agrosshauser@yahoo.com

Member Care Europe
Marion Knell, Coordinator
Email: Marion@Knell.net

Member Care South America
Marcia Tostes, Coordinator
Email: mrast10@uol.com.br

INTERNET RESOURCES

Focus on the Family
Email: www.parsonage.org
www.family.org/postoffice/info/a0000120.html

Provides resources for family life, pastors, children, etc.

Interaction, Inc.
Email: Interaction@compuserve.com
www.tckinteract.net

Provides resources for TCKs and internationally mobile families.

Intercultural Press
Email: books@interculturalpress.com
www.interculturalpress.com

Provides books on many intercultural topics and regions.

International Teams
www.iteams.org/ITeams/resource/crdb

Maintains a resource database on missionary care, MKs, and other ministry related topics.

Missionary Renewal Asia Pacific
Email: mrapag@juno.com
www.mrap.org

Assists Asia Pacific missionaries in locating resources to meet personal and ministry needs.

Missionary Marriages International
Email: info@missionsandmarriages.org
www.missionsandmarriages.org

Offers material to strengthen marriages.

MK Convention
Email: webmaster@mknet.org
www.mknet.org

Provides links and resources for MKs and TCKs.

MK Ministries
www.mkministries.com

A place for MKs to be encouraged, write and receive letters, and learn about other MKs.

New Hope International Ministries
Email: ronald.koteskey@asbury.edu
www.asbury.edu/academ/psych/mis_care

Provides resources on different topics related to member care. Brochures downloaded for free.

OSCAR UK Missions Information Services
www.oscar.org.uk

Provides UK-related information, advice, and resources on missionary/Christian work overseas.

WEA Member Care Web site
Email: MemberCare@kastanet.org
www.membercare.org

Maintains a comprehensive member care Web site. Provides updated information/events, articles, book reviews, and many links.

PUBLICATIONS AND EMAIL FORUMS

Asian MK Care Link – Newsletter
Email: ChanPolly@omf.net

Bimonthly newsletter sponsored by OMF with information and resources for people working with Asian MKs.

BR Anchor Publishing
Beverly D. Roman, Publisher
2044 Montrose Lane
Wilmington, NC 28405
Tel: +1-910-256 9598
Fax: +1-910-256 9579
Email: Broman@branchor.com
Web site: www.branchor.com

A relocation information publishing house. Publishes a free monthly email newsletter on relocation.

Brazil – Pastoral Care Email Forum
Email: carriker@uol.com.br

Portuguese email forum for member care in Brazil.

Brigada
www.brigada.org/others.html

A system of conferences/forums to network with others who share common interests for missions work and training.

COMIBAM Email Forum
Email: iepla@internet.ve

News and discussion email for Latin American member care. Coordinated by the COMIBAM Pastoral Care Working Group.

Dads at a Distance
www.dads.com

Helps fathers who are traveling to maintain and strengthen family relationships.

Encouragement – Barnabas International
Email: Barnabas@barnabas.org
Web site: www.barnabas.org

Produces monthly "Encouragement" hardcopy letters for missionaries.

Link Care
Email: KenRoyer@aol.com

Publishes a monthly email newsletter on pastoral care.

Member Care Africa
member-care-europe-subscribe@
yahoogroups.com

Provides monthly updates about member care in Africa, attached to the Member Care Europe Email Forum.

Member Care Asia
member-care-asia-subscribe@
yahoogroups.com

A biweekly e-info service dedicated to providing information, networking, and discussion on issues related to member care within and from Asia. Sponsored by the Member Care Asia Task Force.

Member Care Europe
member-care-europe-subscribe@
yahoogroups.com

A biweekly e-info service dedicated to providing information, networking, and discussion on issues related to member care within and from Europe. Sponsored by Member Care Europe.

MemCa Member Care Briefing
Email: hoffmannht@compuserve.com

An email newsletter sent three times a year; provides analysis and discussion of current issues/trends in global member care. Coordinated by the WEA Member Care Task Force.

Narramore Christian Foundation
Email: ncf@ncfliving.org

Publishes a free monthly hardcopy magazine, *Psychology for Living*.

NOAHE
Email: guidenoahe@xc.org

Network of Associates for the Health of Expatriates email forum for medical professionals.

Perspektiven
Email: smf@aem.de

German member care email forum, in German and English.

Pastoral Care Email Forum – Brazil
Email: carriker@uol.com.br

Portuguese email forum for all those involved in the care and development of missionaries in/from Brazil.

PTM Care
Email: PTMCAREnet@barnabas.org

A periodic encouraging note to those ministering to men and women in missions, coordinated by Barnabas International.

Toolbox-International Teams
Email: Preston@InternationalTeams.org
Web site: www.iteamspd.org

A collection of resources for personal growth and ministry development, produced every two months in email format.

Women of the Harvest
Email: harvestmag@aol.com
Web site: www.womenoftheharvest.com

A magazine of support and encouragement to women in cross-cultural ministry.

WEF Religious Liberty Commission
Email: MarkAlbrecht@xc.org
Web site: www.worldevangelical.org

An electronic news service that covers persecution of Christians worldwide, with emphasis on religious liberty questions.

***Harry Hoffmann** is a member care facilitator and coach with Youth With A Mission and a member of the WEA Member Care Task Force. He provides member care for workers in restricted access nations, publishes three bimonthly member care email newsletters, and coordinates the ministry of the Member Care Network Chiang Mai. Harry is German and has a master's degree in Chinese studies and cultural anthropology from the Freie Universitaet Berlin. Married to his Austrian wife Tina, they have three daughters and live in Thailand. Correspondence: P.O. Box 290, CMU, 50202 Chiang Mai, Thailand.*
Email: HoffmannHT@compuserve.com.

***Kelly O'Donnell** is a psychologist working with Youth With A Mission and Mercy Ministries International, based in Europe. He co-chairs with Dave Pollock the Member Care Task Force (MemCa), part of the World Evangelical Alliance's Missions Commission. Kelly studied clinical psychology and theology at Rosemead School of Psychology, Biola University, in the United States. Specialties include personnel development, setting up member care affiliations, team building, and crisis care. Together with his wife, Michèle, he has published several articles in the member care field, along with editing **Helping Missionaries Grow** (1988) and **Missionary Care** (1992). They have two daughters: Erin, aged 12, and Ashling, aged 8. Correspondence: Le Rucher, 2067 Route de Tutegny, 01170 Cessy, France. Email: 102172.170@compuserve.com.*

Many thanks to Phil Walters for his help with typing and proofreading this listing.

50

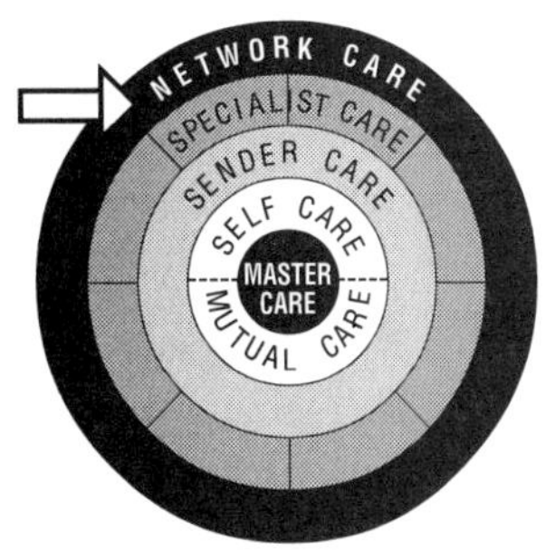

Touring the Terrain: An International Sampler Of Member Care Books

KELLY O'DONNELL

The member care literature continues to expand, informing member care programs, policies, and practice. Here is a compilation of many of the key published materials that have been developed so far. The presence of good literature often reflects the degree to which member care has been developed within a specific region and within a specific type of ministry.

My wife and I work out of an interagency mission center called Le Rucher. The center is nestled at the base of the Jura mountains, not too far from Geneva. Lining the walls of our office are books, articles, journals, and dissertations dealing with missionary care. In this article, I would like to take you on a short tour of the office. Specifically, I want to share a sampling of member care materials that we have found during the course of our geographic and Internet travels. These materials are comprised mostly of books published in English during the last 15 years. Collectively they represent much of the growing international "paper trail" for the field of member care. They are tools to facilitate the life-long learning which can really help missionary longevity (Brewer, 1991).

International Member Care

It is encouraging to see the rising interest in member care within the Newer Sending Countries (NSCs). We can see this in the slow but steady stream of written materials which are being authored by mission leaders and member care workers from these countries, mostly from Asia and Latin America. In many cases, and not surprisingly, their writings are also quite relevant for the global mission community (e.g., *Too Valuable to Lose*, Taylor, 1997).

Member care, like missions, is becoming a two-way street: going from North to South, from East to West, and vice versa. Nonetheless, there is a tremendous need to hear more from NSC colleagues, as they build upon the previous, predominantly Western materials and address many of the issues of particular interest to their own nation and region (O'Donnell, 1997). Older Sending Countries (OSCs) have had quite a head start with regards to publishing member care materials, and this fact is reflected in the quantity of OSC materials (many from American and European authors) which are listed in this article. Over the next few years, we hope to see many more NSC materials (in addition to the ones contained in this book, for example), including compendiums of articles focusing on regional member care issues.

Touring the Literature Terrain

Just as every office needs a good system for organizing its books, so also does a bibliography. I have thus chosen to categorize the materials according to the member care model which has been used to organize this book. The categories are relevant across many organizational and national cultures. As explained in chapter 1, this model consists of five parts, or spheres (see Table 1 below and the diagram in chapter 1). The eight categories (specialist domains) of Sphere 4 provide the main framework to organize the bibliography. Following these categories are some general member care references from NSCs, mostly from periodicals.

Most of the books are still in print, although some may only be available through the authors rather than through a book distributor. I have added some clarifying notes in parentheses after many of the references. I have also added some notes at the end of each of the eight categories (including websites). A few items are included which are not explicitly written for mission contexts yet are still very relevant. At the end of the article, I include additional sources and listings for written member care materials (see Table 2).

Pastoral/Spiritual Care

Huggett, J. (1996). *Embracing God's world*. London, UK: Hodder & Stoughton. (A collection of prayers, many by missionaries.)

Lindquist, L. (1994). *Too soon to quit: Reflections on encouragement*. Rockford, IL, USA: Quadrus Media. (Short, personal chapters on Christian life, filled with Scripture and compassionate insights to encourage Christian workers.)

Rupp, J. (1988). *Praying our good byes: The spirituality of change*. Guildford, Surrey, UK: Eagle. (Explores our relationship to God and others, along with ways to pray in the midst of various types of transitions.)

Note: There are thousands of other devotional books relevant for missionaries, Christian workers, and Christians in general. The Focus on the Family website has a special center for pastors which is also relevant for many mission personnel (www.family.org/pastor).

Physical/Medical Care

Jones, M. (Ed.). *Voluntary Agency Medical Advisors Newsletter*. Published by Care for Mission, Scotland. (A newsletter/journal

Table 1. A member care model. Sphere 4 is used to categorize the literature.

Sphere 1 – Master Care: Care from and for the Master—the *heart* of member care.

Sphere 2 – Self and Mutual Care: Care from oneself and from relationships within the expatriate, home, and national communities—the *backbone* of member care.

Sphere 3 – Sender Care: Care from sending groups (churches and agencies) for all mission personnel, from recruitment through retirement—the *sustainer* of member care.

Sphere 4 – Specialist Care: Care from specialists which is professional, personal, and practical—the *equipper* of member care. There are eight specialist domains of care: **P**astoral/Spiritual, **P**hysical/Medical; **T**raining/Career, **T**eam Building/Interpersonal, **F**amily/MK, **F**inancial/Logistical, **C**risis/Contingency, and **C**ounseling/Psychological.

Sphere 5 – Network Care: Care from international member care networks to help provide and develop strategic, supportive resources—the *facilitator* of member care.

with articles on different aspects of expatriate adjustment, including mental health and tropical medicine updates. Available from: mejones@eihc.org.)

Lankester, T. (1999). *The traveller's good health guide: A guide for backpackers, travellers, volunteers, and overseas workers*. London, UK: Hodder & Stoughton.

Lockie, C., Calvert, L., Cossar, J., Knill Jones, R., Raeside, F., & Walker, E. (Eds.). (2001). *Textbook of travel medicine and migrant health*. London, UK: Churchill Livingstone.

Werner, T. (1992). *Where there is no doctor: A village health care handbook* (Rev. ed.). Palo Alto, CA, USA: Hesperian Foundation. (Practical advice on health care and medical problems, written with simple terms and available in over 50 languages.)

Wilson-Howarth, J., & Ellis, M. (1998). *Your child's health abroad: A manual for travelling parents*. Bradt Publications, UK, and Globe Pequeot Press, USA.

Zuckerman, J., & Zuckerman, A. (Eds.). (2001). *Principles and practices of travel medicine*. Chichester, UK: John Wiley.

Note: Many national health services and international health organizations provide helpful updates, travel advice/warnings, and health care materials for overseas travel/work. TIE is a comprehensive online information exchange for health and medicine, with over 6,500 article citations (www.tie.telemed.org).

Training/Career Care

Austin, C. (1986). *Cross-cultural reentry: A book of readings*. Abilene, TX, USA: Abilene Christian University Press. (A classic collection of articles on reentry for various types of expatriates—military, business, diplomats, missionaries, etc.)

Bacon, D. (1992). *Equipping for missions: A guide to career decisions*. Abilene, TX, USA: Abilene Christian University Press.

Burt, M., & Farthing, P. (Eds.). (1996). *Crossing cultures: How to manage the stress of reentry*. Sydney, Australia: Salvation Army. (A helpful and readable collection of chapters on transitioning back to one's home country.)

Jones, G., & Jones, R. (1991). *Naturally gifted: A self-discovery workbook*. Downers Grove, IL, USA: InterVarsity Press. (Provides tools to explore one's gifts, abilities, temperament, values, and interests, relating these to career choices and job satisfaction; Available from the authors: G.R.Jones@ Libertysurf.co.uk.)

Jordan, P. (1992). *Reentry: Making the transition from missions to life at home*. Seattle, WA, USA: YWAM Publishing. (A practical overview of the process of reentry and advice for successful reentry.)

Lewis, J. (Ed.). (1996). *Working your way to the nations: A guide to effective tentmaking* (2nd ed.). Downers Grove, IL, USA: InterVarsity Press. (Helpful articles, questions, and checklists to help tentmakers prepare for cross-cultural work and living. Also available in Chinese, Spanish, Portuguese, Korean, and Arabic.)

Vella, J., Berardinelli, P., & Burrow, J. (1998). *How do they know? Evaluating adult learning*. San Francisco, CA, USA: Josey-Bass.

Note: The emphasis in this domain is on continuing education, career development, and end-of-service reentry, rather than on pre-field training, cross-cultural preparation, or leadership development. See also the *Manual for Team Recruits* from Team Expansion: www.teamexpansion.org/resources/recruitguide.

Team Building/ Interpersonal Care

Augsburger, D. (1992). *Conflict mediation across cultures: Pathways and patterns*. Louisville, KY, USA: Westminster/John Knox Press.

Benson, I. (1997). *The missionary team: Extending God's kingdom together*. Oswestry, SY, UK: The Missionary Training Service. (Summarizes helpful concepts of team life from several sources. Available from: coordmts@xc.org.)

Chalk, S., & Relph, P. (1998). *Im Team geht alles besser*. Basel, Switzerland: Brunnen Verlag. (Translated from the English version, *Making a team work*. Eastbourne, East Sussex, UK: Kingsway Publications.)

Collier, P., & Lindquist, B. (1999). *Managing conflict on the field: Interpersonal relationships and communication*. Richmond, VA, USA: International Mission Board.

Elmer, D. (1993). *Cross-cultural conflict: Building relationships for effective ministry*. Downers Grove, IL, USA: InterVarsity Press. (Easy to read and practical with suggestions for using indirect methods of conflict resolution.)

Jones, G., & Jones, R. (1995). *Teamwork*. London, UK: Scripture Union. (Practical and filled with team building exercises. Available in English and French from the authors: G.R.Jones@Libertysurf.co.uk.)

Liverman, C. (1999). *Building teams: Moving from conflict to community in cross-cultural ministry*. Mesa, AZ, USA: Frontiers. (Practical suggestions for cross-cultural adjustment within a team context, especially relevant for church planting teams.)

Roembke, L. (2000). *Building credible multicultural teams*. Pasadena, CA, USA: William Carey Library. (Explores team dynamics in a variety of multicultural situations.)

Woodford, B., & Dinnen, S. (Eds.). (n.d.). *Serving together: A manual of intercultural relationships within WEC International*. Gerrards Cross, UK: WEC. (Includes short contributions by missionaries around the world.)

Note: This domain primarily involves team development topics, along with cross-cultural relationships and conflict management. For a bibliography of materials on interpersonal skills, visit: www.relationshipskills.com.

Family/MK Care

Among worlds. (A magazine for empowering and encouraging adult "Third Culture Kids." Available from: www.tckinteract.net/amongworlds.)

Association of Christian Schools International, Office of International Ministries. *World Report*. (Quarterly magazine on MK matters, with recent articles on Asian MK education and the internationalization of MK schools. Edited by David Wilcox. PO Box 35097, Colorado Springs, CO 80935, USA. Email: david_wilcox@acsi.org.)

Association of Christian Schools International. (1999). *Overseas schools profiles*. (A collection of fact sheets on Christian schools worldwide which provide schooling for international students and MKs. Available from ACSI: david_wilcox@acsi.org.)

Baek, R. (Ed.). *MK Journal*. (Published in Korean four times a year by MK Nest, PO Box 144, Yangchun-ku, Seoul, Korea 158-600. Email: hsoooklee@chollian.net.)

Borden, J. (2000). *Confucius meets Piaget: An educational perspective on ethnic Korean children and their parents*. Seoul, Korea: Author. (Available from: jborden@sfs.or.kr.)

Bowers, J. (Ed.). (1998). *Raising resilient MKs: Resources for caregivers, parents, and teachers*. Colorado Springs, CO, USA: Association of Christian Schools International. (An extensive, current compilation of some of the best articles on MK care/education, primarily focusing on Western/American MKs but foundational and relevant for others.)

Brooks, D. (Ed.). (1996). Budapest, Hungary: SHARE. (Practical advice about *Educational Options: Europe and CIS* (2nd ed.) educational issues/choices and a description of schools for MKs and other TCKs.)

Brooks, D., & Blomberg, J. (Eds.). (2001). *Fitted pieces: A guide to parents educating children overseas*. Diósd, Hungary: SHARE. (An outstanding collection of articles on educating children in cross-cultural settings. Available from: sharenet@share-ed-services.org.)

Chan, P. (Ed.). (1997). *Nurturing missionaries' children*. Hong Kong: Hong Kong Association of Christian Missions. (In Chinese; authored by Asians and non-Asians.)

———. (1997). *Nurturing missionaries' children*. Hong Kong: HKACM.

———. (2000). *Kids without borders: Journals of Chinese MKs*. Hong Kong: OMF and HKACM.

CHED. *Parents teaching overseas*. Wycliffe Bible Translators. (A practical source of education resources and methods. Available from: nick_pauls@sil.org.)

Dyer, J., & Dyer, R. (1994). *And bees make honey: An anthology of anecdotes, reflections, and poems by third culture kids*. Torrens Park, SA, Australia: MK Merimna. (The authors also have three other excellent books on Australian TCKs, along with a book to help children with transition into missions, *Harold and Stanley Say Goodbye*. PO Box 205, Mitcaham Centre, Torrens Park, SA 5062, Australia.)

Evangelical Missions Quarterly. (2001, October). (Special issue on missionary families.)

Fraser-Smith, J. (1993). *Love across latitudes: A workbook on cross-cultural marriage*. Worthing, West Sussex, UK: Arab World Ministries.

Groenen, I. (1998). *Vanuit de partner gezien: Leven en werken in de tropen. (Life and work in the tropics, from the spouse's perspective)*. Amsterdam, The Netherlands: Koningklijk Instituut voor de Tropen.

Hoekstra, E. (1998). *Keeping your family close: When frequent travel pulls you apart*. Wheaton, IL, USA: Crossway Books.

Indian Missiology Association. (1998, October). *Indian Journal of Missiology*. (Special issue on care of the missionary family, with Indian and non-Asian authors.)

Interact magazine. (Published since 1993, this magazine is a service of Interaction and covers many current areas about the care and education of MKs. 4 issues/year. PO Box 158, Houghton, NY 14744, USA. See also the special annotated listing of books that parents/teachers can use to help children process their TCK experiences, in the October-November 2001 issue.)

Kaslow, F. (Ed.). (1993). *The military family in peace and war*. New York, NY, USA: Springer. (Excellent book on a variety of military member care topics.)

Loong, H. (2000). *Under the mango tree*. Hong Kong: Hong Kong Association of Christian Missions. (A compilation of the author's articles published in the HKACM Missionary Quarterly on MK care and missionary life; in Chinese. Available from: hloong@hkstar.com.)

Manzano, J., & Manzano, R. (1999). *Filipino MKs: Which schooling option?* Philippine Home Council of OMF Intl. (A booklet reviewing issues/educational options.)

McClure, P. (Ed.). (1999). *Pathways to the future: A review of military family research*. Scranton, PA, USA: Military Family Research Institute. (Outstanding annotated bibliography of several hundred studies.)

McCluskey, K. (Ed.). (1994). *Notes from a traveling childhood: Readings for internationally mobile parents and children*. Washington, DC, USA: Foreign Service Youth Foundation. (Refreshing perspectives and anecdotes by TCKs and sojourning families.)

Park, S. (Ed.). (1999). *Korean MK handbook*. Seoul, Korea: GMF Press. (Resources for Korean parents, caregivers, and MK teachers; in Korean.)

Pollock, D., & Van Reken, R. (1999). *The third culture kid experience: Growing up among worlds*. Yarmouth, ME, USA: Intercultural Press. (A thorough and enlightening description of the challenges and benefits of being raised in more than one culture.)

Romero, D. (1997). *Intercultural marriage: Pitfalls and promises* (2nd ed.). Yarmouth, ME, USA: Intercultural Press.

Rowen, R., & Rowen, S. (1990). *Sojourners: The family on the move*. Farmington, MI, USA: Associates of Urbanus. (Out of print in English, but a Chinese edition was published in 1998 by the Taiwan Chinese Christian Mission.)

Soon, N. (Ed.). (1999). *Korean MK Handbbok*. Seoul, Korea: GMF Press.

Note: There are many other books relevant for missionary families/MKs. Refer also to listings of children's books such as *Books Children Love: A Guide to the Best Children's Literature* by Elizabeth Wilson (1987, Wheaton, IL, USA: Crossway Books). For an excellent list of readings about and resources for MKs, see the appendices in *Raising Resilient MKs* by Joyce Bowers (1998). Some helpful websites are the Association of Christian Schools International (www.acsi.org) and Interact (www.tckinteract.net).

Financial/Logistical Care

Hawthorne, S., et al. (Eds.). (1992). *Stepping out: A guide to short-term missions*. Seattle, WA, USA: YWAM Publishing. (Short stories, advice, agency information, and checklists to prepare for short-term mission trips; primarily for youth.)

Kohls, R. (1996). *Survival kit for overseas living* (3rd ed.). Yarmouth, ME, USA: Intercultural Press. (An all-purpose guide to prepare for and succeed in overseas living.)

Loots, D. (1996). *Short-term outreach in the African context: A practical guide*. Pretoria, RSA: University of Pretoria, Institute for Missiological and Ecumenical Research.

Pirolo, N. (1991). *Serving as senders: Six ways to care for your missionaries*. San Diego, CA, USA: Emmaus Road.

———. (2000). *The reentry team: Caring for your returning missionaries*. San Diego, CA, USA: Emmaus Road.

Quick, J., Quick, J., Nelson, D., & Hurrell, J. (1997). *Preventive stress management in organizations* (Rev. ed.). Washington, DC, USA: American Psychological Association. (A helpful book for organizational development and fostering a more life/work-enhancing environment while on the job.)

Pascoe, R. (2000). *Homeward bound: A spouses guide to repatriation*. Expatriate Press (www.expatriatepress.com).

Townsend, D. (1996). *Stop check go: A short-term overseas projects checklist, and a practical guide for cross-cultural teamwork.* Carlisle, Cumbria, UK: OM Publishing.

Note: Kogan Page (120 Pentonville Road, London N1 9JN, UK; tel. 44 171 837 6348) is an example of a publisher which offers short books on a variety of subjects related to management and personnel issues. One example is in their Better Management Series, *How to Write a Staff Manual*.

Crisis/Contingency Care

Bracken, P., & Petty, C. (Eds.). (1998). *Rethinking the trauma of war*. London, UK: Save the Children. (Insightful analyses of the socio-cultural consequences of war and of rehabilitation programs for war victims.)

Companjen, A. (2000). *Hidden sorrow, lasting joy: The forgotten women of the persecuted church*. London, UK: Hodder & Stoughton. (Short accounts from around the world of Christian women and families who suffer from persecution.)

Cutts, M., & Dingle, A. (1998). *Safety first: Protecting NGO employees who work in areas of conflict* (2nd ed.). London, UK: Save the Children. (Guidelines for orienting staff to the safety practices needed for living in dangerous places.)

Danieli, Y., Rodley, N., & Weisaeth, L. (Eds.). (1996). *International responses to traumatic stress*. Amityville, NY, USA: Baywood Books.

Gist, R., & Lubin, B. (1999). *Response to disaster: Psychological, community, and ecological approaches.* Philadelphia, PA, USA: Taylor & Francis.

Global Missionary Fellowship (1997). *Crisis management for missionaries*. Seoul, Korea: GMF Press.

Humanitarian policy group briefing. London, UK: Humanitarian Policy Group. (Part of the Overseas Development Institute; this regular briefing looks at the organizational structures, management tools, and policies related to the safety and security of staff.)

Kilbourn, P. (Ed.). (1995). *Healing children of war: A handbook for ministry to children who have suffered deep traumas*. Monrovia, CA, USA: MARC.

Lloyd, R., & Bresser, K. (1998). *Healing the wounds of ethnic conflict: The role of the church in healing, forgiveness, and reconciliation*. Rhyl, Wales: Authors. (Available from: rhiannonlloyd@compuserve.com.)

Marsella, A., et al. (Eds.). (1998). *Ethnocultural aspects of post-traumatic stress disorder: Issues, research, and clinical applications*. Washington, DC, USA: American Psychological Association. (Written primarily for health care professionals; an excellent reference work to guide research and helping services.)

Piven, J., & Borgenicht, D. (1999). *The worst-case scenario survival handbook.* San Francisco, CA, USA: Chronicle Books. (Brief, step-by-step instructions for surviving high jumps, escape from animals, being lost at sea, etc. Available from: www.chroniclebooks.com.)

Refugees. (A magazine published by the United Nations High Commissioner of Refugees. Often has material on personnel care. See especially Vol. 4, No. 121, 2000, "Too High a Price?" on security and crisis issues for aid personnel. Available from: www.unhcr.ch.)

Robben, A., & Suarez-Orozco, M. (2000). *Cultures under siege, collective violence, and trauma.* Cambridge, UK: Cambridge University Press.

Roberts, D. (1999). *Staying alive: Safety and security guidelines for humanitarian volunteers in conflict areas*. Geneva, Switzerland: ICRC.

Rogers, C., & Sytsma, B. (1999). *World Vision security manual: Safety awareness for aid workers*. Geneva, Switzerland: World Vision.

Sinclair, D. (1993). *Horrific traumata: A pastoral response to PTSD*. New York, NY, USA: Haworth Pastoral Press. (Written by an Episcopal priest about the spiritual impact of trauma and recovery.)

van Brabant, K. (2000). *Operational security management in violent environments.* London, UK: Humanitarian Practice Network, Overseas Development Institute. (An excellent treatment of the training, precautions, and care needed to work in areas of war/danger.)

World Health Organization. (1996). *Mental health of refugees*. Geneva, Switzerland: Author. (Explores the mental health needs of displaced people and offers practical advice on helping them strengthen their capacity to adjust.)

Note: Most books in this domain are from international and secular sources, although there are a number of excellent articles by authors working with missionaries (a listing of these materials is available through the Mobile Member Care Team: mmctintl@aol.com). I have included the topics of refugee care, reconciliation, and war trauma, as many missionaries are involved in/affected by these areas. Trauma care, stress debriefing, ethnic reconciliation, and contingency planning continue to receive much attention in the literature. An important online source for trauma care/studies is the PILOTS database: www.dartmouth.edu/dms/ptsd/PILOTS.html.

Counseling/ Psychological Care

Ajdukovic, D., & Ajdukovic, M. (Eds.). (2000). *Mental health care of helpers*. Zagreb, Croatia: Society for Psychological Assistance. (An overview of how to support health care workers as they deal with occupational stress.)

Austin, B. (Ed.). (1995). *Personnel development and pastoral care for Youth With A Mission staff: A resource manual* (3rd ed.). UK: Author. (A collection of short checklists and handouts for personnel development areas, developed for YWAM but applicable to other organizations. Available from the author: King's Lodge, Watling St., Nuneaton CV10 0TZ, UK.)

Chung, T. (Ed.). *Counseling and Healing*. (A journal published since 1997, in Korean, by the Christian Healing Ministry Institute in Seoul, Korea.)

Collins, G. (1992). *Christian counseling* (Rev. ed.). Waco, TX, USA: Word. (Translated into several languages; an excellent resource for understanding and helping a variety of problems.)

Currie, J. (1998). *The barefoot counsellor* (Rev. ed.). Bangalore, India: Asian Trading Corp. (A primer in helping relationships.)

Danieli, Y. (2001). *Sharing the front line and the back hills: International protectors and providers, peacekeepers, humanitarian aid workers, and the media in the midst*. Amityville, NY, USA: Baywood Publishing Company.

Deane, H. (1994). *Staying missionary—Missionary attrition: Causes and remedies*. Auckland, New Zealand: Impestus Communications.

Denett, J. (1990). *Personal encouragement and growth for every missionary: A practical approach to biblical caring and counselling*. Pymble, NSW, Australia: Gospel and Missionary Society.

———. (1998). *Thriving in another culture: A handbook for cross-cultural missions*. Brunswick East, VIC, Australia: Acorn Press.

Donovan, K. (1992). *The pastoral care of missionaries: The responsibilities of church and mission.* Bible College of Victoria, Australia: Centre for World Mission.

Fawcett, G. (1999). *Ad-mission: The briefing and debriefing of mission and aid workers*. (Discusses different types of debriefing approaches, with several examples and suggestions drawn primarily from the author's work with YWAM. Available from the author: Highfield Oval, Harpenden, Herts. AL5 4BX, UK.)

Foster, S., Foster, J., & Nyawa-Dall, K. (1990). *An introduction to pastoral counseling: From Africa, for Africa*. Tallahassee, FL, USA: New Focus Publications. (A workbook to train counselors in the African church; see the article in *Evangelical Missions Quarterly*, July 1995.)

Foyle, M. (2001). *Honourably wounded: Stress among Christian workers. Overcoming missionary stress* (Rev. ed.). London, UK, and Grand Rapids, MI, USA: Monarch Books. (The first edition is available in five languages; easy to read and comprehensive, published as *Overcoming Missionary Stress* (first edition) in the USA. A landmark and foundational book in the field.)

Gropper, R. (1996). *Culture and the clinical encounter: An intercultural sensitizer for the health professions.* Yarmouth, ME, USA: Intercultural Press. (Gives short, interactive scenarios involving 23 ethnic groups, to educate health care providers about cross-cultural communication in service delivery.)

Humanitarian Practice Network. *Humanitarian Exchange*. (A quarterly publication from the Overseas Development Institute in the UK dealing with humanitarian aid/action; usually includes articles related to staff care and security. Email: hpn@odi.org.uk.)

International Journal of Frontier Missions. (1995, October). (Special issue on member care, with articles on multinational teams, crisis management, field counseling, etc.)

Jones, M. (Ed.). *Caring for the missionary into the 21st century*. (Two compendiums from the conferences organized by Care for Mission in the UK in 1993 and 1996. Available from: mejones@eihc.org.)

Journal of Psychology and Theology. (Published by Rosemead School of Psychology, Biola University in the USA. There have been four special issues on psychology and missions: 1983, 1987, 1993, and 1999.)

Manalel, G. (1999). *Pastoral counselling*. Mumbai, India: Bombay St. Paul Society.

McNair, R. (1995). *Room for improvement: The management and support of relief and development work*ers. London, UK: Relief and Recovery Network.

Meengs, D. (Ed.). *The Biblical Counselor*. Biblical Counselling Trust of India. (A monthly periodical with information and articles on Christian counseling; Available from: 44 A, Karpagan Ave., R.A. Puram, Chennai, India.)

O'Donnell, K. (Ed.). (1992). *Missionary care: Counting the cost for world evangelization*. Pasadena, CA, USA: William Carey Library. (Contains five sections: overview, counseling/clinical care, team life, mission agencies, and future directions.)

O'Donnell, K., & O'Donnell, M. (Eds.). (1988). *Helping missionaries grow: Readings in mental health and missions*. Pasadena, CA, USA: William Carey Library.

People In Aid Code (1997). *Code of best practice for the management and support of aid personnel.* (A helpful discussion and application of seven principles for staff care, developed by UK/Irish agencies. Contact: 106173.333@compuserve.com.)

Prashantham, B. (1994). *Indian case studies in therapeutic counselling*. Bangalore, India: Asian trading Corporation. (Written by a Christian counselor.)

Steffen, P., & Pennoyer, D. (Eds.). (2001). *Caring for the harvest force in the new millennium*. Evangelical Missiological Society. (Theological foundations, challenges, and context of caring for Christian workers.)

Taylor, W. (Ed.). (1997). *Too valuable to lose: Exploring the causes and cures of missionary attrition*. Pasadena, CA, USA: William Carey Library. (A compilation of 27 articles on attrition and the implications for selection, training, and pastoral care. Written by international authors and also available in Spanish, Portuguese, and Korean.)

Note: This domain includes materials emphasizing missionary mental health/adjustment and general missionary care. There are numerous online sources related to mental health in general. One example is InterPsych (www.interpsych.org), operated by an international organization that maintains numerous professionals forums (e.g., traumatic stress, rural care, etc.) with over 10,000 subscribers from 30 countries. Other missionary care materials online are available from www.iteams.org/Iteams/resource, www.acmc.org/care.html, and www.membercare.org. See also Mental Health Workers Without Borders at www.mhwwb.org/contents.htm.

Some General Member Care Materials From NSC Regions

Latin America

Bertuzzi, F. (1997). *La iglesia latina en misión mundial: Una orientación practica para iglesias y agencias misioneras (The Latin church in world missions: A practical orientation for churches and mission agencies)*. Santa Fe, Argentina: COMIBAM

International. (Contains articles on missions in general and several related to member care, such as training, selection, and pastoral care.)

COMIBAM (Iberoamerican Missions Cooperation). *Ellos Y Nosotros magazine*. (Began in 1995 and usually includes a helpful member care-related article in each issue. Examples: MKs – No. 1, 1995; selection – No. 5, 1997; team building – No. 7, 1999.)

EIRENE International (The Latin American Association for Pastoral and Family Counseling; has published several articles related to family life and personal adjustment, in Spanish and Portuguese. Contact: Carlos Pinto, cpinto@hcjb.org.ec.)

O'Donnell, K. (Ed.). (1997). *En beneficio de la ventana 10-40 del corazón: Un compendio sobre el cuidado pastoral (On behalf of the 10-40 window of the heart: A compendium on pastoral care)*. Author. (A collection of short articles and worksheets prepared for COMIBAM II participants, held in October 1997 in Acapulco, Mexico.)

Table 2
Additional Listings and Sources of Member Care Materials

Additional listings of member care-related books:

- The expanded listing of international literature which I have done, available on the website of the World Evangelical Alliance (www.membercare.org).
- The bibliography of 175 member care articles/dissertations from the 1960s–1987 in the book *Helping Missionaries Grow* (1988).
- The over-500 references listed on the missionary care website for Asbury College, along with several online brochures dealing with topics such as stress, grief, and burnout (www.asbury.edu/academ/psych/mis_care).
- The review of self-help literature in books such as *Authoritative Guide to Self-Help Books* (1994). For evaluative criteria for Christian self-help books, see Johnson, Johnson, and Hillman (1997).

Other sources for member care-related materials:

- Publishers/distributors such as Altheia (38-15 Corporal Kennedy St., Bayside, NY 11361, USA; email: alethpub@aol.com); Intercultural Press (PO Box 700, Yarmouth, ME, USA; email: books@interculturalpress.com); MARC Publications (800 West Chestnut Ave., Monrovia, CA 91016, USA; email: marcpubs@wvi.org); World Evangelical Alliance (Box WEF, Wheaton, IL 60189, USA; email: 102614.502@compuserve.com); and William Carey Library (PO Box 40129, Pasadena, CA 91114, USA; email: orders@wcl.com).
- Proceedings/articles from conferences such as the Mental Health and Missions Conference (organized by Missionary Training International; email: mtipaul@aol.com) and the Pastor to Missionaries Seminar (organized by Barnabas International; email: admin@barnabas.org) in the USA; the European Member Care Consultation (organized by Member Care Europe; email: marion@knell.net); the three regional gatherings of the International Conference on MKs (organized by the Association of Christian Schools International; email: david_wilcox@acsi.org); and other international conferences on travel medicine, tropical medicine, personnel development, and trauma studies.
- Materials/manuals from workshops, including the Interpersonal Skills Workshop developed by Ken Williams, Crisis Response Training offered by Karen Carr and Darlene Jerome, and the Member Care Seminars provided by Richard and Laura Mae Gardner and by Larry and Lois Dodds.
- Websites for various mission journals and magazines, which occasionally include member care articles (for more information, refer to Moreau and O'Rear (1999); for links to mission periodicals, visit www.gmi.org/mislinks/).

Asia

Castillo, M., & Sisco, K. (Eds.). (1998). *Into the 21st century: Asian churches in mission.* Evangelical Fellowship of Asia. (A compendium of presentations from the 1997 Asia Mission Congress II held in Thailand, with some articles related to missionary care. Available from: EFA Missions Commission: gcmtc@pacific.net.pc.)

India Missions Association. *Indian Missions Journal.* (Regularly publishes materials on member care areas: attrition, July 1998; persecution, April 1999; mentoring, July 1999).

Member Care Associates Asia. *Missionary service: Starting well.* (A compilation of several handouts from the Singapore Member Care Consultation 1998. Available from: samkuna@teenchallenge.org.sg.)

Kumar, B. (Ed.). (2000). *Member care handbook.* National Evangelical Christian Fellowship, Missions Commission. (Developed as a result of the first Malaysian member care consultation, October 1999. Available from: sbks@pc.jaring.my.)

Note: Other listings of materials are available from the India Missions Association, the Hong Kong Association of Christian Missions (e.g., *Asian Mission* periodical), and the Global Missionary Fellowship in Korea (e.g., an occasional MK journal; several books have been translated into Korean, such as *Healing for Damaged Emotions* by David Seamands, *Hurt People Hurt People* by Sandra Wilson, and *Counseling Cross-Culturally* by David Hesselgrave; contact: gmfmks@chollia.net). For materials in Central Asia (mostly psychology and self-help books translated into or written in Russian), contact the Moscow School of Psychology (amakhnack@glasnet.ru) and Triad Publishers (triada@glasnet.ru). Few member care materials exist in Central Asian languages apart from Scripture and discipleship helps.

Arabic World

Mallouhi, C. (1994). *Mini-skirts, mothers, and Muslims: Modeling spiritual values in Muslim cultures.* Carlisle, Cumbria, UK: Spear Publications. (STL Distributors, PO Box 300, Carlisle, Cumbria, CA3 0QS, UK.)

Walker, C. (Ed.). (n.d.). *Strangers in a strange land.* Interserve. (Explores issues that affect the well-being of workers in the Islamic world. Available from: mail@link.com.cy.)

Note: Most of the materials in this section are by expatriates living in the Arabic world. A listing of orientation materials to help work in this region is available from: angela@spidernet.com.cy.

Africa

Prins, M., & Willemse, B. (2001a). *Member care for missionaries: A practical guide for senders* (also in Afrikaans: *Sendelingversorging: 'n praktiese gids vir stuurders*). Cape Town, RSA: Member Care Southern Africa. (A manual and workbook to help churches send/support missionaries. Available from: mcsa@xsinet.co.za.)

———. (2001b). *The support team* (also in Afrikaans: *Die Ondersteuningspan*). Cape Town, RSA: Member Care Southern Africa.

Note: I have been unable to find other indigenous member care books from Africa.

References

Brewer, M. (1991). The lifelong learning link: Twelve reasons for continuous education for missionaries. *Missiology: An International Review, 19*, 185-202.

Johnson, W., Johnson, W., & Hillman, C. (1997). Toward guidelines for the development, evaluation, and utilization of Christian self-help materials. *Journal of Psychology and Theology, 25*, 341-353.

Moreau, S., & O'Rear, M. (1999). Missions on the web: Periodically speaking, missions magazines starting to dot the web. *Evangelical Missions Quarterly, 35*, 338-341.

O'Donnell, K. (1997). Member care in missions: Global perspectives and future directions. *Journal of Psychology and Theology, 25*, 143-154.

Santrock, J., et al. (1994). *Authoritative guide to self-help books.* New York, NY, USA: Guilford Press.

This is a revision of an article that first appeared in ***Evangelical Missions Quarterly*** *(2001, vol. 39, pp. 18-29); PO Box 794, Wheaton, IL 60189, USA. Used by permission.*

Many thanks to the colleagues from different regions and organizations who reviewed and added to the references in this article at its various stages.

Index